William Ludden

Pronouncing Musical Dictionary of Technical Words, Phrases and Abbreviations

Including definitions of musical terms used by the ancient Hebrews

William Ludden

Pronouncing Musical Dictionary of Technical Words, Phrases and Abbreviations
Including definitions of musical terms used by the ancient Hebrews

ISBN/EAN: 9783337317911

Printed in Europe, USA, Canada, Australia, Japan

Cover: Foto ©Thomas Meinert / pixelio.de

More available books at **www.hansebooks.com**

PRONOUNCING

MUSICAL DICTIONARY

OF

TECHNICAL WORDS, PHRASES AND ABBREVIATIONS:

INCLUDING

DEFINITIONS OF MUSICAL TERMS USED BY THE ANCIENT HEBREWS, TOGETHER WITH THOSE FOUND IN GREEK AND ROMAN LITERATURE; A DESCRIPTION OF THE VARIOUS KINDS OF INSTRUMENTS, BOTH ANCIENT AND MODERN; ALSO, AN EXPLANATION OF SUCH TECHNICAL TERMS AS ARE EMPLOYED BY THE MOST EMINENT COMPOSERS AND THEORETICAL WRITERS OF ITALY, GERMANY, FRANCE AND AMERICA.

BY W. LUDDEN.

PUBLISHED BY
DITSON & CO.,
Boston, New York, and Philadelphia.

INTRODUCTION.

The method adopted in this work is to give to each word, or musical term, the pronunciation peculiar to the language to which it belongs. It is admitted that it is not unfrequently impossible to express with precision the native pronunciation of foreign languages with English letters, but even in such cases much will be gained by an approximation to the true sound. For the sake of brevity the English terms are, for the most part, only defined, without adding the pronunciation.

One of the most difficult as well as important of the points to be made is that of placing the accent upon the proper syllable. But it is to be borne in mind that in most of the European languages the stress of voice is not thrown so exclusively upon a single syllable as it is in English; and, as a natural consequence, the unaccented syllables are almost invariably pronounced more distinctly than by us. This is specially true in the Italian, French and Spanish languages. In important cases accent is indicated in the word, as pronounced, by placing the accented syllable in Italics.

In the Latin and Greek languages it has been deemed advisable to follow what is known as the *Continental* pronunciation, in preference to the English pronunciation which is adopted in some of our principal Colleges; since it is only by this means that we can conform at all to the usual pronunciation of the same terms by the principal European nations. In this connection it is proper to add, that the Latin words employed in the Catholic church service, as in the *Mass*, *etc.*, are frequently made to conform to the Italian mode of pronunciation. Thus: Dominus, *Dŏm-ĭ-noos;* pacem, *pä-tshĕm;* etc.; but as this system has not been universally adopted by the church choirs of this country, it has seemed best to preserve a uniformity in the pronunciation of all Latin or Greek words, and accordingly no such distinction has been made.

In the preparation of this work, the aim has been rather to practical utility than to great fullness and extent, and no hesitation was felt in discarding over two thousand (so called) musical terms which have appeared in recent publications, as being both useless and illegitimate.

Entered according to Act of Congress, in the year 1875,
By J. L. PETERS,
In the Office of the Librarian of Congress, at Washington, D. C.

ELECTROTYPED BY
MARDER, LUSE & CO.,
CHICAGO.

S. W. GREEN, Printer,
New-York.

RULES

FOR THE

PRONUNCIATION OF THE PRINCIPAL MODERN LANGUAGES.

GERMAN.

VOWELS.

A has the sound of ä as in *far*.
Au is like ou in *house*.
Ai occurs but rarely, and has the sound of I as in *pine*.
Ae or **ä** when long is like a in *mate;* when short it is like ĕ in *met*.
Aeu or **aü** is like oy in *boy*.
E has (1) the sound of ĕ as in *help*, and (2) the sound of a in *hate*.
Ei has always the sound of I in *pine*.
Eu is like oi in *loiter*.
I has the sound of ĭ as in *pin*.
Ie takes the sound of ē as in *tree*.
O has (1) a long sound as in *tone*, and (2) a short sound as in *toss*.
Oe or **ö** has the sound of ō as in *dove*.
U has the sound of oo as in *moon*.
Ue or **ü** has the sound of the French ü.
Y is used only in foreign words, where it does not differ from I.

CONSONANTS.

B and **d** are pronounced as in English.
C is only used in foreign words. Before e, i and y it is pronounced like ts; before other vowels and consonants it is like k.
Ch has nothing corresponding to it in English. It has two sounds; when following a, o, u or au it is a guttural and similar to the Scotch word *Loch;* but when it occurs after e, ei, i, ä, o, au, eu or ü it has a soft palatal aspirate which may be represented by the combinations kh. At the beginning of words ch is like k.
Chs is pronounced like ks or x.
F, l, m, p, t and **x** are the same as in English.
G has the hard sound as in *got*. In some parts of Germany the unaccented, final *ig* is softened into something like *ikh*.
H at the beginning of words is aspirated; between two vowels the aspiration is very weak, and before a consonant or at the end of words it is mute; but in this case it makes the preceding vowel long.
J is equivalent to the English y in *yet*, and is always followed by a vowel.
K is like the English k, but is never mute before n.
Ng sounds like ng in length; but in compound words where the first ends in n and the last begins with g, they are separated.
Q is always joined with u, and together they are pronounced like *kw*.
Ph has the sound of f.
Pf unites the two letters in one sound uttered with compressed lips.
R has a stronger sound than in English, and is the same at the beginning, middle or end of a word.
S is like the English s. It is sounded at the end of words, and between two vowels it frequently takes the sound of z.
Sch is like the English sh in *ship*.
Th takes always the sound of t; h being silent. It has never the sound of th in *thee*.
Tz intensifies the sound of z.
V is pronounced like f.
W answers to the English v.
Z is pronounced like ts in *nets*.

In the German words defined and pronounced in this work, the accented syllable, in words of two or more, will be in Italics.

N. B. For the sake of greater uniformity, most of the German substantives, in the words to be defined in the following pages, are made to conform to English usage by not capitalizing the initial letter.

RULES FOR PRONUNCIATION.

ITALIAN.

VOWELS.

A is always like ä in *father*.

E has (1) the sound of ĕ in *pen*, and (2) the sound of ā in *fate*.

I is pronounced like ē in *me*.

J is always a vowel and at the beginning of a syllable is like y in *you*. At the end of a word it is like ē in *be*.

O has the sound (1) of ō in *tone;* and (2) that of ŏ in *not*.

U has always the sound of oo in *cool*.

CONSONANTS.

B, d, f, l, n, p, q, v, are the same as in English.

C, before a, o and u, has the sound of k; before e, i, and y it has the sound of tsh, or that of ch in the word *cheek*. When doubled (cc) and followed by e, i, or y, the first is pronounced like t and the second takes its usual sound.

Ch, before e or i, has the sound of k.

G, before a, o, or u, is hard as in *go;* before e, or i, it has the sound of j or soft g as in *gem*. When doubled and followed by e, or i, it has the sound of dj; or like dg in *lodge*.

Gh, followed by e, or i, is pronounced like g in *go*.

Gl, followed by i preceding another vowel, is pronounced like ll in *million*.

Gn, followed by a, e, i, o, or u, is like ni in the English word minion.

Gua, gue, gui, are pronounced gwä, gwā, gwē.

Gia, gio, giu, are pronounced djiä, djiō, djioo, in one syllable, giving the i a very faint sound.

S has (1) the hard sound as in *sis*, and (2) the soft sound as in *ease;* usually the latter when occurring between two vowels.

Sc, before e, or i, is like sh in *shall;* before a, o, or u, it has the sound of sk.

Sch is always like sk, or sch in *school*.

Scia, scio, sciu, are pronounced shä, shō, shoo.

R, at the beginning of words, is like the English; but at the end of words or syllables, or when combined with another consonant, it should have a rolling sound.

W and **x** are not found in Italian, except in foreign words.

Z has usually the sound of ts; it is sometimes pronounced like dz.

Italian words are pronounced exactly as written, there being no silent letter except h. The vowels always preserve their proper sounds, forming no dipthongs and being uninfluenced by the consonants with which they may be combined.

In words of two or more syllables there is usually a slight emphasis placed on the penult or ante-penult, but rarely on the last syllable.

FRENCH.

VOWELS.

A has two sounds; ä as in *mass* and ă as in *bar*.

Ai is like ā in *fate*.

An is similar to o in English.

E is (1) like ĕ in *met;* (2) like ā in fate; (3) similar to ŭ in *bud*. It is frequently silent at the end of words.

Ei is nearly like ā in *fate*.

En resembles ŭ in *tub*.

I has the sound (1) of ĭ in *pin*, (2) of ē in *me*.

Ia has nearly the sound of ia in *medial*.

Ie is like ee in *bee*.

O is pronounced like ŏ in *rob;* and like ō in *rope*.

U has no equivalent in English, but resembles the sound of e in *dew*. By prolonging the sound of *e*, taking care not to introduce the sound of *w*, we get an approximate sound of the French u, or ü as it will be marked in this work.

Y, when initial, or coming between two consonants, or standing as a syllable by itself, is the same as the French *i;* but between two vowels it is equivalent to double i, (ii) the first forming a dipthong with the preceding one and the second with the one following.

CONSONANTS.

Final consonants are frequently silent.

B, at the beginning and in the middle of words, is the same as in English.

C has (1) the sound of k before a, o, or u; (2) when written with the cedilla, or before e, or i, it has the sound of s. C final is sounded unless preceded by n.

Ch is pronounced like sh in *she*. In words derived from the Greek ch is pronounced like *k*.

D is the same as in English. It is often silent at the end of words.

F is like the English; when final it is usually sounded.

G, before a, o, or u, is hard, as in *go;* but before e, i, or y, it has the sound of z in the English word *azure*. In the combination gue, or gui, the u is silent, but the g takes its hard sound.

Gn is pronounced like ni in *union*.

H is mute or slightly aspirated.

J is pronounced like z in *azure*.

K has the same sound as in English.

L has (1) the same sound as in English, and (2) the liquid sound as in *million*.

RULES FOR PRONUNCIATION.

M and **n**, when not nasal, have the same sound as in English; if preceded by a vowel in the same syllable, they are always nasal unless immediately followed by a vowel in the next syllable.

Am, an, em, en, are pronounced somewhat like *änh.*

Im, in, aim, ain, eim, ein, are pronounced like *änh.*

Om and **on,** are like *önh.*

Um and **un** are pronounced like *ŭnh.*

P is generally the same as in English. It is sometimes silent; and always when at the end of a word.

Q is usually followed by u, in which case they are together sounded like the letter k.

R is given more roughly than in English. It is often silent when preceded by the vowel *e*.

S has generally the same sound as in English; between two vowels it has generally the same sound as in the English word *rose*.

Sc is the same as in English. S final is generally silent.

T has its hard English sound, but in tial, tiel, and tion, it has the sound of s.

Th is always the same as t alone. T final is usually silent.

V is like the English, only a little softer.

W is found only in foreign words, and is pronounced like *v*.

X, initial, is pronounced like gz; it occurs but in few words.

Ex, at the beginning of words, is sounded like egz. In other places and between two vowels it is pronounced like ks.

Z is like z in *zone*.

Final consonants, which would otherwise be silent, are frequently sounded by carrying them over to the next word when commencing with a vowel.

SPANISH.

VOWELS.

A is pronounced as *ä* in *ah*.

E is generally pronounced like *a* in *mate;* but, when followed by n, r, s, or z, it takes the short sound of *ĕ* as in *met*.

I is pronounced like *ē* as in *me*, and sometimes like *i* as in *pin*.

O takes the same form of pronunciation as in English. It is long as in *nō*, short as in *nŏt*, or close as in *glōve*.

U is pronounced like oo; the only exception to this rule being in syllables, gue, gui, que, qui, when the u becomes silent unless written with two dots over it; thus, ü.

Y is sometimes a vowel and sometimes a consonant. When followed by another vowel it usually unites and forms a dipthong; in most other cases it is a consonant, similar to j in English.

Ay is like the Spanish *i*.

Ei is the same as *i*.

Oy and **uy** are pronounced as *oi*.

CONSONANTS.

B, at the beginning of a word is like the English; but when occurring between two vowels it is sometimes softened to *v*. (This is done by Mexicans, however, and is not regarded as pure Castilian.)

C, before e or i, has the sound of th in *thin;* but followed by a, o, or u, it has the sound of k. When doubled and followed by e, or i, the first is hard and the second soft.

D, at the beginning of a word is the same as in English; but between two vowels it has a peculiar sound not perfectly represented by English characters, but similar to th in *thee*. At the end of a word it has a lisping sound.

F is pronounced as in English.

G, before a, o, u, l, or r, is pronounced as in English; before e, or i, it is an aspirate, as *he, hi*.

H is usually a mute, but is slightly aspirated before *ue*.

Ch is pronounced as in the English word *cheek*.

J is a strong aspirate and is equivalent to the Spanish g before e, or i.

L is pronounced as in English. When double (ll) the last takes the sound of y as in million.

M is the same as the English.

N is like the English, but when it is written ñ, it is pronounced as in the English word *minion*.

P and **q** are pronounced as in English; qu has sometimes the sound of k, the u being mute.

R, at the beginning of words or syllables should be pronounced more roughly than in English; when doubled it is given very harshly.

S has always the hissing sound.

T is pronounced as in *tart, tin*.

V is the same as in English.

X is similar to *ks* in English.

Z is only used before a, o, or u, and is always pronounced with the lisping sound of th; it is the same after a vowel.

In Spanish particular care should be taken to pronounce the letters c, d, r, s, at the end of words. The accent usually falls on the final syllable when the word ends with a consonant. Substantives, ending with a vowel, have usually the accent upon the penultimate or last syllable but one. As exceptions to these rules it may be said that the plurals of nouns and adjectives, though they take on the s, still retain the same accent as in the singular.

SWEDISH.

VOWELS.

A is like the German.

E has the sound of long ä at the beginning of words, when making a syllable by itself, and at the end of words. It has the sound of short ĕ, as in *met*, when followed by f, l, m, n, r, or s.

I is like the German.

O is like oo at the beginning of a word, in a syllable by itself, and at the end of a word or syllable. It has the sound of long ŏ when followed by f, l, m, n, r, s, or t.

U is similar to the long u in English.

Y is like the French ü.

CONSONANTS.

G, before a, o, or u, is hard as in *go*. When followed by i, or y, it is like the English y.

Gjo and **gju** are pronounced like *yo* and *yoo*.

H is aspirated except before v and j, when it becomes silent.

I is like the English y.

K is hard before a, o, and u; but before i and y it has the sound of *ch*.

Kj is like the English *ch*.

Tj has usually the same sound of *ch* only softer.

The remaining consonants are similar to English.

POLISH.

VOWELS.

A, e and **i** correspond to the German.

O, when accented, is like oo in English.

U is like the German.

Y is like short i in *pin*.

CONSONANTS.

B, k, l, m, n, p and **r**, are like English.

C, ch and **w**, are like the German.

Cz is like ch in English.

Sc resembles sts. **Sz** is like the English sh.

DUTCH.

VOWELS.

A, e, i and **o** have the same sounds as in German.

U has the sound of the French ü.

Y or **ij** is equivalent to i in *mind*.

Ui resembles oy in boy.

CONSONANTS.

Consonants are similar to the German, with the following exceptions:

G is always strongly guttural when combined with h.

Sch is not pronounced like sh, but like a*k*.

Gh has the hard sound of g as in go.

DANISH.

VOWELS.

A has two sounds, as in *däh* and *mān*.

E has three sounds as in the German.

I, o and **u** are also like the German.

Y is like the French ü.

CONSONANTS.

D is not sounded after a vowel.

R and **w** are like the German.

J is like the English y; and the remaining consonants like the same in English.

The Norwegian is similar to Danish, except that d is like the English, and o like the Polish.

HUNGARIAN.

VOWELS.

A, when accented, has the Italian ä; but unaccented has the short sound of ŏ.

E has two sounds as in Italian.

I has the two German sounds.

O is similar to English.

U, accented, has the long sound of ō; unaccented, it is like oo.

CONSONANTS.

C is always joined to some other consonant; ca is like *ch*, cz is like *ts*.

G is always hard as in *go*.

H is always aspirate.

S is like *sh;* az is like *ss*.

T and **th** are always hard.

Zs is like the French j.

PRONOUNCING
MUSICAL DICTIONARY.

ā ale, ă add, ä arm, ē eve, ĕ end, ī ice, ĭ ill, ō old, ŏ odd, O dove, oo moon, ū tule, ŭ but, ü French sound.

A

A. 1. The alphabetical name given, in the United States and England, to the sixth tone of the diatonic major scale of C; in France and Italy called *La*.

2. Upon string instruments, the name of the string which, with the open tone, gives the sixth of the natural scale. In tuning, this string is usually first brought to the requisite pitch and from it the others are then regulated; it is the first (smallest) string of the violoncello, the second of the violin, etc.

A, *It.* (äh.) By, for, to, at, in, etc.
Aanes, *Gr.* (ä-nĕz.) A term applied by modern Greeks to modes and tones. (Not in general use.)
Abacus, *Lat.* (ă-bă-kŭs.) An ancient instrument for dividing the intervals of the octave.
A balláta, *It.* (ä bäl-*lä*-tä.) In the style of a dance: see *Ballata*.
Abandon, *Fr.* (ä-bänh-dŏnh.) Without restraint; with self-abandon; with ease.
A battúta, *It.* (ä băt-*too*-tä.) As beaten; strictly in time.
Abat-voix, *Fr.* (ä-bä-vwä.) A voice reflector.
Abbacchiato, *It.* (äb-bät-kē-ä-to.) With a dejected, melancholy expression.
Abbadare, *It.* (äb-bä-dä-rĕ.) Take care; pay attention.
Abbandonási, *It.* (äb-bän-dō-*nä*-zē.) Without restraint; with passionate expression.
Abbandonataménte, *It.* (äb-bän-dō-nä-tä-*män*-tĕ.) Vehemently, violently.
Abbandóne, *It.* (äb-bän-*dō*-nĕ.) Making the time subservient to the expression; despondingly; with self-abandonment.
Abbandonevolménte, *It.* (äb-bän-dō-nĕ-vŏl-*män*-tĕ.) Violently, vehemently; without restraint as to time.
Abbandóno, *It.* (äb-bän-*dō*-nō.) With passionate expression; making the time subservient.
Abbassaménto di mano, *It.* (äb-bäs-sä-*män*-tō dĕ mä-nō.) The down-beat, or descent of the hand, in beating time.
Abbassaménto di vóce, *It.* (äb-bäs-sä-*män*-tō dĕ vō-tshĕ.) Diminishing or lowering of the voice.
Abbelláre, *It.* (äb-bĕl-*lä*-rĕ.) To embellish with ornaments.
Abbelliménti, *It.* (äb-bĕl-lē-*män*-tē.) Ornaments introduced to embellish a plain melody.
Abbelliménto, *It.* (äb-bĕl-lē-*män*-tō.) A grace note, or ornament.

ABBR

Abbellíre, *It.* (äb-bĕl-*lē*-rĕ.) To embellish with ornaments.
Abbellitúra, *It.* (äb-bĕl-lē-*too*-rä.) An ornament, embellishment.
Abbellitúre, *It.* (äb-bĕl-lē-*too*-rĕ.) Ornaments, embellishments.
Abblasen, *Ger.* (äb-blä-z'n.) To sound or flourish the trumpet; to sound the retreat.
Abbreviaménti, *It.* (äb-brä-vē-ä-*män*-tē.) Abbreviations in musical notation.
Abbreviáre, *It.* (äb-brä-vē-*ä*-rĕ.) To abbreviate or shorten the labor of notation.
Abbreviation marks. 1. Oblique strokes which distinguish the *eighth*, *sixteenth* or *thirty-second* notes, when applied to the stem of the *quarter* or *half-note*, signify as many repetitions of the shorter note thus indicated as are equal to the longer note represented. Thus is equivalent to

2. A diagonal stroke with a dot each side signifies a repetition of a group of notes, or sometimes of a complete measure.

3. When the long notes are omitted, the oblique strokes, distinguishing *eighth*, *sixteenth*, etc. notes, are sometimes employed to denote a repetition of such short notes: Thus, indicate a repetition of eighths, sixteenths, thirty-seconds, respectively.

4. A short horizontal line, a row of dots, or a waving line is used to express the repetition, or a continuation of the influence, of the preceding character. Thus,

mi -- sol -- do

5. A combination of rests so written as to denote a long period of silence. These rests indicate a period of eleven measures silence.

6. Figures, when placed upon the staff, or over a measure in which rests are written, serve to indicate the number of whole rests or measures of silence.

PRONOUNCING MUSICAL DICTIONARY.

ă *ale*, ă *add*, ä *arm*, ē *eve*, ĕ *end*, ī *ice*, ĭ *ill*, ō *old*, ŏ *odd*, ȯ *dove*, oo *moon*, ū *lute*, ŭ *but*, ü *French sound*.

ABBR

Abbreviatur, *Ger.* (äb-brä-vĭ-ä-*toor*.) Abbreviation.
Abbreviatúre, *It.* (äb-brä-vē-ä-*too*-rĕ.)
Abbreviaturen, *Ger.* (äb-brä-vē-ä-*too*-r'n.)
Abbreviazióni, *It.* (äb-brä-vē-ä-tsē-ō-nē.) Abbreviations, in musical notation.
Abendglocke, *Ger.* (ä-bĕnd-*glŏk*-ĕ.) Evening bell; curfew.
Abendlied, *Ger.* (ä-bĕnd-lēd.) Evening song, or hymn.
Abendmusik, *Ger.* (ä-bĕnd-*moo*-zĭk.) Evening or night music; serenade.
Abendständchen, *Ger.* (ä-bĕnd-*stănd*-khĕn.) A serenade.
A béne plácito, *It.* (ä bā-nĕ *plä*-tshē-tō.) At pleasure. The time may be retarded or ornaments introduced.
Abermals, *Ger.* (ä-bĕr-mäls.) Once more.
Abertura, *Span.* (ä-bĕr-*too*-rä.) Overture.
Abfassen, *Ger.* (äb-fäs-s'n.) To compose.
Abfasser, *Ger.* (äb-fäs-s'r.) A composer.
Abfiedeln, *Ger.* (äb-fē-d'ln.) To fiddle.
Abfingern, *Ger.* (äb-fĭng-ĕrn.) To finger.
Abflöten, *Ger.* (äb-flō-t'n.) To play the flute.
Abgehen, *Ger.* (äb-gā-ĕn.) To go off, to make an exit, to retire.
Abgeigen, *Ger.* (äb-gbī-g'n.) To play the fiddle.
Abgestossen, *Ger.* (äb-ghĕ-stōs-s'n.) Detached, struck off, staccato.
Abgesetzt, *Ger.* (äb-ghĕ-sĕtst.) Staccato.
Abgurgeln, *Ger.* (äb-goor-g'ln.) To carol.
Abhauchen, *Ger.* (äb-how-kh'n.) To utter softly.
Abilita, *It.* (ä-bē-lē-tä.) Ability.
Ab initio, *Lat.* (äb ĭn-ĭ-shĭ-ō.) An obsolete term, of the same signification as *Da Capo.*
Abkürzen, *Ger.* (äb-kürt-s'n.) To abridge, to abbreviate.
Abkürzung, *Ger.* (äb-kürt-soong.) Abridgment, abbreviation.
Abkürzungen, *Ger.* (äb-kürt-soong-ĕn.) Abbreviations.
Abludo, *Lat.* (äb-lū-dō.) To differ, to play out of tune. (Not used.)
Abnehmend, *Ger.* (äb-nä-mend.) Diminishing.
Abrégé, *Fr.* (ä-brä-zhā.) Abridgment; also, the couples in an organ.
Abréger, *Fr.* (ä-brä-zhā.) To curtail, to abridge.
Abreissung, *Ger.* (äb-rī-soong.) A sudden stop, or pause.
Abrupt Cadence. See *Interrupted Caaence.*
Abrupt modulation. A sudden modulation into keys not closely related to the original key.
Abruptio, *Lat.* (äb-rŭp-shĭ-ō.) Breaking off; a sudden pause.
Absatz, *Ger.* (äb-sätz.) A section or passage of music, usually consisting of four measures; also, a pause or stop.
Absetzen, *Ger.* (äb-sĕt-s'n.) A style of performance similar to *staccato.*
Absingen, *Ger.* (äb-sĭng-ĕn.) To sing, to carol; to fatigue one's self by singing.
Absingung, *Ger.* (äb-sĭng-oong.) Singing, caroling.
Absonus, *Lat.* (äb-sō-nŭs.) Unmusical; incapable of being tuned.
Abspielen, *Ger.* (äb-spē-l'n.) To perform on an instrument; to play a tune; to finish playing.

ACCE

Abstand der Töne, *Ger.* (äb-ständ dĕr tō-nĕ.) Distance of tones.
Absteigende Tonarten, *Ger.* (äb-stī-gĕn-dĕ tō-när-t'n.) Descending scales or keys.
Abstimmen, *Ger.* (äb-stĭm-mĕn.) To tune properly; to lower, or tune down.
Abstimmung, *Ger.* (äb-stĭm-moong.) Discordance; dissonance.
Abstossen, *Ger.* (äb-stŏs-s'n.) Similar in manner of performance to staccato.
Abtönen, *Ger.* (äb-tō-nĕn.) To deviate from the right tone.
Abtrommeln, *Ger.* (äb-trŏm-mĕln.) To beat on the drum; to publish by drumming.
Abtrompeten, *Ger.* (äb-trŏm-pā-t'n.) To perform on the trumpet; to finish trumpeting.
Abub, *Heb.* (ä-bŭb.) A flute, or hautboy.
Abwechselnd, *Ger.* (äb-vĕk-s'lnd.) Alternating, changing. In organ playing, alternately; in choir singing, antiphonally; in dance music, change of movements.
Abyssinian Flute. An instrument resembling the German flute, but with mouth-piece like the clarinet, and played upon lengthwise.
Académie de Musique, *Fr.* (ăk-ăd-ā-mē.) An academy of music, consisting of professors and scholars; a society for promoting musical culture.
Académie Royale de Musique, *Fr.* The name given to the opera-house in Paris.
Académie spirituelle, *Fr.* (ăk-ā-dā-mē spĭr-ē-too-ăl.) A performance or concert of sacred music.
A cappélla, *It.* (ä käp-pāl-lä.) In the church or chapel style.
A cappríccio, *It.* (ä käp-prēt-sbē-ō.) In a capricious style; according to the taste of the performer.
Acatalectic, *Gr.* (ā-kăt-ă-lĕk-tĭk.) A verse having the complete number of syllables without superfluity or deficiency.
Acathistus, *Gr.* (ăk-ă-this-tŭs.) A hymn of praise sung in the ancient Greek church in honor of the Virgin.
Academia, *It.* (ăk-kä-dā-mē-ä.) An academy; the word also means a concert.
Accarezzévole, *It.* (ăk-kä-rĕt-zā-vō-lĕ.) Blandishing; in a persuasive and caressing manner.
Accarezzevolménte, *It.* (ăk-kä-rĕt-zā-vōl-mān-tĕ.) Caressingly; coaxingly.
Accel, *It.* (ät-tshĕl.) An abbreviation of accelerando.
Acceldo. An abbreviation of Accelerando.
Accelerándo, *It.* (ät-tshĕl-ā-rän-dō.) Accelerating the time; gradually increasing the velocity of the movement.
Acceleratamente, *It.* (ät-tshĕl-ä-rä-tä-män-tĕ.) Speedily.
Accelerato, *It.* (ät-tshĕl-ā-rä-to.) Accelerated; increasing in rapidity.
Accent. A stress or emphasis upon a certain note or passage to mark its position in the bar, or its relative importance in regard to the composition.
Accent, dead. An expression of tone resulting from boldly attacking a violin, pressing the bow with heavy dead weight upon the strings.

PRONOUNCING MUSICAL DICTIONARY. 9

ă *ale*, ă *add*, ŭ *arm*, ē *eve*, ĕ *end*, ī *ice*, ĭ *ill*, ō *old*, ŏ *odd*, ō *dove*, oo *moon*, ū *lute*, ŭ *but*, ü *French sound*.

ACCE

Accent, descriptive. An accent which fully illustrates the various expressions or sentiments of a piece in the most minute points.
Accented. Uttered with accent; those notes or parts of a bar on which the emphasis naturally falls.
Accented notes. In common time, the first and third parts, and in triple time the first note, in a measure; notes upon which emphasis is placed.
Accent, false. An accent removed from the first note of the measure to the second or fourth.
Accent, grammatical. The stress laid on the accented part of the measure.
Accent, measured. A regular alternation of strong and weak parts in a measure.
Accénto, *It.* (ät-*tshän*-tō.) Accent or emphasis laid upon certain notes.
Accentor, *It.* (ät-*tshän*-tōr.) An old term, signifying the performer who took the principal part in a duet, trio, etc.
Accent, oratorical. The emphasis dictated by feeling, giving the music its varying expression.
Accent, rhythmical. A uniform succession of small or large groups of figures or notes symmetrical in their relation to each other.
Accénti, *It.* (ät-*tshän*-tē.) }
Accent, *Fr.* (äk-sänh.)   } Accents.
Accentuáre, *It.* (ät-tshēn-too-ä-rē.) To accentuate, to mark with an accent.
Accentuation. The act of accenting; the giving to the several notes of a piece their proper emphasis or expression; the art of placing accents.
Accentnato, *It.* (ät-tshēn-too-ä-to.) Distinctly and strongly accented.
Accentuiren, *Ger.* (äk-tsēn-too-ē-r'n.) To accent.
Accentus, *Lat.* (äk-sēn-tŭs.) Accent.
Accentus Ecclesiastici, *Lat.* The precentor's chant, almost entirely upon one tone. These chants were formerly of seven kinds, viz.: the immutabilia, medius, gravis, acutus, moderatus, interrogatus and finalis.
Accessory notes. Those notes situated one degree above and one degree below the principal note of a turn.
Accessory parts. Accompaniments.
Accessory tones. Harmonics. Tones faintly heard when the principal tone dies away.
Accessory voices. Accompanying voices.
Accia ccare, *It.* (ät-tshē-äk-kä-rē.) A broken and unexpected way of striking a chord.
Acciaccáto, *It.* (ät-tshē-äk-kä-tō.) Violently.
Acciaccatúra, *It.* (ät-tshē-äk-kä-too-rä.) A species of arpeggio; an accessory note placed before the principal note, the accent being on the principal note.
Accidentals. Occasional sharps, flats, or naturals placed before notes in the course of a piece.
Accidénti, *It.* (ät-tshē-dän-tē.) }
Accidents, *Fr.* (äk-sĭ-dänh.)   } Accidentals.
Accidental chords. Chords containing one or more notes foreign to its proper harmony.
Accidental chromatics. Chromatics incidentally employed.

ACCO

Accidental harmonics. The relatives of the key.
Accidental notes. Notes which do not belong to the key.
Accigliaménto, *It.* (ät-tshēl-yē-ä-*män*-tō.) Sadness, melancholy.
Acclamation. A form of words uttered with vehemence, performed in the latter ages of Rome by a choir of singers instructed for the purpose.
Acclamazióne, *It.* (äk-klä-mä-tsē-ō-nē.) Acclamation.
Accodato, *It.* (äk-kō-*dä*-tō.) Accompanied.
Accolade, *Fr.* (äk-kō-*läd*.) The brace which connects two, three or more staves together.
Accom. An abbreviation of accompaniment.
Accom. ad Lib. An abbreviation of Accompaniment ad Libitum.
Accommodáre, *It.* (äk-kōm-mō-*dä*-rē.) To tune an instrument.
Accomp. An abbreviation of Accompaniment.
Accompagnaménto, *It.* (äk-kōm-pän-yē-*män*-tō.) Accompaniment; the figured bass or harmony.
Accompagnaméntó ad Líbitum, *It.* An accompaniment that may be either played or dispensed with.
Accompagnaménto obligáto, *It.* An accompaniment that must be played, being indispensable to the proper effect.
Accompagnando, *It.* (äk-kōm-pän-*yän*-dō.) Accompaniment.
Accompagnáre, *It.* (äk-kōm-pän-*yä*-rē.) To accompany; to play from the figured bass.
Accompagnateur, *Fr.* (äk-kōnh-pänh-yä-tür.) An accompanist.
Accompagnatóre, *It.* (äk-kōm-pän-yä-*tō*-rē.) One who accompanies.
Accompagnato, *It.* (äk-kōm-pän-*yä*-tō.) Accompanied.
Accompagnatríce, *It.* (äk-kōm-pän-ya-*trē*-tshē.) A female accompanist.
Accompagné, *Fr.* (äk-kōnh-pänh-yä.) Accompanied.
Accompagnement, *Fr.* (äk-kōnh-pänh-yü-mänh.) An accompaniment.
Accompagner, *Fr.* (äk-kōmh-pänh-yä.) To accompany.
Accompagnist, *Ger.* (äk-kōm-*päng*-nĭst.) An accompanist.
Accompanied Madrigals. Those madrigals in which the voices are sustained by piano or organ.
Accompanied Recitative. A Recitative having parts arranged for several instruments.
Accompaniment. A part added to a solo or other principal part, to enhance and enrich its effect.
Accompaniments. Vocal or Instrumental parts in a composition which do not include the principal melody but fill up the harmony, sustain the rythm, and, by embellishments, heighten the general effect.
Accompaniment, ad libitum. Use the accompaniment or not at pleasure.
Accompaniment, arpeggio. An accompaniment which consists of the notes of the several chords taken in succession.

ā ale, ă add, ä arm, ē eve, ĕ end, ī ice, ĭ ill, ō old, ŏ odd, o dove, oo moon, ū lute, ŭ but, ü French sound.

ACCO

Accompaniment, obligato. The accompaniment must be used.
Accompaniment of the scale. The harmony assigned to the series of notes forming the diatonic scale, ascending and descending.
Accompaniment, pulsatile. An accompaniment consisting of regular and monotonous repetitions of the chords.
Accompanist. The person playing the accompaniment.
Accompany. The act of performing the accompanying part.
Accomp. Oblto. An abbreviation of accompaniment obligato.
Accopiáto, *It.* (äk-kō-pē-ä-tō.) Bound, tied; joined together.
Accorciare, *It.* (äk-kŏr-tshē-ä-rĕ.) To contract, to abridge.
Accorciatura, *It.* (äk-kŏr-tshē-ä-too-rä.) Abridgment.
Accord, *Fr.* (äk-kŏr.) A chord; a concord; consonance.
Accordamento, *It.* (äk-kŏr-dä-män-tō.) Consonance, unison, harmony of parts.
Accordándo, *It.* (äk-kŏr-dän-dō.) Tuning.
Accordant, *Fr.* (äk-kŏr-dänh.) In concord, in unison.
Accordáre, *It.* (äk-kŏr-dä-rĕ.) To tune, to agree in sound.
Accordáto, *It.* (äk-kŏr-dä-tō.) In harmony, in tune.
Accordatóre, *It.* (äk-kŏr-dä-tō-rĕ.) One who tunes instruments.
Accordatrice, *It.* (äk-kŏr-dä-trē-tshĕ.) A woman who tunes.
Accordatúra, *It.* (äk-kŏr-dä-too-rä.) Concord, harmony. Also, the scale of notes to which the open strings of an instrument are tuned.
Accordeon. An instrument held in the hands the tones of which are produced by a current of air from a bellows acting on metallic reeds.
Accorder, *Fr.* (äk-kŏr-dā.) To tune an instrument; to sing or play in tune.
Accordeur, *Fr.* (äk-kŏr-dŭr.) One who tunes an instrument.
Accordi, *It.* (äk-kŏr-dē.) Play again as before.
According. An harmonious blending of different parts.
Accordion, *Fr.* (äk-kŏr-dĭ-ŏnh.) An accordeon.
Accordiren, *Ger.* (äk-kŏr-dē-r'n.) To accord.
Accórdo, *It.* (äk-kŏr-dō.) A chord, a concord, a consonance.
Accórdo consono, *It.* (äk-kŏr-dō kŏn-sō-nō.) A concord.
Accórdo díssono, *It.* (äk-kŏr-dō dēs-sō-nō.) A discord.
Accordoir, *Fr.* (äk-kŏr-dwä.) A tuning key, tuning hammer.
Accreseéndo, *It.* (äk-krĕ-shän-dō.) Increasing, augmenting in tone and power.
Accrescere, *It.* (äk-krĕ-shä-rĕ.) To increase, to augment.
Accreseiménto, *It.* (äk-krĕ-shē-mān-tō.) Increase, augmentation of sound.
Accresciúto, *It.* (äk-krĕ-shē-oo-tō.) Increased, superfluous, augmented in respect to intervals.

ACUT

Acceleratamente, *It.* (ät-shĕl-ä-rä-tä-män-tĕ.) Speedily, swiftly.
A Cemb. An abbreviation of A Cembalo.
A Cémbalo, *It.* (ä tshäm-bä-lō.) For the harpsichord.
Acento, *Spa.* (ä-thän-tō.) Accent, a modulation of the voice.
Acetabulum, *Lat.* (ä-sĕ-täb-ū-lŭm.) An ancient instrument of music.
Achromatic music. Simple music in which modulations seldom occur and few accidents, flats and sharps are used.
Acht, *Ger.* (äkht.) Eight.
Achtel, *Ger.* (äkh-t'l.) Eighth, quaver or eighth note.
Achtelnote, *Ger.* (ähk-t'l-nōt-ĕ.) A quaver, eighth note.
Achtelpause, *Ger.* (äkh-t'l-pou-sĕ.) A quaver rest.
Achtstimmig, *Ger.* (äkht-stĭm-mĭg.) For eight voices.
A ciula, *It.* (ä koo-lä.) A Portuguese dance similar to the fandango.
A cinque, *It.* (ä tshĕn-quĕ.) For five voices or instruments.
Acolytes. Persons employed in the musical services of the Romish church.
Acolythi, *Gr.* (äk-ō-lē-thē.) Acolytes.
Acolythia, *Gr.* (äk-ō-lē-thī-ä.) The order of service observed in the Greek church.
Acompanamiento, *Spa.* (ä-kŏm-pä-nä-mē-än-tō.) Accompaniment.
Acompanar, *Spa.* (ä-kŏm-pän-yär.) To sing or play in concert with others.
A Compas, *Spa.* (a kŏm-päs.) In true musical time.
Acordar, *Spa.* (ä-kŏr-där.) To tune musical instruments.
Acorde, *Spa.* (ä-kŏr-dä.) Harmony of sounds.
Acostica, *Spa.* (ä-kōs-tĭ-kä.) Acoustics.
Aconsmate, *Fr.* (ä-koos-mät.) The sound of instruments or voices heard in the air.
Acoustics. The science of sound, by a knowledge of which we are enabled to determine the relations of tones and the ratios of intervals produced by vibrations.
Acoustique, *Fr.* (ä-koos-tēk.) Acoustics.
Acte, *Fr.* (äkt.) An act; a part of an opera.
Acte de cadence, *Fr.* (äkt dŭh kä-dänhs.) A cadence, a final part.
Acteur, *Fr.* (äk-tŭr.) An actor, an operatic performer.
Actor. A theatrical or operatic performer.
Actress. A female actor.
Actrice, *Fr.* (äk-trēs.) An actress.
Acts. Parts of an opera or theatrical entertainment.
Act-tunes. The pieces formerly played between the acts of a drama.
Acuite, *Fr.* (äk-weet.) Acuteness.
Acustica, *It.* (ä-kooz-tĭ-kä.) Acoustics, the doctrine of sounds.
Acustice, *Spa.* (ä-koos-tĭk.) Acoustics.
Acustisch, *Ger.* (ä-koos-tĭsh.) Acoustic.
Acuta, *It.* (ä-koo-tä.) Acute, shrill; also, a shrill-toned organ stop.
Acute. High, shrill, sharp as to pitch.

ă ate, ă add, ä arm, ĕ eve, ĕ end, ĭ ice, ĭ ill, ō old, ŏ odd, ô dove, oo moon, ū lute, ŭ but, ü French sound.

ACUT

Acuteness. Elevation or sharpness of sound.
Ad, *Lat.* At, to, for, by.
Adag. An abbreviation of Adagio.
Adagiétto, *It.* (ä-dä-jĕ-ăt-tō.) A short adagio movement.
Adágio, *It.* (ä-dä-jĕ-ō.) A very slow degree of movement, although not the slowest; requiring much taste and expression.
Adágio assái, *It.* (ä-dä-jĕ-ō äs-sä-ĕ.) Very slow and with much expression.
Adágio cantábile e sostenúto, *It.* (ä-dä-jĕ-ō kăn-tä-bĕ-lä ä sōs-tä-noo-tō.) Slow, in a singing style and sustained.
Adágio con gravita, *It.* (ä-dä-jĕ-ō kŏn grä-vĕ-tä.) Slow, with gravity and majesty.
Adágio mólto, *It.* (ä-dä-jĕ-ō mŏl-tō.) Very slow and expressive.
Adágio non tróppo, *It.* (ä-dä-jĕ-ō nŏn trŏp-pō.) Not too slow.
Adágio patético, *It.* (ä-dä-jĕ-ō pä-tă-tĕ-kō.) Slowly and pathetically.
Adágio pesánte, *It.* (ä-dä-jĕ-ō pä-zăn-tĕ.) Slowly and heavily.
Adágio poi allégro, *It.* (ä-dä-jĕ-ō pō-ĕ äl-lä-grō.) Slow, then quick.
Adágio quasi una Fantasia, *It.* (ä-dä-jĕ-ō quä-sĕ oo-nä făn-tä-zĕ-ä.) An adagio similar to a fantasia.
Adágio religióso, *It.* (ä-dä-jĕ-ō rä-lĕ-jĕ-ō-zō.) Slowly, and in a devotional manner.
Adagíssimo, *It.* (ä-dä-jĕs-sĕ-mō.) Extremely slow.
Adaptation. A union of sentiment between the words and the music.
Adasio, *It.* (ä-dă-zĕ-ō.) Adagio.
Adattare, *It.* (ä-dä-tä-rĕ.) Adapted.
Adattazione. *It.* (ä-dät-tä-tsĕ-ō-nĕ.) Adaptation.
Ad captandum, *Lat.* In a light and brilliant style.
Added Lines. Short lines, either above or below the staff; ledger lines.
Added Notes. Notes written on or between the added lines.
Added Sixth. A sixth added to a fundamental chord.
Additáto, *It.* (äd-dĕ-tä-tō.) Fingered.
Additional Keys. Those keys of a pianoforte which extend above F in Alt.
Addolorato, *It.* (äd-dō-lō-rä-to.) With sad and melancholy expression.
Addottrinante, *It.* (äd-dŏt-trĕ-năn-tĕ.) Teacher, professor.
A demi-jeu, *Fr.* (ä dĕ-mĕ-zhū.) } With half
A demi-voix, *Fr.* (ä dĕ-mĕ-vwä.) } the voice or tone. See Mezza Voce.
Adept. A thorough composer, performer or singer.
A deux, *Fr.* (ä dŭh.) For two voices or instruments.
A deux Temps, *Fr.* (ä dŭh tänh.) In *two* time; two equal notes in a measure.
Adiaponon, *Gr.* (ä-dĭ-äp-ō-nŏn.) A species of pianoforte with six octaves; invented in 1820 by Lahuster, a watchmaker of Vienna.
Adiratamente, *It.* (ä-dĕ-rä-tä-măn-tĕ.) } Angrily,
Adiráto, *It.* (äd-ĕ-rä-tō.) } sternly.
A Dirittúra, *It.* (ä dĕ-rĕ-too-rä.) Directly, straight.

ÆOLO

Adjunct notes. Unaccented auxiliary notes.
Adjutant's call. A drum-beat directing the band and field music to take the right of the line
Adjuvant, *Ger.* (ăd-yoo-vănt.) The deputy-master of the choristers; assistant to an organist.
Ad lib. An abbreviation of Ad libitum.
Ad libitum, *Lat.* (äd lĭb-ĭ-tŭm.) At will, at pleasure; changing the time of a particular passage at the discretion of the performer.
Adornaménte, *It.* (ä-dŏr-nä-măn-tĕ.) Gaily, neatly, elegantly.
Adornaménto, *It.* (ä-dŏr-nä-măn-tō.) An ornament, an embellishment.
Adornaménti, *It.* (ä-dŏr-nä-măn-tĕ.) Embellishments.
A dúe, or, A 2, *It.* (ä doo-ĕ.) For two voices or instruments; a duet.
A dúe clarini, *It.* (ä doo-ĕ klä-rĕ-nĕ.) For two trumpets.
A dúe córde, *It.* (ä doo-ĕ kŏr-dĕ.) Upon two strings.
A dúe córi, &c. (ä doo-ĕ kō-rĕ.) For two choirs.
A dúe Soprani, *It.* (ä doo-ĕ sō-prä-nĕ.) For two trebles.
A dúe stroménti, *It.* (ä doo-ĕ strō-măn-tĕ.) For two instruments.
A dúe vóce, *It.* (ä doo-ĕ vō-tshĕ.) For two voices.
Adonia, *Gr.* (ä-dō-nĕ-ä.) A solemn feast of the ancients at which hymns and odes were sung
Adonico, *Spa.* (ä-dō-nĕ-ko.) A Latin verse consisting of a dactyl and spondĕe.
Adonic verse. A verse consisting of one long, two short, and two long syllables.
Adornamento, *It.* (ä-dŏr-nä-măn-tō.) An ornament.
Adoucir, *Fr.* (ä-doo-sĕr.) To soften, to flatten.
Adufazo, *Spa.* (ä-doo-fä-thō.) To strike a timbrel.
Adufe, *Spa.* (ä-doo-fă.) Timbrel, tamborine.
Adnfero, *Spa.* (ä-doo-fă-rō.) A tamborine player.
Adulatoriamente, *It.* (ä-doo-lä-tŏr-ĕ-ä-măn-tĕ.) In a caressing, flattering manner.
Ædophone. A musical instrument invented in the eighteenth century.
A dur, *Ger.* (ä door.) The key of A major.
Ænator. *Lat.* (ĕ-nă-tŏr.) A name given by the ancients to one who blows a brazen horn; a trumpeter.
Æolian. One of the ancient Greek modes; referring to the winds; played upon by the wind.
Æolian Harp. An instrument invented by Kircher about the middle of the seventeenth century. The tones are produced by the strings being so arranged that the air causes vibration among them when it passes through.
Æolian Lyre. The Æolian Harp.
Æolian Mute. A combination of the Æolian pitch-pipe and the mute for the violin.
Æolian Pianoforte. A pianoforte with an Æolian or reed instrument attached in such a way that one set of keys serves for both, or for either singly as the performer desires.
Æolodicon, *Gr.* (ĕ-ō-lō-dĭ-kŏn.) A keyed instrument, the tone of which resembles that of the organ, and is produced by steel springs, which are put in vibration by means of bellows.
Æolodion, *Gr.* (ĕ-ō-lō-dĭ-ŏn.) An Æolodicon.

ā ale, ă add, ä arm, ē eve, ĕ end, ī ice, ĭ ill, ō old, ŏ odd, ô dave, oo moon, ū lute, ŭ but, ü French sound.

ÆOLO

Æolopantalon. An instrument combining the pianoforte and Æolodicon.
Æolsharfe, Ger. (ā-ŏls-här-fĕ.) An Æolian Harp.
Æolus' Harp. An instrument resembling the Æolian Harp, made of strings stretched between pieces of wood.
Æolus modus. The Æolian or fifth. Authentic mode of the Greeks, nearly allied to the Phrygian mode. The scale is the same as the old scale of A minor without any accidentals. See Greek modes.
Æotana, Gr. (ē-ō-tä-nä.) A very small musical instrument made of several short metallic reeds fastened in a frame and played upon by the breath of the performer.
Æquisonans, Lat. (ĕ-quī-sō-näns.) A unison; of the same or like sound.
Æquisonant. A term given to unisons, and also frequently to octaves, as they seem one and the same sound.
Æquisonus. Sounding in unison; concordant.
Æquo animo, Lat. (ē-quō ăni-mō.) Quietly, with serenity.
Ære recurvo, Lat. (ē-rē rē-cŭr-vō.) A military wind instrument resembling a trumpet; the būcēna.
Ærophone. (ē-rō-fōn.) A French reed instrument of the melodeon class.
Æsthetics, Gr. (ēs-thĕt-Iks.) The rules of good taste, the laws of the beautiful. In musical art that which relates to sentiment, expression and the power of music over the soul.
Æusserste Stimmen, Ger. pl. (ois-sērs-tĕ stĭm-mĕn.) The extreme parts.
Ævia, It. (ē-vē-ä.) An abbreviation of the word Alleluia.
Affectacion, Spa. (ā-fĕk-tä-thē-ōn.) Affectation.
Affabile, It. (ăf-fä-bē-lĕ.) In a courteous and pleasing manner.
Affabilita.
Affabilmente, It. (ăf-fä-bē-l-män-tĕ.) With ease and elegance; with freedom; in a pleasing and agreeable manner.
Affannato, It. (ăf-fä-nä-tō.) Sad, mournful, distressed.
Affannoso, It. (ăf-fä-nō-zō.) With mournful expression.
Affectatio, Lat. (ăf-fĕk-tä-shĭ-ō.) Affectation.
Affectation. An attempt to assume or exhibit what is not natural or real.
Affectirt, Ger. (ăf-fĕk-tärt.) With affection.
Affectueux, Fr. (ăf-fĕk-tū-ŭh.) Affectionate.
Affet. An abbreviation of Affetuoso.
Affettatamente, It. (ăf-făt-tä-tä-män-tĕ.) Very affectedly.
Affettazione, It. (ăf-fĕt-tä-tsē-ō-nĕ.) An artificial style.
Affettivo, It. (ăf-fĕt-tē-vō.) Affecting; pathetic.
Affetto, It. (ăf-făt-tō.) Feeling, tenderness, pathos.
Affettuosamente, It. (ăf-fĕt-too-ō-zä-män-tĕ.) With tenderness and feeling.
Affettuosissimo, It. (ăf-fĕt-too-ō-sēs-ss-mō.) With pathos; with tender expression.
Affettuóso, It. (ăf-fĕt-too-ō-zō.) With mournful expression.

AGNU

Affettuóso di molto, It. (ăf-fĕt-too-ō-zō dē mōl-tō.) With much feeling.
Affiche de comédie, Fr. (ăf-fĭsh dŭh kō-mā-dē.) A play-bill.
Affinity. A quality possessed by those chords that admit of an easy and natural progression from one to the other.
Affiocamento, It. (ăf-fē-ō-kä-mān-tō.) Hoarseness.
Affiocato, It. (ăf-fē-ō-kä-tō.) Hoarse.
Afflitto, It. (ăf-flēt-tō.) Sorrowfully,
Afflizióne, It. (ăf-flē-tsē-ō-nĕ.) with mournful expression.
Affreto. An abbreviation of Affrettando.
Affrettándo, It. (ăf-frĕt-tăn-dō.) Hurrying,
Affrettáte, It. (ăf-frĕt-tä-tĕ.) quickening, accelerating the time.
Affrettóso, It. (ăf-frĕt-tō-zō.) Quick, accelerated, hurried.
Aficionado, Spa. (ă-fē-thĭ-ō-nä-dō.) An amateur.
Afinacion, Spa. (ă-fē-nä-thĭ-ōn.) Tuning of instruments.
Afinador, Spa. (ă-fē-nä-dōr.) A key with which stringed instruments are tuned.
Afinar, Spa. (ă-fī-när.) To tune musical instruments.
A Fofa, Por. (ă fō-fä.) A Portuguese dance resembling the Fandango.
After note. A small note occurring on an unaccented part of the measure, and taking its time from the note preceding it.
After notes, double. Two after notes, taking their time from the preceding note.
Agévole, It. (ä-jä-vō-lĕ.) Lightly,
Agevolménte, It. (ä-jä-vōl-män-tĕ.) easily, with agility.
Agevolézza, It. (ä-jä-vō-lā-tsä.) Lightness, ease, agility.
Aggiustaménte, It. (äd-jē-oos-tä-män-tĕ.) In strict time.
Aggiustare, It. (äd-jī-oos-tä-rĕ.) Adjusted,
Aggiustato, It. (äd-jī-oos-tä-tō.) arranged, adapted.
Agilita, It. (ä-jēl-ē-tä.) Lightness, agility.
Agilita, con. It. With agility, with lightness, with rapidity.
Agilménte, It. (ä-jēl-män-tĕ.) Lively, gay.
Aggravér la fugue, Fr. (ăg-grä-vā lä füg.) To augment the subject of a fugue.
Agiren, Ger. (ä-ghē-r'n.) To act, to mimic.
Agitamento, It. (ä-jē-tä-mān-tō.) Agitation, restlessness, motion.
Agitáto, It. (äj-ē-tä-tō.) Agitated, hurried, restless.
Agitato allegro, It. (äj-ē-tä-tō äl-lā-grō.) A nervous, agitated and rapid movement.
Agitato con passióne, It. (äj-ē-tä-tō kōn pässē-ō-nĕ.) Passionately agitated.
Agite, Fr. (ä-zhēt.) Agitated.
Agli, It. pl. (äl-yē.) See Alla.
Agnus Dei, Lat. (äg-nūs dā-ē.) Lamb of God; one of the principal movements in a mass.

ă ale, ă add, ä arm, ē eve, ĕ end, ī ice, ĭ ill, ō old, ŏ odd, ō dove, oo moon, ū lute, ŭ but, ü French sound.

AGOG

Agoge, *Gr.* (ă-gō-ghĕ.) Used by the ancient Greeks. A species of melody in which the notes proceeded by contiguous degrees ascending and descending the scale.
Agoge rhythmica, *Gr.* (ă-gō-ghĕ rĭth-mē-kă.) Time, rhythmical division.
A Grand Chœur, *Fr.* (kūr.) For the entire chorus.
A Grand Orchestre, *Fr.* (ŏr-kĕstr.) For the full or complete orchestra.
Agreménts, *Fr. pl.* (ă-grā-mänh.) Embellishments, ornaments.
Ai, *It.* (ă-ē.) To the; in the style of.
Aigre, *Fr.* (ăgr.) Harsh, sharp.
Aigrement, *Fr.* (ăgr-mänh.) Sharply, harshly.
Aigu, *Fr.* (ă-gü.) Acute, high, sharp, shrill.
A in alt. The A placed upon the first upper added line.
A in altissimo. An octave above A in Alt.
Air. A short song, melody or tune, with or without words. A series of tones bearing a certain relation to each other by their symmetry and regularity, producing a unity of effect, which is called "a tune."
Air a boire, *Fr.* (ār ă bwār.) A drinking song.
Air a reprises, *Fr.* (ār ă rĕh-prēz.) A catch.
Air chantant, *Fr.* (ār shänh-tänh.) An air in graceful, melodious style.
Air détaché, *Fr.* (ār dā-tă-shā.) A single air or melody extracted from an opera or larger work.
Air Ecossais, *Fr.* (ār ă-cōs-sā.) A Scotch air.
Air Irlandais, *Fr.* (ār ēr-länh-dā.) Irish air.
Air Italien, *Fr.* (ār ĭ-tăl-ĭ-änh.) An Italian air.
Air rapide, *Fr.* (ār rā-pēd.) A flourish.
Airs des bateliers Vénétiens, *Fr.* (ār dē bă-tēl-ēr vē-nā-sĭ-änh.) Melodies sung by the Venetian gondoliers or boatmen.
Airs Français, *Fr.* (ār fränh-sā.) French airs.
Airs Russes, *Fr.* (ār rüs) Russian airs.
Airs tendres, (ār tänh-dr.) Amatory airs, love songs.
Air varié, *Fr.* (ār vă-rĭ-ā.) Air with variations; an air embellished and ornamented.
Ais, *Ger.* (ois.) The note A sharp.
Ais-dur, *Ger.* (ois-door.) The key of A$\sharp$ major. This key is not in use, being represented by B♭ major.
Ais-moll, *Ger.* (ois-möll.) The key of A$\sharp$ minor. Not in use, being represented by B♭ minor.
Aisé, *Fr.* (ă-zā.) Glad, joyful; also, easy, facile, convenient.
Aisément, *Fr.* (ā-zā-mänh.) Easily, freely.
Aiyar, *Ara.* (ā-yăr.) Air.
Ajakli-Keman, *Tur.* (ā-yăk-lā kā-mān.) A Turkish instrument resembling the violin.
Akkord, *Ger.* (ăk-kŏrd.) See Accord.
Akromat, *Ger.* (ăk-rō-măt.) A musician, a singer.
Akromatisch, *Ger.* (ăk-rō-mă-tĭsh.) See Achromatic.
Akustik, *Ger.* (ă-koos-tĭk.) See Acoustics.
Al, *It.* (ăl.) To the, in the style of.
Alabado, *Spa.* (ă-lă-bă-dō.) Hymns sung in praise of the sacrament.
A l'abandon, *Fr.* (ă lă-bänh-dōnh.) Without restraint; with passionate expression.

ALLA

A la chasse, *Fr.* (ă lă shäss.) In hunting style.
A la Française, *Fr.* (ă lă fränh-sā.) In the French style.
A la Grecque, *Fr.* (ă lă grĕk.) Choruses introduced by the French at the end of each act of a drama in imitation of the old Greek tragedies.
A la mesure, *Fr.* (ă lă mā-zūr) In time; synonymous with A Tempo.
A la militaire, *Fr.* (ă lă mĭl-ĭ-tār.) In military or march style.
A l'antique, *Fr.* (ă länh-tĕk.) Antique, in the style of the ancients.
A la Polacca, *It.* (ă lă pō-lăk-kă.) In the style of the Polacca.
Alarum trumpet. The trumpet that sounds the alarm or onset in the military service.
A la Savoyarde, *Fr.* (ă lă să-vwă-yărd.) In the style of the airs of Savoy.
Albada, *Spa.* (ăl-bă-dă.) A morning serenade.
Alberti Bass. A species of bass, the chords of which are taken in arpeggios of a particular kind; ex., etc. It was so called because first used by Domenico Alberti.
Albogue, *Spa.* (ăl-bō-gwā.) An instrument belonging to the flute species.
Alboguero, *Spa.* (ăl-bō-gwā-rō.) One who plays on the Albogue.
Alborada, *Spa.* (ăl-bō-rā-dă.) The music of a morning serenade.
Alcaics. Several kinds of verse, so called from Alcaeus, a lyric poet and their inventor.
Alemanian. Pertaining to Aleman, a lyric poet.
Alemanian verse. A verse consisting of six anapests or their equivalents, with the exception of the last two syllables, which are omitted.
Aleluya, *Spa.* (ă-lā-loo-yă.) Hallelujah.
Alemana, *Spa.* (ă-lă-mă-nă.) An old Spanish dance.
Alexandrian verse. A verse consisting of twelve syllables, or twelve and thirteen alternately.
Al fine, *It.* (ăl fē-nē.) To the end.
Al fine, e pói la códa, (ăl fē-nē ă pō-ĕ lă kō-dă.) After playing to where the Fine is marked, go on to the coda.
Aliquot tones. Accessory or secondary sounds; tones indistinctly heard, which are always produced with the principal tone, at harmonic intervals above it.
A l'Italiénne, *Fr.* (ă lĭ-tăl-ē-ănh.) In the Italian style.
A livre ouvert, *Fr.* (ă lēvr oo-vār.) At the opening of the book. To play a piece at first sight.
Al, *It.* (ăl.)
All', *It.* (ăl.)
Alla, *It.* (ăl-lă.) } To the; in the style or manner of.
Alle, *It.* (ăl-lē.)
Agli, *It.* (ăl-yē.)
Allo, *It.* (ăl-lō.)
Alla Bréve, *It.* (ăl-lă brā-vē.) A quick species of common time, formerly used in church music. It is marked ₵ and sometimes ₵. Each bar contains the value of a bréve — equal to two sem-

ă ale, ă add, ă arm, ĕ eve, ĕ end, ī ice, ĭ ill, ō old, ŏ odd, ō dove, oo moon, ū lute, ŭ but, ū French sound.

ALLA

ibreves, or four minims. Modern composers often subdivide these bars into two parts, each containing two minims, and this is called Alla Capélla time to distinguish it from the Alla Bréve, from which it is derived.

Alla cáccia, *It.* (äl-lä kät-tshē-ä.) In the style of hunting music.

Alla cámera, *It.* (äl-lä kä-mē-rä.) In the style of chamber music.

Alla Cappélla, *It.* (äl-lä käp-pāl-lä.) In the church or sacred style; derived from Alla Bréve style, the bar being sub-divided. See Alla Bréve.

Alla dirítta, *It.* (äl-lä dē-rē-tä.) In direct ascending or descending style. With the right hand.

Alla Francése, *It.* (äl-lä frän-tshā-zē.) } In the
Alla Franzése, *It.* (äl-lä frän-tsä-zē.) } French style.

Alla Hanácca, *It.* (äl-lä hä-näk-kä.) A kind of dance resembling the Polonaise.

Alla Mádre, *It.* (äl-lä mä-drē.) To the Virgin Mary. Songs and hymns addressed to the Virgin Mary.

Alla maniera Turka, *It.* (äl-lä mä-nē-ä-ra toor-kä.) In the Turkish style.

Alla márcia, *It.* (äl-lä mär-tshē-ä.) In the style of a march.

Alla militáre, *It.* (äl-lä mē-lē-tä-rē.) In the military style.

Alla modérna, *It.* (äl-lä mō-där-nä.) In the modern style.

Alla Morésco, *It.* (äl-lä mō-rās-kō.) In the Moorish style.

Alla Palestrína, *It.* (äl-lä Pä-lĕs-trē-nä.) In the style of Palestrina; in the ecclesiastical style.

Alla Polácca, *It.* (äl-lä pō-läk-kä.) In the time and style of a Polonaise or Polish dance.

Alla riversa, *It.* (äl-lä rē-vär-sä.) In an opposite direction.

Alla rovérscio, *It.* (äl-lä rō-vär-shī-o.) In a reverse or contrary movement.

Alla Russe, *It.* (äl-lä roos-sē.) In Russian style.

Alla Scozzése, *It.* (äl-lä skō-tsā-zē.) In Scotch style.

Alla Siciliána, *It.* (äl-lä sĭ-tshēl-ĭ-ä-nä.) In the style of the Sicilian shepherd's dance.

Alla strétta, *It.* (äl-lä strāt-tä.) Increasing the time; accelerating the movement. In close, compressed style.

Alla Tedésca, *It.* (äl-lä tē-däz-kä.) In the German style.

Alla Túrka, *It.* (äl-lä toor-kä.) In the Turkish or Oriental style.

Alla uníssono, *It.* (äl-lä oo-nē-sō-nō.) See All' Unisons.

Alla Veneziána, *It.* (äl-lä vē-nä-tsē-ä-nä.) In the Venetian style.

Alla Zíngara, *It.* (äl-lä tsēn-gä-rä.) In the style of gipsy songs.

Alla zóppa, *It.* (äl-lä tsōp-pä.) In a constrained and limping style.

All' antíca, *It.* (äl-län-tē-kä.) In the ancient style.

All' Espagnuóla, *It.* (äl-lĕss-pän-yoo-ō-lä.) In the Spanish style.

All' Inglése, *It.* (äl-lēn-glä-zē.) In the English style.

ALLE

All' Italiána, *It.* (äl-lē-tä-lē-ä-nä.) In the Italian style.

Alla 3 za, *It.* A sign, which, when placed above the staff, indicates that with each note played, a note a third higher must be played, and when placed below the staff, a note a third lower.

Alla 6 ta. A sign, which when placed above the staff indicates that with each note played, a note a sixth higher must be played, and when placed below the staff, a note a sixth lower.

Alle, *It.* (äl-lē.) To the; In the style of.

Alle, *Ger* (äl-lē.) All: alle Instrumente, all the instruments; the whole orchestra.

Allegraménte, *It.* (äl-lē-grä-mān-tē.) } Gaily,
Allégrement, *Fr.* (äl-lē-grĕ-mänh.) } joyfully, quickly.

Allegránte, *It.* (äl-lē-grän-tē.) Joyous, mirthful.

Allegratívo, *It.* (äl-lē-grä-tē-vō.) Gladdening, cheering, blithe.

Allegrettíno, *It.* (äl-lē-grĕt-tē-nō.) A diminutive of Allegrétto and rather slower.

Allegrétto, *It.* (äl-lē-grāt-tō.) Rather light and cheerful but not as quick as Allégro.

Allegrétto Scherzándo, *It.* (äl-lē-grāt-tō skĕr-tsän-dō.) Moderately playful and lively.

Allegrézza, *It.* (äl-lē-grät-zä.) } Joy, gladness,
Allegría, *It.* (äl-lē-grē-ä.) } cheerfulness, gaiety.

Allegrézza, con. *It.* With cheerfulness, joy, animation.

Allegri di bravura, *It.* (äl-lē-grē dē brä-voo-rä.) Compositions written in a brilliant and effective style.

Allegrissimaménte, *It.* (äl-lē-grē-sē-mä-mān-tē.) Very joyfully, with great animation.

Allegríssimo, *It.* (äl-lē-grēs-sē-mō.) Extremely quick and lively; the superlative of Allégro.

Allégro, *Fr. and It.* (äl-lä-grō.) Quick, lively; a rapid, vivacious movement, the opposite to the pathetic, but it is frequently modified by the addition of other words that change its expression: as,

Allégro agitato, *It.* (äl-lä-grō äj-ē-tä-tō.) Quick, with anxiety and agitation.

Allégro appassionato, *It.* (äl-lä-grō äp-päs-sē-ō-nä-tō.) Passionately joyful.

Allégro assái, *It.* (äl-lä-grō äs-sä-ē.) Very quick.

Allégro brillánte, *It.* (äl-lä-grō brēl-län-tē.) Requiring a brilliant style of execution.

Allégro cómodo, *It.* (äl-lä-grō kō-mō-dō.) With a convenient degree of quickness.

Allégro con brío, *It.* (äl-lä-grō kōn brē-ō.) Quick, with brilliancy.

Allégro con briôso, *It.* (äl-lä-grō kōn brē-ō-zō.) Joyful and bold.

Allégro con fuóco, *It.* (äl-lä-grō kōn foo-ō-kō.) Quick, with fire and animation.

Allégro con fuócoso, *It.* (äl-lä-grō kōn foo-ō-kō-zō.) With a great deal of fire and animation.

Allégro con moltissimo moto, *It.* (äl-lä-grō kōn mōl-tēs-sē-mō mō-tō.) A very quick allégro.

Allégro con moto, *It.* Quick, with more than the usual degree of movement.

ă *ale,* ă *add,* ă *arm,* ĕ *eve,* ĕ *end,* ī *ice,* ĭ *ill,* ō *old,* ŏ *odd,* ô *dove,* oo *moon,* ū *lute,* ŭ *but,* ü *French sound.*

ALLE

Allégro con spírito, *It.* (äl-lā́-grō kōn spē-rē-tō.) Quick, with much spirit.
Allégro di bravúra, *It.* (äl-lā́-grō dē brä-voo-rä.) Quick, with brilliant and spirited execution.
Allégro di molto, *It.* (äl-lā́-grō dē mŏl-tō.) Exceedingly quick and animated.
Allégro furioso, *It.* (äl-lā́-grō foo-rē-ō-zō.) Quick, with fury and impetuosity.
Allégro gaio, *It.* (äl-lā́-grō gä-ē-ō.) In a gay and spirited style.
Allégro giústo, *It.* (äl-lā́-grō joos-tō.) Quick, with exactness; in steady and precise time.
Allégro ma grazioso, *It.* (äl-lā́-grō mä grä-tse-ō-zō.) Quick, but gracefully.
Allégro ma non présto, *It.* (äl-lā́-grō mä nōn prăs-tō.) Quick, but not so fast as Presto.
Allégro ma non tánto, *It.* (äl-lā́-grō mä nōn tăn-tō.)
Allégro ma non tróppo, *It.* (äl-lā́-grō mä nōn trop-pō.) Quick and lively, but not too fast.
Allégro moderáto, *It.* (äl-lā́-grō mŏd-ĕ-rä-tō.) Moderately quick.
Allégro mólto, *It.* (äl-lā́-grō mŏl-tō.) Very quick and animated.
Allégro non mólto, *It.* (äl-lā́-grō nōn-mŏl-tō.) Not very fast.
Allégro non tánto, *It.* (äl-lā́-grō nōn tăn-tō.)
Allégro non tróppo, *It.* (äl-lā́-grō nōn trŏp-pō.) Not too fast.
Allégro risoluto, *It.* (äl-lā́-grō rē-zō-loo-tō.) Quick, with vigor and decision.
Allégro velóce, *It.* (äl-lā́-grō vĕ-lō-tshē.) Quick, with extreme velocity.
Allégro vivace, *It.* äl-lā́-grō vē-vä-tshē.) With vivacity, very rapidly.
Allégro vívo, *It.* (äl-lā́-grō vē-vō.) With great life and rapidity.
Allegrúsio, *It.* (äl-lĕ-groo-zē-ō.) Good humored, sprightly.
Alleín, *Ger.* (äl-īn.) Alone, single.
Alleinsang, *Ger.* (äl-īn-säng.) A solo.
Alleinsänger, *Ger.* (äl-īn-sāng-ĕr.) A solo singer.
Alleinspíeler, *Ger.* (äl-īn-spē-lĕr.) One who plays a solo.
Allelnia, *Fr.* (äl-lĕ-loo-yä.) Praise the Lord; Hallelujah.
Allelujah, *Heb.* (äl-lĕ-loo-yä.) An ascription of praise; Hallelujah.
Allemande, *Fr.* (äll-mänhd.) A German air; also, a slow dance or melody of four crotchets in each measure, peculiar to Germany and Switzerland.
Allentaménto, *It.* (äl-lĕn-tä-*măn*-tō.) } Relaxation, giving way, slackening of the time.
Allentáto, *It.* (äl-lĕn-tä-tō.) }
Allentándo, *It.* (äl-lĕn-*tăn*-dō.) Decreasing the time until the close.
Alleramdo, *It.* (äl-lĕr-ä-*măn*-tō.) A breathing time; a respite.
All' Espagnuola, *It.* (äl-lĕs-pän-yoo-ō-lä.) In the Spanish style.
Allied tones. Accessory tones.
Alliévo, *It.* (äl-lē-ā-vō.) A scholar, a pupil.
All' improviso, *It.* (äl-l'ĕm-prō-vē-zō.) }
All' improvista, *It.* (äl-l'ĕm-prō-vēs-tä) } Without previous study; extemporaneously.

ALSE

All' Inglése, *It.* (äl-l'-ōu-*glā*-zē.) In the English style.
All' Italiána, *It.* (äl-l'-ē-tä-lē-ä-nä.) In the Italian style.
Allmählich, *Ger.* (äl-mä-līkh.) Little by little.
Al' lóco, *It.* (äl lō-kō.) To the previous place; a term of reference.
All' Ongarése, *It.* (äl ōn-gä-*rā*-zē.) In the Hungarian style.
Allonger, *Fr.* (äl-lōnh-zhā.) To lengthen, prolong, delay.
Allonger l'archet, *Fr.* (äl-lōnh-zhā l' är-shā.) To lengthen or prolong the stroke of the bow in violin music.
All' ottáva, *It.* (äl ŏt-tä-vä.) In the octave; meaning that one part must play an octave above or below another. It is frequently met with in scores and orchestra parts.
All' ottáva alta, *It.* (äl ŏt-tä-vä äl-tä.) In the octave above.
All' ottáva bassa, *It.* (äl ŏt-tä-vä bäs-sä.) In the octave below.
Alla roversico, *It.* (äl-lä rō-vĕr-sē-kō.) By a contrary movement.
All' unísono. *It.* (äl oo-nē-sō-nō.) In unison; a succession of unisons or octaves.
All' 8va. An abbreviation of All' ottáva.
Alma, *Ara.* (äl-mä.) The name given in the East to singing and dancing girls, who are hired to furnish amusement at public entertainments, and to sing dirges at funerals, etc.
Almain. } The name of an old slow dance of
Alman. } a dignified character.
Almand. }
Almanes, *pl.* See Alman.
Alma Redemptoris, *Lat.* (äl-mä rē-dĕm-tō-rīs.) A hymn to the Virgin.
Almees, *Ara.* (äl-mās.) Arabian dancing girls.
Almehs, *Tur.* (äl-mās.) Turkish singing and dancing girls.
Alpenhorn, *Ger.* (äl-p'n-hōrn.) The Alpine, or cowhorn.
Al piacére, *It.* (äl pē-ä-*tshā*-rĕ.) At pleasure. See A piacére.
Al più, *It.* (äl pē-oo.) The most.
Alphabet. The seven letters used in music, A, B, C, D, E, F, G. When more are required, either ascending or descending, the letters are repeated in the same order.
Alpine Horn. An instrument made of the bark of a tree, and used by the Alpine shepherds for conveying sounds a long distance.
Al rigóre di tempo, *It.* (äl rē-gō-rē dē *tĕm*-pō.) In very rigorous and strict time.
Al rigóre del tempo, *It.* (äl rē-gō-rē dĕl *tĕm*-pō.) In very rigorous and strict time.
Al riverso, *It.* (äl rē-vĕr-sō.) Reverse, backward motion.
A la Russe, *Fr.* (ä lä rües.) In the Russian style.
Al Seg. An abbreviation of Al Segno.
Al Segno, *It.* (äl săn-yō.) To the sign; meaning that the performer must return to the sign 𝄋 in a previous part of the piece and play from that place to the word Fine, or the mark ⁀ over a double bar.

ā ale, ă add, ä arm, ē eve, ĕ end, ī ice, ĭ ill, ō old, ŏ odd, ô dove, oo moon, ū lute, ŭ but, ü French sound.

ALT

Alt, *It.* (ält.) High. This term is applied to the notes which lie between F on the fifth line of treble staff and G on the fourth added line below.
Alta, *It.* (äl-tä.) High, or higher; Ottáva álta, an octave higher.
Alta, *Spa.* (äl-tä.) A dance formerly used in Spain.
Alta-Viola, *It.* (äl-tä vē-ō-lä.) A counter tenor viol.
Alt Clarinet, *Ger.* (ält klär-ĭu-ĕt.) A large clarinet, a fifth deeper than the ordinary clarinet.
Al Tedésco, *It.* (äl tĕ-däs-kō.) In the German style.
Altera prima donna, *It.* (äl-tĕ-rä prē-mä dôn-nä.) One of two principal female singers.
Alteratio, *Lat.* (äl-tĕ-rā-shī-o.)
Alteráto, *It.* (äl-tĕ-rä-tō.)
Altéré, *Fr.* äl-tĕ-rā.)
Changed, angmented. In composition it means doubling the value of a note.
Alterati suoni, *It.* (äl-tĕ-rä-tē swō-nē.) Sounds raised or lowered by sharps and flats.
Altered notes, Notes changed by accidentals.
Altered triads. The diatonic dissonant triad, with its third sometimes sharped and sometimes flatted.
Alternaménte, *It.* (äl-tĕr-nä-mān-tĕ.) Alternating, by turns.
Alternándo, *It.* (äl-tĕr-nän-dō.) See Alternaménte.
Alternations. Melodies composed for bells.
Alternativo, *It.* (äl-tĕr-nä-tē-vō.) Alternating one movement with another.
Altgeige, *Ger.* (ält-ghī-ghĕ.) The viola, or tenor violin.
Alti, *It.* (äl-tē.) High; the plural of Alto.
Altieraménte, *It.* (äl-tē-ĕr-ä-mān-tĕ.) With grandeur, haughtily.
Altisonante, *It.* (äl-tē-zō-nän-tä.) Loud sounding.
Altisono, *It.* (äl-tē-sō-nō.) Sonorous.
Altisonous. High sounding. A term formerly used to denote the highest part intended for the natural adult male voice.
Altiso, *It.* (äl-tē-zō.) An abbreviation of Altissimo.
Altissimo, *It.* (äl-tēs-sē-mō.) The highest; extremely high as to pitch. It is applied to all the high treble notes which are more than an octave above F, on the fifth line of the treble staff.
Altist. An alto singer.
Altista, *It.* (äl-tēs-tä.) One who has an alto
Altiste, *Fr.* (äl-tēst.) voice.
Altitonans, *Lat.* (äl-tī-tō-näns.) The alto, or highest part under the treble; used in choral music in the sixteenth century.
Alto, *It.* (äl-tō. (High. In vocal music the highest male voice, sometimes called the counter tenor. In *mixed chorus* it is the part next below the soprano sung by low female voices.
Alto Basso, *It.* (äl-tō bäs-sō.) A Venetian stringed instrument, not in use at the present day.
Alto clef. The C clef on the third line of the staff.
Alto concertina. A concertina having the compass of a viola.

AMAT

Alto Flauto, *It.* (äl-tō flä-oo-tō.) An alto flute; used in bands.
Alt' ottáva, *It.* (äl-t' ōt-tä-vä.) The same notes an octave higher.
Alto primo, *It.* (äl-tō prē-mō.) The highest alto.
Alto secondo, *It.* (äl-tō sĕ-kōn-dō.) The lowest alto.
Alto tenore, *It.* (äl-tō tĕn-ō-rĕ.) The highest tenor.
Alto Trombone. A trombone with the notation on the alto clef. Its compass is from the small c, or e, to the one lined a or two lined c.
Alto Viola, *It.* (äl-tō vē-ō-lä.) The viola, or tenor violin.
Alto Violino, *It.* (äl-tō vē-ō-lē-nō.) Small tenor violin on which the alto may he played.
Altra, *It.* (äl-trä.)
Altro, *It.* (äl-trō.) } Other, another.
Altri, *It.* (äl-trē.) Others.
Altro modo, *It.* (äl-trō mō-dō.) Another mode or manner.
Altsänger, *Ger.* (ält-säng-ĕr.) Alto singer, counter tenor singer.
Altschlüssel, *Ger.* (ält-shlūs-s'l.) The alto clef; the C clef on the third line.
Altus, *Lat.* (äl-tūs.) The alto or counter tenor.
Altviole, *Ger.* (ält-fī-ō-lĕ.) The viola, or tenor violin.
Altzeichen, *Ger.* (ält-tsī-k'n.) See Altschlüssel.
Alzaménto, *It.* (äl-tsä-mān-tō.) An elevating of the voice; lifting up.
Alzaménto di máno, *It.* (äl-tsä-mān-tō dē mä-nō.) To elevate the hand in beating time.
Alzaménto di voce, *It.* (äl-tsä-mān-tō dē vō-tshĕ.) Elevation of the voice.
Alzándo, *It.* (äl-tsän-dō.) Raising, lifting up.
Al Zop. An abbreviation of Alla Zoppa.
Amábile, *It.* (ä-mä-bē-lĕ.) Amiable, gentle, graceful.
Amabilitá, *It.* (ä-mä-bē-lē-tä.) Tenderness, amiability.
Amabilitá, con. With amiability.
Amabilménte, *It.* (ä-mä-bēl-mān-tĕ.) Amiably, gently.
A major. That key in modern music in which the fundamental tone is the sixth distonic tone in the scale of C major.
Amarévole, *It.* (ä-mä-rā-vō-lĕ.) Amiably, affectionately.
Amarézza, *It.* (ä-mä-rät-zä.) Bitterness, sadness.
Amarézza, con. *It.* With bitterness; with sorrow.
Amarissiménte, *It.* (ä-mä-rēs-sē-mä-mān-tĕ.)
Amaríssimo, *It.* (ä-mä-rēs-sē-mō.) Very bitterly, in a very mournful, sad and afflicted manner.
Amáro, *It.* (ä-mä-rō.) Grief, bitterness, affliction.
Amateur, *Fr.* (äm-ä-tūr.) One who has taste and proficiency in music, but does not practice it as a profession.
Amati. A name applied to violins made by the brothers Amati, in Italy, in the middle of the seventeenth century. They are smaller than the ordinary violin, and distinguished for their peculiar sweetness of tone.

ă ale, ă add, ă arm, ē eve, ĕ end, ī ice, ĭ ill, ō old, ŏ odd, ô dove, oo moon, ū lute, ŭ but, ü French sound.

AMAN

Amantes. Persons who composed the songs and plays used by the old Incas of Peru.
Ambitus, Lat. (ăm-bǐ-tŭs.) Compass or range of sounds; also, the distance between the highest and lowest sounds.
Ambo, Lat. (ăm-bō.) The desk at which the canons were sung in the middle ages.
Ambon. Fr. (ănh-bōnh.) The Ambo.
Ambrosian Chant. A series of sacred melodies or chants collected and introduced into the church by St. Ambrose, Bishop of Milan, in the fourth century, and supposed to have been borrowed from the ancient Greek music.
Ambrosianus Cantus, Lat. (ăm-brō-sǐ-ā-nŭs kă'-tŭs.) Ambrosian chant.
Ambubaje, Gr. (ăm-bū-bā-jē.) The name of a society of strolling flute players among the ancient Greeks.
Ambulant, Fr. (ănh-bū-lănh.) Wandering; an itinerant musician.
Ame, Fr. (ăm.) The sound-post of a violin, viola, etc.
Amen, Heb. (ă-mĕn.) So be it. A word used as a termination to psalms, hymns, and other sacred music.
Amen Chorus. A chorus in which the word *amen* forms the principal language.
Ameno, It. (ă-mā-nō.) Charming, pleasing, sweet.
Amenochord. An instrument resembling a pianoforte.
American fingering. That style of fingering in which the sign x is used to indicate the thumb in piano playing, in distinction from the German or foreign fingering, in which the thumb is called the first finger.
American organ. A variety of the harmonium which differs from the European harmonium in in the arrangement of the bellows, and for producing varieties of expression.
A mezza aria, It. (ă măt-sä ä-rō-ä.) An air partly in the style of a recitative; between speaking and singing.
A mezza voce, It. (ă măt-sä vō-tshě.)   } In a
A mezza di voce, It. (ă măt-sä dē vō-tshě.) } soft subdued tone; with half the power of the voice. The term is also applied to instrumental music.
A mezza manico, It. (ă măt-sä mä-nē-kō.) In violin playing, the placing the hand near the middle of the neck.
Ammaestratore, It. (ăm-mă-ĕs-trä-tō-rĕ.) An instructor.
Ammaestratrice, It. (ăm-mă-ĕs-trä-trē-tshĕ.) An instructress.
Ammodulato, It. (ăm-mō-doo-lä-tō.) Tuned.
A moll, Ger. (ă mōll.) The key of A minor.
A molto cori, It. (ă mōl-tō kō-rē.) Full choruses; a collection of choruses.
A monocorde, Fr. (ă mŏnh-ō-kŏrd.) On one string only.
Amóre, It. (ă-mō-rĕ.) Tenderness, affection, love.
Amóre, con, It. With tenderness and affection.
Amorévole, It. (ă-mō-rā-vō-lĕ.) Tenderly, gently, lovingly.
Amorevolménte, It. (ă-mō-rä-vōl-mĕn-tĕ.) With extreme tenderness.

ANCH

A morésco, It. (ă mō-rās-kō.) In the Moorish style; in the style of a morésco or Moorish dance.
Amorosaménte, It. (ă-mō-rō-zä-mĕn-tĕ.) In a tender and affectionate style.
Amoróso, It. (ă-mō-rō-zō.) See Amarosaménte.
Amonsikos, Gr. (ă-moo-sǐ-kōs.) Unmusical; a term used by the ancient Greeks implying a deficiency in the organs of sound or want of cultivation.
Amphibrach, Ger. (ăm-fǐ-brăk.) A musical foot, comprising one short, one long and one short note or syllable, accented and marked thus,‿—‿
Amphimacer, Gr. (ăm-fǐ-mă-sĕr.) A musical foot, comprising one long, one short and one long note, or syllable, accented and marked thus,—‿—
Amphion, Gr. (ăm-fǐ-ŏn.) The most ancient Greek musician. He played upon the lyre.
Ampollosaménte, It. (ăm-pōl-lō-zä-mĕn-tĕ.) ⎫
Ampollóso, It. (ăm-pōl-lō-zō.)   ⎬
In a bombastic and pompous manner.
Ampoulé, Fr. (ănh-poo-lā.) High flown, bombastic.
Amusement, Fr. (ă-mūz-mănh.) A light and pleasing composition frequently employed as an exercise in a course of piano studies.
Anabasis, Gr. (ă-nä-bä-sǐs.) A succession of ascending tones.
Anacamptic. (ăn-ă-kămp-tǐk.) The name given by the ancient Greeks to sounds produced by reflection, as echoes.
Anacamptos, Gr. (ăn-ă-kămp-tōs.) A course of retrograde or reflected notes; notes proceeding downwards or from acute to grave.
Anaclastic glass. A thin glass vial of the form of a tunnel which when blown upon by the performers is capable of producing a very loud noise.
Anacreontic, Gr. (ăn-ăk-rē-ŏn-tǐk.) In the Bacchanalian or drinking style.
Anafil, Spa. (ă-nä-fēl.) A musical pipe used by the Moors.
Anaflero, Spa. (ă-nä-fē-lē-rō.) A player on the anafil.
Anagaza, Spa. (ă-nä-gä-thä.) A bird call.
Anakara, It. (ăn-ă-kä-rä.) The kettle drum.
Anakarista, It. (ăn-ă-kä-rēs-tä.) A tympanist, or kettle-drum player.
Anakrusis. (ăn-ă-kroo-sǐs.) The up stroke in conducting, or beating time.
Análisi, It. (ă-nä-lē-zē.)   ⎫ An analysis.
Analyse, Fr. (ăn-ä-lēz.)   ⎬
Analyzation. The resolution of a musical composition into the elements which compose it for the sake of ascertaining its construction.
Ananes, Gr. (ă-nä-nēs.) The modes or tones of the ancient Greek church.
Anapest, Gr. (ăn-ă-pĕst.) A musical foot, containing two short notes, or syllables and a long one, accented and marked thus, ‿‿—
Anapesto, Spa. (ăn-ă-pĕs-tō.) An anapést.
Anaphona, Gr. (ăn-ă-fō-nä.) An old term implying the immediate repetition of a passage that has just been played.
Anarmonia. Dissonance, false harmony.
Anche, Fr. (ănhsh.) The reed, or mouth-piece of the oboe, bassoon, clarionet, etc.; also the various reed stops in an organ.

2

ā ale, ă add, ä arm, ē eve, ĕ end, ī ice, ĭ ill, ō old, ŏ odd, ō dove, oo moon, ū tute, ŭ but, ü French sound.

ANCK — ANHA

Anche d'orgue, *Fr.* (änhsh d'ōrg.) A reed stop of an organ.

Ancher, *Fr.* (ähn-shā.) To put a reed to a musical instrument.

Ancia, *It.* (än-tshē-ā.) See Anche.

Ancient flute. An instrument composed of two tubes with a mouth-piece attached.

Ancient modes. The modes or scales of the ancient Greeks and Romans.

Ancient signatures. Old signatures in which the last sharp or flat was suppressed and used as an accidental note when required.

Ancilla, *Gr.* (än-sĕl-lä.) Shields, by the beating of which, the ancient Greeks marked the measure of their music on festive occasions.

Ancora, *It.* (än-kō-rä.) Once more, repeat again; also, yet, still, etc.

Ancora da capo, *It.* (än-kō-rä dä kä-pō.) From the commencement again.

Ancōr piu mósso, *It.* (än-kōr pē-oo mōs-sō.) Still more motion, quicker.

Andacht, *Ger.* (än-däkht.) Devotion.

Andächtig, *Ger.* (än-däkh-tĭg.) Devotional.

Andaménto, *It.* (än-dă-mĕn-to.) A rather slow movement; also, an accessory idea or episode introduced into a fugue to produce variety.

Andante, *It.* (än-dän-tē.) A movement in moderate time but flowing steadily, easily, gracefully. This term is often modified both as to time and style by the addition of other words; as,

Andánte affettuóso, *It.* (än-dän-tē äf-fĕt-too-ō-zō.) Moderately, and with much pathos.

Andánte amabile, *It.* (än-dän-tē ä-mä-bē-lĕ.) An andante expressive of affection.

Andánte cantabile, *It.* (än-dän-tē cän-tä-bē-lĕ.) Slowly, and in a singing and melodious style.

Andánte con móto, *It.* (än-dän-tē kŏn mō-tō.) Moving easily, with motion or agitation; rather lively.

Andánte graziōso, *It.* (än-dän-tē grä-tsē-ō-zō.) Moderately slow in time and in graceful easy style.

Andánte largo, *It.* (än-dän-tē lär-gō.) Slow, distinct and exact.

Andánte maestóso, *It.* (än-dän-tē mä-ĕs-tō-zō.) Moving rather slowly and in majestic style.

Andánte ma non troppo, e con tristéza, *It.* (än-dän-tē mä nŏn trop-pō, ä kŏn trĕs-tät-sä.) Not too slow, and with pathos.

Andánte non troppo. Moving slowly but not too much so.

Andánte pastorále, *It.* (än-dän-tē päa-to-rä-lē.) Moderately slow and in simple pastoral style.

Andánte piu tosto allegretto, *It.* (än-dän-tē pē-oo tōs-tō äl-lĕ-grät-tō.) Andante, or rather allegretto.

Andánte quasi allegretto, *It.* An andante nearly as rapid as allegretto.

Andanteménte, *It.* (än-dän-tē-mān-tĕ.) See Andante.

Andantíno, *It.* (än-dän-tē-nō.) A little slower than andante.

Andantíno sostenúto e simpliceménte, il cánto e pocó piú forte. (än-dän-tē-no sōs-tĕ-noo-to ä sĕm-plē-tshĕ-mān-to, ĕl kän-to ä po-ko pē-oo fōr-tĕ.) In a sustained and simple manner, with the melody a little louder than the other notes.

Andno. An abbreviation of Andantino.

Andár diritto, *It.* (än-där dē-rēt-tō.) To go straight on.

Andáre a tempo, *It.* (än-dä-rĕ ä tĕm-pō.) To play or sing in time.

Androïdes. A musical automaton figure which by means of certain springs can play on some instruments.

Andte. An abbreviation of andante.

Aneanes, *Gr.* (än-ē-ä-nĕs.) The modes and tones of the ancient Greeks.

Anelanteménte, *It.* (än-ä-län-tē-män-tĕ.) Anxiously, ardently.

Anelánza, *It.* (än-ä-län-tsä.) } Shortness of
Anélito, *It.* (än-ä-lē-tō.)   } breath.

Anemochord. A species of Eolian Harp.

Anemometer. A wind guage, or machine for weighing the wind in an organ.

Anfang, *Ger.* (än-fäng.) Beginning, commencement.

Anfänger, *Ger.* (än-fäng-ĕr.) A beginner.

Anfangsgründe, *Ger.* (än-fängs-grün-dĕ.) Rudiments, elements, principles.

Anfangsritornell, *Ger.* (än-fängs-rē-tōr-nĕll.) Introductory symphony to an air.

Anfibraco, *Spa.* (än-fē-brä-kō.) See Amphibrach.

Anfiteátro, *It.* (än-fē-tĕ-ä-trō.) See Amphitheatre.

Anführer, *Ger.* (än-fü-rĕr.) A conductor, director, leader.

Angeben, *Ger.* (än-gä-b'n.) To give a sound; to utter a tone; den Ton angeben, to give out the tune.

Angelica, *Ger.* (än-jĕ-lĭ-kä.) } An organ stop:
Angélique, *Fr.* (änh-zhä-lĕk.) } also an Angelot.

Angelot. An old musical instrument somewhat similar to the lute.

Angélus, *Fr.* (änh-zhä-lü.) Ave Maria; prayer time.

Angemessen, *Ger.* (än-ghĕ-mĕs-s'n.) Conformable, suitable, fit.

Angenehm, *Ger.* (än-ghĕn-äm.) Agreeable, pleasing, sweet.

Angkloung, *Jav.* (änk-loong.) A rude instrument of the Javanese, made of different lengths of bamboo fastened to a strip of wood.

Anglaise, *Fr.* (änh-gläz.) } In the English
Anglico, *It.* (än-glē-kō.) } style ; a tune adapted for an English air or country dance.

Angóre, *It.* (än-gō-rĕ.) Distress, anguish, passion, grief.

Angoscévole, *It.* (än-gōs-tshā-vō-lĕ.) Sad, sorrowful.

Angóscia, *It.* (än-gōs-tshē-ä.)

Angosciaménte, *It.* (än-gōs-tshē-ä-män-tĕ.) } Anxiety, anguish, grief.

Angosciosaménte, *It.* (än-gōs-tshē-ō-zä-män-tĕ.) Apprehensively, anxiously, sorrowfully.

Angosciōso, *It.* (än-gōs-tshē-ō-zō.) Afflicted, ..distressed.

Ängstlich, *Ger.* (ängst-lĭkh.) Uneasy, timid, anxious.

Anhaltend, *Ger.* (än-häl-tĕnd.) Continuous, constant, holding out.

Anhaltende Cadenz, *Ger.* (än-häl-tĕn-dĕ kä-dĕntz.) A pedal note or organ point; a protracted cadence.

PRONOUNCING MUSICAL DICTIONARY. 19

ă *ale,* ă *add,* ä *arm,* ē *eve,* ĕ *end,* Ī *ice,* ĭ *ill,* ō *old,* ŏ *odd,* ô *dove,* oo *moon,* ū *lute,* ŭ *but,* û *French sound.*

ANHA

Anhang, *Ger.* (än-häng.) A postscript, an appendix, a coda.
Anhänglich, *Ger.* (än-häng-lĭkh.) Attached.
Anima, *It.* (än-ē-mä.) Soul, feeling; animated, lively.
Anima, con., *It.* With life and animation.
Animas, *Spa.* (än-ē-mäs.) The ringing of a bell in the Roman Catholic church for prayers for souls in purgatory.
Animato, *It.* (än-ē-mä-to.) Animated; with life and spirit.
Animazióne, *It.* (än-ē-mä-tsē-ō-nĕ.) Animation.
Animé, *Fr.* (änh-ē-mä.) } Animated, lively,
Animo, *It.* (ä-nē-mō.) } spirited.
Animo, con., *It.* With boldness.
Animo corde, *Lat.* (än-ē-mō kôr-dĕ.) An instrument invented in 1789, by Jacob Schnell, of Paris. The tone is produced by wind passing over the strings.
Animosaménte, *It.* (än-ē-mō-zä-män-tĕ.) Boldly, resolutely.
Animosissimaménte, *It.* (äu-ē-mō-zēs-sē-mä-män-tĕ.) Exceedingly bold and resolute.
Animosissimo, *It.* (äu-ē-mō-zĕs-sē-mō.) Exceedingly bold and resolute.
Animóso, *It.* (än-ē-mō-zō.) In an animated manner; lively, energetic.
Aniversario, *Spa.* (än-ē-vĕr-sä-rĭ-ō.) A mass celebrated on the anniversary of a person's death.
Anklang, *Ger.* (än-kläng.) Accord, harmony, sympathy.
Anklingeln, *Ger.* (än-klĭng-ĕln.) To ring a bell.
Anklingen, *Ger.* (än-klĭng-ĕn.) To accord in sound.
Anlage, *Ger.* (än-lä-ghĕ.) The plan or outline of a composition.
Anlaufen, *Ger.* (än-lou-f'n.) To increase in sound, to swell.
Anleitung, *Ger.* (än-lī-toong.) An introduction, a preface.
Anmuth, *Ger.* (än-moot.) Sweetness, grace.
Anmuthig, *Ger.* (än-moo-tĭg.) Agreeable, sweet, pleasant.
Anomalies. False scales or intervals which are found in keyed instruments; they are so called because incapable of being perfectly tempered.
Anomalous chord. A chord whose intervals are sometimes greater and sometimes less.
Anomalous triads. See Altered Triads.
Anonner, *Fr.* (än-nŏnh-nā.) To hesitate, blunder or stammer.
Anpfeifen, *Ger.* (än-pfī-f'n.) To whistle at; to hiss at.
Ansatz, *Ger.* (än-säts.) The embouchure of a wind instrument.
Anschlag, *Ger.* (än-shläg.) A stroke, the percussion of a cord; the striking of a chord or key; the touch in piano playing.
Ansingĕn, *Ger.* (än-sĭng-ĕn.) To welcome with a song.
Anspielen, *Ger.* (än-spē-l'n.) To play first.
Anspràche, *Ger.* (än-sprä-khĕ.) Intonation.
Ansprechen, *Ger.* (än-sprĕ-kh'n.) To sound, to emit or give forth a sound.
Anstimmen, *Ger.* (än-stĭm-mĕn.) To strike up, to begin to sing, to tune.

ANTI

Anstimmung, *Ger.* (än-stĭm-moong.) Intonation, tuning.
Antecedent. (än-tē-sē-dĕnt.) The subject of a fugue or of a point of imitation.
Ante-chapel. That portion of the chapel leading to the choir.
Antanzen, *Ger.* (än-tän-ts'n.) To begin to dance.
Anth. An abbreviation of anthem.
Anthem. A vocal composition, the words of which are usually selected from the Bible. Used in church and generally accompanied on the organ.
Anthema. An ancient Greek dance.
Anthem, choral. An anthem in a slow measured style, after the manner of a choral.
Anthem, full. An anthem consisting wholly of chorus.
Anthem, solo. An anthem consisting of solos and choruses.
Anthologue, *Gr.* (än-thō-lŏg.) A collection of choice pieces.
Anthologium, *Gr.* (än-thō-lŏg-I-ŭm.) See Antiphonarium.
Anthropoglossa, *Gr.* (än-thrō-pō-glŏs-sä.) The vox humana, an organ stop somewhat resembling the human voice.
Antibacchius. (än-tĭ-băk-kĭ-ŭs.) A musical foot of three syllables, the first two long or accented and the last short or unaccented, thus, — — ᴗ.
Antica, *It.* (än-tē-kä.) Ancient.
Anticipaménto, *It.* (än-tē-tshē-pä-män-tō.) Anticipation.
Anticipation. The taking of a note or chord before its natural and expected place.
Anticipazione, *It.* (än-tē-tshē-pä-zē-ō-nĕ.) See Anticipation.
Antico, *It.* (än-tē-kō.) Ancient.
Antico, all', *It.* (än-tē-kō, äll'.) In the ancient style.
Antienne, *Fr.* (änh-tēn.) An anthem.
Antifona, *It.* (än-tē-fō-nä.) } An anthem.
Antifona, *Spa.* (än-tē-fō-nä.) }
Antifonal, *Spa.* (än-tē-fō-näl.) } A book of
Antifonario, *It.* (än-tē-fō-nä-rē-ō.) } anthems;
an anthem singer.
Antifonero, *Spa.* (än-tē-fō-nĕ-rō.) A precentor.
Antifoni snoni, *It.* (än-tē-fō-nē swō-nē.) Notes, which although one or more octaves apart are yet concords among themselves.
Antipasto, *Spa.* (än-tē-päs-tō.) A foot consisting of four syllables the first and last of which are short and the second and third long.
Antiphon. The chant or alternate singing in churches and cathedrals.
Antiphona, *Gr.* (än-tē-fō-nä.) An anthem.
Antiphonaire, *Fr.* (änh-tē-fō-nār.) A book of anthems, responses, etc.
Antiphonarium, *Gr.* (än-tĭ-fō-nä-rĭ-ŭm.) The collection of Antiphons used in the Catholic church; they are sung responsively by the priest and congregation.
Antiphonary. Book of anthems, responses, etc. in the Catholic church.
Antiphone, *Gr.* (än-tē-fō-ne.) The response made by one part of the choir to another, or by the congregation to the priest in the Roman Catholic service; also, alternate singing.

ă ale, ă add, ä arm, ē eve, ĕ end, ī ice, ĭ ill, ō old, ŏ odd, ô dove, oo moon, ū lute, ŭ but, ü French sound.

ANTI — APPO

Antiphonic, *Gr.* (ăn-tĭf-ŏ-nē.) Name applied to music sung responsively. See Antiphone.
Antiphonies, *Fr.* (ănh-tĭ-fō-nē.) A book of anthems.
Antiphonizing. Singing in octaves in the ancient Greek church; singing responsively.
Antiphonon, *Gr.* (ăn-tĭf-ō-nŏn.) In ancient Greek music, accompaniment in the octave.
Antiphon. Alternate singing or chanting in choirs. See Antiphone.
Antiphony. The response of one choir to another when an anthem or psalm is sung by two choirs; alternate singing or chanting.
Antistrofa, *Spa.* (ăn-tēs-trō-fä.) An ancient Spanish dance.
Antistrophe. } The second couplet of each period in the ancient Greek odes
Antistrophy. } sung in parts; that part of a song or dance which was performed by turning from left to right, in opposition to the *strophe* which turns from right to left.
Antithesis. In fugues, this term is applied to the *answer*; it generally signifies contrast.
Antönen, *Ger.* (ăn-tō-nĕn.) To begin to sound.
Antrommeln, *Ger.* (ăn-trŏm-mĕln.) To begin to drum.
Antrompeten, *Ger.* (ăn-trŏm-pā-t'n.) To publish by sound of trumpet.
Anwachsend, *Ger.* (ăn-văkh-sĕnd.) Swelling, increasing.
A otto voci, *It.* (ä ŏt-tō vō-tshē.) For eight voices.
Apagador, *Spa.* (ä-pä-gä-dōr.) A piece of cloth used to deaden the echo of the tones of the harpsichord.
Apagar la voz, *Spa.* (ä-pä-gär lä vōth.) To put a mute on a stringed instrument.
A parte, *It.* (ä pär-tē.) On the side of.
A parte equale, *It.* (ä pär-tē ā-quä-lē.) A term applied to a musical performance where the voices or instruments sustain an equally prominent part; where two or more performers sustain parts of equal difficulty.
A passo a passo, *It.* (ä päs-sō ä päs-sō.) Step by step, regularly.
Apelde, *Spa.* (ä-păl-dĕ.) The morning bell in Franciscan convent.
Apérto, *It.* (ä-pār-tō.) Open; in pianoforte music it signifies that the damper or open pedal is to be pressed down.
Apertus, *Lat.* (ä-pĕr-tŭs.) Open; as, open diapason, open canon, etc.
Apfelregal, *Ger.* (äp-fĕl-rĕ-gäl.) Apple-register, a reed stop in old organs no longer in use.
Aphonie, *Fr.* (ä-fō-nē.) Aphony, want of voice.
Aphonous. Being destitute of voice.
Aphony. (ăn-tĭf-ō-ny.) Dumbness, loss of voice.
A piacere, *It.* (ä pē-ä-tshā-rĕ.) At pleasure.
A piacimento, *It.* (pē-ä-tshē-mĕn-tō.) At the pleasure or taste of the performer.
Apieni, *It.* (ä-pē-ā-nē.) Sounds which are one or more octaves apart, but not discordant.
A piena Orchestra, *It.* (ä pē-ā-nä ōr-kās-trä.) For full orchestra.
A pino, *Spa.* (ä pē-nō.) Upright; a term applied to bells when exactly reversed in ringing.
Aplomb, *Fr.* (ä plŏnh.) Firm, in exact time, with precision.

Apnœa, *Gr.* (ăp-nē-ä.) } Want of breath, weakness of lungs.
Apnéa, *It.* (ăp-nā-ä.) }
A póco, *It.* (ä pō-kō.) By degrees, gradually.
A póco a póco, *It.* (ä pō-kō ä pō-kō.) By little and little.
A póco pin lénto, *It.* (ä pō-kō pē-oo lĕn-tō.) A little slower.
A póco piu mósso, *It.* (ä pō-kō pē-oo mōs-sō.) A little quicker.
Apollino, *Gr.* (ăp-ŏl-lē-nō.) An harmonic invention or contrivance combining the different qualities and powers of several kinds of instruments, and capable of playing them separately or all together.
Apollo. In ancient mythology, the god of music and said to be the inventor of the lyre.
Apollo Lyra. An instrument shaped like a lyre with a brass mouth-piece like a horn; now obsolete.
Apollonicon. A large organ, invented in the present century, with immense self-acting machinery which brings the whole power of the instrument into operation at once, producing the effect of a full orchestra. It has six keyboards and can be played upon by six performers at the same time.
Apopemptic. A song or hymn among the ancients sung or addressed to a stranger.
Apotome, *Gr.* (ăp-ō-tōme.) That portion of a major tone that remains after deducting from it an interval less by a comma, than a major semitone.
Apotome major, *Gr.* An enharmonic interval.
Apotome minor, *Gr.* An interval smaller than the Apotome Major.
Apotomy. See Apotome.
Apotropœa, *Gr.* (ăp-ō-trō-pē-ä.) Hymns written by the ancients for the purpose of appeasing the wrath of incensed divinities.
Appassionataménte, *It.* (ăp-păs-sē-ō-nä-tä-mān-tĕ.)
Appassionatamento, *It.* (ăp-păs-sē-ō-nä-tä-mān-tō.)
Appassionáto, *It.* (ăp-päs-sē-ō-nä-tō.) Passionately, with intense emotion and feeling.
Appeau. (ăp-pō.) Tones which resemble the singing of birds.
Appel, *Fr.* (ăp-pāl.) Call of the drum.
Appenáto, *It.* (ăp-pĕ-nä-tō.) Grieved, distressed; an expression of suffering and melancholy.
Applaudissement, *Fr.* (ăp-plō-dēss-mŏnh.) } Applause.
Applauso, *It.* (ăp-plä-oo-zō.) }
Applicatur, *Ger.* (ăp-plĭ-kä-toor.) The art of fingering.
Appoggiándo, *It.* (ăp-pŏd-jē-ăn-do.) } Leaning
Appoggiáto, *It.* (ăp-pŏd-jē-ä-tō.) } upon, dwelt upon, drawn out.
Appoggiatura, *It.* (ăp-pŏd-jē-ä-too-rä.) Leaning note, grace note, note of embellishment.
Appoggiatura, compound. An appoggiatura consisting of two or more grace notes or notes of embellishment.
Appoggiatura, inferior. An appoggiatura situated one degree below its principal note.
Appoggiatura, superior. An appoggiatura situated one degree above its principal note.

ā ale, ă add, ä arm, ē eve, ĕ end, ī ice, ĭ ill, ō old, ŏ odd, ô dove, oo moon, ū lute, ŭ but, ü French sound.

APPO

Appoggiatura, It. (ăp-pŏd-jē-ă-too-rĕ.) See Appoggiatura.
Apprestáre, It. (ăp-prĕs-tă-rĕ.) To prepare, or put in a condition to be played.
A première vue, Fr. (ă prĕm-ĭ-ăr vü.) } At
A prima vista, It. (ă prē-mă vēz-tă.) } first sight.
Apre, Fr. (ăpr.) Harsh.
Aprement, Fr. (ăpr-mŏnh.) Harshly.
Apreté, Fr. (ăp-rĕ-tă.) Harshness.
Apuntacion, Spa. (ă-poon-tă-thē-ŏn.) The act of marking musical notes.
A púnta d'arco, It. (ă poon-tă d'ăr-kō.) With the point ot the bow.
Apuntador, Spa. (ă-poon-tă-dōr.) A prompter.
A púnto, It. (ă poon-tō.) Punctually, exactly, correctly.
Apycnos, Gr. (ă-pĭk-nōs.) A term applied to the diatonic genus, in distinction from the chromatic and enharmonic.
A quatre mains, Fr. (ă kătr mănh.) } For
A quáttro máni. It. (ă quăt-trō mă-nē.) } four hands. For two performers on one pianoforte.
A quáttro, or a 4, It. For four voices or instruments; a quartette.
A quáttro parti, It. (ă quăt-trō păr-tă.) In four parts.
A quatre voix, Fr. (ă kătr vwă.) } For
A quáttro vóci, It. (ă quăt-trō vō-tshē.) } four voices.
A quattre seuls, Fr. (ă kătr sŭl.) } For four
A quáttro sóli. It. (ă quăt-trō sō-lē.) } solo voices or instruments.
A quáttro tempi staccati e vivace, It. (ă quăt-trō tĕm-pē stăk-kă-tē ă vē-vă-tshē.) The measure in four time to be taken with spirit and animation.
Ar, Por. (ăr.) Air.
Arbitrii, Lat. (lă-bĭt-rĭ-ē.) Certain points or embellishments which a singer introduces or improvises at pleasure while singing an aria or tune.
Arbítrio, It. (ăr-bē-trē-ō.) At the will or pleasure of the performer.
Arc, It. (ărk.) The bow; an abbreviation of Arco.
Arcata, It. (ăr-kă-tă.) Manner of bowing.
Arcáto, It. (ăr-kă-tō.) Bowed, played with the bow.
Arch. A curve formerly placed over a bass note to show that it was accompanied by the imperfect fifth.
Arch-chanter. The leader of the chants, the chief chanter.
Arche, Ger. (ăr-khĕ.) The sounding board of an organ.
Archeggiaménto, It. (ăr-kĕd-jē-ă-măn-to.) The management of the bow in playing the violin, etc.
Archeggiare, It. (ăr-kĕd-jē-ă-rĕ.) To use the bow, to fiddle.
Archet, Fr. (ăr-shā.)
Archettino, It. (ăr-kĕt-tē-nō.) } A violin bow.
Archétto, It. (ăr-kăt-tō.)
Archicéllo, It. (ăr-kē-tshăl-lō.) } A little bow.
Archilnth, Fr. (ăr-shē-lŭt.) } See Archlute.
Arcilúdto, It. (ăr-tshĕl-yoo-tō.) }
Archilochian line. The third line of an alcaic stanza.
Archlute. A theorbo or lute with two nuts and

ARIE

sets of strings, one for the bass. The strings of the theorbo were single, but in the bass, strings were doubled with an octave and the small strings with an unison.
Arco, It. (ăr-kō.) The bow.
Ardénte, It. (ăr-dăn-tĕ.) With fire, glowing, vohement.
Ardentemente, It. (ăr-dĕn-tĕ-măn-tĕ.) Ardently, vehemently.
Ardentíssimo, It. (ăr-dĕn-tēs-sē-mō.) Very ardently.
Arditaménte, It. (ăr-dē-tă-măn-tĕ.) Boldly, with ardor.
Arditezza, It. (ăr-dē-tăt-să.) Boldness.
Ardíto, It. (ăr-dē-tō.) Bold, with energy.
Ardíto di molto, It. (ăr-dē-tō dē mŏl-tō.) Passionately with much force.
Aretinian syllables. The syllables ut, re, me, fa, sol, la, introduced by Guido d'Arezzo for his system of hexachords or six notes.
Argentin, Fr. (ăr-zhăn-tănh.) Silver toned.
Arghool, Tur. (ăr-gool.) A musical instrument of the Turks, of the flute species.
Argives. Ancient people of Argos, celebrated for their love of music.
Argute. Acuteness of sound, sharp, shrill. (Little used.)
Aria, It. (ă-rē-ă.) An air, a song, a tune; sung by a single voice either with or without an accompaniment.
Aria buffa, It. (ă-rē-ă boof-fă.) A comic or humorous air.
Aria cantábile, It. (ă-rē-ă kăn-tă-bē-lĕ.) An air in a graceful and melodious style.
Aria concertáta, It. (ă-rē-ă kŏn-tshĕr-tă-tă.) An air with orchestral accompaniments in a Concertánte style; a concerted air.
Aria d'abilità, It. (ă-rē-ă d'ă-bĕl-lē-tă.) A difficult air requiring great skill and musical ability in the singer.
Aria di bravúra, It. (ă-rē-ă dē bră-voo-ră.) A florid air in bold, marked style and permitting great freedom of execution.
Aria di cantábile, It. See Aria Cantábile.
Aria fugáta, It. (ă-rē-ă foo-gă-tă.) An air accompanied in the fugue style.
Aria d'ostinazione, It. (ă-rē-ă d'ŏs-tē-nă-tsē-ō-nĕ.) Obligato air.
Aria parlánte, It. (ă-rē-ă păr-lăn-tĕ.) An air in the declamatory style; a recitative a tempo.
Aria tedésca, It. (ă-rē-ă tĕ-dăs-kă.) An air in the German style.
Ariadne dance. A Grecian dance.
Aria und chor, Ger. (ă-rē-ă oond kōr.) Air and chorus.
Arie, It. pl. (ă-rē-ĕ.) } Airs or songs.
Arien, Ger. pl. (ă-rē-ĕn.) }
Arie aggiúnte, It. (ă-rē-ĕ ăd-jē-oon-tĕ.) Airs added to or introduced into an opera, or other large work.
Ariétta, It. (ă-rē-ăt-tă.) } A short air or melody.
Ariette, Fr. (ă-rē-ĕt.) }
Ariétta alla Venezíana, It. (ă-rē-ăt-tă ăl-lă vĕn-ă-tsē-ă-nă.) A short air in the style of the Venetian Barcarolles.
Ariettína, It. (ă-rē-ĕt-tē-nă.) A short air or melody.

PRONOUNCING MUSICAL DICTIONARY.

ă *ale*, ă *add*, ä *arm*, ĕ *eve*, ĕ *end*, ī *ice*, ĭ *ill*, ō *old*, ŏ *odd*, ô *dove*, oo *moon*, ū *lute*, ŭ *but*, ü *French sound*.

ARIG — ARTI

A rigore del tempo, *It.* (ä rē-gō-rĕ dĕl tĕm-pō.) In strict time.
Arigot, *Fr.* (ä-rē-gō.) A fife.
Arion. An ancient harp player and poet of Greece who lived 618 B. C.
Ariosa, *It.* (ä-rē-ō-zä.) In the movement of an aria or tune.
Ariose cantáte, *It. pl.* (ä-rē-ō-zĕ kän-tä-tĕ.) Airs in a style between a song and recitative, introducing frequent changes in time and manner.
Arióso, *It.* (ä-rē-ō-zō.) Melodious, graceful; a short piece in the style of an aria, but less symmetrical in construction.
Arm. A small piece of iron at the end of the roller of an organ.
Armayon, *Spa.* (är-mä-yōn.) A bell frame.
Armer la clef, *Fr.* (är-mä lä klä.) The signature; or, the flats and sharps placed immediately after the clef.
Armoneggiáre, *It.* (är-mō-nĕd-jĕ-ä-rē.) To sound in harmony.
Armonía, *It.* (är-mō-nē-ä.) Harmony, concord.
Armoniáco, *It.* (är-mō-nē-ä kō.) Harmonized.
Armoniále, *It.* (är-mō-nē-ä-lē.) Harmonious, concordant.
Armoniáto, *It.* (är-mō-nē-ä-tō.) See Armoniáco.
Armónica, *It.* (är-mō-nē-kä.) The earliest form of the accordion; a collection of musical glasses so arranged as to produce exquisite effects.
Armonica, guida, *It.* (är-mō-nē-kä gwē-dä.) A guide to harmony.
Armonici, *It.* (är-mō-nē-tshē.) Harmonic.
Armónico, *It.* (är-mō-nē-kō.) Harmonious.
Armoniosaménte, *It.* (är-mō-nē-ō-zä-män-tē.) Harmoniously.
Armonióso, *It.* (är-mō-nē-ō-zō.) Concordant, harmonious.
Armonísta, *It.* (är-mō-nēs-tä.) One who is acquainted with the principles of harmony.
Armonizzaménto, *It.* (är-mō-nēt-zä-män-tō.) Agreement, concord.
Armonizzánte, *It.* (är-mō-nēt-tsän-tē.) That is harmonious, musical.
Armonizzáre, *It.* (är-mō-nēt-tsä-rē.) To harmonize, to make harmony.
Arm viol. The viola, called by the Italians, Viola di Braccio, because it rested on the arm.
A rovescio, *It.* (ä rō-vä-shē-ō.) Reversed, in an opposite direction.
Arpa, *It.* (är-pä.) }
Arpa, *Spa.* (är-pä.) } The harp.
Arpa, *Port.* (är-pä.) }
Arpe, *It.* (är-pĕ.) }
Arpa d' Eolo, *It.* (är-pä d' ā-ō-lō.) An Eolian harp.
Arpa dóppia, *It.* (är-pä dōp-pē-ä.) The double action harp; it meant formerly a harp with two strings to each note,
Arpador, *Spa.* (är-pä-dōr.) A harp player.
Arpa eolica, *It.* (är-pä ā-ō-lē-kä.) Eolian harp or lyre.
Arpanétta, *It.* (är-pä-nät-tä.) } A small harp or
Arpinélla, *It.* (är-pē-nĕl-lä.) } lute.
Arpeg. An abbreviation of Arpeggio.
Arpegement, *Fr.* (är-päzh-mänh.) An arpeggio.

Arpeger, *Fr.* (är-pĕ-zhä.) To play arpeggios.
Arpeggi, *It.* (är-pĕd-jē.) Arpeggios.
Arpeggiaménto, *It.* (är-päd-jĕ-ä-män-tō.) In the style of the harp; arpeggio.
Arpeggiándo, *It.* (är-päd-jĕ-än-dō.) } Music
Arpeggiáto, *It.* (är-päd-jĕ-ä-tō.) } played arpeggio, in imitation of the harp; harping, harp music.
Arpeggiáre, *It.* (är-päd-jĕ-ä-rē.) To play upon the harp.
Arpeggiatúra, *It.* (är-päd-jĕ-ä-too-rä.) Playing arpeggio, or in the style of the harp.
Arpéggio, *It.* (är-päd-jē-ō.) Playing the notes of a chord quickly one after another in the harp style, thus,

Arpeggio accompaniment. An accompaniment which consists chiefly of chords played in arpeggio style.
Arpicórdo, *It.* (är-pē-kōr-dō.) A Harpsichord.
Arpista, *Spa.* (är-pēs-tä.) A harper, a minstrel.
Arp'o. An abbreviation of Arpeggio and Arpeggiato.
Arqueada, *Spa.* (är-kä-ä-dä.) The stroke of a violin bow.
Arr. }
Arrang. } Abbreviations of *arrangement*.
Arrangement. The selection and adaptation of a composition or parts of a composition to instruments for which it was not originally designed, or for some other use for which it was not at first written.
Arranger, *Fr.* (är-ränh-zhä.) } To arrange music for particular voices or instruments; to arrange
Arrangiren, *Ger.* (är-ränh-zhē-r'n.) } orchestral music for the pianoforte.
Arrendajo, *Spa.* (är-rĕn-dä-hō.) A buffoon.
Arrullo, *Spa.* (är-rool-yō.) A lullaby.
Ars canendi, *Lat.* (ärs kä-nĕn-dē.) The art of singing with taste and expression.
Ars componentis, *Lat.* (ärs kŏm-pō-nĕn-tis.) The art of composing.
Arsis, *Gr.* (är-sĭs.) The upstroke of the hand in beating time.
Ars musica, *Lat.* (ärs mū-sĭ-kä.) The art of music.
Art, *Ger.* (ärt.) Species, kind; quality.
Art de l'archet, *Fr.* (ärt düh l'är-shä.) The art of bowing.
Articoláre, *It.* (är-tē-kō-lä-rē.) } To pronounce
Articuler, *Fr.* (är-tē-kü-lä.) } the words distinctly; to articulate each note.
Articulate. To utter distinct separate tones; to sing with a distinct and clear enunciation.
Articulation. A distinct and clear utterance; a clear and exact rendering of every syllable and tone.
Articoláto, *It.* (är-tē-kō-lä-tō.) Articulated, distinctly enunciated.
Articolazione, *It.* (är-tē-kō-lä-tsē-ō-nē.) Exact and distinct pronunciation.
Artificial. Not natural; a term applied to notes or chords when chromatics are introduced.
Artificial scale. A scale in which there are chromatic tones. In contradistinction to the natural scale which has neither flats nor sharps.

ă ale, ă add, ä arm, ĕ eve, ĕ end, ī ice, ĭ ill, ō old, ŏ odd, ô dove, oo moon, ū lute, ŭ but, ü French sound.

ARTI

Artikuliren, Ger. (ăr-tĭk-oo-lă-r'n.) To articulate.
Artista, It. (ăr-tĭs-tă.) } An artist; one who
Artiste, Fr. (ăr-tēst.) } excels in the composition or performance of music.
Arzillo, It. (ăr-tsēl-lō.) Lively, sprightly.
As, Ger. (äs.) The note A flat.
Assamblea, Spa. (ä-săm-blä-ä.) A drum beat to call soldiers together.
Asclepiad, Gr. (ăs-klĕp-ĭ-ăd.) In ancient poetry a verse of four feet.
Asclepiadeo, Spa. (ăs-klä-pē-ä-dĕ-ō.) An asclepiad.
Ascoltatore, It. (äs-kōl-tä-tō-rĕ.) An auditor, a hearer.
Asculæ, Gr. (äs-koo-lē.) A name given by the ancients to performers on the organ.
As dur, Ger. (äs door.) The key of A♭ major.
Asheor, Heb. ă-shē-ōr.) A ten stringed instrument of the Hebrews.
As moll, Ger. (äs mōll.) The key of A♭ minor.
Asperges me, Lat. (äs-pĕr-gĕs mā.) The opening of the Mass in the Catholic service.
Aspiracion, Spa. (äs-pē-rä-thē-ōn.) Aspiration; breathing; a short pause in singing.
Aspirare, It. (äs-pē-rä-rĕ.) To breathe loudly; to use too much breath in singing.
Asprézza, It. (äs-prād-să.) Roughness, dryness, harshness.
Assái, It. (äs-sä-ē.) Very, extremely, in a high degree, as Allégro Assái, very quick.
Assái più, It. (äs-sä-ē pē-oo.) Much more.
Assemblage, Fr. (äs-sänh-blăzh.) Doubletongueing on the flute; executing rapid passages on wind instruments.
Assez, Fr. (äs-sä.) Enough, sufficiently.
Assez lent, Fr. (äs-sä länh.) Rather slowly.
Assoluto, It. (äs-sō-loo-tō.) Absolute, free; alone, one voice.
Assonant, Having a resemblance of sounds.
Assonánte, It. (äs-sō-nän-tĕ.) Harmonious, consonant.
Assonanz, Ger. (äs-sō-nän-ts.) Similarity, or
Assonánza, It. (äs-sō-nän-tsä.) } consonance of tone.
Assono, Lat. (äs-sō-nō.) To sound like a bell.
Assourdir, Fr. (äs-soor-dēr.) To muffle, to deafen, to stun.
Assourdissant, Fr. (äs-soor-dēs-sänh.) Deafening, stunning.
A súo arbítrio, It. (ä swō är-bē-trē-ō.)
A súo béne plácito, It. (ä swō bā-nĕ plătshē-tō.)
A súo cómodo, It. (ä swō kō-mō-dō.)
At pleasure, at will, at the inclination or discretion of the performer; synonymous with ad libitum.
A súo béne placimento, It. (ä swō bā-nĕ plă-tshē-mān-tō.) An old term signifying at the will or pleasure of the performer.
Asynartete verse. A verse consisting of two members having different rhythms.
A súo luógo, It. (ä swō loo-ō-gō.) Synonymous with Loco.
Asymphonie, Ger. (ä-sĭm-fō-nē.) Dissonance.
Atabal, Spa. (ä-tä-bäl.) A kettle drum; a species of tabor used by the Jews.

ATTA

Atabalear. Spa. (ät-ä-băl-ĕ-är.) To imitate the noise of kettle drums.
Atabalejo, Spa. (ät-ä-bä-lĕ-hō.) } A small
Atabalillo, Spa. (ät-ä-bä-lēl-yō.) } kettle drum.
Atabalero, Spa. (ät-ä-bä-lā-rō.) A kettle drum player.
A table sec, Fr. (ä tăbl sĕk.) } The prac-
A table séche, Fr. (ä tăbl säsh.) } tice of vocal exercises unaccompanied by an instrument.
Atellanus, Lat. (ă-tĕl-lă-nŭs.) A style of ancient comedy, consisting mostly of low songs.
A tēm, It. } Abbreviations of A Tempo.
A temp, It. }
A témpo, It. (ä tĕm-pō.) In time; a term used to denote that after some deviation or relaxation of the time, the performers must return to the original movement.
A tempo dell' allegro, It. (ä tĕm-pō dăll' äl-lā-grō.) In allegro time.
A tempo cómodo, It. (ä tĕm-pō kō-mō-dō.) In convenient time; an easy moderate time.
A tempo di gavótta, It. (ä tĕm-pō dē gävōt-tä.) In the time of a gavot; moderately quick.
A tempo giústo, It. (ä tĕm-pō joos-tō.) In just, strict, exact time.
A tempo ordinário, It. (ä tĕm-pō ōr-dē-nä-rē-ō.) In ordinary, moderate time.
A tempo rubáto, It. (ä tĕm-pō roo-bä-tō.) Irregular time; deviation in time so as to give more expression, but so that the time of each bar is not altered on the whole.
Athem, Ger. (ä-tĕm.) Breath, breathing, respiration.
Athemholen, Ger. (ä-tĕm-hō-l'n.) To breathe, to respire.
Athmen, Ger. (ät-mĕn.) To blow softly.
Athemzug, Ger. (ä-tĕm-tsoog.) Act of respiration, breathing.
Atabal, A kind of tabour used by the Moors.
Atiplar, Spa. (ä-tē-plär.) To render a sound more acute; to sharpen a tone very much.
A ton basse, Fr. (ä tōnh bäss.) In a low tone of voice.
A tre, or a 3, It. (ä trā.) For three voices or instruments; a Trio or Terzétto.
A tre córde, It. (ä trā kōr-dĕ.) For three strings; with three strings.
A tre máni, It. (ä trā mä-nē.) For three hands.
A tre párti, It. (ä trā pär-tē.) In three parts.
A tre soli, It. (ä trā sō-lē.) For three solo voices.
A tre soprani, It. (ä trā sō-prä-nē.) For three soprano voices.
A tre voci, It. (ä trā vō-tshē.) For three voices.
Atril, Spa. ä-trēl.) A missal stand.
A trois, or a 3, Fr. (ä trwä.) For three voices or instruments.
A trois mains, Fr. (ä trwä mănh.) For three hands.
A trois parties, Fr. (ä trwä pär-tē.) In three parts.
A trois voix, Fr. (ä trwä vwä.) For three voices.
A trompa tanida, Spa. (ä trōm-pä tä-nē-dä.) At the sound of the trumpet.
Attable, Fr. (ät-tăbl.) A kind of Moorish drum.

ā *ale,* ă *add,* ä *arm,* ē *eve,* ĕ *end,* ī *ice,* ĭ *ill,* ō *old,* ŏ *odd,* ô *dove,* oo *moon,* ū *lute,* ŭ *but,* ü *French sound.*

ATTA — AUME

Attácca, *It.* (ät-täk-kä.) At-
Attácca súbito, *It.* (ät-täk-kä soo-bē-tō.) tack or commence the next movement immediately.
Attacca l'allegro, *It.* (ät-täk-kä l' äl-lā-grō.) Commence the allegro immediately.
Attaccáre. *It.* (ät-täk-kā-rē.) To attack or com-
Attaquer, *Fr.* (ät-täk-ā.) mence the performance.
Attastáre, *It.* (ät-täs-tä-rē.) To touch, to strike.
Attempered system. A system of temperament founded on the diminution of some intervals, and the augmentation of others.
Attendant keys. Those scales having most sounds in common with the scale of any given key; the relative keys. In C major the attendant keys are, its relative minor A, the dominant G, and its relative minor E, the sub-dominant F and its relative minor D.
Attibbel. (ät-tĕb-bĕl.) A drum.
Attillatamente, *It.* (ät-tĕl-lä-tä-män-tĕ,) With affectation.
Atto, *It.* (ät-tō.) An act of an opera or play.
Atto di cadenza, *It.* (ät-tō dē kä-dän-tsä.) The point in a piece where a cadence may be introduced.
Atto primo, *It.* (ät-tō prē-mō.) The first act.
Attóre, *It.* (ät-tō-rē.) An actor or singer in an opera or play.
Attóri, *It.* (ät-tō-rē.) The principal actors or singers in an opera.
Atto secóndo, *It.* (ät-tō sĕ-kŏn-dō.) The second act.
Atto terzo, *It.* (ät-tō tĕr-tsō.) The third act.
Attríce, *It.* (ät-trē-tshĕ.) An actress or singer.
Aubade, *Fr.* (ō-bäd.) Morning music; a morning concert in the open air.
Au commencement, *Fr.* (ō cŏm-mänhamänh.) At the beginning.
Andáce, *It.* (ä-oo-dä-tshĕ.) Bold, spirited, audacious.
Auf, *Ger.* (ouf.) On, upon, in, at, etc.
Auf-blasen, *Ger.* (ouf-blä-z'n.) To sound a wind instrument.
Auf dem claviere spielen, *Ger.* (ouf dĕm kläf-ēr spē-l'n.) To play on the piano.
Auf dem klavier trommeln, *Ger.* (ouf dĕm kläf-ĕr trŏm-mĕln.) To drum on the piano.
Auf dem oberwerk, *Ger.* (ouf dĕm ō-bĕr-värk.) Upon the *upper-work* or highest row of keys in organ playing.
Auf der trommel wirbeln, *Ger.* (ouf dĕr trŏm-m'l vēr-b'ln.) To beat on the drum.
Auf der trompete blasen, *Ger.* (ouf dĕr trŏm-pāt-ĕ blä-z'n.) To play on the trumpet.
Auf einer trommel, *Ger.* (ouf ī-nĕr trŏm-m'l.) To beat on the drum.
Auflöten, *Ger.* (ouf-flō-t'n.) To play on a flute.
Aufgeigen, *Ger.* (ouf-ghī-gh'n.) To play on a fiddle.
Aufgeweekt, *Ger.* (ouf-ghĕ-vĕkt.) Lively, sprightly, cheerful.
Aufgeweektheit, *Ger.* (ouf-ghĕ-vĕkt-hīt.) Liveliness, cheerfulness.
Aufhalten, *Ger.* (ouf-häl-t'n.) To stop, to retard, to keep back.
Anfhaltung, *Ger.* (ouf-häl-toong.) Keeping back; a suspension.

Auflage, *Ger.* (ouf-lä-ghĕ.) Edition.
Auflösung, *Ger.* (ouf-lō-zoong.) The resolution of a discord.
Auforgeln, *Ger.* (ouf-ōr-g'ln.) To play for one on the organ.
Aufpfeifen, *Ger.* (ouf-pfī-f'n.) To play on a pipe, fife or flute.
Aufs, *Ger.* (oufs.) To the, on the.
Aufschlag, *Ger.* (ouf-shläg.) Up beat; the unaccented part of a bar. [londly.
Aufschallen, *Ger.* (ouf-shäl-l'n.) To sound
Aufsingen, *Ger.* (ouf-sing-ĕn.) To sing to, to awaken by singing.
Aufspielen, *Ger.* (ouf-spē-l'n.) To play upon, to play for the dance.
Aufsteigende tonarten, *Ger.* *pl.* (ouf-stī-ghĕn-dĕ tōn-är-t'n.) Ascending scales or keys.
Aufstrich, *Ger.* (ouf-strīkh.) An up-bow.
Auftakt, *Ger.* (ouf-täkt.) See Aufschlag.
Auftrompeten, *Ger.* (ouf-trŏm-pā-t'n.) To play on a trumpet.
Augmentatio, *Lat.* (aug-mĕn-tä-shī-ō.) Augmentation.
Augmentation. In counterpoint this signifies that the notes of the subject are repeated or imitated with notes of double their original value.
Augmenté, *Fr.* (ōg-mänh-tā.) Augmented.
Ingmentazione, *It.* (oug-mĕn-tä-tsē-ō-nĕ.) Increase.
Augmented. An epithet applied to such intervals as are more than a major or perfect.
Augmented fifth. An interval containing four whole tones or steps.
Augmented fourth. An interval containing three whole tones or steps.
Augmented intervals. Those which include a semitone more than major or perfect intervals; as,

Augmented octave. An interval containing five whole tones or steps, and two semitones or half steps.
Augmented second. An interval containing one whole and one semitone equal to three half steps.
Augmented sixth. An interval containing four whole tones or steps and one semitone or half step.
Augmented unison. A semitone, or half step.
Augménto, *It.* (oug-mān-tō.) Augmentation.
Auletes, *Gr.* (ou-lē-tĕs.) A flute player, a piper.
Auletic. Pertaining to a pipe; (little used.)
Au lever du rideau, *Fr.* (ō lĕ-vä dü rē-dō.) At the rising of the curtain.
Aullar, *Spa.* (oul-lär.) To howl, to utter a cry of distress.
Aullido, *Spa.* (oul-lē-dō,) Howl; the cry of a
Aullo, *Spa.* (oul-lō.) wolf or dog; a cry of terror.
Aulo, *It.* (ou-lō.) A species of ancient flute.
Aulos, *Gr.* (ou-lōs.)
Aulodia. *It.* (ou-lō-dī-ä.) Singing accompanied by the flute.
Aumentazióne, *It.* (ou-mĕn-tä-tsē-ō-nē.) Augmentation.

PRONOUNCING MUSICAL DICTIONARY.   25

ă ale, ă add, ä arm, ē eve, ĕ end, ī ice, ĭ ill, ō old, ŏ odd, ô dove, oo moon, ū tute, ŭ but, ü French sound.

AUNA

A úna córda, *It.* (ä oo-nä kōr-dä.) On one string.
Aus, *Ger.* (ous.) From, out of.
Ausarbeitung, *Ger.* (ous-är-bī-toong.) The last finish or elaboration of a composition.
Ausblänken, *Ger.* (ous-blän-k'n.) To play the closing chords of a piece on a wind instrument.
Ausblasen, *Ger.* (ous-blä-z'n.) To blow out; to publish by sound of trumpet.
Ausdehnung, *Ger.* (ous-dā-noong.) Expansion, extension, development.
Ausdruck, *Ger.* (ous-drook.) Expression.
Ausdrucksvoll, *Ger.* (ous-drooks-föll.) Expressive.
Ausführung, *Ger.* (ous-fū-roong.) Performance.
Ausfüllung, *Ger.* (ous-fül-loong.) The filling up, the middle parts.
Ausgabe, *Ger.* (ous-gä-bě.) Edition.
Ausgang, *Ger.* (ous-gäng.) Going out, exit, conclusion.
Ausgehalten, *Ger.* (ous-ghě-häl-t'n.) Sostenuto.
Ausgeigen, *Ger.* (ous-ghī-g'n.) To play to the end.
Ausgelassen, *Ger.* (ous-ghě-läs-s'n.) Wild, ungovernable.
Ausgelassenheit, *Ger.* (ous-ghě-läs-s'n-hīt.) Extravagance, wantonness.
Aushalten, *Ger.* (ous-häl-t'n.) To hold on, to sustain a note.
Aushaltung, *Ger.* (ous-häl-toong.) The sustaining of a note.
Aushaltungszeichen, *Ger.* (ous-häl-toongs-tsī-kh'n.) A pause. (⌒)
Auslauten, *Ger.* (ous-lou-t'n.) To emit a sound.
Ausklingeln, *Ger.* (ous-klīng-ĕln.) To publish by ringing a bell.
Ausklingen, *Ger.* (ous-klīng-ĕn.) To cease sounding.
Ausposaunen, *Ger.* (ous-pō-sou-nĕn.) To trumpet forth; to proclaim.
Aussingen, *Ger.* (ous-sīng ĕn.) To sing out, to sing to the end.
Ausstimmen, *Ger.* (ous-stĭm-mĕn.) To tune thoroughly.
Austrommeln, *Ger.* (ous-tröm-mĕln.) To drum out, to publish by the drum.
Austrompeten,*Ger.* (ous-tröm-pā-t'n.) To trumpet, to publish by sound of the trumpet.
Ausweichen, *Ger.* (ous-vī-kh'n.) To make a transition from one key to another.
Ausweichung, *Ger.* (ous-vī-khoong.) A transient modulation or change of key.
Auténtico, *It.* (ou-tän-tē-kō.) Authentic.
Anteur, *Fr.* (ō-tŭr.) An author, a composer.
Anteur d' hymnes, *Fr.* (ō-tŭr d'ĕmn.) A hymnologist, one who writes hymns.
Authentic. A name given to those church modes whose melody was confined within the limits of the tonic, or final, and its octave.
Authentic cadence. The old name for a perfect cadence; the harmony of the dominant followed by that of the tonic, or the progression of the dominant to the tonic.
Authentic keys. Among the ancient Greeks, those keys whose tones extended from the tonic to the fifth and octave above.

AZIO

Authentic melodies. Those melodies whose notes are chiefly confined within the limits of the tonic and its octave.
Authentique, *Fr.* (ō-tĕn-tēk.) Authentic.
Autor, *Spa.* (on-tōr.) } An author, a composer.
Autóre, *It.* (ou-tō-rĕ.) }
Antos sacramentales, *Spa.* (ou-tōs säk-rä-mĕn-tä-lĕs.) Dramatic representations formerly used by the Spaniards at religious festivals.
Auxiliary notes. Notes standing on the next degree above or below an essential note; the harmony remaining stationary and not moving from one essential note to another.
Auxiliary scales. This name is sometimes given to the *relative* or *attendant* keys.
Avant-dernier, *Fr.* (ä-vänh dĕr-nē-ä.) The penultimate; the last but one.
Avant-scene, *Fr.* (ä-vänh sän.) Before the opening of the opera or scene.
Ave, *Lat.* (ä-vě.) Hail.
Avec, *Fr.* (ä-vĕk.) With.
Avec allegresse, *Fr.* (ä-vĕk äl-lĕ-grĕss.) Lively, sprightly.
Avec ame, ou gout, *Fr.* (ä-vĕk äm, oo goot.) With feeling or grace.
Avec douleur, *Fr.* (ä-vĕk doo-lŭr.) With grief, with sadness.
Avec feu, *Fr.* (ä-vĕk fŭ.) With spirit.
Avec force, *Fr.* (ä-vĕk förss.) With power.
Avec gout, *Fr.* (ä-vĕk goo.) With taste.
Avec grande expression, *Fr.* (ä-vĕk granh dĕx-prä-sī-önh.) With great expression.
Avec lenteur, *Fr.* (ä-vĕk länh-tŭr.) With slowness, lingering.
Avec les pieds, *Fr.* (ä-vĕk lā pē-ä.) With the feet, in organ playing.
Avec liaison, *Fr.* (ä-vĕk lī-ā-sönh.) With smoothness.
Avec mouvement, *Fr.* (ä-vĕk moov-mönh.) With movement.
Ave Maria, *Lat.* (ä-vě mä-rē-ä.) Hail Maria! A hymn or prayer to the Virgin Mary.
Avemmaría, *It.* (ä-vĕm-mä-rē-ä.) A short prayer or hymn to the Virgin Mary; also, the tolling of a bell, in Roman Catholic countries, morning, noon, and at dusk, as a call to prayer.
Avéna, *It.* (ä-vā-nä.) A reed, a pipe.
A vicénda, *It.* (ä vē-tshĕn-dä.) Alternately, by turns.
A vide, *Fr.* (ä vēd.) Open.
A vista, *It.* (ä vē-tä.) At sight.
Avivadamente, *Spa.* (ä-vē-vä-dä-mān-tĕ.) In a lively manner, briskly.
A vóce sóla, *It.* (ä vō-tshĕ sō-lä.) For one voice alone.
Avoir du retentissement, *Fr.* (ä-vwär dŭ rā-tänh-tēss-mänh.) To be repeated.
A-voir le vois haut, *Fr.* (ä vwär lĕh vwä sō.) To have a loud voice.
A voix forte, *Fr.* (ä vwä fört.) With a loud voice.
A volonté, *Fr.* (ä vō-lönh-tā.) At will, at pleasure.
A vue, *Fr.* (ä vū.) At sight.
Ayre, *Spa.* (ä-rĕ.) Air.
Azióne sacra, *It.* (ä-tsē-ō-nĕ sä-krä.) An Oratorio; a sacred musical drama.

ā ale, ă add, ä arm, ē eve, ĕ end, ī ice, ĭ ill, ō old, ŏ odd, ô dove, oo moon, ū tute, ŭ but, ü French sound.

B

B. The seventh note of the modern scale of C. It is called in France and Italy *Si*, and by the Germans *H*. The Germans use the letter *B* to indicate *B flat*.

Baazas, *Fr.* (bä-zü.) A species of guitar.

Babara, *Spa.* (bär-bä-rä.) A Spanish country dance.

Babel. A confused mixture of sounds.

Bacas, *Spa.* (bä-käs.) A quick tune on the guitar.

Bacchia. A Kamschatka dance in 2–4 time.

Bacchanalian songs. Drinking songs; songs pertaining to drunkenness and revelry.

Bacchins, *Gr.* (băk-kĭ-ŭs.) A musical foot, consisting of one short, unaccented, and two long, accented notes or syllables marked ‿ ‒ ‒.

Bacchuslied, *Ger.* (băkh-oos-lēd.) A Bacchanalian song.

Bacciocolo, *It.* (bät-tshē-ō-kō-lō.) A musical instrument common in some parts of Tuscany.

Bachelor of Music. The first musical degree taken at the universities.

Badajada, *Spa.* (bä-dä-hä-dä.) The stroke of a bell.

Badajo, *Spa.* (bä-dä-hō.) The tongue of a bell.

Badinage, *Fr.* (bä-dĭ-näzh.) Playfulness, sportiveness.

Bagatelle, *Fr.* (băg-ă-tĕl.) A trifle, a toy, a short, easy piece of music.

Bagpipes. A favorite Scotch instrument, one of whose pipes is a *drone*, producing always the same sound, which serves as a perpetual bass for every tune. It is a very ancient instrument, and in one form or another has been in general use not only in England and Scotland, but many European countries.

Baguette. *Fr.* (bä-ghĕt.) A drumstick.

Baguettes de tambour, *Fr.* (bä-ghĕt düh täm-boor.) Drumsticks.

Baile, *Spa.* (bä-ē-lĕ.) The national dances of Spain.

Baisser, *Fr.* (bäs-sä.) To lower or flatten the pitch or tone.

Baisser le rideau, *Fr.* (bäs-sä lŭh rē-dō.) To drop the curtain.

Bajon, *Spa.* (bä-hōn.) The bassoon.

Balada. *Spa* (bä-lä-dä.) A ballad.

Balalaika, *Rus.* (bä-lä-lä-kä.) A rude instrument of the Russians, with three strings.

Bälgetreter, *Ger.* (bäl-ghĕ-trĕt-ĕr.) Organ blower or bellows treader in old German organs.

Balgzug, *Ger.* (bälg-tsoog.) In an organ, the bellows stop.

Balansé, *Fr.* (bä-länh-sä.) A step or figure in dancing.

Balancement, *Fr.* (băl-änks-mänh.) Quivering motion; a tremolo.

Balcken, *Ger.* (băl-k'n.) The bass bar placed under the fourth string in a violin.

Baldaménte, *It.* (bäl-dä-män-tĕ.) Boldly.

Baldánza, *It.* (bäl-dän-tsä.) } Audacity, boldness.
Baldézza, *It.* (bäl-dät sä.) }

Balken, *Ger.* (băl-k'n.) See Balcken.

Ballábile, *It.* (bäl-lä-bē-lĕ.) In the style of a dance.

Ballad. A short simple song of natural construction, usually in the narrative or descriptive form. It formerly had a wider signification and was applied to music set to romance or historical poem, and also to a light kind of music used both in singing and dancing. The word Ballad means, now, any unvaried simple song, each verse being sung to the same melody.

BALLO

Ballade, *Ger.* (băl-lä-dĕ.) } A dance, dancing;
Balláta, *It.* (băl-lä-tä.) } also, a Ballad.

Balladendichter, *Ger.* (băl-lăd'n-dĭkh-tĕr.) A ballad writer.

Balladensänger, *Ger.* (băl-lăd'n-säng-ĕr.) A ballad singer.

Balladenverkäufer, *Ger.* (băl-lăd'n-fär kof-fr.) A ballad vender.

Balladist. A writer of ballads.

Ballad of Ballads. The designation given in an old version of the Bible to Solomon's Song.

Ballad opera. Light opera; an opera in which ballads and dances predominate.

Balladry. The subject or style of ballads.

Ballad singer. One whose employment is to sing ballads.

Ballad style. In the manner or style of a ballad.

Balláre. *It.* (băl-lä-rĕ.) To dance.

Ballatélla, *It.* (băl-lä-tĕl-lä.) } A short Balláta.
Ballatétta, *It.* (băl-lä-tĕt-tä.) }

Ballatóre, *It.* (băl-lä-tō-rĕ.) A dancer, a male dancer.

Ballatríce, *It.* (băl-lä-trē-tsĕ.) A female dancer.

Ballan. *Wel.* (băl-län.) A bell.

Ballematia. *It.* (băl-lĕ-mä-tē-ä.) } Songs or mel-
Ballistia, *It.* (băl-ĭs-tē-ä.) } odies in the dance style.

Ballerína, *It.* (băl-lĕ-rē-nä.) A dancing mistress, a female dancer.

Ballerino, *It.* (băl-lĕ-rē-nō.) A dancing master, a male dancer.

Balleronzolo. *It.* (băl-lĕ-rōn-tsō-lō.) A little dance.

Ballet. *Fr.* (băl-lā.) } A theatrical represen-
Balletto, *It.* (băl-lĕt-tō.) } tation of some story or fable, by means of dances or metrical action, accompanied with music. In England the second or concluding piece of the evening's entertainment is generally a ballet. In the sixteenth century the term *ballet*, *ballad*, or *ballette* was applied to a light kind of music which was both sung and danced.

Ballet Master. The person who superintends the rehearsals of the ballet, and who frequently invents the fable and its details.

Ballette. A ballet.

Balletti, *It.* (băl-lĕt-tē.) Dance airs.

Bálli, *It. pl.* (băl-lē.) Dances.

Bálli della Stíria, *It. pl.* (băl-lē dĕl-lä stē-rē-ä.) Styrian dances resembling waltzes.

Bálli Inglési, *It. pl.* (băl-lē ēn-glä-zē.) English country dances.

Bálli Ungarési, *It. pl.* (băl-lē oon-gä-rä-zē.) Hungarian dance in 2–4 time, generally syncopated, or accented on the weak part of the bar.

Bállo, *It.* (băl-lō.) A dance or dance tune.

Ballónchio, *It.* (băl-lōn-kē-ō.) An Italian country dance.

Ballonzáre, *It.* (băl-lōn-tsä-rĕ.) To dance artistically.

ā ale, ă add, ä arm, ē eve, ĕ end, ī ice, ĭ ill, ō old, ŏ odd, ô dove, oo moon, ū lute, ŭ but, ü French sound.

BAMB

Bambalina, *Spa.* (bäm-bä-lē-nä.) The proscenium of an opera house.
Band. A number of instrumental performers associated together for the purpose of playing in concert on their respective instruments.
Bánda, *It.* (bän-dä.) A band.
Band, brass. A band where only brass instruments are played.
Band, chamber. A band whose performances consist only of chamber music.
Band, choral. Orchestral performers.
Band, full. Where all the instruments proper to a band are employed.
Band, marine. A band located in a garrison or employed on ships of war.
Band master. The leader or conductor of a band.
Bandola, *Spa.* (bän-dō-lä.) An instrument resembling a lute.
Bandóra, *It.* (bän-dō-rä.) } An ancient stringed
Bandóre, *It.* (bän-dō-rē.) } instrument of the lute or cither species.
Band, reed. A band with only reed instruments.
Band, regimental. A band belonging to a regiment; a military band.
Band, string. A band with only stringed instruments.
Bandurría, *Spa.* (bän-door-rē-ä.) A species of Spanish guitar; a *Bandóra*.
Banjo. A species of guitar and tambourine united, used by the negroes.
Bänkelsänger, *Ger.* (bän-k'l-säng-ĕr.) A ballad singer.
Baqueta, *Spa.* (bä-kĕ-tä.)
Baquetas del tambor, *Spa.* (bä-kĕ-täs dĕl tän-bôr.) } Drumsticks.
Baquico, *Spa.* (bä-kē-kō.) Bacchanalian.
Bar. Lines drawn perpendicularly across the staff to divide it into small and equal portions; the term is also applied to each of these small and equal portions by European usage.
Barbarism. In music it relates to false harmony or false modulation.
Barbiton, *Gr.* (bär-bī-tŏn.) A name formerly applied to the viol and violin.
Barbitos, *Lat.* (bär-bī-tŏs.) An ancient instrument of the lyre species.
Barcaróla, *It.* (bär-kä-rō-lä.) } A song or air
Barcarolle, *Fr.* (bär-kä-rōl.) } sung by the Venetian *gondoliers*, or boatmen, while following their avocations.
Barcaruola, *It.* (bär-kä-roo-ō-lä.) The song of the gondolier.
Bard. A poet and singer among the ancient Celts. The bard was a person of great importance and received great attention from high and low.
Bardd, *Wel.* (bärd.) A bard, a poet and musician.
Bardd alan, *Wel.* (bärd ä-län.) A professor of music.
Bardgan, *Wel.* (bärd-gän.) A song.
Bardo, *It.* (bär-dō.) A bard among the ancient Celts.
Bárdahī. (bär-dä-hē.) The Hindoo name for a bard.
Bardóne, *It.* (bär-dō-nĕ.) See Bourdon.
Bar, dotted double. A double bar with dots

BARR

preceding it, shows that the music before it is to be repeated; the dots after the double bar show that the following music is to be repeated. Dots each side of the double bar show that both the preceding and following music are to be repeated
Bar, double. Heavy lines drawn across the staff to divide off different parts of the movement or show the end of the piece.
Bardus, *Cel.* (bär-düs.) A singer.
Barem. A stopped register, of soft 8 or 16 feet tone, in German organs.
Bari. An abbreviation of Baritone.
Bari-basso. A deep baritone voice.
Bariolage, *Fr.* (bär-ĭ-ō-läzh.) A passage for the violin, etc., in which the open strings are more especially used.
Baripicni, *Gr.* (bä-rĭ-pĕk-nē.) A term applied by the ancient Greeks to low tones in general.
Baripicni suoni, *It.* (bä-rē-pĕk-nē swō-nē.) Fixed sounds.
Bari-tenor. The deeper sort of tenor voice.
Bariton-clef. The F clef, placed upon the third line; now obsolete.
Bariton, *Fr.* (bä-rĭ-tŏnh.) } A male voice in-
Baritono, *It.* (bär-rē-tō-nō.) } termediate in re-
Baritone. } spect to pitch between the bass and tenor, the compass usually extending from B flat to F.
Baritono, *It.* (bä-rē-tō-nō.) Baritone.
Barócco, *It.* (bä-rōk-kō.) } A term applied to
Baroque, *Fr.* (bä-rōk.) } music in which the harmony is confused and abounding in unnatural modulations.
Bärpfeife, *Ger.* (bär-pfī-fĕ.) Bear pipe; an obsolete reed stop of soft intonation.
Barquarde, *Fr.* (bär-kärd.) An obsolete term for *barcarolle*.
Barrage, *Fr.* (bär-räzh.) See *Barré*.
Barre, *Fr.* (bär.) A bar, in music.
Barré, *Fr.* (bär-rā.) In guitar playing, a temporary nut formed by placing the forefinger of the left hand across some of the strings.
Barred C. C with a bar across it; one of the marks of common time, thus, ₵.
Barre de luth, *Fr.* (bär düh loot.) The bridge of the lute.
Barre de mesure, *Fr.* (bär düh mĕ-zür.) A bar-line.
Barre de répétition, *Fr.* (bär düh rā-pā-tē-sĭ-ōnh.) A dotted double bar; also, a thick line used as an abbreviation to mark the repetition of a group of notes.
Barred semicircle. See Barréd C; a character that denotes a quicker movement than the sign without a bar, and called alla breve, because it was formerly written with one breve in a measure.
Barrel. The body of a bell.
Barrel chime. The cylindrical portion of the mechanism sometimes used for the purpose of ringing a chime of bells.
Barrel organ. An organ, the tones of which are produced by the revolution of a cylinder. The tunes are produced by an arrangement of pins and staples with which the cylinder is studded.

ā ale, ă add, ä arm, ē eve, ĕ end, ī ice, ĭ ill, ō old, ŏ odd, ô dove, oo moon, ū lute, ŭ but, ü French sound.

BARR

Barrer. The act of employing the forefinger of the left hand as a nut in guitar playing.
Barrer, great. The act of pressing all the strings of the guitar at the same time, with the forefinger of the left hand.
Barrer, small. The act of pressing two or three strings of a guitar with the forefinger of the left hand.
Barrure, Fr. (băr-rür.) The bar of a lute, etc.
Baryphonus. (bă-rĭf-ō-nŭs.) A man with a very deep or very coarse voice.
Barypicni, Gr. (bā-rĭ-pĭk-nē.) A name given by the ancients to five of the tones of their system.
Baryton. Fr. (bā-rĭ-tônh.) A kind of bass viol, now obsolete. A brass instrument.
Barytone. See Baritone.
Barz, Wel. (bärz.) A poet musician, a bard.
Bas, Fr. (bäh.) Low.
Bas dessus, Fr. (bäh däs-sü.) A mezzo soprano, or second treble voice.
Base. The lowest or deepest male voice; the
Bass. lowest part in a musical composition.
Basilica, It. (bä-zēl-ē-kä.) A cathedral.
Bássa, It. (băs-sä.) Low, deep; 8va bássa, play the notes an octave lower.
Bass alberti. A bass formed by taking the notes of chords in arpeggios.
Bassanello, It. (bäs-sä-nāl-lō.) An obsolete musical instrument.
Bássa ottáva, It. (băs-sä ōt-tä-vä.) Play the passage an octave lower than written.
Bass beam. The small beam inside the viol, nearly under the bass string.
Bassbläser, Ger. (bäs-s-blä-z'r.) A bassoonist.
Bass bridge. The bass beam.
Bass chantante, Fr. (bäs shōnb-tônht.) The vocal bass.
Bass clef. The bass or F clef, placed upon the fourth line.
Bass concertina. A concertina having the compass of a violincello.
Bass, continued. Bass continued through the whole piece; the figured bass.
Bass, contra, It. (bäss kōn-trä.) The lower bass.
Bass cornet. An ancient instrument consisting of a tube four or five feet long and increasing in size from the mouth to the end.
Bass, counter. The under bass; part performed by the double basses.
Bass, double. The double bass viol; the lowest toned instrument of the viol kind.
Bass drone. The monotonous bass produced by the large tube of the bagpipe.
Basse, Fr. (bäss.) The bass part.
Basse chantante, Fr. (bäss shänh-tänht.) Vocal bass; see Bass Chantante.
Bass chiffree, Fr. (bäss shēf-frā.) A figured bass.
Bass continue, Fr. (bäss kōnh-tēn-ü.) Thorough bass.
Bass contrainte, Fr. (bäss kōnh-tränht.) The constrained or ground bass.
Bass contre, Fr. (bäss kōntr.) Bass counter, double bass; also, the deep bass voice called by the Italians *basso profóndo*.

BASS

Bass figuree. Fr. (bäss fē-gü-rā.) The figured bass.
Bass fondamentale, Fr. (bäss fōnh-dä-mänh-täl.) The fundamental bass.
Bass taille, Fr. (bäss tä-yüh.) Baritone voice; low tenor voice.
Basset horn. An instrument resembling a clarinet; the scale is extensive and intermediate between those of the clarinet and bassoon.
Bassett. A little bass, generally somewhat higher than the usual bass.
Bassétto, It. (bäs-sāt-tō.) The little bass; also, an obsolete instrument with four strings; also, a 4 feet reed organ stop of bright tone.
Bassetto horn. A species of clarinet a fifth lower than the C clarinet.
Bass, figured. A bass figured, or accompanied by numerals, denoting the harmony to be played by the other parts of the composition.
Bass, first. High bass.
Bass-flöte, Ger. (bäss flō-tē.) An old instru-
Bass-flute. ment of the bassoon species; also, the name of an organ stop on the pedal of 8 feet tone.
Bass, fundamental. The bass which contains the roots of the chords only. This bass is not intended to be played, but serves as a test of the correctness of the harmony.
Bass-geige, Ger. (bäss-ghī-ghē.) Bass-viol; the contra-basso.
Bass, given. A bass to which harmony is to be placed.
Bass, grace. A small note like a short appoggiatura struck at the same time with the principal chord but immediately left. It is frequently used in organ playing to strengthen the parts and supply the want of pedals.
Bass, ground. A bass consisting of a few notes or bars containing a subject of its own, repeated throughout the movement and each time accompanied by a new or varied melody.
Bass, high. A baritone, a voice midway between bass and tenor.
Bass horn. An instrument resembling the ophicleide, formerly much used in bands.
Bassi, It. (bäs-sē.) A term implying the entrance of the brass instruments.
Bassist, Ger. (bäs-sĭst.) } A bass singer.
Bassista, It. (bäs-sēs-tä.) }
Bass, low. Second bass.
Básso, It. (bäs-sō.) The bass part.
Básso, buffo, It. (bäs-sō boof-fō.) The principal bass singer in the comic opera.
Básso cantante, It. (bäs-sō kän-tän-tē.) The vocal bass part; also, the principal bass singer in an opera.
Básso comico, It. (bäs-sō kō-mē-kō.) A comic bass singer in an opera.
Básso concertánte, It. (bäs-sō kōn-tshěr-tän-tē.) The principal bass; also, the lighter and more delicate parts performed by the violincello or bassoon.
Básso construtto, It. (bäs-sō kōn-stroot-tō.) Ground bass, constrained bass.
Básso continuo, It. (bäs-sō kōn-tē-noo-ō.) The continued bass; a bass that is figured to indicate the harmony.

ă ale, ă add, ă arm, ĕ eve, ĕ end, ī ice, ĭ ill, ō old, ŏ odd, ō dove, oo moon, ū lute, ŭ but, ū French sound.

BASS

Básso contra, *It.* (bäs-sō kŏn-trä.) ⎱ A double
Básso contro, *It.* (bäs-sō kŏn-tro.) ⎰ bass viol;
the lowest or gravest part of a musical composition.
Básso d'accompagnamento, *It.* (bäs-sō d' äk-kŏm-pän-yä-män-tō.) An accompanying bass.
Básso figuráto, *It.* (bäs-sō fē-goo-rä-tō.) The figured bass.
Básso fondamentále, *It.* (bäs-sō fŏn-dä-män-tä-lĕ.) The fundamental bass.
Básso numeráto, *It.* (bäs-sō noo-mě-rä-tō.) Figured bass.
Básso ostináto, *It.* (bäs-sō ōs-tē-nä-tō.) A ground bass.
Básso primo, *It.* (bäs-sō prē-mo.) The first bass.
Básso recitánte, *It.* (bäs-sō rā-tahē-tän-tē.) Bass of the small chorus.
Básso ripiéno, *It.* (bäs-sō rē-pē-ā-nō.) A bass part only intended to be played in the full or tutti passages.
Básso rivoltáto, *It.* (bäs-sō rē-vōl-tä-tō.) An inverted bass.
Básso secondo, *It.* (bäs-sō sĕ-kŏn-dō.) The second bass.
Básso tenúto, *It.* (bäs-sō tĕ-noo-tō.) Continued bass.
Básso violino, *It.* (bäs-sō vē-ō-lē-nō.) A small bass viol.
Bass oder F Schlussel, *Ger.* (bäss ō-dĕr F shloos-a'l.) The bass, or F clef.
Basson, *Fr.* (bäs-sŏnh.) Bassoon.
Bassoon. A wind instrument of wood, consisting of a perforated tube and a reed through which it is blown. It is not very agreeable as a solo instrument, but indispensable in full orchestra. The lower tones are strong and rough, but the middle rich and pleasing. Its compass extends from double B flat to B flat in alt.
Bassoonist. A performer on the bassoon.
Basson quinte, *Fr.* (bäs-sŏnh känht.) A small bassoon of the same compass as the ordinary bassoon, but the tones are a fifth higher.
Basson quart, (bäs-sŏnh kär.) An instrument whose tones are a fourth lower than the ordinary bassoon.
Bassoon stop, A reed stop in the organ which imitates the tones of the bassoon.
Bass-pfeife, *Ger.* (bäss pfī-fĕ.) Bass-pipe, bassoon.
Bass posaune, *Ger.* (bäss pō-zou-nĕ.) Bass trombone, sackbut.
Bass, radical. The fundamental bass.
Bass-saite. *Ger.* (bäss sot-tĕ.) Bass string.
Bass-schlüssel, *Ger.* (bäss shlūs-a'l.) The bass clef.
Bass staff. The staff marked with the bass clef.
Bass-stimme, *Ger.* (bäss stĭm-mĕ.) Bass voice, bass part.
Bass string. The string of any instrument upon which the lowest note is sounded.
Bass, sub. The lowest notes of an organ; the ground bass.
Bass, thorough. The art of writing out harmony for different parts or voices through the bass alone, it being the only part given; the fundamental rules of musical composition.

BAYL

Bass trombone. A trombone having a compass from the great C to the one lined e, and noted in the F clef.
Bass tuba, *Lat.* (bäss tū-bä.) See Tuba.
Bass viol. An old name for the viol da gámba, now often given to the violincello.
Bass viol, double. A stringed instrument, the largest and deepest toned of its class.
Bass voice. The lowest or deepest of male voices.
Bass-zeichen, *Ger.* (bäss tsī-k'n.) The bass clef.
Básta, *It.* (bäs-tä.) ⎱ Enough, sufficient,
Bastánte, *It.* (bäs-tän-tĕ.) ⎰ proceed no further unless directed by the conductor.
Bastardilla, *Spa.* (bäs-tär-dēl-yä.) A species of flute.
Batillus, *Lat.* (bä-tĭl-lūs.) An instrument used by the Armenians in their church service.
Batócchie, *It.* (bät-tŏk-kē-ō.) ⎱ The tongue of
Battáglio, *It.* (bät-täl-yē-ō.) ⎰ a bell.
Battant, *Fr.* (bät-tänh.)
Battement, *Fr.* (bät-mŏnh.) ⎱ An old name
Battiménto, *It.* (bät-tē-män-tō.) ⎰ for that kind of short-shake called a beat.

Báttere, *It.* (bät-tā-rĕ.) The down stroke in beating time.
Báttere a ricolta, *It.* (bät-tā-rĕ ä rē-kŏl-tä.) To beat a retreat.
Batterie, *Fr.* (bät-trē.) The roll of the drum; also, a particular way of playing the guitar by striking the strings instead of pulling them.
Baton, *Fr.* (bä-tŏnh.)
Baton de mesure, *Fr.* (bä-tŏnh dūh mĕ-sūr.) The stick used by the conductor in beating time.
Batoon. A term denoting a rest of four semi-breves.
Battitúra, *It.* (bät-tē-too-rä.) The act of beating time.
Battle hymn. A war song composed to be sung before or during a battle.
Battre, *Fr.* (bättr.) To beat.
Battre la caisse, *Fr.* (bätr lä käss.)
Battre le tambour, *Fr.* (bätr lūh tämboor.) ⎱ To beat the drums.
Battre la mesure, *Fr.* (bätr lä mä-sūr.) To beat time; to mark the time by beating with the hand or with a stick.
Battísta, *It.* (bät-tēs-ta.) Time or measure; the accented part of a bar.
Bau, *Ger.* (bou.) The structure, the fabric, the construction of musical instruments.
Bäuerisch, *Ger.* (boy-ĕr-ish.) Rustic, coarse.
Bauernflöte, *Ger.* (bou-ĕrn-flōt-ĕ.) Rustic flute; a stopped register in an organ.
Bauernlied, *Ger.* (bou-ĕrn-lēd.) A rustic ballad.
Baxo, *Spa.* (bäk-sō.) Bass; a player on the bass-viol or bassoon.
Baxon, *Spa.* (bäk-sŏn.) A bassoon. See Bajon.
Baxonsillo, *Spa.* (bäk-sŏn-sēl-yō.) A little bassoon; also, an organ stop equivalent to the open diapason.
Bayladero, *Spa.* (bä-lä-dā-rō.) Suited to dancing.

ă ale, ă add, ă arm, ē eve, ĕ end, ī ice, ĭ ill, ō old, ŏ odd, ô dove, oo moon, ū tute, ŭ but, ü French sound.

BAYL

Bayle, *Spa.* (bā-lē.) An interlude between the second and third act; a dance.
Baylecito, *Spa.* (bē-lē-thē-tō.) A little dance.
B, cancellatum, *Lat.* (B kăn-sĕl-lā-tŭm.) The old name for a *sharp,* (♯).
B, double. The B below G gamut; the twelfth below the bass clef note.
B dur, *Ger.* (BĂ door.) The key of B flat major.
B durum, *Lat.* (B dū-rŭm.) B *hard* or B major.
Bearbeitet, *Ger.* (bĕ-ăr-bī-tĕt.) Arranged, adapted.
Bearbeitung, *Ger.* (bĕ-ăr-bī-toong.) Adaptation.
Bearing notes. In tuning instruments those erroneous or falsely tempered fifths on which "the wolf" is said to be thrown.
Bearpipe. See Bärpfeife.
Beat. The rise or fall of the hand or *bâton* in marking the divisions of time in music; an important musical embellishment, consisting of the principal note and the note *below* it, resembling a short trill.
Beat, down. The falling of the hand in beating time.
Beatings. Regular pulsations produced in an organ by pipes of the same key when they are not exactly in unison.
Beating time. Marking the divisions of the bar by means of the hand, foot or bâton.
Beat, left. The movement of the hand toward the left in beating time.
Beat, right. A motion to the right in beating time.
Beat, up. The elevation of the hand in beating time.
Beben, *Ger.* (bā-b'n.) To tremble, to shake, to vibrate.
Bebende stimme, *Ger.* (bā-bĕn-dĕ stĭm-mĕ.) A trembling voice.
Bebung, *Ger.* (bā-boong.) A shaking, a vibration; also, a German organ stop.
Bec, *Fr.* (bĕk.) The mouthpiece of a clarinet.
Bécarre, *Fr.* (bā-kăr.) The mark called a natural, (♮).
Bécco, *It.* (băk-kō.) The mouthpiece of a clarinet, flageolet, etc.
Becco polacco, *It.* (băk-kō pō-lăk-kō.) A large species of bagpipe used in some parts of Italy.
Becken, *Ger.* (bĕk'n.) Cymbals.
Beckenschläger, *Ger.* (bĕk'n-shläg-ĕr.) A cymbal player.
Bedon, *Fr.* (bĕ-dônh.) An old name for a tabret, or drum.
Be, *Ger.* (bā.) Flat, b flat.
Been, *Ger.* (bān.) A stringed instrument of the guitar species, used in India.
Befabemi, *Spa.* (bĕf-ă-bā-mē.) A musical sign.
Beffroi, *Fr.* (bĕf-frwă.) The frame that supports the bell in a belfry; a belfry.
Begeisterung, *Ger.* (bĕ-ghīs-tĕ-roong.) Inspiration, animation, enthusiasm.
Begl. An abbreviation of *begleitung.*
Begleiten, *Ger.* (bĕ-glī-t'n.) To accompany.
Begleitende stimmen, *Ger. pt.* (bĕ-glī-tĕn-dĕ stĭm-mĕn.) The accompanying parts.
Begleiter, *Ger.* (bĕ-glī-tĕr.) An accompanist.

BELL

Begleitung, *Ger.* (bĕ-glī-toong.) An accompaniment.
Beharrlich, *Ger.* (bĕ-hăr-lĭkh.) Perseveringly.
Beherzt, *Ger.* (bĕ-hărtst.) Courageous.
Beifallklatschen, *Ger.* (bī-făl-klăt-sh'n.) Applauding; applause.
Beinahe, *Ger.* (bī-nă-ĕ.) Almost.
Beisp. An abbreviation of *beispiel.*
Beispiel, *Ger.* (bī-spēl.) Example.
Beit, *Per.* (bīt.) A distich.
Beitöne, *Ger.* (bī-tō-nĕ.) Accessory tones.
Beizeichen, *Ger.* (bī-tsī-kh'n.) An accidental.
Belfry. A tower in which a bell or bells are hung.
Belieben, *Ger.* (bĕ-lē-b'n.) Pleasure; at pleasure.
Beliebig, *Ger.* (bĕ-lē-bĕg.) To one's liking, or pleasure.
Bélière, *Fr.* (bā-lī-ăr.) The tongue of a bell.
Bell. A vessel or hollow body of cast metal, used for making sounds. It consists of a barrel or hollow body enlarged or expanded at one end, an ear or cannon by which it is hung to a beam, and a clapper inside. 2. A hollow body of metal perforated, and containing a solid ball to give sounds when shaken. 3. The wide circular opening at the end of a trumpet, horn, and similar instruments.
Bells, *Sax.* (bĕl-lă.) A bell.
Bell chamber. That portion of the tower or steeple in which the bell hangs, the belfry.
Bellézza, *It.* (bĕl-lăt-să.) Beauty of tone and expression.
Bellézza della vóce, *It.* (bĕl-lăt-să dĕl-lă vō-tshĕ.) Beauty or sweetness of voice.
Bell gamba. A gamba stop in an organ, the top of each pipe spreading out like a bell.
Bell harp. An old instrument, probably the lyra or cithera of the ancients. 2. A stringed instrument, so named from its being swung like a bell when played.
Bellicosaménte, *It.* (bĕl-lē-kō-ză-măn-tĕ.) In a martial and warlike style.
Bellicóso, *It.* (bĕl-lē-kō-zō.)
Bellicum, *Lat.* (bĕl-lī-kŭm.) The sound of a trumpet calling to battle.
Bell, mass. A small bell used in the Roman Catholic service to call attention to the more solemn parts of the mass.
Bell metronome. A metronome with a small bell that strikes at the beginning of each bar.
Bellows. A pneumatic appendage for supplying organ pipes with air.
Bellows, exhaust. A kind of bellows used on organs and other reed instruments; the air, when the chamber is exhausted, being drawn in through the reeds.
Bellows, panting. A style of bellows designed to prevent all jerkings and to produce a regular flow of wind in the pipes of an organ.
Bell-ringers. Performers who, with bells of different sizes, ranging from smallest to largest, are able to produce very pleasing and effective music.
Bell, sacring. A small bell used in the Roman Catholic church. See Bell, mass.
Bell scale. A diapason with which bell founders measure the size, thickness, weight and tone of their bells.

ă ale, ă add, ä arm, ē eve, ĕ end, ī ice, ĭ ill, ō old, ŏ odd, ô dove, oo moon, ū tute, ŭ but, ü French sound.

BELL

Bell, vesper. The sounding of a bell about half an hour after sunset, in Roman Catholic countries, calling the people to vespers.
Belly. The sound-board of an instrument, that part over which the strings are distended.
Bel metállo di vóce, *It.* (běl mĕ-tăl-lo dē vō-tchĕ.) A clear and brilliant voice.
Bemerkbar, *Ger.* (bĕ-märk-bär.) Observable, marked; to be played in a prominent manner.
Bémol, *Fr.* (bā-mŏl.) The mark called a
Bemólle, *It.* (bă-mŏl-lĕ.) } flat, (♭).
Bemolado, *Spa.* (bă-mō-lá-do.) Having B flat.
Bemol, double. B double flat.
Bemolise, *Fr.* (bă-mō-lēz.) Marked with a flat.
Bemolisée, *Fr.* (bĕ-mō-lī-zā.) A note preceded by a flat.
Bemoliser, *Fr.* (bĕ-mō-lī-zā.) } To flat-
Bemollizzáre, *It.* (bă-mŏl-lēt-sä-rĕ.) } ten notes; to lower the pitch by putting a flat before them.
Bemolle, *It.* (bă-mol.) Flat.
Bén, *It.* (băn.) } Well, good.
Béne, *It.* (bā nĕ.) }
Benedicite, *Lat.* (bĕn-ĕ-dĕ-sī-tĕ.) A canticle used at morning prayer, in the church, after the first lesson.
Benedictus, *Lat.* (bĕn-ĕ-dĭk-tŭs.) One of the principal movements in a mass.
Béne plácito, *It.* (bā-nĕ plă-tshē-tō.) At will, at pleasure, at liberty to retard the time and ornament the passage.
Ben marcáto, *It.* (băn mär-kă-tō.) } Well
Béne marcáto, *It.* (bā-nĕ mär-kă-tō.) } marked, in a distinct and strongly accented manner.
Ben marcáto il cánto, *It.* (băn mär-kă-tō ĭl kăn-tō.) Mark well the melody.
Ben moderáto, *It.* (băn mŏd-ĕ-rä-tō.) Very moderate time.
Ben pronunciato, *It.* (băn prō-noon-tshē-ä-tō.) }
Ben pronunziato, *It.* (băn prō-noon-tsē-ä-tō.) } Pronounced clearly and distinctly.
Ben tenuto, *It.* (băn tĕ-noo-tō.) Held on; fully sustained.
Be quádro, *It.* (bā quă-drō.) } The mark called
Bé quarré, *Fr.* (bā kăr-rā.) } a natural, (♮).
Bequem, *Ger.* (bĕ-quěm.) Convenient.
Bergamásca, *It.* (bĕr-gă-mäs-kă.) A kind of rustic dance.
Bergeret, (bĕr-jĕ-rĕt.) An old term signifying a song.
Bergomask. A rustic dance. See Bergamásca.
Bergreigen. *Ger.* (bĕrg-rī-ghĕn.) Alpine melody.
Berlingozza, *It.* (bĕr-lĕn-gŏt-sä.) A country dance.
Berloque, *Fr.* (bĕr-lŏk.) In military service the drum calling to meals.
Bes, *Ger.* (bĕs.) The note B double flat, B♭♭.
Besaiten, *Ger.* (bĕ-sol-t'n.) To string an instrument.
Beschleunigend, *Ger.* (bĕ-shloi-nĕ-gĕnd.) Hastening.
Beschreibung, *Ger.* (bĕ-shrī-boong.) A description.
Befiedern, *Ger.* (bĕ-fē-dĕrn.) To quill a harpsichord.
Besingen, *Ger.* (bĕ-sĭng-ĕn.) To sing, to celebrate in song.
Bestimmt, *Ger.* (bĕs-tĭmt.) Distinct.

BISC

Bestimmtheit, *Ger.* (bĕs-tĭmt-hīt.) Precision, certainty.
Betglocke, *Ger.* (bāt-glŏk-ĕ.) Prayer bell.
Betonend, *Ger.* (bĕ-tō-nĕnd.) } Accented.
Betont, *Ger.* (bĕ-tōnt.) }
Betónung, *Ger.* (bĕ-lō-noong.) Accentuation.
Betrübniss, *Ger.* (bĕ-trüb-nĭss.) Grief, sadness.
Betrübt, *Ger.* (bĕ-trübt.) Afflicted, grieved.
Bewegung, *Ger.* (bĕ-vā-goong.) Motion, movement.
Beweglich, *Ger.* (bĕ-vā-glĭkh.) Movable.
Bewegt, *Ger.* (bĕ-vāgt.) Moved, rather fast.
Beyspiel, *Ger.* (bī-spēl.) An example.
Bezeichnung. *Ger.* (bĕ-tsĭkh-noong.) Mark, accentuation.
Bezifferte bass, *Ger.* (bĕr-tsĭf-fĕr-tĕ bäss.) The figured bass.
B flat. The flat seventh of the key of C.
Bhát. (bät.) The Hindoo name for a *bard*.
Bi. (bē.) A syllable applied by the Spaniards to the letter B of the scale, called by other nations *si*.
Bianca, *It.* (bē-än-kă.) A minim or half note.
Bichord, *Lat.* (bē-kŏrd.) A term applied to instruments that have two strings to each note.
Bichordon, *Lat.* (bī-kŏr-dŏn.) An instrument with only two strings. See *Colachon*.
Bisinium *Lat.* (bī-sĭn-ī-ŭm.) A composition in two parts; a duet, or two part song.
Bien attaquer une note, *Fr.* (bī-ănh ăt-tăk-ā ŭn nōt.) To strike a note firmly.
Bifara, *Lat.* (bī-fă-rä.) An organ stop, each pipe having two mouths, causing gentle waves or undulations.
Bimmólle, *It.* (bēm-mŏl-lĕ.) The mark called a flat, (♭).
B in alt, *It.* (bē ĭn ält.) The third in alt; the tenth above the treble clef note.
B in altissimo, *It.* (bē ĭn äl-tĭs-sē-mō.) The third note in altissimo; the octave above *B in alt*.
Binary measure. Common time of two in a bar.
Bind. A tie uniting two notes on the same degree of the staff.
Binde, *Ger.* (bĕn-dĕ.) A tie or bind.
Binding notes. Notes held together by the tie or bind.
Bindung, *Ger.* (bĭn-doong.) Connection.
Bindungszeichen, *Ger.* (bĭn-doongs-tsī-kh'n.) A tie or bind.
Biniou. (bĭn-yŏu.) Bagpipes.
Binotonus, *Lat.* (bī-nō-tō-nŭs.) Consisting of two notes.
Biol, *Iri.* (bī-ŏl.) A viol.
Biquadro, *It.* (bē-quä-drō.) A natural, (♮).
Bird organ. A small organ used in teaching birds to sing.
Birn, *Ger.* (bĭrn.) That part of the clarinet, basset horn, etc., into which the mouthpiece is inserted.
Bis, *Lat.* (bĭs.) Twice; indicating that the passage marked is to be repeated.
Biscantáre, *It.* (bĕs-kăn-tā-rĕ.) }
Biscantorellare, *It.* (bĕs-kăn-tŏ-rĕl-lä-rĕ.) }
To sing often, to sing and sing again.

ă ale, ă add, ă arm, ĕ eve, ĕ end, ī ice, ĭ ill, ō old, ŏ odd, ō dove, oo moon, ū lute, ŭ but, ü French sound.

BISCA

Biscánto, *It.* (bēs-kän-tō.) A kind of duet, where two are singing.
Bischero, *It.* (bēs-kā-ro.) A peg of a violin, violincello or similar instrument; the pin of any instrument.
Biscróma, *It.* (bēs-krō-mä.)
Biscrome, *Fr.* (bis-krŏm.) } A semiquaver, or sixteenth note.
Bis-diapason, *Lat.* (bis dī-ă-pā-sŏn.) A double octave, or fifteenth; a compass of two octaves.
Biseau, *Fr.* (bĕ-zō.) The stopper of an organ pipe to make the tone sharper or flatter.
Bisinia, *Lat.* (bī-sĕn-ī-ä.) A term applied to a pianoforte passage where the notes played by one hand are regularly repeated by the other.
Bis unca, *Lat.* (bis ŭn-kā.) An old name for a semiquaver.
Bissex, *Lat.* (bis-sĕx.) A species of guitar with twelve strings.
Bitterkeit, *Ger.* (bĭt-tĕr-kīt.) Bitterness.
Bizzarraménte, *It.* (bēt-sär-rä-mān-tĕ.) Oddly, in a whimsical style.
Bizzarría, *It.* (bēt-sär-rē-ä.) Written in a capricious, fantastic style; sudden, unexpected modulations.
Bizzárro, *It.* (bēt-sär-ro.) Whimsical, odd, fantastical.
Blanche, *Fr.* (blänsh.) A minim or half note.
Blanche pointée, *Fr.* (blänsh pwänh-tă.) A dotted minim.
Bläsebalg, *Ger.* (blä-zĕ-bälg.) The bellows of an organ.
Blasegeräth, *Ger.* (blä-zĕ-ghĕ-rät.) A wind instrument.
Blasehorn, *Ger.* (blä-zĕ-hŏrn.) Bugle horn, hunter's horn.
Blase-instrument, *Ger.* (blä-zĕ in-stroo-mĕnt.) A wind instrument.
Blase-musik, *Ger.* (blä-z'n.) Music for wind instruments.
Blasen, *Ger.* (blä-z'n.) To blow, to sound.
Bläser, *Ger.* (blä-z'r.) A blower; an instrument for blowing.
Blast. The sudden blowing of a trumpet or other instrument of a similar character.
Blatant. Bleating, bellowing.
Blech-instruménte, *Ger.* (blĕkh-in-stroo-mĕn-tĕ.) The brass instruments, as trumpets, trombones, etc.
Blockflöte, *Ger.* (blŏk-flö-tĕ.) An organ stop, composed of large scale-pipes, the tone of which is full and broad.
Blower, clarino. One who plays the first trumpet part.
Blower, organ. One who works the bellows of an organ.
Bluette. A short brilliant piece.
B-mol, *Fr.* (bă-mŏl.) The character called a flat, (♭). See Bé mol.
B moll, *Ger.* (bĕ mŏl.) The key of B flat minor.
B molle, *Lat.* (bĕ mŏl-lĕ.) B *soft* or Minor.
Bobibation, (bŏ-bĭ-bă-shŭn.) } Solféggi
Bocedisation. (bŏ-sĕ dĭ-să-shŭn.) } adapted to the syllables of the Flemish or Belgian language.
Boans, *Lat.* (bŏ-äns.) Echoing, resounding.
Board, finger. The key-board of a pianoforte,

BOMB

organ or similar instrument. 2. That part of a stringed instrument which the fingers press in playing.
Board, fret. That part of a guitar or similar instrument on which the frets are placed.
Board, key. The rows of keys of a pianoforte, organ, or similar instrument. See Finger board.
Board, sound. In the organ a broad shallow box, extending almost the whole width of the instrument and divided into as many grooves as there are keys, and upon which are placed the rows of pipes forming the stops. 2. A thin board designed to contribute to the vibration of tone in musical instruments.
Board, sounding. See Sound board.
Boat songs. Gondolier songs.
Bobo, *Spa.* (bō-bō.) A buffoon.
Bocal, *Fr.* (bō-kăl.) } The mouth-piece of a
Bócca, *It.* (bōk-kä.) } horn, trumpet, trombone and similar instruments.
Bócca ridente, *It.* (bōk-kä rē-dĕn-tĕ.) *Smiling mouth.* A term in singing, applied to a peculiar opening of the mouth approaching to a smile, believed to be conducive to the producing of a pure tone.
Bocchino, *It.* (bōk-kē-no.) Mouth-piece of a horn.
Bociaccia, *It.* (bōt-tshē-ät-tshē-ä.) A loud, strong voice.
Bocciuola, *It.* (bōt-tshē-oo-ō-lä.) A small mouthpiece.
Bocina, *Spa.* (bō-thē-nä.) A species of large trumpet, a bugle horn.
Bocina de cazador, *Spa.* (bō-thē-nä dĕ kä-thä-dōr.) A huntsman's horn.
Bocinar, *Spa.* (bō-thē-när.) To sound the trumpet or horn.
Bocinero, *Spa.* (bō-thī-nā-ro.) A trumpeter.
Bocinilla. A small speaking trumpet.
Bockpfeife, *Ger.* (bōk-pfī-fĕ.) A bagpipe.
Bockstriller, *Ger.* (bōks-trĭl-lĕr.) A bad shake, with false intonation.
Boden, *Ger.* (bō-d'n.) The back of a violin, viola, etc.
Boehm Flute. (bōhm.) An instrument with the holes arranged in their natural order, and with keys, by means of which the fingers are enabled to act with greater facility. Invented by Boehm.
Bogen, *Ger.* (bō-g'n.) The bow of a violin, etc.
Bogenflügel, *Ger.* (bō-g'n-flü-g'l.) An instrument resembling a piano forte.
Bogenführung, *Ger.* (bō-g'n-fü-roong.) The management of the bow; the act of bowing.
Bogen-Instrument, *Ger.* (bō-g'n in-stroo-mĕnt.) A bow instrument; an instrument played with a bow.
Bogenstrich, *Ger.* (bō-g'n-strĭkh.) A stroke of the bow.
Bogiganga, *Spa.* (bō-hē-gän-gä.) A company of strolling singers.
Boléro, *Spa.* (bō-lā-ro.) A lively Spanish dance, in 3-4 time, with castanets.
Bomb. A stroke upon a bell; tō sound.
Bombarde, *Fr.* (bōnh-bärd.) } A powerful reed
Bombárdo, *It.* (bōm-bär-dō.) } stop in an organ of 16 feet scale; also a old wind instrument of the hautboy species.

ā ale, ă add, ä arm, ē eve, ĕ end, ī ice, ĭ ill, ō old, ŏ odd, ō dove, oo moon, ū lute, ŭ but, ü French sound.

BOMB

Bombardon, *Ger.* (bŏm-bär-dŏn.) A large bass wind instrument of brass, with valves, something like the ophicleide.
Bombilation. Sound, report, noise (little used).
Bombilatus, *Lat.* (bŏm-bĭ-lä-tūs.) To make a humming noise.
Bombix, *Gr.* (bŏm-bĭx.) An ancient Greek instrument, formed of a long reed or tube.
Bombo, *Spa.* (bŏm-bō.) A large drum.
Bombus, *Lat.* bŏm-būs.) A species of applause used by the ancients—humming, buzzing, clapping.
Bomme, *Dut.* (bŏm-mĕ.) A drum.
Bommen, *Dut.* (bŏm-mĕn.) To drum.
Bonang, *Jav.* (bŏ-năng.) A Javeneee instrument, consisting of a series of gongs placed in two lines on a frame.
Bones. A name sometimes given to castanets; castanets made of bone.
Bons Temps de la mesure, *Fr.* (bŏnh tŏnh däh lä mĕ-sūr.) The accented parts of a measure.
Book, choral. A collection of choral melodies.
Book, mass. The Missal, the Roman Catholic service book.
Boom. To roll and roar as the waves of the sea.
Boquilla, *Spa.* (bō-kēl-yä.) Mouth-piece of a wind instrument.
Bora, *Tur.* (bō-rä.) A tin trumpet used by the Turkish military.
Border tunes. Melodies sung on the English border.
Bordóne, *It.* (bŏr-dō-nĕ.) ⎫ An organ stop, the
Bourdon, *Fr.* (boor-dŏnh.) ⎭ pipes of which are stopped or covered, and produce the 16 feet, and sometimes the 32 feet tone; also a drone bass.
Bordun. See Bourdon.
Bordone, falso, *It.* (bŏr-dō-nĕ fäl-zō.) A term formerly used for harmony having a drone bass, or one of the other parts continuing in the same pitch.
Borduu flöte, *Ger.* (bŏr-doon flō-tĕ.) An organ stop; see Bordóne.
Bourdon de cornemuse, *Fr.* (boor-dŏnh düh körn-mūz.) The drone of a bagpipe.
Bourdon de musette, *Fr.* (boor-dŏnh düh mū-zĕt.) The drone of a bagpipe.
Boree, *Fr.* (bō-rä.) A dance introduced from Biscay.
Borrowed harmony. Chords of the added ninth derived from the dominant seventh, by substituting the ninth in the place of the eighth.
Botasela, *Spa.* (bō-tä-sā-lä.) A trumpet signal for cavalry to saddle.
Botto, *It.* (bŏt-tō.) The tolling of a bell.
Boudoir piano. (boo-dwär.) An upright piano.
Bouffe, *Fr.* (boof.) A buffoon.
Bourdon de l'orgue, *Fr.* (boor-dŏnh düh l'org.) The drone of an organ.
Bourdonnement, *Fr.* (hoor-dŏnh-mŏnh.) Humming, singing.
Bourree, *Fr.* (boor-rä.) A step in dancing; see Boree.
Boutade, *Fr.* (boo-täd.) An impromptu ballet in a fanciful, capricious style.
Bow. The instrument used to play upon the violin, violincello and other similar instruments.

BRAT

Its present length is from 27 to 30 inches, but formerly it was shorter.
Bow, contrary. A reversed stroke of the bow.
Bow hair. Hair used in making the bows of violins, violincellos, etc.; it is usually horse hair.
Bow hand. The right hand; the hand which holds the bow.
Bow harpsichord. An instrument invented at Konigsburg by Garbrecht.
Bowing. The art of using the bow, playing with the bow.
Bow instruments. All instruments whose tones are produced by the bow.
Box, music. A small box producing tunes by the revolution of a cylinder moved by a spring in which steel pins are fixed that touch steel points at such intervals as to produce the variations of a tune.
Boyandier, *Fr.* (bō-yŏ-dĭ-ä.) A maker of violin strings.
Boy-choir. A choir of boys, from eight to fourteen years of age. Such organizations are confined mostly to Episcopal and Catholic churches.
B quadratum, *Lat.* (b quăd-rā-tŭm.) ⎫ An old
B quadrum, *Lat.* (b quăd-rŭm.) ⎭ name for the natural, ♮; formerly, this was applied to the note B.
B-quarre, *Fr.* (bä-kär.) See Béquarre.
Brace. A character curved or straight used to connect together the different staves.
Brachycatalectic, *Gr.* (brăk-ĭ-kăt-ă-lĕk-tĭk.) In Greek and Latin poetry a verse wanting two syllables and its termination.
Brachygraphy, musical. The art of writing music in short hand, by means of signs, characters, etc.
Braccio, *It.* (brä-tshē-ō.) A term applied to the violin and other instruments of a similar character that are held up to the neck with the left hand, and played with a bow.
Bramadera, *Spa.* (brä-mä-dä-rä.) A rattle, a shepherd's horn.
Branches. Those parts of a trumpet that conduct the wind.
Bran de Inglaterra, *Spa.* (brän dĕ ĕn-glä-tĕr-rä.) An old Spanish dance.
Braudo, *Spa.* (brän-dō.) A tune adapted to a dance.
Branle, *Fr.* (brănhl.) A lively old dance performed in a circle.
Bransle, *Fr.* (brănhl.) An old dance, slow and resembling the *Alman*.
Bransle de poictou, *Fr.* (brănhl düh pwäk-tōō.) A dance in quicker time than the Bransle.
Bransle double. (brănhl doo-bl.) A dance in a quicker time than the Bransle.
Bransle simple, *Fr.* See Bransle.
Brass band. A number of performers whose instruments are exclusively brass.
Brass instrument. Wind instruments made of brass and used chiefly for field service.
Bratsche, *Ger.* (brä-tshĕ.) The viola or tenor violin.
Bratschen, *Ger.* (brä-tshĕn.) Violas.
Bratschenspieler, *Ger.* (brä-tchĕn-spä-lĕr.) Violist, one who plays on the viola.

ă *ale*, ă *add*, ă *arm*, ĕ *eve*, ĕ *end*, ī *ice*, ĭ *ill*, ō *old*, ŏ *odd*, ô *dove*, oo *moon*, ū *lute*, ŭ *but*, ü *French sound*.

BRAT

Bratschenstimme, *Ger.* (*brä*-tchĕn-*stĭm*-mĕ.) The viol part of any composition.
Braul. See Brawl.
Braut-lied, *Ger.* (*brout*-lēd.) A bridal hymn, a wedding song.
Braut-messe, *Ger.* (*brout*-mĕs-sĕ.) Music before the wedding ceremony; the ceremony itself.
Bráva, *It. fem.* (*brä*-vä.) ⎫ An exclamation of
Brávi, *It. pl.* (*brä*-vē.) ⎬ approval often used
Bravo, *It. mas.* (*brä*-vō.) ⎭ in theatres; excellent, very good, etc.
Bravíssima, *It. fem.* (brä-*vēs*-sĕ-mä.) ⎫ Exceed-
Bravíssimi, *It. pl.* (brä-*vēs*-sĕ-mē.) ⎬ ingly
Bravíssimo, *It. mas.* (brä-*vēs*-sĕ-mō.) ⎭ good, exceedingly well done.
Bravour-arie, *Ger.* (brä-voor-ä-rē-ĕ.) An *aria di bravúra*.
Bravúra, *It.* (brä-voo-rä.) Spirit, skill, requiring great dexterity and skill in execution.
Bravúra, con., *It.* (brä-voo-rä kŏn.) With spirit and boldness of execution.
Bravúra mezza, *It.* (brä-voo-rä mĕt-sä.) A song requiring a moderate degree of skill.
Brawl. ⎫ A shaking, or swinging motion. 2.
Brawle. ⎭ An old round dance in which the performers joined hands in a circle; the balls were usually opened with it.
Bray. The harsh sound of a trumpet or similar instrument.
Brazen instruments. Brass instruments.
Brazzo, *It.* (brät-sō.) Instruments played with a bow.
Breit, *Ger.* (brīt.) Broad.
Brelocque, *Fr.* (brĕ-lŏk.) In military service the call of a drum for breakfast or dinner.
Bretador, *Spa.* (brä-tä-dōr.) A bird call.
Brett-geige, *Ger.* (brĕt-ghī-ghĕ.) A small pocket fiddle.
Bréve, *It.* (brä-vĕ.) Short; formerly the Breve was the shortest note. The notes then used were the Large, the Long and the Breve. The Breve is now the longest note; it is equal to two *semibreves* or whole notes. 2. A Double note.
Bréve alla, *It.* (brä-vĕ äl-lä.) A term to indicate a quick species of common time; formerly employed in church music.
Breve rest. A rest equal in duration to a Bréve or Double note.
Breviario, *It.* (brĕv-ē-ä-rē-ō.) A breviary.
Breviary. A book containing the matins, lauds, and vespers of the Catholic church.
Brevis, *Lat.* (brä-vīa.) A breve.
Bridge. That part of a stringed instrument that supports the strings.
Bridge, bass. The bass beam; the small beam inside a viol nearly under the bass.
Brief. An upright piece of wood over which the strings of a bass viol are drawn.
Brill. An abbreviation of Brillánte.
Brillador, *Spa.* (brēl-yä-dōr.) Brilliant, sparkling.
Brillánte, *It.* (brēl-län-tĕ.) ⎱ Bright, sparkling,
Brillante, *Fr.* (brē-yänht.) ⎰ brilliant.
Brilláre, *It.* (brēl-lä-rĕ.) To play or sing in a brilliant style.
Brimbaler, *Fr.* (bränh-bä-lā.) To ring.
Brío, *It.* (brē-ō.) Vigor, animation, spirit.

BUFF

Brío ed animato, con, *It.* (brē-ō ĕd än-ē-*mä*-tō.) With animation and brilliancy.
Brióso, *It.* (brē-ō-zō.) Lively, vigorously, with spirit.
Brisé, *Fr.* (brē-zä.) Split; broken into an *arpéggio*.
Broach. An old musical instrument, played by turning a handle.
Broderies, *Fr.* (brō-dē-rē.) Ornaments, embellishments.
Broken cadence. See *Interrupted cadence*
Broken chords. Chords whose notes are not taken simultaneously, but in a broken and interrupted manner.
Brokking. An old term, signifying quavering.
Bronce, *Spa.* (brŏn-thĕ.) A trumpet made of brass.
Bronco, *Spa.* (brŏn-kō.) Harsh, unpleasant to the ear.
Bronquedad, *Spa.* (brŏn-kĕ-dād.) Harshness, roughness of sound.
B rotundum, *Lat.* (b ro-*tŭn*-dŭm.) The character called a flat, ♭; formerly this was applied only to the note B.
Bruit, *Fr.* (brü-ē.) Noise, rattle, clatter.
Brümmen, *Gr.* (broom-mĕn.) To hum, to drum.
Brümmton, *Ger.* (broom-tōn.) A humming sound.
Brunette, *Fr.* (brü-nĕt.) A love song.
Bruscaménte, *It.* (broos-kä-*män*-tĕ.) Abruptly, coarsely.
Brusquement, *Fr.* (brŭsk-mŏnh.) Brusque, rough, rude.
B sharp. The sharp seventh of the diatonic scale of C; in keyed instruments the same as C natural.
Bual-gorn, *Wel.* (boo-äl-gŏrn.) A hunting or military horn.
Búccina, *It.* (boot-tshē-nä.) An ancient wind instrument of the trumpet species.
Buccinal, *Lat.* (bŭk-sī-näl.) Sounding like a horn or trumpet.
Buccinateur, *Fr.* (bŭk-sī-nä-tŭr.) A trumpeter.
Buccino, *Lat.* (bŭk-sī-nō.) To sound a trumpet.
Buccinum, *Lat.* (buk-sī-nŭm.) A trumpet.
Bucinador, *Spa.* (boo-thē-nä-dōr.) A trumpeter.
Bucólica, *It.* (book-kŏ-lē-kä.) ⎱ Pastoral songs
Bucolic, *Lat.* (bū-kŏl-īk.) ⎰ or verses.
Bucolique, *Fr.* (bü-kŏl-ēk.) ⎱
Bucolical, *Lat.* (bū-kŏl-ī-käl.) In the pastoral style.
Bucolico, *Spa.* (boo-kŏl-ī-kō.) Relating to pastoral songs.
Buffa, *It.* (boof-fä.) ⎱ Comic, humorous, in the
Buffo, *It.* (boof-fō.) ⎰ comic style; also a singer who takes comic parts in the opera.
Buffa caricáta, *It.* (boof-fä kär-ē-kä-tä.) ⎱
Buffo caricáto, *It.* (boof-fō kär-ē-kä-tō.) ⎰ comic character in Italian opera.
Buffet d' orgue, *Fr.* (boof-fĕ d' ōrg.) An organ case.
Buffet organ. A very small organ.
Buffo burlesco, *It.* (boof-fō boor-lĕs-kō.) A buffo singer and caricaturist.
Buffóne, *It.* (boof-fō-nĕ.) Comic singer in an opera.

ā ale, ă add, ä arm, ē eve, ĕ end, ī ice, ĭ ill, ō old, ŏ odd, ō dove, oo moon, ū lute, ŭ but, ü French sound.

BUFF

Buffonescaméute, *It.* (boof-fō-nĕs-kă-mān-tĕ.) In a burlesque and comical manner.
Buffo, opera, *It.* (boof-fō ŏ-pĕ-rä.) A comic opera, a burletta.
Bufo, *Spa.* (boo-fō.) Comic opera.
Bufonazo, *Spa.* (boo-fō-nā-thō.) A great buffoon.
Bugle. A hunting horn. 2. An instrument of copper or brass, similar to the French horn, but higher and more piercing. There are different kinds; one furnished with keys, and another kind with pistons or cylinders.
Bugle horn. A hunting horn.
Buloso, *It.* (boo-ē-ŏ-zō.) In a gloomy and obscure manner.
Bünge, *Ger.* (boon-ghĕ.) A drum; a kettle drum.
Büngen, *Ger.* (boon-ghĕn.) To drum.
Buon, *It.* (bwōn.) Good.
Buonaccordo, *It.* (bwōn-năk-kŏr-dō.) An instrument resembling a pianoforte, but smaller, to accommodate children.
Buóna nota, *It.* (bwō-nä nō-tä.) Accented note.
Buón cantánte, *It.* (bwōn kăn-tăn-tĕ.) An accomplished singer.
Buón gusto, *It.* (bwōn goos-tō.) Good taste, refinement of style.
Buóna máno, *It.* (bwō-nä mä-nō.) A good hand, a brilliant performer.
Buonocardo, *It.* (bwō-nō-kăr-dō.) An instrument like the spinet.
Burden. A regular return of the theme in a song at the close of each verse; the chorus.

BYMI

Burla, *It.* (boor-lä.)
Burlándo, *It.* (boor-lăn-dō.)
Burlésco, *It.* (boor-lĕs-kō.)
Burlescaménte, *It.* (boor-lĕs-kă-mān-tĕ.)
Facetious, droll, comical; in a playful manner.
Burlesque music. A musical composition or performance, in which light and trifling matters are treated with great gravity and solemnity, and serious matters turned into ridicule.
Burlétta, *It.* (boor-lăt-tä.) A comic operetta; a light musical and dramatic piece, somewhat in the nature of the English farce.
Burasca, *It.* (boor-răs-kä.) A composition descriptive of a tempest.
Burre, *Fr.* (bür.) A dance melody.
Burthen. See *Burden.*
Busaun, *Ger.* (boo-soun.) A sackbut; a reed stop in an organ.
Busna, *It.* (boos-nä.) A species of trumpet.
Bussóne, *It.* (boos-sō-nĕ.) A bassoon, a wind instrument, (obsolete.)
Buxum, *Lat.* (bŭx-ŭm.) A pipe.
Buxus, *Lat.* (bŭx-ŭs.) A pipe with two rows of holes.
Buzz. A low humming noise.
Buzain, *Ger.* (boo-tsīn.) See Busaun.
Byma, *Sax.* (bī-mä.) A trumpet.
Bymian, *Sax.* (bĭm-ĭ-ăn.) To blow, or to sound a trumpet.

ă ale, ă add, ä arm, ē eve, ĕ end, ī ice, ĭ ill, ō old, ŏ odd, ô dove, oo moon, ū lute, ŭ but, ü French sound.

C

C. The first note of the modern scale, called by the French *ut*, and by the Italians Do. The major scale of C is called the *natural* scale, because it has no flats or sharps.

C C The lowest note on the manuals of an organ, and is called an 8 feet note; that being the length of the open pipe required to produce it.

C C C. This note is an octave below C C, and requires a 16 feet pipe.

C C C C. A note an octave below C C C; it requires a 32 feet pipe.

C with *one stroke*; the German method of indicating middle C. The six notes above it are marked in the same manner.

C with *two strokes*; an octave above C with one stroke.

C with *three strokes*; an octave above C with two strokes.

C with *four strokes*; an octave above C with three strokes.

₵ Indicates common time of four crotchets or quarter notes in a bar.

₵ This character indicates *álla brève*, or *álla capélla* time.

C. A. The initials of *Col Arco*; sometimes used in abbreviation.

Cabalétta, *It.* (kä-bä-lăt-tä.) A simple melody of a pleasing and attractive character; an operatic air like the rondo in form: a cavaletta.

Cabinet d'orgue, *Fr.* (kăh-ĭ-nä d'ŏrg.) The case or cabinet in which the keys of an organ are sometimes placed.

Cabinet pianoforte. An upright pianoforte.

Cabiscola. The ancient name of the leader of the choristers in a church.

Cáccia, *It.* (kät-tshē-ä.) See Alla Cáccia.

Cáccia, alla, *It.* (kät-tshē-ä äl-lä.) In the hunting style.

Cachucha, *Spa.* (kä-tchoo-tchä.) A popular Spanish dance in triple time.

Cacofonía, *It.* (kä-kō-fō-nē-ä.) ⎫ Want of harmony, cacophony.
Cacophonie, *Fr.* (kăk-ō-fō-nē.) ⎭

Cacofónico, *It.* (kä-kō-fō-nē-kō.) Cacophonous, discordant.

Cacophony. (kă-kŏf-ō-ny.) A combination of discordant sounds, false intonation, bad tones.

Cad. An abbreviation of *Cadenza*.

Cadence, *Fr.* (kă-dänhs.) A shake or trill; also a close in harmony.

Cadence. A close in melody or harmony, dividing it into numbers or periods, or bringing it to a final termination. 2. An ornamental passage.

Cadence, authentic. A perfect or final cadence; the harmony of the dominant followed by that of the tonic or the progression of the dominant to the tonic.

Cadence, church. The plagal cadence.

Cadence, complete. A full cadence; when the final sound of a verse in a chant is on the key-note.

Cadence, deceptive. When the dominant chord resolves into another harmony instead of the tonic.

Cadence, demi. A half cadence.

CAIS

Cadence, false. An imperfect or interrupted cadence.

Cadence, Greek. Plagal cadence.

Cadence, half. A cadence that is imperfect; a close on the dominant.

Cadence, imperfaite, *Fr.* (änh-pĕr-fä.) An imperfect cadence.

Cadence, imperfect. When the dominant harmony is preceded by the common chord of the tonic.

Cadence, interrompue, *Fr.* (änh-tĕr-rŏnh-pü.) An interrupted cadence.

Cadence, interrupted. Similar to the perfect cadence, except that in place of the final tonic harmony some other chord is introduced.

Cadence, irregular. See *Imperfect* cadence.

Cadence marks. Short lines placed perpendicularly to indicate the cadence notes in chanting.

Cadence, parfaite, *Fr.* (pär-fät.) A perfect cadence.

Cadence, perfect. Where the dominant passes into the harmony of the tonic.

Cadence perlée, *Fr.* (pĕr-lä.) A brilliant cadence.

Cadence, plagal. When tonic harmony is preceded by subdominant.

Cadence, radical. The cadence resulting when the basses of both chords are the roots of their respective triads.

Cadence, rompue. *Fr.* (rŏnh-pü.) A broken or interrupted cadence.

Cadence, suspended. Where the cadence passes through several modulations from the dominant to the tonic chord.

Cadencia, *Spa.* (kä-dĕn-thē-ä.) ⎫ Cadence.
Cadens, *Lat.* (kä-dĕns.) ⎭

Cadenz, *Ger.* (kä-dĕnts.) ⎫ A cadence; an ornamental passage introduced near the close of a song or solo either by the composer or extemporaneously by the performer.
Cadénza, *It.* (kä-dän-tsä.) ⎭

Cadenza d'ingánno, *It.* (kä-dän-tsä dĕn-gän-nō.) An interrupted or deceptive cadence.

Cadenza fiorita, *It.* (kä-dän-tsä fē-ō-rē-tä.) An ornate, florid cadence with graces and embellishments.

Cadenza sfuggita, *It.* (kä-dän-tsä sfoog-ghē-tä.) An avoided or broken cadence.

Cadénza sospésa, *It.* (kä-dän-tsä sŏs-pā-zä.) A suspended cadence.

Cesura, *Fr.* (sē-sür.) ⎫ 1. A pause in verse, so introduced as to aid the recital and make the versification more melodious. 2. A break or section in rhythm. 3. The rhythmic termination of any passage consisting of more than one musical foot. 4. The last accented note of a phrase, section or period.
Cesura, *It.* (tshē-soo-rä.)
Cesura, *Lat.* (sē-sū-rä.) ⎭

Cæsural, *Lat.* (sē-sū-räl.) Relating to the *cesura* or to the pause in the voice.

Cahier de chant, *Fr.* (kä-l-ā düh shănh.) A singing-book.

Cahier de musique, *Fr.* (kä-l-ā düh mü-zēk.) A music book.

Caisse, *Fr.* (käss.) A drum.

PRONOUNCING MUSICAL DICTIONARY. 37

ă *ate*, ă *add*, ä *arm*, ē *eve*, ĕ *end*, ī *ice*, ĭ *ill*, ō *old*, ŏ *odd*, ȯ *dove*, oo *moon*, ū *lute*, ŭ *but*, ü *French sound*.

CAIS

Caisse roulante, *Fr.* (käse roo-länht.) The side drum, the body being of wood and rather long.
Caisses claires, *Fr.* (käss klär.) The drums.
Cal. An abbreviation of *Calando.*
Calamist. (*kal-ă*-mist.) A piper; one who plays on a pipe or a fife.
Calamo, *Spa.* (kä-*lä*-mō.) A kind of flute.
Calamus pastoralis, *Lat.* (kă-*lä*-mŭs pās-tō-rä-lĭs.) A reed or pipe used by shepherds.
Caland, *It.* (kä-*lănd*.) } Gradually diminish-
Calándo, *It.* (kä-*lăn*-dō.) } ing the tone and retarding the time; becoming softer and slower by degrees.
Calándo nella forza. (kä-*lăn*-dō näl-lä fōr-tsä.) A decrease in the power or strength of a tone.
Calándo nel tempo e nella forza. (kä-*lăn*-dō näl tĕm-pō ā näl-lä fōr-tsä.) Diminishing both the strength and time of a movement.
Calascione, *It.* (kä-lä-shō-ĭ-nē.) A species of guitar.
Calathumpian music. A discordant combination of sounds. A low and grotesque performance upon instruments unmusical and out of tune.
Calàta, *It.* (kä-*lä*-tä.) An Italian dance in 2-4 time.
Caleándo, *It.* (kăl-*kăn*-dō.) Pressing forward and hurrying the time.
Calcant, *Ger.* (käl-känt.) The bellows treader, in old German organs.
Call. The beat of a drum.
Call, adjutant's. A drum beat directing the band and field music to take the right of the line.
Calliope, (käl-*lē*-ō-pē.) In pagan mythology the muse that presided over eloquence and heroic poetry. 2. An instrument formed of metal pipes, with keys like an organ; they are placed on steam engines sometimes, and the tones are produced by currents of steam instead of air.
Calma, *It.* (*käl*-mä.)
Calmáte, *It.* (käl-*mä*-tē.) } Calmness, tranquility, repose.
Calmáto, *It.* (käl-*mä*-tō.) }
Calo. An abbreviation of *Calándo.*
Calóre, *It.* (kä-*lō*-rē.) Warmth, animation.
Caloróso, *It.* (käl-ō-rō-zo.) Very much animation and warmth.
Calumean, (*käl*-ŭ-mō.) A reed or pipe.
Cambaleo, *Spa.* (käm-bä-lē-ō.) A company of comedians among the ancients, consisting of five men and five women.
Cambiáre, *It.* (käm-bē-*ä*-rē.) To change, to alter.
Camena, *Lat.* (kä-*mā*-nä.) } The muse.
Camoena, *Lat.* (kä-*mō*-nä.) }
Cámera, *It.* (kä-mē-rä.) Chamber; a term applied to music composed for private performance or small concerts.
Cámera musica, *It.* (kä-mē-rä moo-zē-kä.) Chamber music.
Caminándo, *It..* (kä-mē-*năn*-dō.) Flowing, with easy and gentle progression.
Campána, *It.* (käm-*pä*-nä.) A bell.
Campanada, *Spa.* (käm-pä-*nä*-dä.) Sound of a bell.

CANC

Campana de rebato, *Spa.* (käm-*pä*-nä dē rĕ-bä-tō.) An alarm bell.
Campana funebrio, *Lat.* (käm-*pä*-nä fū-nä-brĭ-ō.) A funeral bell.
Campanájo, *It.* (käm-pä-*nä*-yō.) A bell-ringer; a bell founder; a performer upon the *campanétta*.
Campanario, *Spa.* (käm-pä-*nä*-rĭ-ō.) A belfry; a place where bells are rung.
Campanarum, *Lat.* (käm-pä-*nä*-rŭm.) Clock chimes.
Campanarum concentus, *Lat.* (käm-pä-*nä*-rŭm kŏn-*sĕn*-tŭs.)
Campanarum modulatio, *Lat.* (käm-pä-*nä*-rŭm mŏd-ū-*lä*-shĭ-ō.) Ringing of bells or chimes; chiming of bells.
Campanarum pulsator, *Lat.* (käm-pä-*nä*-rŭm pŭl-*sä*-tōr.) A ringer of bells.
Campanélla, *It.* (käm-pä-*näl*-lä.) }
Campanéllo, *It.* (käm-pä-*näl*-lō.) } A little bell.
Campanellíno, *It.* (käm-pä-něl-*lē*-nō.) A very little bell.
Campaneo, *Spa.* (käm-*pä*-nē-ō.) Chiming, bell ringing.
Campanero, *Spa.* (käm-*pä*-nē-rō.) A bell ringer.
Campaneta, *Spa.* (käm-pä-*nä*-tä.) A small bell.
Campanétta, *It.* (käm-pä-*nät*-tä.) A set of bells tuned diatonically, and played with keys like a pianoforte.
Campaníle, *It.* (käm-pä-*nē*-lē.) A belfry.
Campanílla, *Spa.* (käm-pä-*nēl*-yä.) A small bell.
Campanillazo, *Spa.* (käm-pä-něl-yä-thō.) A violent ringing of bells.
Campanésta, *It.* (käm-pä-*näs*-tä.) A player upon the *campanétta.*
Cámpanologist. (käm-pä-*nŏl*-ō-jĭst.) A bell ringer.
Campanology. (käm-pä-*nŏl*-ō-gy.) The art of ringing bells.
Campanóne, *It.* (käm-pä-*nō*-nē.) A great bell.
Campanula sacra, *Lat.* (käm-pä-*nū*-lä sä-krä.) A saint's bell.
Can, *Wel.* (kän.) A song.
Cana, *Arm.* (kä-nä.) To sing.
Canarder, *Fr.* (kä-när-dä.) To imitate the tones of a duck.
Canarie, *Fr.* (kä-nä-rē.) } An old dance, in
Canaries, *Eng.* (kä-*nā*-rēs.) } lively 3-8 or 6-8,
Canário, *It.* (kä-*nä*-rē-ō.) } and sometimes 12-8 time of two strains. It derives its name from the Canary Islands, from whence it is supposed to have come.
Cancelling sign. A natural, (♮) employed to remove the effect of a previous flat or sharp.
Cancion, *Spa.* (kän-thē-*ŏn*.) A song; words set to music.
Cancioncilla, *Spa.* (kän-thē-ŏn-*thēl*-yä.) A canzonet; a little song.
Cancionéro, *Spa.* (kän-thē-ō-*nä*-rō.) A book of songs.
Cancionista, *Spa.* (kän-thē-ō-*nēs*-tä.) A singer of songs; a song writer.
Cancrizans, *It.* (kän-*krē*-tsäns.) } Retrograde
Cancrizante, *It.* (kän-krē-*tsän*-tē.) } movement; going backward.

ă ale, ă add, ä arm, ĕ eve, ĕ end, ī ice, ĭ ill, ō old, ŏ odd, ô dove, oo moon, ū lute, ŭ but, ū French sound.

CAND

Candamo, *Spa.* (kän-dä-mō.) An ancient rustic dance.
Canere, *Lat.* (kän-ĕ-rĕ.) To sing; to play upon an instrument.
Canere ad tibiam, *Lat.* (kän-ĕ-rĕ ăd tĭb-ĭ-ăm.) To sing to the pipe.
Canere receptui, *Lat.* (kän-ĕ-rĕ rē-sĕp-tū-ē.) To sound a retreat.
Canere tibiā, *Lat.* (kän-ĕ-rĕ tĭb-ĭ-ā.) To play upon pipes.
Canevas, *Fr.* (kän-ĕ-vā.) Unconnected words set to music. 2. The rough sketch or draft of a song, indicating the measure of the verses required.
Can-can. (kän-kän.) A vulgar kind of dance.
Candora. A species of Spanish guitar.
Cangiáre, *It.* (kän-jē-ä-rē.) To change, to alter.
Cánna, *It.* (kän-nä.) A reed or pipe.
Canna d' órgano, *It.* (kän-nä d'ōr-gä-nō.) The pipe of an organ.
Cannien, *Arm.* (kän-nĕn.) To chant.
Cannon. The portion of a bell by which it is suspended.
Cannon drum. The tom-tom used by the natives of the East Indies.
Cano, *Lat.* (kä-nō.) To produce melodious artistic sounds; to sing, to play.
Canon. (kăn-ŏn.) In *ancient music*, a rule or method for determining the intervals of notes. 2. In *modern music*, a kind of perpetual fugue, in which the different parts, beginning one after another, repeat incessantly the same air.
Cánone, *It.* (kä-nō-nĕ.) } A canon.
Canónico, *It.* (kä-nŏn-ē-kō.) }
Cánone al sospiro, *It.* (kä-nō-nĕ äl sōs-pē-rō.) A canon whose different parts commence at the distance of a crochet rest from each other.
Cánone apérto, *It.* (kä-nō-nĕ ä-pàr-tō.) An *open canon;* a canon of which the solution or development is given.
Cánone chiúso, *It.* (kä-nō-nĕ kē-oo-zō.) A *close* or *hidden* canon, the solution or development of which must be discovered; also an enigmatical canon.
Cánone in corpo, *It.* (kä-nō-nĕ ēn-kŏr-pō.) A perpetual fugue.
Cánone partito, *Lat.* (kä-nō-nĕ pär-tī-tō.) A perpetual fugue, in which all the parts are written in partitions or different lines, or in separate parts, with the proper pauses which each is to observe.
Canoneria, *Spa.* (kän-ō-nä-rī-ä.) All the pipes in an organ.
Cánone sciólto, *It.* (kä-nō-nĕ shē-ōl-tō.) A free canon, not in the strict style.
Canon, free. A canon not in strict conformity to the rules, the melody of the first part not being followed throughout.
Canon, harmonical. The monochord.
Canon, hidden. A close canon. See *Cánone Chiúso.*
Canonical mass. A mass in which the different parts of the musical service are in strict canonical order.
Canon, infinite. A canon, the end of which leads to the beginning; a perpetual fugue.

CANT

Canon perpetuus, *Lat.* (kän-ŏn pĕr-pĕt-ū-ŭs.) See canon, infinite.
Canon, mixed. A canon of several voices, beginning at different intervals.
Canon, strict. A canon in which the rules of this form of composition are strictly followed.
Canore, *Fr.* (kä-nōr.) } Musical, tuneful,
Canóro, *It.* (kä-nō-rō.) } harmonious.
Canorus, *Lat.* (kä-nō-rŭs.) }
Canos o canones del organo, *Spa.* (kä-nōs ō kä-nō-nĕs dĕl ōr-gä-nō.) Tubes or pipes of an organ.
Cant. An abbreviation of canto and cantate.
Cantab. An abbreviation of *cantabile.*
Cantábile, *It.* (kän-tä-bĕ-lĕ.) That can be sung; in a melodious, singing and graceful style, full of expression.
Cantábile ad libitum, *It.* (kän-tä-bĕ-lĕ äd lē-bē-tŭm.) In singing style, at pleasure.
Cantábile con molto portamento, *It.* (kän-tä-bĕ-lĕ kŏn mōl-tō pōr-tä-mĕn-tō.) In singing style, with a great deal of *portamento;* in a melodious style, with embellishments at pleasure, but few and well chosen.
Cantable, *Spa.* (kän-tä-blĕ.) Tunable, harmonious, musical.
Cantacchiáre, *It.* (kän-täk-kē-ä-rĕ.) To sing often and badly; to hum.
Cantada, *Spa.* (kän-tä-dä.) A cantata.
Cantadour, *Fr.* (känh-tä-door.) A singer of songs and ballads in the tenth and following centuries.
Cantaféra, *It.* (kän-tä-fä-rä.) The air, the melody. See *Cantiléna.*
Cantajuólo, *It.* (kän-tä-yoo-ō-lō.) } A street
Cantambánca, *It.* (kän-täm-bän-kä.) } singer; an itinerant musician; a contemptuous name for a singer.
Cantaménto, *It.* (kän-tä-mĕn-tō.) Tune, air.
Cantándo, *It.* (kän-tän-dō.) In a melodious, singing style.
Cantans, *Lat.* (kän-täns.) Singing.
Cantánte, *It.* (kän-tän-tĕ.) A singer; also a part intended for the voice.
Cantánte ariose, *It.* (kän-tän-tĕ ä-rē-ō-zĕ.) A species of melody which, by its frequent changes of measure and conversational style, first served to mark the distinction between air and recitative.
Cantar, *Spa.* (kän-tär.) To sing, or to chant.
Cantar a la almohadilla, *Spa.* (kän-tär ä lä äl-mō-ä-dĕl-yä.) To sing alone, and without being accompanied by instruments.
Cantarcico, *Spa.* (kän-tär-thē-kō.) } A little
Cantarcillo, *Spa.* (kän-tär-thăl-yō.) } song.
Cantáre, *It.* (kän tä-rĕ.) To sing, to celebrate, to praise.
Cantáre a ária, *It.* (kän-tä-rĕ ä ä-rē-ä.) To sing without confining one's self strictly to the music as written.
Cantáre a libro, *It.* (kän-tä-rĕ ä lē-brō.) To sing from notes.
Cantáre a orécchio, *It.* (kän-tä-rĕ ä ō-rät-kē-o.) To sing by ear, without a knowledge of musical notation; singing by rote.
Cantáre di maniéra, *It.* (kän-tä-rĕ dē mä-nē-

PRONOUNCING MUSICAL DICTIONARY. 39

ă *ale,* ă *add,* ä *arm,* ō *eve,* ĕ *end,* ī *ice,* ĭ *ill,* ō *old,* ŏ *odd,* ô *dove,* oo *moon,* ū *lute,* ŭ *but,* ü *French sound.*

CANT

ä-rā.) To sing in a correct style, with grace and expression.
Cantáre manieráta, *It.* (kän-tä-rĕ mä-nĕ-ĕ-rä-tä.) To sing with too many embellishments, without taste or judgment.
Cantarín, *Spa.* (kän-tä-rēn.) One who is constantly singing.
Cantarína, *Spa.* (kän-tä-rē-nä.) A woman who sings in public.
Cantáta, *It.* (kän-*tä*-tä.) ⎫ A poem set to music; a vocal composition of several movements, comprising airs and recitatives; a short oratorio or operetta without action.
Cantate, *Fr.* (känh-*tät.*) ⎬
Cantate, *Ger.* (kän-*tä*-tĕ.) ⎭
Cantáta amoróse, *It.* (kän-*tä*-tä ä-mō-rō-zĕ.) A cantata having love for its subject.
Cantáta moráli o spirituáli, *It.* (kän-*tä*-tä mō-rä-lē ō spē-re-too-ä-lē.) A cantata designed for the church.
Cantatílla, *It.* (kän-tä-*tēl*-lä.) ⎫ A short cantata; an air pre-ceded by a recitative.
Cantatílle, *Fr.* (känh-tä-*tēl.*) ⎬
Cantatína, *It.* (kän-tä-*tē*-nä.) ⎭
Cantátor, *Lat.* (kän-*tä*-tōr.) A singer, a chanter.
Cantatóre, *It.* (kän-tä-*tō*-rĕ.) A male singer.
Cantatórium, *Lat.* (kän-tä-*tō*-rĭ-ŭm.) The book from which the priests in the Roman Catholic service chant or recite the responses.
Cantatríce, *It.* (kän-tä-*trē*-tshĕ.) A female singer.
Cantratíce buffa, *It.* (kän-tä-trē-tshĕ *boof*-fä.)
Cantatrix, *Lat.* (kän-*tä*-trix.) A female singer; a woman who sings in comic opera.
Cantazzáre, *It.* (kän-tät-zä-rĕ.) To sing badly.
Cantellerándo, *It.* (kän-tĕl-lĕ-rän-dō.) Singing with a subdued voice; murmuring, trilling.
Canterelláre, *It.* (kän-tä-rĕl-lä-rĕ.) To chant or sing.
Canteríno, *It.* (kän-tĕ-rē-nō.) A singer; a chanter.
Cántica, *It.* (kän-tĕ-kä.) ⎫ Canticles; the ancient *l a u d i,* or sacred songs of the Roman Catholic church.
Canticse, *Lat.* (kän-tĭ-sĕ.) ⎬
Cántici, *It. pl.* (kän-tĕ-tshĕ.) ⎪
Cantico, *Spa.* (kän-tē-kō.) ⎭
Cánti carnascialéschi, *It.* (*kän*-tē cär-näs-tshĕ-ä-läs-kē.)
Cánti charneváli, *It.* (*kän*-tē kär-nĕ-vä-lē.) Songs of the *carnival* week.
Canticchiáre, *It.* (kän-tē-kĕ-ä-rĕ.) To sing; to hum.
Canticio, *Sp.* (kän-tä-thĭ-o.) Constant or frequent singing.
Canticle. A sacred hymn or song. 2. A canto, a division of a song.
Cántico, *It.* (kän-tē-kō.) ⎫ A canticle.
Canticum, *Lat.* (*kän*-tĭ-kŭm.) ⎬
Cantíga, *Spa.* (kän-tä-gä.) To chant, to sing.
Cantillate. (*kän*-tĭl-lāte.) To chant, or to recite with musical tones.
Cantillátion. A chanting, a recitation with musical modulations.
Cantillátio. *Lat.* (kän-tĭl-*lä*-shĭ-o.) A singing style of declamation.
Cantiléna, *It.* (kän-tĭ-*lä*-nä.) The melody, air or principal part in any composition; generally the highest vocal part.

CANT

Cantilenáccia, *It.* (kän-tĕ-lĕ-*nät*-tshĕ-ä.) A bad song.
Cantilenáre, *It.* (kän-tĕ-lĕ-*nä*-rĕ.) To sing little songs; a term of contempt.
Cantiléna scótica, *It.* (kän-tĕ-*lä*-nä skō-tĕ-kä.) A Scotch air or tune.
Cantiléne, *It.* (kän-tĕ-*lä*-nĕ.) A *cantiléna.*
Cantína, *Spa.* (kän-*tä*-nä.) A vulgar song.
Cantinéla, *Spa.* (kän-tĕ-*nä*-lä) A ballad.
Cantíno, *It.* (kän-*tē*-nō.) The smallest string of the violin, guitar, etc.
Cantio, *Lat.* (*kän*-tĭ-o.) A song.
Cantion. A song or number of verses.
Cantiónes sacræ, *Lat.* (kän-shĭ-*ō*-nēs sä-krä.) Sacred songs.
Cantique, *Fr.* (känh-*tēk.*) A canticle or hymn of praise.
Cantique des Cantiques. *Fr.* (känh-*tēk* dĕ känh-*tēk.*) Solomon's Song.
Cantiúncula, *Lat.* (kän-tĭ-*ŭn*-kū-lä.) A ballad, a catch.
Cánto, *It.* (*kän*-tō.) Song, air, melody, the highest vocal part in choral music. 2. A part or division of a poem.
Cánto armónico, *It.* (*kän*-tō är-*mō*-nē-kō.) A part-song for two, three or more voices.
Cánto clef. The C clef when placed on the first line.
Cánto concertánte, *It.* (*kän*-tō kŏn-tshär-*tän*-tĕ.) The treble of the principal concerting parts.
Cánto cromático, *It.* (*kän*-tō krō-*mä*-tē-kō.) Singing in semitones.
Cánto férmo, *It.* (*kän*-tō *fār*-mō.) A chant or melody. 2. Choral singing in unison on a plain melody. 3. Any subject consisting of a few long plain notes, given as a theme for counterpoint.
Cánto figuráto, *It.* (*kän*-tō fē-goo-*rä*-tō.) A figured melody.
Cánto florítto, *It.* (*kän*-tō fē-*ō*-rēt-tō.) A song in which many ornaments are introduced.
Cánto fúnebre, *It.* (*kän*-tō foo-*nä*-brĕ.) A funeral song.
Cánto Gregoriáno, *It.* (*kän*-tō grĕ-gō-rē-*ä*-nō.) The Gregorian chant.
Cánto lláno, *Spa.* (*kän*-tō *lyä*-nō.) ⎫ The plain chant or song.
Cánto pláno, *It.* (*kän*-tō *plä*-nō.) ⎬
Cánto necessário, *It.* (*kän*-tō nä-tshĕs-*sä*-rē-o.) A term indicating those parts that are to sing through the whole piece.
Cánto prímo, *It.* (*kän*-tō prē-mō.) The first treble or soprano.
Cantór, *It.* (kän-*tōr.*) A singer, a chanter.
Cantor, *Lat.* (*kän*-tōr.) ⎫
Cantor choralis, *Lat.* (*kän*-tōr kō-*rä*-lĭs.) ⎬ A *precentor;* a leader of the choir.
Cantoráte, *It.* (kän-tō-*rä*-tĕ.) A leading singer of a choir.
Cantorcíllo, *Spa.* (kän-tōr-*thēl*-yō.) A poor, worthless singer.
Cantóre, *It.* (kän-*tō*-rĕ.) A singer, a chanter, a poet.
Cánto recitatívo, *It.* (*kän*-tō rä-tshĕ-tä-*tē*-vō.) Recitative, declamatory singing.
Cantória, *It.* (kän-*tō*-rē-ä.) ⎫ A singing gallery, a musical can to, singing.
Cantória, *Spa.* (kän-*tō*-rē-ä.) ⎭

ă ale, ă add, ă arm, ĕ eve, ĕ end, ĭ ice, ĭ ill, ō old, ŏ odd, ō dove, oo moon, ū lute, ŭ but, ū French sound.

CANT

Cantorei, *Ger.* (kăn-tō-rī.) The dwelling-house of the cantor. 2, A class of the choristers in the public school.
Cantoren, *Ger.* (kăn-tō-r'n.) Chanters, a choir of singers.
Cantor figuralis, *Lat.* (kăn-tōr fĭg-ū-rā-lĭa.) Oratorio singer, conductor of the choir.
Cantor in choro, *Lat.* (kăn-tōr ĭn kō-rō.) A chorister.
Canto ripieno, *It.* (kăn-tō rē-pē-ā-nō.) The treble of the grand chorus; the part that sings or plays only in the grand chorus.
Cantoris, *Lat.* (kăn-tō-rĭs.) A term used in cathedral music to indicate the passages intended to be sung by those singers who are placed on that side of the choir where the *cantor* or *precentor* sits. This is usually on the left hand side on entering the choir from the nave.
Cánto rivoltato, *It.* (kăn-tō rē-vōl-tā-tō.) The treble changed.
Cánto secondo, *It.* (kăn-tō sē-kŏn-dō.) The second treble.
Cánto simplice, *It.* (kăn-tō sēm-plā-tshĕ.) A plain song.
Cantrice, *It.* (kāu-trē-tshĕ.) } A female singer,
Cantrix, *Lat.* (kăn-trĭx.) } a songstress.
Canturia, *Spa.* (kăn-too-rĭ-ā.) Musical composition, method of performing music, vocal music.
Cantus, *Lat.* (kăn-tūs.) A song, a melody; also, the treble or soprano part.
Cantus ambrosianus, *Lat.* (kăn-tūs ăm-brō-sĭ-ā-nūs.) The four chants or melodies, introduced into the church by St. Ambrose, Bishop of Milan, in the fourth century, and which are supposed to be derived from ancient Greek melodies.
Cantus durus, *Lat.* (kăn-tūs dū-rūs.) A song written in a major key.
Cantus ecclesiasticus, *Lat.* (kăn-tūs ĕk-klē-sĭ-ăs-tĭ-kūs.) Sacred song; ecclesiastical or church music.
Cantus figuratus, *Lat.* (kăn-tūs fĭg-ū-rā-tūs.) Embellished or figurative chants or melodies.
Cantus firmus, *Lat.* (kăn-tūs fĭr-mūs.) The plain song or chant. See *cánto férmo*.
Cantus Gregorianus, *Lat.* (kăn-tūs Grē-gō-rĭ-ā-nūs.) Those four chants or melodies introduced into the church by St. Gregory and which with the Ambrosian chants, formed a series of eight *modes* or *tones* as they were called.
Cantus mensurabilis, *Lat.* (kăn-tūs mĕn-sūr-ā-bĭ-lĭs.) A regular or measured melody.
Cantus mollis, *Lat.* (kăn-tūs-mŏl-lĭs.) A song written in the minor key.
Canu, *Wel.* (kă-noo.) To sing.
Canum, *Tur.* (kă-nŭm.) A Turkish musical instrument on which the ladies play.
Canzóna, *It.* (kăn-tsō-nă.) } Song, ballad, can-
Canzóne, *It.* (kăn-tsō-nĕ.) } zonet. 2. A graceful and somewhat elaborate air in two or three strains or divisions. 3. An air in two or three parts with passages of fugue and imitation, somewhat similar to the madrigal.
Canzonáccea, *It.* (kăn-tsō-năt-tshĕ-ă.) A low, trivial song, a poor canzone.
Canzoncína, *It.* kăn-tsōn-tshă-nă.) A short canzóne or song.

CAPR

Canzóne sácra, *It.* (kăn-tsō-nĕ să-krā.) A sacred song.
Canzonet. A short song in one, two or three parts.
Canzonnétta, *It.* (kăn-tsō-năt-tă.) A short canzóne.
Canzoni, *It.* (kăn-tsō-nē.) A sonata; in connection with a passage of music it has the same meaning as *allégro*.
Canzoniére, *It.* (kăn-tsō-nē-ā-rō.) A song book.
Canzonina, *It.* (kăn-tsō-nē-nă.) } A can-
Canzonuccia, *It.* (kăn-tsō-noot-tshē-ă.) } zonet ; a little song.
Caoinan, *Iri.* An ancient Irish requiem.
Capelle, *Ger.* (kă-pĕl-lĕ.) A chapel, a musical band.
Capell-meister, *Ger.* (kă-pĕl-mīs-tĕr.) The director, composer or master of the music in a choir.
Capilla, *Spa.* (kă-pĕl-yă.) A band of chapel musicians.
Capiscol, *Spa.* (kă-pĕs-kōl.) } The *chanter*
Capiscolus, *Lat.* (kă-pĭs-kō-lŭs.) } or *precentor* of a choir.
Capistrum, *Ger.* (kă-pĭs-troom.) An implement used by the ancient trumpeters, to relieve the strain on their cheeks. It was almost universally used.
Capitular, *Spa.* (kă-pĕt-oo-lăr.) To sing prayers at service.
Capitulario, *Spa.* (kă-pĕt-oo-lă-rĭ-ō.) A book of prayers.
Capo, *It.* (kă-pō.) The head or beginning; the top.
Capodastro, *It.* (kă-pō-dăs-trō.) See Capotásto.
Cápo d' instrumenti, *It.* (kă-pō d' ĕn-ĕs-atroo-mān-tĕ.) The leader or director of the instrumental performers.
Cápo d' opera, *It.* (kă-pō d' ō-pĕ-ră.) The masterpiece of a composer.
Cápo d' orchestra, *It.* (kă-pō d' ōr-kĕs-tră.) The leader of the orchestra.
Capona, *Spa.* (kă-pō-nă.) A spanish dance.
Capotásto, *It.* (kă-pō-tăs-tō.) The nut or upper part of the fingerboard of a violin, violincello, etc. 2. A small instrument used by guitar players to form a temporary nut upon the finger board, to produce certain effects.
Capo violino, *It.* (kă-pō vē-ō-lē-nō.) The first violin.
Cappélla, *It.* (kăp-pĕl-lă.) A chapel or church. 2. A band of musicians that sing or play in a church.
Cappélla alla, *It.* (kăp-păl-lă ăl-lă.) In the the church style.
Cappélla músíca, *It.* (kăp-păl-lă moo-zē-kă.) Chapel or church music.
Capriccietto, *It.* (kă-prēt-shē-ăt-tō.) A short *capriccio*.
Capriccio, *It.* (kă-prēt-shē-ō.) A fanciful and irregular species of composition; a species of *fantasia*; in a capricious and free style.
Capricciosamente, *It.* (kă-prēt-shē-ō-ză-mān-tĕ.) Capriciously.
Capriccioso, *It.* (kă-prēt-shē-ō-zō. In a fanciful and capricious style.
Capricci, *It.* (kă-prēt-shē.) } A caprice. See *Ca-*
Caprice, *Fr.* (kă-prēs.) } *príccio*.

ă ale, ă add, ă arm, ē eve, ĕ end, ī ice, ĭ ill, ō old, ŏ odd, ō dove, oo moon, ū lute, ŭ but, ü French sound.

CAPR

Caprice. A whimsical, fanciful style of composition. See *Capriccio*.
Capricho, *Spa.* (kä-prē-kō.) A caprice.
Capricieusement, *Fr.* (kä-prē-sŭs-mōnh.) Capriciously.
Capricieux, *Fr.* (kä-prē-sŭ.) In a fanciful and capricious style.
Car. *It.* (kär.) An abbreviation of Carta.
Caracteres de musique, *Fr.* (kär-äk-tār dŭh mū-zēk.) A term applied to musical signs; all the marks or symbols belonging to musical notation.
Caramillar, *Spa.* (kär-ä-mēl-yär.) To play on a flageolet.
Caramillo, *Spa.* (kär-ä-mēl-yō.) A flageolet, a small flute.
Carâttere, *It.* (kä-rät-tā-rĕ.) Character, quality, degree.
Carâttere, mezzo, *It.* (kä-rät-tā-rĕ mĕt-sō.) A term applied to music of moderate difficulty.
Caressant, *Fr.* (kä-rĕs-sänh.) Caressing, tenderly.
Carezzándo, *It.* (kä-rĕt-tsän-dō.) } In a careas-
Carezovóle, *It.* (kä-rät-sō-vō-lĕ.) } sing and tender manner.
Caricáto, *It.* (kä-rē-kä-tō.) Exaggerated, caricature.
Caricatura, *It.* (kä-rē-kä-too-rä.) A caricature, an exaggerated representation.
Carillon, *Fr.* (kä-rē-yōnh.) Chime. See *Carillons*.
Carillon a clavier, *Fr.* (kä-rē-yōnh ä kläv-ī-ā.) A set of keys and pedals acting upon the bells.
Carillonement, *Fr.* (kä-rē-yōnh-mänh.) Chiming.
Carillonner, *Fr.* (kä-rē-yō-nā.) To chime or ring bells.
Carillonneur, *Fr.* (kä-rē-yo-nŭr.) A player or ringer of bells or *carillons*.
Carillons, *Fr. pl.* (kä-rē-yōnh.) Chimes; a peal or set of bells, upon which tunes are played by the machinery of a clock, or by means of keys, like those of a pianoforte. 2. Short simple airs adapted to such bells. 3. A mixture stop in an organ, to imitate a peal of bells.
Carita, *It.* (kä-rē-tä.) Tenderness, feeling.
Carita, con. *It.* (kä-rē-tä kōn.) With tenderness.
Carmen, *Ger.* (kär-mĕn.) } A tune, a song, a
Carmen, *Lat.* (kär-mĕn.) } poem.
Carmen natalitium, *Lat.* (kär-mĕn nä-tä-lē-ahī-ŭm.) A carol.
Carol. A song. 2. A song of joy and exultation, a song of devotion. 3. Old ballads sung at Christmas and Easter.
Carola, *It.* (kä-rō-lä.) A ballad, a dance with singing.
Caroláre, *It.* (kä-rō-lä-rĕ.) To sing in a warbling manner, to carol.
Carolétta, *It.* (kä-rō-lāt-tä.) A little dance.
Caroli, *Wel.* (kä-rō-lē.) To carol.
Carolle, *Fr.* (kä-rōl.) A carol.
Carracca, *Spa.* (kär-räk-kä.) A rattle.
Carracon, *Spa.* (kär-rä-kōn.) A large rattle.
Carrure des phrases, *Fr.* (kär-rŭr dĕ fräz.) The quadrature or balancing of the phrases.
Cart. *It.* An abbreviation of *Carta*.
Carta, *It.* (kär-tä.) A page, a folio.

CAVA

Cartel, *Fr.* (kär-tĕl.) The first sketch of a composition, or of a full score. (Obsolete.)
Cartellóne, *It.* (kär-tĕl-lō-nĕ.) A large play bill; the printed catalogue of operas to be performed during the season.
Carrol, *Wel.* A carol, a ballad.
Cascabel-ada, *Spa.* (käs-kä-bĕ-lä-dä.) A jingling of small bells.
Case, organ. The frame or outside of an organ.
Cássa, *It.* (käs-sä.) Chest or box.
Cássa grande. *It.* (käs-sä grän-dĕ.) } The
Cássa militare, *It.* (käs-sä mē-lē-tä-rĕ.) } great drum in military music.
Castagnet. Castanet.
Castagnétta, *It.* (käs-tän-yāt-tä.) } Snappers;
Castagnettes, *Fr.* (käs-tänh-yĕt.) } castanets,
Castagnole, *Spa.* (käs-tän-yō-lĕ.) } used in
Castanétas, *Spa.* (käs-tän-yä-täs.) } dancing.
See *Castanets.*
Castanets. Snappers used to accompany dancing; an instrument of music formed of small concave shells of ivory, or hard wood, shaped like spoons. Castanets are used by dancers in Spain and other southern countries to mark the rhythm of the *boléro*, cachucha, etc.
Castanheta, *Por.* (käs-tän-ā-tä.) } Casta-
Castanuélas, *Spa.* (käs-tän-yoo-ā-läs.) } nets.
Castorion, *Gr.* (käs-tō-rī-ōn.) A martial melody used by the Greeks just before battle.
Castráto, *It.* (käs-trä-tō.) A male singer with a soprano voice, formerly very frequent, but now seldom to be met with.
Catacoustics. (kät-ä-koos-tīks.) } That part of
Cataphonics. (kät-ä-fōn-īks.) } accoustics that treats of reflected sounds.
Catalectic. Pertaining to metrical composition or to measure.
Catalectic verses. Verses that want either feet or syllables.
Catch. A humorous composition for three or four voices, supposed to be of English invention and dating back to the Tudors. The parts are so contrived, that the singers catch up each other's words, thus giving them a different sense from that of the original reading.
Caténa di trilli, *It.* (kä-tā-nä dē trēl-lē.) A chain, or succession of shakes.
Catgut. A small string for violins and other instruments of a similar kind, made of the intestines of sheep and lambs, and sometimes cats.
Cathédrale. *Fr.* (kät-ä-drdl.) } A cathedral.
Cattedrále, *It.* (kät-tĕ-drä-lĕ.) }
Catling. A lute string.
Cattivo, *It.* (kät-tē-vō.) Bad, unfit.
Cattivo tempo, *It.* (kät-tē-vō tĕm-pō.) A part of a measure where it is not proper to end a cadence, place a long syllable, etc.
Cauda, *Lat.* (kau-dä.) Coda.
Cavalletta, *It.* (kä-väl-lĕt-tä.) } A cabalétta.
Cavallétto, *It.* (kä-väl-lĕt-tō.) }
Cavalquet, *Fr.* (käv-äl-kā.) Trumpet signal for the cavalry.
Cavata, *It.* (kä-vä-tä.) A small song, sometimes preceded by a recitative; a cavatina.
Cavatína, *It.* (kä-vä-tē-nä.) } An air of one
Cavatine, *Fr.* (käv-ä-tēn.) } strain only, of dramatic style sometimes preceded by a recitative.

ä ale, ă add, ä arm, ē eve, ĕ end, ī ice, ĭ ill, ō old, ŏ odd, ō dove, oo moon, ü lute, ü but, ü French sound.

CAXA

Caxa, *Spa.* (käx-ä.) A drum; the wooden case of an organ.
Caxon, *Spa.* (käx-ŏn.) A mould for casting organ pipes.
C. B. The initials of *col basso* and *contra basso*.
C barré, *Fr.* (bär-rā.) } The character ₵ used
C barred.   } to indicate *alla brève* or *alla cappélla* time.
C clef. The *tenor* clef. It is called the C clef, because, on whatever line it is placed, it gives to the notes of that line the name and pitch of *middle* C. Is used also for Sop. and Alt.
C dur, *Ger.* (tsā door.) The key of C major.
Cebell. The name of an old air in common time, characterized by a quick and sudden alternation of high and low notes.
Ceja, *Spa.* (thā-hā.) Bridge of a violin or similar instrument.
Celebrer, *Fr.* (sä-lĕ-brā.) To celebrate, to extol, to praise.
Célere, *It.* (tshā-lĕ-rĕ.) Quick, rapid, with velocity.
Celeridad, *Spa.* (thā-lā-rĕ-däd.) } Celerity, ve-
Celeritá, *It.* (tshā-lā-rĕ-tä.)   } locity, rapid-
Célérité, *Fr.* (sä-lā-rĕ-tā.)   } ity.
Céleste, *Fr.* (sä-lĕst.) Celestial, heavenly; in some passages it indicates the employment of the pedal which acts on the *celestina* or soft stop.
Celestial music. Among the ancients, the harmony of sounds supposed to result from the movements of the heavenly bodies.
Celestina, *It.* (tshā-lĕs-tē-nä.) An organ stop of small 4 feet scale, producing a very delicate and subdued tone.
'Célli, *It.* (tshāl-lē.) An abbreviation of *violincelli*.
'Céllist, *It.* (tshāl-lēst.) An abbreviation of *violincellist*.
'Céllo, *It.* (tshāl-lō.) An abbreviation of *violincello*.
Cemb. An abbreviation of *Cémbalo*.
Cembalista, *It.* (tshĕm-bä-lăz-tä.) A player on the harpsichord; also, a player on the cymbals.
Cémbalo, *It.* (tshăm-bä-lō.) } A harpsichord;
Cémbolo, *It.* (tshăm-bō-lō.) } also the name for a cymbal.
Cembanélla, *It.* (tshĕm-bä-nĕl-lä.) } A bag-
Cemmanélla, *It.* (tshĕm-mä-nĕl-lä.) } pipe, a
Cemmenéllo, *It.* (tshĕm-bä-nĕl-lō.) } pipe, a
Cennamella, *It.* (tshĕn-nä-mĕl-lä.) } flute, a flageolet.
Cemmamélla, *It.* (tshĕm-mä-mĕl-lä.) A cymbal.
Cencerrear, *Spa.* (thĕn-thä-rĕ-är.) To play on an untuned guitar.
Cencerro, *Spa.* (thĕn-thar-rō.) An ill tuned guitar.
Cenobites. Monks of a religious order who live in a convent and perform the services of the choir.
Cento, *Lat.* (sĕn-tō.) The title of a poem made up of various verses of another poem; a cento.
Cento. A composition formed by verses and passages from other authors and disposed in a new order.
Centone, *Lat.* (sĕn-tō-nĕ.) A cento, or medley of different tunes or melodies.

CHAM

Cercár délla nóta, *It.* (tehĕr-kär dăl-lä nō-tä.) To seek or feel for the note; a gliding from one note to another, in singing, by anticipating the proper time of the second note.
Cerdana, *Spa.* (thär-dä-nä.) A dance in Catalonia.
Cerdear, *Spa.* (thär-dĕ-är.) To emit harsh and discordant sounds.
Cervalet. An ancient wind instrument resembling in tone the bassoon.
Ces, *Ger.* (tsĕs.) The note C.flat.
Ces dur, (tsĕs door.) The key of C flat major.
C. Espr. An abbreviation of Con Espressione.
Cesura. } A pause in verse introduced to aid the
Cesure. } recital and render the versification more melodious. See *Caesura*.
Cétera, *It.* (tshā-tĕ-rä.) A cittern, a guitar.
Ceteránte, *It.* (tshā-tĕ-rän-tĕ.) A player upon the cittern or guitar.
Ceteráre, *It.* (tshā-tĕ-rä-rĕ.) To play upon the cittern or guitar.
Ceteratojo, *It.* (tshā-tĕ-rä-tō-yō.) A song accompanied upon the cittern.
Ceteratóre, *It.* (tshā-tĕ-rä-tō-rĕ.) } A player
Ceterista, *It.* (tshā-tĕ-räs-tä.)   } upon the cittern or guitar.
Ceterizzare, *It.* (tshā-tĕ-rĕt-zä-rĕ.) To sing with or play upon the cittern.
Cetra, *It.* (tshā-trä.) A small harp.
Cetrarciéro, *It.* (tshĕt-rär-tshĕ-ā-rō.) A harp with the bow and lyre.
Cetráre, *It.* (tshĕt-rä-rĕ.) See Ceteráre.
Ch. An abbreviation of *choir* and *chorus*.
Cha Chi. (kä, kē.) A Chinese instrument similar to the *kin*, but having the chromatic scale.
Chabatis. (kä-bä-tĭs.) The name of the favorite melodies sung by the Arabian singing girls.
Chacóna, *Spa.* (tshä-kō-nä.) } A chacone, a
Chaconne, *Fr.* (shä-kŏnh.)   } graceful, slow Spanish movement in 3-4 time, and composed upon a ground bass. It is always in the major key and the first and third beats of each bar are strongly accented.
Chacoon. A dance like a carsband. See *Chacóna*.
Chair organ. Found in old organ music. See *choir organ*.
Chal. An abbreviation of *Chalumeau*.
Chalil, *Heb.* (kä-lĭl.) An old Hebrew instrument similar to a pipe or flute.
Chalmey. See Chalumeau.
Chalotte. A tube of brass made to receive the reed of an organ pipe.
Chalmeau, *Fr.* (shäl-mō.)   } An ancient rus-
Chalumeau, *Fr.* (shä-lü-mō.)   } tic flute resembling the hautboy, and blown through a *calamus*, or reed. The term is also applied to some of the low notes of the clarinet.
Chamade, *Fr.* (shä-mäd.) Beat of drum declaring a surrender or parley.
Chamber band. A company of musicians whose performances are confined to chamber music.
Chamber music. Music composed for private performance or for small concerts; such as instrumental duets, trios, quartets, etc.
Chamberga, *Spa.* (tshäm-bĕr-gä.) A Spanish dance accompanied by a song.

ă ale, ă add, ä arm, ē eve, ĕ end, I ice, Ĭ ill, ō old, ŏ odd, Ō dove, oo moon, ū lute, ŭ but, ü French sound.

CHAM

Chamber voice. A voice especially suited to the execution of parlor music.
Changeable. A term applied to chants which may be sung either in the major or minor mode of the key or tonic in which they are written.
Change, enharmonic. A passage where the notation is changed, but the same keys of the instrument are employed.
Changer de jeu, *Fr.* (shänh-zhă dŭh zhŭ.) To change the stops or registers in an organ.
Changes. The various alterations and different passages produced by a peal of bells.
Changing notes. A term applied by some theorists to passing notes or discords, which occur on the *accented* parts of a bar.
Chans. An abbreviation of *Chanson*.
Chanson, *Fr.* (shänh-sŏnh.) A song.
Chason bachique, *Fr.* (shänh-sŏnh băk-ēk.) A drinking song.
Chanson des rues, *Fr.* (shänh-sŏnh dĕ rü.) A street song; a vaudeville.
Chansonner, *Fr.* (shäh-sŏnh-nā.) To make songs.
Chansonnette, *Fr.* (shänh-sŏnh-nĕt.) A little or short song, or canzonet.
Chansonnier, *Fr.* (shänh-sŏnh-nĭ-ā.) A maker of songs or ballads.
Chansonniere, *Fr.* (shänh-sŏnh-nĭ-är.) A female song writer.
Chansons de geste, *Fr.* (shänh-sŏnh dŭh zhĕst.) The romances formerly sung by the wandering minstrels of the middle ages.
Chant. A simple melody, generally harmonized in four parts, to which lyrical portions of the Scriptures are set, part of the words being recited *ad libitum*, and part sung in strict time. 2. To recite musically, to sing.
Chant, (shänh.) The voice part; a song or melody, singing.
Chant, Ambrosian. The chant introduced by St. Ambrose into the church at Milan, in the fourth century.
Chant amoureux, *Fr.* (shänh ă moo-rŭh.) A love song, an amorous ditty.
Chantant, *Fr.* (shänh-tänh.) Adapted to singing; in a melodious and singing style.
Chantante, *Fr.* (shänh-tänht.) Singing.
Chantante, bass, *Fr.* (shänh-tänht bāss.) Vocal bass.
Chant d' allegresse, *Fr.* (shänh d' äl-lĕ-grās.) A song of joy.
Chant d' eglise, *Fr.* shänh d' ĕ-glēz.) Church singing.
Chant de noel. *Fr.* (shänh dŭh nō-āl.) A Christmas carol.
Chant des oiseaux, *Fr.* (shänh dĕ swä-zō.) Singing of the birds.
Chant de triomphe, *Fr.* (shänh dŭh trē-ŏnhf.) A triumphal song, a song of victory.
Chant dorian, *Fr.* (shänh dō-rĭ-änh.) A grave chant, with which the harp was sometimes associated.
Chant, double. A chant extending through two verses of a psalm.
Chant du soir, *Fr.* (shänh dŭ swär.) Evening chant.
Chantée, *Fr.* (shän-tā.) Sung.

CHAN

Chanter. One who chants. 2. The pipe that sounds the treble or tenor in a bagpipe.
Chanter. *Fr.* (shänh-tā.) To sing, to celebrate, to praise.
Chanter a livre ouvert, *Fr.* (shänh-tā ä lĕvr oo-vār.) To sing at sight.
Chanter a pleine voix, *Fr.* (shänh-tā ä plān vwä.) To be in full voice.
Chanter, arch. The chief chanter, the leader of the chants.
Chanterelle, *Fr.* (shänh-tĕ-rāl.) Treble string; the smallest string of the violin.
Chanter en choeur, *Fr.* (shänh-tā änh kŭr.) To sing in chorus.
Chanter faux. *Fr.* (shänh-tā fō.) To sing out of tune.
Chanterie, *Fr.* (shänh-tĕ-rē.) The chanter's place.
Chanter juste, *Fr.* (shänh-tā zhüst.) To sing with correct intonation.
Chanter la note, *Fr.* (shänh-tā lă nōt.) To sing the notes, but without expression.
Chanterres, *Fr.* (shänh-tĕ-rā.) The singers of songs and ballads in the tenth and following centuries.
Chanter toujours la meme antienne, *Fr.* (shänh-tā too-zhoor lă mām änh-sĭ-ānh.) To sing the same song over and over again.
Chanteur, *Fr.* (shänh-tŭr.) A singer.
Chanteur des rues, *Fr.* (shänh-tŭr dĕ rü.) A street singer.
Chanterie, *Fr.* (shänh-trē.) } Institutions established and endowed for the purpose of singing the souls of the
Chantry. } founders out of purgatory. A church or chapel endowed with revenue for the purpose of saying mass daily for the souls of the donors.
Chantry priests. Priests selected to sing in the chantry.
Chanteuse, *Fr.* (shänh-tŭs.) A female vocalist.
Chant funebre, *Fr.* (shänh fü-nābr.) Dirge, a funeral song.
Chant, Gregorian. See *Cantus Gregorianus*.
Chant sur le livre, *Fr.* (shänh sür lŭh lēvr.) A barbarous kind of counterpoint or *descant*, as it was termed, performed by several voices, each singing ex tempore.
Chant, lugubre, *Fr.* (shänh lü-gūbr.) A dismal, doleful song.
Chant, Lydian. A melody in a sad style, sung in a languid and melancholy manner.
Chant, monotone. A monotonous song.
Chant, Phrygian. A chant intended to excite the hearers to fury and rage.
Chant, plain. A single chant, seldom extending beyond the limits of an octave, or through more than one verse.
Chant, Roman. The Gregorian chant.
Chant, sacre, *Fr.* (shänh säkr.) Sacred music.
Chant, single. A simple harmonized melody, extending only through one verse of a psalm.
Chant sub Phrygian. A chant employed to appease the fury excited by the *Phrygian chant*.
Chantonner, *Fr.* (shänh-tŏnh-nā.) To hum a tune.
Chantonnerie, *Fr.* (shänh-tŏnh-nĕ-rē.) Humming.

ă ale, ă add, ä arm, ĕ eve, ĕ end, ī ice, ĭ ill, ō old, ŏ odd, ȯ dove, oo moon, ū lute, ŭ but, ü French sound.

CHAN

Chantor. A singer in a cathedral choir.
Chantre, *Fr.* (shäntr.) A chorister, a chanter, a singing boy.
Chanzoneta, *Spa.* (tshän-thō-nā-tä.) A ballad, a little song.
Chapeau chinois, *Fr.* (shä-pō shē-nwä.) A crescent or set of small bells used in military music.
Chapel, ante. That portion of the chapel leading to the choir.
Chapelle, *Fr.* (shäp-ěl.) A chapel. See Cappella.
Chapier, *Fr.* (shä-pī-ā.) A cope bearer; a singer in his cope.
Characteristic chord. The leading or principal chord.
Characteristic note. A leading note.
Characters. A general name for musical signs.
Charfreitag, *Ger.* (kär-frī-täg.) Good Friday.
Chariot air. A musical air of the ancient Greeks.
Charivari, *Fr.* (shä-rī-vä-rē.) Noisy music made with tin dishes, horns, bells, etc.; clatter; a mock serenade.
Charlatan, *Fr.* (shär-lä-tänh.) A quack, an imposter; a superficial artist who makes great pretensions, which are not justified in performance.
Chasse, *Fr.* (shäss.) Hunting; in the hunting style.
Chatsoteroth, *Heb.* (kăt-sō-tě-rōth.) } The silver trumpet of the ancient Hebrews.
Catzozerath, *Heb.* (kăt-zō-zě-räth.) }
Chaunt. See *Chant*.
Chaunter. A person who sings in a choir; a *chantor*.
Che, *It.* (kā.) Than, that, which.
Che Chi. (kā kē.) One of the eight species into which the Chinese divide their musical sounds.
Chef, *Fr.* (shā.) Leader, chief.
Chef-d'attaque, *Fr.* (shā d'ät-täk.) The leader, or principal first violin performer; also, the leader of the chorus.
Chef-d'œuvre, *Fr.* (shā d'oovr.) A master piece, a capital performance; the principal or most important composition of an author.
Chef-d'orchestre, *Fr.* (shā d'ōr-kästr.) The leader of an orchestra.
Chelpour, *Per.* A Persian trumpet used in military service.
Chelys, *Gr.* (kā-lĭs.) A species of lute or viol.
Cheng Chi. (kěng kē.) One of the eight species into which the Chinese divide their musical sounds.
Cherubical hymn. A hymn of great importance in the early Christian church; the Trisagium.
Chest of viols. An old expression applied to a set of viols, two of which were basses, two tenors and two trebles, each with six strings. These instruments were particularly adapted to those compositions called *fantasias*.
Chest tones. } The lowest register of the voice.
Chest voice. }
Chest, wind. A reservoir in an organ for holding the air, which is conveyed from thence into the pipes by means of the bellows.

CHIR

Chevalet, *Fr.* (shěv-ă-lā.) The bridge of a violin, viola, etc.
Cheville, *Fr.* (shē-věl.) The peg of a violin, viola, etc.
Chevrotement, *Fr.* (shē-vrōt-mönh.) A tremor or shake in singing.
Chevroter, *Fr.* (shē-vrō-tā.) To sing with a trembling voice; to make a bad or false shake.
Chiamare, *It.* (kē-ä-mä-rě.) To chime.
Chiamere, a racolta, *It.* (kē-ä-mä-rě ä räk‚kōl-tä.) To beat a drum.
Chiamata, *It.* (kē-ä-mä-tä.) To beat a parley.
Chiara, *It.* (kē-ä-rä.) } Clear, brilliant, pure as
Chiaro, *It.* (kē-ä-rō.) } to tone.
Chiaramente, *It.* (kē-ä-rä-měn-tě.) Clearly, brightly, purely.
Chiarentana, *It.* (kē-ä-rěn-tä-nä.) An Italian country dance.
Chiarezza, *It.* (kē-ä-rāt-sä.) Clearness, neatness, purity.
Chiarina, *It.* (kē-ä-rē-nä.) A clarion.
Chiaroscuro, *It.* (kē-ä-rōs-koo-rō.) Light and shade; the modifications of piano and forte.
Chiáve, *It.* (kē-ä-vě.) A clef, or key.
Chiáve maestro, *It.* (kē-ä-vě mä-ěs-trō.) The fundamental key or note.
Chickera, *Hin.* (chĭ-kē-rä.) An instrument used in India having four or five strings and played with a bow.
Chiésa, *It.* (kē-ā-zä.) A church.
Chiffres, *Fr.* (shěfr.) Figures used in Harmony and Thorough Bass.
Chifla, *Spa.* (tshē-flä.) } A whistle.
Chifladera, *Spa.* (tshē-flä-dě-rä.) }
Chifladura, *Spa.* (shē-flä-doo-rä.) Whistling.
Chiflar, *Spa.* (tshē-flär.) To whistle.
Chifle, *Spa.* (tshē-flě.) A bird call.
Chillido, *Spa.* (tshěl-yē-dō.) A shrill sound.
Chimbe. An old word signifying *chime*.
Chime. A set of bells tuned to a musical scale; the sound of bells in harmony; a correspondence of sound.
Chime barrel. The cylindrical portion of the mechanism sometimes used for ringing a chime of bells.
Chimney. In an organ, a small tube passing through the cap of a stopped pipe.
Chindara, *Per.* (tshĭn-dä-rä.) A fabulous fountain of the Persians at which it was said the sounds of instruments are constantly heard.
Chinese flute. An instrument used by the Chinese made of bamboo.
Chinese musical scale. A scale consisting of five notes without semitones, the music being written on five lines in perpendicular columns, and the elevation and depression of tones indicated by distinctive names.
Chinnor, *Heb.* (kěn-nōr.) } An instrument of
Chinor, *Heb.* (kē-nōr.) } the harp or psaltery species, supposed to have been used by the ancient Hebrews.
Chirie, *It.* (kē-rē-ě.) Lord. See Kyrie.
Chirm. To sing as a bird.
Chirimia, *Sp* (tshē-rē-mī-ä.) The hautboy.
Chirogymnast, *Gr.* (kē-rō-ghĭm-năst.) } A
Chirogymnaste, *It.* (kē-rō-gĭm-näs-tě.) } square board on which are placed various mechanical

CHIR

contrivances for exercising the fingers of a pianist.
Chiroplast, *Gr.* (kĕ-rō-plăst.) A small machine invented by Logier, to keep the hands and fingers of young pianoforte players in the right position.
Chirriar, *Spa.* (tshē-rĭ-ăr.) To sing out of time or tune.
Chisporroteo, *Spa.* (tshĕs-pŏr-rō-tĕ-ō.) Sibillation, hissing.
Chitarone, *It.* (kē-tā-rō-nĕ.) A large or double guitar.
Chitárra, *It.* (kē-tăr-rā.) A guitar, a cithara.
Chittárra coll' arco, *It.* (kē-tăr-rā kŏll' är-kō.) A species of guitar played with a bow like a violin.
Chitarriglia, *It.* (kē-tăr-rēl-yā.) A small guitar.
Chittarrína, *It.* (kēt-tăr-rē-nā.) The small Neapolitan guitar.
Chittarrino, *It.* (kēt-tăr-rē-nō.)
Chitarrista, *It.* (kēt-ăr-rēs-tā.) One who plays on the guitar.
Chinechiurlája, *It.* (kē-oot-kē-oor-lā-yā.) A buzzing or humming sound.
Chiudéndo, *It.* (kē-oo-dăn-dō.) Closing, ending with.
Chiudéndo col aria, *It.* (kē-oo-dăn-dō kōl ā-rē-ā.) Ending with the air.
Chiudéndo col motívo, *It.* (kē-oo-dăn-dō kōl mō-tē-vō.) Concluding with the subject.
Chiudéndo col ritornello, *It.* (kē-oo-dăn-dō kōl rē-tŏr-nĕl-lō.) Ending with the symphony.
Chiuláre, *It.* (kē-oo-lā-rĕ.) The singing of a cuckoo.
Cho. Abbreviation of *chorus.*
Choeur, *Fr.* (kur.) The choir or chorus.
Choice notes. Notes placed on different degrees in same measure either or all of which may be sung.
Choir. That part of a cathedral or church set apart for the singers. 2. The singers themselves taken collectively.
Choir, boy. A choir formed of boys from eight to fourteen years of age. These choirs are confined mostly to the Episcopal church.
Choir, grand. In organ playing, the union of all the reed stops.
Choir organ. In a large organ, the lowest row of keys is called the choir organ, which contains some of the softer and more delicate stops and is used for accompanying solos, duets, etc.
Choir, trombone. Among the Moravians, a number of musicians whose duty it is to announce from the steeple of the church the death of one of the members, and assist at the funeral solemnities.
Choliambic. A verse in poetry having an iambic foot in the fifth place, and a spondee in the sixth or last.
Choor, *Dan.* (koor.) ⎱ Choir, chorus; chōir of a
Chor, *Ger.* (kōr.) ⎰ church.
Choragus, *Lat.* (kō-rā-gŭs.) The leader of the ancient dramatic chorus.
Choral. Belonging to the choir; full, or for many voices.
Choral, *Ger.* (kō-răl.) Psalm or hymn tune; choral song or tune.
Choral anthem. An anthem in a simple, measured style in the manner of a choral.

CHOR

Choral book. A collection of choral melodies either with or without a prescribed harmonic accompaniment.
Choral-Buch, *Ger.* (kō-răl-hookh.) Choral book; a book of hymn tunes.
Chorále, *Ger. pl.* (kō-rā-lĕ.) Hymn tunes.
Choraleon. *Pot.* (kō-rā-lĕ-ŏn.) An instrument invented at Warsaw, of similar construction to an organ.
Choral hymn. A hymn to be sung by a chorus.
Choralist. Chorister, choir singer.
Choraliter, *Ger.* (kō-răl-ĭ-tĕr.) ⎱ In the
Choralmässig, *Ger.* (kō-răl-mās-sĭg.) ⎰ style or measure of a psalm tune or choral.
Choral service. A form of religious service in which the priest sings in response to the choir.
Chor-alter, *Ger.* (kōr-ăl-tĕr.) The high or great alter.
Chor-amt, *Ger.* (kōr-ămt.) Cathedral service, choral service.
Choraula, *Gr.* (kō-raw-lā.) The flute player who accompanied the Greek chorus.
Choraules, *Lat.* (kō-raw-lēs.) Flute players.
Chorantus, *Lat.* (kō-raw-tŭs.) The name given by the ancient Romans to the bagpipe.
Chord. The union of two or more sounds heard at the same time.
Chorda, *Lat.* (kŏr-dā.) A string of a musical instrument.
Chord, accidental. A chord produced either by anticipation or suspension.
Chordæ vocales, *Lat.* (kŏr-dē vō-kā-lēs.) Vocal chords.
Chord, anomalous. A chord in which one or more of the intervals are greater or less than of those of the fundamental chord.
Chord a vido, *It.* (kōrd ā vē-dō.) A name formerly given to a sound drawn from the open string of a violin, violincello, or similar instrument.
Chorda characteristica, *Lat.* (kŏr-dā kăr-ăk-tĕr-ĭs-tĭ-kā.) The leading, or characteristic note or tone.
Chord, characteristic. The principal chord; the leading chord.
Chord, chromatic. A chord that contains one or more chromatic signs.
Chord, common. A chord consisting of a fundamental note together with its third and fifth.
Chord, dominant. A chord that is found on the dominant of the key in which the music is written. 2. The *leading* or *characteristic* chord.
Chorda dominant septima. The dominant chord of the seventh.
Chord, equivocal. A name sometimes given to the *diminished seventh*.
Chordæ essentiales, *Lat.* (kŏr-dē ĕs-sĕn-ahl-ĭ-lēs.) These are the tonic, third and fifth of each diatonic mode or scale.
Chordaulodian. ⎱ The name given to a mu-
Chordomelodion. ⎰ sical instrument resembling a large barrel organ, self-acting. It was invented by Kaufmann of Dresden.
Chor-dienst, *Ger.* (kōr-dīnst.) Choir or choral service.
Chordometer. An instrument for measuring strings.

ā ale, ă add, ä arm, ē eve, ĕ end, ī ice, ĭ ill, ō old, ŏ odd, ô dove, oo moon, ū lute, ŭ but, ü French sound.

CHOR

Chord, fundamental. A chord consisting of the fundamental tone with its third and fifth and its inversions.
Chordienst, *Ger.* (kōr-dīnst.) Choir service.
Chord, imperfect, common. A chord founded on the leading tone. It has a *minor third* and *diminished fifth*.
Chord, inverted. A chord whose lowest tone is not the fundamental but the third, fifth, or seventh from the lowest or bass note.
Chord, leading. The *dominant* chord.
Chord nona. Chord of the *Ninth*.
Chord of the eleventh. A chord founded on the chord of the ninth by adding the interval of the eleventh.
Chord of the fifth and sixth. (⁶⁄₅) The first inversion of the chord of the seventh, formed by taking the third of the original chord for the base, and consisting of that together with its *third, fifth* and *sixth*.
Chord of the fourth and fifth. (⁵⁄₄) Chord of the *eleventh*, with the seventh and ninth omitted.
Chord of the fourth and sixth. (⁶⁄₄) The second inversion of the common chord.
Chord of the ninth. (9) A chord consisting of a third, fifth, seventh and ninth with its root.
Chord of the second and fourth. (⁴⁄₂) The third inversion of the *seventh*.
Chord of the seventh. (7) A chord consisting of the root together with the third, fifth and seventh.
Chord of the sixth. (6) The first inversion of the common chord.
Chord of the third, fourth and sixth. (⁶⁄₄⁄₃) The second inversion of the chord of the *seventh*.
Chord of the thirteenth. Founded on the chord of the ninth by adding the eleventh and the thirteenth.
Chord of the tritone. Third inversion of the *dominant seventh* containing a superfluous fourth.
Chords, derivative. Chords derived from the fundamental chords.
Chords, diminished. Chords with less than *perfect* intervals.
Chords, sensible. The dominant chord.
Chords, imperfect. Those which do not contain all the intervals belonging to them.
Chords, small threefold. A common chord with a minor third.
Chords, relative. Chords which by reason of affinity admit of an easy and natural transition from one to the other.
Chord, threefold. The common chord.
Chord, transient. A chord in which, in order to smooth the transition from one chord to another, notes are introduced which do not form any component part of the fundamental harmony.
Chöre, *Ger. pl.* (kö-rĕ). Choirs, choruses.
Chorea, *Lat.* (kō-rē-ä.) A dance in a ring; a dance.
Choree, *Gr.* (kō-rā.) In ancient poetry a foot of two syllables, the first long, the second short; the trochee.
Choreus, *Lat.* (kō-rĕ-ŭs.) The choree or trochee.

CHRO

Choriambus. A musical foot, accented thus: –◡◡–.
Chorion, *Gr.* (kō-rī-ŏn.) A hymn in praise of Cybele.
Chori, Præfectus, *Lat.* (kō-rē prē-fĕk-tŭs.) A chanter.
Chorist, *Ger.* (kō-rĭst.) } A chorister, a choral
Choriste, *Fr.* (kō-rēst.) } singer.
Chorister. A leader of a choir; a singer.
Chorknabe, *Ger.* (kōr-knä-bĕ.) Singing boy.
Chorocitharistæ, *Lat.* (kō-rō-sĭth-ä-rĭs-tē.) A concert of instruments and voices; those who play to dancing.
Chor-regent, *Ger.* (kōr-rĕ-ghĕnt.) Leader or director of the choristers.
Chor-sänger, *Ger.* (kōr-săng-ĕr.) } A chorista.
Chor-schüler, *Ger.* (kōr-shü-lĕr.) } ter, a choral singer; a member of the choir.
Chor-ton, *Ger.* (kōr-tōn.) *Choral-tone;* the usual pitch or intonation of the organ, and therefore of the choir. A choral tune.
Chorus. A company of singers; a composition intended to be sung by a number of voices. 2. Among the ancient Greeks the chorus was a band of singers and dancers who assisted at the performance of their dramas.
Chorus, cyclic. (sĕ-klĭk.) The chorus among the ancient Athenians which performed at some of their dramatic representations, dancing in a circle around the altar of Bacchus.
Choruses, martial. Choruses in commemoration of warlike deeds.
Chorus singer. One who sings in a chorus.
Chorus-tone. See *Chor-ton*.
Christe eleison, *Gr.* (krĭs-tĕ ā-lī-sŏn.) O Christ, have mercy; a part of the kyrie or first movement in a mass.
Christmas carols. Light songs, or ballads, commemorating the birth of Christ, sung during the Christmas holidays.
Christmesse. *Ger.* (krĭst-mĕs-sĕ.) } Christmas
Christmette. *Ger.* (krĭst-mĕt-tĕ.) } matins.
Chroma, *Gr.* (krō-mä.) The chromatic signs; a *sharp ♯*, or *flat ♭*.
Chroma diesis, *Gr.* (krō-mä dī-ā-sĭs.) A semitone, or half tone.
Chroma duplex. The *double-sharp,* marked by the sign ×, or ♯♯.
Chromameter. (krō-mä-mē-ter.) A tuning fork.
Chromatic. Proceeding by semitones.
Chromatic depression. The lowering a note by a semitone.
Chromatic elevation. The elevation of a note by a semitone.
Chromatic horn. The French horn.
Chromatic instruments. All instruments upon which chromatic tones and melodies can be produced.
Chromatic keyboard. An attachment applied to the ordinary keys of a piano, for the purpose of enabling players of moderate skill to execute with greater facility the simple chromatic scale, chromatic runs, cadenzas, etc.
Chromatic keys. The black keys of a pianoforte. 2. Every key in the scale of which one or more chromatic tones occur.

ă ale, ă add, ă arm, ē eve, ĕ end, ī ice, ĭ ill, ō old, ŏ odd, ô dove, oo moon, ū lute, ŭ but, ü French sound.

CHRO

Chromatic melody. A melody the tones of which move by chromatic intervals.
Chromatic scale. A scale which divides every whole tone of the diatone scale, and consists of twelve semitones or half-steps in an octave.
Chromatic signature. The flats or sharps placed after the clef at the beginning of the staff.
Chromatic signs. Accidentals; sharps, flats, and naturals.
Chromatic tuning fork. A tuning fork sounding all the tones and semitones of the octave.
Chromatici suoni, *It.* (krō-mä-tē-tehē swō-nĕ.) Sounds raised above their natural pitch a semitone.
Chromatics, accidental. Chromatics employed in preparing the leading note of the minor scale; chromatics incidentally employed.
Chromatique, *Fr.* (krō-măt-ēk.) } Chromatic,
Chromatisch, *Ger.* (krō-măt-ish.) } moving by semitones.
Chromatiquement, *Fr.* (krō-măt-ēk-mŏnh.) Chromatically.
Chromatisches klanggeschlecht, *Ger.* (krō-măt-ĭ-shēs kläng-ghĕ-shlĕkht.) The chromatic genus or mode.
Chromatische tonleiter, *Ger.* (krō-măt-ĭ-shē tōn-lī-tĕr.) The chromatic scale.
Chronometer, *Gr.* (krō-nŏm-ĕ-tĕr.) The name given to any machine for measuring time.
Chronometer, Weber. An invention of Godfrey Weber, similar to a metronome, but simpler in construction, consisting of a chord marked with fifty five inch spaces, and having a weight attached to its lower end. The degree of motion is varied by the length of the cord.
Chrotta, *It.* (krōt-tä.) The primitive fiddle, differing from the modern in the absence of a neck; the crowle.
Church cadence. Another name for the *Plagal Cadence.*
Church modes. See Gregorian modes.
Churumbela, *Spa.* (tshoo-rŭm-bā-lä.) A wind instrument resembling the hautboy.
Ciaccóna, *It.* (tshĕ-ăt-kō-nä.) } A slow Spanish
Ciaccónne, *It.* (tshĕ-ăt-kŏn-nĕ.) } ish dance generally constructed on a ground bass. See Chaconne.
Ciaramélla, *It.* (tshĕ-ăr-ă-mĕl-lä.) A bagpipe.
Cicuta, *Lat.* (sĕ-kū-tä.) A pipe or flute made from the hollow stalks of the hemlock; a shepherd's pipe.
Cicutrénna, *It.* (tshĕ-koo-trĕn-nä.) A musical pipe.
Ciguena, *Spa.* (thĕ-gwä-nä.) The crank of a bell.
Cimbale. See Cimbel.
Cimbali, *It. pl.* (tshĕm-bä-lē.) } Cymbals; military
Cimballes, *Fr. pl.* (sĭm-băl.) } tary instruments used to mark the time.
Cimbalello, *Spa.* (thĕm-bä-lä-yō.) A small bell.
Cimbalo, *Spa.* (thĕm-bä-lō.) A cymbal.
Cimbel, *Ger.* (tsĭm-bĕl.) A mixture stop of acute tone.
Cimbal-stern, *Ger.* (tsĭm-bĕl stărn.) *Cymbal star.* An organ stop consisting of five bells, and composed of circular pieces of metal cut in the

CITH

form of a star, and placed at the top of the instrument in front.
C in alt. The eleventh above the G, or treble clef note; the fourth note in alt.
C in altissimo. The octave above C in alt; the fourth note in altissimo.
Cinelle, *Tur.* } A cymbal; a Turkish musical
Cinellen, *Tur.* } instrument more noisy than musical.
Cinnara, *It.* (tshĕn-nä-rä.) The harp of the Romans.
Cink, *Ger.* (tsĭnk.) A small reed stop in an organ; see Kinkhorn.
Cinq, *Fr.* (sănhk.) } Five; the fifth voice
Cinque, *It.* (tshēn-quĕ.) } or part in a quintet.
Cinyra. (sĭn-ē-rä.) An old name for the harp.
Ciphering. (sī-fĕr-ĭng.) The sounding of the pipes of the organ when the keys are not touched.
Circular canon. A canon which goes through the twelve major keys.
Circle, half. A melodic figure consisting of four tones, the second and fourth of which are the same.
Circle of fifths. A method of modulation which conveys us round through all the scales back to the point from which we started.
Circular scale. The row of tuning pins and the wrest-plank of a piano made in a curved form.
Cis, *Ger.* (tsĭs.) The note C♯.
Cis-cis, *Ger.* (tsĭs-tsĭs.) The note C double sharp, C𝄪. C✗.
Cis dur, *Ger.* (tsĭs-door.) The key of C♯ major.
Cis moll, *Ger.* (tsĭs mŏll.) The key of C♯ minor.
Cisne, *Spa.* (thĕs-nĕ.) A good musician.
Cistella, *Lat.* (sĭs-tĕl-lä.) A small chest or box, triangular in shape aud strung with wires which are struck with little rods. See Dulcimer.
Cistre, *Fr.* (sēstr.) A cithern, a small harp.
Cistrum. See Cittern.
Citara, *It.* (tshē-tä-rä.) A cittarn, a guitar.
Citaredo, *It.* (tshē-tä-rā-dō.) } A minstrel, a
Citarista, *It.* (tshē-tä-rēs-tä.) } player upon the harp or cittarn.
Citarizar, *Spa.* (thĕt-ă-rē-thăr.) } To play
Citárizzáre, *It.* (tshē-tä-rē-tsä-rē.) } upon the cittern.
Cithar, *Dan.* (tsĭth-ăr.) A cittern.
Cithara, *Lat.* (sĭth-ä-rä.) } The lute, an old in-
Cithara, *Spa.* (thĕt-ä-rä.) } strument of the guitar kind.
Cithara bijuga, *Lat.* (sĭth-ä-rä bī-jū-gä.) A cithara, so called from its having two necks which determine the length of the strings.
Cithára hispánica, *Sp.* (thĕt-ä-rä hĭs-pän-ĭ-kä.) The Spanish guitar.
Cithara, keyed. The clavicitherium.
Citharista, *Lat.* (sĭth-ä-rĭs-tä.) A player upon the harp.
Citharizo, *Lat.* (sĭth-ä-rē-zō.) To play or strike upon the cithara.
Citharodia, *Gr.* (sĭth-ä-rō-dĭ-ä.) The art of singing to the lyre.
Citharoedus, *Lat.* (sĭth-ä-rē-dŭs.) He who plays upon a harp or cithara.
Citharoeda, *Lat.* (sĭth-ä-rē-dä.) A female singer and player upon the cithara.

48 PRONOUNCING MUSICAL DICTIONARY.

ă ale, ă add, ä arm, ĕ eve, ĕ end, ĭ ice, ĭ ill, ō old, ŏ odd, ô dove, oo moon, ū lute, ŭ but, ü French sound.

CITH

Cither. ⎫ An old instrument of the lute or
Cithera. ⎪ guitar species; the oldest on record
Cithern. ⎬ had three strings, which were after-
Cittern. ⎪ ward increased to eight, nine, and up
Cythorn. ⎭ to twenty-four. The *cither* was very
popular in the sixteenth century. The cittern and guitar seem to be derived from the same Greek word.
Citole, *Lat.* (sĭt-ō-lē.) An old instrument of the dulcimer species, and probably synonymous with it.
Cittam. The ancient English name of the guitar.
Civetteria, *It.* (tshĕ-vĕt-tă-re-ă.) Coquetry; in a coquettish manner.
Clair, *Fr.* (klăr.) Clear, shrill, loud.
Claircyliudre. (klăr-sĭ-lănhdr.) An instrument invented by Chladni, in 1787, for the purpose of experimenting in accoustics.
Clairon, *Fr.* (klă-rŏnh.) Trumpet; also, the name of a reed stop in the organ.
Clam. In bell ringing, to nuite sounds on the peal.
Clamor. In bell ringing, a rapid multiplication of strokes.
Clamor de campanas, *Spa.* (klă-mŏr dŭh kăm-pă-năs.) A solemn peal upon the bells.
Clamorear, *Spa.* (klă-mō-rĕ-ăr.) To toll the passing bell.
Clamoroso, *Spa.* (klă-mō-rō-zō.) Plaintive sounds.
Clamosus, *Lat.* (klă-mō-sŭs.) Full of clamor or noise.
Clang. A sharp, shrill noise.
Clango, *Lat.* (klăn-gō.) To clang, to sound.
Clangor, *Lat.* (klăn-gŏr.) A sound, noise; the clang of the trumpet when blown powerfully.
Clangor tubarum, *Lat.* (klăn-gŏr tū-bă-rŭm.) A military trumpet used by the ancient Romans, consisting of a large tube of bronze surrounded by seven smaller tubes, all terminating in one point, or a single mouth piece.
Clan marches. These are composed for the Scotch bagpipe, with a strong accent and marked rhythm.
Clapper. The tongue of a bell.
Claquebois, *Fr.* (klăk-bwă.) A three stringed viol.
Clar. An abbreivation of *Clarinet*.
Clara voce, *Lat.* (klă-ră vō-sĕ.) A clear, loud voice.
Clarabella, *Lat.* (klă-ră-bĕl-lă.) An organ stop of eight feet scale, with a powerful, fluty tone; the pipes are of wood and not stopped.
Claribella. The name of an organ stop tuned in unison with the diapasons.
Claribel-flute. An organ stop of the flute species.
Clarichord. See *Ctavichord*.
Clarichorde. *Fr.* (klăr-ĭ-kŏrd.) The clarichord or clavichord.
Clarim, *Por.* (klă-rĕm.) ⎫ A clarion.
Clarin, *Spa.* (klă-rēn.) ⎭
Clarin, *Ger.* (klă-rēn.) A clarion; also the name of a four feet reed stop in German organs.
Clarinblasen, *Ger.* (klăr-ĕn-blă-zĕn.) Soft notes or tones upon the trumpet.
Clarinero, *Spa.* (klă-rē-nă-rō.) A trumpeter.

CLAU

Clarinet. A rich and full toned wind instrument of wood, with a reed mouth piece.
Clarinet, alto. A large clarinet, curved near the mouth piece, and a fifth deeper than the ordinary clarinet.
Clarinet, bass. A clarinet whose tones are an octave deeper than those of the C or B flat clarinet.
Clarinette, *Fr.* (klăr-ĭ-nāt.) The clarinet; also the name of an organ stop.
Clarinettista, *It.* (klă-rē-nĕt-tĭs-tă.) ⎫ A per-
Clarinettiste, *Fr.* (klăr-ĭ-nĕt-tēst.) ⎭ former upon the clarinet.
Clarinétto, *It.* (klă-rē-nĕt-tō.) A clarinet.
Clarinétto d'amore, *It.* (klă-rē-nĕt-tō d'ä-mō-rĕ.) A species of clarinet a fifth lower than the C clarinet.
Clarinétto dolce, *It.* (klă-rē-nĕt-tō dōl-tshĕ.) A species of clarinet a fifth lower than the C clarinet.
Clarinétto secondo, *It.* (klă-rē-nĕt-tō sĕ-kŏn-dō.) The second clarinet.
Clarino, *It.* (klă-rē-nō.) ⎫ A small; or octave
Clárion. ⎭ trumpet; also the name of a 4 feet organ reed stop, tuned an octave above the trumpet stop. The term is also used to indicate the trumpet parts in a full score.
Clarion harmonique, *Fr.* (klă-rĭ-ŏuh hăr-mōnh-nēk.) An organ reed stop; see Harmonique.
Clarionet. A wind instrument of the single reed species, of a full, rich tone; also an organ reed stop of 8 feet scale and soft quality of tone; see *Clarinet*.
Clarionet-flute. An organ stop of a similar kind to the stopped diapason.
Charone, *It.* (klă-rō-nĕ.) A clarinet.
Clarus, *Lat.* (klă-rŭs.) Loud, clear, bright.
Clarté de voix, *Fr.* (klăr-tă dŭh vwă.) Clearness of voice.
Classical music. Standard music; music of first rank, written by composers of the highest order.
Classicum, *Lat.* (klăs-sĭ-kŭm.) A field or battle signal given with the trumpet.
Classicum canere, *Lat.* (klăs-sĭ-kŭm kăn-ĕ-rĕ.) To sound an alarm.
Clause. A *phrase*.
Clausel, *Ger.* (klou-z'l.) ⎫ A close, a ca-
Clausula, *Lat.* (klau-sŭ-lă.) ⎭ dence, a concluding musical phrase.
Clausula affinalis, *Lat.* (klau-sŭ-lă ăf-fī-nă-lĭs.) A cadence in a key nearly related to the original key of the piece.
Clausula dissecta, *Lat.* (klau-sŭ-lă dĭs-sĕk-tă.) A half cadence.
Clausula dominans, *Lat.* (klau-sŭ-lă dŏm-ĭ-năns.) A cadence on the dominant.
Clausula falsa, *Lat.* (klau-sŭ-lă făl-să.) A false or deceptive cadence.
Clausula finalis, *Lat.* (klau-sŭ-lă fī-nă-lĭs.)
Clausula primaria, *Lat.* (klau-sŭ-lă prī-mă-rĭ-ă.)
Clausula principalis, *Lat.* ktau-sŭ-lă prĭn-sĭ-pă-lĭs.)
A final cadence or close in the original key.
Clausula peregrina, *Lat.* (klau-sŭ-lă pĕr-ĕ-grē-nă.) A cadence in a key whose fundamental tone is not in the scale of the principal key.

ă ale, ā add, ä arm, ĕ ere, ē end, ĭ ice, ĭ ill, ō old, ŏ odd, ô dove, oo moon, ū lute, ŭ but, ü French sound.

CLAU

Clausula propria, *Lat.* (klau-sū-lä prō-prĭ-ä.) }
Clausula pura, *Lat.* (klau-sū-lä pū-rä.) }
A proper or natural close.
Clausula impropria, *Lat.* (klau-sū-lä ĭm-prō-prĭ-ä.) An uncommon, or deviating cadence.
Clausula secundaria, *Lat.* (klau-sū-lä sĕ-kŭn-dä-rĭ-ä.) A cadence on the dominant.
Clausus, *Lat.* (klaw-sŭs.) A close canon.
Clav. An abbreviation of Clavecembalo, Clavicord, and Clavecin.
Clave, *Lat.* (klā-vĕ.) A key; a clef.
Clavecin, *Fr.* (klăv-ĕ-sănh.) The harpsichord.
Clavecin acoustique, *Fr.* (klăv-ĕ-sănh ä-koo-zĭk.) An instrument of the harpsichord or pianoforte class.
Clavecin a peau de buffle, *Fr.* (klăv-ĕ-sănh ä pō düh büf-fl.) An instrument of the harpsichord or pianoforte class.
Clavecin d'amour, *Fr.* (klăv-ĕ-sănh d'ä-moor.) An instrument of the harpsichord or pianoforte class.
Clavecin harmonieux, *Fr.* (klăv-ĕ-sănh här-mō-nĭ-ŭh.) An instrument of the harpsichord or pianoforte class.
Clavecin organise, *Fr.* (klăv-ĕ-sănh ōr-găn-ēz.) An instrument of the harpsichord or pianoforte class.
Clavicymbalum, *Lat.* (klăv-ĭ-sym-bä-lŭm.) The harpsichord; spinet.
Clavicymbel, *Ger.* (klăf-ĭ-tsym-b'l.) A clavichord.
Claveciniste, *Fr.* (klä-vĕ-sănh-ēst.) A harpsichord player, or maker.
Claveoline, *Fr.* (klăv-ĭ-ō-lēn.) An instrument of the harpsichord or pianoforte class.
Claves, *Lat.* (klā-vēs.) A word formerly used for clefs.
Claves intellectæ, *Lat.* (klā-vēa ĕn-tĕl-lĕk-tē.) A term applied to those notes whose pitch could be known without being marked.
Claves non signatæ, *Lat.* (klā-vēa nŏn sĭg-nā-tē.) Notes without signature.
Claves signatæ, *Lat.* A term applied by Guido to colored lines used before the invention of clefs, to mark the situation of the notes.
Clavessin, *Fr.* klăv-ĕs-sănh.) The harpsichord. (See Clavecin.)
Claviary. An index of keys or a scale of lines and spaces.
Claviatus. An harmonica furnished with a set of keys.
Claviatur, *Ger.* (klä-vē-ä-toor.) The keys of a harpsichord, piano, etc.
Clavicémbalo, *It.* (klä-vē-tshäm-bä-lō.) }
Clavicembalum, *Lat.* (klä-vĭ-sĕm-bä-lŭm.) }
The harpsichord.
Clavichord. A small, keyed instrument, like the spinet, and the forerunner of the pianoforte. The tone of the clavichord was agreeable and impressive but not strong.
Clavichordium, *Lat.* (klăv-ĭ-kŏr-dĭ-ŭm.) See *Clavichord.*
Clavicytherium, *Lat.* (klăvĭ-sē-thē-rĭ-ŭm.) A species of upright harpsichord, said to have been originally in the form of a harp or lyre. It was invented in the thirteenth century and was the earliest approach to the modern pianoforte.

CLEF

Clavicordio, *Spa.* (klăv-ē-kŏr-dĭ-ō.) A harpsichord.
Clavicylinder. An instrument exhibited in Paris in 1806. It was supposed to consist of a series of cylinders which were operated upon by bows set in motion by a crank and brought in contact with the cylinders by means of the keys of a finger-board.
Clavier, *Fr.* (klăv-ēr.) } The keys or key-board
Clavier, *Ger.* (klă-fēr.) } of a pianoforte, organ, etc. Also, an old name for the *clavichord.*
Clavier-auszug, *Ger.* (klă-fēr ous-tsoog.) An arrangement of a full score for the use of piano players.
Clavier-drath, *Ger.* (klă-fēr drät.) Wire for the pianoforte, etc.
Clavier-lehrer, *Ger.* (klă-fēr lā-rēr.) A pianoforte teacher.
Clavieren, *Ger. pl.* (klăf-ă-rĕn.) The keys: see *clavier.*
Clavierschule, *Ger.* (klăf-ēr-shoo-lĕ.) A pianoforte instruction book.
Clavierspieler, *Ger.* (klăf-ēr-spē-lēr.) A pianoforte player.
Clavierstimmer, *Ger.* (klăf-ēr-stĭm-mēr.) A pianoforte tuner.
Clavierübung, *Ger.* (klăf-ēr-ü-boong.) Exercises for the clavichord.
Clavierunterricht, *Ger.* (klăf-ēr-oon-tēr-rĭkht.) Lessons or instruction on the pianoforte.
Clavigero, *Spa.* (klä-vē-hä-rō.) Bridge of a harpsichord.
Clavija, *Spa.* (klăv-ē-hä.) Peg of a stringed instrument.
Claviorgano, *Spa.* (klăv-ē-ōr-gä-nō.) A harpsichord having strings and pipes.
Clavis, *Lat.* (klā-vĭs.) } A key; a clef.
Clavis, *Ger.* (klă-fĭs.) }
Clear-flute. An organ stop of 4 feet scale, the tone of which is very clear and full.
Clé, *Fr.* (klā.) } A key; a character used to determine the name and pitch of the notes on the staff to which it is prefixed.
Clef, *Fr.* (klā.) }
Clef, alto. The C clef on the third line of the staff.
Clef, baritone. The F clef when placed on the third line.
Clef, bass. The character at the beginning of the staff, where the lower or bass notes are written, and serving to indicate the pitch and name of those notes. The F clef.
Clef, C. So called because it gives its name to the notes placed on the same line with itself.
Clef, counter tenor. The C clef when placed on the third line in order to accommodate the counter tenor voice.
Clef d'accordeur, *Fr.* (klā d'ăk-kōr-dūr.) A tuning hammer.
Clef de fay, *Fr.* (klā düh fā.) The F, or base clef.
Clef descant. The treble or soprano clef.
Clef d'ut, *Fr.* (klā d'oot.) The C clef.
Clef, F. The base clef.
Clef, French treble. The G clef on the bottom line of the staff; formerly much used in French music for the violin, flute, etc.

4

ă ale, ă add, ä arm, ĕ eve, ĕ end, ī ice, ĭ ill, ō old, ŏ odd, ô dove, oo moon, ū lute, ŭ but, ü French sound.

CLEF

Clef, German soprano. The C clef placed on the first line of the staff for soprano.

Clef, mean. The tenor clef 𝄢 or 𝄡

Clef, mezzo soprano. The C clef when placed on the second line of the staff.

Clef note. The note indicated by the clef.

Clef note, bass. The note which is on the same line with the bass clef.

Clef note, treble. The note which is on the same line with the treble clef.

Clef sol, *Fr.* (klä sŏl.) The G, or treble clef.

Clef, soprano. The C clef placed on the first line.

Clef, tenor. See *Mean clef.* The C clef when on the fourth line of the staff.

Clef, treble. The G clef; soprano clef.

Cerizon, *Spa.* (thĕr-ē-thŏn.) A chorister, a singing boy in a cathedral.

Clinis, *Gr.* (klī-nĭs.) A name given by the Greek musicians of the middle ages to one of their notes.

Cloche, *Fr.* (klŏsh.) A bell.

Cloche de l'elevation, *Fr.* (klŏsh dŭh l'ĕl-ĕ-vā-sĭ-ŏnh.) Saint's bell, rung at *elevation* in mass.

Cloche funebre, *Fr.* (klŏsh fü-nābr.) Death bell.

Cloche mortuaire, *Fr.* (klŏsh mŏr-tŭ-ār.) The passing, funeral bell.

Clocher, *Fr.* (klō-shā.) A belfry.

Cloche sourde, *Fr.* (klŏsh soord.) A muffled bell.

Clocheton, *Fr.* (klŏsh-tōnh.) A bell turret.

Clochette, *Fr.* (klō-shĕt.) A little bell, a hand bell.

Clocks, musical. Clocks containing an arrangement similar to a barrel organ, moved by weights and springs and producing various tunes.

Clorone. A species of clarinet which is a fifth lower than the clarinet.

Close. A cadence; the end of a piece or passage.

Close harmony. Harmony in which the notes or parts are kept as close together as possible.

C major. The diatonic scale or key of C without flats or sharps.

C minor. The diatonic scale or key of C with the third and sixth flatted.

C moll, *Ger.* (tsā mŏll.) The key of C minor.

C natural. C without flat or sharp.

C. O. An abbreviation of *choir organ.*

Co, *It.* (kō.)
Col, *It.* (kō-ĕ.) } With, with the.
Coll, *It.* (kŏl.)

Coalottino, *It.* (kō-ä-lŏt-tē-nō.) See *Concertino.*

Cocchiáta, *It.* (kŏt-kē-ä-tä.) A serenade in a coach.

Cocchina, *It.* (kŏt-kē-nä.) An Italian country dance.

Códa, *It.* (kō-dä.) The *end;* a few bars added to the end of a piece of music to make a more effective termination.

Códa brillante, *It.* (kō-dä brēl-län-tĕ.) A brilliant termination.

COLL

Codétta, *It.* (kō-dĕt-tä.) A short coda or passage added to a piece, or serving to connect one movement with another.

Codon. A bell.

Coffre, *Fr.* (kŏfr.) The frame of a lute, guitar, etc.

Cogli, *It.* (kŏl-yē.) With the.

Cogli stromenti, *It. pl.* (kŏl-yē strō-mān-tē.) With the instruments.

Cognoscente, *It.* (kōn-yō-shān-tē.) One well versed in music; a *connoisseur.*

Coi bassi, *It.* (kō-ē bäe-sē.) With the basses.

Coi fagotti, *It.* (kō-ē fä-gŏt-tē.) With the bassoons.

Cor violini, *It.* (kōr vē-ō-lē-nē.) With the violins.

Cola, *Spa.* (kō-lä.) Coda.

Colachon, *Fr.* (kō-lä-shŏnh.) An Italian instrument, much like a lute, but with a longer neck.

Col árco, *It.* (kŏl-är-kō.) *With the bow;* see *Coll' árco.*

Colasciónè, *It.* (kō-lä-shē-ō-nē.) An instrument like the guitar, with two strings only.

Col basso, *It.* (kŏl bäs-sō.) With the bass.

Col C. An abbreviation of *Col Canto.*

Col Cánto, *It.* (kŏl kän-tō.) With the melody or voice; see *Colla Vóce.*

Coliseo, *Spa.* (kō-lēs-kō.) An opera house, a stage upon which operas or dramatic performances are given.

Coll, *It.* (kŏl.)
Colla, *It.* (kŏl-lä.) } With the.
Collo, *It.* (kŏl-lō.)

Colla déstra, *It.* (kŏl-lä dās-trä.) With the right hand.

Colla massima discrezione, *It.* (kŏl-lä mäs-sē-mä dēz-krā-tsē-ō-nē.) With the greatest discretion.

Colla párte, *It.* (kŏl-lä pär-tē.) *With the part;* indicating that the time is to be accommodated to the solo singer or player.

Colla piu gran fórza e prestézza, *It.* (kŏl-lä pē-oo grän fōr-zä ā prĕs-tāt-zä.) As loud and as quickly as possible.

Colla púnta d'arco, *It.* (kŏl-lä poon-tä d'är-kō.) With the point or tip of the bow.

Colla sinistra, *It.* (kŏl-lä sē-nēs-trä.) With the left hand.

Colla vóce, *It.* (kŏl-lä vō-tshē.) *With the voice;* implying that the accompanist must accommodate and take the time from the singer.

Coll' árco, *It.* (kŏl-l' är-kō.) *With the bow;* the notes are to be played with the bow, and not *pizzicáto.*

College songs. Songs for the use, and sung by, college students, usually of a convivial and spirited character.

College youths. A name given to a society of London bell-ringers, formerly of high repute.

Collegiáta, *It.* (kŏl-lā-jē-ä-tä.) A collegiate church.

Collegiat-kirche, *Ger.* (kŏl-lā-ghē-ät-kēr-shē.) A collegiate church.

Col legno, *It.* (kŏl lān-yō.) *With the bow stick.*

Col légno dell' arco, *It.* (kŏl län-yō dĕl-l'är-kō.) With the bow stick; strike the strings with the wooden side of the bow.

ă *ale*, ă *add*, ă *arm*, ĕ *eve*, ĕ *end*, ī *ice*, ĭ *ill*, ō *old*, ŏ *odd*, ȯ *dove*, oo *moon*, ū *lute*, ŭ *but*, ü *French sound*.

COLL

Colle parti, *It.* (kŏl-lĕ pär-tē.) With the principal parts.
Colle trombe, *It.* kŏl-lĕ trōm-bĕ.) With the trumpets.
Collinet. Flageolet.
Coll' ottava, *It.* (kŏl-l' ōt-tä-vä.) With the octave.
Colofane, *Fr.* (kŏl-ŏ-fāne.)
Colofónia, *It.* (kŏl-ŏ-fō-nē-ä.)
Colophane, *Fr.* (kŏl-ŏ-fāne.)
Colophon, *Fr.* (kŏl-ŏ-fōnh.)
Colophonium. *Ger.* (kŏl-ŏ-fō-nĭ-oom.)
Colophony, *Eng.*
Resin; used for the hair in the bow of a violin, etc., to enable the performer to get a better hold upon the strings.
Coloratúra, *It.* (kō-lō-rä-*too*-rä.)   Orna-
Colorature, *It.* (kō-lō-rä-*too*-rĕ.) } mental
Coloraturen, *Ger.* (kō-lō-rä-*too*-rĕn.) } passages, roulades, embellishments, etc., in vocal music.
Coma, *Spa.* (kŏ-mä.) A comma.
Combination pedals. See *Composition pedals*.
Come, *It.* (*kŏ*-mē.) As, like, the same as.
Comédie, *Fr.* (kŏm-ä-dē.) Comedy, play.
Comédien, *Fr.* (kŏm-ä-dĭ-*änh*.)   } A com-
Comediante, *Spa.* (kō-mä-dē-*än*-tē.) } edian, an actor.
Comédienne, *Fr.* (kŏm-ä-dĭ-*änh*.) An actress.
Comedy, lyric. A comedy specially adapted for singing.
Cóme il primo témpo, *It.* (kō-mĕ ēl prē-mō tĕm-pō.) In the same time as the first.
Cóme prima, *It.* (kō-mĕ prē-mä.) As before, as at first.
Comes, *Lat.* (kō-mĕs.) A *companion;* this term was used by old theorists to indicate the *answer*, in a fugue.
Cóme sópra, *It.* (kō-mĕ sō-prä.) *As above; as before;* indicating the repetition of a previous or similar passage.
Cóme sta, *It.* (kō-mĕ stä.) *As it stands;* perform exactly as written.
Cóme témpo del téma. *It.* (kō-mĕ tĕm-pō dĕl tä-mä.) In the same time as the theme.
Cómico, *It.* (kō-mē-kō.)   { Comic; also, a comic
Comique, *Fr.* (kŏm-ēk.) { actor, and a writer of comedies.
Comic opera. Burlesque opera; an opera interspersed with light songs, dances and jests.
Comic song. A song set to comical, humorous words.
Comiquement, *Fr.* (kŏm-ēk-mänh.) Comically, jocosely.
Cominciánte, *It.* (kō-mēn-tshē-*än*-tē.) A beginner in music, etc.
Cominciáre, *It.* (kō-mēn-tshē-*ä*-rĕ.) To begin.
Cominciáta, *It.* (kō-mēn-tshē-*ä*-tä.) The beginning, the commencement.
Cómma, *It.* (kŏm-mä.) The smallest of all the sensible intervals of tone, and used in treating or analyzing musical sounds. As an illustration, the difference between D♯ and E♭ as played upon the violin by the best performers. A *tone* is divided into *nine* almost imperceptible intervals, called *commas*, five of which constitute the major semitone, and four the minor semitone.

COMP

Commédia, *It.* (kŏm-*mä*-dē-ä.) A play, a comedy; also, a theatre.
Commediánte, *It.* (kŏm-*mä*-dē-*än*-tē.) A comedian.
Comme il-faut, *Fr.* (kŏm ēl fō.) As it should be.
Commençant. *Fr.* (kŏm-mänh-sänh.) A beginner in music, etc.
Commencer, *Fr.* (kŏm-mänh-sā.) To begin, to commence.
Commodamente, *It.* (kŏm-mō-dä-*män*-tĕ) With ease and quietude.
Commodo, *It.* (kŏm-mō-dō.) Quietly, composedly.
Common chord. A chord consisting of a bass note with its third and fifth, to which its octave is usually added.
Common chord, imperfect. A chord consisting of a bass, accompanied by its minor third and imperfect fifth.
Common hallelujah metre. A stanza of six lines of iambic measure, the syllables of each being in number and order as follows: 8, 6, 8, 6, 8, 8.
Common measure. That measure which has an even number of parts in a bar.
Common metre. A verse or stanza of four lines in iambic measure, the syllables of each being in number and order, thus, 8, 6, 8, 6.
Common particular measure. A stanza of six lines in iambic measure, the number and order of syllables as follows: 8, 8, 6, 8, 8, 6.
Common time. That time which has an even number of parts in a bar; *common measure*.
Common time, compound. Sextuple time.
Common time, half. A measure containing only two crotchets or their equivalents.
Common time, simple. There are two species, the first containing one semibreve in each bar, and the second a minim.
Common turn. A turn consisting of the *principal* note, the note *above* it and the note *below* it.
Commune, *Lat.* (kŏm-*mū*-nĕ.) One of the modes of the ancients.
Comodaménte, *It.* (kō-mō-dä-*män*-tē.) } Con-
Cómodo, *It.* (kō-mō-dō.)   } veniently, easily, quietly, with composure.
Compania, *Spa.* (kŏm pä-nī-ä.) A company of players.
Comparses, *Fr.* (kŏnh-pär-sä.) Supernumeraries; persons who appear upon the stage to swell the numbers without taking active part.
Compas, *Spa.* (kŏm-*päs*.) Capability of voice, time.
Compasillo, *Spa.* (kŏm-pä-sēl-yō.) Quick time, in music.
Compass. The range of notes or sounds of which any voice or instrument is capable.
Compasso, *Por.* (cŏm-*päs*-sō.) A beating of time.
Compensating piano. An English piano with heavy strings by means of which full power is obtained from a small or cottage piano.
Compensation mixture. An organ mixture stop, in the pedals, and intended to assist the intonation of the pedal pipes.

ā ale, ă add, ä arm, ē eve, ĕ end, ī ice, ĭ ill, ō old, ŏ odd, ô dove, oo moon, ū lute, ŭ but, ü French sound.

COMP

Compiacévole, *It.* (kŏm-pē-ä-tshä-vō-lĕ.) }
Compiacimento, *It.* (kŏm-pē-ä-tshē-män-tō.) }
Agreeable, pleasing, attractive.
Complacevolmente, *It.* (kŏm-pē-ä-tshĕ-vŏl-män-tĕ.) In a pleasant and agreeable style.
Compléta, *It.* (kŏm-pē-ā-tä.) Complin; evening prayers.
Complainte, *Fr.* (kŏm-plänht.) A religious ballad.
Complement. That quantity which is wanting to any interval to fill up an octave.
Complementary part. That part which is added to the subject and counter-subject of a fugue.
Compiésso, *It.* (kŏm-plās-sō.) A term applied to a chord which is complete.
Complete cadence. A full cadence.
Complin, *Lat.* (kŏm-plĭn.) Evening service during Lent in the Catholic church.
Componaster, *Ger.* (kŏm-pō-näs-tĕr.) A bad composer.
Compónere, *It.* (kŏm-pō-nā-rĕ.) }
Componiren, *Ger.* (kŏm-pō-nē-r'n.) } To compose music.
Compórre, *It.* (kŏm-pŏr-rĕ.) } sic.
Componedor, *Spa.* (kŏm-pō-nā-dŏr.) A composer, an author.
Componitóre, *It.* (kŏm-pō-nē-tō-rĕ.) }
Componista, *It.* (kŏm-pō-nĕs-tä.) }
Componitríce, *It.* (kŏm-pō-nē-trē-tshĕ.) A female composer.
Comparre per l'organo, *It.* (kŏm-pär-rĕ pĕr l'ŏr-gä-nō.) To set to the organ.
Composer, *Fr.* (kŏnh-pō-zā.) To compose music.
Composer. One who composes, one who writes an original work.
Composicion, *Spa.* (kŏm-pō-sē-thē-ŏn.) Musical composition.
Composite intervals. Those intervals which consist of two or more semitones.
Compositeur, *Fr.* (kŏm-pōs-ĭ-tŭr.) } A composer of music.
Compositóre, *It.* (kŏm-pōs-ē-tō-rĕ.) }
Componist, *Ger.* (kŏm-pō-nĭst.) }
Compositeur de fugues, *Fr.* (kŏm-pōs-ĭ-tŭr dŭh fŭg.) A composer of fugues.
Composition. Any musical production; the art of inventing or composing music, according to the rules of harmony.
Composition, free. That which deviates somewhat from the rules of composition.
Composition, erotic. That which has *love* for its subject.
Composition, strict. A composition that adheres rigidly to the rules of art.
Composition pedals. Pedals connected with a system of mechanism for arranging the stops of an organ. Invented by J. C. Bishop.
Compositor, music. A person who sets music type.
Compositúra, *It.* (kŏm-pōs-ē-too-rä.) } A composition, or musical work.
Composizióne, *It.* (kŏm-pōs-ē-tsē-ō-nĕ.) }
Composizióne di tavolíno, *It.* (kŏm-pōs-ē-tsē-ō-nĕ dē täv-ō-lē-nō.) Table music, music sung at table, as glees, catches, rounds.
Compósso, *It.* (kŏm-pōs-sō.) } Composed, set to music.
Compósto, *It.* (kŏm-pōs-tō.) }
Compostura, *Spa.* (kŏm-pōs-too-rä.) Musical composition.

CONC

Compound appoggiatura. An appoggiatura consisting of two or more small notes.
Compound harmony. Simple harmony with an octave added.
Compound harpsichord. An instrument invented in 1774, having hammers like a pianoforte.
Compound intervals. Those which exceed the extent of an octave; as a ninth, tenth, etc.
Compound stops. Where three or more organ stops are arranged so that by pressing down one key, they all sound at once.
Compound times. Those which include, or exceed *six* parts in a measure, and contain *two*, or more, principal accents, as, 6-4, 6-8, 9-4, 9-8, 12-8, etc.
Compressed harmony. See *Close Harmony*.
Compntatrices, *Lat.* (kŏm-pŭ-tā-trĭ-sĕs.) Women whom the ancients employed to sing and weep over the dead at funerals.
Con, *It.* (kŏn.) With.
Con abbandóno, *It.* (kŏn ä-bän-dō-nō.) With passion, with ardent feeling.
Con abbandóno ed espressióne, *It.* (kŏn ä-bän-dō-nō ĕd ĕs-präs-sē-ō-nĕ.) With passionate feeling and self-abandon.
Con affétto, *It.* (kŏn äf-fāt-tō.) } In an affecting manner, with warmth.
Con affezióne, *It.* (kŏn äf-fā-tsē-ō-nĕ.) }
Con afflizióne, *It.* (kŏn äf-flē-tsē-ō-nĕ.) With affliction, mournfully.
Con agilità, *It.* (kŏn ä-jēl-ē-tä.) With agility, neatly.
Con agitazióne, *It.* (kŏn äj-ē-tä-tsē-ō-nĕ.) With agitation, hurriedly.
Con alcúna licénza, *It.* (kŏn äl-koo-nä lē-tshän-tsä.) With a certain degree of license as regards time and expression.
Con allégrezza, *It.* (kŏn äl-lē-grät-sä.) With lightness, cheerfully.
Con alterézza, *It.* (kŏn äl-tĕ-rät-sä.) With an elevated and sublime expression.
Con amabilità, *It.* (kŏn ä-mä-bēl-ē-tä.) With gentleness and grace.
Con amarézza, *It.* (kŏn ä-mä-rät-sä.) With affliction, with a sense of grief.
Con amóre, *It.* (kŏn ä-mō-rĕ.) With tenderness and affection.
Con anima, *It.* (kŏn än-ē-mä.) } With animation and boldness.
Con animo, *It.* (kŏn än-ē-mō.) }
Con animazióne, *It.* (kŏn än-ē-mä-tsē-ō-nĕ.) With animation, decision, boldness.
Con audáce, *It.* (kŏn on-dä-tshĕ.) With boldness, audacity.
Con bellézza, *It.* (kŏn bĕl-lāt-zä.) With beauty of tone and expression.
Con bizarria, *It.* (kŏn bē-tsär-rē-ä.) Capriciously, at the fancy of the player or composer.
Con bravura, *It.* (kŏn brä-voo-rä.) With bravery, with boldness.
Con brío, *It.* (kŏn brē-ō.) With life, spirit, brilliancy.
Con brío ed animáto, *It.* (kŏn brē-ō ĕd än-ē-mä-tō.) With brilliancy and animation.
Con cálma, *It.* (kŏn käl-mä.) With calmness and tranquility.

ā *ale*, ă *add*, ä *arm*, ē *eve*, ĕ *end*, ī *ice*, ĭ *ill*, ō *old*, ŏ *odd*, ō *dove*, oo *moon*, ū *lute*, ŭ *but*, ü *French sound*.

CONC

Con calóre, *It.* (kŏn kä-lō-rĕ. With warmth, with fire.
Con carita, *It.* (kŏn kä-rē-tä.) With tenderness.
Con celerita, *It.* (kŏn tshā-lĕr-ē-tä.) With celerity, with rapidity.
Concatenazióne armónica, *It.* (kŏn-kät-ē-nä-tsē-ō-nĕ· är-mō-nē-kä.) Harmony in which some of the parts are changed or moving, while others are held on or sustained.
Concent. Concord of sounds, harmony.
Concentio, *Lat.* (kŏn-sĕn-shĭ-o.) ⎱ Concord,
Concénto, *It.* (kŏn-*tshăn*-to.) ⎰ agreement, harmony of voices and instruments.
Concentrāre, *It.* (kŏn-tshĕn-trä-rĕ.) To concentrate the sounds. It also means to veil the sounds in mystery.
Concentual. Harmonious.
Concentus, *Lat.* (kŏn-sĕn-tŭs.) Harmonious blending of sounds; concord.
Concert. A performance in public of practical musicians, either vocal or instrumental, or both. 2. Harmony, unison.
Concert, amateur. A concert of non-professional musicians.
Concertando, *It.* (kŏn-tshĕr-*tăn*-dō.) A concertante.
Concertant, *Fr.* (kŏnh-sĕr-*tänh*.) Performer in a concert, a musician.
Concertánte, *It.* (kŏn-tshĕr-*tän*-tĕ.) A piece in which each part is alternately principal and subordinate, as in a *dúo concertánte*. 2. A concerto for two or more instruments, with accompaniments for a full band. 3. A female concert singer.
Concertáto, *It.* (kŏn-tshĕr-tä-tō.) In an irregular and extemporaneous manner; see also *Concertánte.*
Concertata, messa, *It.* (kŏn-tshĕr-tä-tä mĕs-sä.) A concerted mass.
Concertate, madrigali, *It.* (kŏn-tshĕr-tä-tĕ mäd-rē-gä-lē.) Accompanied madrigals.
Concerted music. Music in which several voices or instruments are heard at the same time; in opposition to *sólo* music.
Concerter, *Fr.* (kŏn-sĕr-tä.) To give a concert, to practice for a concert.
Concert-geber, *Ger.* (kŏn-*tsĕrt*-gä-bĕr.) One who gives a concert.
Concert-grand pianoforte. The largest grand pianoforte.
Concertina, *It.* (kŏn-tshĕr-tē-nä.) A small instrument, hexagonal in shape, held in the hands. The sounds are produced by pressing the fingers upon the keys, which are placed upon each side of the instrument, and working the bellows at the same time, to produce the requisite supply of wind.
Concertina, alto. A concertina having the compass of the viola.
Concertina, bass. A concertina having the compass of the violincello.
Concertina, soprano. A concertina having the compass of the violin.
Concertíno, *It.* (kŏn-tshĕr-tē-nō. A short concerto. 2. A principal part in a concerto, or other full orchestral piece. 3. The principal instrument in a concert.

CONC

Concertiren, *Ger.* (kŏn-tsĕr-tē-r'n.) To accord, to agree in sound; also, a soli movement where each instrument or voice has in its turn the principal part.
Concertizing. Giving concerts.
Concert-meister, *Ger.* (kŏn-*tsĕrt* mīs-tĕr.) Master or conductor of a concert.
Concérto, *It.* (kŏn-tshĕr-tō.) A composition for a solo instrument with orchestral accompaniments. 2. A concert; harmony.
Concérto a solo. A concerto written for the purpose of displaying the powers of a particular instrument, without accompaniment.
Concérto di chiesa, *It.* (kŏn-tshĕr-tō dē kē-ĕ-zä.) A concert of church music.
Concérto doppio, *It.* (kŏn-tshĕr-tō dŏp-pē-ō.) A concerto for two or more instruments.
Concérto grande, *Fr.* (kŏn-tshĕr-tō gränd.) ⎱
Concérto grosso, *It.* (kŏn-tshĕr-tō grōs-sō.) ⎰ A grand orchestral composition for many instruments; a grand concert.
Concérto spirituále, *It.* (kŏn-tshĕr-tō spē-rē-too-ä-lĕ.) A miscellaneous concert consisting chiefly of sacred or classical music.
Concertone, *It.* (kŏn-tshĕr-tō-nĕ.) A concertánte.
Concert, operatic. A performance of music selected from operas.
Concert-saal, *Ger.* (kŏn-*tsĕrt* säl.) Concert hall.
Concert-spieler, *Ger.* (kŏn-*tsĕrt* spē-lĕr.) A solo player, concerto player.
Concert spirituel, *Fr.* (kŏn-*tsĕrt* spē-rē-too-ĕl.) See *Concérto Spirituále.*
Concert-stück, *Ger.* (kŏn-*tsĕrt* stük.) A concert-piece; a concerto.
Concert pitch. The pitch adopted by general consent for some one given note, and by which every other note is governed.
Concha, *Lat.* (kŏn-kä.) The Triton's trumpet.
Conches. A species of trumpet used among the Himalayan mountains.
Conocinidad, *Spa.* (kŏn-ō-thē-nē-däd.) Harmony, just proportion of sound.
Concinnity. Fitness, suitableness, neatness: (little used.)
Concinnus, *Lat.* (kŏn-sĭn-nŭs.) Harmonizing, coinciding in effect.
Concino, *Lat.* (kŏn-sē-nō.) To sing or play harmoniously.
Concitáto, *It.* (kŏn-tshē-tä-tō.) Agitated, perturbed.
Concomitant sounds. *Accessory sounds.*
Con civetteria, *It.* (kŏn tshē-vĕt-tä-rē-ä.) With coquetry, in a coquettish manner.
Conclusione, *It.* (kŏn-kloo-zē-ō-nĕ.) The conclusion, or winding up.
Con cómodo, *It.* (kŏn kō-mō-dō.) With ease, in convenient time.
Concord. A harmonious combination of sounds; the opposite to a *discord.*
Concordabilis, *Lat.* (kŏn-kŏr-dä-bĕ-lĭs.) Easily according, harmonizing.
Concordáncia, *Spa.* (kŏn-kŏr-dän-thē-ä.) Concord, harmony.
Concordant. Agreeing, correspondent, harmonious.

ă ale, ă add, ă arm, ē eve, ĕ end, ī ice, ĭ ill, ō old, ŏ odd, ō dove, oo moon, ū lute, ŭ but, ū French sound.

CONC

Concordante, *It.* (kŏn-kŏr-dăn-tĕ.) Concordant.
Concordanten, *Ger.* (kŏn-kŏr-dăn-t'n.) Those sounds which, in combination, produce a concord.
Concordanza, *It.* (kŏn-kŏr-dăn-tsă.) } Concord.
Concorde, *Fr.* (kŏn-kŏrd.) } harmony.
Concórdia, *It.* (kŏn-kŏr-dē-ă.) }
Concord, consonant. The perfect concord and its derivatives.
Concord, imperfect. A term sometimes applied to the third and eighth concords.
Concords, dissonant. An inconsistent expression at times applied to discordant combinations.
Concord, simple. That in which only *two* notes in consonance are heard.
Concords, perfect. The perfect fourth, fifth, and eighth.
Con delicatézza, *It.* (kŏn dĕl-ĕ-kă-tăt-să.) With delicacy and sweetness.
Con desidério, *It.* (kŏn dă-zĕ-dă-rē-ō.) With desire and ardent longing.
Con devozióne, *It.* (kŏn dă-vō-tsē-ō-nĕ,) With devotion, devoutly.
Con diligenza, *It.* (kŏn dē-lĕ-jĕn-tsă.) With care and diligence.
Con discrezióne, *It.* (kŏn dĕs-krā-tsē-ō-nĕ.) With discretion; at the discretion of the performer.
Con disperazióne, *It.* (kŏn dĕs-pĕ-rā-tsē-ō-nĕ.) With despair, violence of expression.
Con divozióne, *It.* (kŏn dē-vō-tsē-ō-nĕ.) With religious feeling; in a devotional manner.
Con dólce maniéra, *It.* (kŏn dŏl-tshĕ mă-nē-ā-rā.)
Con dolcézza, *It.* (kŏn dŏl-tsăht-să.) }
In a simple, delicate manner; with softness, sweetness, delicacy.
Con dolóre, *It.* (kŏn-dō-lō-rĕ.) Mournfully, with grief and pathos.
Conducidor, *Spa.* (kŏn-doo-thĕ-dōr.) A conductor.
Conduciménto, *It.* (kŏn-doo-tshĕ-măn-tō.) A melody consisting of a regular succession of conjoined degrees.
Conduciménto circoncorrente, *It.* (kŏn-doo-tshĕ-măn-tō tshĕr-kŏn-kŏr-răn-tĕ.) A species of modulation of the ancient Greeks, in which the sounds rise by sharps and fall by flats.
Conduciménto recto, *It.* (kŏn-doo-tshĕ-măn-tō rĕk-tō.) Another species of modulation where the sounds move from grave to acute.
Conduciménto ritornante, *It.* (kŏn-doo-tshĕ-măn-tō rē-tŏr-năn-tĕ.) Still another species of modulation where the sounds move from acute to grave.
Conductor. The master or chief of an orchestra, who directs the time and performance of every piece with his *baton*.
Conductus, *Lat.* (kŏn-dŭk-tŭs.) A very old species of descant which, instead of being founded upon some popular melody, was entirely original, both descant and harmony, and entirely independent of everything but the imagination of the composer.
Con duólo, *It.* (kŏn doo-ō-lō.) Mournfully, with grief.
Conduttóre, *It.* (kŏn-doot-tō-rĕ.) A conductor.

CONG

Con elegánza, *It.* (kŏn ā-lĕ-găn-tsă.) With elegance.
Con elevatezza, *It.* (kŏn ā-lĕ-vă-tăt-să.) }
Con elevazióne, *It.* (kŏn ā-lĕ-vă-tsē-ō-nĕ.) }
With elevation of style; with dignity.
Con energía, *It.* (kŏn ā-nĕr-jē-ă.) } With energy and emphasis.
Con enérgico, *It.* (kŏn ā-nĕr-jē-kō.) }
Con entusiásmo, *It.* (kŏn ĕn-too-zē-ăs-mō.) With enthusiasm.
Con equalianza, *It.* (kŏn ā-quăl-lē-ăn-tsă.) With smoothness and equality.
Con e senza stromenti, *It.* (kŏn ā sĕn-tsă strō-mĕn-tĕ.) With and without instruments.
Con e senza violini, *It.* (kŏn ā sĕn-tsă vē-ō-lē-nē.) With and without violins.
Con esp. An abbreviation of *Con Espressione.*
Con espres. }
Con espressióne, *It.* (kŏn ās-prĕs-sē-ō-nĕ.) With expression.
Con facilitá, *It.* (kŏn fă-tshē-lē-tă.) With facility and ease.
Con espressióne dolorósa, *It.* (kŏn ās-prĕs-sē-ō-nĕ dō-lō-rō-ză.) With a sad expression.
Con éstro poético, *It.* (kŏn ās-trō pō-ā-tē-kō.) With poetic fervor.
Con fermézza, *It.* (kŏn fĕr-măt-să.) With firmness.
Con festivitá, *It.* (kŏn fĕs-tē-vē-tă.) With festive gaiety.
Con fidúcia, *It.* (kŏn fē-doo-tshē-ă.) With hope, with confidence.
Con fierézza, *It.* (kŏn fē-ĕ-răt-să.) With fire, fiercely.
Con fiochézza, *It.* (kŏn fē-ō-kăt-să.) With hoarseness, hoarsely, as occasionally in *Lŭffo* parts.
Conflation. The act of blowing two or more instruments together.
Con flessibilitá, *It.* (kŏn flĕs-sē-bē-lē-tă.) With freedom, flexible.
Confogotto obligato, *It.* (kŏn fō-gŏt-tō ōh-lē-gă-tō.) Must be played with a bassoon.
Con forza, *It.* (kŏn fŏr-tsă.) With force; with vehemence.
Con freddezza, *It.* (kŏn frĕd-dăt-tsă.) With coldness and apathy.
Confrérie de St. Julien, *Fr.* (kŏn-frā-rē dūh sŏnh jū-lē-ănh.) An ancient French association or club of ballad singers and itinerant fiddlers.
Con frétta, *It.* (kŏn frăt-tă.) Hurriedly, with an increase of time.
Con fuóco, *It.* (kŏn foo-ō-kō.) With fire and passion.
Con fúria, *It.* (kŏn foo-rē-ă.) } With fury, rage, vehemence.
Con furóre, *It.* (kŏn foo-rō-rĕ.) }
Con gárbo, *It.* (kŏn găr-bō.) With simplicity and elegance.
Con gentilézza, *It.* (kŏn jĕn-tē-lăt-tsă.) With grace and elegance.
Con giustezza, *It.* (kŏn djoos-tăt-tsă.) With justness and precision.
Con giustézza dell' intonazióne, *It.* (kŏn djoos-tăt-tsă dĕll' ēn-tō-nă-tsē-ō-nĕ.) With just and correct intonation.
Con gli, *It. pl.* (kŏn glē.) With the.

ā *ale*, ă *add*, ä *arm*, ē *eve*, ĕ *end*, ī *ice*, ĭ *ill*, ō *old*, ŏ *odd*, ö *dove*, oo *moon*, ū *lute*, ŭ *but*, ü *French sound*.

CONG

Con gli stromenti, *It.* (kŏn glē strō-*măn*-tē.) With the instruments.
Con gradazione, *It.* (kŏn grä-dä-tsē-ō-ně.) With gradual increase and decrease.
Con gránde espressióne, *It.* (kŏn *grän*-dĕ ĕs-prĕs-sē-ō-ně.) With much expression.
Con grandézza, *It.* (kŏn grän-dăt-tsä.) With dignity and grandeur.
Con gravità, *It.* (kŏn grä-vē-*tä*.) With gravity.
Con grázia, *It.* (kŏn *grä*-tsē-ä.) With grace and elegance.
Con gústo, *It.* (kŏn *goos*-tō.) With taste.
Con ímpeto, *It.* (kŏn *ĕm*-pā-tō.)
Con impetuosita, *It.* (kŏn ĕm-pē-too-ō-sē-*tä*.)
With impetuosity and vehemence.
Con ímpeto doloróso, *It.* (kŏn *ĕm*-pē-tō dō-lō-rō-zō.) With pathetic force and energy.
Con indifferénza, *It.* (kŏn ĕn-dēf-fē-*rän*-tsä.) In an easy and indifferent manner.
Con innocénza, *It.* (kŏn ĕn-nō-*tshän*-tsä.) In a simple, artless style.
Con intimíssimo sentiménto, *It.* (kŏn ĕn-tē-*mēs*-sē-mō sĕn-tē-*män*-tō.) With very much feeling; with great expression.
Con intrepidézza, *It.* (kŏn ĕn-trä-pē-*dăt*-tsä.) With intrepidity, boldly.
Con íra, *It.* (kŏn *ē*-rä.) With anger.
Con isdegno, *It.* (kŏn ĕs-dăn-yō.) With anger, angrily.
Con ismania, *It.* (kŏn ĕs-mä-nē-ä.) In a frenzied style.
Con istrepito, *It.* (kŏn ĕs-trä-pē-tō.) With noise and bluster.
Conjoint degrees. Two notes which immediately follow each other in the order of the scale.
Conjoint tetrachords. Two tetrachords or fourths of which the highest note of one is the lowest of the other.
Conjunct, *Lat.* (kŏn-*jŭnkt*.) A term applied by the ancient Greeks to tetrachords, or fourths, when the highest note of the lower tetrachord was also the lowest note of the tetrachord next above it.
Conjunct degree. A degree in which two notes form the interval of a second.
Conjunct succession. Where a succession of tones proceed regularly upward or downward through several degrees.
Con jústo, *It.* (kŏn *joos*-tō.) With exactness.
Con leggerézza, *It.* (kŏn lĕd-jĕ-rät-tsä.) } With
Con leggierezza,*It.*(kŏn lĕd-jē-ĕ-*rät*-tsä.) } lightness and delicacy.
Con lenézza, *It.* (kŏn lē-*nät*-tsä.) With mildness, sweetness.
Con lentézza, *It.* (kŏn lĕn-*täd*-tsä.) With slowness, lingering.
Con maesta, *It.* (kŏn mä-ĕs-*tä*.) With majesty and grandeur.
Con malanconia, *It.* (kŏn mä-län-*kō*-nē-ä.)
Con malenconia, *It.* (kŏn mä-lĕn-*kō*-nē-ä.) }
Con malinconia, *It.* (kŏn mä-lĕn-*kō*-nē-ä.)
With an expression of melancholy and sadness.
Con máno déstra, *It.* (kŏn *mä*-nō *dās*-trä.) }
Con máno dritta,*It.* (kŏn *mä*-nō *drät*-tä.) }
With the right hand.
Con máno sinistra, *It.* (kŏn *mä*-nō sē-*näs*-trä.) With the left hand.

CONS

Con mistério, *It.* (kŏn měz-*tä*-rē-ō.) With mystery, with an air of mystery.
Con moderazióne, *It.* (kŏn mŏd-ĕ-rä-tsē-ō-ně.) With a moderate degree of quickness.
Con mólto espressióne, *It.* (kŏn *mŏl*-tō ĕs-prĕs-sē-ō-ně.) With much expression.
Con mólto caráttere, *It.* (kŏn *mŏl*-tō kär-*ät*-tē-rě.) With much character and emphasis.
Con mólto passióne, *It.* (kŏn *mŏl*-tō päs-sē-ō-ně.) With much passion and feeling.
Con mólto sentiménto, *It.* (kŏn *mŏl*-tō sĕn-tē-*män*-tō.) With much feeling or sentiment.
Con morbidézza, *It.* (kŏn mŏr-bē-dăt-tsä.) With excess of feeling or delicacy.
Con móto, *It.* (kŏn *mō*-tō.) With motion; not dragging.
Connecting note. A note held in common by two successive chords.
Con negligénza, *It.* (kŏn näl-yē-jän-tsä.) In a negligent manner, without restraint.
Con nobilita, *It.* (kŏn nō-bē-lē-*tä*.) With nobility.
Connaisseur, *Fr.* (kŏn-nä-*sŭr*.) } One skilled
Connoisseur, *Fr.* (kŏn-wä-*sŭr*.) } in music; a good judge and critic of musical composition and performance.
Conocedor, *Sp.* (kŏn-ō-thĕ-*dŏr* (A connoisseur.
Con osservánza, *It.* (kŏn ŏs-sĕr-vän-zä.) With great care and exactness in regard to time and expression.
Con ottáva, *It.* (kŏn ŏt-*tä*-vä.) } With the oc-
Con 8va. } tave; to be played in octaves.
Con passióne, *It.* (kŏn päs-sē-ō-ně.) In an impassioned manner, with great emotion.
Con piacevolézza, *It.* (kŏn pē-ä-tshěv-o-*lät*-tsä.) With pleasing and graceful expression.
Con piu moto, *It.* (kŏn pē-oo mō-tō.) With increased motion.
Con precipitazióne, *It.* (kŏn prĕ-tshē-pē-tä-tsē-ō-ně.) With precipitation; in a hurried manner.
Con precisióne, *It.* (kŏn prē-tshē-zē-ō-ně.) With exactness and precision.
Con prestézza, *It.* (kŏn prěs-*täd*-tsä.) With precision and exactness.
Con rábbia, *It.* (kŏn *räb*-bē-ä.) With rage, with fury.
Con rapidità, *It.* (kŏn rä-pē-dē-*tä*.) With rapidity.
Con réplica, *It.* (kŏn *rä*-plē-kä.) With repetition.
Con risoluzióne, *It.* (kŏn rē-zō-loo-tsē-ō-ně.) With firmness and resolution.
Con scioltézza, *It.* (kŏn shē-ŏl-*täd*-tsä.) Freely, disconnectedly.
Con sdégno, *It.* (kŏn *sdän*-yō.) With wrath; in an angry and scornful manner.
Consecutive. A term applied to two or more similar intervals or chords, immediately following one another.
Consecutive fifths. Two or more perfect fifths, immediately following one another in similar motion. Consecutive fifths are disagreeable to the ear and forbidden by the laws of harmony.
Consecutive intervals. Where two parallel

PRONOUNCING MUSICAL DICTIONARY.

ă ale, ă add, ä arm, ĕ eve, ĕ end, ĭ ice, ĭ ill, ō old, ŏ odd, ō dove, oo moon, ū lute, ŭ but, ū French sound.

CONS

parts or voices of a score proceed in succession by similar motion.

Consecutive octaves. Two parts moving in unison or octaves with each other.

Consecutives covered. Passages in which consecutive fifths may be imagined, though they do not really exist; as, where a third or a sixth moves to a fifth.

Consecutives hidden. Such as occur in passing, by similar motion, from an imperfect to a perfect concord, or from one perfect concord to another of a different kind.

Con semplicità, *It.* (kŏn sĕm-plē-tshē-tă.) With simplicity.

Con sensibilità, *It.* (kŏn sĕn-sē-bō-lē-tă.) With sensibility and feeling.

Con sentiménto, *It.* (kŏn sĕn-tē-mān-tō.) With feeling and sentiment.

Consequent, *Lat.* (kŏn-sĕ-qnĕnt.) ⎫ An old
Consequente, *It.* (kŏn-sĕ-qŭăn-tĕ.) ⎭ term, meaning the *answer* in a fugue, or of a point of imitation.

Conservatoire, *Fr.* (kŏn-sĕr-vă-twŭr.) ⎫
Conservatória, *It.* (kŏn-sĕr-vă-tō-rē-ă.) ⎪
Conservatório, *It.* (kŏn-sĕr-vă-tō-rō-ō.) ⎬
Conservatorium, *Ger.* kŏn-sĕr-fă-to-rĭ-ŭm.) ⎪
Conservatory. ⎭
A school or academy of music, in which every branch of musical art is taught.

Con severita, *It.* (kŏn sĕ-vĕr-ĕ-tă.) With strict and severe style.

Consolánte, *It.* (kŏn-sō-lăn-tĕ.) In a cheering and consoling manner.

Consolataménte, *It.* (kŏn-sō-lă-tă-mān-tĕ.) Quietly, cheerfully.

Con solennita, *It.* (kŏn sō-lĕn-nē-tă.) With solemnity.

Con sómma espressione, *It.* (kŏn sŏm-mă ĕs-prĕs-sē-ō-nĕ.) With very great expression.

Consonance. An accord of sounds agreeable and satisfactory to the ear; the opposite to a discord or dissonance.

Consonance, perfect. A consonance in which the interval is invariable; octaves and fifths, are called *perfect* consonances.

Consonances, imperfect. The major and minor thirds and sixes.

Consonant. Accordant, harmonious.

Consonancia, *Spa.* (kŏn-sō-năn-thō-ă.) Consonance.

Consonant concord. The *perfect concord* and its derivitaves.

Consonante, *It.* (kŏn-sō-năn-tĕ.) Harmonious, consonant.

Consonantaménte, *It.* (kŏn-sō-năn-tă-mān-tĕ.) Accordantly.

Consonantia, *Lat.* (kŏn-sō-năn-shĭ-ă.) Accord, agreement of voices.

Consonant sixths. The major and minor sixths.

Consonant thirds. The major and minor thirds.

Consonanz, *Ger.* (kŏn-sō-năntz.) ⎫ A conso-
Consonánza, *It.* (kŏn-sō-năn-tsă.) ⎭ nance, a concord.

Consonar, *Spa.* (kŏn-sō-năr.) To sing or play in concord or unison.

CONT

Consonáre, *It.* (kŏn-sō-nă-rĕ.) To tune in unison with another.

Consones, *Spa.* (kŏn-sō-nĕs.) Concordant sounds.

Consoni suoni, *It.* (kŏn-sō-nē swō-nē.) Concords.

Consono, *Spa.* (kŏn-sō-nō.) Harmonious; consonant.

Consoniren, *Ger.* (kŏn-sō-nē-r'n.) To harmonize; to agree in sound.

Con sonorità, *It.* (kŏn sō-nō-rē-tă.) With a sonorous, vibrating kind of tone.

Con sordini, *It. pl.* (kŏn sŏr-dē-nē.) *With mutes*, in violin playing; in pianoforte music, *with dampers*, indicating that the dampers are not to be raised by the pedal.

Con sordino, *It.* (kŏn sŏr-dē-no.) *With the mute;* meaning that a mute or damper is to be affixed to the bridge of the violin, viola, etc.

Con spirito, *It.* (kŏn spē-rē-tō.) With spirit, life, energy.

Con strepito, *It.* (kŏn strĕ-pē-tō.) In a boisterous manner, with impetuosity.

Con stromenti, *It. pl.* (kŏn strō-măn-tē.)
Con strumenti, *It. pl.* (kŏn stroo-măn-tē.)
With the instruments: meaning that the orchestra and voices are together.

Con suavézza, *It.* (kŏn swă-vāt-tsă.) ⎫ With
Con suavità, *It.* (kŏn swă-vē-tă.) ⎭ sweetness and delicacy.

Consueta, *Spa.* (kŏn-soo-ă-tă.) A prompter.

Cont. An abbreviation of *Contano*.

Contadina, *It.* (kŏn-tă-dē-nă.) A country dance.

Contadinésco, *It.* (kŏn-tă-dē-nās-kō.) Rustic, in a rural style.

Contano, *It.* (kŏn-tă-nō.) To count or rest; a term applied to certain parts not played for the time being, while the other parts move on.

Con tenerézza, *It.* (kŏn tĕ-nĕ-rāt-tsă.) With tenderness.

Con tepidità, *It.* (kŏn tĕ-pē-dē-tă.) With coldness and indifference.

Contera, *Spa.* (kŏn-tă-ră.) Prelude.

Con timedézza, *It.* (kŏn tē-mō-dăt-tsă.) With timidity.

Con tinto, *It.* (kŏn tēn-tō.) With various shades of expression.

Continuáto, *It.* (kŏn-tē-noo-ă-tō.) Continued, held on, sustained.

Continued bass. See *Básso Continuo*.

Continued harmony. A harmony that does not change, though the bass varies.

Continued rest. A rest continuing through several successive measures, the number of measures being indicated by a figure over a whole rest.

Continuo, *It.* (kŏn-tē-noo-ō.) Without cessation.

Continuous horizontal line. A line indicating that the passages are to be played as unisons.

Contra, *It.* (kŏn-tră.) Low, under.

Contrabássist. A double bass player.

ă ale, ă add, ä arm, ĕ eve, ĕ end, ĭ ice, ĭ ill, ō old, ŏ odd, ö dove, oo moon, ū lute, ŭ but, ü French sound.

CONT

Cóntra-basś, *It.* (kŏn-trä-bäs.) The
Cóntra-basso, *It.* (kŏn-trä-bäs-sō.)
Contra-bass viol.
Contrabaxo, *Spa.* (kŏn-trä-bäk-sō.)
double bass, the deepest-toned stringed instrument of the bow species.
Contraction. When two parts in a fugne compress the subject, counter-subject, or an intervening subject.
Contraddánza, *It.* (kŏn-träd-dän-tsä.) A country dance.
Cóntra fagótto, *It.* (kŏn-trä-fä-gŏt-tō.) The double bassoon; also, the name of an organ stop of 16 or 32 feet scale.
Cóntra fuga, *It.* (kŏn-trä foo-gä.) Counter fugne.
Contr' alti, (kŏn-träl-tē.) The higher male voices, usually called counter tones.
Contrálto, *It.* (kŏn-träl-tō.) The deepest species of female voice.
Con tranquillézza, *It.* (kŏn trän-quĕl-lät-tsä.)
Con tranquillita, *It.* (kŏn trän-quĕl-lē-tä.)
With tranquillity; with calmness.
Contrapasso, *Spa.* (kŏn-trä-päs.) A Spanish dance.
Contra-posaune, *Ger.* (kŏn-trä-pō-zou-nĕ.) Double trombone; a 16 or 32 reed stop in an organ.
Contrappuntísta, *It.* (kŏn-träp-poon-tēz-tä.) One skilled in counter point.
Contrappúnto, *It.* (kŏn-träp-poon-tō.) Counterpoint.
Contrappúnto alla decima, *It.* (kŏn-träp-poon-tō äl-lä dä-tshē-mä.) A species of double counterpoint, where the principal counterpoint may rise a tenth above, or fall as much below, the subject.
Contrappúnto alla mente, *It.* (kŏn-träp-poon-tō äl-lä män-tē.) See Chant sur le Livre.
Contrappúnto dóppio, *It.* (kŏn-träp-poon-tō dŏp-pē-ō.) Double counterpoint.
Contrappúnto dóppio alla duodécima, *It.* (kŏn-träp-poon-tō dŏp-pē-ō äl-lä doo-o-dä-tshē-mä.) Double counterpoint in the twelfth.
Contrappúnto sciolto, *It.* (kŏn-träp-poon-tō shē-ōl-tō.) A free counterpoint.
Contrappúnto sópra il soggétto, *It.* (kŏn-träp-poon-tō sō-prä ēl sōd-jät-tō.) Counterpoint *above* the subject.
Contrappúnto sotto il soggétto, *It.* (kŏn-träp-poon-tō sŏt-tō ēl sōd-jät-tō.) Counterpoint *below* the subject.
Contrappúnto syncopato, *It.* (kŏn-träp-poon-tō sĕn-kō-pä-tō.) The syncopation of one part for the purpose of producing discord.
Contrapunkt, *Ger.* (kŏn-trä-poonkt.) Counterpoint.
Contrapunctum floridum, *Lat.* (kŏn-trä-pŭnk-tum flō-rī-dŭm.) Ornamental counterpoint.
Contrapunctum in decima gravi, *Lat.* (kŏn-trä-pŭnk-tum in dĕs-ī-mä grä-vē.) A term given to double counterpoint when the parts move in tenths or thirds below the subject.
Contrapuntal. Relating to counterpoint.
Contrapuntist.
Contrapuntísta, *It.* (kŏn-trä-poon-tēz-tä.)
One skilled in counterpoint.
Contrapuntus simplex, *Lat.* (kŏn-trä-pŭn-tŭs sim-plĕx.) Simple counterpoint.

CONV

Contr' árco, *It.* (kŏn-tr' är-kō.) Bowing an instrument in a manner contrary to rule.
Contrário, *It.* (kŏn-trä-rē-o.) Contrary.
Contrary bow. A reversed stroke of the bow.
Contrary motion. Motion in an opposite direction to some other part; one rising as the other falls.
Contras, *Spa.* (kŏn-träs.) The bass pipes in an organ.
Contrassoggetto, *It.* (kŏn-träs-sōd-jĕt-tō.) The counter subject of a fugue.
Con trasporto, *It.* (kŏn träs-pŏr-tō.) With anger, excitement, passion.
Contra témpo, *It.* (kŏn-trä tĕm-pō.) *Against the time;* syncopation, one part moving in a slower progression than the other parts.
Contra-tenor. See *Counter tenor*.
Contra túne, *Ger.* (kŏn-trä tō-nĕ.) A term applied to the deeper tones of the bass voice.
Cóntra violóne, *It.* (kŏn-trä vē-ō-lō-nĕ.)
Contre-basse, *Fr.* (kŏntr-bäss.)
The double bass.
Contredance, *Fr.* (kŏntr-dänhs.) A country dance, a dance in which the parties engaged stand in two opposite ranks.
Contre partie, *Fr.* (kŏntr pär-tē.) The second part.
Contrepoint, *Fr.* (kŏntr-pwänh.) Counterpoint.
Contre-sujet, *Fr.* (kŏntr-sü-zhä.) The countersubject, or second subject in a fugue.
Contre-temps, *Fr.* (kŏntr-tänh.) Syncopation, driving notes, notes tied and accented contrary to the natural rhythmic flow of the measure.
Contretems, *Fr.* (kŏntr-tänh.) Counter time, against the time, a deviation from strict time.
Contretenour, *Fr.* (kŏntr-tĕ-noor.) Counter tenor.
Con tristézza, *It.* (kŏn trĕz-tät-tsä.) With sadness, with heaviness.
Contro, *It.* (kŏn-trō.) Counter, low.
Contro basso, *It.* (kŏn-trō bäs-sō.) Properly written, *contra basso.* A double bass viol, the lowest part of a musical composition.
Contro fagotto. See *Contra fagotto.*
Contro fugue. Counter fugue.
Controviolone. See *Contraviolone.*
Con tútta fórza, *It.* (kŏn toot-tä fŏr-tsä.)
Con tútta la fórza, *It.* (kŏn toot-tä lä fŏr-tsä.)
With all possible force, with the whole power, as loud as possible.
Con un díto, *It.* (kŏn oon dē-tō.) With one finger.
Con variazione, *It.* (kŏn vä-rē-ä-tsē-ō-nĕ.) With variations.
Con veeménza, *It.* (kŏn vē-män-tsä.) With vehemence, force.
Con velocita, *It.* (kŏn vē-lō-tshē-tä.) With velocity.
Conversio, *Lat.* (kŏn-vĕr-sī-ō.) Inversion in counterpoint.
Con vigóre, *It.* (kŏn vē-gō-rĕ.) With vigor, sprightliness, strength.
Con violénza, *It.* (kŏn vē-ō-län-tsä.) With violence.
Con vivacitá, *It.* (kŏn vē-vä-tshē-tä.)
Con vivézza, *It.* (kŏn vē-vät-tsä.)
With liveliness, vivacity, animation.

ă ale, ă add, ä arm, ĕ eve, ē end, ĭ ice, ĭ ill, ŏ old, ō odd, ô dove, oo moon, ŭ lute, ŭ but, ü French sound.

CONV

Con vóce ránca, *It.* (kŏn *vō*-tsbĕ *rä*-oo-kä.) With a hoarse or rough voice.
Con volubilità, *It.* (kŏn vō-loo-bē-lē-*tä*.) With volubility, with fluency and freedom of performance.
Con zélo, *It.* (kŏn tsā-lō.) With zeal.
Con 8va. An abbreviation of Con Ottava.
Con 8va ad libitum. With octaves at pleasure.
Copérto, *It.* (kō-*pär*-tō.) Covered. muffled.
Copist, *It.* (kō-*pĕst*.) ⎫
Copiste, *Fr.* (kō-*pēst*.) ⎬ A music copyist.
Coplero, *Spa.* (kō-plā-*rō*.) A ballad seller.
Coplica, *Spa.* (kō-plē-*kä*.) A little ballad.
Coppel-flüte, *Ger.* (*kŏp*-p'l *flō*-tĕ.) *Coupling flute*; an organ stop of the clarabella, or stopped diapason species, intended to be used in combination with some other stop.
Cópula, *It.* (*kō*-poo-lä.) ⎫ A coupler. An ar-
Copule, *Fr.* (kō-*pūl*.) ⎬ rangement by which two rows of keys can be connected together, or the keys connected with the pedals.
Copyright. The exclusive right of an author or his representative to print, publish, or sell his work during a specified term of years.
Cor. An abbreviation of *cornet*.
Cor, *Fr.* (kōr.) A horn, commonly called the French horn.
Cor, *Wel.* (kōr.) A choir.
Cora, *Ital.* (kō-*rä* lē.) A chorus.
Coràle, *It.* (kō-*rä* lē.) Choral; the plain chant.
Coranash, *Gae.* A funeral song or dirge.
Cor Anglaise, *Fr.* (kōr änh-glās.) *English horn;* the tenor hautboy, also a reed stop in an organ.
Coránte, *It.* (kō-*rän*-tĕ.) ⎫ A slow dance in 3-2
Corúnto, *It.* (kō-*rän*-tō.) ⎬ or 3-4 time.
Corchea, *Spa.* (*kōr*-kā-ä.) A crotchet. 𝄽

Córda, *It.* (*kōr*-dä.) A string; *una córda*, one string.
Cordatúra, *It.* (kōr-dä-*too*-rä.) The scale or series of notes by which the strings of any instrument are tuned.
Corde, *Fr.* (kōrd.) A string.
Corde a boyau, *Fr.* (kōrd ä bwä-yō) Catgut; strings for the violin, harp, etc.
Corde à jour, *Fr.* (kōrd ä zhoor.) ⎫ An open
Corde a vide, *Fr.* (kōrd ä vēd.) ⎬ string on the violin, vio'n, etc.
Cor de chasse, *Fr.* (kōr düh shäss.) The hunting horn; the French horn.
Corde de luth, *Fr.* (kōrd düh loot.) A lute string.
Corde fausse, *Fr.* (kōrd fōss.) A false or dissonant string.
Cor de postillon, *Fr.* (kōr düh pōs-tē-yōnh.) Postillion's horn.
Cordes de Naples, *Fr.* (kōrd düh Nä-pl.) The strings imported from Naples, for the violin, harp, etc.
Cor de signal, *Fr.* (kōr düh sēn-yäl.) A bugle.
Cor de vaches, *Fr.* (kōr düh vä-shä.) The cowboy's horn.
Corde vuide, *Fr.* (kōrd vwēd.) An open string on the violin, viola, etc.

COKN

Cordiéra, *It.* (kōr-dē-*ā*-rä.) The tail piece of a violin, viola, etc.
Cordon de sonnette, *Fr.* (kōr-*dōnh* düh sŏn-*nät*.) A bell rope.
Corea, *Spa.* (*kō*-rā-ä.) Dance accompanied by a chorus.
Corear, *Spa.* (kō-rä-*är*.) To sing or play in a chorus.
Coregrafía, *It.* (kō-rĕ-*grä*-fē-ä.) The method of describing the figures of a dance.
Coreo, *Spa.* (*kō*-rā-ō.) A foot in Latin verse.
Coriambus, *Gr.* (kō-rē-*äm*-bŭs.) In ancient poetry, a foot consisting of four syllables, the first and last long and the others short.
Córica, *It.* (*kō*-rē-kä.) ⎫ Choral.
Córico, *It.* (*kō*-rē-kō.) ⎬
Corifėo, *It.* (kō-rē-*fā*-ō.) The leader of the dances in a ballet.
Corillo, *Spa.* (*kō*-rēl-yō.) A small choir.
Corimagistro, *It.* (kō-rēm-ä-*jēs*-trō.) The leader of a choir.
Coriphæus, *Gr.* (kō-*rīf*-ē-ŭs.) A leader, chief; head; see *Coriféo.*
Corista, *It.* (kō-*rēs*-tä.) A chorister.
Cormorne. A soft-toned horn; also a reed stop in English organs. See *Oremōna.*
Corn, *Wel.* (kōrn.) A horn.
Cornamúsa. *It.* (kōr-nä-*moo*-zä.) A species of bagpipe.
Cornamusáre, *It.* (kōr-nä-moo-zä-*rē*.) To play on the bagpipe.
Cornamute. A wind instrument, a species of bagpipe.
Cornáre, *It.* (kōr-*nä*-rē.) To sound a horn or cornet.
Cornatóre, *It.* (kōr-nä-*tō*-rē.) One who sounds, or plays on a horn.
Corno, *Fr.* (kōrn.) A horn.
Corne, de chasse, *Fr.* (kōrn düh shäss.) See *Cor de Chasse.*
Corneous Instruments. Instruments belonging to the horn species.
Cornemuse, *Fr.* (kōrn-üh-müz.) See *Carnamúsa.*
Corner, *Fr.* (kōr-nä.) To sound a horn, or cornet.
Cornet. The name of an organ stop consisting of several ranks of pipes. Also, a small horn, of the nature of a trumpet used in brass bands.
Corneta, *Spa.* (kōr-nä-*tä*.) Cornet, a French horn.
Corneta. ⎫ A name sometimes applied to a
Cornetto. ⎬ reed stop in an organ of 16 feet scale.
Cornet a bouquin, *Fr.* (kōr-nět ä boo-*kănh*.) Cornet; bugle horn.
Cornet a pistons. *Fr.* (kōr-nět ä pēs-tōnh.) A species of trumpet, but shorter and softer, with valves or pistons to produce the semitones.
Cornet dreifach, *Ger.* (kōr-*nět* drī-fäkh.) Cornet with three ranks in German organs.
Cornete, *Spa.* (kōr-*nä*-tě.) ⎫
Cornett, *Ger.* (kōr-*nět*.) ⎬ A cornet.
Cornetta, *It.* (kōr-*nät*-tä.) ⎭
Cornetica, *Spa.* (kōr-nä-*tē*-kä.) ⎫ A small cor-
Cornettino, *It.* (kōr-nät-*tē*-nō.) ⎬ net.
Cornétto, *It.* (kōr-*nět*-tō.) A cornet.
Cornet stop. An organ stop, consisting of five pipes to each note.

ā ale, ă add, ä arm, ē eve, ĕ end, ī ice, ĭ ill, ō old, ŏ odd, ô dove, oo moon, ū lute, ŭ but, ü French sound.

CORN

Cornet, tenor. An old style of cornet consisting of a curved tube, and increasing in diameter from the mouth-piece to the end.
Cornet, treble. See *Cornet tenor.*
Corneus, *Fr.* (kŏr-nūs.) A post-boy, a horn blower.
Corneznelo, *Spa.* (kŏr-nā-thoo-ā-lō.) A bugle.
Corni, *It. pl.* (kŏr-nē.) The horns.
Cornicello, *It.* (kŏr-nē-tshāl-lō.) A small horn or cornet.
Cornist. } A performer on the cornet or horn.
Corneter. }
Corniste. *Fr.* (kŏr-nēst.) A player upon the horn.
Cornmuse. A Cornish pipe, similar to a bagpipe.
Córno, *It.* (kŏr-nō.) A horn.
Córno alto, *It.* (kŏr-nō ăl-tō.) A horn of a high pitch.
Córno básso, *It.* (kŏr-nō bäs-sō.) A bass horn, a horn of a low pitch.
Córno cromático, *It.* (kŏr-nō krō-mä-tē-kō.) The chromatic horn.
Córno di bassétto, *It.* (kŏr-nō dē bäs-sāt-tō.) The basset horn. A species of clarinet a fifth lower than the C clarinet. 2. A delicate toned reed organ stop of 8 feet scale.
Córno di cáccia, *It.* (kŏr-nō dē kät-tshē-ä.) The hunting or French horn.
Córno dólce, *It.* (kŏr-nō dŏl-tshē.) Soft-horn; an organ stop, occurring both in the manuals and pedals.
Córno flute. An organ stop of 8 feet scale of soft, agreeable tone.
Córno in B básso, *It.* A low B horn.
Córno Inglése, *It.* (kŏr-nō ēn-glā-zē.) The English horo.
Cornopean. An organ reed stop of 8 feet scale; also, a wind instrument of the trumpet species.
Córno primo, *It.* (kŏr-nō prē-mō.) The first horn.
Córno quarto, *It.* (kŏr-nō quär-tō.) The fourth horn.
Córno quinto, *It.* (kŏr-nō quēn-tō.) The fifth horn.
Córno secóndo, *It.* (kŏr-nō sē-kŏn-dō.) The second horn.
Córno sordo, *It.* (kŏr-nō sŏr-dō.) A horn with dampers.
Córno ventile, *It.* (kŏr-nō vēn-tē-lū.)
Cor omnitonique, *Fr.* (kŏr ŏnh-nit-ō-nĕk.) } Chromatic horn with valves or keys for producing the semitones.
Coro, *It.* (kō-rō.) } A choir, a chorus, a piece
Coro, *Spa.* (kō-rō.) } for many voices.
Corobasnas, *Iri.* An ancient brass instrument used for marking time.
Coromeion, *Gr.* (kō-rō-mē-ŏn.) A brazen bell much used by the ancients.
Coróna, *It.* (kō-rō-nä.) }
Coronata, *It.* (kō-rō-nä-tä.) } A pause or hold, ⌒.
Coronach, *It.* (kō-rō-näk.) Funeral hymn.
Coro primo, *It.* (kō-rō prē-mō.) The first chorus.
Coro spezzato, *It.* (kō-rō spět-sä-tō.) A composition for two or more choruses.
Corps, *Fr.* (kŏr.) The body of a musical instrument. 2. A band of musicians.
Corps de ballet, *Fr.* (kŏr dŭh bäl-lā.) A general name for the performers in a ballet.

COUN

Corps de voix, *Fr.* (kŏr dŭh vwä.) Body or fullness of tone.
Corrénte, *It.* (kŏr-rän-tē.) An old dance tune in slow triple time; see *Coránto.*
Corrépétiteur, *Fr.* (kŏr-rā-pä-tī-tür.) } A mu-
Corripetitore, *It.* (kŏr-rē-pä-tē-tō-rē.) } sician who instructs the chorus singers of the opera.
Corrido, *Spa.* (kŏr-rē-dō.) A lively song accompanied by the guitar.
Corybant, *Gr.* (kō-rī-bănt.) A priest of Cybele, whose rites were celebrated with dances to the sound of the drum and cymbal.
Coryphæns, *Gr.* (kō-rĭf-ē-ŭs.) The conductor of the chorus; see *Corifēo.*
Coryphée, *Fr.* (kō-rĭ-fā.) The leader or chief of the group of dancers in a *ballet.*
Cosaque, *Fr.* (kō-säk.) The Cossack dance.
Cote de luth, *Fr.* (kōt dŭh lüt.) A part of the lute.
Cotil. An abbreviation of *cotillon.*
Cotillon, *Fr.* (kō-tē-yōnh.) A lively, old dance in 6-8 time.
Couac, *Fr.* (quäk.) The quacking sound produced by bad playing of hautbois or clarinet.
Couched harp. The original name of the spinet.
Coulé, *Fr.* (koo-lā.) A group of two notes, connected by a slur.
Couler. *Fr.* (koo-lā.) To slide, to slur.
Counter. A name given to an under part, as *counter tenor.*
Counter bass. A second bass.
Counter dance. See *Contredanse.*
Counter fugue. A fugue in which the subjects move in contrary directions.
Counterpart. The part to be applied to another, as the bass is the counterpart of the treble.
Counterpoint, *Point against point.* The art of adding one or more parts to a given theme or subject. Before the invention of notes, the various sounds were expressed by *points.*
Counterpoint, double. A counterpart that admits of an inversion of the parts.
Counterpoint, equal. Where the notes are of equal duration.
Counterpoint, fugued. Counterpoint consisting of four, five, six, or seven parts; the only counterpoint in use before the eighteenth century.
Counterpoint, inverted. Where the parts are not only reversed toward each other, but move in a contrary direction.
Counterpoint, quadruple. Counterpoint in four parts.
Counterpoint, single. Where only two parts are inverted.
Counterpoint, triple. A counterpoint in three parts, all of which are inverted.
Counter subject. The second subject in a fugue composed on two subjects.
Counter tenor. High tenor; the highest male voice. It is generally *a fatsétto.*
Counter tenor clef. The C-clef, when placed on the third line.
Counter theme. See *Counter Subject.*
Country-dance. An old English dance, dating from about the fifteenth century. See *Contredance.*

ă *ale,* ă *add,* ă *arm,* ĕ *eve,* ĕ *end,* Ī *ice,* Ĭ *ill,* ō *old,* ŏ *odd,* ō *dove,* oo *moon,* ū *lute,* ŭ *but,* ü *French sound.*

COUP

Coup de baguette, *Fr.* (koo dŭh bă-gwĕt.) Beat of the drum.
Coup de cloche, *Fr.* (koo dŭh klōsh.) Stroke of the clock.
Couper le sujet, *Fr.* (koo-pā lŭh soo-jā.) To curtail or contract the subject or theme.
Coupler. See *Cópula.*
Couplet, *Fr.* (koo-plā.) } A stanza, or verse;
Couplet. } two verses or lines of poetry forming complete sense.
Coupleter, *Fr.* (koo-plĕ-tā.) To lampoon, to satirize.
Coupling flute. A name given to a stop that may be coupled with any other register.
Coups d'archet, *Fr.* (koo d'är-ehā.) Strokes of the bow; ways or methods of bowing.
Courante, *Fr.* (koo-rănht.) *Running;* an old dance in triple time.
Courtal, *Fr.* (koor-tăl.) } An old instrument;
Courtaud, *Fr.* (koor-tō.) } a species of short bas-
Courtaut, *Fr.* (koor-tō.) } *soon.*
Covered consecutives. See *Hidden Consecutives.*
Covered octaves. Consecutive octaves that are not apparent until the interval between the two parts is filled up with unimportant notes.
C. P. Abbreviation of *Colla Parte.*
Cr.
Cres. } Abbreviations of Crescendo.
Cresc.
Cracovienne, *Fr.* (krä-kō-vē-ĕnn.) A Polish dance in 3-4 time.
Cravicembalo, *It.* (krā-vē-tshĕm-*bä*-lō.) A general name for all instruments of the harpsichord species.
Credo, *Lat.* (krā-dō.) I *believe;* one of the principal movements of the mass.
Crembala. An ancient instrument, resembling the castanets.
Cremóna, *It.* (krē-*mō*-nä.) An organ stop; the name of a superior make of violins.
Cremorn. A reed organ stop of 8 feet scale.
Crepitaculum, *Lat.* (krĕp-ĭ-*tăk*-ū-lŭm.) A timbrel, a rattle.
Cres. al forte, or al ff. Increasing as loud as possible.
Cres. al fortissimo. Increasing to very loud.
Crescéndo, *It.* (krē-*shān*-dō.) A word denoting an increasing power of tone; it is often indicated by the sign,
Crescéndo al fortissimo, *It.* (krē-*shān*-dō äl fōr-tĭs-sē-mō.) Increase the tone until the greatest degree of power is obtained.
Crescéndo al diminuendo, *It.* (krē-*shān*-dō äl dē-mēn-oo-ĕn-dō.)
Crescéndo e diminuendo, *It.* (krē-*shān*-dō ā dē-mēn-oo-ĕn-dō.)
Crescéndo pói diminuendo, *It.* (krē-*shān*-dō pō-ē dē-mēn-oo-ĕn-dō.)
Increase and then diminish the tone; indicated often by the sign,
Crescéndo e incaleándo póco a póco, *It.* (krē-*shān*-dō ā ēn-käl-kän-dō pō-kō ä pō-kō.) Increasing the tone and hurrying the time by degrees.
Crescéndo póco a póco, *It.* (krē-*shān*-dō pō-kō ä pō-kō.) Increasing the tone by little and little.
Crescéndo il tempo, *It.* (krē-*shān*-dō ēl tĕm-pō.) Increase the time of the movement.
Crescéndo nel tempo e nella forza, *It.* (krē-*shān*-dō nĕl tĕm-pō ā nĕl-lä fōr-tsä.) Increase in time and power.
Crescent. A Turkish instrument made of small bells hung on an inverted crescent.
Cres. dim. An abbreviation of Crescéndo e Diminuéndo.
Cres. e legato, *It.* (krĕs ā lĕ-gä-tō.) Crescéndo and *legato.*
C. reversed. A sign in old music of a diminution of one half the value of the notes.
Criard, *Fr.* (krē-är.) Bawling, shouting; relating to the quality of the tone of the voice.
Crier, *Fr.* (krē-ā.) To bawl, to shriek, to sing badly.
Crincrin, *Fr.* (krănh-krănh.) A squeaking fiddle.
Croche, *Fr.* (krōsh.) A quaver, or eighth note.
Croche, double, *Fr.* (krōsh doobl.) A semiquaver, or sixteenth note.
Croche, pointee, *Fr.* (krōsh pwăn-tā.) A dotted quaver.
Croche, quadruple, *Fr.* (krōsh quä-drū-pl.) A hemidemisemiquaver or sixty-fourth note.
Croche, triple, *Fr.* (krōsh trēpl.) A demisemiquaver or thirty-second note, thus,
Crochet, *Fr.* (krō-shā.) The *hook* of a quaver, semiquaver, etc.
Croma, *It.* (krō-mä.) A quaver, or eighth note.
Cromática, *It.* (krō-*mä*-tē-kä.) } Chromatic, re-
Cromático, *It.* (krō-*mä*-tē-kō.) } ferring to intervals and scales.
Cróme, *It. pl.* (krō-mē.) Quavers; when written under crotchets or minims, it shows that those notes are to be divided into quavers.
Crom-horn, *Ger.* (krŏm-hŏrn.) A reed stop in an organ.
Crómmo, *It.* (krŏm-mō.) A choral dirge or lamentation.
Cromorna stop. (krō-mōr-nä.) } The name of
Cromorne, *Fr.* (krō-mōrn.) } a reed stop in an organ.
Crooked flute. An Egyptian instrument in the shape of a bull's horn.
Crooked horn. } The *buccina;* a wind in-
Crooked trumpet. } strument of the ancients.
Crooks. Small curved tubes applied to horns, trumpets, etc., to change their pitch, and adapt them to the key of the piece in which they are to be used.
Croque-note, *Fr.* (krōk-nōt.) } An unskillful
Croque-sol, *Fr.* (krōk-sōl.) } musician.
Cross. The head of a lute; a mark for the thumb, placed over a note.
Cross flute. A transverse flute, a German flute.

ā ale, ă add, ä arm, ē eve, ŭ end, I ice, ĭ ill, ō old, ŏ odd, ō dove, oo moon, ū lute, ŭ but, ü French sound.

CROT

Crotale, *Fr.* (krō-tāl.) } An ancient musical instrument,
Crótalo, *It.* (krō-tä-lō.) used by the priests
Crotalum, *Gr.* (krō-tä-lŭm.) of Cybele. From the reference made to it by different authors, it seems to have been a small cymbal or a species of *castanet*.
Crotales. Little bells.
Crotalistria, *Gr.* (krō-tăl-ĕs-trī-ä.) A woman who plays upon an instrument called crotalon; a female minstrel.
Crotchet. A note equal in value to half a minim.
Crotchet rest. A rest equal in duration to a crotchet.
Crowd. An old name for the violin: see *Crwth*.
Crowder. An old term for a performer on the *crowd*, afterwards applied to a common fiddler.
Crowle. An old English wind instrument of the bassoon species.
Crowth. The English name of the *Crwth*.
Crowther. See *Crowder*.
Crucifixus, *Lat.* (krū-sĭ-fĭx-ŭs.) Part of the *Credo* in a mass.
Cruit, *Iri.* (krū-ĭt.) An ancient musical instrument of the Irish.
Crupezia, *Gr.* (krū-pā-zī-ä.) Wooden clogs worn by the Greek musicians in beating time.
Crusma, *Gr.* (krooz-mä.) A timbrel, a tabor.
Crutchetam. Name originally given to the crotchet.
Cruth. See *Crwth*.
Crwth. *Welsh.* (krūth.) An old Welsh instrument, having six strings, resembling the violin.
C. S. The initials of *Con Sordino*.
Csardas, *Hun.* (tsär-däs.) Hungarian dance.
C Schlüssel. *Ger.* (tsā shlüs-s'l.) The C clef.
Cto. Abbreviation of *Concerto*.
Cuclear, *Spa.* (koo-klā-är.) To sing as the cuckoo.
Cue. *The tail, the end of a thing.* The last words of an actor on a stage, serving as an intimation to the one who follows, when to speak and what to say.
Cuerno, *Spa.* (kwār-nō.) A horn, a cornet.

CWIZ

Cumbe, *Spa.* (koom-hĕ.) A negro dance.
Cum cantu, *Lat.* (kŭm kăn-tū.) *With song, with singing.*
Cum discantu, *Lat.* (kŭm dĭs-kăn-tū.) A phrase used in the Catholic church service.
Cum Sancto Spiritu, *Lat.* (kŭm sănk-tō spĭr-ĭ-tū.) Part of the *Gloria* in a mass.
Currendaner, *Ger.* (koor-rĕn-dä-nĕr.) } School
Currende. *Ger.* (koor-rĕn-dĕ.) } boys, or young choristers chanting in procession through the streets.
Currendschüler, *Ger.* (koo-rĕnd-shü-lĕr.) See *Currendaner*.
Currens saltatio, *Lat.* (kŭr-rĕns säl-tä-shĭ-ō.) See *Coranta*.
Curtail. A wind instrument of the bassoon species.
Curtle, A term applied to the lowest note of the bassoon.
Curule song. A song said to have been composed by Olympus.
Custo, *It.* (koos-to.) } *A direct* ∿. A mark
Custos, *Lat.* *kŭs-tōs.*) sometimes placed at the end of a staff to indicate the note next following.
Cyclic chorus. See *Chorus, Cyclic*.
Cyclicus, *Lat.* (sĭk-lĭ-kŭs.) An itinerant maker and singer of ballads. A cyclic poet.
Cymbales, *Fr.* (sănh-bäl.) } Circular metal
Cymbals. } plates used in bands, usually in combination with the great drum; they are clashed together, producing a ringing, brilliant effect.
Cymbalum, *Lat.* (sĭm-bă-lŭm.) The cymbal.
Cymbale, *Fr.* (sănh-bäl.) } A mixture organ
Cymbel, *Ger.* (tsĭm-b'l.) } stop of a very acute quality of tone.
Cypher system. An old system of musical notation, in which the notes were represented by numerals.
Cytara. The cithara.
Cyter, *Dan.* (sū-tĕr.) A cithern or cithera.
Cythorn. (sĭth-ōrn.) A cithern or cithera.
Cwibian, *Wel.* (kwē-bĭ-än.) To quaver, to trill.
Cwizaro, *Wel.* (kwē-thä-rō.) Cadence.

ă *ate*, ă̄ *add*, ä *arm*, ĕ *eve*, ĕ *end*, ī *ice*, ĭ *ill*, ō *old*, ŏ *odd*, ō *dove*, oo *moon*, ū *lute*, ŭ *but*, ü *French sound*.

D

D. The second note in the diatonic scale of C; the syllable *re* is applied to this note.
Da, *It.* (dă) By, from, for, through, etc.
Da ballo, *It.* (dă *băl*-lō.) In the style of a dance, like a dance.
Dabbuda, *It.* (dăb-boo-*dă*.) A psaltery, a species of harp.
D'abord tres lentement, et avec egalité, *Fr.* (d'ä-bōr trä länht-mänh ă tă-vĕk ĕ-*găl*-ĭ-tă.) At first very slow and equal.
Da camera, *It.* (dă *kă*-mĕ-rä.) For the chamber; in the style of chamber music.
Da cappella, *It.* (dă kăp-*pĕl*-lä.) For the church; in the style of church or chapel music.
Da capo, *It.* (dă *kă*-pō.) *From the beginning;* an expression placed at the end of a movement to indicate that the performer must return to the first strain.
Da capo al fine, *It.* (dă *kă*-pō äl *fē*-nĕ.) Return to the beginning and conclude with the word *Fine.*
Da capo, sin' al fine, *It.* (dă *kă*-pō sĕn äl *fē*-nĕ.) Return to the beginning and conclude with the word *Fine.*
Da capo al segno, *It.* (dă *kă*-pō äl *săn*-yō.) Repeat from the sign 𝄋.
Da capo fin al segno, *It.* (dă *kă*-pō fēn äl *săn*-yō.) Return to the beginning and end at the sign 𝄋.
Da capo e pói la códa, *It.* (dă *kă*-pō ā *pō*-ē lä *kō*-dä.) Begin again and then play to the *Códa.*
Da capo senza repetizióne, e pói la códa, *It.* (dă *kă*-pō sĕn-tsă rā-pē-tē-tsē-ō-nĕ ā *pō*-ē lä *kō*-dä.) Begin again, but without repetition, and then proceed to the *Coda.*
Da capo sin' al ségno, *It.* (dă *kă*-pō sĕn äl *săn*-yō.) Return to the beginning and conclude at the sign 𝄋.
D' accord, *Fr.* (d' äk-*kōrd*.) } In tune, in
D' accordo, *It.* (d' äk-kōr-dō.) } concord, in harmony.
Da chiésa, *It.* (kă kē-ā-zä.) For the church.
Dactilo, *Spa.* (dăk-*tē*-lō.) A dactyl.
Dactyl, *Lat.* (*dăk*-tĭl.) A metrical foot, consisting of one long syllable followed by two short ones, marked thus, — ◡ ◡.
Dactylic flute. A flute consisting of unequal intervals.
Dactylion, *Gr.* (dăk-*tĭl*-ĭ-ŏn.) A machine invented by Henri Hertz, for strengthening the fingers and rendering them independent of each other in pianoforte playing.
Dactylus, *Lat.* (*dăk*-tĭl-ŭs.) See Dactyl.
Dada. A term used in drum music to indicate the left hand.
Daina. (dä-ē-nä.) } A term in Lithuania for
Dainos. (dä-ē-nōs.) } little love songs.
Daire. The tambourine, or hand drum.
Daktylus, *Gr.* (*dăk*-tĭl-oos.) A *dactyl.*
Dal, *Hun.* (Däl.) A song.
Dal, *It.* (däl.)
Dall', *It.* (däll'.)
Dalla, *It.* (*däl*-lä.) } From the, by the, of the, etc.
Dalle, *It.* (*däl*-lĕ.)
Dallo, *It.* (*däl*-lō.)
Da lontano, *It.* (dä lōn-*tä*-nō.) *At a distance;* the music is to sound as if far away.

DAQU

Dal ségno, *It.* (däl *săn*-yō.) *From the sign,* 𝄋. A mark directing a repetition from the sign.
Dal ségno alla fine, *It.* (däl *săn*-yō äl-lä *fē*-nĕ) From the sign to the end.
Dal ségno fin al ségno, *It.* (däl *săn*-yō fēn äl *săn*-yō) From sign to sign.
Dal teatro, *It.* (däl tē-ă-trō.) In the style of theatre music.
Dama, *Spa.* (dä-mä.) An ancient Spanish dance.
Damenisation. *Solfeggi,* to which are adapted the syllables, da, me, ni, po, tu, la, be.
Damper pedal. That pedal in a pianoforte which raises the dampers from the strings and allows them to vibrate freely. Its use is indicated by the abbreviation *ped.*
Dampers. A portion of the movable mechanism of the pianoforte covered with cloth, and, by means of a pedal, brought in contact with the wires in order to stop their vibration and prevent a confusion of sounds.
Dämpfen, *Ger.* (*däm*-pfĕn.) To muffle, or deaden the tone of an instrument.
Dämpfer, *Ger.* (*däm*-pfĕr.) A mute, or damper, used to deaden the tone of a violin, or other similar instrument.
Dämpfung, *Ger.* (*däm*-pfoong.) Damping, smothering the tone.
Dance, ariadne. A Grecian dance.
Dance, country. A quadrille; any lively, pointed melody suitable for dancing.
Dance, morrice. } A dance in imitation of
Dance, morris. } the Moors, usually performed
Dance, morriske. } by young men dressed in loose frocks, adorned with bells and ribbons, and accompanied by castanets, tambours, etc.
Dances. Certain tunes composed especially for dancing.
Danklied, *Ger.* (*dănk*-lēd.) A thanksgiving song.
Danse, *Fr.* (dänhs.) A dance tune.
Danser, *Fr.* (dänh-*să*.) To dance.
Danseries, *Fr.* (dänh-sä-*rē*.) A name formerly given to all collections of dance tunes.
Danseur, *Fr.* (dänh-*sŭr*.) A male dancer.
Danseuse, *Fr.* (dänh-*sŭs*.) A female dancer.
Danse, contre, *Fr.* (dänhs kōntr.) A country dance, a quadrille.
Danse de matelot, *Fr.* (dänhs dŭh măt-ä-lō.) A dance resembling the hornpipe.
Dánza, *It.* (dän-tsä.) } A dance.
Danza, *Spa.* (dän-thä.) } A dance.
Danzánte, *It.* (dän-*tsän*-tĕ.) A dancer.
Danzáre, *It.* (dän-*tsä*-rĕ.) To dance.
Danzatore, *It.* (dän-tsä-*tō*-rĕ.) A male dancer.
Danzatrice, *It.* (dän-tsä-*trē*-tshĕ.) A female dancer.
Danzétta, *It.* (dän-tsĕt-tä.) A little dance, a short dance.
Da prima, *It.* (dä *prē*-mä.) At first; from the beginning.
Da quésta párte fino al maggióre, póco a póco piu animáto e piu fórte, *It.* (*gudz*-tä *pär*-tĕ *fē*-nō äl mäd-jĕ-ō-rĕ *pō*-kō ā *pō*-kō pē-oo ä-nē-*mä*-to ā pē-oo *fōr*-tĕ.) From this place, as far as the major, gradually more animated and louder.

ă ale, ă add, ă arm, ĕ eve, ĕ end, ĭ ice, ī ill, ŏ old, ŏ odd, ô dove, oo moon, ū lute, ŭ but, ü French sound.

DARA

Darabukkeh, (dă-rä-*boo*-kĕh.) A small drum used by the Egyptians.
Dar fiato alla tromba, *It.* (där fē-ä-tō äl-lä trŏm-bä.) To blow the trumpet.
Dar la voce, *It.* (där lä vō-tshĕ.) To strike or give the key note.
Darm-saite, *Ger.* (*därm*-soī-tĕ.) A gut-string, cat gut.
Darm-saiten, *Ger. pl.* (*därm*-soī-t'n.) Gut-strings used for the harp, violin, guitar, etc.
Darsteller, *Ger.* (*där*-stĕl-lĕr.) A performer.
Da scherzo, *It.* (dä skärt-sō.) In a lively, playful manner.
Das harpeggiren, *Ger.* (däs här-pĕ-*jē*-r'n.) The arpeggio.
Das lob Gottes singen, *Ger.* (däs lōb gŏt-tĕs sĭn-ghĕn.) To sing to the praise of God.
Das positiv einer orgel, *Ger.* (däs pōz-ĭ-tĭf ī-nĕr ōr-g'l.) Choir organ.
Dasselbe, *Ger.* (däs-*sĕl*-bĕ.) The same.
Das setzen der ton-zeichen, *Ger.* (däs sĕt-tsĕn dĕr tōn-tsī-kh'n.) The *tonic*.
Das singen, *Ger.* (däs sĭng-ĕn.) Singing, chanting.
Das solfeggiren, *Ger.* (däs sōl-fĕ-*jē*-i'n.) Solfaing.
Das trillern, *Ger.* (däs trĭl-lĕrn.) To make a shake or trill.
Das trommeln, *Ger.* (däs trŏm-mĕln.) Drumming.
Da suonar, *It.* (dä swō-när.) To sound or play.
Das waldhorn blasen, *Ger.* (däs vǎld-hōrn blä-z'n.) To wind the horn.
Das wirbeln, *Ger.* (däs vēr-bĕln.) The roulade; trilling, warbling.
Da teatro, *It.* (dä tē-ä-trō.) For the theatre; music composed for the theatre.
Datis, *Gr.* (dä-tis.) A song of mirth.
Dáttilo, *It.* (dăt-tē-lō.) A dactyl.
Dauer, *Ger.* (*dou*-ĕr.) The length or duration of notes.
Daul, *Tur.* A large drum used by the Turkish soldiers.
Daum, *Ger.* (doum.) } The thumb.
Daumen, *Ger.* (*dou*-mĕn.) }
Daumenklapper, *Ger.* (dou-mĕn-kläp-pĕr.) Castanet, snapper.
D. C. The initials of Da Capo.
D dur, *Ger.* (dä-door.) D major; the key of D major.
Debander, *Fr.* (dĕ-bän-dā.) To unbrace a drum.
Débile. *It.* (dā-bē-lĕ.) } Weak, feeble, faint.
Débole. *It.* (dā-bō-lĕ.) }
Debit, *Spa.* (dĕ-bēt.) A recitative.
Début, *Fr.* (dā-bü.) First appearance; the first public performance.
Débutant. *Fr.* (dā-bü-tänh.) } A singer or performer who appears for the first time before the public.
Débutante, *Fr.* (dā-bü-tänht.) }
Débuter, *Fr.* (dā-bü-tā.) To begin, to play first.
Decachord, (dĕk-ă-kōrd.) } An ancient musical instrument of the harp or psaltery species, with ten strings. It was called by the Hebrews *Hasur*.
Decachordon, *Lat.* (dĕk-ă-kŏr-dŏn.) }
Decacórdo, *It.* (dĕk-ă-*kŏr*-dō.) }
Decameróne, *It.* (dĕk-ă-mĕ-rō-nĕ.) A period of ten days; a collection of ten musical pieces.

DECR

Decani, *Lat. pl.* (dĕ-*kā*-nē.) In cathedral music this term implies that the passages thus marked must be taken by the singers on the side of the choir where the *Dean* usually sits.
Decanto, *Lat.* (dĕ-kän-tō.) To sing, to chant.
Decastich. A poem consisting of ten lines.
Decena, *Spa.* (dĕ-*thā*-nä.) A consonance made of an octave and a third.
Deceptive cadence. A cadence which, instead of closing upon the tonic, or a chord bearing a close relation to it, takes the ear wholly by surprise, and terminates with a chord foreign to the harmony of the tonic.
Deceptive modulation. A modulation by which the ear is deceived and led into unexpected harmony.
Décidé, *Fr.* (dĕ-sē-dā.) } With decision,
Décidément, *Fr.* (dĕ-sē-dā-mänh.) } with resolution.
Decima, *Lat.* (*dĕs*-ĭ-mä.) A *tenth*; an interval of ten degrees in the scale, also the name of an organ stop sounding the tenth.
Decima, *Spa.* (dä-*thē*-mä.) A Spanish stanza of ten verses of eight syllables.
Decima acuta, *Lat.* (*dĕs*-ĭ-mä ă-*kū*-tä.) Tenth above.
Decima gravis, *Lat.* (*dĕs*-ĭ-mä grä-vĭs.) Tenth below.
Decima quarta, *Lat.* (*dĕs*-ĭ-mä quăr-tä.) The interval of a fourteenth.
Decima quinta, *Lat.* (*dĕs*-ĭ-mä quĭn-tä.) The interval of a fifteenth.
Decima tertia, *Lat.* (*dĕs*-ĭ-mä tĕr-shĭ-ä.) The interval of a thirteenth.
Décime, *Fr.* (dā-sēm.) A tenth; see Decima.
Decimole. A musical figure formed out of the division of any note or chord into ten parts or notes of equal value.
Décisif, *Fr.* (dā-sē-sĭf.) Decisive, clear, firm.
Decisióne, *It.* (dā-tshē-zē-ō-nĕ.) Decision, firmness.
Décisivement, *Fr.* (dā-sē-zēv-mōnh.) Decisively.
Decisivo, *It.* (dä-tshē-zē-vō.) } In a bold and
Deciso, *It.* (dä-tshē-zō.) } decided manner.
Decke, *Ger.* (dĕk-ĕ.) The sound board of a violin, violincello, etc.; also, the cover or top in those organ stops which are *covered* or *stopped*.
Declamándo, *It.* (dĕk-lä-*män*-dō.) With declamatory expression.
Declamátio, *It.* (dĕk-lä-*mä*-tē-ō.) Declamation, recitative.
Declamation. Dramatic singing; the art of rendering words set to music in a correct and effective style.
Declamazióne, *It.* (dĕk-lä-mä-tsē-ō-nĕ.) Declamation.
Déclaver, *Fr.* (dā-klä-vā.) To go out of the key.
Décomposé, *Fr.* (dā-kōm-pō-zā.) Incoherent, unconnected.
Décoration, *Fr.* (dā-kō-rä-sĭ-ōnh.) Used by some French theorists to indicate the *signature*.
Decorative notes. Notes of embellishment, appoggiaturas, etc.
Decr. } Abbreviations of *decrescendo*.
Decres. }

ă *ale,* ă *add,* ă *arm,* ĕ *eve,* ĕ *end,* ī *ice,* ĭ *ill,* ō *old,* ŏ *odd,* ô *dove,* oo *moon,* ū *tute.* ŭ *but,* ü *French sound.*

DECR

Decrescéndo, *It.* (dă-krĕ-*shăn*-dō.) Gradually diminishing in power of tone ➤.

Decrescéndo sin al pianissimo, *It.* (dă-krĕ-*shăn*-dō sēn äl pē-ăn-ĕs-sē-mō.) Diminishing to the softest possible sound.

Dedicáto, *It.* (dĕd-ē-kă-tō.) } Dedicated.
Dédié, *Fr.* (dă-dī-ā.)

Deduccion, *Spa.* (dă-dook-thē-*ŏn.*) The natural progression of sounds.

Deductio, *Lat.* (dĕ-*dŭk*-shĭ-ō.) The ascending scale in the Aretinian form of solmisation.

Dedutttone, *It.* (dĕ-doot-tē-ō-nĕ.) A term applied by Guido to the rise of the voice in singing the scale.

Defettiva quinta, *It.* (dă-fēt-*tē*-vă *quĕn*-tă.) A defective or false fifth.

Deficiéndo, *It.* (dă-fē-tshē-*ăn*-dō.) Dying away.

Degli, *It.* (dăl-yē.) Of the.

Degré, *Fr.* (dĕ-*grā*.) A degree of the staff.

Degree. The step between two notes; each line and space of the staff.

Degree, conjunct. A degree in which two notes form the interval of a second.

Degree, disjunct. A degree in which two notes form a third or any greater interval.

Degree, half. A semitone.

Der Lehrer, *Ger.* (dār *lā*-rĕr.) The teacher.

Del, *It.* (dĕl.) Of the.

Délassement, *Fr.* (dā-lăss-mănh.) An easy and agreeable composition.

Deliberataménte, *It.* (dĕ-lē-bĕ-rā-tā-*măn*-tĕ.) }
Deliberáto, *It.* (dĕ-lē-bā-*rā*-tō.)
Deliberately.

Delicataménte, *It.* (dĕl-ē-kă-tā-*măn*-tĕ.) Delicately, smoothly.

Délicatesse, *Fr.* (dă-lē-kă-tĕss.) } Delicacy,
Delicatézza, *It.* (dĕl-ē-kă-*tăt*-ză.) } refined execution.

Delicatissimaménte, *It.* (dĕl-ē-kă-tēs-sē-mă-*măn*-tĕ.) } With extreme delicacy.
Delicatíssimo, *It.* (dĕl-ē-kă-*tĕs*-sē-mō.)

Delicáto, *It.* (dĕl-ē-*kă*-tō.) Delicately, smoothly.

Delirio, *It.* (dĕ-*lē*-rē-ō.) Frenzy, excitement.

Delivery. The act of controlling the respiration and using the vocal organs so as to produce a good tone.

Deliziosaménte, *It.* (dĕ-lēt-sē-ō-ză-*măn*-tĕ.) Deliciously, sweetly.

Dell', *It.* (dĕll.)
Della, *It.* (*dăl*-lă.)
Delle, *It.* (*dăl*-lĕ.) } Of the, by the, etc.
Dello, *It.* (*dăl*-lo.)

Delyn, *Wel.* (dē-*lün*.) The Welsh harp.

Dem, *Ger.* (dĕm.) To the.

Démancher, *Fr.* (dā-mănh-shā.) To change or alter the position of the hand; to shift on the violin, etc.; to cross hands on the pianoforte, making the left hand play the part of the right, and *vice versa.*

Demande, *Fr.* (dĕ-*mănhd*.) The question, or proposition of a fugue; called also, *dux,* or lead-in subject.

Demi, *Fr.* (dĕ-*mē*.) Half.

Demi baton, *Fr.* (dĕ-*mē bā*-tŏnh.) A breve rest.

Demi cadence, *Fr.* (dĕ-*mē* kă-*dănhs*.) A half cadence, or cadence on the dominant.

DERI

Demi ditone, *Fr.* (dĕ-*mē* dī-*tōn*.) A minor third.

Demi croche, *Fr.* (dĕ-*mē* krōsh.) A quaver, a half crotchet.

Demi legato. A style of playing indicated by dots placed under a legato mark showing that the hand is to be raised from the wrist and the fingers to be pressed with a slight accent on the keys, holding the notes about three-fourths their true time.

Demi jeu, *Fr.* (dĕ-*mē* jhū.) Same as *mezzo forte.*

Demi mesure, *Fr.* (dĕ-*mē* mĕ-*zūr*.) } A minim or half rest.
Demi pause, *Fr.* (dĕ-*mē* pōz.)

Demi quart de soupir, *Fr.* (dĕ-*mē* kär dŭh soo-*pēr*.) A demi-semiquaver rest.

Demi-semiquaver. A short note, equal in duration to one-half the semiquaver, made thus, or thus,

Demi-semiquaver rest. A mark of silence, equal in duration to a demi-semiquaver, made thus,

Demi soupir, *Fr.* (dĕ-*mē* soo-pēr.) A quaver rest.

Demi-ton, *Fr.* (dĕ-*mē*-tŏnh.) } An interval of a half tone.
Demi-tone. (dĕ-*mē*-tōn.)

Demitrule, *Gr.* (dĕm-ĭ-*troo*-lĕ.) Harvest hymn of the Greeks and Romans in honor of Ceres and Bacchus.

Dénoument, *Fr.* (dā-noo-mănh.) Conclusion, the catastrophe of an opera, play, etc.

Den ton aendern, *Ger.* (dĕn tōn *ăn*-dĕrn.) To beat time.

Den ton anfechten, *Ger.* (dĕn tōn *ăn*-fĕkh-t'n.)

Den ton angeben, *Ger.* (dĕn tōn *ăn*-gā-b'n.) To give the tone, to sound the key note.

Den ton nicht halten, *Ger.* (dĕn tōn nĭkht *hăl*-t'n.) To get out of tune.

Den ton verstärken, *Ger.* (dĕn tōn fŭr-*stăr*-k'n.) To swell the sound.

Den zapfenstreich trommeln, *Ger.* (dĕn tsā-pf'n-strīkh *trŏm*-mĕln.) To beat the tattoo.

De plus en plus vite, *Fr.* (dŭh plū zănh plū vēt.) More and more quickly.

Depressio, *It.* (dĕ-*prĕs*-sē-ō.) The fall of the hand in beating time.

Depression. The lowering of a tone.

Depression, chromatic. The depression of a tone by a chromatic sign.

De profundis, *Lat.* (dē prō-*fŭn*-dĭs.) One of the seven penitential psalms.

Der bezifferte bass, *Ger.* (dĕr bĕ-*tsĭf*-fĕrtĕ băss.) The figured bass.

Der bezolleneiner geige, *Ger.* (dĕ bĕ-tsŏl-lĕ-nī-nĕr ghī-ghĕ.) The strings of a violin.

Derbouka, *Ara.* (dĕr-boo-kă.) A musical instrument among the Arabs.

Der fiedelbogen, *Ger.* (dĕr *fē*-d'l-bō-g'n.) The bow of a violin.

Der f schlussel, *Ger.* (dĕr f shlüs-s'l.) The bass clef.

Dergleichen, *Ger.* (dĕr-*glī*-kh'n.) The same.

Dérivé, *Fr.* (dā-rē-vā.) Derivative.

Derivative chords. Chords derived from others by inversion.

PRONOUNCING MUSICAL DICTIONARY. 65

ă ale, ă add, ă arm, ē eve, ĕ end, I ice, ĭ ill, ō old, ŏ odd, ō dove, oo moon, ū lute, ŭ hut, ü French sound.

DERS

Der schüler, *Ger.* (dĕr shü̆-lĕr.) The scholar.
Der ton, *Ger.* (dĕr-tōn.) The tone.
Des, *Ger.* (dĕs.) The note D flat.
Désaccordé, *Fr.* (dāz-ăk-kŏr-dā.) Untuned; put out of tune.
Désaccorder, *Fr.* (dāz-ăk-kŏr-dā.) To untune, to put out of tune.
Descant. A composition containing several parts; harmony, extemporaneous or otherwise, sung or played to a given melody or theme.
Descant clef. The treble or soprano clef.
Descant, double. An arrangement of the parts of a composition that admits of the treble or any high part being converted into the bass, and *vice versa*.
Descant, figured. A form of descant consisting of a free and florid melody.
Descant, plain. Simple counterpoint.
Descend. To pass from a higher to a lower tone.
Descendant, *Fr.* (dĕ-sănh-dănh.) Descending.
Descendere, *It.* (dĕ-shĕn-dā-rĕ.) } To descend.
Descendre, *Fr.* (dĕ-sănhdr.)
Descender, *Spa.* (dĕ-sŏnh-dā.) Descending.
Descendre d'un ton, *Fr.* (dĕ-sănhdr d'ŭnh tōnh.) To sing a note lower.
Deschant, *Fr.* (dĕ-shānh.) Descant.
Des dur, *Gr.* (dĕs-door.) D flat major.
Desenclavijar, *Spa.* (dā-sĕn-klāv-ē-hăr.) To take the pins or pegs from an instrument.
Desentonacion, *Spa.* (dā-sĕn-tō-nă-tnē-ōn.) Dissonance, a harsh, rude tone of voice.
Desentonamiento, *Spa.* (dā-sĕn-tō-nă-mē-ăn-tō.) Dissonance, a harsh, rude tone of voice.
Descentono, *Spa.* (dā-sĕn-tō-nō.) Dissonance, a harsh, rude tone of voice.
Deshecha, *Spa.* (dĕ-shā-kā.) The burden of a song.
Desinvolturáto, *It.* (dā-zĕn-vōl-too-rā-tō.) See Disinvolturato.
Design. The general sketch or idea and arrangement of a musical composition.
Des moll, *Ger.* (dĕs mōll.) The key of D flat minor.
De soie filée d'argent, *Fr.* (dŭh sŏ-ă fē-lā d'är-zhānh.) Covered strings.
Desperazióne, *It.* (dĕs-pĕ-rā-tsē-ō-nĕ.) See Disperazione.
Dessauer marsch, *Ger.* (dĕs-sou-ĕr mărsh.) A famous instrumental march, one of the national airs of Germany.
Dessin, *Fr.* (dĕs-sănh.) The design or sketch of a composition.
Dessiner, *Fr.* (dĕs-sī-nā.) To make the sketch or design of a composition.
Dessus, *Fr.* (dĕs-sü.) The treble or upper part.
Destemple, *Spa.* (dĕs-tăm-plā.) Discordance.
Desterita, *It.* (dās-tĕr-ē-tā.) Dexterity.
Désto, *It.* (dās-tō.) Brisk, sprightly.
Déstra, *It.* (dās-trā.) Right; *dēstra māno*_r the right hand.
Détaché, *Fr.* (dā-tā-shā.) Detached, staccato.
Determinatíssimo, *It.* (dā-tĕr-mē-nā-tĭs-sē-mō.) Very determined, very resolutely.
Determináto, *It.* (dā-tĕr-mē-nā-tō.) Determined, resolute.
Determinazióne, *It.* (dā-tĕr-mē-nā-tsē-ō-nĕ.) Determination, resolution.

DIAP

Détonnation, *Fr.* (dā-tōnh-nă-sē-ōnh.) False intonation.
Détonner, *Fr.* (dā-tōnh-nā.) To sing or play out of tune.
Détto, *It.* (dāt-tō.) The same.
Deutlich, *Ger.* (doit-lĭkh.) Distinctly.
Deutsche flöte, *Ger.* (doit-shĕ flō-tĕ.) A German flute.
Deux, *Fr.* (dŭ.) Two.
Deux cors, *Fr.* (dŭ kŏr.) Two horns.
Deux fois, *Fr.* (dŭ fwä.) Twice.
Deuxieme, *Fr.* (dŭ-zĭ-ăm.) Second.
Deuxieme position, *Fr.* (dŭ-zĭ-ăm pō-zē-sĭ-ōnh.) The second position of the hand or fingers in playing the violin, etc.
Devóto, *It.* (dā-vō-tō.) Devout, religious.
Devozióne, *It.* (dā-vō-tsē-ō-nĕ.) Devotion, religious feeling.
Dextra, *Lat.* (dĕx-trā.) }
Dextre, *Fr.* (dĕxtr.) } The right hand.
Dextræ, *Lat. pl.* (dĕx-trē.) Name given by the Romans to those flutes played with the right hand. Those played with the left were called *sinistræ*.
Dhu, *Hin.* (doo.) A syllable applied to the sixth note of the Hindoo scale in solfaing.
Di, *It.* (dē.) Of, with, for, etc.
Dia, *Gr.* (dĭ-ā.) Through, throughout.
Diachisma, (dĭ-ā-kĭs-mā.) An interval produced by the division of another interval.
Diaconicon, *Gr.* (dĭ-ā-kŏn-ĭ-kŏn.) The set of collects chanted in the service of the Greek church.
Diadrom. The tremulance or variation of sounds.
Diafoni suoni, *It.* (dē-ā-fō-nē swō-nē.) Discordant sounds.
Diagrámma, *It.* (dē-ā-grăm-mā.) The ancient Greek scale or system of sounds.
Dialogue. A composition in which two parts or voices respond alternately to each other.
Diálogo, *It.* (dē-ā-lō-gō.) } A dialogue.
Dialogue, *Fr.* (dē-ā-lōg.) }
Diána, *It.* (dē-ā-nā.) } The reveille; the beat
Diane, *Fr.* (dĭ-ăn-ŭh.) } of drums at daybreak.
Diap. An abbreviation of *diapason*.
Diapase, *Gr.* (dē-ā-pā-sĕ.) Diapason.
Diapason, *Lat.* (dē-ā-pā-sŏn.) } *The whole oc-*
Diapason, *Eng.* (dĭ-ā-pā-sŏn.) } *tave.* 2. Among musical instrument makers, a rule or scale by which they adjust the pipes of organs, the holes of flutes, etc., in order to give the proper proportion for expressing the tones and semitones. 3. Certain important stops and registers in the organ.
Diapason, bis. Twice through the octave; a double octave.
Diapason cum diapente, *Gr.* An *octave* and *fifth;* the interval of a twelfth.
Diapason cum diatessaron, *Gr.* An *octave and fourth;* the interval of a *eleventh*.
Diapason stop, open. An organ stop, the pipes of which are open at the top and generally made of metal.
Diapason stops. Stops that run through the whole register of the keyboard of an organ.
Diapason stop, stopped. An organ stop having its pipes closed at their upper end with a wooden plug by which it is tuned.

5

ă *ale,* ă *add,* ä *arm,* ĕ *eve,* ĕ *end,* ī *ice,* ĭ *ill,* ō *old,* ŏ *odd,* ô *dove,* oo *moon,* ū *lute,* ŭ *but,* ü *French sound.*

DIAP

Diapente, *Gr.* (dē-ä-pĕn-tē.) A perfect *fifth;* also, an organ stop.
Diapente col ditono, *Gr.* (dē-ä-pĕn-tē kōl dī-tō-nō.) A major seventh.
Diapente col semiditono. *Gr.* (dē-ä-pĕn-tē kōl sĕm-I-dī-tō-nō.) A minor seventh.
Diapentisare, *Gr.* (dē-ä-pĕn-tī-sä-rĕ.) To *descant,* or modulate in fifths.
Diaphonie. (dē-äf-ō-nē.) } Clear, transparent;
Diaphony. (dē-äf-ō-ny.) } two sounds heard together.
Diaphonics, *Gr.* (dē-ä-fŏn-īks.) The science of refracted sounds.
Diaschisma, *Gr.* (dē-äs-kĭs-mä.) An interval forming the half of a minor semitone.
Diastaltic, *Gr.* (dē-äs-tăl-tĭk.) Dilating; a term applied by the ancient Greeks to the major third, major sixth, and major seventh because they are extended or dilated intervals.
Diastema, *Gr.* (dē-äs-tē-mä.) An interval, a space.
Diastolik, *Gr.* (dē-äs-tŏl-ĭk.) The system of musical division and periods.
Diatessaron, *Gr.* (dē-ä-tĕs-sä-rŏn.) A perfect fourth.
Diatonic, *Gr.* (dē-ä-tŏn-ĭk.) *Naturally;* proceeding in the order of the degrees of the natural scale, including tones and semitones.
Diatonic flute. A flute capable of producing the various shades or differences of pitch of the major and minor scales.
Diatonic melody. A melody in which no tones foreign to the key are used.
Diatonico, *It.* (dē-ä-tŏn-ē-kō.)
Diatonique, *Fr.* (dē-ä-tōnh-nēk.) } Diatonic.
Diatonisch, *Ger.* (dī-ä-tŏn-ĭsh.)
Diatoniquement, *Fr.* (dē-ä-tōnh-nēk-mänh.) Diatonically.
Diatonic scale. The different gradations of tone of the scale or gamut arranged in proper order in conformity to some particular key.
Diatonic scale, major. Where the semitones fall between the third and fourth and seventh and eighth both in ascending and descending.
Diatonic scale, minor. That in which the semitones occur between the second and third, and seventh and eighth ascending, and between the fifth and sixth and second and third descending.
Diatoni, *Lat. pl.* (dē-ä-tō-nī.) The natural or diatonic series of notes; the diatonic scale.
Diatonum intensum, *Lat.* (dē-ä-tō-nŭm ĭn-tĕn-sŭm.) The name given to the proportions of musical intervals in Ptolemy's system.
Diazeutic, *Gr.* (dē-ä-zoo-tĭk.) In the ancient Greek system, a tone located between two fourths, and which being joined to either forms a fifth.
Diazieuxis, *Gr.* (dē-ä-zoox-ĭs.) Division; a name given by the ancients to the tone which separates two tetrachords.
Dibattitojo, *It.* (dē-bät-tē-tō-yō.) A cithern or lute.
Di bel nuóvo, *It.* (dē-bĕl noo-ō-vō.) Again.
Di bravúra, *It.* (dē brä-voo-rä.) In a brilliant, florid style.
Dicélie, *It.* (dē-tshä-lē-ĕ.) Farces.
Dicht, *Dut.* (dĭkt.) A ditty, a little song.

DIEW

Di chiáro, *It.* (dē kē-ä-rō.) Clearly.
Dichord, *Ger.* (dī kŏrd.) Two stringed lyre: see *Bichord.*
Dichten, *Ger.* (dĭhk-t'n.) To compose metrically.
Dichter, *Ger.* (dĭhk-tĕr.) A poet, a minstrel.
Di cólto, *It.* (dē kōl-tō.) At once, instantly, suddenly.
Didactic. That which is calculated to instruct.
Didactic exercises. Scale exercises and compositions designed to give a correct knowledge of musical execution.
Die vierte, *Ger.* (dē fēr-tĕ.) The subdominant.
Die erste violine, *Ger.* (dē ärs-tĕ fī-ō-lē-nĕ.) The first violin.
Die gesammten stimmen, *Ger.* (dē ghĕ-säm-t'n stĭm-m'n.) The chorus.
Die grosse bassgeige, *Ger.* (dē grōs-sĕ bäss-ght-ghĕ.) The double bass.
Die grosse sechste, *Ger.* (dē grōs-sĕ sĕx-tĕ.) The major sixth.
Die grosse terze, *Ger.* (dē grōs-sĕ tär-tsĕ.) The major third.
Die kleine bassgeige, *Ger.* (dē klī-nĕ bäss-ght-ghĕ.) The violincello.
Die kleine sechste, *Ger.* (dē klī-nĕ sĕx-tĕ.) The minor sixth.
Die kleine terze, *Ger.* (dē klī-nĕ tär-tsĕ.) The minor third.
Die note hervorgehoben, *Ger.* (dē nō-tĕ här-fōr-ghĕ-hō-b'n.) The note must be accented.
Diesáre, *It.* (dē-ä-zä-rĕ.) } To raise the pitch
Diéser, *Fr.* (dī-ä-zä.) } of a note, either at the signature or in the course of a composition by means of a sharp.
Diese, *Fr.* (dī-äz.) A sharp, (♯).
Diesi, *Spa.* (dī-ä-zē.) The smallest division of a tone.
Dies iræ, *Lat.* (dī-äz ē-rä.) A principal movement in a requiem.
Diésis, *Gr. and It.* (dē-ä-sĭs.) } A quarter of a
Diesis, *Fr.* (dī-ä-sĭs.) } tone; half a semitone; a small interval used in the mathematical computation of intervals. The ancient Greeks applied it to the smallest interval used in their music. In modern music it means a *sharp.*
Diesis chromatica, *Gr.* (dī-ä-sĭs krō-mät-ĭ-kä.) The third part or fraction of a whole tone.
Diesis enharmonica, *Gr.* (dī-ä-sĭs ĕn-här-mŏn-ĭ-kä.) A quarter tone. As an illustration, the difference between G♯ and A♭, or between D♯ and E♭, on the violin.
Diesis magna, *Gr.* (dī-ä-sĭs mäg-nä.) A semitone.
Dies, music. Steel punches for the purpose of stamping music plates.
Die stimme einer geige, *Ger.* (dē stĭm-mĕ ī-ner ghī-ghĕ.) Sounding post of a violin.
Die stimmen ausschreiben, *Ger.* (dē stĭm-m'n ous-shrī-b'n.) To copy the parts.
Diestra, *Spa.* (dē-äs-trä.) The right hand.
Die tiefe weiberstimme, *Ger.* (dē tē-fĕ vī-bĕr-stĭm-mĕ.) Counter tenor. Alto.
Der ton-abstand, *Ger.* (dĕr tōn-äb-ständ.) To be played staccato.
Die walze, *Ger.* (dē vält-sĕ.) The barrel of a hand organ.

ă als, ă add, ă arm, ē eve, ĕ end, Ī ice, ĭ ill, ō old, ŏ odd, ô dove, oo moon, ū lute, ŭ but, ü French sound.

DIEZ | DIRE

Diese, *Fr.* (dĭ-ăz.) A sharp, (♯).
Diese, double, *Fr.* (dĭ-ăz doobL.) A double sharp, (𝄪).
Die zeugmenon, *Gr.* (dĕ zoog-mĕ-nŏn.) The third tetrachord disjoined from the second.
Diezeutic, *Gr.* (dĕ-zoo-tĭk.) See *Diazeutic.*
Die zunge einer hoboe, *Ger.* (dĕ tsoon-ghĕ ī-nĕr hō-bō-ĕ.) The reed or mouth-piece of a hautboy.
Diff, *Tur.* (dĕff.) An oriental instrument resembling the tambourine.
Differentia, *Gr.* (dĭf-fĕ-rĕn-shĭ-ă.) A ratio measuring an interval.
Difficile, *It.* (dĕf-fē-tshĕ-lĕ.) Difficult.
Di gala, *It.* (dĕ gä-lä.) Merrily, cheerfully.
Digital exercises. Exercises for strengthening the fingers and rendering them independent of each other.
Dignità, *It.* (dĕn-yĕ-tä.) ⎫ Dignity, gran-
Dignitàde, *It.* (dĕn-yĕ-tä-dĕ.) ⎬ deur, greatness.
Dignitàte, *It.* (dĕn-yĕ-tä-tĕ.) ⎭
Di grádo, *It.* (dĕ-grä-dō.) By *degrees;* step by step; in opposition to *di salto.*
Di grádo ascendente, *It.* (dĕ grä-dō ä-shĕn-dän-tĕ.) A series of notes of regular ascent.
Di grádo descendente, *It.* (dĕ grä-dō dä-shĕn-dän-tĕ.) A series of notes descending regularly.
Digressing. Moving from one key into another to return to the first.
Digressione, *It.* (dē-grĕs-sē-ō-nĕ.) A deviation from the regular course of a piece.
Diiambus, (dē-ĭ-ăm-bŭs.) A metrical foot consisting of two iambic feet.
Di leggiére, *It.* (dĕ lĕd-jĕ-ā-rĕ.) ⎫ Easily,
Di leggiéro, *It.* (dĕ lĕd-jĕ-ā-rō.) ⎬ lightly.
Dilettant, *Ger.* (dĕ-lē-tănt.) ⎫ A lover of art;
Dilettánte, *It.* (dĕ-lĕt-tän-tĕ.) ⎬ an amateur who composes or performs without making music a profession.
Dilettársi di musica, *It.* (dĕ-lĕt-tär-sē dē moo-zē-kä.) To love music.
Dilettosamente, *It.* (dĕ-lĕt-tō-zä-mān-tĕ.) Agreeably, pleasantly.
Dilicataménte, *It.* (dĕ-lē-kä-tä-mān-tĕ.) Delicately, softly; see *Delicataménte.*
Dilicatézza, *It.* (dĕ-lē-kä-tāt-sä.) Delicateness, softness, neatness.
Dilicatissimaménte, *It.* (dĕ-lē-kä-tēs-sē-mä-mān-tĕ.) With extreme softness and delicacy.
Dilicatíssimo, *It.* (dĕ-lē-kä-tēs-sē-mō.) With extreme softness and delicacy.
Dilicáto, *It.* (dĕ-lē-kä-tō.) Soft, delicate.
Diligénza, *It.* (dĕ-lē-jän-tsä.) Diligence.
Diligénza, con, *It.* (dĕ-lē-jän-tsä kōn.) In a diligent and careful manner.
Dilúdium, *Lat.* (dĭ-lū-dĭ-ŭm.) An interlude.
Dilúendo, *It.* (dē-lōo-än-dō.) Diminishing, a gradual dying away of the tone until it is extinct.
Dim. ⎫ Abbreviations of *diminuéndo.*
Dimin. ⎭
Dimeter. A poetic measure of four feet; a series of two metres.
Diminished. This word is applied to intervals or chords, which are less than minor or perfect intervals.

Diminished chords. Chords that are composed of diminished intervals.
Diminished fifth. An interval containing two whole tones and two semitones.
Diminished fourth. One whole tone and two semitones.
Diminished imitation. A style of imitation in which the answer is given in notes of less value than that of the subject.
Diminished intervals. Those which are one semitone less than minor or perfect intervals.
Diminished octave. One semitone less than a full octave.
Diminished seventh. One semitone less than a minor seventh.
Diminished sixth. One semitone less than a minor sixth.
Diminished third. One semitone less than a minor third.
Diminished triad. A chord composed of the minor third, and the diminished or imperfect fifth.
Diminucion, *Spa.* (dĭm-ē-noo-thē-ōn.) A diminishing.
Diminué, *Fr.* (dĭ-mĕn-oo-ā.) Diminished: see *diminuito.*
Diminuéndo, *It.* (dē-mē-noo-än-dō.) Diminishing gradually the intensity or power of the tone.
Diminuer, *Fr.* (dĭ-mē-noo-ā.) To diminish.
Diminuir, *Spa.* (dē-mē-noo-ēr.) To diminish, as applied to intervals, chords, etc.
Diminuito, *It.* (dē-mĭ-noo-ē-tō.) ⎫ Diminished,
Diminúto, *Lat.* (dē-mē-noo-tō.) ⎬ lessened, in speaking of intervals or chords.
Diminútio, *Lat.* (dĭm-ĭ-nū-shĭ-ō.) Diminution.
Diminution. In counterpoint this means the imitation of a given subject or theme, in notes of shorter length, or duration; in opposition to *augmentation.*
Diminuzióne, *It.* (dē-mē-noo-tsē-ō-nĕ.) Diminution.
Di molto, *It.* (dĕ mōl-tō.) *Very much;* an expression which serves to augment the meaning of the word to which it is applied.
D in alt, *It.* The fifth note in alt; the twelfth above the G. or treble clef note.
D in altíssimo, *It.* The fifth note in altissimo; the twelfth above G in alt.
D'inganno, *It.* (d'ĕn-gän-nō.) An unexpected ending.
Di nétto, *It.* (dĕ nāt-tō.) Neatly, cleverly.
Di nuóvo, *It.* (dĕ noo-ō-vō.) Anew, once more, again.
Dioxia. A perfect fifth; the fifth tone, or sound.
Di peso, *It.* (dĕ pā-zō.) At once.
Diphonium. A vocal duet.
Di pósta, *It.* (dĕ pōs-tä.) At once.
Di quiéto, *It.* (dĕ quē-ā-tō.) Quietly.
Direct. A mark sometimes placed at the end of a staff to indicate the note next following, (⤳)
Directeur, *Fr.* (dĭ-rĕk-tŭr.) The director or conductor of a musical performance.
Direct intervals. Intervals reckoned from their fundamental tones upward, on which any kind of harmony may be produced.
Direct motion. Similar or parallel motion; the parts rising or falling in the same direction.

ă ale, ă add, ä arm, ĕ eve, ĕ end, ī ice, ĭ ill, ō old, ŏ odd, ô dove, oo moon, ū lute, ŭ but, ü French sound.

DIRE

Director. The conductor or manager of a musical performance.
Directrice, *Fr.* (dĭ-rĕk-trĕss.) A female director or manager.
Direct turn. A turn consisting of four notes, viz., the note above that over which the sign is placed, the principal note, Written. Played. the note below it, and ending with the principal note,
Dirétto, *It.* (dē-rāt-tō.) Directed, conducted.
Direttóre, *It.* (dĕ-rĕt-tō-rĕ.) A director: see *directeur*.
Direttrice, *It.* (dĕ-rĕt-trē-tshĕ.) See *directrice*.
Direttore della musica, *It.* (dĕ-rĕt-tō-rĕ dāl-lā moo-zē-kā.) A musical director.
Dirge. A musical composition, either vocal or instrumental, designed to be performed at a funeral or in commemoration of the dead.
Diritta, *It.* (dē-rēt-tā.) Direct; straight on, in ascending or descending intervals.
Dirizzatóre, *It.* (dē-rēt-tsā-tō-rĕ.) A director.
Dis, *Ger.* (dēz.) The note D♯.
Disaccentáto, *It.* (dēz-āt-tshān-tā-tō.) Unaccented.
Disaccordáre, *It.* (dēz-āk-kōr-dā-rĕ.) To be out of tune.
Di salto, *It.* (dē sāl-tō.) By *leaps* or by *skips*; in opposition to *di grádo*.
Disarmonía, *It.* (dēz-ār-mō-nē-ā.) Discord, want of harmony.
Disarmonichíssimo, *It.* (dēz-ār-mō-nē-kēs-sē-mō.) Extremely discordant.
Disarmónico, *It.* (dēz-ār-mō-nē-kō.) Inharmonious, discordant.
Discant. The upper part; see also, *descant*.
Discant schlüssel, *Ger.* (dīz-känt shlü-s'l.) The soprano; the C clef placed upon the first line — the note upon that line being called C. It is seldom used now.
Discantar, *Spa.* (dēz-kän-tär.) To discant, to sing in parts, to chant.
Discante, *Spa.* (dēs-kän-tĕ.) The upper part; concert of stringed instruments; a small guitar.
Discant-geige, *Ger.* (dĭs-känt ghī-ghĕ.) An obsolete term for the violin.
Discantist, *Ger.* (dĭs-kän-fĭst.) Treble, or soprano singer.
Discant-saite, *Ger.* (dĭs-känt sī-tĕ.) Treble string.
Discant-sänger, *Ger.* (dĭs-känt säng-ĕr.) Treble, or soprano singer.
Discantus, *Lat.* (dĭs-kăn-tŭs.) Descant; singing in parts; a piece of music in parts.
Discendere, *It.* (dē-shān-dā-rĕ.) To descend.
Discépola, *It.* (dē-shā-pō-lā.) A female pupil.
Discépolo, *It.* (dē-shā-pō-lō.) Disciple, pupil, scholar.
Disciólto, *It.* (dē-shē-ōl-tō.) Skillful, dexterous.
Disconcórdia, *It.* (dēs-kōn-kōr-dē-ā.) Discord.
Discord. A dissonant or inharmonious combination of sounds. In harmony it requires to be resolved into a concord or proceed to a concord in order to satisfy the ear.
Discordant. A term applied to all discordant or inharmonious sounds.
Discordánte, *It.* (dēs-kōr-dān-tĕ.) Discordant.

DISS

Discordanteménte, *It.* (dēs-kōr-dān-tĕ-mān-tĕ.) Discordantly.
Discordánza, *It.* (dēs-kōr-dān-tsā.) Discord.
Discordáre, *It.* (dēs-kōr-dā-rĕ.) } To be out
Discorder, *Fr.* (dīs-kōr-dā.) } of tune.
Discorde, *Fr.* (dīs-kōrd.)
Discordia, *Lat.* (dīs-kōr-dī-ā.) } Discord.
Discord, prepared. Where the ear has been prepared for the discordant note in a previous concord.
Discréto, *It.* (dēs-krā-tō.) Discreetly.
Discrezióne, *It.* (dēs-krāt-tsē-ō-nĕ.) Discretion, judgment, moderation.
Dis-diapason, *Gr.* (dēz dī-ā-pā-sōn.) A double octave; an interval of two octaves; a fifteenth.
Dis dur, *Ger.* (dĭs door.) The key of D♯ major.
Diseurs, *Fr. pl.* (dēz-ûr.) A name formerly given to French itinerant vocalists who recited ballads and romances.
Disharmonie, *Ger.* (dĭs-hār-mō-nē.) Disharmony.
Disharmonisch, *Ger.* (dĭs-hār-mō-nĭsh.) Unharmonious.
Disharmony. Discord, want of harmony.
Disinvólto, *It.* (dēz-ēn-vōl-tō.) }
Disinvolturáto, *It.* (dēz-ēn-vōl-too-rā-tō.) } Off hand, bold, not forced, naturally.
Disjunct. A term applied by the Greeks to those tetrachords where the lowest sound of the upper one was one degree higher than the acutest sound of the one immediately beneath it.
Disjunct degree. Where two notes form the interval of a third or any greater interval.
Disjunct succession. A succession of sounds passing from one degree to another, without touching the intermediate degrees.
Dis moll, *Ger.* (dĭs mōl.) The key of D sharp minor.
Disonancia, *Spa.* (dēz-ō-nän-thē-ä.) } Dissonance.
Disonanza, *It.* (dēz-ō-nän-tsä.) }
Disonare, *It.* (dēz-ō-nä-rĕ.) To sound discordantly.
Di soppiano, *It.* (dē sōp-pē-ā-nō.) Low; with a low voice.
Di sopra, *It.* (dē sō-prā.) Above.
Disperáto, *It.* (dēz-pĕ-rā-tō.) *Despaired* of; with desperation.
Disperazióne, *It.* (dēz-pĕ-rāt-sē-ō-nĕ.) Despair, desperation.
Dispersed harmony. Harmony in which the notes forming the various chords are separated from each other by wide intervals.
Dispondee. In Greek and Latin poetry, a double spondee, comprising four long syllables.
Disposition. The arrangement of the stops in an organ, disposing them according to power, quality of tone, etc.
Disruption of chords. Harmonic figuration; the progression of a chord from one tone to another of the same chord, thence passing in the same way through successive different chords.
Dissolution. A term used in ancient Greek music, when a sound in the enharmonic genus is lowered three diescs.
Dissonance. A discord; an interval or chord displeasing to the ear and requiring to be fol-

ă *ale,* ă *add,* ă *arm,* ĕ *eve,* ĕ *end,* ī *ice,* ĭ *ill,* ō *old,* ŏ *odd,* ô *dove,* oo *moon,* ū *lute,* ŭ *but,* ū *French sound.*

DISS

lowed by another in which the dissonant note is resolved.
Dissonant. An inharmonious combination of sounds.
Dissonant chords. All the chords except the perfect concord and its derivatives.
Dissonant, *Fr.* (dĕs-sō-nänh.) } Dissonant,
Dissonánte, *It.* (dĕs-sō-nän-tĕ.) } out of tune, discordant.
Dissonant sixths. The diminished and superfluous sixths.
Dissonanz, *Ger.* (dĭs-sō-*nänts*.) } Dissonance;
Dissonánza, *It.* (dĕs-sō-*nän*-tsä.) } discord.
Dissonáre, *It.* (dĕs-sō-*nä*-rĕ.) } To sound
Dissoner, *Fr.* (dĕs-sō-*nä*.) } out of tune;
Dissoniren, *Ger.* (dĭs-sō-*nē*-r'n.) } to be discordant.
Dissoni suoni, *It.* (dĕs-sō-nē swō-nē.) Inharmonious sounds; discords.
Distance. The interval between any two sounds differing in pitch.
Distánza, *It.* (dĕz-tän-tsä.) Distance, space between.
Distich. A couplet; a couple of verses, or poetic lines making complete sense.
Distico, *Spa.* (dĕs-tē-kō.) A distich.
Distinti suoni, *It. pl.* (dĕs-*tĕn*-tē swō-nē.) Distinct sounds.
Distínto, *It.* (dĕs-*tēn*-tō.) Clear, distinct.
Distique, *Fr.* (dĭs-*tēk*.) A distich.
Distonáre, *It.* (dĕs-tō-nä-rĕ.) To be out of tune.
Distoniren, *Ger.* (dĭs-tō-*nē*-r'n.) To get out of tune; to produce discord either in singing or playing.
Distrop, *It.* (dĕz-trŏp.) A song of two stanzas
Distune. To throw out of tune (obsolete).
Di testa, *It.* (dē-*tās*-tä.) Of the head, in speaking of the voice.
Dithyrambe, *Fr.* (dē-tĭ-*rähmb*.) } A song or
Dithyrambe, *Ger.* (dē-tĭ-*räm*-bĕ.) } ode sung in ancient times in honor of *Bacchus;* a wild rhapsodical composition.
Dithyrambic, *Gr.* (dē-thĭ-*räm*-bĭk.) A song in honor of Bacchus; any poem written in a wild rhapsodical manner.
Dithyrambique, *Fr.* (dē-tĭ-ränh-*bēk*.) }
Dithyrambisch, *Ger.* (dē-tĭ-*räm*-bĭsh.) } Dithyrambic.
Dithyrambus, (dĭ-thĭ-*räm*-bŭs.) See *Dithyrambe.*
Ditirámbica, *It.* (dē-tē-*räm*-bē-kä.) } Dithy-
Ditirámbico, *It.* (dē-tē-*räm*-bē-kō.) } rambic.
Ditirámbo, *It.* (dē-tē-*räm*-bo.) See *Dithyrambe.*
Díto, *It.* (dē-tō.) The finger.
Dito grósso, *It.* (dē-tō grōs-sō.) The thumb.
Diton, *Fr.* (dē-tōnh.) } Of two parts or
Ditone, *Gr.* (dē-tōn.) } tones; a major third
Ditono, *It.* (dē-tō-nō.) } or interval of two
Ditonus, *Lat.* (dĭ-tō-nŭs.) } whole tones.
Ditrochee. A double trochee; a foot made up of two trochees.
Dittanaclasis. An instrument of the harpsichord and pianoforte class.
Ditty. A song, a sonnet; a little poem to be sung.
Divan, *Per.* (dē-vän.) Among the Persians, a term applied to a series of poems with the distichs

DOL

ending in every letter successively; a collection of the writings of a single author.
Diverberation. A sounding through.
Diverbia, *Lat.* (dī-vĕr-bĭ-ä.) } A musical dia-
Divérbio, *It.* (dē-*vär*-bē-ō.) } logue, often used by the ancients to enrich their drama.
Divertiménto, *It.* (dē-vĕr-tē-*män*-tō.) A short, light composition, written in a pleasing and familiar style.
Divertissement, *Fr.* (dī-vĕr-*tēss*-mänh.) A series of airs and dances resembling a short ballet, introduced between the acts or at the conclusion of an opera; also, a composition in a light and pleasing style.
Divided accompaniment. A form of accompaniment in which the intervals are taken by both hands, always maintaining the distance required by the rules.
Divinare. A stopped organ register of a beautiful tone.
Divisi, *It.* (dē-vē-zē.) Divided, separated. In orchestral parts this word implies that one-half the performers must play the upper notes and the others the lower notes. The term has a similar meaning when it occurs in vocal music.
Division. A series of notes sung to one syllable. Formerly this word implied a sort of variation upon a given subject.
Division, *It.* (dĭ-vē-zē-ōnh.) A double bar.
Division du temps, *Fr.* (dĭ-vē-zē-ōnh dŭ tänh.) Time table.
Division marks. Figures with a curved line above them, showing the number of equal parts into which the notes are divided ♩ ♩ ♩ ♩, etc.
Divotaménte, *It.* (dē-vō-tä-*män*-tĕ.) } Devoutly, in a solemn style.
Divóto, *It.* (dē-vō-tō.) }
Divozione, *It.* (dē-vot-sē-ō-nĕ.) Devotion, religious feeling.
Dix huitiéme, *Fr.* (dēz wē-tĭ-*äm*.) The *eighteenth,* or double octave to the fourth.
Dixiéme, *Fr.* (dēz-ĭ-*äm*.) The *tenth,* or octave to the third.
Dix-neuvieme, *Fr.* (dēz nŭv-ĭ-*äm*.) The *nineteenth,* or double octave to the fifth.
Dix-septieme, *Fr.* (dēz sĕt-ĭ-*äm*.) The *seventeenth,* or the double octave to the third.
Dizain, *Fr.* (dēz-änh.) Stanza of ten verses.
D. M. The initials of *Destra Máno.*
D moll, *Ger.* (dä mŏll.) The key of D minor.
Do, *It.* (dō.) A syllable applied to the first note of a scale in solfaing.
Doble, *Spa.* (dō-blĕ.) A step in a Spanish dance.
Dochimus, *Lat.* (dō-kĭ-mŭs.) A metrical foot consisting of five syllables.
Docke, *Ger.* (dō-kĕ.) The *jack* of a harpsichord.
Doctor of music. The highest musical degree conferred by the universities.
Dodedachordon, *Gr.* (dō-dĕd-ä-*kŏr*-dŏn.) The twelve ancient modes.
Dóglia, *It.* (dŏl-yĕ-ä.) Grief, affliction, sadness.
Doigt, *It.* (dwä.) Finger.
Doigté, *Fr.* (dwä-tä.) Fingered.
Doigter, *Fr.* (dwä-tä.) To finger; the art of fingering any instrument.
Doigts fixes, *Fr.* (dwä fēk-sĕ.) Fixed fingers.
Dol. An abbreviation of *dolce.*

ă ale, ă add, ä arm, e eve, ĕ end, ī ice, ĭ ill, ō old, ŏ odd, ô dove, oo moon, ū lute, ŭ but, ü French sound.

DOLC

Dolcan. An organ stop of 8 feet scale, the pipes of which are of larger diameter at the top than at the bottom.
Dólce, *It.* (dōl-tshĕ.) Sweetly, softly, delicately.
Dólce con gústo, *It.* (dōl-tshĕ kŏn goos-tō.) Softly, sweetly, with taste and expression.
Dólce e cantabile, *It.* (dōl-tshĕ ā kän-tā-bē-lĕ.) Sweet, soft, in singing style.
Dólce e lusingándo, *It.* (dōl-tshĕ ā loo-sēn-gän-dō.) In a soft and insinuating style.
Dólce e piacevolménte espressivo, *It.* (dōl-tshĕ ā pē-ā-tshĕ-vŏl-män-tĕ äs-prĕs-sē-vō.) Soft and with pleasing expression.
Dólce ma marcáto, *It.* (dōl-tshĕ mä mär-kä-tō.) Soft and delicate but marked and accented.
Dólce maniéra, *It.* (dōl-tshĕ mä-nē-ā-rä.) A delicate and expressive manner of delivery.
Dolceménte, *It.* (dōl-tshĕ-mān-tĕ.) Sweetly, gently, softly.
Dolcézza, *It.* (dōl-tshāt-zä.) Sweetness, softness of tone.
Dolciáno, *It.* (dōl-tshĕ-ā-nō.)) A small bassoon,
Dolcíno, *It.* (dōl-tshē-nō.) formerly much used as a tenor to the hautboy.
Dolcicanóro, *It.* (dōl-tshē-kä-nō-rō.) Harmonious.
Dolcimello, *It.* (dōl-tshē-mäl-lō.) A dulcimer.
Dolciss. An abbreviation of *dolcissimo.*
Dolcíssimo, *It.* (dōl-tshēs-sē-mō.) With extreme sweetness and delicacy.
Dolemment, *Fr.* (dō-lĕm-mänh.) Dolefully, mournfully.
Dolent, *Fr.* (dō-länh.)) Sorrowful, mournful,
Dolénte, *It.* (dō-län-tĕ.) pathetic.
Dolentemént e, *It.* (dō-län-tĕ-män-tĕ.) Sorrowfully, mournfully.
Dolentíssimo, *It.* (dō-län-tēs-sē-mō.) With extreme sadness; with very pathetic and mournful expression.
Dolóre, *It.* (dō-lō-rĕ.) Grief, sorrow.
Dolorosaménte, *It.* (dō-lō-rō-zä-män-tĕ.))
Doloróso, *It.* (dō-lō-rō-zō.)
Dolorously, sorrowfully, sadly.
Dolzaína, *It.* (dōlt-sä-ē-nä.)) The hautboy.
Dolzaíno, *It.* (dōlt-sä-ē-nō.)
Dom, *Ger.* (dōm.) A cathedral.
Dom-chor, *Ger.* (dōm-kōr.) The cathedral choir.
Dominant. The name applied by theorists to the *fifth* note of the scale.
Dominant chord. A chord found on the dominant or *fifth* note of the scale and introducing a perfect cadence.
Dominante, *Fr.* (dŏm-ī-nänht.)) The dom-
Dominante, *It.* (dŏm-ī-nän-tĕ.) inant.
Dominant harmony. Harmony on the dominant or *fifth* of the key.
Dominant section. A section terminating on the common chord of the dominant.
Domine salvum fac, *Lat.* (dō-mī-nĕ säl-vüm fäk.) A prayer for the reigning sovereign, sung after mass.
Dominicali psalmi, *Lat.* (dō-mī-nē-kä-lē säl-mō.) Certain psalms of the Roman Catholic church, sung in the vespers.)
Dom-kirche, *Ger.* (dōm kēr-khĕ.) A cathedral.
Dona nóbis pacem, *Lat.* (dō-nä nō-bīs pä-sĕm.) The concluding movement of the mass.

DOTT

Dónna, *It.* (dŏn-nä.) Lady; applied to the principal female singers in an opera.
Dónne, *It. pl.* (dŏn-nĕ) Ladies: see *dónna.*
Donner du cor, *Fr.* (dŏn-nä dü kōr.) To blow a French horn.
Donner une serenade, *Fr.* (dŏn-nä ün sĕr-ĕn-äd.) To serenade.
Dópo, *It.* (dō-pō.) After.
Doppel, *Ger.* (dŏp-p'l.) Double.
Doppel-be, *Ger.* (dŏp-p'l bä.) A double flat, (♭♭) lowering a note two semitones.
Doppelblasebass. *Ger.* (dŏp-p'l-blä-zĕ-bäss.) A counter bassoon.
Doppel-flöte, *Ger.* (dŏp-p'l flö-tĕ.) *Double flute.* a stop in an organ the pipes of which have two mouths.
Doppel-fuge, *Ger.* (dŏp-p'l-foo-ghe.) Double fugue.
Doppelgedeckt, *Ger.* (dŏp-p'l-gĕ-dĕkt.) Double-stopped diapason.
Doppelgeige, *Ger.* (dŏp-p'l-ghī-ghĕ.) An organ stop. See *Viola d'Amour.*
Doppelgriffe, *Ger.* (dŏp-p'l-grĭf-fĕ.) Double stop on the violin, etc.
Doppelkreuz, *Ger.* (dŏp-p'l-kroitz.) A double sharp, ⤪, or ×, raising a note two semitones.
Doppelschlag, *Ger.* (dŏp-p'l-shläg.) A mordent.
Doppelschritt, *Ger.* (dŏp-p'l-shrit.) A quick march.
Doppelt, *Ger.* (dŏp-p'lt.) Double.
Doppelten noten, *Ger.* (dŏp-p'l-tĕn nō-t'n.) Double notes.
Doppelter trillerlauf, *Ger.* (dŏp-p'l-tĕr trĭl-lĕr-louf.) Double cadence.
Doppelt gestrichene note, *Ger.* (dŏp-pĕlt ghĕ-strī-kh'nĕ nō-tĕ.) A semiquaver.
Doppia lyra, *It.* (dŏp-pē-ä lē-rä.) A double lyre.
Dóppio, *It.* (dŏp-pē-ō.) Double, twofold; sometimes indicating that octaves are to be played.
Dóppio moviménto, *It.* (dŏp-pē-ō mō-vē-män-tō.) Double movement or time, that is, *as fast again.*
Dóppio pedále, *It.* (dŏp-pē-ō pĕ-dä-lĕ.) Playing a bass passage on the organ with the pedals moving in octaves, etc.; that is, using both feet at the same time.
Dóppio tempo, *It.* (dŏp-pē-ō tĕm-pō.) Double time, *as fast again.*
Dóppo, *It.* (dŏp-pō.) After: see *Dópo.*
Dorian, *Gr.* (dō-rī-än.)) The name of one of
Dorien, *Fr.* (dō-rī-änh.) the ancient modes or scales.
Doric mode. The first of the authentic Greek modes.
Dossologia, *It.* (dōs-sō-lō-jē-ä.) Doxology.
Dot. A mark, which when placed *after* a note increases its duration one-half. When the dot is placed *over* a note it signifies that the note is to be played *staccáto.*
Dot, double. Two dots placed after a note to increase its duration three-fourths of its original value.
Dots. When placed at the side of a bar, or double bar, they show that the music on that side is to be repeated.
Dotted double bar. A double bar with dots preceding it, indicates that the preceding strain

ā ale, ă add, ä arm, ē eve, ĕ end, ī ice, ĭ ill, ō old, ŏ odd, ō dove, oo moon, ü lute, ŭ but, ü French sound.

DOUB

is to be repeated; when the dots are *after* the double bar, it shows that the following strain is to be repeated; a double bar with dots both sides indicates that both the preceding and following strains are to be repeated.

Double. The old name for a *variation;* used by Handel, Scarlatti, and others.

Double A, or AA. In England the term *double* is applied to all those bass notes from G to F inclusive. In Germany the rule is different. See *Double G.*

Double action harp. A harp with pedals, by which each string can be raised two semitones.

Double after-note. Two after notes, taking their time from the previous note.

Double appoggiatura. A union of two short appoggiaturas.

Double B, or BB. See *Double G.*

Double bar, Two thick strokes drawn down through the staff, to divide one strain or movement from another.

Double bass. The largest and deepest toned of all bow instruments.

Double bassoon. A large bassoon, the sounds of which are an octave deeper than the bassoon; also, a 16 or 32 feet organ reed stop, of smaller scale and softer tone than the double trumpet.

Double bemol, *Fr.* (bă-mōl.) Double flat.

Double C, or CC. See *Double G.*

Double chant. A simple harmonized melody in four strains or phrases, and extending to *two* verses of a psalm or canticle.

Double chorde, *Fr.* (doobl kŏrd.) Playing one and the same note, on the violin, upon two strings at once.

Double counterpoint. A counterpart which admits of the parts being inverted.

Double croche, *Fr.* (doobl krŏsh.) *Double hooked;* a semiquaver.

Double curtail. A wind instrument similar to to a bassoon.

Doubled. A term applied when one of the notes of a chord is repeated in a different part of the same chord.

Double D, or DD. See *Double G.*

Double-demisemiquaver. A note equal in duration to one-half of a demisemiquaver; a sixty-fourth note. It is written thus:

Double-descant. Where the treble or any high part can be converted into the bass, and *vice versa.*

Double dipason. An organ stop tuned an octave below the diapasons. It is called a 16 feet stop on the manuals; on the pedals it is a 32 feet stop.

Double diese, *Fr.* (doobl dī-ăz.) A double sharp, ♯♯, or ×.

Doubled letters. Capital letters doubled, indicating that the tone is an octave lower than where the letters stand single.

Double drum. A large drum used in military bands and beaten at both ends.

Double dulciana. An organ stop of small 16 feet scale and delicate tone.

Double E, or EE. See *Double G.*

DOUB

Double F, or FF. See *Double G.*

Double flageolet. A flageolet consisting of two tubes, blown in through one mouthpiece, and producing two sounds at one time.

Double flat. A character (♭♭) which, placed before a note, signifies that it is lowered two semitones.

Double flute. A flute so constructed that two tones may be produced from it at the same time; a stop in an organ. See *Doppel Flöte.*

Double fugue. A fugue on two subjects.

Double G. The octave below G gamut; the lowest G on the pianoforte. In England the term *double* is applied to all those bass notes from G to F inclusive.

Double grand pianoforte. An instrument with a set of keys at each end, invented by James Pierson, of New York.

Double hautboy. A 16 feet reed organ stop of small scale.

Double lyre. The *Lyria Doppia,* an old instrument of the viol kind.

Double note. A breve; a note twice the length of a whole note.

Double octave. An interval of two octaves; a fifteenth; the bis-diapason of the ancient Greeks.

Double quartet. A composition written for eight instruments or voices.

Double reed. The mouthpiece of the hautboy, bassoon, etc., formed of two pieces of cane joined together.

Double-reed melodeon. A melodeon containing two sets of reeds.

Doubles. An old term for variations. See *Double.*

Double shake. Two notes shaken simultaneously; they must form sixths or thirds.

Double sharp. A character which, when placed before a note, raises that note two semitones. It is usually written as follows: ♯♯, or ×.

Double sonata. A sonata composed for two instruments concertante; as, the pianoforte and violincello.

Double stopped-diapason. An organ stop of 16 feet tone on the manuals; the pipes are stopped or covered at the top.

Double suspension. A suspension that retards two notes and requires a double preparation and resolution.

Double tierce. An organ stop tuned a tenth above the diapasons, or a major third above the principal.

Double time. A time in which every measure is composed in two equal parts. It is marked by letting the hand fall and rise alternately.

Double tongueing. A method of articulating quick notes used by flute players.

Double trill. See *Double Shake.*

Double triplet. The union of two triplets; a sextole, thus:

Double trumpet. A organ stop of 16 feet scale; sometimes the lowest octave of pipes is omitted, and it is then called the *Tenoroon* trumpet.

Double twelfth. An organ stop, sounding the fifth above the foundation stops; it is generally composed of stopped pipes.

ă ate, ă add, ä arm, ē eve, ĕ end, ī ice, ĭ ill, ō old, ŏ odd, ô dove, oo moon, ū lute, ŭ but, ü French sound.

DOUB

Doublette, *Fr.* (doob-lĕt.) An organ stop tuned an octave above the principal; in England it is called the *fifteenth*.
Doucet, *Fr.* (doo-sā.) Sweet, soft, gentle.
Doucement, *Fr.* (doos-mänh.) Sweetly, softly, pleasingly.
Donleur, *Fr.* (doo-lŭr.) Grief, sorrow, pathos.
Douloureusement, *Fr.* (doo-loor-ŭs-mänh.) Plaintively, sorrowfully.
Douloureux, *Fr.* (doo-loor-ŭh.) Sorrowful, tender, plaintive.
Doux, *Fr.* (dooz.) Sweet, soft, gentle.
Douzieme, *Fr.* (doo-zhĭ-ăm.) A twelfth.
Down beat. The falling of the hand or baton in beating or marking time.
Down bow sign. A sign used in violin music indicating that the bow is to be drawn down; thus, |—|.
Doxologia, *Lat.* (dŏx-o-lō-jĭ-ā.) } Doxology.
Doxologie, *Fr.* (dŏx-ŏl-ō-zhē.)
Doxology. A form of praise sung in divine service, usually at the close of a prayer, psalm or hymn.
Draht-saite, *Ger.* (drāt-soi-tē.) Music wire; wire string.
Drama. A poem accompanied by action; a play, a tragedy or comedy.
Dramatic. A term applied to music written for the stage and to all other music representing passion.
Dramaticamente, *It.* (drä-mä-tē-kä-män-tē.) } Dramatically.
Dramatiquemente, *Fr.* (drä-mä-tēk-mänht.)
Dramatique, *Fr.* (drä-mä-tēk.) } Dramatic.
Dramatisch, *Ger.* (drä-mā-tish.)
Dramatischer dichter, *Ger.* (drä-mā-tĭ-shĕr dĭkh-tĕr.) A dramatist; a writer for the stage.
Dramatis personæ, *Lat.* (drä-mä-tĭs pĕr-sō-nē.) The characters of an opera or play.
Dramaturge, *Fr.* (drăm-ä-türzh.) } A dramatist.
Dramaturgo, *It.* (drä-mä-toor-gō.)
Drame, *Fr.* (dräm.) } A drama.
Drámma, *It.* (dräm-mä.)
Drámma burlésca, *It.* (drä-mä boor-lĕs-kä.) A comic or humorous drama.
Drámma lírico, *It.* (drä-mä lē-rē-kō.)
Dránima per musica, *It.* (drä-mä pär moo-zē-kä.) An opera or musical drama.
Drammaticaménte, *It.* (dräm-mä-tē-cä-män-tē.) Dramatically, in a declamatory style.
Drammático, *It.* (dräm-mä-tē-kō.) Dramatic.
Draw-stops. In an organ, stops placed on each side of the rows of keys by moving which the player opens or closes the stops within the organ.
Dreh-orgel, *Ger.* (drā-ōrg'l.) Barrel organ.
Drehsessel, *Ger.* (drā-sĕs-s'l.) } A music stool.
Drehstuhl, *Ger.* (drā-atool.)
Dreher, *Ger.* (drā-ĕr.) A slow waltz, or German dance.
Drei. *Ger.* (drī.) Three.
Dreiachtel, *Ger.* (drī-äkh-t'l.) Three quavers, or eighth notes.
Dreiachteltact, *Ger.* (drī-äkh-t'l-täkt.) Measure in 3-8 time.
Dreihändig, *Ger.* (drī-hän-dĭg.) For three hands.
Dreiangel, *Ger.* (drī-än-g'l.) Triangle.

DRUM

Dreichörig. *Ger.* (drī-kōr-ĭg.) A grand pianoforte with three strings to each note.
Dreidoppelt, *Ger.* (drī-dŏp-p'lt.) } Three-fold.
Dreifach, *Ger.* (drī-fäkh.) } triple.
Dreigesang, *Ger.* (drī-ghĕ-säng.) Trio for three voices.
Dreiklang, *Ger.* (drī-kläng.) A triad, a chord of three sounds.
Dreiling, *Ger.* (drī-lĭng.) A third.
Dreimal, *Ger.* (drī-mäl.) Thrice.
Dreireim, *Ger.* (drī-rīm.) A triplet, a stanza of three verses.
Dreisang, *Ger.* (drī-säng.) } A trio.
Dreispiel, *Ger.* (drī-spēl.)
Dreist, *Ger.* (drīst.) Brave, bold, confident.
Dreistigkeit, *Ger.* (drīs-tĭg-kīt.) Boldness, confidence, resolution.
Dreistimmig, *Ger.* (drīs-tĭm-mĭg.) See *Dreystimmig*.
Dreivierteltact, *Ger.* (drī-fēr-t'l-täkt.) Measure in 3-4 time.
Dreizehn, *Ger.* (drī-tsēn.) Thirteen.
Dreizehnte, *Ger.* (drī-tsēn-tē.) Thirteenth.
Dreizweiteltact, *Ger.* (drī-tsvī-t'l-täkt.) Measuring 3-2 time, or a measure of three minims.
Dreyklang, *Ger.* (drī-kläng.) See *Dreiklang*.
Dreystimmig, *Ger.* (drī-stĭm-mĭg.) In three parts; for three voices.
Dringend, *Ger.* (drĭng-ĕnd.) Pressing.
Dritta, *It.* (drēt-tä.) } Right; *máno drítta*, the
Dritto, *It.* (drēt-tō.) } right hand.
Dritte, *Ger.* (drĭt-tē.) Third.
Driving notes. An old term applied to a passage consisting of long notes placed between shorter notes in the same measure and accented contrary to the usual and natural flow of the rhythm.
Drohne, *Ger.* (drō-nē.) A heavy tone, a drone.
Droite, *Fr.* (drwät.) Right; *main droite*, the right hand.
Drommete, *Ger.* (drŏm-mā-tē.) A trumpet.
Drommeten, *Ger.* (drŏm-mā-t'n.) To sound a trumpet.
Drommeter, *Ger.* (drŏm-mā-tĕr.) A trumpeter.
Drone. The largest of the three tubes of the bagpipe. It only sounds one deep note, which answers as a perpetual bass to every tune.
Drönen, *Ger.* (drō-nĕn.) To give a low, dull sound; to drone.
Drum. An instrument of percussion formed of a cylinder made of thin wood or metal, over each end of which is drawn a skin, tightened by means of cords.
Druma, *Irl.* (droo-mä.) A drum.
Drum, bass. A large drum used in military bands. See *Double drum*.
Drum-bass. A term applied to the mere use of the tonic and dominant in playing upon the double bass.
Drum, kettle. A bass drum of a cup-like shape, over the top of which the parchment head is stretched. These drums are used in pairs, one being tuned to the key note and the other to the fifth of the key.
Drum major. The principal drummer in a military band; the officer directing the band.
Drumslade. An old name for a drummer.

ā ale, ă add, ä arm, ē eve, ĕ end, ī ice, ĭ ill, ō old, ŏ odd, ō dove, oo moon, ū lute, ŭ but, ü French sound.

DRUM

Drum, snare. The small drum, so called on account of having strings of twisted hide drawn over its lower head, and to distinguish it from the bass drum; the side drum.
Drum, side. The common drum, the snare drum.
D. S. The initials of *Dal Segno*.
Duan, *Gae. and Iri.* (doo-awn.) A poem suited to music, a song.
Dudeler, *Ger.* (doo-dlĕr.) One who plays or sings badly.
Dudelkasten, *Ger.* (doo-d'l-käs-t'n.) Barrel organ; a hurdy-gurdy.
Dudelkastensack, *Ger.* (doo-d'l-käs-t'n-säk.) A bagpipe, a cornamuse, a hornpipe.
Dudeln, *Ger.* (doo-d'ln.) To play on the bagpipe; also a contemptuous term for playing badly on the flute, etc.
Dúe, *It.* (doo-ĕ.) Two; in two parts.
Dúe clarini, *It.* (doo-ĕ klä-rē-nē.) Two trumpets.
Dúe córde. *It.* (doo-ĕ kōr-dĕ.) Two strings; see *Adùe còrde*.
Dúe córi, *It.* (doo-ĕ kō-rē.) Two choirs or choruses.
Dúe pedáli, *It.* (doo-ĕ pĕ-dä-lē.) The two pedals are to be used.
Duet. A composition for two voices or instruments.
Due trombe, *It.* (doo-ĕ trŏm-bĕ.) Two trumpets.
Duett, *Ger.* (doo-ĕt.) A duet.
Duette, *Ger. pt.* (doo-ĕt-tĕ.) } Duets.
Duetti, *It. pl.* (doo-ĕt-tē.) }
Duettino, *It.* (doo-ĕt-tē-nō.) A short and easy duet.
Duétto, *It.* (doo-ăt-tō.) A duet.
De volte, *It.* (doo-ĕ vōl-tĕ.) Twice.
Dulcana, *Spa.* (dool-thä-nä.) } A small
Dulcaynas, *Spa.* (dool-thē-näs.) } bassoon; formerly much used; see *Dolciádo*.
Dulce, *Spa.* (dool-thĕ.) Soft.
Dulcet. Soft, sweet, musical; an organ stop.
Dulcian, *Fr.* (dŭl-sē-änh.) A small bassoon; see Dolciáno. An organ stop.
Dulciana stop. An 8 feet organ stop, of a soft and sweet quality of tone.
Dulciana principal. A 4 feet organ stop of delicate tone.
Dulcimer. An instrument usually of a triangular shape, the strings of which are struck with little rods held in each hand. The name of an ancient Hebrew instrument, the qualities of which we are ignorant, but probably of the wind species.
Dulcino, *It.* (dool-tshē-nō.) } A small bas-
Dulzain, *Spa.* (dool-thä-ēn.) } soon; see *Dolciano*.
Dulcisono, *Spa.* (dool-thē-sō-nō.) Sweet toned.
Dulzaina, *Spa.* (dool-thä-ē-nä.) The dulcimer; also a fiute or pipe.
Dulz-flöte, *Ger.* (doolts-flŏ-tĕ.) An open organ stop of 8 or 4 feet scale and pleasant, sweet tone.
Dumb spinnet. Another name for the *Clavichord*.
Dumpf, *Ger.* (doompf.) } Of a dull, hol-
Dumpfig, *Ger.* (doomp-fĭg.) } l o w, muffled sound.
Dumpfigkeit, *Ger.* (doomp-fĭg-kīt.) Hollowness, dullness of sound.

DURC

Dúo, *It.* (doo-ō.) Two; in two parts; a composition for two voices or instruments; a duet.
Duo concertante, *It.* (doo-ō kŏn-tshĕr-tän-tĕ.) A duo in which each part is alternately principal and subordinate.
Duodécima, *It.* (doo-ō-dä-tshē-mä. {
Duodécimo, *It.* (doo-ō-dä-tshē-mō.) }
The twelfth; the twelfth note from the tonic; the name is also applied to an organ stop tuned a twelfth above the diapasons.
Duodecima acuta, *Lat.* (dū-ō-děs-ē-mä ä-kū-tä.) A twelfth above.
Duodecima gravi, *Lat.* (dū-ō-děs-ē-mä grä-vē.) A twelfth below.
Duodecimóle, *It.* (doo-ō-dä-tshē-mō-lĕ.) A musical phrase, formed by a group of twelve notes.
Duodrámma, *It.* (doo-ō-drăm-mä.) A kind of melodrama in which only two persons act and sing.
Duol, *It.* (dwō-ĕ.) Two.
Duólo, *It.* (dwō-lō.) Sorrow, sadness, grief.
Duómo, *It.* (dwō-mō.) A cathedral.
Dupla, *Lat.* (doo-plä.) Double.
Duple time. Double time.
Duplex longa. *Lat.* (dū-plĕx lŏn-gä.) Maxima, one of the notes in the old system of music.
Duplication. Doubling; where one or more of the intervals of a chord are repeated in different parts.
Duplo, *It.* (doo-plō.) Double.
Dur, *Ger.* (door.) Major, in speaking of keys and modes; as, C *dur*, C *major*.
Dúra, *It.* (doo-rä.) Delay, stop, stay.
Durale, *It.* (doo-rä-lĕ.) Hard, harsh, sharp.
Duraménte, *It.* (doo-rä-měn-tĕ.) Harshly, roughly; also, meaning that the passage is to be played in a firm, bold style, and strongly accented.
Duráte, *It.* (doo-rä-tĕ.) Hard, rough; also implying false relations in harmony.
Durchblasen, *Ger.* (doorkh blä-z'n.) To play, or practice on a wind instrument.
Durchbrummen, *Ger.* (doorkh-broom-m'n.) To hum through.
Durchcomponiren, *Ger.* (doorkh-kŏm-pō-nē-r'n.) To set a song, through all its stanzas, to music.
Durchdringend, *Ger.* (doorkh-drĭng-ĕnd.) Penetrating, piercing.
Durchdringende stimme, *Ger.* (doorkh-drĭng-ĕn-dĕ stĭm-mĕ.) A shrill voice or tone.
Durchführung, *Ger.* (doorkh-fü-rŏŏng.) Development.
Durchgängig, *Ger.* (doorkh-gäng-ĭg.) }
Durchgänglich, *Ger.* (doorkh-gäng-lĭkh.) }
Throughout.
Durchgehend, *Ger.* (doorkh-gā-ĕnd.) Passing, transient; passing through.
Durchschallen, *Ger.* (doorkh-shäl-l'n.) To sound through, to penetrate with sound.
Durchschlagend, *Ger.* (doorkh-shlä-gĕnd.) A term applied to some organ stops, indicating that they extend through the whole compass of the manual; it also signifies a *free reed* stop.
Durchspielen, *Ger.* (doorkh-spē-l'n.) To play to the end; to perform a musical piece thoroughly.

ă ale, ă add, ä arm, ē eve, ŏ end, ī ice, ĭ ill, ō old, ŏ add, ô dove, oo moon, ū tute, ŭ but, ü French sound.

DUR

Durchstimmen, *Ger.* (*doorkh-*stĭm-měn.) To tune thoroughly.
Durchtrillen, *Ger.* (*doorkh-*trĭl-l'n.) To trill from beginning to end.
Durée, *Fr.* (dü-rā.) Length, duration of notes.
Durement, *Fr.* (dür-mänh) Hard, harsh.
Dureté, *Fr.* (dü-rĕ-tā.) See *Durāte.*
Durézza, *It.* (doo-rāt-zā.) Hardness, harshness of tone or expression.
Dúro, *It.* (doo-ro.) Rude, harsh.
Durum, *Gr.* (dū-rŭm.) One of the tetrachords in the Guidonian scale.
Dur und moll tonleiter, *Ger.* (door oond mōl tōn-lī-tĕr.) The major and minor scales.

EDUR

Düster, *Ger.* (düs-tĕr.) Gloomy.
Dnten, *Ger.* (doo-t'n.) } A contemptuous term,
Düten, *Ger.* (dü-t'n.) } meaning to *toot,* or blow on a horn.
Dux, *Lat.* (dŭx.) *Leader, guide;* the subject, or leading melody of a fugue.
Dynamics. This term in music has reference to expression and the different degrees of power to be applied to notes.
Dystonie, *Gr.* (dĭs-tō-nē.) } Discord, or false
Dystonie, *Ger.* (dis-tō-nă.) } intonation.
Dzwick, *Pol.* (dzvěk.) Sound.

E.

E, called in France and Italy *mi;* the third note of the modern scale of Guido d'Arezzo.
E. Ed, *It.* (ĕd.) *And.*
E. The smallest and most acute string on the violin and guitar.
Eccedente, *It.* (ĕt-tshĕ-dän-tĕ.) *Augmented,* in speaking of intervals.
Eccheggiánte, *It.* (ĕk-kăd-jĕ-än-tĕ.) Resounding, echoing.
Eccheggiáre, *It.* (ĕk-kăd-jĕ-ä-rĕ.) To resound, to echo.
Eechus, *Gr.* (ĕk-kŭs.) An echo of the voice.
Ecclésia, *It.* (ĕk-klā-zē-ă.) Church.
Ecclesiastical. A term applied to all music written for the church.
Ecclesiastical modes. See *Church modes.*
I'ecclesiastico stilo, *It.* (ĕk-klā-zē-ăs-tē-kō stē-lō.) In the church or ecclesiastical style.
Eeco, *It.* (ĕk-kō.) An echo.
Echar el compas, *Spa.* (ā-kär ĕl kŏm-pās.) To beat time.
Echeggiare, *It.* (ā-kĕd-jĕ-ä-rĕ.) To echo, to resound.
Echeia, *Gr.* (ĕ-kī-ă.) Harmonic vases used by the ancients at their dramatic performances, etc., to increase the effect of their voices.
Echelle, *Fr.* (āshĕll.) The scale, or gamut.
Echelle chromatique, *Fr.* (āshĕll krō-mät-ēk.) The chromatic scale.
Echelle diatonique, *Fr.* (āshĕll dī-ă-tōnh-ēk.) The diatonic scale.
Echelon, *Fr.* (āshē-lōnh.) Step, or degree of the scale.
Echo. *Fr.* (ā-kō.) In organ music, this term means a repetition, or imitation of a previous passage, with some striking modification in regard to tone.

Echo cornet. An organ stop, the pipes of which are of small scale, with a light, delicate tone. It is usually placed in the swell.
Echometre. An instrument for measuring the powers of echoes and other sounds.
Echometry. The art of measuring the duration of sounds.
Eclat, *Fr.* (ā-klä.) A burst of applause, expressions of approbation.
Eclatante, *Fr.* (ā-klă-tänht.) Piercing, loud.
Eclisses, *Fr.* (ā-klēss.) The sides or hoops of a violin, guitar, etc.
Eloga, *Spa.* (ĕk-lō-gă.) } An eclogue, selection,
Eclogue, *Gr.* (ĕk-lŏg.) } choice.
Eclogue. A pastoral song or poem.
Ecmeli suoni, *It. pl.* (ĕk-mā-lē swŏ-nē.) Unmelodious sounds.
Eco, *It.* (ā-kō.) An echo; the repetition of a previous passage in a softer tone.
Ecole, *Fr.* (ā-kŏl.) A school, a method or course of instruction, a style formed by some eminent artist.
Ecole de chant, *Fr.* (ā-kŏl düh shänh.) A singing school.
Ecolier, *Fr.* (ā-kō-lī-ā.) A pupil.
Ecometria, *It.* (ā-kō-mât-rē-ă.) Echometry; the art of measuring the duration of sounds.
Ecometro, *It.* (ā-kō-mât-rō.) An echometre.
Ecossais, *Fr.* (ā-kōs-sā.) } Scotch: a dance,
Ecossaise, *Fr.* (ā-kōs-sāz.) } tune or air, in the Scotch style.
Ecossäse, *Ger.* (ā-kŏs-ā-zĕ.) See *Ecossaise.*
Ecoutants, *Fr.* (ā-koo-tänh.) Auditors, listeners.
Ed. *It.* (ĕd.) And.
E dur, *Ger.* (ă door.) The key of E major.

EFFE — ELEG

ă *ale*, ă *add*, ă *arm*, ē *eve*, ĕ *end*, I *ice*, ĭ *ill*, ō *old*, ŏ *odd*, ô *dove*, oo *moon*, û *lute*, ŭ *but*, ü *French sound*.

Effet, *Fr.* (ĕf-fĕ.) Effect ; the effect of
Effétto, *It.* (ĕf-*fā*-to.) music upon an audience·
E flat. The flat seventh of F, and the second flat introduced in modulating by fourths from the natural diatonic scale.
Egalement, *Fr.* (ā-gäl-mänh.) Equally, evenly, smoothly.
Egalité, *Fr.* (ā-gäl-ĭ-*tā*.) Equality, evenness.
Eglise, *Fr.* (ā-glēz.) Church.
Egloga, *It.* (*āl*-yō-gä.) An eclogue; a pas-
Eglogue, *Fr.* (ā-*glōg*.) toral poem.
Egnaglianza, *It.* (ā-gwäl-yē-*dnt*-sä.) Equality, evenness.
Eguále, *It.* (ā-*gwä*-lē.) Equal, even, alike; also applied to a composition for several voices or instruments of one kind, as, male voices only, female voices only.
Egualézza, *It.* (ā-gwä-*lät*-zä.) Equality, evenness
Egualménte, *It.* (ā-gwäl-*män*-tē.) Equally, evenly, alike.
Eighth. An octave.
Eighth-note. A quaver.
Eighth semibreve rest. A rest equal in duration to eight semibreves. ≡
Ein, *Ger.* (īn) A ; an ; one.
Eine, *Ger.* (ī-nĕ.)
Einblasen, *Ger.* (īn-blä-z'm.) To blow into.
Ein dreistimmiger gesang, *Ger.* (īn drī-stĭm-mĭ-ghĕr ghē-säng.) A trio.
Eine viertelsnote, *Ger.* (īn-ĕ fēr-tēls-nō-tĕ.) A crotchet.
Eine flötenähnliche stimme, *Ger.* (īn-ĕ flō-t'n-*än*-lĭ-khĕ stĭm-mĕ.) A soft, musical voice.
Eine geige dämpfen, *Ger.* (īn-ĕ ghī-ghē dämp-f'n.) To apply a mute to a violin.
Eine kreischende stimme, *Ger.* (īn-ĕ krī-sh'n-dĕ stĭm-mē.) A shrill voice.
Einen, *Ger.* (ī-nĕn.) A, one.
Einfach, *Ger.* (īn-fākh.) Simple, plain, ornamented.
Einfacher choral, *Ger.* (īn-fākh-ĕr kō-*räl*.) Plain choral, without variation or ornament.
Eingang, *Ger.* (īn-gäng.) Introduction, preface, prelude.
Eingang der messe, *Ger.* (īn-gäng dĕr *mĕs*-sĕ.) The entrance or beginning of a mass; the introit.
Eingang einer musik, *Ger.* (īn-gäng ī-nĕr moo-zīk.) Prelude.
Eingangs-schlüssel, *Ger.* (īn-gängs-*shlüs*-s'l.) Introductory key.
Eingestrichen, *Ger.* (īn-ghē-strī-kh'n.) Note of the treble marked with *one stroke*. This refers to the octave from middle C to the B above.
Eingestrichene octave, *Gr.* (īn-ghē-strī-kh'n-ĕ ŏk-*tä*-fē.) The notes from middle C to the B above, both inclusive.
Einglied, *Ger.* (īn-glēd.) *One-linked* or *one chord*, in speaking of sequences.
Einhällig, *Ger.* (īn-häl-līg.) Unison, harmonious.
Einhalt, *Ger.* (īn-hält.) A pause.
Einhalten, *Ger.* (īn-häl-t'n.) To pause.
Einhauchen, *Ger.* (īn-hou-kh'n.) To breathe into.
Einheit, *Ger.* (īn-hīt.) Unity.

Einhelfen, *Ger.* (īn-hĕl-f'n.) To prompt.
Einhelfer, *Ger.* (īn-hĕl-fĕr.) Prompter.
Einigen, *Ger.* (ī-nĭ-ghĕn.) Some, any.
Einigkeit, *Ger.* (ī-nĭg-kīt.) Concord, harmony, unity.
Einklang, *Ger.* (īn-kläng.) Consonance, harmony.
Einklingen, *Ger.* (īn-klīng-ĕn.) To accord.
Einlaut, *Ger.* (īn-lout.) Monotonous.
Einleitung, *Ger.* (īn-lī-toong.) Introduction, prelude.
Einleitungs-satz, *Ger.* (īn-lī-toongs-sätz.)
Einleitungs-spiel, *Ger.* (īn-lī-toongs-spēl.)
Introductory movement; overture, prelude.
Einmal, *Ger.* (īn-mäl.) Once.
Einmüthigkeit, *Ger.* (īn-mü-tĭg-kīt.) Concord, unanimity.
Einsang, *Ger.* (īn-säng.) A solo.
Finschlafen, *Ger.* (īn-shlä-f'n.) To die away, to slacken the time and diminish the tone.
Einschmeichelnd, *Ger.* (īn-shmī-khĕlnd.) Flattering, insinuating.
Einschnitt, *Ger.* (īn-shnĭt.) A phrase, or incomplete musical sentence.
Einsperrnspielen, *Ger.* (īn-spär-r'n-*spē*-l'n.) To practice on an instrument.
Einstimmen, *Ger.* (īn-stĭm-m'n.) To agree in tune, to be concordant.
Eistimmener gesang, *Ger.* (īn-stĭm-mē-nĕr ghē-*säng*.) A solo.
Einstimmigkeit, *Ger.* (īn-stĭm-mīg-kīt.) A concord, agreement.
Eintönig, *Ger.* (īn-tō-nĭg.) Monotonous.
Eintracht, *Ger.* (īn-träkht.) Concord, unity.
Einträchtig, *Ger.* (īn-trĕkh-tīg.) Concordant, harmonious.
Einträchtigkeit, *Ger.* (īn-trĕkh-tīg-kīt. Concordance, harmony.
Eintretend, *Ger.* (īn-trē-tĕnd.) Entering, beginning.
Eintritt, *Ger.* (īn-trĭt.) Entrance, entry, beginning.
Einverständniss, *Ger.* (īn-fĕr-stĕnd-nīss.) Harmony, concord.
Ein vollkommener tonkünstler, *Ger.* (īn *fŏl*-kŏm-mĕ-nĕr *tōn*-künst-lĕr.) A scientific musician; a virtuoso.
Ein zweistimmiger gesang, *Ger.* (īn tzvī-stĭm-mĭ-gĕr ghē-*säng*.) A duet.
Eis, *Ger.* (īs.) The note E sharp.
Eisteddfod, *Welsh.* A bardic congress, an assemblage of bards first held in 1078.
Ejacucion, *Spa.* (ā-häk-oo-thĭ-*ŏn*.) Execution or performance of music, vocal or instrumental.
Ela. The name originally given to the highest note in the scale of Guido.
Elami, *Spa.* (ā-*lä*-mē.) The sixth ascending note of the scale.
Electric piano. A piano invented in 1851, the wires of which were vibrated by electro-magnetism.
Elégamment, *Fr.* (ĕl-ā-gäm-mänh.)
Eleganteménte, *It.* (ĕl-ā-gän-tĕ-*män*-tē.)
Elegantly, gracefully.
Elegánte, *It.* (ĕl-ā-*gän*-tē.) Elegant, graceful.
Elegánza, *It.* (ĕl-ā-*gän*-tsä.) Elegance, grace.

ă *ale,* ă *add,* ä *arm,* ē *eve,* ĕ *end,* Ī *ice,* ĭ *ill,* ō *old,* ŏ *odd,* ô *dove,* oo *moon,* ū *lute,* ŭ *but,* ü *French sound.*

ELEG — ENDE

Elegía, *It.* (ĕl-ā-jē-ä.) An elegy, or monody; music of a mournful or funereal character.
Elegiac. Plaintive, mournful, sorrowful.
Elegiaco, *It.* (ĕl-ā-jē-ä-kō.) } Mournful, plaintive, elegiac.
Elégiaque, *Fr.* (ĕl-ā-zhǐ-ăk.) }
Elégie, *Fr.* (ĕl-ā-zhē.) An elegy.
Elego, *Spa.* (ĕl-ā-gō.) Mournful, plaintive.
Elegus, *Lat.* (ĕl-ē-gŭs.) An elegy, a mournful ditty.
Elegy. A mournful or plaintive poem, or a funeral song.
Elementary music. Exercises and studies specially adapted to beginners in the study of music.
Elémens, *Fr.* (ĕl-ā-mănh.) } The rudiments, elements of musical science.
Elementi, *It.* (ĕl-ē-mĕn-tē.) }
Elements. The first or constituent principles or parts of any thing; the priciples or rudiments of musical science.
Eleutheria, *Gr.* (ĕ-lū-thā-rǐ-ä.) A festival of liberty; a song or hymn of liberty.
Elevaménto, *It.* (ĕl-ĕ-vä-mĕn-tō.) } Grandeur, sublimity, loftiness of expression.
Elevatezza, *It.* (ĕl-ĕ-vä-tĕt-zä.) }
Eleváto, *It.* (ĕl-ĕ-vä-tō.) Elevated, exalted, sublime.
Elevazióne, *It.* (ĕl-ĕ-vä-tsē-ō-nĕ.) Elevation, grandeur.
Élève, *Fr.* (ā-lāv.) A pupil.
Eleventh. An interval comprising an octave and a fourth.
Elever, *Fr.* (ā-lĕ-vä.) To raise or lift up the hand in beating time.
Elf, *Ger.* (ĕlf.) Eleven.
Elfte, *Ger.* (ĕlf-tĕ.) Eleventh.
Eline, *Gr.* (ā-tē-nĕ.) The ancient song of the weavers.
Ellenlänge, *Ger.* (ĕl-lĕn-lăng-ĕ.) } Ell-length, or *two foot* size, speaking of the scale of pipes.
Ellig, *Ger.* (ĕl-lĭg.) }
Eloge, *Fr.* (ā-lōzh.) } Praise, eulogy.
Elogio, *Spa.* (ā-lō-hǐ-ō.) }
Elogy. See Eulogy.
Embellir, *Fr.* (änh-bĕl-lēr.) To embellish, to adorn, to ornament.
Embellissement, *Fr.* (änh-bĕl-lēss-mŏnh.) Embellishment.
Embellishment. Ornament, decoration, notes added for the purpose of heightening the effect of a piece.
Embocadura, *Spa.* (ĕm-bō-kä-doo-rä.) Mouthpiece of an instrument; embouchure.
Embouchure, *Fr.* (änh-boo-shoor.) The mouthpiece of a flute, hautboy, or other wind instrument; that part to which the lips are applied to produce the sound. It also refers to the position which the mouth must assume in playing the instrument.
Emérite, *Fr.* (ē-mār-ēt.) Said of a professor who has honorably retired from the duties of his profession.
Emettre, *Fr.* (ē-mătr.) To utter sounds.
Emmeli suoni, *It. pl.* (ĕm-mā-lē swō-nē.) Melodious sounds.
E moll, *Ger.* (a mŏll.) The key of E minor.

Emozióne, *It.* (ĕm-ŏt-sē-ō-nĕ.) Emotion, agitation.
Empâter les sons, *Fr.* (önh-pä-tā lĕ sönh.) To sing or play in a masterly manner, without defects or imperfections.
Empfindung, *Ger.* (ĕmp-fĭn-doong.) Emotion, passion, feeling.
Emphase, *Ger.* (ĕm-fä-zĕ.) Emphasis.
Emphatique, *Fr.* (änh-fä-tēk.) } Emphatical.
Emphatisch, *Ger.* (ĕm-fä-tĭsh.) }
Emphatiquement, *Fr.* (änh-fä-tēk-mănh.) Emphatically.
Emphasis. Marked expression; particular stress or accent on any note, indicated thus: > V ∧ fz., sf., etc.
Emphasize. To sing with marked accent.
Empfindsam, *Ger.* (ĕm-pfĭnd-säm.) Sensitive, sentimental.
Empito, *It.* (ĕm-pē-tō.) Impetuosity.
Empituosaménte, *It.* (ĕm-pĕ-two-zä-mĕn-tĕ.) Impetuously.
Emplumer, *Fr.* (änh-plü-mä.) To *pen*, or put quills into the *jacks* of a spinet, etc.
Empneousta, *Gr.* (ĕmp-nĕ-oos-tä.) Wind instruments.
Emporkirche, *Ger.* (ĕm-pōr-kĭrkh-ĕ.) An organ loft.
Emporté, *Fr.* (änh-pōr-tā.) Passionate, hurried.
Emportement, *Fr.* (änh-pōrt-mănh.) Passion, transport.
Empressé, *Fr.* (änh-prĕs-sā.) In haste, eager, hurried.
Empressement, *Fr.* (änh-prĕss-mănh.) Eagerness, zeal.
En, *Fr.* (änh.) In.
En accélérant, *Fr.* (änh näk-sā-lā-ränh.) Accelerating.
Enarmónico, *It.* (ĕn-är-mō-nē-kō.) } Enharmonic, a scale proceeding by quarter tones.
Enarmonico, *Spa.* (ĕn-är-mō-nē-kō.) }
En augmentant la force peu a peu, *Fr.* (änh ōg-mănh-tänh lä fōrs pŭh ä pŭh.) Increasing in power little by little.
En augmentant legerement, *Fr.* (änh nōg-mănh-tänh lĕ-zhār-mănh.) Gently forcing the sound.
En chantant, *Fr.* (änh shänh-tänh.) In a singing style.
En chœur, *Fr.* (änh kŭr.) In a chorus.
Enchorda, *Gr.* (ĕn-kōr-dä.) Stringed instruments.
Encorda, *Spa.* (ĕn-kōr-dä.) To string an instrument.
Encore, *Fr.* (änh-kōr.) Again, once more; demand for the repetition of a piece.
Endecasíllabo, *It.* (ĕn-dĕ-kä-zēl-lä-bō.) Consisting of eleven syllables; a metrical line of eleven syllables.
Endecha, *Spa.* (ĕn-dā-kä.) A dirge, a doleful song.
Endechar, *Spa.* (ĕn-dā-kär.) To sing funeral songs in honor and praise of the dead.
Endechoso, *Spa.* (ĕn-dā-kō-zō.) Mournful, doleful.
En descendant, *Fr.* (änh dĕ-sänh-dänh.) In descending.

ā ale, ă add, ä arm, ē eve, ĕ end, ī ice, ĭ ill, ō old, ŏ odd, ô dove, oo moon, ū lute, ŭ but, û French sound.

ENDI

En diminuant la force, *Fr.* (änh dĭ-mēn-oo-änh lä fôrs.) Diminishing the force of a tone.
Ende, *Ger.* (ĕnd-ĕ.) End, conclusion, concluding piece.
Energeticaménte, *It.* (ĕn-ĕr-jă-tĕ-kä-mān-tĕ.) Energetically, forcibly.
Energético, *It.* (ĕn-ĕr-jä-tĕ-kō.) Energetic, with emphasis.
Energía, *It.* (ĕn-ĕr-jē-ä.) } Energy, force, em-
Energie, *Fr.* (ĕn-ĕr-zhē.) } phasis.
Energicaménte, *It.* (ĕn-ĕr-jĕ-kä-mān-tĕ.) Energetically, forcibly.
Enérgico, *It.* (ĕn-ār-jĕ-kō.) Energetic, vigorous, forcible.
Energique, *Fr.* (ĕn-ĕr-zhēk.) } Energetic,
Energisch, *Ger.* (ĕn-ār-ghĭsh.) } with emphasis.
Energiquement, *Fr.* (ĕn-ĕr-zhēk-mänh.) Energetically, forcibly.
Enfant de chœur, *Fr.* (änh-fänh dŭh kûr.) Singing boy.
Enfasi. *It.* (ĕn-fä-zē.) Emphasis, earnestness.
Enfaticaménte, *It.* (ĕn-fä-tĕ-kä-mān-tĕ.) Emphatically.
Enfático, *It.* (ĕn-fä-tĕ-kō.) Emphatical, with earnestness.
Enflataménte, *It.* (ĕn-fē-ä-tä-mān-tĕ.) Proudly, pompously.
Enfler, *Fr.* (änh-flā.) To swell, to increase the tone.
En forçant subitement le son, *Fr.* (änh fŏr-sänh sū-bēt-mänh lŭh sŏnh.) Increasing the sound suddenly.
Enge, *Ger.* (ĕng-ĕ.) Close, condensed, compressed; this term is applied to the *stretto* in a fugue. In speaking of organ pipes, it means narrow, straight.
Enge harmonie, *Ger.* (ĕng-ĕ här-mō-nē.) Contracted or close harmony, the intervals or sounds being close together.
English fingering. In pianoforte music the use of a sign (×) to designate the thumb, in distinction from the German fingering, where the thumb is designated as the first finger.
English horn. A species of oboe, a fourth or a fifth lower than the instrument usually designated by that name.
Enguichure, *Fr.* (änh-ghē-shûr.) The mouthpiece of a trumpet.
Enharmonic, *Gr.* (ĕn-här-mŏn-ĭk.) One of the ancient scales or modes, proceeding by quarter tones. On the pianoforte these cannot be expressed; but on the violin, 'cello, etc., they may be described as something like the difference between G♯ and A♭, or between D♯ and E♭, etc. In modern music it also means such a change in the nature of an interval or chord, as can be effected by merely altering the notation of one or more notes, thus:
Enharmonic change. A passage in which the notation is changed, but the same keys of the instrument are employed.
Enharmonic diesis, *Lat.* (ĕn-här-mŏn-ĭk dĭ-ä-sĭs.) The difference between the greater and lesser semitone; the least sensible interval in music.

ENTG

Enharmonic genus. A style of melody constructed from a scale of tones nominally about one-fourth as far from each other as those of the common diatonic scale.
Enharmonic intervals. Such as have only a nominal difference; for instance, the minor third C, E♭, and the extreme second, C. D♯; or, the extreme fifth, C, G♯, and the minor sixth, C, A♭, etc.
Enharmonici suoni, *It.* (ĕn-här-mŏn-ē-tshē swō-nē.) Sounds raised above their natural pitch by means of the enharmonic diesis.
Enharmonic keys. They include (in the pianoforte) the same notes, and have the same scales, but under different names; for instance, the scales of F♯ and G♭:—B♯ and C♭:—D♯ and E♭:—E♯ and F, etc.
Enharmonic modulation. A modulation produced by altering the notation of one or more intervals belonging to some chord, and thus changing the key into which the chord would naturally have resolved.
Enharmonic organ. An organ in which the octave, instead of being limited to a division of twelve intervals, contains from seventeen to twenty-four.
Enharmonic relation. The relation existing between two chromatics, when, by the elevation of one and depression of the other, they are united into one.
Enharmonic scale. A scale proceeding by quarter tones.
Enharmonicus, *Lat.* (ĕn-här-mŏn-ĭ-kŭs.)
Enharmonique, *Fr.* (änh-när-mŏnh-ēk.)
Enharmonisch, *Ger.* (ĕn-här-mŏn-ĭsh.)
Enharmonic.
Enjoné, *Fr.* (änh-zhoo-ā.) Cheerful, gay.
Enjouement, *Fr.* (änh-zhoo-mönh.) Cheerfulness, gaiety.
Eulever, *Fr.* (ŭnh-lĕ-vā.) To lift up the hand in beating time.
Enoncer, *Fr.* (ā-nŏnh-sā.) To enunciate, to proclaim.
Enonciation, *Fr.* (ā-nŏnh-sē-ā-sē-ŏnh.) Enunciation, declaration.
En mesure, *Fr.* (änh mĕ-sûr.) In time.
Enoplia, *Gr.* (ĕn-ō-plĭ-ä.) War songs of the ancient Spartans.
En passant, *Fr.* (änh päs-sänh.) In passing, by the way.
En ralentissant, *Fr.* (änh rāl-länh-tēs-sänh.) Slackening the time.
En rondeau, *Fr.* (änh-rŏnh-dō.) After the style of *a rondeau*.
Ensayo, *Spa.* (ĕn-sā-yō.) Rehearsal of a piece.
Enseignement, *Fr.* (änh-sān-mänh.) Instructions.
Enseigner, *Fr.* (änh-sān-yā.) To instruct, to teach.
Ensemble, *Fr.* (änh-sänh-bl.) *Together, the whole;* applied to concerted music when the whole is given with perfect smoothness and oneness of style.
Entata, *Gr.* (ĕn-tä-tä.) Stringed instruments.
Entgegen, *Ger.* (ĕnt-gā-gh'n.)
Entgegengesetzt, *Ger.* (ĕnt-gā-g'n-ghĕ-sĕtzt.) }
Contrary, opposite speaking of motion.

ă ale, ă add, ä arm, ĕ eve, ĕ end, ĭ ice, ĭ ill, ō old, ŏ odd, ô dove, oo moon, ū lute, ŭ but, ü French sound.

ENTH

Enthousiasme, *Fr.* (ănh-too-zē-ăsm.) \
Enthusiasmus, *Ger.* (ĕn-too-zē-ăz-moos.) }
Enthusiasm.
Enthusiastisch, *Ger.* (ĕn-too-zē-ăs-tĭsh.) Enthusiastically.
Entonacion, *Spa.* (ĕn-tō-nä-thē-ŏn.) Modulation; blowing the bellows of an organ.
Entonador, *Spa.* (ĕn-tō-nä-dŏr.) An organ blower.
Entoner, *Fr.* (änh-tō-nā.) | To begin to
Entonner, *Fr.* (ănh-tōuh-nā.) } chant, to begin to sing; to intonate.
Entr' acte, *Fr.* (änh-tr' ăkt.) Between the acts; music played between the acts of a drama.
Entránte, *It.* (ĕn-trän-tĕ.) \ An entrance,
Entráta, *It.* (ĕn-trä-tä.)   } introduction, pre-
Entráda, *It.* (ĕn-trä-dä.)   } lude.
Entráre, *It.* (ĕn-trä-rĕ.) To enter, to begin.
Entráre in ballo, *It.* (ĕn-trä-rĕ ĕn băl-lō.) To begin to dance.
Entrée, *Fr.* (änh-trā.) Entry, entrance, beginning.
Entremes, *Spa.* (ĕn-trā-mĕs.) A short interlude.
Entremets, *Fr.* (änh-trĕ-mā.) Movements introduced for the sake of variety.
Entretaille, *Fr.* (änhtr-lă-yŭh.) The interchange of the foot in dancing.
Entries. Name formerly given to operatic scenes, burlettas, etc.
Entscheidung, *Ger.* (ĕnt-shī-doong.) Decision, determination.
Entschieden, *Ger.* (ĕnt-shē-d'n.) Decided, in a determined manner.
Entschlafen, *Ger.* (ĕnt-shlä-f'n.) To die away, to diminish.
Entschliessung, *Ger.* (ĕnt-shlēs-soong.) Resolution, determination.
Entschlossen, *Ger.* (ĕnt-shlōs-s'n.) Determined, resolute.
Entschlossenheit, *Ger.* (ĕnt-shlōs-s'n-hīt.) Resoluteness, firmness.
Entschluss, *Ger.* (ĕnt-shlooss.) Resolution.
Entusiasmo, *It.* (ĕn-too-zē-äs-mō.) Enthusiasm.
Entwurf, *Ger.* (ĕnt-woorf.) Sketch, outline of a composition.
Enunciáre, *It.* (ā-noon-tshē-ä-rĕ.) To enunciate, to declare, to proclaim.
Enunciatíva, *It.* (ā-noon-tshē-ä-tē-vä.) Enunciation, declaration.
Enuncíato, *It.* (ā-noon-tshē-ä-tō.) Enunciated, proclaimed.
Enunciazione, *It.* (ā-noon-tshē-ät-sē-ō-nĕ.) Enunciation, declaration.
Envoys. Old English ballads.
En voz, *Spa.* (ĕn vōth.) In voice.
Eólia, *It.* (ā-ō-lē-ä.) \ One of the most
Eolian, *Gr.* (ē-ō-lǐ-än.) } ancient modes; see
Eolien, *Fr.* (ā-ō-lē-änh.) } Greek modes.
Eólio, *It.* (ā-ō-lē-ō.)
Eolic. Pertaining to Æolia.
Eolique, *Fr.* (ā-ō-lēk.) Eolic; see *Eolian*.
Eoli harpe, *Fr.* (ā-ō-lē härp.) The Æolian harp.
Eolodion, *Ger.* (ā-ō-lō-dǐ-ōn.) A German melodian.
Epandoran, *Gr.* (ĕ-păn-dō-răn.) An ancient stringed instrument.

EPOI

Epiaula, *Gr.* (ĕp-ē-ou-lä.) The ancient Greek song of the millers.
Epic. A poem in the narrative style.
Epicamente, *It.* (ĕp-ē-kä-mān-tĕ.) In the epic style.
Epicédio, *It.* (ĕp-ē-tshā-dē-ō.) \ An elegy,
Epicedion, *Gr.* (ĕp-ĭ-sĕ-dĭ-ōn.) } dirge, funeral song or ode.
Epico, *It.* (ĕp-ē-kō.) Epic, heroic.
Epidotonos, *Gr.* (ĕp-ĭ-dō-lō-nŏs.) The third above.
Epigonion, *Gr.* (ĕp-ĭ-gō-nĭ-ŏn.) \ An ancient
Epigonium, *Lat.* (ĕp-ĭ-gō-nĭ-ŭm.) } Greek instrument with forty strings, so named from Epigonius, its inventor.
Epilenia, *Gr.* (ĕp-ĭ-lā-nĭ-ä.) | The ancient
Epilenion, *Gr.* (ĕp-ĭ-lā-nĭ-ŏn.) } song of the grape gatherers.
Epilogue. A speech or short poem addressed to the spectators by one of the actors, after the conclusion of the play.
Epinette, *Fr.* (ā-pē-nĕt.) A spinet.
Epinicia, *Lat.* (ĕp-ĭn-ē-shĭ-ä.) \ Triumphal
Epinicion, *Gr.* (ĕp-ĭn-ē-shĭ-ŏn.) } songs, songs of victory.
Episode. An incidental narrative or digression; A portion of a composition not founded upon the principal subject or theme.
Episodicamente, *It.* (ĕp-ē-sō-dē-kä-män-tĕ.) In the manner of an episode.
Episódico, *It.* (ĕp-ē-sō-dē-kō.) Episodic, digressive.
Episódio, *It.* (ĕp-ē-sō-dē-ō.) Episode, digression.
Episodisch, *Ger.* (ĕp-ĭ-sō-dĭsh.) In the manner of an episode.
Epistrophe, *Gr.* (ĕp-ĭ-strō-fĕ.) A repetition of the concluding melody.
Epistolario, *Spa.* (ĕp-ĭs-tō-lä-rĭ-ō.) A collection of epistles read or sung at the mass.
Epistolero, *Spa.* (ĕp-ĭs-tō-lā-rō.) The priest who reads or sings the epistles.
Epitachordo maggiore, *It.* (ĕp-ē-tä-kŏr-dō mäd-jē-ō-rĕ.) Major seventh.
Epitachordo minore, *It.* (ĕp-ē-tä-kŏr-dō mē-nō-rĕ.) Minor seventh.
Epitalámio, *It.* (ĕp-ē-tä-lä-mē-ō.) \ Epithala-
Epithalme, *Fr.* (ĕp-ĭ-tăl-mĕ.)   } mium.
Epithalamion, *Gr.* (ĕp-ĭ-thä-lä-mĭ-ŏn.) \
Epithalamium, *Gr.* (ĕp-ĭ-thä-lä-mĭ-ŭm.) }
Epithalamium, *Eng.*
Epithalamy, *Eng.*
A marriage song; a nuptial song or ode.
Epitonium, *Lat.* (ĕp-ĭ-tō-nĭ-ŭm.) A tuning hammer; a peg or pin to which the strings of an instrument are fastened.
Epitrite, *Gr.* (ĕp-ĭ-trī-tĕ.) A metrical foot consisting of three long syllables and one short.
Epode, *Gr.* (ĕp-ō-dĕ.) \ Conclusion of a cho-
Epodo, *Spa.* (ĕp-ō-dō.) } rus; a short lyric poem.
Epode. In lyric poetry, the third or last part of the ode; that which follows the strophe and antistrophe. The word is now used for any little verse or verses, that follow one or more great ones; thus a pentameter after a hexameter is an epode.
E poi, *It.* (ā-pō-ē.) And then.
E poi la coda, *It.* (ā pō-ē lä kō-dä.) And then the coda.

ă ate, ă add, ä arm, ē eve, ĕ end, ī ice, ĭ ill, ō old, ŏ odd, ô dove, oo moon, ū lute, ŭ but, ü French sound.

EPOP

Epopee, *Gr.* (ĕp-ō-pā.) An epic poem.
Epopeja, *It.* (ĕp-ō-pā-yä.) } An epic or hero-
Epopeya, *Spa.* (ĕp-ō-pā-yä.) } ic poem.
Epos, *Gr.* (ĕp-ōz.)
Epoumoner, *Fr.* (ĕ-poo-mō-nā.) To tire the lungs.
Eptachordo, *Gr.* (ĕp-tä-kŏr-dō.) The seventh.
Eptacorde, *Fr.* (ĕp-tä-kŏrd.) A heptachord, a lyre with seven strings.
Equábile, *It.* (ĕ-quä-bē-lĕ.) Equal, alike, uniform.
Equabilménte, *It.* (ĕ-quä-bĕl-mān-tĕ.) Equally, smoothly, evenly.
Equal counterpoint. A composition in two, three, four, or more parts, consisting of notes of equal duration.
Equal temperament. That equalization, or tempering of the different sounds of an octave which renders them all of an equal degree of purity; the imperfection being divided among the whole: see *Wolf and Unequal Temperament.*
Equal voices. Compositions in which either all male or all female voices are employed.
Equisonant. Of the same or like sound; a unison. In guitar music the term is used to express the different ways of stopping the same note.
Equisono, *It.* (ā-quē-zō-nō.) Having the same sound.
Equi suoni, *It. pl.* (ā-quē swō-nē.) Unisons.
Equivocal. Such chords as may by a slight change in the notation belong to more than one key.
Equivocále, *It.* (ā-quē-vō-kā-lĕ.) Equivocal.
Equivocal chord. A name sometimes applied to the diminished seventh.
Erblasen, *Ger.* (ĕr-blä-z'n.) To play on a wind instrument.
Ergeigen, *Ger.* (ĕr-ghī-g'n.) To play on the violin.
Erhaben, *Ger.* (ĕr-hä-b'n.) Elevated, sublime, in a lofty and exalted style.
Erheben, *Ger.* (ĕr-hā-b'n.) To raise, to elevate, to lift up the hand in beating time.
Erhebung, *Ger.* (ĕr-hā-boong.) Elevation, raising the hand in beating time.
Erhöhen, *Ger.* (ĕr-hō-ĕn.) See Erheben.
Erhöhung, *Ger.* (ĕr-hō-oong.) See Erhebung.
Erhöhungs-zeichen, *Ger.* (ĕr-hō-oongs tsī-kh'n.) An expression for raising a note a semitone.
Erklingen, *Ger.* (ĕr-kling-ĕn.) To ring, to resound.
Erlehren, *Ger.* (ĕr-lā-r'n.) To acquire by teaching.
Erniedrigung, *Ger.* (ĕr-nē-drī-goong.) The depression of a note by means of a flat or natural.
Erniedrigungszeichen, *Ger.* (ĕr-nēd-rī-goongs-tsī-kh'n.) A flat, or other sign for lowering a note a semitone.
Ermunterung, *Ger.* (ĕr-moon-tĕ-roong.) Animation, excitement.
Ernst, *Ger.* (ĕrnst.) Earnest, serious; in a grave
Ernsthaft, *Ger.* (ĕrnst-häft.) } and earnest style.
Ernsthaftigkeit, *Ger.* (ĕrnst-häf-tĭg-kīt.) Earnestness, seriousness.

ESPI

Ernstlich, *Ger.* (ĕrnst-lĭkh.) Earnest, serious, grave.
Ernstlichkeit, *Ger.* (ĕrnst-lĭkh-kīt.) Earnestness.
Ernst, und mit steigender Lebhaftigkeit, *Ger.* (ĕrnst oond mit stī-ghĕn-der lāb-häf-tĭg-kīt.) Earnestly, and with increasing vivacity.
Erntelied, *Ger.* (ĕrn-tĕ-lēd.) Harvest song.
Eröffnung, *Ger.* (ĕr-ŏf-moong.) Opening, beginning.
Eröffnungs-stück, *Ger.* (ĕr-ŏf-noongs-stük.) Overture.
Eroico, *Gr.* (ĕr-ō-ī-kō.) Heroic.
Erotic. (ĕr-ŏt-ĭk.) An amorous composition or poem.
Erotical. (ĕr-ŏt-ĭ-kăl.) Pertaining to love.
Erótica, *It.* (ĕr-ō-tē-kä.) Love songs, amatory ditties.
Erotic songs. Love songs.
Erst, *Ger.* (ĕrst.) First.
Erstemal, *Ger.* (ĕrs-tĕ-mäl.) First time.
Ersterben, *Ger.* (ĕr-stĕr-b'n.) To die away.
Ertönen, *Ger.* (ĕr-tō-nĕn.) To sound, to resound.
Erweckung, *Ger.* (ĕr-vĕk-oong.) Animation, excitement.
Erweitert, *Ger.* (ĕr-vī-tĕrd.) Expanded, developed.
Es, *Ger.* (ĕz.) The note E flat.
Esàcordo, *It.* (ĕz-ä-kŏr-dō.) Hexachord.
Esámetro, *It.* (ĕz-ä-mĕt-rō.) Hexameter.
Esátta, *It.* (ĕz-ät-tä.) Exact, strict.
Esátta intonazióne, *It.* (ĕz-ät-tä ĕn-tō-nät-sē-ō-nĕ.) Exact intonation.
Escuela, *Spa.* (ās-koo-ā-lä.) A school.
Es dur, *Ger.* (ĕz door.) The key of E flat major.
Esecutóre, *It.* (ĕz-ā-koo-tō-rĕ.) A performer.
Esecuzióne, *It.* (ĕz-ā-koot-sē-ō-nĕ.) Execution, facility of performance.
Esecutrice, *It.* (ĕz-ā-koo-trē-tshĕ.) A female performer.
Eseguire, *It.* (ĕz-ā-gwē-rĕ.) To execute, or perform, either vocally or on an instrument.
Esémpio, *It.* (ĕz-ām-pē-ō.) Example.
Esercízio, *It.* (ĕz-ār-ĭshät-sē-ō.) An exercise, a study.
Esercízi, *It. pl.* (ĕz-ār-tshĕt-sē.) } Exercises.
Esercízj, *It. pl.* (ĕz-ār-tshĕt-sē.) }
Es es, *Ger.* (ĕz ĕz.) The note E double-flat (E♭♭.)
Esitaménto, *It.* (ĕz-ē-tä-män-tō.) } Hesitation.
Esitazióne, *It.* (ĕz-ē-tät-sē-ō-nĕ.) }
Es moll, *Ger.* (ĕz mŏll.) The key of E flat minor.
Esonáre, *It.* (ĕz-ōr-nä-rĕ.) To adorn, to embellish.
Espace, *Fr.* (ĕs-päs.) A space; the interval between two lines of the staff.
Espacio, *Spa.* (ĕs-pä-thē-ō.) An interval.
Espagnol, *Fr.* (ĕs-pän-yōl.) } Spanish,
Espagnuólo, *It.* (ĕs-pän-yoo-ō-lō.) } in the Spanish style.
Espagnuola, all', *It.* (ĕs-pän-yoo-ō-lä.) In the Spanish style.
Espanoleta, *Spa.* (ĕs-pä-nō-lā-tä.) An old Spanish dance.
Espérto, *It.* (ĕs-pĕr-tō.) Skillful, expert.
Espinela, *Spa.* (ĕs-pē-nä-lä.) A species of Spanish poetry consisting of ten lines of eight syllables.

ā ale, ă add, ä arm, ē eve, ĕ end, ī ice, ĭ ill, ō old, ŏ odd, ô dove, oo moon, ū lute, ŭ but, ü French sound.

ESPI   EUPH

Espineta, *Spa.* (ĕs-pē-nä-tä.) A spinet.
Espirando, *Spa.* (ĕs-pē-rän-dō.) Diminishing to the end.
Esplendor, *Spa.* (ĕs-plĕn-dŏr.) Splendor, brilliancy.
Espondeo, *Spa.* (ĕs-pŏn-dā-ō.) A spondee.
Espr. ⎫ Abbreviations of *Espressivo*.
Espress. ⎭
Espressióne, *It.* (ĕs-prās-sē-ō-nĕ.) Expression, feeling.
Espressivo, *It.* (ĕs-prās-sē-vō.) Expressive, to be played or sung with expression.
Espirándo, *It.* (ĕs-pē-rän-dō.) Breathing deeply; with great endeavor.
Esquilla, *Spa.* (ĕs-kēl-yä.) A small bell.
Essai, *Fr.* (ĕs-sā.) An essay, a trial.
Essay. An effort, an attempt; a trial of musical performance.
Essémpio, *It.* (ĕs-sĕm-pē-ō.) See Esémpio.
Essential harmonies. The three harmonies of the key; tonic, dominant and subdominant.
Essential notes. The real, component notes of a chord; in contradistinction to all merely accidental, passing, or ornamental notes.
Essential seventh. The dominant seventh.
Essodio, *It.* (ĕs-sō-dē-ō.) Interlude.
Estancia, *Spa.* (ĕs-tän-thē-ä.) A stanza.
Estemporále, *It.* (ĕs-tĕm-pō-rä-lĕ.) ⎫ Ex-
Estemporáneo, *It.* (ĕs-tăm-pō-rä-nē-ō.) ⎬ temporaneous.
Estilo, *Spa.* (ĕs-tē-lo.) Style.
Estinguéndo, *It.* (ĕs-tĕn-guän-dō.) ⎫ Becom-
Estinte, *It.* (ĕs-tĕn-tĕ.) ⎬ ing ex-
Estinto, *It.* (ĕs-tĕn-tō.) ⎭ tinct, dying away gradually in time and strength of tone.
Estrangul, *Spa.* (ĕs-trän-gool.) Mouthpiece of a wind instrument.
Estravagánte, *It.* (ĕs-träv-ä-gän-tĕ.) ⎫
Estravagánza, *It.* (ĕs-träv-ä-gäni-sä.) ⎬ Extravagant.
Estremaménte, *It.* (ĕs-trā-mä-mĕn-tĕ.) Extremely.
Estribilho. A popular Portuguese song in 6-8 time.
Estribillo, *Sp.* (ĕs-trē-bĕl-yō.) A verse often repeated, the burden of the song.
Estrinienda, *It.* (ĕs-trē-nē-ĕn-dä.) A close, binding style of performance; extremely *legáto*.
Estrinciendo, *It.* (ĕs-trēn-tshē-ĕn-dō.) Playing a passage with force and precision.
Estro, *It.* (ĕs-trō.) Elegance and grace.
Estro poético, *It.* (ĕs-trō pō-ĕ-tē-kō.) Poetic inspiration; imaginative power in a composer.
Estrofa, *Spa.* (ĕs-trō-fä.) A strophe.
Estudiante, *Spa.* (ĕs-too-dē-än-tĕ.) A prompter.
Esultazióne, *It.* (ĕs-ool-tät-sē-ō-nĕ.) Exultation.
Et, *Lat.* (ĕt.) And.
Eteinte, *Fr.* (ĕ-tănht.) See Estinte.
Etendre, *Fr.* (ĕ-tänhdr.) To extend, to spread.
Etendue, *Fr.* (ĕ-tänh-dü.) The extent or compass of an instrument or voice.
Ethologus, *Lat.* (ĕ-thŏl-ō-gūs.) A buffoon; a comic actor.
Et Incarnatus, *Lat.* (ĕt ĭn-kär-nä-tūs.) A portion of the Credo.

Etouffé, *Fr.* (ă-toof-fā.) Stifled, smothered; a word used in harp playing to signify a deadening of the tones; in pianoforte music it means an exceedingly soft style of playing.
Etouffer, *Fr.* (ă-toof-fā.) To stifle, to deaden the tone.
Etouffoirs, *Fr. pl.* (ă-too-fwăr.) The dampers.
Etrc en repetition, *Fr.* (ĕtr ănh rĕp-ĭ-tä-sĭ-ōnh.) To be in rehearsal.
Et resurrexit, *Lat.* (ĕt rĕs-ŭr-ĕx-ĭt.) A part of the Credo.
Etta, *It.* (ĕt-tä.) ⎫ *Little;* an Italian final diminu-
Etto, *It.* (ĕt-tō.) ⎭ tive; as, *Trombétta*, a little trumpet.
Etrurian. Etruscan.
Etruscan. The music of Etruria, where the people were noted for their musical talent.
Ettachordo, *It.* (ĕt-tä-kŏr-dō.) Instruments having seven strings.
Ettasillabo, *It.* (ĕt-tä-sĕl-lä-bō.) Of seven syllables.
Etude, *Fr.* (ă-tüd.) A study, an exercise.
Etudier, *Fr.* (ă-tü-dē-ā.) To study, to practice.
Etui de luth, *Fr.* (ă-twē düh lüt.) Lute case.
Et vitam, *Lat.* (ĕt-vē-täm.) A part of the Credo, in the mass.
Etwas, *Ger.* (ĕt-väs.) Some, somewhat, a little.
Etwas langsamer, *Ger.* (ĕt-väs läng-sä-mĕr.) A little slower.
Eufonia, *It.* (yoo-fō-nē-ä.) ⎫ Euphony; an
Eufonia, *Spa.* (yoo-fō-nē-ä.) ⎭ agreeable sound.
Eufónico, *It.* (yoo-fō-nē-kō.) Harmonious, well-sounding.
Euphone, *Fr.* (üh-fōn.) A reed stop in an organ of 16 feet scale.
Euphonie, *Fr.* (üh-fō-nē.) ⎫ Euphony, sweet-
Euphonie, *Ger.* (oi-fō-nē.) ⎭ ness of tone. Sounds agreeable to the ear.
Euphony. Agreeable sound; an easy, smooth enunciation of sounds.
Euharmonic. Producing harmony or concordant sounds.
Euharmonic organ. An ingenious instrument of American origin invented about the year 1848. It contains three or four times the usual number of distinct sounds within the compass of an octave, furnishing the precise intervals for every key. The name is not to be confounded with *enharmonic*.
Eumolpides, *Gr.* (yū-mŏl-pĭ-dēs.) A name applied by the ancient Greeks to their priests and singers, from *Eumolpus*.
Euphoniad. (yū-fō-nĭ-ăd.) An instrument of American origin, containing thirty keys with their semitones, and combining in its tones those of the organ, horn, bassoon, clarinet and violin.
Euphonicon, *Gr.* (yū-fō-nĭ-kŏn.) An instrument of the pianoforte kind.
Euphonious. (yū-fō-nĭ-ŭs.) Smooth and melodious.
Euphonique, *Fr.* (üh-fō-nēk.) Euphonious.
Euphonism. (yū-fō-nĭsm.) An agreeable combination of sounds.
Euphonium. A bass wind instrument of modern invention, used in military bands,

ă ale, ă add, ä arm, ē eve, ĕ end, ī ice, ĭ ill, ō old, ŏ odd, ô dove, oo moon, ū lute, ŭ but, ü French sound.

EUPH

Euphonon. A musical instrument resembling the upright piano, and having the tones of the organ.

Eurythmy. (yū-rĭth-my.) Harmony; regular, symmetrical measure.

Euterpe, Gr. (yū-tĕr-pĕ.) The seventh muse, celebrated for the sweetness of her singing.

Euthia, Gr. (yū-thī-ä.) A term used in the ancient Greek music and signifying a regularly ascending succession of sounds.

Eutimia, It. (yoo-tē-mē-ä.) Alacrity, vivacity.

Evangelista, Spa. (ĕv-ăn-jä-lēs-tä.) One who chants the gospels in church.

Eveillé, Fr. (ā-vā-yā.) Lively, gay, sprightly.

Eviráti, It. (ĕv-ō-rä-tē.) Men with soprano voices among the Italians, who formerly took the treble parts in the church and theatre. They are now nearly, if not quite, extinct.

Evoe, It. (ĕv-ō-ē.) An acclamation to Bacchus.

Evolutio, Lat. (ĕv-ō-lū-shĭ-ō.) Inversion of the parts in double counterpoint.

Exaltation, Fr. (ĕx-äl-tä-sē-ōnh.) In an exalted, dignified manner.

Exametro, Spa. (ĕx-äm-ä-trō.) Hexameter verse.

Exécutant, Fr. (ĕx-ā-koo-tänh.) A performer, either vocal or instrumental.

Executer, Fr. (ĕx-ā-koo-tā.) To perform, to execute.

Execute. To sing or play a piece of music.

Exerciren, Ger. (ĕx-ār-tsē-r'n.) To practice.

Execution. Dexterity and skill, either vocal or instrumental; agility in performance.

Exemple, Fr. (ĕx-änh-pl.) Example.

Exequiæ, Lat. (ĕx-ā-quī-ē.) Dirge.

Exequien, Ger. (ĕx-ā-quē-ĕn.) Masses for the dead.

Exercice, Fr. (ĕx-ĕr-sēss.) Exercise.

Exercice de l'archet, Fr. (ĕx-ĕr-sēss dŭh l'är-shā.) Practice of the bow in violin playing.

Exercise. A musical composition calculated to improve the voice or fingers of the performer.

Exercises, didactic. Exercises for the purpose of imparting instruction in musical execution.

Exercises, digital. Exercises for the purpose of acquiring an independent action of the fingers.

Exercitium, Ger. (ĕx-ĕr-tsĭt-sē-oom.) An exercise.

Exercitien, Ger. pl. (ĕx-ĕr-tsĭt-sē-ĕn.) Exercises.

Exercizi, It. pl. (ĕx-ār-tshēt-sē.) See Eserciaj.

Exility. Fineness, thinness of voice.

Exit, Lat. (ĕx-ĭt.) A word set in the margin of operas or plays, to mark the time when the actor is to leave the stage.

Explosive tone. A tone produced by sounding a note suddenly and with great emphasis and suddenly diminishing; indicated thus >∨∧, or Sf.

Expresion, Spa. (ĕx-prā-sē-ōn.) With expression.

EXTR

Expressif, Fr. (ĕx-press-sĭf.) Expressive.

Expressio, Lat. (ĕx-prĕs-sī-ō.) Indicates that the passage is to be executed with expression.

Expression. That quality in a composition or performance which appeals to our feelings; taste or judgment displayed in rendering a composition and imparting to it the sentiment of the author.

Expressivo, It. (ĕx-press-sē-vō.) See Espressivo.

Extemporaneous. Without premeditation.

Extempore, Lat. (ĕx-tĕm-pō-rē.) Unpremeditated, improvised.

Extemporize. To perform extemporaneously, without premeditation.

Extended harmony. See Dispersed Harmony.

Extended phrase. Whenever, by repeating one of the feet, or by any other variation of the melody, three measures are employed instead of two, the phrase is termed *extended*, or irregular.

Extended section. A section containing from five to eight bars.

Extension pedal. The loud pedal of a pianoforte.

Extraneous. Foreign, far-fetched, belonging to a remote key.

Extraneous modulation. A modulation into some remote key, far distant from the original key and its relatives.

Extravagánza, It. (ĕx-träv-ä-gänt-sä.) A cadence or ornament, which is in bad taste; an extravagant and eccentric composition.

Extreme. A term referring to the most distant parts, as the treble and bass. Relating also to intervals in an augmented state; as *extreme sharp sixth*, etc.

Extreme flat eighth. The octave diminished by the chromatic semitone.

Extreme flat fourth. The perfect fourth diminished by a chromatic semitone.

Extreme flat seventh. The minor seventh diminished, consisting of three tones and three diatonic semitones, forming seven degrees.

Extreme flat third. Two diatonic semitones; composed of three degrees and is the minor third diminished by the chromatic semitone.

Extreme intervals. Intervals larger than those denominated major and smaller than those called minor.

Extreme sharp fifth. The perfect fifth increased by the chromatic semitone.

Extreme sharp second. A tone and a chromatic semitone, forming two degrees.

Extreme sharp sixth. The major sixth increased by the chromatic semitone, consisting of five tones and forming six degrees.

Extreme keys. An old term implying those keys which have many sharps or flats, as, B, F♯, D♭, G♭.

ă *ale*, ă *add*, ä *arm*, ē *eve*, ĕ *end*, ī *ice*, ĭ *ill*, ō *old*, ŏ *odd*, ô *dove*, oo *moon*, ü *lute*, ŭ *but*, ü *French sound*.

F

F. The name of the fourth note in the natural diatonic scale of C.
Fa. A syllable applied in solfaing to the fourth degree of every scale.
Fabella, *Lat.* (fă-bĕl-lă.) An interlude.
Fa bémol, *Fr.* (fä bā-mōl.) The note F flat.
Fabot, *Spa.* (fä-bōt.) A species of wind instrument.
Fa-burden. A term applied by the old English musical writers to a certain species of counterpoint.
Façade d'orgue, *Fr.* (fä-sād d'ōrg.) The front of an organ case.
Facciata, *It.* (fät-tshē-ä-tä.) Page; folio.
Faces d'un accord, *Fr.* (fäss d'ûn äk-kōr.) The various positions of a chord.
Fach, *Ger.* (fäkh.) Ranks; thus *fünf-fach*, five ranks.
Fácile, *Fr.* (fä-sēl.) } Light, easy.
Facile, *It.* (fä-tshĕ-lĕ.) }
Facilita, *It.* (fä-tshēl-ē-tä.) } Facility; an easier
Facilité, *Fr.* (fä-sēl-ĭ-tä.) } arrangement or adaptation.
Facilement, *Fr.* (fä-sēl-mänh.) } Easily, with
Facilménte, *It.* (fä-tshēl-*män*-tĕ.) } facility
Fackel-tanz, *Ger.* (fäk'l-tänts.) Dance with flambeaux.
Facistol, *Spa.* (fä-thēs-tōl.) A stand upon which choir books are placed; a music stand.
Facteur de pianos, *Fr.* (fäk-tŭr düh pī-ă-nō.) A piano maker.
Facteur d'orgue, *Fr.* (fäk-tŭr d'ōrg.) An organ maker.
Facture, *Fr.* (fäk-tŭr.) The composition, or workmanship of a piece of music.
Facture d'orgues, *Fr.* (fäk-tŭr d'ōrg.) Dimensions or scale of the pipes of an organ.
Fa dièse, *Fr.* (fä dĭ-äz.) The key of F sharp.
Fa dièse majeur, *Fr.* (fä-dĭ-*äz* mä-*zhŭr*.) The key of F♯ major.
Fa dièse mineur, *Fr.* (fä dĭ-*äz* mĭ-*nŭr*.) The key of F♯ minor.
Faggiólo, *It.* (fäd-jē-ō-lō.) The *flänto piccolo;* the flageolet.
Fagott, *Ger.* (fä-gŏtt.) A bassoon.
Fagottino, *It.* (fä-gŏt-tē-nō.) A small bassoon.
Fagottist, *Ger.* (fä-gŏt-tĭst.) } A performer on
Fagottista, *It..* (fä-gŏt-tēs-tä.) } the bassoon.
Fagótto, *It.* (fä-gŏt-tō.) A bassoon, also an organ stop.
Fagótto, contro, *It.* (fä-gŏt-tō kōn-trō.) A large bassoon, an octave, a fifth, or a fourth lower than the common bassoon.
Fagóttone, *It.* (fä-gŏt-*tō*-nĕ.) A large bassoon formerly in use, an octave lower than the *fagótto*.
Fahnen-marsch, *Ger.* (fä-nĕn märsh.) The march or tune that is played when the colors are lodged.
Faible, *Fr.* (*fä*-bl.) Weak, feeble, thin.
Faiblement, *Fr.* (fä-bl-mänh.) Feebly, weakly.
Faire, *Fr.* (fär.) To do, to execute.
Faire chorus, *Fr.* (fär kō-rüs.) To join in the chorus.
Faire des fredons, *Fr.* (fär dō frä-dōnh.) To run a division, to trill.
Faire retentir, *Fr.* (fär rä-tänh-*tär*.) To resound.

FAND

Faites bien sentir la mélodie, *Fr.* (fät bĭ-änh sänh-*tär* lä-*mā*-lō-dē.) Play the melody very distinctly.
Fa, la. The burden, chorus, or refrain of many old songs. Fa, la, etc., were much in fashion in the seventeenth century, and are to be found in the works of some eminent composers.
Falalella, *It.* (fä-lä-*lĕl*-lä.) A nonsensical song.
Falótico, *It.* (fä-*lō*-tē-kō.) Fantastical, whimsical.
Falsa, *It.* (fäl-sä.) } False, wrong, inharmo-
Falsch, *Ger.* (fälsh.) } nious.
Falsch singen, *Ger.* (fälsh *sing*-ĕn.) To sing out of tune.
False. Those intonations of the voice that do not truly express the intended intervals are called *false*, as well as all ill-adjusted combinations. The term *false* is applied in music to any violation of acknowledged or long-established rules, or to any thing imperfect or incorrect.
False accent. When the accent is removed from the first beat of the bar to the second or fourth, it is called *false* accent.
False cadence. An imperfect or interrupted cadence.
False chords. An epithet applied by theorists to certain chords, because they do not contain *all* the intervals appertaining to those chords in their perfect state.
False closes. Closes so called to distinguish them from the full or final close.
False fifth. An old term for an imperfect or diminished fifth; a fifth containing only *six* semitones, as C, G♭.
False harmony. Harmony contrary to established rules.
False intonation. Incorrect intonation; where the voice does not express the intended or correct intervals.
False relation. When a note which has occurred in one chord, is found chromatically altered in the followed chord, but in a *different part.*
False triad. The diminished triad, formerly so called on account of its having a false fifth.
Falsett, *Ger.* (fäl-sĕt.) }
Falsétto, *It.* (fäl-*sät*-tō.) } Falsetto.
Falsette. } A false or artificial voice; that part
Falsetto. } of a person's voice that lies above its natural compass.
Falso, *It.* (fäl-sō.) False.
Fálso bordóne, *It.* (*fäl*-sō bōr-dō-nĕ.) A term formerly applied to such counterpoint as had a drone bass, or some part constantly moving in the interval with it.
Fa majeure, *Fr.* (fä mä-*zhŭr*.) } The key of F
Fa majore, *It.* (fä mä-*zhōr*.) } major.
Fa mineur, *Fr.* (fä mĭ-*nŭr*.) Key of F minor.
Fanático, *It.* (fä-nä-tē-kō.) A fanatic or passionate admirer.
Fancies. An old name for little lively airs or tunes.
Fandángo, *Spa.* (fän-dän-gō.) A dance much used in Spain, in 3-4 time, generally accompanied with castanets and having a strong emphasis upon the second beat of each bar.
Fandanguéro, *Spa.* (fän-dän-*gwä*-rō.) One who is skillful in dancing the fandango.

ă *ale*, ă *add*, ä *arm*, ĕ *eve*, ĕ *end*, ī *ice*, ĭ *ill*, ō *old*, ŏ *odd*, ō *dove*, oo *moon*, ū *lute*, ŭ *but*, ü *French sound*.

FANF

Fanfare, *Fr.* (fănh-făr.) A short, lively, loud and warlike piece of music, composed for trumpets and kettle drums. Also short, lively pieces performed on hunting horns in the chase.
Fanfaron, *Fr.* (fănh-fă-rŏnh.) A boaster.
Fantaisie, *Fr.* (făn-tā-zē.) } Fancy, imagina-
Fantasia, *It.* (făn-tā-zē-ă.) } tion, caprice; a spe-
Fantasie, *Ger.* (făn-tā-zē.) } cies of music in which the composer yields to his imagination and gives free scope to his ideas, without regard to those restrictions by which other productions are regulated.
Fantasiosaménte, *It.* (făn-tā-zē-ō-zā-*măn*-tĕ.) Fantastically, critically.
Fantasióso, *It.* (făn-tā-zē-ō-zō.) Fantastic, capricious.
Fantasiren, *Ger.* (făn-tā-zē-r'n.) To improvise, to play extemporaneously.
Fantasticaménte, *It.* (făn-tās-tē-kă-*măn*-tĕ.) In a fantastic style.
Fantástico, *It.* (făn-*tăs*-tē-kō.) } Fantastical,
Fantastique, *Fr.* (făn-tăs-*tēk*.) } whimsical,
Fantastisch, *Ger.* (făn-*tăs*-tish.) } capricious in relation to style, form, modulation, etc.
Farandole, *Fr.* (fă-rănh-*dōl*.) } A lively
Farandoule, *Fr.* (fă-rănh-*dool*.) } dance in 6-8 time, peculiar to Provence.
Farce. A short, extravagant comedy, interspersed with airs or songs with instrumental accompaniments.
Farcical. Belonging to a farce.
Fares, *Spa.* (fä-rēs.) Choral service sung in the holy week.
Far fiásco, *It.* (făr fē-ās-kō.) To fail, to make no impression, to displease the public.
Far furóre, *It.* (făr foo-rō-rĕ.) To excite a high degree of admiration.
Far il capotasto, *It.* (făr ĕl kă-pō-*tăs*-tō.) In violincello playing, the art of making a bridge by means of the thumb.
Farneticaménto, *It.* (făr-nā-tē-kă-*măn*-tō.) Frenzy, madness.
Fársa, *It.* (făr-sā.) } Farce.
Farsa, *Spa.* (făr-sā.) }
Fársa in música, *It.* (făr-sā ĕn moo-zē-kă.) Musical farce; a species of little comic opera, in one act.
Fáscie, *It. pl.* (făs-tshē-ĕ.) The sides or hoops of a violin, viola, etc.
Fastosaménte, *It.* (făs-tō-zā-*măn*-tē.) Pompously, proudly.
Fastóso, *It.* (făs-tō-zō.) Proud, stately, in a lofty and pompous style.
Faucette, *Fr.* (fō-sĕt.) } Falsetto.
Fausset, *Fr.* (fō-sā.) }
Faux, *Fr.* (fō.) False, out of tune.
Faux accord, *Fr.* (fō zăh-kōrd.) A dissonance.
Faux bourdon, *Fr.* (fō boor-dōnh.) See Faburden.
F clef. The bass clef; a character placed on the fourth line of the staff so that the two dots are in the third and fourth spaces.
F dur, *Ger.* (f door.) The key of F major.
Feathering. A term sometimes applied to a particularly delicate and lightly detached manner of bowing certain rapid passages on the violin.
Fedel, *Dan.* (fā-dĕl.) A fiddle

FEST

Feder-bret, *Ger.* (fā-der-brĕt.) The spring board of an organ.
Feeders. Small bellows sometimes employed to supply the large bellows of an organ with wind.
Feier, *Ger.* (fī-ĕr.) Festival, celebration.
Feier-gesang, *Ger.* (fī-ĕr ghĕ-*săng*.) Solemn hymn, anthem.
Feierlich, *Ger.* (fī-ĕr-lĭkh.) Solemn, festive.
Feierlichkeit, *Ger.* (fī-ĕr-lĭkh-kīt.) Solemnity, pomp.
Feigned voice. A *falsetto* voice.
Feine stimme, *Ger.* (fī-nĕ *stĭm*-mĕ.) A fine voice.
Feinte. An old name for a semitone; an accidental.
Feldgesang, *Ger.* (fĕld-ghĕ-*săng*.) A rural song.
Feldkunstpfeifer, *Ger.* (fĕld-*koonst*-pfī-fĕr.) A military musician.
Feld-musik, *Ger.* (fĕld-moo-zĭk.) Military music.
Feldrohr, *Ger.* (fĕld-rōr.) A rural pipe.
Feldton, *Ger.* (fĕld-tōn.) The tone or key note of the trumpet and other military wind instruments.
Feld-trompete, *Ger.* (fĕld-trōm-*pā*-tĕ.) Military trumpet.
Férma, *It.* (făr-mā.) Firm, resolute, steady.
Fermaménte, *It.* (făr-mā-*măn*-tĕ.) Firmly, steadily.
Fermáta, *It.* (făr-mā-tā.) } A pause or hold
Fermate, *Ger.* (făr-mā-tĕ.) } marked thus, ⌢.
Fermáte, *It.* (făr-mā-tĕ.) } Firmly, steadily,
Fermáto, *It.* (făr-mā-tō.) } resolutely.
Fermement, *Fr.* (făr-mĕ-mănh.) Firmly, resolutely.
Fermeté, *Fr.* (făr-mĕ-tā.) } Firmness, resolu-
Fermézza, *It.* (făr-*mĕt*-zā.) } tion.
Férmo, *It.* (făr-mō.) Firm, resolute.
Fern-werk, *Ger.* (fĕrn-vărk.) Distant, or remote work; a term applied to a particular row of keys in German organs.
Feróce, *It.* (fā-rō-tshĕ.) } Fierce,
Feroceménte, *It.* (fā-rō-tshĕ-*măn*-tĕ.) } with an expression of ferocity.
Ferocita, *It.* (fā-rō-tshĕ-tā.) Fierceness, roughness.
Fertig, *Ger.* (fĕr-tĭg.) Quick, nimble, dexterous.
Fertigkeit, *Ger.* (fĕr-tĭg-kīt.) Quickness, dexterity.
Fervemment, *Fr.* (făr-vă-mănh.) Fervently, vehemently.
Fervénte, *It.* (făr-văn-tĕ.) Fervent, vehement.
Ferventeménte, *It.* (făr-văn-tĕ-*măn*-tĕ.) } Fer-
Fervidaménte, *It.* (făr-vĕ-dā-*măn*-tĕ.) } vently, vehemently.
Férvido, *It.* (făr-vĕ-dō.) Fervent, vehement.
Fes, *Ger.* (fĕs.) The note F flat.
Fescennina, *It.* (fĕs-tshĕn-nē-nā.) A name given to the first nuptial songs.
Fescennine verses. So called from the town of Fescennia in Etruria. They were in the form of a dialogue between two persons; also, a sort of dramatic poem.
Fescue. An old name for a plectrum, or instrument for playing on the harp.
Fest, *Ger.* (fĕst.) Feast, festival; also, firm, steady.

ă ale, ă add, ä arm, ĕ eve, ĕ end, ī ice, ĭ ill, ō old, ŏ odd, ȯ dove, oo moon, ū lute, ŭ but, ü French sound.

FEST — FILE

Feste, *Ger.* (fĕs-tĕ.) Firmness, steadiness.
Festigkeit, *Ger.* (fĕs-tĭg-kīt.) steadiness.
Festiglich, *Ger.* (fĕs-tĭg-līkh.) Firmly, steadily.
Festivaménte, *It.* (fĕs-tē-vă-män-tĕ.) Gaily, brilliantly.
Festivita, *It.* (fĕs-tē-vē-tä.) Festivity, gaiety.
Festivo, *It.* (fes-tē-vō.) Merry, cheerful, gay.
Festlich, *Ger.* (fĕst-līkh.) Festive, solemn.
Festlichkeit, *Ger.* (fĕst-līkh-kīt.) Festivity, solemnity.
Festlied, *Ger.* (fĕst-lēd.) A festive song.
Festóso, *It.* (fes-tō-zō.) Merry, cheerful, gay.
Fest-overture, *Ger.* (feat ō-ver-tūr.) Festival overture; an overture in a vigorous, brilliant style.
Festzeit, *Ger.* (fĕst-tsīt.) Festival.
F. F. Fortissimo; very loud.
F. F. F. Very fortissimo, as loud as possible.
F. p., principalménte il basso, *It.* (f̄, prĕn-tsĕ-päl-män-tĕ ēl bäs-sō.) Very loud, especially in the bass.
Feuer, *Ger.* (foi-ĕr.) Fire, ardor, passion.
Feurig, *Ger.* (foi-rīg.) Fiery, ardent, passionate.
Feyer, *Ger.* (fī-ĕr.) Festival, celebration.
Fiacca, *It.* (fē-äk-kä.) Feeble, weak, languish.
Fiacco, *Ger.* (fē-äk-kō.) ing, speaking of the tone,
Fiasco, *It.* (fē-äs-kō.) The technical term for a failure; a complete *break down* in a musical performance.
Fiáto, *It.* (fē-ä-tō.) The breath, the voice.
Fiddle. A common name for a violin.
Fiddler. A common name for a violinist, usually applied to a poor player.
Fiddle-stick. A violin bow.
Fidicen, *Lat.* (fē-dī-sĕn.) A harper; one who plays upon a stringed instrument.
Fidicina, *Lat.* (fē-dī-sē-nä.) A woman who plays upon a stringed instrument.
Fidicula, *Lat.* (fē-dī-koo-lä.) A small lute, or guitar.
Fidicinal. A term applied to all stringed instruments.
Fiducia, *It.* (fē-doo-tshē-ä.) Confidence.
Fiedel, *Ger.* (fē-d'l.) A fiddle, a violin.
Fiedel-bogen, *Ger.* (fē-d'l-bō-g'n.) A fiddle stick, a violin bow.
Fiedelbrett, *Ger.* (fē-d'l-brĕt.) A squeaking fiddle.
Fiedeln, *Ger.* (fē-d'ln.) To play upon the fiddle, to scrape.
Fiedler, *Ger.* (fēd-lĕr.) A fiddler.
Fiel. An old name for the fiddle or violin.
Field music. Music for military instruments; martial music.
Fieraménte, *It.* (fē-ĕr-ä-män-tĕ.) Fiercely, vehemently, boldly.
Fiére, *Fr.* (fī-är.) Proud, lofty, fierce.
Fièrement, *Fr.* (fī-är-mänh.) In a fierce manner.
Fieramente assai, *It.* (fē-ä-rä-män-tĕ äs-sä-ē.) Very bold and energetic.
Fiéro, *It.* (fē-ä-rō.) Bold, energetic, lively.
Fierté, *Fr.* (fēr-tā.) Fierceness, boldness.
Fife. A small, shrill-toned instrument, used only in martial music.
Fifer. One who plays on the fife.
Fiffaro, *It.* (fēf-fä-rō.) A fife.

Fifre, *Fr.* (fēfr.) A fife, also a fifer; the name is also applied to one of the stops in a harmonium.
Fifteenth. An interval of two octaves; also, the name of an organ stop, tuned two octaves above the diapasons.
Fifth. A distance comprising four diatonic intervals; that is, three tones and a semitone.
Fifth, augmented. An interval containing four whole tones.
Fifth, diminished. An interval containing two whole tones and two semitones.
Fifth, perfect. An interval containing three whole tones and one semitone.
Fifths, consecutive. Two or more perfect fifths immediately following one another in two parallel parts of the score.
Fifth, sharp. An interval consisting of eight semitones.
Figur, *Ger.* (fī-goor.) A musical figure, phrase, or idea.
Figura, *It.* (fē-goo-rä.) Note employed as an ornament.
Figural-gesang, *Ger.* (fī-goo-räl-ghĕ-säng.) Varied and ornamented chant as opposed to plain chant.
Figural-gesänge, *Ger. pt.* (fī-goo-räl-ghĕ-säng-ĕ.) Varied and ornamented chant as opposed to plain chant.
Figurántes, *Fr.* (fē-gü-ränht.) Those dancers in a ballet who do not dance singly, but in groups and many together. In the drama, people who figure without having anything to say.
Fignrate counterpoint. Where there is a mixture of discords with concords.
Figuration. An ornamental treatment of a passage; a mixture of concords and discords.
Figuration, harmonic. The progression of a chord from one tone to another of the same chord, and similarly through successive different chords.
Figuráto, *It.* (fē-goo-rä-tō.) } Figured, florid,
Figuré, *Fr.* (fī-gü-rā.) } embellished.
Figured. Free, florid; a term applied to an air which, instead of moving note by note with the bass, consists of a free and florid melody. It also means indicated or noted by figures.
Figured bass. A bass with figures placed over or under the notes to indicate the harmony; see *Thorough bass.*
Figured harmony. Where one or more of the parts of a composition move during the continuance of a chord, through certain notes which do not form any of the constituent parts of that chord.
Figures. Numerical characters written upon the staff, usually in the form of a fraction, to denote the measure.
Figures of diminution. Numerical characters which change the time of the notes over which they are placed, one-third of their relative length. The notes with a figure three are called *triplets*; where there are two triplets a figure six is used.
Filar la vóce, *It.* (fē-lär lä vō-tshĕ.) To spin out, to prolong the tone, gradually augmenting and diminishing the sound of the voice.
Filarmónico, *It.* (fē-lär-mō-nē-kō.) Philharmonic, music loving.
Filer, *Fr.* (fī-lā.) To spin, to draw out.

PRONOUNCING MUSICAL DICTIONARY. 85

ă *ale,* ă *add,* ä *arm,* ĕ *eve,* ŏ *end,* ī *ice,* ĭ *ill,* ō *old,* ŏ *odd,* ô *dove,* oo *moon,* ū *lute,* ŭ *but,* ü *French sound.*

FILE

Filer le son, *Fr.* (fī-lā lŭh sŏnh.) See Filăr la voce.
Filet de voix, *Fr.* (fī-lā dŭh vwä.) A very thin voice.
Fileur, *Fr.* (fī-lŭr.) A spinner; a string maker.
Filum, *Lat.* (fē-lŭm.) A name formerly given to the *stem* of a note.
Fin, *Fr.* (fănh.) } The end.
Fin, *Spa.* (fēn.) }
Fin al, *It.* (fēn äl.) End at; play as far as.
Final. An old application given to the last sound of a verse in a chant which, if complete, is on the key note of the chant; if incomplete, on some other note in the scale of that key.
Final close. Final cadence.
Finále, *It.* (fē-nä-lē.) Final, concluding; the last piece of any act of an opera or of a concert; or, the last movement of a sonata or symphony, etc.
F in alt. The seventh above G in alt; the seventh note in alt.
F in altissimo. The octave above F in alt; the seventh note in altissimo.
Fin a qui, *It.* (fēn ä quē.) To this place.
Fine, *It.* (fē-nē.) The end, the termination.
Fine del aria, *It.* (fē-nē dĕl ä-rē-ä.) The end of the air.
Fine del atto, *It.* (fē-nē dĕl ät-tō.) The end of the act.
Finement, *Fr.* (fēnh-mănh.) Finely, acutely.
Finger board. That part of a stringed instrument on which the fingers press; the keyboard or manual of a pianoforte, organ, etc.
Fingered. A term applied to piano music, signifying that figures or other characters are applied to the notes to show the method of fingering.
Fingering, American. The use of the sign (×) to indicate the thumb in pianoforte playing, in distinction from the German or foreign fingering, in which the thumb is called the first finger.
Fingering, foreign. } A method of fingering
Fingering, German. } piano music which designates the thumb as the first finger.
Fingern, *Ger.* (fĭng-ĕrn.) To play, to finger.
Finger-leiter, *Ger.* (fĭng-ĕr-lī-tĕr.) Finger-guides.
Finger-satz, *Ger.* (fĭng-ĕr-sätz.) Fingering.
Finiménto, *It.* (fē-nē-mān-tō.) Conclusion, end.
Finished. A term applied to those vocal or instrumental performers who have attained an advanced and artistic execution.
Finita, *It.* (fē-nē-tä.) } Finished, ended, concluded.
Finito, *It.* (fē-nē-tō.) }
Finite canon. A canon which is not repeated.
Fino al, *It.* (fē-nō äl.) Play as far as, stop at, end at.
Fin qui, *It.* (fēn quē.) To this place.
Fint, *It.* (fēnt.) } Feigned, false, interrupted,
Finto, *It.* (fēn-tō.) } in respect to cadences; a feint, or deceptive close.
Fiŏca, *It.* (fē-ō-kä.) } Hoarse, faint, feeble.
Fiŏco, *It.* (fē-ō-kō.) }
Fiochézza, *It.* (fē-ō-kāt-zä.) Hoarseness.
Floreggiánte, *It.* (fē-ō-rĕd-jē-än-tē.) Too ornate, decorated with roulades, cadences, etc.
Florétti, *It.* (fē-ō-rät-tē.) Little graces or ornaments, in vocal music.

FLAG

Florisçénte, *It.* (fē-ō-rē-shän-tē.) } Florid,
Floríto, *It.* (fē-ō-rē-tō.) } abounding with ornaments.
Florita cadenza, *It.* (fē-ō-rē-tä kä-dänt-sä.) A cadenza whose last note but one is divided into many notes.
Florittezza, *It.* (fē-ō-rē-tät-sä.) Embellishment; a florid style of performance.
Floritúre, *It.* (fē-ō-rē-too-rē.) } Literally, *little*
Floritúri, *It.* (fē-ō-rē-too-rē.) } *flowers;* graces and embellishments in singing.
Fiŏtola, *It.* (fē-ō-tō-lä.) A flute.
First. A word applied to the upper part of a duet, trio, quartet, or any other composition, vocal or instrumental; such parts generally express the air.
First bass. High bass.
First inversion. A term applied to a chord when the bass takes the third.
First soprano. The high soprano.
First tenor. The high tenor.
Fis, *Ger.* (fĭs.) The note F sharp.
Fischiare, *It.* (fē-skē-ä-rē.) To whistle, to hiss.
Fis dur, *Ger.* (fĭs door.) The key of F♯ major.
Fis fis, *Ger.* (fĭs fĭs.) The note F double sharp.
Fis moll, *Ger.* (fĭs mŏll.) The key of F♯ minor.
Fistel, *Ger.* (fĭs't'l.) Feigned voice, falsetto.
Fistola, *It.* (fĭs-tō-lä.) } A reed, a pipe.
Fistula, *Lat.* (fĭs-tū-lä.) }
Fistula dulcis, *Lat.* (fĭs-tū-lä dŭl-sĭs.) This was once a common flute and was blown at the end; see *Flute a Bec.*
Fistula Germanica, *Lat.* (fĭs-tū-lä gĕr-män-ĭ-kä.) German flute.
Fistula Panis, *Lat.* (fĭs-tū-lä pä-nĭs.) The Pandean pipes; wind instruments of the ancients.
Fistula pastoralis, *Lat.* (fĭs-tū-lä päs-tō-rä-lĭs.) The Pandean pipes; wind instruments of the ancients.
Fistula pastorica, *Lat.* (fĭs-tū-lä päs tō-rē-kä.) Name given by Cicero and other classical writers to the oaten pipe used by the audience in the Roman theatres to express their disapprobation.
Fistulator, *Lat.* (fĭs-tū-lä-tŏr.) } A piper, a
Fistulatóre, *It.* (fĭs-too-lä-tō-rē.) } player on a flute or flageolet.
Fistuliren, *Ger.* (fĭs-too-lēr'n.) To sing in a feigned voice.
Fithele. The old English name for the fiddle.
Fixed syllables. Syllables which do not change with the change of key. The Italians use fixed syllables.
Flach-flöte, *Ger.* (fläkh-flō-tē.) Shallow *flute;* flageolet; also an organ stop of rather thin tone.
Flageolet, *Fr.* (flä-zhē-ō-lā.) } A small pipe
Flageolet, *Ger.* (flä-ghē-ō-lĕt.) } or flute, resembling a small hautboy, the notes of which are exceedingly clear and shrill. It is generally made of box or other hard wood, but sometimes of ivory. Also an organ stop of 2 feet scale and wood pipes.
Flageolet, double. A flageolet having two tubes.
Flageolet tones. Tones produced on instruments of the violin species by drawing the bow very lightly and merely touching the strings with the fingers. See *Harmonics.*
Flagiolétta, *It.* (flä-jē-ō-lāt-tä.) See Flageolet.

ă *ale*, ă *add*, ä *arm*, ĕ *eve*, ĕ *end*, ī *ice*, ĭ *ill*, ō *old*, ŏ *odd*, ô *dove*, oo *moon*, ū *lute*, ŭ *but*, ü *French sound*.

FLAM

Flam. In drum music a grace note or stroke corresponding with the appoggiatura in other compositions.
Flaschinett, *Ger.* (flä-shĭ-nĕt.) The flageolet.
Flat. A character which lowers a note one semitone, (♭).
Flat, double. A character composed of two flats which lowers a note two semitones, (♭♭).
Flat eighth, extreme. The octave diminished by the chromatic semitone.
Flat fifth. An interval consisting of five degrees and containing two tones and two semitones.
Flat fourth, extreme. The perfect fourth diminished by a chromatic semitone.
Flat seventh. The minor seventh, containing four tones and two diatonic semitones.
Flat third, extreme. The minor third diminished by the chromatic semitone.
Flatter la corde, *Fr.* (flăt-tä lä kôrd.) To play the violin, etc., in a soft, expressive manner.
Flauta, *Spa.* (flä-oo-tä.) A flute.
Flauta amabilis, *Lat.* (flaw-tä ä-mä-bĭ-lĭs.) See Flauto Amábile.
Flautándo, *It.* (flä-oo-tăn-dō.) } *Flute-like tone;*
Flautáto, *It.* (flä-oo-tä-tō.) } that quality of tone obtained by drawing the bow smoothly and gently across the strings over that end of the finger-board nearest the bridge.
Flautero, *Spa.* (flä-oo-tä-rō.) One who makes flutes; a flute-player.
Flautina, *It.* (flä-oo-tē-nä.) } A small flute, an
Flautino, *It.* (flä-oo-tē-nō.) } octave flute; a piccolo.
Flautista, *It.* (flä-oo-tēs-tä.) A performer on the flute.
Flauti unisoni, *It.* (flä-oo-tē oo-nē-sō-nē.) The flutes in unison.
Fláuto, *It.* (flä-oo-tō.) A flute.
Fláuto a becco, *It.* (flä-oo-tō ä băk-kō.) A beaked flute; a flute having a mouth-piece like a flageolet.
Fláuto ad libitum, *It.* (flä-oo-tō.) The flute part may be played or omitted.
Fláuto, alto, *It.* (flä-oo-tō äl-tō.) A tenor flute used in bands.
Fláuto amábile, *It.* (flä-oo-tō ä-mä-bē-lĕ.) The name of an organ stop of soft and delicate tone.
Fláuto amoróso, *It.* (flä-oo-tō ä-mō-rō-zō.) A 4 feet organ stop of delicate tone.
Fláuto di Pan, *It.* (flä-oo-tō dē pän.) *Pan's flute;* an organ stop of small size.
Fláuto dolce, *It.* (flä-oo-tō dōl-tshĕ.) An organ stop of soft, agreeable tone.
Fláuto doris, *It.* (flä-oo-tō dō-rĕs.) } See
Fláuto douce, *It.* (flä-oo-tō doo-tshĕ.) } Flâuto Dolce and Flûte Douce.
Fláuto e violino, *It.* (flä-oo-tō ā vē-ō-lē-nō.) Flute and violin.
Fláuto gráve, *It.* (flä-oo-tō grä-vĕ.) An organ stop of 8 feet tone.
Flautóne, *It.* (flä-oo-tō-nĕ.) The bass flute, not in use; also a 16 feet pedal stop in an organ, of soft tone.
Fláuto o violino, *It.* (flä-oo-tō ō vē-ō-lē-nō.) Flute or violin.
Fláuto piccolo, *It.* (flä-oo-tō pĭk-kō-lō.) An

FLUT

octave flute, a small flute of very shrill tone; a flageolet.
Fláuto tacere. *It.* (flä-oo-tō tä-tshä-rĕ.) The flute is not to play.
Fláuto tedesco, *It.* (flä-oo-tō tĕ-dăs-kō.) A German flute.
Fláuto terzo, *It.* (flä-oo-tō tărt-sō.) The third flute.
Fláuto transverso, *It.* (flä-oo-tō träns-vär-sō.) }
Fláuto travérso, *It.* (flä-oo-tō trä-vär-sō.) }
The *transverse flute*, thus named because it is held *across*, and blown at the side, contrary to the *flûte a bec;* it is also often called the German flute. The name is also applied to an organ stop.
Flébile, *It.* (flā-bē-lĕ.) Mournful, sad, doleful.
Flebilménte, *It.* (flä-bĕl-măn-tĕ.) Mournfully, dolefully.
Flessíbile, *It.* (flĕs-sē-bē-lĕ.) Flexible, pliant.
Flessibilita, *It.* (flĕs-sē-bē-lē-tä.) Flexibility.
Fleut, *Arm.* A flute.
F-löcher, *Ger.* (ĕf lŏkh-ĕr.) The f holes, or sound holes of a violin, etc.
Flon-flon, *Fr.* (flŏnh flŏnh.) Bad music, trash; also, the burden of certain old vandevilles.
Floreo, *Spa.* (flō-rā-ō.) A flourish.
Florid. Ornamental, figured, embellished.
Florid counterpoint. Figured counterpoint.
Flötchen, *Ger.* (flŏt-khĕn.) A little flute, a pipe, a flageolet.
Flöten, *Ger.* (flŏ-t'n.) To play upon the flute.
Flöten-begleitung, *Ger.* (flŏ-t'n bĕ-glī-toong.) Flute accompaniment.
Flöten-bläser, *Ger.* (flŏ-t'n blā-z'r.) Flute player.
Flöten-duo, *Ger.* (flŏ-t'n doo-ō.) Flute duet.
Flötenfutter, *Ger.* (flŏ-t'n-foot-tĕr.) A flute case.
Flötenspieler, *Ger.* (flŏ-'n-spē-lĕr.) A flute player.
Flötenstimme, *Ger.* (flŏ-t'n-stĭm-mĕ.) A soft, sweet voice; the part for the flute.
Flötenzug, *Ger.* (flŏ-t'n-tsoog.) A flute stop in an organ.
Flöte traverso, *Ger.* (flŏ-tĕ trä-vĕr-sō.) The German flute; also, an organ stop; see *Fláuto Tráverso.*
Flötist, *Ger.* (flō-tĭst.) A flute player.
Flourish. An appellation sometimes given to the decorative notes which a performer adds to a passage, with the double view of heightening the effect and showing his own dexterity and skill.
Flüchtig, *Ger.* (flükh-tĭg.) Lightly, nimbly.
Flüchtigkeit, *Ger.* (flükh-tĭg-kīt.) Lightness, fleetness.
Flugblatt, *Ger.* (floog-blăt.) A fugitive piece, a circular.
Flügel, *Ger.* (flü-g'l.) A harpsichord, a grand piano.
Flügel-pianoforte. Grand pianoforte, in the form of a harpsichord.
Fluit, *Dut.* (floit.) } A flute.
Fluta, *Lat.* (floo-tä.) }
Flute. A common and well known wind instrument, generally made of wood, but sometimes of metal, consisting of a tube closed at one end and being furnished with holes and keys at its side for

ā ale, ă add, ä arm, ē eve, ĕ end, ī ice, ĭ ill, ō old, ŏ odd, ō dove, oo moon, ū lute, ŭ but, ü French sound.

FLUT — FORT

the purpose of varying the sounds. The compass extends from middle C to the third C above, three octaves with the semitones.
Flute. An organ stop of the diapason species, the tone of which resembles that of the flute.
Flute, *Fr.* (floot.) A flute; see that word.
Flute a bec, *Fo.* (floot ă bĕk.) *Flute with a beak;* the old English flute, with a lip or *beak;* it was blown at the end.
Flute allemande, *Fr.* (floot ăl-mänhd.) The German flute.
Flute, ancient. An instrument which had some sort of a mouthpiece and was double as well as single. It also frequently was composed of two tubes both played together.
Flute, Boehm, (bŏm.) An instrument invented by M. Boehm, of Germany, in 1832. It differs from the common flute in having the size and location of the holes arranged in their natural order with keys.
Flute conique, *Fr.* (floot kŏn-ēk.) Conical flute; an organ stop.
Fluted. A term applied to the upper notes of a soprano voice, when they are of a thin and flute-like tone.
Flute d'allemande, *Fr.* (floot d'ăl-mänhd.) A German flute.
Flute d'amour, *Fr.* (floot d'ă-moor.) A flute, the compass of which is a minor third below that of the German flute; the name is also applied to an organ stop of 8 or 4 feet scale.
Flute, diatonic. A flute capable of producing all the different tones of the major and minor diatonic scales.
Flute, dolce, *It.* (floo-tē dōl-tshē.) A flute with a mouthpiece like that of a flageolet.
Flute douce, *Fr.* (floot dooss.) *Soft flute;* the *flûte à bec;* there were four kinds, the treble, alto, tenor and bass.
Flutée, *Fr.* (floo-tā.) Soft, sweet.
Flute, German. A wind instrument of German invention, consisting of a tube formed of several joints or pieces, with holes at the side and furnished with movable metal keys which, by opening and closing certain holes, serve to give the required tones.
Flute, harmonique, *Fr.* (floot här-mŏnhn-ēk.) See Harmonic flute.
Flute, octave. A flute the tones of which range an octave higher than the German flute.
Flute, octaviante, *Fr.* (floot ŏk-tă-vĭ-änht.) Octave flute, an organ stop.
Flute, ouverte, *Fr.* (floot oo-vär.) An organ stop of the diapason species.
Flute, pastoral. } A flute shorter than the
Flute, shepherd's. } transverse flute and blown through a lip piece at the end.
Fluter, *Fr.* (floo-tā.) To play the flute.
Flute transverse. The German flute.
Flute traversière, *Fr.* (floot trăv-ĕr-sĭ-âr.) The transverse or German flute.
Fluteur, *Fr.* (floo-tur.) A flute player.
Flutist. } A flute player.
Flutiste, *Fr.* (floo-tēst.) }
Fluttuan. An organ stop with a tone resembling a horn.
Flying cadence. See *False Cadence.*

F moll, *Ger.* (ĕf mŏll.) The key of F minor.
Fóco, *It.* (fō-kō.) Fire, ardor, passion.
Focosamente, *It.* (fō-kō-zä-män-tē.) Ardently, vehemently.
Focosissimo, *It.* (fō-kō-sē-sē-mō.) Very ardently, with a great deal of passion.
Focóso, *It.* (fō-kō-zo.) Fiery, passionate.
Fogliétta, *It.* (fōl-yē-ăt-tō.) Copy of the first violin part, in which the *sōlo* passages of the other instruments, and the voice parts are indicated for the use of the leader.
Fois, *Fr.* (fwä.) Time.
Fois, première, *Fr.* (fwä prĕm-ĭ-ār.) The first time.
Fois, duexieme, *Fr.* (fwä dū-zĭ-ăm.) The second time.
Folatre, *Fr.* (fō-lătr.) Frolicsome, wild, playful.
Folia, *Spa.* (fō-lĭ-ä.) A species of Spanish dance
Folio, music. A case for holding loose sheets of music; a wrapper used in a music store for the convenience of classifying the music.
Follia di spagna, *Spa.* (fōl-yĭ-ä dē spän-yä.) A species of composition invented by the Spaniards, consisting of variations on a given air.
Fondamentále, *It.* (fōn-dä-mĕn-tä-lē.) }
Fondamentale, *Fr.* (fōnh-dä-mänh-tăl.) }
Fundamental; fundamental bass.
Fondaménto, *It.* (fōn-dä-män-tō.) The fundamental bass; the roots of the harmony.
Fond d'orgue, *Fr.* (fōnh d'ōrg.) The most important stop in an organ, called in England the open diapason, 8 feet scale. In Germany this is called the 8 feet principal.
Fonologia, *It.* (fōn-ō-lō-jē-ä.) Phonology; the science or doctrine of sounds.
Foot. A certain number of syllables constituting a distinct metrical element in a verse. In very old English music it was a kind of drone accompaniment to a song which was sustained by an other singer.
Foramina, *Lat.* (fō-răm-ĭ-na.) The name given by the Romans to the holes made in the pipe or flute.
Fork, tuning. A small steel instrument with two tines and a handle, used for ascertaining the pitch of any given tone.
Forlána, *It.* (fōr-lä-nä.) } A lively Venitian
Forlane, *Fr.* (fōr-lăn.) } dance in 6-8 time.
Formula. A rule or method of musical instruction, or performance.
Fórte, *It.* (fōr-tē.) Loud, strong.
Fortement, *Fr.* (fōrt-mänh.) } Loudly,
Forteménte, *It.* (fōr-tĕ-män-tē.) } powerfully, vigorously.
Forte, mezzo, *It.* (fōr-tē mät-zō.) With medium power.
Fortézza, *It.* (fōr-tĕt-zä.) Force, power, strength
Forte-piano, *It.* (fōr-tĕ-pĕ-ă-nō.) } The pia-
Forte-piano, *Fr.* (fōrt pĭ-ă-nō.) } noforte; a
Forte-piano, *It.* (fōr-tĕ pĭ-ă-nō.) } keyed instrument of German invention, so called from its capability of expressing different degrees of power or intensity of tone.
Fórte possibile, *It.* (fōr-tĕ pōs-sē-bē-lē.) As loud as possible.
Fortgeigen, *Ger.* (fōrt-ghī-g'n.) To fiddle.

ă ale, ä add, ă arm, ē eve, ĕ end, ī ice, ĭ ill, ō old, ŏ odd, ô dove, oo moon, ū lute, ŭ but, ü French sound.

FORT

Fortiss. An abbreviation of *Fortissimo.*
Fortissimo, *It.* (fōr-tĭs-sē-mō.) Very loud.
Fortissimo quanto possibile, *It.* (fōr-tĭs-sē-mō quän-tō pōs-sē-bē-lē.) As loud as possible.
Fortsetzung, *Ger.* (fōrt-sĕt-soong.) A continuation.
Fortsingen, *Ger.* (fōrt-sĭng-ĕn.) To continue singing.
Fórza, *It.* (fōrt-sä.) Force, strength, power.
Forzándo, *It.* (fōr-tsän-dō.) } Forced; laying a
Forzáto, *It.* (fōr-tsä-tō.) } stress upon one note or chord; sometimes marked ∨∧>.
Forzare, *It.* (fōr-tsä-rĕ.) To strengthen.
Fourchette tonique, *Fr.* (foor-shĕt tōnh-ēk.) A tuning fork.
Four-part song. A song arranged for four parts.
Fourth. A distance comprising three diatonic intervals; that is two tones and a half.
Fourth, augmented. An interval containing three whole tones.
Fourth flute. A flute sounding a fourth higher than the concert flute.
Fourth, perfect. An interval containing two whole tones and a semitone
Fourth shift. The last shift in violin playing.
Française, *Fr.* (fränh-sĕdz.) A graceful dance in 3-4 time.
Franchézza, *It.* (frän-kāt-zä.) Freedom, confidence, boldness.
Française, *Fr.* (fränh-sĕdz.) } French;
Franzése, *It.* (frän-tsā-zĕ.) } in the
Französisch, *Ger.* (fränt-sö-ǵĭsh.) } French style.
Franzton, *Ger.* (fränts-tōn.) An intonation below that of the received concert pitch.
Frappé, *Fr.* (fräp-pā.) Stamping, striking; a particular manner of beating time or striking notes with force.
Frapper, *Fr.* (fräp-pā.) To beat the time, to strike.
Frási, *It.* (frä-zē.) Phrases, short musical passages.
Frauenstimme, *Ger.* (frow-ĕn-stĭm-mĕ.) A female voice.
Freddaménte, *It.* (frĕd-dä-män-tĕ.) Coldly, without animation.
Freddézza, *It.* (frĕd-dā-tsä.) Coldness, frigidity.
Fréddo, *It.* (frād-dō.) Cold, devoid of sentiment.
Fredon, *Fr.* (frĕ-dōnh.) Trilling; a flourish, or other extemporaneous ornament.
Fredonner, *Fr.* (frĕ-dōnh-nā.) To trill, to shake; also, to hum, to sing low.
Free composition. In a free style; a composition not in strict accordance with the rules of musical art.
Free-men's songs. Little compositions for three or four voices, in use about 1600.
Free reed. A reed stop in an organ, in which the tongue by a rapid vibratory motion to and fro produces the sound. The tone of a *free* reed is smooth and free from rattling, but not usually so strong as that of the *striking* reed.
Fregiáre, *It.* (frā-jē-ä-rĕ.) To adorn, to embellish.

FUGA

Fregiáto, *It.* (frā-jē-ä-tō.) Embellished, ornamented.
Fregiatúra, *It.* (frā-jē-ä-too-rä.) An ornament, an embellishment.
Frei, *Ger.* (frī.) Free.
Frémissement, *Fr.* (frĕ-mĕss-mänh.) Humming, singing in a low voice.
French horn. See *Horn.*
French sixth. One form of an augmented sixth; a chord composed of a major third, extreme fourth, and extreme sixth.
French treble clef. The G clef on the hottom line of the staff, formerly much used in French music for violin, flute, etc.
Frescaménte, *It.* (frĕs-kä-män-tĕ,) } Freshly,
Frésco, *It.* (frĕs-kō.) } vigorously, lively.
Frétta, *It.* (frāt-tä.) Increasing the time; accelerating the movement.
Frets. Short pieces of wire fixed on the finger-board of guitars, etc., which, as the strings are brought in contact with them by the pressure of the fingers, serve to vary and determine the pitch of the tones.
Freude, *Ger.* (froy-dĕ.) Joy, rejoicing.
Freuden-gesang, *Ger.* (froy-d'n gĕ-säng.) A song of joy.
Freudig, *Ger.* (froy-dĭg.) Joyfully.
Freudig keit, *Ger.* (froy-dĭg kīt.) Joyfulness, joyousness.
Frei, *Ger.* (frī.) Free, unrestrained as to style.
Freie schreibart, *Ger.* (frī-ĕ shrīb-ärt.) Free style of composition.
Friedens marsch, *Ger.* (frē-d'ns märsh.) A march in honor of peace.
Frisch, *Ger.* (frĭsh.) Freshly, briskly, lively.
Frivolo, *It.* (frē-vō-lō.) Frivolous, trifling, trashy.
Frohgesang, *Ger.* (frō-ghĕ-säng.) A joyous song.
Fröhlich, *Ger.* (frö-lĭkh.) Joyous, gay.
Fröhlichkeit, *Ger.* (frö-lĭkh-kīt.) Joyfulness, gaiety.
Frohnamt, *Ger.* (frōn-ämt.) High mass.
Frosch, *Ger.* (frŏsh.) The lower part or nut of a violin bow.
Fróttola, *It.* (frŏt-tō-lä.) A ballad, a song.
Frottoláre, *It.* (frŏt-tō-lä-rĕ.) To compose ballads.
Frühlingslied, *Ger.* (frü-lĭngs-lēd.) Spring song.
Frühmesse, *Ger.* (frü-mĕs-sĕ.) } Matins, early
Frühstück, *Ger.* (frü-stük.) } mass.
F schlüssel, *Ger.* (ĕf shlüs-s'l.) The F or bass clef.
Fúga, *It.* (foo-gä.) A *flight*, a chase; see *Fugue.*
Fúga authentica, *Lat.* (fū-gä aw-thĕn-tĭ-kä.) A fugue with an *authentic* theme or subject.
Fúga canonica, *Lat.* (fū-gä kä-nŏn-ĭ-kä.) A canon.
Fúga contraria, *Lat.* (fū-gä kŏn-trä-rĭ-ä.) A fugue in which the answer is generally *inverted.*
Fúga doppia, *It.* (foo-gä dŏp-pē-ä.) A double fugue.

PRONOUNCING MUSICAL DICTIONARY. 89

ă ale, ă add, ä arm, ĕ eve, ĕ end, ī ice, ĭ ill, ō old, ŏ odd, ô dove, oo moon, ū lute, ŭ but, ü French sound.

FUGA — FURL

Fúga irreguláris, *Lat.* (fū-gä ĭr-rĕg-ū-lä-rĭs.) An irregular fugue.
Fúga líbera, *Lat.* (fū-gä lĭb-ĕ-rä.) A free fugue.
Fúga mixta, *Lat.* (fū-gä mĭx-tä.) A mixed fugue.
Fúga obligáta, *Lat.* (fū-gä ŏb-lĭ-gä-tä.) A strict fugue.
Fúga partiális, *Lat.* (fū-gä pär-shĭ-ä-lĭs.) The common form of the fugue intermixed with passages of a different character.
Fúga própria, *Lat.* (fū-gä prŏ-prĭ-ä.) A regular fugue strictly according to rule.
Fúga plagále, *It.* (foo-gä plä-gä-lĕ.) A fugue with a *plagal* theme or subject.
Fúga ricercáta, *It.* (foo-gä rē-tshär-kä-tä.) An artificial fugue.
Fúga sciólta, *It.* (foo-gä shē-ŏl-tä.) } A free
Fúga soluta, *Lat.* (fū-gä sō-lū-tä.) } fugue.
Fúga totális, *Lat.* (fū-gä to-tä-lĭs.) A canon.
Fugára, *Lat.* (fū-gä-rä.) An organ stop of the gamba species.
Fugáto, *It.* (foo-gä-tō.) In the style of a fugue.
Fuge, *Ger.* (foo-ghē.) A fugue.
Fuge galánte, *Ger.* (foo-ghē gä-län-tē.) A free fugue in the style of chamber music.
Fúgha, *It.* (foo-gä.) A fugue.
Foghétta, *It.* (foo-gāt-tä.) A short fugue.
Fug etten, *Ger.* (foo-ghĕt-t'n.) Fugues.
Fugírtes, *Ger.* (foo-gēr-tĕs.) } In the fugue
Fugírt, *Ger.* (foo-gērt.) } style; *fugirt* is also applied to the ranks of a mixture stop in an organ.
Fugitive pieces. Ephemeral, short lived compositions.
Fugue, (fūg.) A term derived from the Latin word *fuga,* a flight. It is a composition in the strict style, in which a subject is proposed by one part and answered by other parts, according to certain rules. There are three distinct kinds of fugues, the *simple, double* and *counter.*
Fugue, counter. A fugue in which the subjects move in contrary directions.
Fugue, double. A fugue on two subjects.
Fugue renversée, *Fr.* (fūg rănh-vĕr-sā.) A fugue, the answer in which is made in contrary motion to that of the subject.
Fugue, strict. A fugue in which the fugal form and its laws are strictly observed.
Fugue, perpetual. A canon so constructed that its termination leads to its beginning, and hence may be continually repeated.
Fugue, simple. A fugue containing but a single subject.
Fuguist. A composer or performer of fugues.
Führer, *Ger.* (füh-rĕr.) Conductor, director; also the subject or leading theme in a fugue.
Full. For all the voices or instruments.
Full anthem. An anthem in four or more parts, without verses or solo passages; to be sung by the whole choir in chorus.
Full band. A band in which all the instruments are employed.
Full cadence. See *Perfect Cadence.*
Full flöte, *Ger.* (fūl flō-tĕ.) *Filling-flute;* a stopped organ register of 4 feet tone.
Full orchestra. An orchestra in which all the stringed and wind instruments are employed.

Full organ. An organ with all its registers or stops in use.
Full score. A complete score of all the parts of a composition, vocal or instrumental, or both combined, written on separate staves placed under each other.
Full service. A service for the whole choir in chorus.
Fundamental. An epithet applied to a chord when its lowest note is that from which the chord is derived.
Fundamental bass. The name given to any bass note when accompanied with the chord derived from that note.
Fundamental chord. A chord whose lowest note is that from which the chord is derived.
Fundamental note. The note on which the chord is constructed.
Fundamental tones. The tonic, dominant, and sub-dominant of any scale or key.
Fúnebre, *Fr.* (fū-nābr.) } Funereal, mourn-
Funeràle, *It.* (foo-nĕ-rä-lĕ.) } ful.
Funéreo, *It.* (foo-nā-rē-ō.)
Funestaménte, *Sp a.* (foo-nĕs-tä-mĕn-tē.) Mournfully.
Fünf, *Ger.* (fünf.) Five.
Fünf-fach. *Ger.* (fünf fäkh.) *Five-fold;* five ranks; speaking of organ pipes.
Fünf-stimmig, *Ger.* (fünf stĭm-mĭg.) For five voices.
Fünfte, *Ger.* (fünf-tē.) Fifth.
Fünfzehnte, *Ger.* (fünf-tsĕn-tē.) Fifteenth.
Funzióne, *It.* (foont-sē-ō-nĕ.) Function, or ceremony in a church.
Funzióni, *It. pl.* (foont-sē-ō-nē.) Oratorios, masses and other sacred musical performances in the Roman Catholic church.
Fuóco, *It.* (foo-ō-kō.) Fire, energy, passion.
Fuocóso, *It.* (foo-ō-kō-zō.) Fiery, ardent, impetuous.
Für, *Ger.* (für.) For.
Für beibe hände zusammen, *Ger.* (für bī-bĕ hän-dĕ tsoo-zäm-mĕn.) For both hands together.
Für das ganze werk, *Ger.* (für däs gänt-sĕ värk.)
Für das volle werk, *Ger.* (für däs fŏl-lĕ värk.)
For the full organ.
Für die linke hand allein, *Ger.* (für dē lĭn-kĕ händ äl-līn.) For the left hand alone.
Für die rechte hand allein, *Ger.* (für dē rĕkh-tĕ händ äl-līn.) For the right hand alone.
Fureur, *Fr.* (fū-rŭr.) } Fury, passion, rage.
Fúria, *It.* (foo-rē-ä.) }
Furibóndo, *It.* (foo-rē-bōn-dō.) Furious, mad, extreme vehemence.
Fúrie, *Fr.* (fū-rē.) Fury, passion.
Furieusement, *Fr.* (fū-rŭz-mänh.) } Furi-
Furiosaménte, *It.* (foo-rē-ō-zä-mĕn-tē.) } ously, madly.
Furiosíssimo, *It.* (foo-rē-ō-sēs-sē-mō.) Very furiously.
Furióso, *It.* (foo-rē-ō-zō.) Furious, vehement, mad.
Furlándo, *It.* (foor-län-dō.) } An antiquated
Furláno, *It.* (foor-lä-nō.) } dance.

ă ale, ă add, ä arm, ē eve, ĕ end, Ī ice, ĭ ill, ō old, ŏ odd, ô dove, oo moon, ū lute, ŭ but, ü French sound.

FURN

Furniture stop. An organ stop, consisting of several ranks of pipes, of very acute pitch.
Furóre, *It.* (foo-rō-rĕ.) Fury, rage, passion.
Für zwei manuale, *Ger.* (für tsvī măn-oo-ä-lĕ.) For two manuals; in organ playing.
Fusa, *Lat.* (fū-sä.) A quaver.
Fusée, *Fr.* (fū-zā.) A very rapid roulade or passage; a skip, etc.
Fusella, *Lat.* (fū-sĕl-lä.) Name formerly applied to the demisemiquaver.

GAMM

Fuss, *Ger.* (foos.) Foot; the lower part of an organ pipe.
Füsse, *Ger. pl* (füs sĕ.) Feet.
Füssig, *Ger.* (füs-sig.) Footed: 8-füssig, of 8 feet size, or scale.
Fusston, *Ger.* (foos-tōn.) The *tone,* or *pitch;* as 8 *Fusston,* a pipe of 8 feet tone.
Fut, *Fr.* (foo.) The barrel of a drum.
Fz. An abbreviation of *Forzando.*

G.

G. The nominal of the fifth note in the natural diatonic scale of C, to which is applied the syllable *sol;* it is also one of the names of the highest or treble clef.
Gagliárda, *It.* (găl-yĕ-är-dä.) A *galliard.*
Gagliardaménte, *It.* (găl-yĕ-är-dä-*mĕn*-tĕ.) Briskly, gaily.
Gagliárdo, *It.* (găl-yĕ-är-do.) Brisk, merry, gay.
Gai, *Fr.* (gā.) Gay, merry.
Gaiement, *Fr.* (gā-mănh.) } Merrily, lively, gay.
Gaiment, *Fr.* (gā-mănh.) }
Gaillarde, *Fr.* (gā-yärd.) Merry, brisk; also a *galliard.*
Gaillardement, *Fr.* (gā-yärd-mănh.) Merrily, briskly.
Gaio, *It.* (gă-ē-ō.) With gayety and cheerfulness.
Gaita, *Spa.* (gä-ē-tä.) A bagpipe; also a kind of flute; a street organ.
Gaitéro, *Spa.* (gä-ē-tä-rō.) A player upon the bagpipe.
Gája, *It.* (gä-yä.) } Gay, merry, lively.
Gájo, *It.* (gä-yo.) }
Gajamente, *It.* (gä-yä-*mĕn*-tĕ.) Gaily, cheerfully.
Galánte, *It.* (gä-län-tĕ.) }
Galanteménte, *It.* (gä-län-tĕ-*mĕn*-tĕ.) } Gallantly, boldly.
Galanterie-fugue, *Ger.* (gä-län-tĕ-rē foo-gū.) A fugue in the free style.
Galanterien, *Ger. pl.* (gä-län-tĕ-rē-ĕn.) The ornaments, turns, trills, etc., with which the old harpsichord music was embellished.
Galanterie-stücke, *Ger. pl.* (gä-län-tĕ-rē stü-kĕ.) Pieces in the free ornamental style.
Galanterstyl, *Ger.* (gä-länt-ĕr-stēl.) Free style, ideal style.
Galliambus, *Lat.* (găl-lĭ-ăm-bŭs.) A species of Latin verse.
Galliard. A lively old dance in triple time, formerly very popular.

Galop, *Fr.* (găl-ō.) A quick dance, generally in 2-4 time.
Galopade, *Fr.* (găl-ō-päd.) }
Galopp, *Ger.* (găl-ŏp.) } A *galop.*
Galóppo, *It.* (gä-lŏp-pō.) }
Galoubé, *Fr.* (gä-loo-bā.) } A small flute with
Galoubet, *Fr.* (gä-loo-bā.) } three holes, sometimes to be met with in France.
Gámba, *It.* (găm-bä.) The *viol di gámba,* or *bass viol;* see that term.
Gamba-bass. A 16 feet organ stop, on the pedals.
Gámba major. A name given to a 16 feet organ stop or double gamba.
Gambe, *Ger.* (găm-bĕ.) Viol di gamba.
Gambeta, *Spa.* (găm-bĕ-tä.) An ancient Spanish dance.
Gambette, *Ger.* (găm-bĕt-tĕ.) A small, or octave gamba stop in an organ.
Gambist. A performer upon the *viol di gamba.*
Gamb-viole. *Ger:* (gămb fē-ō-lĕ.) An instrument resembling the violincello.
Games, panathenean. Ancient Greek games in which singers and players on the flute and cithara competed for prizes.
Gámma, *It.* (găm-mä.) } The gamut or scale.
Gamme, *Fr.* (găm.) }
Gamme chromatique, *Fr.* (găm krō-mät-ēk.) The chromatic scale.
Gamme descendante, *Fr.* (găm dĕ-sänh-dänht.) Descending scale.
Gamme de sol majeur, *Fr.* (găm düh sol mä-zhür.) Scale of G major.
Gamme d'ut majeur, *Fr.* (găm d'üt mä-zhür.) Scale of C major.
Gammes en bemols, *Fr.* (găm sänh bä-mōl.) Scales with flats.
Gamme majeure montante, *Fr.* (găm mä-zhür mŏnh-tänht.) An ascending major scale.
Gammes. Exercises on the scale.

ă *ate,* ă *add,* ä *arm,* ĕ *evs,* ē *end,* ĭ *ice,* ī *ill,* ŏ *old,* ŏ *odd,* ô *dove,* oo *moon,* ŭ *lute,* ŭ *but,* ü *French sound.*

GAMU

Gamut. The scale of notes belonging to any key; the lines and spaces on which the notes are placed.

Gamut G. That G which is on the first line of the bass staff.

Gamut, Guido's. The table or scale introduced by Guido, and to which he applied the syllables ut, ra, mi, fa, sol, la. It consisted of twenty notes, namely, two octaves and a major sixth, the first octave distinguished by the capital letters, G, A, B. etc., the second by the small letters, g, a, b, etc., and the major sixth by double letters, gg, aa, bb, etc.

Ganascióne, *It.* (gän-ä-shē-ō-nĕ.) An Italian lute.

Gang. *Ger.* (gäng.) Pace, rate of movement or motion.

Ganiles, *Spa.* (gä-nī-lĕa.) Fauces, organs of the voice.

Ganz, *Ger.* (gänts.) Whole, entire; also, all, very.

Ganz langsam, *Ger.* (gänts läng-säm.) Very slowly.

Ganze note, *Ger.* (gän-tsĕ nō-tĕ.) A *whole note,* or semibreve.

Ganzer ton, *Ger.* (gän-tsĕr tōn.) A whole tone.

Ganzes-werk, *Ger.* (gän-tsĕs värk.) The full organ.

Ganzverhallend, *Ger.* (gänts-fĕr-häl-lĕnd.) Entirely dying away.

Garbataménte, *It.* (gär-hä-tä-män-tĕ.) Gracefully.

Garbáto, *It.* (gär-bä-tō.) Graceful.

Garbo, *It.* (gär-bō.) Simplicity, grace, elegance.

Gargantear, *Spa.* (gär-gän-tē-är.) To quaver, to warble.

Garganteo, *Spa.* (gär-gän-tē-ō.) Quavering, a tremulous modulation of the voice.

Garibo, *It.* (gä-rē-bō.) A dance, a ball.

Gariglione, *It.* (gä-rēl-yē-ō-nĕ.) Chime, musical bells.

Garnir un violin de cordes, *Fr.* (gär-nēr ūnh vē-ō-länh düh kŏrd.) To string a violin.

Garrire, *It.* (gär-rē-rē.) To chirp, to warble like a bird.

Gastrollen, *Ger.* (gäs-trŏl-l'n.) A term applied to a singer or actor on a starring expedition.

Gauche, *Fr.* (gōzh.) Left.

Gauche, main, *Fr.* (gōzh mänh.) The left hand.

Gaudénte, *It.* (goo-dän-tĕ.) Blithe, merry, sprightly.

Gaudeteménte, *It.* (goo-dĕn-tĕ-män-tĕ.) Merrily, joyfully.

Gaudioso, *It.* (goo-dē-ō-zō.) Merry, joyful.

Gavot, *Eng.* (gä-vŏt.) } A dance consisting
Gavótta, *It.* (gä-vŏt-tä.) } of two light, lively
Gavotte, *Fr.* (gä-vŏt.) } strains in common time.

Gayménte, *Spa.* (ghē-män-tĕ.) Gayly, briskly, lively.

Gaytero, *Spa.* (ghē-tä-rō.) One who plays on a bagpipe; a piper.

Gazzarra, *It.* (gät-zär-rä.) Rejoicings with music and cannon.

G clef. The treble clef; a character composed of the letters G and S, for the syllable *Sol,* which invariably turns on the second line of the staff.

GEIG

G double or double G. The octave below G gamut.

G dur, *Ger.* (gä door.) The key of G major.

Geberdenspiel, *Ger.* (ghĕ-bär-d'n-spēl.) Pantomime.

Geblase, *Ger.* (ghĕ-blä-zĕ.) Trumpeting, blowing.

Gebläse, *Ger.* (ghĕ-blä-zĕ.) Bellows, apparatus for blowing.

Gebrochen, *Ger.* (ghĕ-brō-kh'n.) Broken.

Gebrochene akkorde, *Ger.* (ghĕ-brō-kh'n-ĕ äk-kŏr-dĕ.)

Gebróchener accord, *Ger.* (ghĕ-brō-kh'n-ĕr äk-kŏrd.) Broken chords, chords played in arpeggio.

Gebrochene stimme, *Ger.* (ghĕ-brō-kh'n-ĕ stĭm-mĕ.) A broken voice.

Gebunden, *Ger.* (ghĕ-boon-d'n.) Connected, syncopated, in regard to the style of playing or writing.

Gebundene note, *Ger.* (ghĕ-boon-dĕ-nĕ nō-tĕ.) A tied note, a note which is to be held and not repeated.

Gebundener stil, *Ger.* (ghĕ-boon-dĕn-ĕr stēl.) Style of strictly connected harmony; style of counterpoint.

Geburts-lied, *Ger.* (ghĕ-boorts lēd.) Birth-day song.

Gedackt, *Ger.* (ghĕ-däkht.) } Stopped, in opposition to the open
Gedeckt, *Ger.* (ghĕ-däkht.) } pipes in an organ.

Gedact. See Gedackt.

Gedackt-flöte, *Ger.* (ghĕ-däkht flō-tĕ.) Stopped flute, in an organ.

Gedeckte stimmen, *Ger. pl.* (ghĕ-dĕk-tĕ stĭm-mĕn.) Stops with covered pipes, as the stopped diapason.

Gedehnt, *Ger.* (ghĕ-dänt.) Lengthened.

Gedicht, *Ger.* (ghĕ-dĭkht.) A poem, tale, fable.

Gefährte, *Ger.* (ghĕ-fär-tĕ.) The answer in a fugue.

Gefällig, *Ger.* (ghĕ-fäl-lĭg.) Pleasingly, agreeably.

Gefiedel, *Ger.* (ghĕ-fē-d'l.) Fiddling, playing on the fiddle.

Gefühl, *Ger.* (ghĕ-fühl.) Sentiment, expression.

Gegenbewegung, *Ger.* (gä-g'n-bĕ-vä-goong.) Contrary motion.

Gegengesang, *Ger.* (gä-g'n-ghĕ-säng.) Antiphony.

Gegenhall, *Ger.* (gä-g'n-häll.) } Resonance,
Gegenschall, *Ger.* (gä-g'n-shäll.) } echo.

Gegenpunkt, *Ger.* (gä-g'n-poonkt.) Counterpoint.

Gegenstimme, *Ger.* (gä-g'n-stĭm-mĕ.) Counter-tenor, or alto part.

Gegenstimmig, *Ger.* (gä-g'n-stĭm-mĭg.) Dissonant, discordant.

Gegensubject, *Ger.* (gä-g'n-soob-jĕct.) Counter-subject, in a fugue.

Gehend, *Ger.* (gä-ĕnd.) A word referring to movement and having the same meaning as *andante.*

Gehör-spielen, *Ger.* (ghĕ-hör spē-l'n.) To play by ear.

Gehörlehre, *Ger.* (ghĕ-hör-lä-rĕ.) Acoustics

Geige, *Ger.* (ghī-ghĕ.) The violin.

ă ale, ă add, ă arm, ĕ eve, ĕ end, ĭ ice, ĭ ill, ō old, ŏ odd, ô dove, oo moon, ū lute, ŭ but, ü French sound.

GEIG

Geigen, *Ger.* (ghī-g'n.) To play on the violin.
Geigen-blatt, *Ger.* (ghī-g'n blăt.) The fingerboard of a violin.
Geigen-bogen, *Ger.* (ghī-g'n bō-g'n.) Violin bow.
Geigen-clavicymbel. An instrument similar to a harpsichord or pianoforte.
Geigen-förmig, *Ger.* (ghī-g'n fōr-mĭg.) Having the form of a violin.
Geigen-futter, *Ger.* (ghī-g'n foot-tĕr.) Case for a violin.
Geigen-hals, *Ger.* (ghī-g'n häls.) The neck of a violin.
Geigen-harz, *Ger.* (ghī-g'n härts.) Spanish resin, hard resin.
Geigen-holz, *Ger.* (ghī-g'n hōlts.) The wood used in making violins.
Geigen-macher. (ghī-g'n mä-khĕr.) A violin maker.
Geigen-principal, *Ger.* ghī-g'n prĭn-tsĭ-pȧl.) A German organ diapason stop with a tone like that of the gamba, but fuller.
Geigen-saite, *Ger.* (ghī-g'n say-tĕ.) Violin string.
Geigen-sattel, *Ger.* (ghī-g'n sät-t'l.) } The
Geigen-steg, *Ger.* (ghī-g'n stēg.) } bridge of a violin.
Geigen-schule, *Ger.* (ghī-g'n shoo-lĕ.) A violin school, or method of instruction.
Geigen-strich, *Ger.* (ghī-g'n strĭkh.) A stroke of the violin bow.
Geigen-stück, *Ger.* (ghī-g'n stŭk.) A tune for the violin.
Geigen-werk, *Ger.* (ghī-g'n värk,) The celestina, an organ stop of 4 feet scale.
Geigen-wirbel, *Ger.* (ghī-g'n vēr-b'l.) A violin peg.
Geigen-zug, *Ger.* (ghī-g'n tsoog.) A violin stop.
Geiger, *Ger.* (ghī-gher.) Violin player.
Geistlich, *Ger.* (ghīst-lĭkh.) Ecclesiastical, clerical.
Geistliche gesänge, *Ger.* (ghīst-lĭkh-ĕ gĕ-sän-ghĕ.)
Geistliche lieder, *Ger.* (ghīst-lĭkh-ĕ lē-dĕr.) } Psalms, hymns, spiritual songs.
Geistreich, *Ger.* (ghīst-rīkh.) } Spirited, full
Geistvoll, *Ger.* (ghīst-fōl.) } of life and animation.
Geklingel, *Ger.* (ghĕ-klĭng-'l.) Tinkling, ringing of a bell.
Gelassen, *Ger.* (ghĕ-läs-s'n.) Calmly, quietly.
Gelassenheit, *Ger.* (ghĕ-läs-s'n-hīt.) Calmness, tranquility.
Geläufe, *Ger.* (ghĕ-loy-fĕ.) } Running pas-
Geläufen, *Ger.* (ghĕ-loy-f'n.) } sages, scale passages, rapid movements.
Geläufig, *Ger.* (ghĕ-loy-fĭg.) Easy, fluent, rapid.
Geläufigkeit, *Ger.* (ghĕ-loy-fĭg-kīt.) Fluency, ease.
Geläut, *Ger.* (ghĕ-loyt.) A peal of bells, ringing of bells.
Gelinde, *Ger.* (ghĕ-lĭn-dĕ.) Softly, gently.
Gelindigkeit, *Ger.* (ghĕ-lĭn-dĭg-kīt.) Softness, gentleness, sweetness.
Gellen, *Ger.* (ghĕl-l'n.) To sound loudly.
Gellenflöte, *Ger.* (ghĕl-l'n-flō-tĕ.) Clarionet.
Geltung, *Ger.* (ghĕl-toong.) The value or proportion of a note.

GENU

Gemächlich, *Ger.* (ghĕ-mäkh-lĭkh.) } Quietly;
Gemachsam, *Ger.* (ghĕ-mäkh-säm.) } in a calm, slow manner.
Gemählig, *Ger.* (ghĕ-mä-lĭg.) Gradually, by degrees.
Gemisch, *Ger.* (ghĕ-mĭsh.) Mixed; mixture, or compound stops in an organ.
Gemsen horn. An instrument formed of a small pipe made of the horn of a chamois, or wild goat.
Gems-horn, *Ger.* (ghĕms hŏrn.) An organ stop with conical pipes. The tone is light but very clear.
Gems-horn-quint, *Ger.* (ghĕms hŏrn kwĭnt.) An organ stop with conical pipes, sounding a fifth above the foundation stops.
Gemüth, *Ger.* (ghĕ-müt.) Mind, soul.
Gemüthlich, *Ger.* (ghĕ-müt-lĭkh.) Agreeable, expressive.
Genera, *Lat.* (ĭn-ĕ-rä.) } A term used by the
Genus, *Lat.* (jā-nŭs.) } ancients to indicate the modes according to which they divided their tetrachords. The different methods of dividing the octave: when both tones and semitones are employed, according to the natural arrangement of the diatonic scale, it is called the *diatonic* or natural genus; when it is divided by semitones only, it is called the *chromatic* genus, and the *enharmonic* genus when quarter tones alone are used.
General bass. Thorough bass, figured bass.
General pause. A general cessation or silence of all the parts.
Generateur, *Fr.* (zhā-nĕ-rä-tūr.) The fundamental note of the common chord.
Generator. The principal sound or sounds by which others are produced; the fundamental note of the common chord.
Génere, *It.* (jā-nĕ-rĕ.) See Genera.
Generoso, *It.* (jā-nĕ-rō-zō.) Noble, in a dignified manner.
Genialia, *Lat.* (jā-nĭ-ä-lĭ-ä.) The name given by the ancient Romans to cymbals, because they were used in the celebration of weddings.
Génie, *Fr.* (zhā-nē.) }
Génis, *It.* (jā-nēs.) } Genius, talent, spirit.
Genre, *Fr.* (zhänhr.) Style, manner.
Genre chromatique, *Fr.* (zhänhr krō-mä-tēk.) The chromatic genus.
Genre diatonique, *Fr.* (zhänhr dī-ä-tŏnh-ēk.) The diatonic, or natural genus.
Genre enharmonique, *Fr.* (zhänhr änh-här-mŏnh-ēk.) The enharmonic genus.
Genre expressif, *Fr.* (zhänhr ĕks-prĕs-sĭf.) The expressive style.
Gentile, *It.* (jĕn-tē-lĕ.) Pleasing, graceful, elegant.
Gentilezza, *It.* (jĕn-tĕl-lät-zä.) Grace, elegance, refinement of style.
Gentilménte, *It.* (jĕn-tĕl-mān-tĕ.) Gracefully, elegantly.
Genus, *Lat.* (jā-nŭs.) See *Genera*.
Genus chromaticum, *Lat.* (jā-nŭs krō-mät-ĭ-kŭm.) The chromatic genus or mode.
Genus diatonicum, *Lat.* (jā-nŭs dĭ-ä-tŏn-ĭ-kŭm.) The diatonic genus or mode.

ă *ale*, ă *add*, ä *arm*, ē *eve*, ĕ *end*, ī *ice*, ĭ *ill*, ō *old*, ŏ *odd*, ô *dove*, oo *moon*, ū *lute*, ŭ *but*, ü *French sound*.

GENU

Genus enharmonicum, *Lat.* (jā-nŭs ĕn-här-mŏn-ĭ-kŭm.) The enharmonic genus or mode.
Genus inflatile, *Lat.* (jā-nŭs ĭn-flā-tĕ-lĕ.) Wind-instruments.
Genus percussibile, *Lat.* (jā-nŭs pĕr-kŭs-sĭ-bĕ-lĕ.) Instruments of percussion.
Genus syntonum, *Lat.* (jā-nŭs sĭn-tō-nŭm.) An old term of the diatonic scale.
Genus tensile, *Lat.* (jā-nŭs tĕn-sĕ-lĕ.) Stringed instruments.
Gerade bewegung, *Ger.* (ghĕ-rā-dĕ bĕ-vā-goong.) Similar motion.
Gerade taktart, *Ger.* (ghĕ-rā-dĕ täkt-ärt.) Common time.
Geriesel, *Ger.* (ghĕ-rē-z'l.) A soft, murmuring sound.
German fingering. A method of fingering piano music which designates the thumb as the first finger, in distinction from the English or American mode, which indicates the use of the thumb by a sign.
German flute. See *Flàuto Travèrso*.
German scale. A scale of the natural notes, consisting of A, H, C, D, E, F, G, instead of A, B, C, etc., the B being always reserved to express B flat.
German sixth. A name given to a chord composed of a major third, perfect fifth, and extreme sixth, as—
German soprano clef. The C clef placed on the first line of the staff for soprano, instead of the G clef on the second line of that part.
Ges, *Ger.* (ghĕs.) The note G flat.
Gesang, *Ger.* (ghĕ-säng.) Singing; the art of singing, a song, melody, air.
Gesang-buch, *Ger.* (ghĕ-säng bookh.) Song book, hymn book.
Gesang der vögel, *Ger.* (ghĕ-säng dĕr fō-g'l.) Singing of birds.
Gesänge, *Ger. pl.* (ghĕ-säng-ĕ.) Songs, hymns.
Gesangsweise, *Ger.* (ghĕ-sängs-vī-zĕ.) In the style of a song.
Gesangweise, *Ger.* (ghĕ-säng-vī-zĕ.) Melody, tune.
Gesause, *Ger.* (ghĕ-sou-zĕ.) Humming, whistling.
Geschick, *Ger.* (ghĕ-shĭk.) Skill, dexterity.
Geschleift, *Ger.* (ghĕ-shlīft.) Slurred, legato.
Geschwänzte noten. (ghĕ-shvänts-tĕ.) A quaver, or flag notes.
Geschwind, *Ger.* (ghĕ-shvĭnd.) Quick, rapid.
Geschwindigkeit, *Ger.* (ghĕ-shvĭnd-ĭg-kīt.) Swiftness, rapidity, speed.
Geschwindmarsch, *Ger.* (ghĕ-shvĭnd-märsh.) A quickstep.
Ges dur, *Ger.* (ghĕs door.) The key of G flat major.
Gesinge, *Ger.* (ghĕ-sĭng-ĕ.) Constant singing, bad singing.
Gestossen, *Ger.* (ghĕ-stōs-s'n.) Separated, detached.
Gestrichene, *Ger.* (ghĕ strĭ-khĕ-nĕ.) A quaver.
Getern. } Old names for the *cittern*.
Getron. }
Getön, *Ger.* (ghĕ-tŏn.) Repeated sounds, clamor.

GIUB

Getragen, *Ger.* (ghĕ-trä-g'n.) Well sustained, carried.
Getrost, *Ger.* (ghĕ-trōst.) Confidently, resolutely.
Geübtere, *Ger.* (ghĕ-üb-tĕ-rĕ.) Expert performers.
Gewirbel, *Ger.* (ghĕ-vĭr-b'l.) The roll of drums.
Gewiss, *Ger.* (ghĕ-vĭss.) Firm, resolute.
Gewissheit, *Ger.* (ghĕ-vĭss-hīt.) Firmness, resolution.
Geziert, *Ger.* (ghĕ-tsērt.) With affectation.
G flat. The flat seventh of A flat; the fifth flat introduced in modulating by fourths from the natural diatonic mode.
G gamut. The G on the first line of the bass staff.
Ghijghe. An old name for the fiddle: see *Geige*.
Ghiribizzi, *It.* (ghē-rē-bĕt-zē.) Unexpected intervals, eccentric, fantastical passages.
Ghiribizzóso, *It.* (ghē-rē-bĕt-sō-zō.) Fantastical, whimsical.
Ghirónda, *It.* (ghē-rōn-dä.) A hurdy-gurdy.
Ghittern. An old name for the cittern.
Gia maestro di cappella, *It.* (ghē-ä mä-ĕs-trō dĕ kä-pĕl-lä.) Before the master of music.
Giambo, *It.* (jē-äm-bō.) Iambic.
Gicheróso, *It.* (jĕ-kĕ-rō-zō.) Merry, playful.
Giga, *It.* (jē-gä.) } A jig, or lively species
Gigue, *Fr.* (zhĕg.) } of dance. The name is
Gigue, *Ger.* (ghĕg.) } supposed to be derived from the German word *geig*, or *geige*, meaning a fiddle, the music is particularly adapted to instruments of that class.
Gighárdo, *It.* (jē-gär-dō.) A sort of jig.
G in alt. The first note in alt; the octave above the G, or treble clef note.
G in altissimo. The first note in altissimo; the fifteenth above the G or treble clef note.
Ginglarns. A small Egyptian flute.
Giochévole, *It.* (jē-ō-kā-vō-lĕ.) Merry, sportive, gay.
Giochevolménte, *It.* (jē-ō-kā-vōl-mān-tĕ.) }
Giocolarménte, *It.* (jē-ō-kō-lär-mān-tĕ.) } Merrily, sportively.
Giocondaménte, *It.* (jē-ō-kŏn-dä-mān-tĕ.) Merrily, joyfully, gayly.
Giocóndo, *It.* (jē-ō-kŏn-dō.) Cheerful, merry, gay.
Giocosaménte, *It.* (jē-ō-kō-zä-mān-tĕ.) } Humor-
Giocóso, *It.* (jē-ō-kō-zō.) } ously, sportively.
Gioja, *It.* (jō-yä.) Joy, gladness.
Giojánte, *It.* (jē-ō-yän-tĕ.) } Blithe, joyful, gay.
Giojóso, *It.* (jē-ō-yō-zō.) }
Giojosaménte, *It.* (jē-ō-yō-zä-mān-tĕ.) Joyfully, merrily.
Gioviále, *It.* (jē-ō-vē-ä-lĕ.) Jovial.
Giovialitá, *It.* (jē-ō-vē-ä-lē-tä.) Joviality, gayety.
Giraffe. (jĭ-ràf.) A species of ancient *spinet*.
Gis, *Ger.* (ghĭs.) The note G sharp.
Gis moll, *Ger.* (ghĭs mŏll.) The key of G♯ minor.
Gitana, *It.* (jē-tä-nä.) A Spanish dance.
Gittern. (jĭt-tĕrn.) A species of *cittern*.
Gitteth, *Heb.* (jĭt-tĕth.) An instrument which David brought from Gath, of the harp kind.
Giubbilóso, *It.* (joob-bē-lō-zō.) Jubilant, exulting.

94 PRONOUNCING MUSICAL DICTIONARY.

ă *ale,* ă *add,* ä *arm,* ĕ *eve,* ĕ *end,* ĭ *ice,* ĭ *ill,* ō *old,* ŏ *odd,* ȯ *dove,* oo *moon,* ū *lute,* ŭ *but,* ü *French sound.*

GUBI — GOND

Gubilazióne, *It.* (joo-bē-lät-sē-ō-nĕ.) } Jubilation, rejoicing.
Giubilio, *It.* (joo-bē,lē-ō.)
Giubilo, *It.* (joo-bē-lō.)
Giucante, *It.* (joo-kän-tĕ.) } Merry, joyful; see *Giojante.*
Giuchevole, *It.* (joo-kā-vō-lĕ.)
Giulivaménte, *It.* (joo-lē-vä-män-tĕ.) Joyfully, lively.
Giulivissimo, *It.* (joo-lē-vēs-sē-mō.) Very joyful.
Giulivo, *It.* (joo-lē-vō.) Cheerful, joyful.
Giullari, *It.* (jool-lä-rē.) Bands of dancers, actors, or singers.
Giuocante, *It.* (joo-ō-kän-tĕ.) With sport and gayety.
Giuoco, *It.* (joo-ō-kō.) An organ stop.
Giuocóso, *It.* (joo-ō-kō-zō.) See Giocoso.
Giustaménte, *It.* (joos-tä-män-tĕ.) Justly, with precision.
Giústo, *It.* (joos-tō.) A term signifying that the movement indicated is to be performed in an equal, steady and just time.
Giustezza, *It.* (joos-tăt-zä.) Precision.
Given bass. A bass given, to which the harmony is to be added.
Giving out. The prelude by which the organist announces to the congregation the tune they are to sing.
Glais, *Fr.* (glä.) The passing bell.
Glais funébre, *Fr.* (glä fü-näbr.) A funeral knell.
Glapissant. *Fr.* (glä-pis-sänh.) Shrill, squeaking.
Glasses, musical. An instrument formed of a number of glass goblets shaped like finger glasses, tuned by filling them with more or less water, ``∙`` `` `` played upon with the fingers ``..`` listene.
Glatt, *Ger.* (glät.) Smooth, even.
Glätte, *Ger.* (glät-tĕ.) Smoothness, evenness.
Glee. A vocal composition in three or four parts, generally consisting o more than one movement, the subject of which may be grave, tender, or gay and bacchanalian. The glee, in its present form, first appeared in the middle of the eighteenth century, and is a composition peculiar to England.
Gleek. A. o ɑ Anglo Saxon word, signifying *music* or *musician.*
Gleemen. An ancient name for minstrels.
Gleich, *Ger.* (glīkh.) Equal, alike, consonant.
Gleichklang, *Ger.* (glīkh-kläng.) Consonance of sound.
Gleichstimmig, *Ger.* (glīkh-stĭm-mĭg.) Harmonious, accordant.
Gleiten, *Ger.* (glī-t'n.) To slide the fingers.
Gli, *It. pl.* (glē.) The.
Glide. Portamento.
Gliding. In flute playing, a sliding movement of the fingers for the purpose of blending the tones.
Glie, (glee.) An old Anglo Saxon word signifying a *glee.*
Glied, *Ger.* (glēd.) *Link;* the term is used to express a *chord,* as Einglied, *one chord;* Zweiglied, *two chords.*
Glissade, *Fr.* (glĭs-säd.) Gliding; the act of passing the fingers in a smooth, unbroken manner over the keys or strings.

Glissándo, *It.* (glēs-sän-dō.) } Slurred,
Glissáto, *It.* (glēs-sä-tō.) } smooth, in a
Glissement, *Fr.* (glēs-mönh.) } gliding manner.
Glisser, *Fr.* (glēs-sā.) An embellishment which is executed by turning the nail and drawing the thumb or finger rapidly over the keyboard.
Glissez le pouce, *Fr.* (glēs-sā lūh poos.) Slide the thumb.
Glissicándo, *It.* (glēs-sē-kän-dō.) } Slurred;
Glissicáto, *It.* (glēs-sē-kä-tō.) } smooth; in a gliding manner; see also *Glisser.*
Gli stroménti, *It.* (glē strō-män-tĕ.) The instruments.
Glitschen, *Ger.* (glĭt-shĕn.) To glide the finger; see *Glisser.*
Glöckchen, *Ger.* (glŏk-kh'n.) A little bell.
Glocke, *Ger.* (glŏk-ĕ.) A bell.
Glöckeln, *Ger.* (glĕ-kĕln.) To ring little bells.
Glockengeläute, *Ger.* (glŏk'n-gĕ-loy-tĕ.) The ringing or chiming of bells.
Glockenist, *Ger.* (glŏk-ĕn-ĭst.) } Player on the
Glöckner, *Ger.* (glŏk-nĕr.) } chimes, or bell ringer.
Glockenklang, *Ger.* (glŏk-ĕn-kläng.) The sound of bells.
Glockenklöppel, *Ger.* (glŏk-'n-klŏp-p'l.) Bell clapper.
Glockenmass, *Ger.* (glŏk-ĕn-mäss.) Bell founder's diapason.
Glockenläuter, *Ger.* [(glŏk-ĕn-loy-tĕr.) Bell ringer.
Glockenspiel, *Ger.* (glŏk-ĕn-spēl.) Chimes; also, a stop in imitation of bells, in German organs.
Glockenzug, *Ger.* (glŏk-ĕn-tsoog.) The ringing of bels.
Glöcklein-ton, *Ger.* (glŏk-līn tōn.) An organ atop of very small scale and wide measure.
Gloria, *Lat.* (glō-rĭ-a.) A principal movement in a mass.
Glosa, *Spa.* (glō-zä.) A variation.
Glosar, *Spa.* (glō-zär.) To vary the notes.
Glottis, *Gr.* (glŏt-tĭs.) The narrow opening at the upper part of the trachea or windpipe, which by its dilation and contraction contributes to the modulation of the voice. The name is also applied to a kind of reed used by the ancient flute players, which they held between their lips, and blew through in performance.
Glühend, *Ger.* (glū-ĕnd.) Ardent, glowing.
Glyconic, *Lat.* (glī-kŏn-ĭk.) A verse in Greek and Latin poetry of three feet.
G moll, *Ger.* (jă mōl.) The key of G minor.
Gnacchera, *It.* (näk-kā-rä.) A tambourin, a tabor.
Gnugab, *Heb.* (noo-gäb.) The name given by the ancient Hebrews to the organ.
Gol, *Iri.* (gōl.) A funeral dirge of the Irish peasantry.
Góla, *It.* (gō-lä.) The throat; also, a gutteral voice.
Goll trompa. A trumpet used by the ancient Irish, Danes, Normans and English.
Golpe de musica, *Spa.* (gŏl-pĕ dūh moo-zā-kä.) A band of music.
Gondellied, *Ger.* (gŏn-d'l-lēd.) A gondolier song.

ā ate, ă add, ä arm, ē eve, ĕ end, ī ice, ĭ ill, ō old, ŏ odd, ô dove, oo moon, ū lute, ŭ but, ü French sound.

GOND

Gondolier songs. Songs composed and sung by the Venitian gondoliers, of a very graceful and pleasing style; barcarolles.

Gong. A Chinese instrument of the pulsatile kind, consisting of a large, circular plate of metal, which, when struck, produces an exceedingly loud noise.

Gorgear, *Spa.* (gör-hē-är.) To quaver, to warble.

Gorgeo, *Spa.* (gŏr-hē-ō.) Trilling.

Gorghéggi, *It. pl.* (gŏr-gäd-jē.) Rapid divisions, or passages, as exercises for the voice to acquire facility.

Gorgheggiaménto. *It.* (gŏr-gäd-jē-ä-mĕn-tō.) Trilling, quavering.

Gorgheggiáre, *It.* (gŏr-gäd-jē-ä-rĕ.) To trill, to shake.

Gorgéggio; *It.* (gŏr-gäd-jē-ō.) A trill; a shake of the voice in singing.

Gout, *Fr.* (goo.) Taste, style, judgment.

Governing key. The principal key; that key in which a piece is written.

Grab-gesang, *Ger.* (gräb gē-säng.)) Dirge, fu-
Grab-lied, *Ger.* (gräb lēd.) } neral song.

Graces. Ornamental notes and embellishments, either written by the composer, or introduced by the performer. The principal embellishments are the *appoggiatúra*, the *turn* and the *shake*.

Grace note. Any note added to a composition as an embellishment.

Gracieux, *Fr.* (grä-sĭ-ŭh.) Graceful.

Grácile, *It.* (grä-tshē-lĕ.) Thin, weak, small: referring to the tone.

Grazioso, *Spa.* (grä-thē-ō-zō.) Graceful.

Grad, *Ger.* (gräd.) Steps, degree; see *Grado*.

Gradacion, *Spa.* (grä-dä-thē-ŏn.) Gradation of tone.

Gradáre, *It.* (grä-dä-rĕ.) To descend step by step.

Gradataménte, *It.* (grä-dä-tä-mān-tĕ.) } By de-
Gradation, *Fr.* (grä-dä-sē-ŏoh.) } grees,
Gradazióne, *It.* (grä-dä-tsē-ō-nĕ.) } a gradual increase, or diminution of speed, or intensity of tone.

Gradévole, *It.* (grä-dā-vō-lĕ.) }
Gradevolménte, *It.* (grä-dä-vōl-mān-tĕ.) }
Gracefully, pleasingly.

Gradíre, *It.* (grä-dē-rĕ.) To ascend, step by step.

Graditaménte, *It.* (grä-dē-tä-mān-tĕ.) In a pleasing manner.

Graditissimo, *It.* (grä-dē-tēs-sē-mō.) Very sweetly, most gracefully.

Gradleiter, *Ger.* (gräd-lī-tĕr.) A scale.

Grádo, *It.* (grä-dō.) A degree, or single step on the staff; *di grado* means that the melody moves by degrees, ascending or descending, in opposition to *di salto*, by skips of greater intervals.

Grádo ascendénte, *It.* (grä-dō ä-shĕn-dān-tĕ.) An ascending degree.

Grado descendénte, *It.* (grä-dō dä-shĕn-dān-tĕ.) A descending degree.

Grados, *Spa.* (grä-dōs.) Musical intervals.

Gradual. That part of the Roman Catholic service that is sung between the Epistle and the Gospel, and which was anciently sung on the steps of the altar.

Gradualménte, *It.* (grä-doo-äl-mān-tĕ.) }
Graduataménte, *It.* (grä-doo-ä-tä-mān-tĕ.) }
Gradually, by degrees or steps.

GRAP

Gradual modulation. Modulation in which some chord is taken before the modulating chord, which may be considered as belonging to the original key or the new key.

Graduare, *It.* (grä-doo-ä-rĕ.) To divide into degrees.

Graduazióne, *It.* (grä-doo-ä-tsē-ō-nĕ.) See *Gradasione*.

Graduellement, *Fr.* (grä-dwäl-mänb.) } Grad-
Gradweise, *Ger.* (gräd-vī-zĕ.) } ually, by degrees.

Grail. (grāl.) The gradual.

Graillement, *Fr.* (grä-mänh.) A hoarse sound.

Grammar, musical. The rules by which musical compositions are governed.

Grammatical accent. The common measure accent, marked by the length of the words, and a regular succession of strong and weak parts.

Gran, *It.* (grän.) } Great, grand.
Grande, *It.* (grän-dĕ.) }

Gran cantore, *It.* (grän kän-tō-rĕ.) A fine singer.

Gran cássa, *It.* (grän käs-sä.) The great drum.

Grand-barré, *Fr.* (gränh bär-rā.) In guitar playing this means laying the first finger of the left hand upon all the six strings of the guitar at once.

Grand bourdon. Great or double bourdon; an organ stop of 32 feet tone in the pedal.

Grand chantre, *Fr.* (gränh shäntr.) A precentor.

Grand choir. In organ playing, the union of all the reed stops.

Grand cornet. This name is sometimes given to a reed stop of 16 feet scale on the manuals of an organ.

Grande messe, *Fr.* (gränhd mäss.) High mass.

Grande mesure a deux temps, *Fr.* (gränhd mā-zhūr ä dū tänh.) Common time of *two beats* in a bar, marked 2-2, or sometimes 4-4, or ₵; see also *Alla Cappella*.

Grandézza, *It.* (grän-dāt-sä.) Grandeur, dignity.

Grandióso, *It.* (grän-dē-ō-zō.) Grand, noble.

Grandisonánte, *It.* (grän-dē-zō-nän-tĕ.) Very sonorous, full sounding.

Grand jeux, *Fr.* (gränh zhŭ.) Full organ, all the stops in organ playing.

Grand opera. Italian opera; a full opera with an intricate plot and full cast of performers.

Grand orgue, *Fr.* (gränh dŏrg.) Great organ.

Grand pianoforte. A pianoforte in which nearly all the octaves have three strings to each tone, tuned in unison, and struck at once by the same hammer.

Grand sonata. An extended sonata, consisting generally of four movements.

Gran gústo, *It.* (grän goos-tō.) In a lofty, elevated manner, a full, rich, high-wrought composition. The manner of a fine and great singer is said to be in the *gran gusto*.

Gran prova, *It.* (grän prō-vä.) The last rehearsal.

Gran tambúro, *It.* (grän täm-boo-rō.) The great drum.

Gráppa, *It.* (gräp-pä.) The brace, or character used to connect two or more staves.

ā *ale,* ă *add,* ä *arm,* ē *eve,* ĕ *end,* ī *ice,* ĭ *ill,* ō *old,* ŏ *odd,* ô *dove,* oo *moon,* ū *lute,* ŭ *but,* ü *French sound.*

GRAT

Gratias agimus, *Lat.* (grä-ahl-ăs ăj-ĭ-mŭs.) Part of the gloria in a mass.
Grave, *It.* (grä-vĕ.) A slow and solemn movement, also a deep low pitch in the scale of sounds.
Gravecembalum, *Lat.* (grä-vĕ-sĕm-bä-lüm.) An old name for the harpsichord.
Gravement, *Fr.* (gräv-mänh.) } With gravity, in a dignified and solemn manner.
Gravemente, *It.* (grä-vĕ-mĕn-tĕ.) }
Gravĕzza, *It.* (grä-vĕt-tsä.) Gravity, solemnity.
Gravicémbalo, *It.* (grä-vĕ-tshăm-bä-lō.) } An old name for the harpsichord.
Gravicémbolo, *It.* (grä-vĕ-tshăm-bō-lō.) }
Gravisonante, *It.* (grä-vĕ-zō-nän-tĕ.) Loud sounding.
Gravità, *It.* (grä-vĕ-tä.) }
Gravität, *Ger.* (grä-fĭ-tät.) } Gravity, majesty.
Gravité, *Fr.* (grä-vĭ-tä.) }
Gravity. That modification of any sound by which it becomes deep or low in respect to some other sound. The gravity of sounds depends in general on the mass, extent, and tension of the sonorous bodies. The larger and more lax the bodies, the slower will be the vibrations and the graver the sounds.
Grăzia, *It,* (grä-tsē-ä.) } Grace, elegance.
Grazie, *Ger.* (grä-tsī-ĕ.) }
Graziosamente, *It.* (grä-tsē-ō-zä-mĕn-tĕ.) Gracefully, smoothly.
Graziōso, *It.* (grä-tsē-ō-zō.) In a graceful style.
Greater scale. Major scale.
Greater sixth. A name sometimes given to the major sixth.
Greater third. A name sometimes given to the major third.
Great octave. The name given in Germany to the notes between C and B inclusive; these notes are expressed by capital letters.
Great organ. In an organ with three rows of keys, usually the middle row, so called because containing the greatest number of stops, and having its pipes voiced louder than those in the swell or choir organ.
Great sixth. The appellation given to the chord of the fifth and sixth when the fifth is perfect and the sixth major.
Grecian lyre. A lyre of the ancient Greeks, having but seven strings and quite small, being held in the hand when played upon.
Greek modes. The ancient Greek modes or scales were twelve in number; of these, six were *authentic,* and six plagal. The sounds are supposed to have been somewhat similar to those in the scale of C.
Gregorian chant. A style of choral music, according to the eight celebrated church modes introduced by Pope Gregory in the sixth century.
Gregorianisch, *Ger.* (grĕ-gō-rĭ-än-ĭsh.) Gregorian.
Gregorianischer Gesang, *Ger.* (grĕ-gō-rĭ-än-ĭsh.) The Gregorian chant.
Gregorian modes. } Those chants or melodies
Gregorian tones. } used for the Psalms in the Roman Catholic service, and also in many English churches. They are taken from the ancient Greek modes, and the sounds are supposed to

GRUN

have been somewhat similar to those in the modern or natural scale of C.
Gregoriáno, *It.* (grä-gō-rĕ-ä-nō.) } Gregorian.
Gregorien, *Fr.* (grä-gō-rĭ-änh.) }
Grell, *Ger.* (grĕll.) Shrill, acute.
Grellheit, *Ger.* (grĕll-hīt.) Sharpness, shrillness.
Grelot, *Fr.* (grä-lō.) A small bell.
Grex, *Lat.* (grĕx.) The chorus in a play.
Griffbret, *Ger.* (grĭff-brĕt.) The finger-board of a violin, violincello, etc.
Griffloch, *Ger.* (grĭff-lōkh.) The holes of a flute and like instruments.
Grillig, *Ger.* (grĭl-lĭg.) Capricious, fanciful.
Gringotter, *Fr.* (gränh-gō-tä.) To quaver, to warble.
Grisoller, *Fr.* (grĕ-zō-lä.) To sing like a lark.
Grob, *Ger.* (grōb.) Deep, low voice, bass.
Grob-gedackt, *Ger.* (grōb ghĕ-däkht.) Large stopped diapason of full tone.
Groppétto, *It.* (grōp-pä-tō.) See *Gruppétto.*
Grōppo, *It.* (grōp-pō.) A group of notes, a rapid vocal passage.
Gros-fa. A name formerly given to old church music in square notes, semibreves and minima.
Grossartig, *Ger.* (grōs-är-tĭg.) Grand.
Grosse, *Ger.* (grōs-ĕ.) Major, speaking of intervals; also grand in respect to style.
Grosse caisse, *Fr.* (grōs käss.) The great drum.
Grosse nazard, *Ger.* (grōs-ĕ nä-tsärd.) An organ stop, sounding a fifth above the diapasons.
Grosse principal, *Ger.* (grōs-ĕ prĭn-tsĭ-päl.) An organ stop of 32 feet scale of the open diapason species.
Grosse quint, *Ger.* (grōs-ĕ quĭnt.)
Grosse quinten-bass, *Ger.* (grōs-ĕ quĭn-t'n bäss.) } An organ stop in the pedals sounding a fifth or twelfth to the great bass of 32 feet or 16 feet.
Grosse sonate, *Ger. pl.* (grōs-ĕ sō-nä-tĕ.) Grand sonatas.
Grosse tierce, *Ger.* (grōs-ĕ tĕr-sĕ.) Great third sounding stop in an organ, producing the third or tenth, above the foundation stops.
Grosse trommel, *Ger.* (grōs-ĕ trŏm-m'l.) The great drum.
Gross-gedacht, *Ger.* (g'rōs ghĕ-däkht.) Double stopped diapason of 16 feet tone in an organ.
Grōsso, *It.* (grōs-sō.) Full, great, grand.
Grossvatertanz, *Ger.* (grōs-fä-tĕr-tänts.) Grandfather's dance; an old fashioned dance.
Gros tambour, *Fr.* (grō tänh-boor.) The great drum.
Grottésco, *It.* (grŏt-tās-kō.) Grotesque.
Ground. The name of any composition in which the bass, consisting of a few bars of independent notes, is perpetually repeated to an ever-varying melody.
Ground bass. A bass consisting of a few simple notes, intended as a theme, on which, at each repetition, a new melody is constructed.
Gromp. Several short notes tied together.
Grund-stimme, *Ger.* (groond stĭm-mĕ.) The bass part.
Grund-ton, *Ger.* (groond tōn.) The bass note; fundamental, or principal tone.

ă ale, ă add, ă arm, ĕ eve, ĕ end, ī ice, ĭ ill, ō old, ŏ odd, ô dove, oo moon, ū lute, ŭ but, ü French sound.

GRUP

Gruppétto, *It.* (groop-pā́-tŏ.) A turn; also, a small group of grace, or ornamental notes.
Gruppe, *Ger.* (groop-pĕ.) } A group of notes;
Grúppo, *It.* (groop-pŏ.) } formerly it meant a trill, shake or turn.
G-schlüssel, *Ger.* (gā-shlüs-s'l.) The G, or treble clef.
Guarácha, *Spa.* (gwär-äk-ä.) A Spanish dance.
Guarnerius. (gwär-nā-rĭ-ŭs.) A make of violin highly prized, so called from the name of the manufacturer.
Guddok, *Rus.* (goo-dŏk.) A rustic violin, with three strings, used among the Russian peasantry.
Guerriéro, *It.* (gwĕr-rē-ā-rō.) Martial, warlike.
Guet, *Fr.* (gā.) A military trumpet piece.
Guia, *Spa.* (ghē-ä.) Fugue, conductor, leader.
Guída, *It.* (gwē-dä.) Guide; also, the mark called a *direct*.
Guída armónica, *It.* (gwē-dä är-mō-pē-kä.) A guide to harmony.
Guída musica, *It.* (gwē-dä moo-zē-kä.) An instruction book in music.
Guide. That note in a fugue which leads off and announces the subject.
Guide-main, *Fr.* (ghēd mănh.) The hand guide, an instrument invented by Kalkbrenner, for assisting young players to acquire a good position of the hands on the pianoforte.
Guidon, *Fr.* (ghē-dŏnh.) The mark called a *direct*.
Guidonian hand. The figure of a left hand used by Guido and upon which was marked the names of the sounds forming his three hexachords.
Guidonian syllables. The syllables ut, re, mi, fa, sol, la, used by Guido d'Arezzo, and called the Aretinian scale.
Guido's gamut. The table or scale introduced by Guido Aretinus in 1204, and to the notes of which he applied the syllables, ut, re, mi, fa, sol, la. It consisted of twenty notes, viz., two octaves and a major sixth, the first octave being distinguished by capital letters, the second by small letters and the sixth by double small letters.
Guigue, *It.* (gwē-ghē.) See Giga.
Guiltern. See *Gittern*.
Guimbarde, *Fr.* (ghĕm-bärd.) A Jew's harp,

GYNA

Guion, *Spa.* (ghē-ōn.) A sign indicating that the piece or passage is to be repeated.
Guitar. (ghĭt-är.) An instrument with six strings, the body of which is somewhat oval in form and the neck somewhat similar to the violin. The strings are tuned in *fourths*, with the exception of the third string which is tuned a third below the second. There are three kinds: the German, Italian and Spanish guitar. It is supposed to be of Spanish invention and is very popular in that country.
Guitare, *Fr.* (ghĭt-är.)
Guitárre, *Spa* (ghē-tär-rä.) } A guitar.
Guitarre, *Ger.* (ghĭt-är-rĕ.)
Guitárre d'amour, *Fr.* (ghē-tär d'ä-moor.) A modification of the German guitar.
Guitarre, lyre, *Fr.* (ghē-tär lērh.) A French instrument having six strings and formed somewhat like an ancient lyre.
Guitarrero, *Spa.* (ghē-tär-rā-rō.) A guitar maker.
Guitarfila, *Spa.* (ghē-tä-rēl-yä.) A little guitar.
Guitarrista, *Spa.* (ghē-tär-rēs-tä.) A guitar player.
Guitarron, *Spa.* (ghē-tär-rōn.) A large guitar.
Guiterne, *Fr.* (ghē-tärn.) An ancient species of lute or guitar.
Gunst, *Ger.* (goonst.) Grace, tenderness, favor.
Gurácho, *Spa.* (goo-rä-kō.) See *Guarácha*.
Gusto, *It.* (goos-tō.) Taste, expression.
Gustosaménte, *It.* (goos-tō-zä-mǟn-tĕ.) Tastefully, expressively.
Gustóso, *It.* (goos-tō-zō.) Expressive, tasteful.
G, ut. A name applied by Guido to the tone large G, because this tone was the lowest of the whole system of tones.
Gutdünken, *Ger.* (goot-dün-k'n.) At pleasure, according to the taste of the performer.
Guttural. Formed in the throat, pertaining to the throat.
Gutturalmente, *It.* (goot-too-räl-mǟn-tĕ.) Gutturally.
Gummastikos, *Gr.* (gŭm-näs-tĭ-kōs.) Contests of skill among the ancients, in which the performance of music formed a principal part.
Gynaikites, *Tur.* A female choir; the place designed for female singers in a mosque.

ă ale, ă add, ă arm, ĕ eve, ĕ end, ĭ ice, ĭ ill, ō old, ŏ odd, ō dove, oo moon, ŭ lute, ŭ but, ü French sound.

H

H. This letter is used by the Germans for B natural, which note is called by the French and Italians, *si*.
Habanera, *Spa.* (hä-bän-ĕ-rä.) A slow Spanish dance in 3–4 time; a dance.
Haber-rohr, *Ger.* (hä-bĕr rōr.) Shepherd's flute.
Hackbrett, *Ger.* (häk-brĕt.) The dulcimer.
Halb, *Ger.* (hälb.) Half.
Halb-cadence, *Ger.* (hälb kä-dĕn-tsĕ.) Half cadence.
Halb-note, *Ger.* (hälb nō-tĕ.) A minim or half note.
Halb-ton, *Ger.* (hälb tōn.) Half tone, semitone.
Half-cadence. An imperfect cadence, a close on the dominant.
Half-note. A minim.
Half-note rest. A pause equal in duration to a half note.
Half-shift. The first shift on a violin; that on the fifth line.
Half-step. The smallest interval used in music.
Half-tone. A semitone.
Hall, *Ger.* (häll.) } Sound, clangor, clang.
Halle, *Ger.* (häl-lĕ.) }
Hall-drommete, *Ger.* (häll drōm-mä-tĕ.) A powerful trumpet.
Hallelujah, *Heb.* (häl-lĕ-loo-yäh.) *Praise ye the Lord;* a song of thanksgiving.
Hallelujah metre. A stanza in six lines of iambic measure, the syllables of each being in number and order as follows: 6, 6, 6, 6, 8, 8.
Hallen, *Ger.* (häl-l'n.) To sound, to clang.
Hall-trompete, *Ger.* (häll trōm-pä-tĕ.) A powerful trumpet.
Halmpfeife, *Ger.* (hälm-pfī-fĕ.) Shepherd's pipe.
Hals, *Ger.* (häls.) Neck of a violin, viola, etc.
Hammer. That part of the *action* or mechanism of a pianoforte, which strikes the strings and thus produces the sound.
Hammer, tuning. An instrument by which pianos and harps are tuned, by tightening or loosening the strings.
Hanche, *Fr.* (hänh-shĕ.) See *Anche*.
Hand drum. A tamborine.
Hände, *Ger.* (hän-dĕ.) Hands.
Händespiel, *Ger.* (hän-dĕ-spēl.) Organ keys.
Hand-glocke, *Ger.* (händ glŏ-kĕ.) Hand bell.
Hand-guide. See *Guide-main*. [tanet.
Hand-klapper, *Ger.* (händ kläp-pĕr.) A castanet.
Hand-harmonica. An accordean.
Handlage, *Ger.* (händ-lä-ghĕ.) The position of the hand.
Handleiter, *Ger.* (händ-lī-tĕr.) Hand-guide; See *Guide*.
Hand organ. A portable instrument consisting of a cylinder, on which by means of wires, pins and staples are set the tunes, the revolution of the cylinder causing the pins, etc., to act on the keys and also to give admission to the wind.
Hardiment, *Fr.* (här-dī-mänh.) Boldly firmly.
Harfe, *Ger.* (här-fĕ.) A harp.
Harfen, *Ger.* (här-f'n.) To play on the harp.
Harfener, *Gr.* (här-f'n-ĕr.) Harp player.
Harfenett, *Ger.* (bär-f'nĕt.) A little harp.
Harfenist, *Ger.* (här-f'nĭst.) Harp player.
Harfen-saite, *Ger.* (här-f'n sī-tĕ.) Harp string.

HARM

Harfen-spieler, *Ger.* (här-f'n spē-lĕr.) Harp player.
Harmatian air. This term is derived from the Greek, and is the name given by the ancients to a certain air composed by Olympus, and used to animate horses that drew the chariot during battle.
Harmonia, *Lat.* (här-mō-nĭ-ä.) A daughter of Mars and Venus. Her name was first used to indicate music in general.
Harmonic. Concordant, musical.
Harmonica. A musical instrument invented by Benjamin Franklin, consisting of glasses, sometimes globular, and sometimes flat. The tone is produced by rubbing the edge of the globular glasses with a moistened finger, or striking the flat ones with small hammers. The name is also applied to an organ stop of delicate tone.
Harmonica-ätherisch, *Ger.* (här-mō-nĭ-kä ä-tĕr-ĭsh.) A mixture stop of very delicate scale in German organs.
Harmonical trumpet. An instrument very much like a trumpet, except that it is longer and consists of more branches; the sackbut.
Harmonic figuration. The progression from one tone to another of the same chord, thence passing in the same manner through successive different chords.
Harmonic flute. An open metal organ stop, of 8 or 4 feet pitch; the pipes are of double length, that is, 16 or 8 foot, and the bodies have a hole bored in them midway between the foot and the top; the tone is exceedingly full, fluty and powerful.
Harmonic hand. The Guidonian hand.
Harmonichord. An instrument having the form of an upright piano, but a tone something like that of a violin, produced by the friction of a cylinder covered with leather upon the strings. It was invented in 1785, by Fr. Kaufman.
Harmonici, *It. pl.* (här-mō-nē-tshē.) Harmonics in violin music.
Harmonic mark. A sign used in violin, harp music, etc., to indicate that certain passages are to be played upon such parts of the open strings as will produce the harmonic sounds, O.
Harmonic modulation. A change in the harmony from one key to another.
Harmonicon. A small instrument held in the hand, the sounds being produced from small metal springs, set in motion by blowing from the mouth.
Harmonics. An epithet applied to those concomitant, accessory sounds accompanying a principal, and apparently simple tone. Harmonics are also artificially produced from the harp, violin, etc., by lightly touching the strings at certain points.
Harmonic triad. The common chord, consisting of a fundamental note, its third and fifth.
Harmonie, *Fr.* (här-mō-nē.) } Harmony.
Harmonie, *Ger.* (här-mō-nē.) }
Harmonie-musik, *Ger.* (här-mō-nē moo-zēk.) Music for wind instruments only.
Harmonie-regeln, *Ger.* (här-mō-nē rā-g'ln.) The rules or laws of harmony.
Harmonieusement, *Fr.* (här-mō-nĭ-ŭs-mänh.) Harmoniously.

ā ale, ă add, ä arm, ē eve, ĕ end, ī ice, ĭ ill, ō old, ŏ odd, ô dove, oo moon, ū lute, ŭ but, ü French sound.

HARM

Harmonie-verständiger, *Ger.* (här-mō-nē fĕr-stän-dĭ-ghĕr.) Harmonist; one versed in harmony.

Harmonieux, *Fr.* (här-mō-nĭ-ŭh.) Harmonious.

Harmonious. A term applicable to any two or more sounds which form a consonant or agreeable union.

Harmoniphon. A small instrument with a keyboard like a pianoforte, invented in 1837, and intended to supply the place of hautboys in an orchestra. The sounds are produced from small metal tongues acted upon by a current of air through a flexible tube.

Harmonique, *Fr.* (här-mō-nēk.) Harmonic; the relation of sounds to each other; also applied to organ pipes of double length.

Harmoniquement, *Fr.* (här-mō-nēk-mänh.) Harmonically.

Harmoniren, *Ger.* (här-mō-nē-r'n.) To harmonize, to be in unison.

Harmonisch, *Ger.* (här-mō-nĭsh.) Harmonious, harmonical.

Harmonische theilung, *Ger.* (här-mō-nĭ-ahĕ tī-loong.) Harmonical division.

Harmonist. One acquainted with the science of harmony.

Harmonista, *Spa.* (här-mō-nĕs-tä.) A harmonist, a musician.

Harmonium. An instrument played upon by means of keys, like a pianoforte, and furnished with bellows, the tones being produced by the vibration of metallic reeds.

Harmonize. To combine two or more parts according to the laws of harmony.

Harmonized. A melody is said to be *harmonized* when additional parts are subjoined in order to give it more fullness.

Harmonizer. A practical harmonist; in an extended sense a composer, but usually limited to mean one who supplies additional parts to the compositions of others.

Harmonometre, *Fr.* (här-mō-nō-mătr.) An instrument to measure the proportion of sounds, a species of monochord.

Harmony. The agreement or consonance of two or more united sounds. The art of combining sounds into chords and treating those chords according to certain rules.

Harmony, borrowed. Chords of the added ninth derived from the dominant seventh, by substituting the ninth in place of the eighth.

Harmony, close. A harmony whose tones are compact and nearly allied in regard to pitch.

Harmony, compound. Simple harmony with the harmony of another octave added.

Harmony, dispersed. A harmony in which the notes forming the different chords are separated by wide intervals.

Harmony, dominant. Harmony on the fifth of the key.

Harmony, false. A harmony contrary to the received rules.

Harmony, figured. Harmony in which, for the purpose of melody, one or more of the parts of a composition move, during the continuance of a chord, through certain notes that do not form any of the constituent parts of that chord,

HARP

Harmony, natural. The harmonic triad or common chord.

Harmony, simple. A harmony in which there is no concord to the fundamental above an octave; it is sometimes termed *close* harmony.

Harmony, suspended. One or more notes of a chord retained in the following chord.

Harp. A stringed instrument of very ancient origin, consisting of a triangular frame, having strings extended in parallel sections from the upper part to one of its sides, and played with the fingers.

Harp, Æolian. An instrument consisting of wire or catgut drawn in parallel lines over a box of thin wood and placed so that a current of air may cause the strings to vibrate.

Harp, couched. Name originally given to the spinet.

Harp, double action. A harp with pedals that can be used in two positions, the first, raising the instrument a half tone, and the second a whole tone.

Harpe, *Fr.* (härp.) A harp.

Harpechorde, *Fr.* (härp-kŏrd.) A old French name for the harpsichord.

Harpe Eolienne, *Fr.* (härp ā-ō-lĭ-ĕnu.) Æolian harp.

Harpeggiate, *It.* (här-pĕd-jē-ä-tĕ.) In the style of a harp, arpeggiately.

Harpeggiato, *It.* (här-pĕd-jē-ä-tō.) Causing the sounds of a chord, to be played not together but distinctly one after another. See *Arpeggiato.*

Harpeggiren, *Ger.* (här-pĕ-ghē-r'n.) Arpeggiate.

Harper. } A performer upon the harp.
Harpist. }

Harp, Jew's. A small instrument made of brass or steel with a flexible metal tongue, played upon by placing it between the teeth and vibrating the tongue by striking it with the finger: the action of the breath determines the power of the tone.

Harp lute. An instrument having twelve strings, and resembling the guitar.

Harp pedal. The pedal of a pianoforte, sometimes called the soft pedal.

Harpsecol. See Harpsichord.

Harpsichord. An instrument much used before the invention of the pianoforte. In shape it resembled the grand pianoforte and had sometimes two rows of keys, but it was very inferior to that instrument in capacity for power and expression: the various shades of loud or. soft could only be obtained by changing from one set of keys to the other, or by moving certain stops as in the organ. The compass was about four octaves.

Harpsichord, double. A harpsichord with two unison strings and an octave.

Harpsichord, harmonica. A harmonica, the sounds of which are produced by means of keys similar to the pianoforte, invented at Berlin.

Harpsichord, viol. An old French instrument resembling a viol, played with a wheel.

Harpsichord, single. A harpsichord with two unison strings.

Harpsichord, vis-a-vis. A harpsichord arranged for two performers at the same time, A double harpsichord.

ă ale, ă add, ă arm, ē eve, ĕ end, ī ice, ĭ ill, ō old, ŏ odd, ô dove, oo moon, ū lute, ŭ but, ü French sound.

HARP

Harpsicon. An old name for the harpsichord.
Harp, single action. A harp whose pedals can be used in one position only, raising the sounds of the instrument a half tone.
Harp style. In the arpeggio style.
Harp treadle. The pedal of the harp.
Harp, triangular. An ancient instrument of Phrygian invention.
Harp, wels. An ancient instrument having about one hundred strings.
Harsur, *Heb.* (här-soor.) An instrument of ten strings, used by the Hebrews.
Harte. *Ger.* (här-tĕ.) Major, in respect to intervals and scales.
Hart-klingend, *Ger.* (härt klĭng-ĕnd.) Hard sounding; harsh.
Hasur, *Heb.* (hä-zoor.) An ancient instrument with ten strings.
Hate, *Fr.* (hawt.) Haste, speed.
Haubois, *Fr.* (hō-bwä.) See *Hautbois*.
Haupt, *Ger.* (houpt.) Head, principal.
Haupt-kirche, *Ger.* (houpt kĭr-khĕ.) Cathedral.
Haupt-manual, *Ger.* (houpt mä-noo-ăl.) The great or principal manual, the great organ.
Haupt-note, *Ger.* (houpt no-tĕ.) The principal note in a shake or turn; that note over which the —, or the tr is placed.
Haupt-periode, *Ger.* (houpt pĕ-rĭ-ō-dĕ.) Capital period; the principal period in a musical phrase.
Haupt-satz, *Ger.* (houpt sätz.) Principal theme, or subject; the *motive*, or leading idea.
Haupt-schluss, *Ger.* (houpt shloos.) A final cadence.
Haupt-tonart, *Ger.* (houpt tō-närt.) The principal key of a composition.
Haupt-stimme, *Ger.* (houpt stĭm-mĕ.) Principal voice; principal part.
Haupt-ton, *Ger.* (houpt tōn.) Fundamental, or principal tone; the tonic.
Haupt-werk, *Ger.* (houpt värk.) Chief work, or manual; the great organ.
Hausse, *Fr.* (hōss.) The nut of a bow.
Hausser, *Fr.* (hōs-sā.) To raise, or sharpen the pitch.
Haut, *Fr.* (hō.) Acute, high, shrill.
Hautb. An abbreviation of Hautboy.
Hautbois, *Fr.* (hō-bwä.) The *oboè* or hautboy.
Hautbois d'amour, *Fr.* (hō-bwä d'a-moor.) A species of hautboy with a pleasing tone, but difficult to play in tune, and now nearly obsolete; also an organ stop.
Hautboy, (hō-boy.) A portable wind instrument of the reed kind, with a *double reed*, consisting of a tube gradually widening from the top toward the lower end, and furnished with keys and circular holes for modulating its sounds: the tone is penetrating and slightly nasal, and peculiarly adapted to express soft and plaintive passages. The name is also given to an 8 feet organ reed stop, the tone of which resembles that of the hautboy.
Hautboy-clarion. See *Octave Hautboy*.
Hautboyist. A performer on the hautboy or oboe.

HEPT

Haute-contre, *Fr.* (hōt-kōntr.) High or counter tenor.
Haute-dessus, *Fr.* (hōt-dĕs-sū.) High treble, first treble.
Hautement, *Fr.* (hōt-mänh.) Haughtily; in a dignified manner.
Haute-taille, *Fr.* (hōt tā-yŭh.) High tenor.
H bes, *Ger.* (hä bĕs.) B double flat.
H dur, *Ger.* (hä door.) B major.
Head. That part of a note which determines its position on the staff and to which the stem is joined.
Head tones. Tones produced by the upper register of the voice.
Head voice. The upper or highest register of the voice; the falsetto in men's voices.
Hearsal. An old name for rehearsal.
Hebdomadarie, *Spa.* (hĕb-dō-mä-dä-rē-o.) A person who officiates a week in a choir.
Hebdomadary. A member of a convent whose weekly turn it is to officiate in the choir, rehearse the anthems, prayers, etc.
Heer-horn, *Ger.* (här hōrn.) A military trumpet.
Heer-pauke, *Ger.* (här pou-kĕ.) Kettle-drum, tymbal.
Herr-pauker, *Ger.* (här pou-kĕr.) Kettle drummer, military drummer.
Heftig, *Ger.* (hĕf-tĭg.) Vehement, boisterous.
Heftigkeit, *Ger.* (hĕf-tĭg-kīt.) Vehemence, impetuosity.
Heiss, *Ger.* (hīss.) Hot, ardent.
Heiter, *Ger.* (hī-tĕr.) Serene, bright.
Helden-lied, *Ger.* (hĕl-d'n lēd.) Heroic song.
Heldenmüthig, *Ger.* (hĕl-d'n-mū-tĭg.) Heroic.
Helikon, *Ger.* (hĕl-ĭ-kōn) ⎫ The name of an
Helicon, *Eng.* (hĕl-ĭ-kŏn.) ⎭ ancient instrument said to be invented by Ptolemy, for demonstrating, or measuring consonances.
Hell, *Ger.* (hĕl.) Clear, bright.
Helle stimme, *Ger.* (hĕl-lĕ stĭm-mĕ.) A clear voice.
Hemi. *Gr.* (hă-mĭ.) Half.
Hemidemisemiquaver. A sixty-fourth note.
Hemidemisemiquaver rest. A sixty-fourth rest.
Hemidiapente, *Gr.* (hĕm-ĭ-dē-ä-păn-tĕ.) Diminished, or imperfect fifth.
Hemiditonos, *Gr.* (hĕm-ĭ-dē-tō-nōs.) Lesser or minor third.
Hemiope, *Gr.* (hä-mē-ō-pĕ.) An ancient flute consisting of a tube with three holes.
Hemi phrase. A member of a phrase consisting of only one bar.
Hemistitch. Half a poetic verse, or a verse not completed.
Hemistiquio, *Spa.* (hĕ-mĭe-tē-kĭ-ō.) A hemistitch.
Hemitone. A half tone, called now a *semitone*.
Hemitonium, *Gr.* (hä-mĭ-tō-nĭ-ŭm.) A semitone or half tone.
Heptachord. A scale or system of seven sounds. In ancient poetry verses sung or played on seven chords or different notes; a lyre or cithera having seven strings.

ā ale, ă add, ä arm, ē eve, ĕ end, ī ice, ĭ ill, ō old, ŏ odd, ô dove, oo moon, ū lute, ŭ but, ü French sound.

HEPT

Heptachordon, *Gr.* (hĕp-tä-kŏr-dŏn.) The major seventh.
Heptameris, *Gr.* (hĕp-tä-mā-rĭs.) In ancient music the seventh part of a *meris*, or forty-third part of an octave.
Heptaphonos, *Gr.* (hĕp-tä-fō-nŏs.) The name given to each of the ten musical notes used during the middle ages.
Herabstrich, *Ger.* (hăr-ăb-strĭkh.) A down-bow.
Heralds, or "Des herauts," *Fr.* (dā-zĕr-ō.) An appellation formerly applied by the French to minstrels, because on account of the strength and clearness of their voices, they were qualified for that duty.
Heraufgehen, *Ger.* (hăr-ouf-gā'n.) To ascend.
Hergeigen, *Ger.* (hăr-ghī-g'n.) To fiddle.
Hersingen, *Ger.* (hăr-sĭn-g'n.) To recite in a singing manner.
Herstrich, *Ger.* (hăr-strĭkh) A down bow.
Hervorgehoben, *Ger.* (hăr-fōr-ghĕ-hō-b'n.)
Hervorhebend, *Ger.* (hăr-fōr-hā-bĕnd.)
Hervortretend, *Ger.* (hăr-fōr-trĕ-tĕnd.)
Play the notes very prominently and distinctly.
Herzlich, *Ger.* (hĕrts-līkh.) Tenderly, delicately.
Hesychiastic, *Gr.* (hā-sĭ-kī-ăs-tĭk.) A chord in ancient music equivalent to a modern sixth.
Hexachord, *Ger.* (hĕx-ă-kŏrd.) A scale or system of six sounds; an interval of a sixth; a lyre having six strings.
Hexachordon, *Gr.* (hĕx-ă-kŏr-dŏn.) A major sixth.
Hexachorde, *Fr.* (hĕx-ă-kŏrd.) A *hexachord*. See that word.
Hexameron, *Gr.* (hĕx-ăm-ĕ-rŏn.) Set of six musical pieces or songs.
Hexameter. In ancient poetry, a verse of six feet, the first four of which may be either dactyls or spondees, the fifth always a dactyl and the sixth a spondee.
Hexametro, *Spa.* (hĕx-ăm-ĕ-trō.) Hexameter.
Hexaphonic. Composed of six voices.
Hexastich, *Gr.* (hĕx-ăs-tĭch.) A poem of six verses.
Hialemos, *Gr.* (hī-ăl-ĕ-mŏs.) An elegy, a lament.
Hiatus, *Lat.* (hī-ă-tŭs.) A gap, imperfect harmony.
Hibernian melodies. Irish melodies.
Hidden. A term applied to octaves and fifths when the harmony moves in such a manner that consecutive octaves and fifths may be imagined, although they do not really occur.
Hidden canon. A close canon.
Hidden consecutives. Such as occur in passing by similar motion from an imperfect to a perfect concord.
Hief-horn, *Ger.* (hēf hŏrn.) Bugle horn, hunting horn.
Hief, *Ger.* (hēf.) } Sound given by
Hief-stoss, *Ger.* (hēf stōes.) } the bugle or hunting horn.
Hierophon, *Gr.* (hē-rō-fŏn.) A singer of sacred music.
Higgaion selah, *Heb.* (hĭg-gă-ŏn sā-läh.) A term employed in ancient Hebrew music to indicate the use of stringed instruments with the trumpets.
High. Acute in pitch, speaking of sounds.

HOCK

High bass. A voice between bass and tenor; a baritone.
Higher rhythm. A rhythmical form which is larger than a single measure.
High mass. The mass celebrated in the Roman Catholic churches by the singing of the choristers, distinguishing it from the low mass in which the prayers are read without singing.
High soprano. The first soprano.
High tenor. Counter tenor voice; the highest male voice.
High treble clef. In old French music, the G clef, placed on the first line.
Hilarodi, *Gr. pl.* (hĭl-ă-rō-dē.) Itinerant poet musicians among the ancient Greeks who went from one place to another singing poems or songs.
Hilarodia, *Gr.* (hĭl-ă-rō-dĭ-a.) Songs, or short lyric poems sung by the *hilarodi*.
Himno, *Spa.* (hĭm-nō.) A hymn.
Hinaufstrich, *Ger.* (hĭn-ouf-strĭkh.) } An up
Hinstrich, *Ger.* (hĭn-strĭkh.) } bow.
Hinchar, *Spa.* (hĕn-kăr.) To fill a musical instrument with air.
Hindudeln, *Ger.* (hĭn-doo-dĕln.) To hum a tune.
Hirten-flöte, *Ger.* (hĭr-t'n flō-tĕ.) Shepherd's flute.
Hirten-gedicht, *Ger.* (hĭr-t'n ghĕ-dĭkht.) Pastoral poem, idyl.
Hirten-lied, *Ger.* hĭr-t'n lēd.) A pastoral song.
Hirtlich, *Ger.* (hĭrt-līkh.) Pastoral, rural.
Hirten-pfeife, *Ger.* (hĭr t'n-pfī-fĕ.) Rural pipe, pastoral pipe.
His, *Ger.* (his.) The note B sharp.
Histrio, *Lat.* (hĭs-trĭ-ō.) } Stage actor or
Histrion, *Spa.* (bĭs-trē-ōn.) } singer.
Histrionisa, *Spa.* (hēs-trĭ-ō-nē-zä.) An actress.
Hiven, *Chi.* (hē-vĕn.) One of the eight species of sound in the musical system of the Chinese.
Hlud, *Sax.* (lood.) Loud.
H moll, *Ger.* (hä mŏl.) The key of B minor.
Hoboe, *Ger.* (hō-bō-ĕ.) } Oboe, hautboy.
Hoboy, *Ger.* (hō-boy.) }
Hoboen, *Ger. pl.* (hō-bō-ĕn.) Oboes, hautboys.
Hoboist, *Ger.* (hō-hō-ĭst.) Hautboy player.
Hoch, *Ger.* (hŏkh.) High.
Hoch-amt, *Ger.* (hŏkh-ämt.) High mass.
Hochfeierlich, *Ger.* (hŏkh-fī-ĕr-līkh.) Exceedingly solemn.
Hoch-gesang, *Ger.* (hŏkh ghĕ-zăng.) Ode, hymn.
Hoch-horn, *Ger.* (hŏkh hŏrn.) Hautboy.
Hoch-horn-bläser, *Ger.* (hŏkh-hŏrn-blā-zĕr.) Player on the hautboy.
Hoch-lied, *Ger.* (hŏkh lēd.) Ode, hymn.
Hoch-messe, *Ger.* (hŏkh mĕs-sĕ.) High mass.
Hochmuth, *Ger.* (hŏkh-moot.) Dignity, elevation, pride.
Höchsten, *Ger.* (hŏkh-stĕn.) Highest.
Hochzeits-gedicht, *Ger.* (hŏkh tsīts-ghĕ-dĭkht.) }
Hochzeits-lied, *Ger.* (hŏkh-tsīts lēd.) }
Epithalamium nuptial poems; wedding song.
Hochzeits-marsch, *Ger.* (hŏkh-tsīts marsh.) Wedding march.
Hocket. A name formerly given to a *rest;* or cutting short a note without accelerating the time. It corresponds to the term *staccato*. It is no longer used.

ā ale, ă add, ä arm, ē eve, ĕ end, ī ice, ĭ ill, ō old, ŏ odd, ô dove, oo moon, ū tute, ŭ but, ü French sound.

HOFC — HUMM

Hof-capelle, Ger. (hŏf kä-pĕl-lä.) Court chapel.
Hof-concert, Ger. (hŏf kŏn-tsĕrt.) Court concert.
Hof-dichter, Ger. (hŏf dĭkh-tĕr.) Poet laureate.
Hof-kirche, Ger. (hŏf kĭrkh-ĕ.) Court church.
Höflich, Ger. (hŏf-lĭkh.) In a pleasing
Höflichkeit, Ger. (hŏf-lĭkh-kīt.) and graceful style.
Hof-musikant, Ger. (hŏf moo-zĭ-känt.) Court musician.
Hof-organist, Ger. (hŏf ŏr-gän-ĭst.) Court organist.
Hoheit, Ger. (hō-hīt.) Dignity, loftiness.
Hohen, Ger. (hō-ĕn.) High, upper.
Hohe-lied, Ger. (hō-hē lēd.) The Song of Solomon.
Hohle und heisere stimme, Ger. (hō-lĕ oond hī-zā-rĕ stĭm-mĕ.) Hollow and hoarse voice.
Hohl-flöte, Ger. (hŏl-flō-tĕ.) Hollow-toned flute; an organ stop producing a thick and powerful hollow tone. Each pipe has two holes in it, near the top and opposite each other.
Hohl-quinte, Ger. (hŏl quĭn-tĕ.) A quint stop of the hohl-flute species.
Hold, Ger. (hōld.) Pleasing, agreeable.
Hold. A character (⌢) indicating that the time of a note or rest is to be prolonged.
Holding-note. A note that is sustained or continued while the others are in motion.
Holding. The burden or chorus of a song. (Found in Shakespeare.)
Holz-flöte, Ler. (hŏlts flō-tĕ.) Wood-flute; an organ stop.
Homologous. (hō-mŏl-ō-gŭs.) A term applied by the ancients to certain correspondences in their tetrachords.
Homophone. A letter or character expressing a like sound with another.
Homophonie, Fr. (hō-mō-fo-nē.) Homophony.
Homophonous. Of the same pitch, in unison.
Homophonoi suoni, It. (hō-mō-fō-nō-ē swō-nē.) Unisons.
Homophony. Unison: two or more voices singing in unison.
Hoorn, Dut. (hoorn.) A horn.
Hopser, Ger. (hŏp-sĕr.) A German dance, a lively waltz.
Hops-tanz, Ger. (hŏps-tänts.) Hop-dance.
Hops-walzer, Ger. (hŏps-väl-tsĕr.) Quick waltzes.
Horæ, Lat. (hō-rē.)
Horæ regulares, Lat. (hō-rē rĕg-ū-lä-rēs.) Hours: chants sung at prescribed hours, in convents and monasteries.
Horizontal lines. Used in connection
Horizontal strokes. with the figured bass, they usually show the continuation of the same harmony, the bass note being unchanged, but they are sometimes used to abbreviate the expression of figures, in which case, if the bass part moves, the harmony must necessarily be changed.
Horn. A wind instrument chiefly used in hunting.
Horn, alpine. An instrument made of the bark of a tree and used to convey sounds to a great distance.

Horn, bass. An instrument formerly much used in bands, resembling the ophicleide, by which it has in a great measure been superseded.
Horn, basset. An instrument resembling the clarinet, but of greater compass, embracing nearly four octaves.
Horn, bassetto. A species of clarinet a fifth lower than the C clarinet.
Horn-blawere, A. S. A horn blower.
Horn, bugle. A trumpet with keys.
Horn, chromatic. The French horn.
Horn, English. A species of oboe, a fourth or a fifth lower than the ordinary oboe.
Horn, French. An orchestral instrument of brass or silver, consisting of a long tube twisted into several circular folds, and gradually increasing in diameter from the mouth-piece to the end. Also an 8 feet organ stop of a smooth, full tone.
Horn, gemsen. An instrument formed of a small pipe made of the horn of the chamois, or wild goat.
Horn, hunting. A bugle.
Horn, kent. A horn having six keys, four of which are used by the right hand and two by the left.
Horn, klappen. The kent-horn.
Horn, valve. A horn in which a portion of the tube is opened or closed by the use of valves, by means of which a higher or lower pitch is obtained.
Horner. One who blows a horn.
Hörner, Ger. pl. (hŏr-ner.) The horns
Hörnerschall, Ger. (hŏr-nĕr-shall.) Sound of horns.
Hornpipe. An old dance, in triple time, peculiar to the English nation. It is supposed to have received its name from the instrument played on during its performance. Modern hornpipes are usually in common time and of a more lively character than the ancient hornpipe.
Hosanna, Lat. (hō-zän-nä.) Part of the Sanctus in a mass.
Houl, Per. (howl.) A common drum of the Persian soldiery.
Hreol, Dan. (wrā-ōl.) A Danish peasant dance, similar to the reel.
Huchet, Fr. (hū-shā.) A huntman's or postman's horn.
Huer, Fr. (hwā.) To shout.
Hüft-horn, Ger. (hŭft hŏrn.) Bugle horn.
Huggab, Heb. (hoog-gäb.) An organ of the Hebrews; Pan's pipes.
Huitain, Fr. (hwē-tănh.) A stanza of eight lines.
Hülfslinien, Ger. (hŭlfs-lĭn-ĭ-ĕn.) Ledger lines.
Hülfs-note, Ger. (hŭlfs-nōt-ĕ.) Auxiliary note,
Hülfs-ton, Ger. (hŭlfs-tōn.) accessory note, a note standing one degree above, or below the principal note.
Hülfs-stimme, Ger. (hŭlfs stĭm-mĕ.) Obligato voice.
Humorous songs. Songs full of mirth and humor.
Hummel, Ger. (hoom-mĕl.) A sort
Hummelchen, Ger. (hoom-mĕl-khĕn.) of bagpipe; in organs the thorough bass drone.
Hummen, Ger. (hoom-m'n.) Humming, singing in a low voice.

ă *ale,* ă *add,* ä *arm,* ō *eve,* ĕ *end,* ī *ice,* ĭ *ill,* ō *old,* ŏ *odd,* ō *dove,* oo *moon,* ū *lute,* ŭ *but,* û *French sound.*

HUNT

Hunting horn. A bugle, a horn used to cheer the hounds.
Hunting song. A song written in praise of the chase.
Hurdy gurdy. An old instrument consisting of four strings, which are acted upon by a wheel rubbed in resin powder which serves as a bow. Two of the strings are affected by certain keys which stop them at different lengths and produce the *tune,* while the others act as a drone bass.
Hurtig, *Ger.* (*hoor-tĭg.*) Quick, swiftly; same meaning as Allégro.
Hurtigkeit, *Ger.* (*hoor-tĭg-kĭt.*) Swiftness, quickness, agility.
Hydraulicon, *Gr.* (hĭ-*draw*-lĭ-kŏn.) An ancient instrument whose tones were produced by the action of water.
Hydraulic organ. An organ whose motive power was water, and. the invention of which is of much greater antiquity than the pneumatic or wind organ. It is supposed to have been invented by Ctesibius, a mathematician of Alexandria.
Hydraulon, *Gr.* (hĭ-*draw*-lŏn.) } An organ
Hydraulus, *Lat.* (hĭ-*draw*-lŭs.) } blown by the action of water.
Hymee, *Gr.* (hē-mā.) A song of the millers, so called by the ancient Greeks.
Hymenæa, *Gr.* (hĭm-ĕn-ē-ä.)
Hymenæus, *Ger.* (hĭm-ĕn-ā-oos.) } A marriage
Hymenaion, *Gr.* (hĭm-ĕn-ā-ŏn.) } song.
Hymeneal. (hī-mē-nē-ăl.)
Hymenean. (hī-mē-nē-ăn.) } A marriage song.
Hymn. A song of praise or adoration to the Deity; a short, religious lyric poem intended to be sung in church. Anciently, a song in honor of the gods or heroes.
Hymnal. } A compilation, or collection of
Hymn book. } hymns.
Hymn, cherubical. A hymn highly prized in the early Christian church.
Hymn, choral. A hymn to be performed by a chorus.
Hymne, *Fr.* (ĕmn.) } A hymn, sacred song,
Hymne, *Ger.* (*hĭm*-nĕ.) } an anthem.
Hymne de louange, *Fr.* (ĕmn dŭh loo-ănzh.) Doxology, hymn of praise.
Hymnic. Relating to hymns.
Hymni saliares, *Lat.* (hĭm - nē săl-ĭ-ā-rēs.) Songs of the ancient Romans, which the salii, or priests of Mars sung on the feast days of that deity.
Hymn of battle. A song of supplication constantly used by the ancients just before an engagement.
Hymnologie, *Fr.* (ĕmn-nŏl-ō-jē.) Hymnology.
Hymnologist. A writer or composer of hymns.
Hymnology. The art of composing hymns.
Hymns, Orphic. A hymn pertaining to Orpheus.
Hymns, fountain. Songs of the wells, so called by the ancients and still known in the Greek isles.

HYPO

Hymns, theurgic. Songs of incantation; the first hymns of Greece.
Hymnus, *Lat.* (*hĭm*-nŭs.) A hymn.
Hymnus, ambrosianus, *Lat.* (*hĭm*-nŭs ăm-brō-zhĭ-ā-nŭs.) The Ambrosian chant.
Hymn, vesper. A hymn sung in the vesper service of the Catholic church.
Hypate, *Gr.* The first or most grave string in the lyre; the lowest of the Greek tetrachords.
Hypathoides. The lower sounds in the ancient Greek scale.
Hyper, *Gr.* (*hī*-pĕr.) *Above.* This word in connection with the name of any mode or interval, signifies that it is higher than when without it.
Hyper-Æolian, *Gr.* (*hī*-pĕr ē-ō-lĭ-ăn.) The *Authentic* Æolian mode.
Hyper-diapason, *Gr.* (*hī*-pĕr dī-ă-pā-sŏn.) The upper octave.
Hyper-ditonos, *Gr.* (*hī*-pĕr-dĭ-*tō*-nŏs,) The third above.
Hyper-Dorian, *Gr.* (*hī*-pĕr-dō-rĭ-ăn.) The *Authentic* Dorian mode.
Hyper-Ionian, *Gr.* (*hī*-pĕr-ē-ō-nĭ-ăn.) The *Authentic* Ionian mode.
Hyper-Lydian, *Gr.* (*hī*-pĕr-*lĭd*-ĭ-ăn.) The *Authentic* Lydian mode.
Hyper-mixo-Lydian, *Gr.* (*hī*-pĕr-mĭx-o-*lĭd*-ĭ-ăn.) The *Authentic* mixo-Lydian mode.
Hyper-Phrygian, *Gr.* (*hī*-pĕr frĭj-ĭ-ăn.) The *Authentic* Phrygian mode.
Hyperoche, *Gr.* (*hī*-pĕr-ō-kē.) A word used by the ancient authors to signify the difference between the enharmonic and chromatic diesies.
Hypo. *Below.* The word prefixed to the name of any ancient mode or interval, signifies that it is lower than when without it.
Hypo-Æolian, *Gr.* (hī-pō ē-ō-lĭ-ăn.) The *plagal* Æolian mode.
Hypo-diapason, *Gr.* (hī-pō dē-ā-pā-sŏn.) The lower octave.
Hypo-diapente, *Gr.* (hī-pō dē-ā-*pĕn*-tē.) The fifth below.
Hypo-ditonos, *Gr.* (hī-pō dē-*tō*-nŏs.) The third below.
Hypo-Dorian, *Gr.* (hī-pō dō-rĭ-an.) The *plagal* Dorian mode.
Hypo-Ionian, *Gr.* (hī-pō ē-ō-nĭ-ăn.) The *plagal* Ionian mode.
Hypo-Lydian, *Gr.* (hī-pō *lĭd*-ĭ-ăn.) The *plagal* Lydian mode.
Hypo-mixo-Lydian, *Gr.* (hī-pō mĭx-o *lĭd*-ĭ-an.) The *plagal* mixo-Lydian mode.
Hypo-Phrygian, *Gr.* (hī-pō *frĭj*-ĭ-ăn.) The *plagal* Phrygian mode.
Hypocritic, *Gr.* (hī-pō-*krĭt*-ĭc.) An epithet applied by the ancients to the art of gesticulation, which was prominent in their public vocal performances.
Hypocritic music. Among the ancient Greeks all music intended for the stage or theatre; in modern times, all music adapted to pantomimic representation.

ă ale, ă add, ä arm, ĕ eve, ĕ end, ī ice, ĭ ill, ō old, ŏ odd, ô dove, oo moon, ū lute, ŭ but, ü French sound.

IAMB

Iambe, *Fr.* (ē-ănh-bŭh.) Iambus
Iambic. ⎱ A poetical and musical foot, consist-
Iambus. ⎰ ing of one short unaccented, and one long accented note or syllable.
Iambics. Certain songs or satires which are supposed to have been the precursors of the ancient comedy; they were of two kinds, one for singing and one for recitation, accompanied by instruments.
Iastian. *Gr.* (ē-ăs-tĭ-ăn.) One of the ancient Greek modes.
Ictus, *Gr.* (ĭk-tŭs.) A stroke of the foot, marking the point of emphasis in music.
Idillio, *It.* (ēd-ĭl-lĭ-ō.) An idyl.
Idyl. A short poem in pastoral style; an eclogue.
Idylle, *Fr.* (ē-dĭll.) ⎱ An idyl.
Idylle, *Ger.* (ĭd-ĭl-lē.) ⎰
Il, *It.* (ēl.) The.
Ilarita, *It.* (ē-lär-ē-tä.) Hilarity, cheerfulness, mirth.
Il basso, *It.* (ēl bäs-sō.) The fundamental tone; the lowest note of a chord.
Il canto, *It.* (ēl kän-tō.) The song.
Il dito grósso, *It.* (ēl dē-tō grōe-sō.) The thumb.
Il colorito, *It.* (ēl kō-lō-rē-tō.) A term used in dramatic singing to denote the adaptation of the performance to the character represented.
Il ditono con diapente, *It.* (ēl dē-tō-nō kŏn dē-ä-pän-tĕ.) A major seventh.
Il dóppio moviménto, *It.* (ēl dōp-pē-o mō-nĕ-män-tō.) Double movement; that is, as fast again.
Il fine, *It.* (ēl fē-nĕ.) The end.
Il passo tempo, *It.* (ēl päs-sō tĕm-pō.) Name sometimes given to a collection of light, familiar, and amusing pieces.
Il piu, *It.* (ēl pē-oo.) The most.
Il piu fórte possíbile, *It.* (ēl pē-oo fŏr-tĕ pōs-sē-bē-lĕ.) As loud as possible.
Il piu piáno possíbile, *It.* (ēl pē-oo pē-ä-nō pōs-sē-bē-lĕ.) As soft as possible.
Il ponticello, *It.* (ēl pōn-tē-tshäl-lō.) The *little bridge;* an appellation given by the Italians to that particular part of the voice where the natural tone forms a junction with the falsetto.
Il sdrucciolare, *It.* (ēl sdroot-tshē-ō-lä-rĕ.) A sliding movement over the keys of a piano.
Il témpo crescéndo, *It.* (ēl tĕm-pō krĕ-shän-dō.) Increasing the time.
Il térzo dito a tútte le nóte di básso, *It.* (ēl tär-tsō dē-tō ä too-tĕ lĕ nō-tĕ dē bäs-sō.) The third finger on all the notes in the bass.
Il violíno, *It.* (ēl vē-ō-lē-nō.) The violin.
Il volteggiare, *It.* (ēl vō-tĕd-jē-ä-rĕ.) Crossing the hands in piano playing.
Im, *Ger.* (ĕm.) In the.
Imboccatúra, *It.* (ēm-bōt-kä-too-rä.) Mouthpiece, *embouchure.*
Imbrices, *Lat.* (ĭm-brī-sĕs.) A species of applause among the ancients made by beating a kind of sounding vessel.
Imbróglio, *It.* (ēm-brōl-yō.) Confusion, want of distinct ideas.
Imitándo, *It.* (ēm-ē-tän-dō.) Imitating.
Imitándo la voce, *It.* (ēm-ē-tän-dō lä vo-tchĕ.) Imitating the inflections of the voice.
Imitatio, *Lat.* (ĭm-ĭ-tä-shĭ-ō.) Imitation, in counterpoint.

IMPE

Imitation. A species of fugue, in which the parts imitate each other, though not in the same intervals, or according to the strict laws of a fugue or canon.
Imitation, augmented. A style of imitation in which the answer is given in notes of greater value than those of the subject.
Imitation, diminished. A style of imitation in which the answer is given in notes of less value than those of the subject.
Imitation, freely inverted. Where the order of successive notes is not strictly retained.
Imitation, in contrary motion. That in which the answers invert the subject so that the rising intervals descend, and the falling intervals ascend.
Imitation, in similar motion. Where the answer retains the same order of notes as the subject.
Imitation, in different divisions. That in which the subject is answered in a different division of the bar; for instance, the subject beginning on the accented division, is answered on the unaccented.
Imitation, retrograde. A form of imitation in which the subject is commenced backwards in the answer.
Imitation, reversed retrograde. A form of imitation in which the subject is commenced backwards in the answer and in contrary motion.
Imitation, simple. A simple fugue.
Imitation, strictly inverted. That form of imitation in which half and whole tones must be precisely answered in contrary motion.
Imitative music. Music written to imitate some of the operations of nature, art, or human passion, as, the firing of cannon, the rolling of thunder, love, joy, grief, etc.
Imitato, *It.* (ĕm-ē-tä-tō.) Imitation.
Imitazióne, *It.* (ĕm-ē-tä-tsē-ō-nĕ.) Imitation, referring to counterpoint.
Immediate cadence. Cadence that occurs immediately after the dominant harmony.
Immer, *Ger.* (ĭm-mĕr.) Always, ever.
Immusical. Unmusical. (Not used.)
Imparfait, *Fr.* (änh-pär-fä.) Imperfect.
Impaziénte, *It.* (ĕm-pä-tsē-än-tĕ.) Impatient, hurried.
Impazienteménte, *It.* (ĕm-pä-tsē-ĕn-tĕ-män-tĕ.) Impatiently, hurriedly.
Imperfect. Not perfect, less than perfect in speaking of intervals and chords.
Imperfect cadence. A cadence which ends on a triad of the dominant; the preceding chord may be either that of the tonic or subdominant or in minor keys the sixth of the scale; the triad of the dominant always being *major*.
Imperfect close. Imperfect Cadence.
Imperfect common chord. A chord consisting of a bass note accompanied by its minor third and imperfect fifth.
Imperfect concords. Thirds and sixths are called imperfect concords because they are liable to change from major to minor or the contrary, still remaining consonant.
Imperfect consonances. The major and minor third and the major and minor sixth.

ā ale, ă add, ä arm, ē eve, ĕ end, ī ice, ĭ ill, ō old, ŏ odd, ô dove, oo moon, ū lute, ŭ but, ü French sound.

IMPE

Imperfect intervals. Those which include one semitone less than the perfect interval of the same name.
Imperfect measure. An old term for two-fold measure.
Imperfect time. A term by which the ancients designated common time, indicated by the letter C or a semicircle.
Imperfect triad. The chord of the third, fifth and eighth, taken on the seventh of the key, consisting of two minor thirds.
Imperfetto, *It.* (ĕm-pĕr-fät-tō.) Imperfect.
Imperiosaménte, *It.* (ĕm-pā-rē-ō-zä-mān-tĕ.) Imperiously, pompously.
Imperiosità, *It.* (ĕm-pā-rē-ō-zē-tä.) Stateliness, pomposity.
Imperióso, *It.* (ĕm-pā-rē-ō-zō.) Imperious, pompous.
Imperturbábile, *It.* (ĕm-pĕr-toor-bä-bē-lĕ.) Quietly, easily.
Impeto, *It.* (ĕm-pĕ-tō.) Impetuosity, vehemence.
Impeto doloroso, *It.* (ĕm-pĕ-tō dō-lō-rō-zō.) Pathetic force and energy.
Impetuosaménte, *It.* (ĕm-pā-too-ō-zä-mān-tĕ.) Impetuously.
Impetuosità, *It.* (ĕm-pā-too-ō-zē-tä.) Impetnosity, vehemence.
Impetuóso, *It.* (ĕm-pā-too-ō-zō.) Impetuous, vehement.
Imponénte, *It.* (ĕm-pō-nän-tĕ.) Imposingly, haughtily.
Impresário, *It.* (ĕm-prĕ-zä-rē-ō.) A term applied by the Italians to the manager or conductor of operas or concerts.
Imprómptu, *Fr.* (änh-prŏmp-too.) An extemporaneous production.
Improvisare, *It.* (ĕm-prō-vē-zä-rĕ.) To compose, or sing extemporaneously.
Improvisateur, *Fr.* (änh-prō-vē-zä-tŭr.) ⎱ See
Improvisator, *Ger.* (Im-prō-fī-zä-tōr.) ⎰ *Improvisatôre.*
Improvisation. The act of singing, playing or composing music without previous preparation; extemporaneous performance.
Improvisatrice, *Fr.* (änh-prō-vē-zä-trĕss.) A female who plays or sings extemporaneously.
Improvise. To sing or play without premeditation.
Improviser, *Fr.* (änh-prō-vē-zā.) To improvise.
Improvisé, *Fr.* (änh-prō-vē-zā.) Extemporaneous.
Improvvisaménte, *It.* (ĕm-prō-vē-zä-mān-tĕ.) Extemporaneously.
Improvvisare, *It.* (ĕm-prō-vē-zä-rĕ.) To improvise.
Improvvisáta, *It.* (ĕm-prō-vē-zä-tä.) An extempore composition.
Improvviso, *It.* (ĕm-prōv-vē-zō.) Extemporaneous.
Improvvissatóre, *It.* (ĕm-prō-vēs-sä-tō-rĕ.) One who sings or declaims in verse extemporaneously.
Improvvissatóri, *It. pl.* (ĕm-prōv-vēs-sä-tō-rē.) Persons gifted with the power of singing or reciting verses extemporaneously.
Im tact, *Ger.* (Im täkt.) In time.
In, *It. and Lat.* (ēn.) In, into, in the.

INFI

Inacutíre, *It.* (ĕn-ä-koo-tē-rĕ.) To sharpen, to make sharp.
In alt, *It.* (ĕn Ält.) Notes are said to be *in alt* when they are situated above F on the fifth line of the treble staff.
In altíssimo, *It.* (ĕn äl-tēs-sē-mō.) A term applied to all notes which run higher than F above the third leger line in the treble, or F *in alt.*
Inbrunst, *Ger.* (In-broonst.) Fervor, ardor, warmth of passion.
Inbrünstig, *Ger.* (In-brüns-tIg.) Ardent, fervent, passionate.
Incantable, *Spa.* (ĕn-kän-tä-blĕ.) Cannot be sung.
Incantation. Enchantment; a form of words pronounced or sung in connection with certain ceremonies, for the purpose of enchantment.
Incantazione, *It.* (ĕn-kän-tä-tsē-ō-nĕ.) Songs of incantation.
Incisóre di nóte, *It.* (ĕn-tshē-zō-rĕ dä nō-tĕ.) An engraver of notes or music.
Incomposite, (In-kŏm-pŏs-it.) A term applied to those intervals which are simply constituted, and in the calculation of which we take no notice of the intermediaries, but only consider the terms.
Inconsoláto, *It.* (ĕn-kōn-sō-lä-tō.) In a mournful style.
Inconsonance. The effect of two discordant or disagreeing sounds.
Inconsonant. Discordant.
Incordaménto, *It.* (ĕn-kōr-dä-mān-tō.) Tension of the strings of an instrument.
Incordáre, *It.* (ĕn-kōr-dä-rĕ.) To string an instrument.
Indeciso, *It.* (ĕn-dĕ-tshē-zō.) Undecided, wavering, hesitating; slight changes of time and a somewhat capricious value of the notes.
Indegnataménte, *It.* (ĕn-dän-yä-tä-mān-tĕ.) ⎱
Indegnáto, *It.* (ĕn-dän-yä-tō.) ⎰
Angrily, furiously, passionately.
Index. A direct ⁓; also, the forefinger.
Indications sceniques, *Fr.* (änh-dē-kä-sē-ōnh sā-nēk.) Stage directions.
Indifferente, *It.* (ĕn-dēf-fē-rän-tĕ.)
Indifferenteménte, *It.* (ĕn-dēf-fē-rän-tĕ-mān-tĕ.) ⎱
Coldly, with indifference.
Indifferenza, *It.* (ĕn-dēf-fē-rän-tsä.) Indifference.
In disparte, *It.* (ĕn dĕs-pär-tĕ.) A term used in operatic music, signifying that the part is to be addressed to some one aside, or not taking part in the performance.
In distánza, *It.* (ĕn dĕs-tän-tsä.) A distance.
Infantíle, *It.* (ĕn-fän-tē-lĕ.) Childlike, infantine; the thin quality of tone in the upper notes of some female voices.
Infernále, *It.* (ĕn-fĕr-nä-lĕ.) Infernal, diabolic.
Infervoráto, *It.* (ĕn-fĕr-vō-rä-tō.) Fervent, impassioned.
Infiammaménte, *It.* (ĕn-fē-äm-mä-tä-män-tĕ.) Ardently, impetuously.
Infinite canon. An epithet given to those canons which are so constructed that the end leads to the beginning, and the performance may be indefinitely repeated; also called *circular* or *endless canon.*

ā ale, ă add, ä arm, ē eve, ĕ end, ī ice, ĭ ill, ō old, ŏ odd, ô dove, oo moon, ū lute, ŭ but, ü French sound.

INFI

Infinito, *It.* (ēn-fē-nē-tō.) Perpetual.
Inflatile. An epithet applied to wind instruments, as a hautboy or flute.
Inflection. Any change or modification in the pitch or tone of the voice.
Infra, *Lat.* (in-frä.) Beneath.
In frétta, *It.* (ĕn frāt-tä.) In haste, hastily.
In fugue, *It.* (ĕn foo-ghē.) An expression applied to any composition constructed on a given subject.
Infuriánte, *It.* (ēn-foo-rē-ān-tē.) } Furious, raging.
Infuriáto, *It.* (ēn-foo-rē-ä-tō.) }
Ingánni, *It. pl.* (ēn-gän-nē.) See *Ingánno*.
Ingánno, *It.* (ēn-gän-nō.) A *deception;* applied to a deceptive or interrupted cadence; also, to any unusual resolution of a discord, or an unexpected modulation.
Ingégno, *It.* (ēn-gān-yō.) Art, skill, discretion.
Inharmonic. Wanting harmony.
Inharmonic relation. The introduction of a dissonant sound, not heard in the preceding chord.
Inharmoniously. Discordantly.
Iniziato, *It.* (ēn-ē-tsē-ä-tō.) Initiated; a term applied to those advanced in music, in distinction from beginners.
Iniziatore, *It.* (ēn-ē-tsē-ä-tō-rē.) A beginner.
Innario, *It.* (ēn-nä-rē-ō.) Hymn book.
Inneggiare, *It.* (ēn-nād-jē-ä-rē.) To compose or sing hymns.
Inni, *It. pl.* (ēn-nē.) Hymns.
Innig, *Ger.* (ĭn-nĭg.) Sincere, cordial.
Inno, *It.* (ēn-nō.) A hymn, canticle, ode.
Innocénte, *It.* (ēn-nō-tshän-tē.)
Innocenteménte, *It.* (ēn-nō-tshän-tē-mān-tē.) } Innocently, in an artless and simple style.
Innocénza, *It.* (ēn-nō-tshän-tsä.) Innocence.
Innodia, *It.* (ēn-nō-dē-ä.) Hymn singing.
Innografo, *It.* (ēn-nō-grä-fo.) A writer of hymns.
Innologo, *It.* (ēn-nō-lō-gō.) Hymnologist.
Ino, *It.* (ē-nō.) An Italian final diminutive.
In órgano, *It.* ĕn ôr-gä-nō.) An old term for music in more than two parts.
In pálco, *It.* (ĕn pāl-kō.) On a stage; applied to musical performances *on the stage*.
Inquiéto, *It.* (ēn-quē-ā-tō.) Restless, uneasy, agitated.
Insegnaménto, *It.* (ēn-sān-yä-mān-tō.) Instruction.
Insegnatóre, *It.* (ēn-sān-yä-tō-rē.) Teacher, instructor.
Insensíbile, *It.* (ēn-sĕn-sē-bē-lē.)
Insensibilménte, *It.* (ēn-sān-sē-bēl-mān-tē.) } Insensibly, by small degrees, by little and little.
Instanteménte, *It.* (ēn-stän-tē-mān-tē.) Vehemently, urgently.
Instrument. A musical instrument is any sonorous body, artificially constructed for the production of musical sounds.
Instrument à l'archet, *Fr.* (änh-strü-mänh ä l'är-kā.) Instrument played with a bow.
Instrumental. A term applied to music composed for or performed on instruments.
Instrument à cordes, *Fr.* (änh-strü-mänh ä kōrd.) A stringed instrument.
Instrumentále, *It.* (ēn-stroo-mēn-tä-lē.) Instrumental.

INST

Instrumentalist. One who plays on an instrument.
Instrumental score. A score in which the instrumental parts are given in full.
Instrumentare, *It.* (ēn-stroo-mēn-tä-rē.) To compose instrumental music.
Instrumentation. The act of writing for an orchestra, with a practical knowledge of each instrument, and of the distribution of harmony among the different instruments.
Instrument à vent, *Fr.* (änh-strü-mänh ä vänh.) A wind instrument.
Instrumentazióne, *It.* (ēn-stroo-mēn-tä-tsē-ō-nē.) Instrumentation.
Instrumentiren, *Ger.* (In-stroo-mēn-tē-r'n.) }
Instrumentirung, *Ger.* (In-stroo-mēn-tē-roong.) } Instrumentation.
Instrumenten-macher, *Ger.* (In-stroo-mēnt-ĕn mäkh-ēr.) An instrument maker.
Instruménto, *It.* (ēn-stroo-mān-tō.) An instrument.
Instruménto a campanélla, *It.* (ēn-stroo-mān-tō ä käm-pä-nāl-lä.) A small case, containing one or more octaves of small bells, tuned diatonically, and played with a key-board like the pianoforte.
Instruménto a corda, *It.* (ēn-stroo-mān-tō ä kōr-dä.)
Instruménto da arco, *It.* (ēn-stroo-mān-tō dä är-kō.) } A stringed instrument.
Instruménto da fiáto, *It.* (ēn-stroo-mān-tō dä fē-ä-tō.) A wind instrument.
Instruménto da pénna, *It.* (ēn-stroo-mān-tō dä pān-nä.) *Instrument with the quill;* an old name for the spinet.
Instruménto da percotiménto, *It.* (ēn-stroo-mān-tō dä pĕr-kō-tē-mān-tō.) A instrument of percussion.
Instruménto da tasto, *It.* (ēn-stroo-mān-tō dä tās-tō.) A keyed instrument.
Instruments, bow. All instruments whose tones are produced by means of a bow.
Instruments, brass. Wind instruments formed of brass and used chiefly for military purposes.
Instruments, inflatile. Wind instruments.
Instruments, keyed. All instruments the sounds of which are produced by the pressure of the fingers upon the keys.
Instruments, mechanical. Instruments which produce tunes by the means of some mechanical contrivance, as, crank, springs, weights, etc.
Instruments, percussive. } Instruments
Instruments, pulsatile. } whose sounds are produced by being struck.
Instruments, pneumatic. Instruments, the tones of which are produced by the action of the wind.
Instruments, reed. Instruments whose tones are produced by the action of air upon reeds of metal or wood.
Instruments, stringed. Instruments whose tones are produced by striking or drawing strings or the friction of a bow.
Instruments, tensile. A general name for

ă ale, ă add, ä arm, ō eve, ĕ end, ī ice, ĭ ill, ō old, ŏ odd, ō dove, oo moon, ū lute, ŭ but, ü French sound.

INST

all instruments dependent upon the tension of strings for their tone.
Instruments, tubular. Instruments consisting of one or more tubes of wood or metal.
Instruments, wind. Instruments the sounds of which are produced by the breath or the wind of bellows.
Instrument vent, Fr. (änh-strü-mänh vänh.) A wind instrument.
Intavoláre, It. (ĕn-tä-vō-lä́-rĕ.) To write notes, to copy music.
Intavolatúra, It. (ĕn-tä-vō-lä-too-rä.) Musical notation.
In témpo, It. (ĕn tăm-pō.) In time.
In tempore justo, Lat. (ĕn tĕm-pō-rĕ jūs-tō.) A direction to sing or play in equal, just and exact time.
Intendant, Fr. (änh-tänh-dänh.) } Director,
Intendénte, It. (ĕn-tĕn-dän-tĕ.) } conductor. See Impresário.
Intentio, Lat. (ĭn-tăn-shĭ-ō.) The word *intentio* was used in the ancient music, to denote the passage of the voice from grave to acute.
Intercaláre, It. (ĕn-tĕr-kä-lä-rĕ.) A verse interlaced or often repeated; the burden of a song.
Interlude. A short musical representation, introduced between the acts of any drama, or between the play and afterpiece; an intermediate strain or movement played between the verses of a hymn.
Interluder. A performer in an interlude.
Interludium, Lat. (ĭn-tĕr-lū-dĭ-ŭm.) } An interlude;
Intermede, Fr. (änh-tĕr-mĕd.) } interlude;
Intermédio, It. (ĕn-tĕr-mä-dē-ō.) } inter-
Intermezzo, It. (ĕn-tĕr-mĕt-sō.) } mediate, placed between two others; detached pieces introduced between the acts of an opera.
Intermediate. A term applied to those flats and sharps which do not form any part of the original key of a composition, and which are also called *Accidentals*.
Intermediate subject. Ideas not unlike the principal, or counter subject in a fugue, introduced for embellishment.
Intermediate tuning. That method of tuning in which every key deviates a little from perfect tune for the common good.
Intermézzi, It. pl. (ĕn-tĕr-mĕt-tsĕ.) Interludes, detached pieces or dances.
Intermediétto, It. (ĕn-tĕr-mä-dē-ĕt-tō.) A short interlude, or *intermezzo*.
Interrótto, It. (ĕn-tĕr-rōt-tō.) Interrupted, broken, speaking of cadence, accent or rhythm.
Interrupted cadence. A cadence in which the triad of the dominant is followed by some chord which changes the progression of the harmony.
Interruzióne, It. (ĕn-tĕr-root-sē-ō-nĕ.) Interruption.
Interval. The distance, or difference of pitch between tones.
Interval, augmented. An interval which is a semitone, or half-step, greater than a major or perfect interval.
Interval, consecutive. An interval passing in the same direction in two parallel parts.

INTR

Interval, diminished. An interval less than a perfect interval by a half-step or semitone.
Interval, direct. An interval which forms any kind of harmony on the fundamental sound which produces it.
Interval, enharmonic. An interval which is only nominal, as from G♯ to A♭.
Interval, extreme. A larger interval than the major, or a smaller than the minor.
Interval, false. An incorrect interval, according to the received rules.
Interval, imperfect. An interval that does not contain its full number of degrees.
Interval, major. An interval containing the greater number of semitones under the same denomination.
Interval, prepared. An interval changed from large to small, and *vice versa*, by the aid of intermediate tones.
Interval, redundant. An interval greater than that of the major by a minor semitone.
Interval, superfluous. See Redundant Interval.
Intervall, Ger. (ĭn-tĕr-fäll.)
Intervalle, Fr. (änh-tĕr-väll.) } An in-
Intervállo, It. (ĕn-tĕr-väl-lō.) } terval.
Intervallum, Lat. (ĭn-tĕr-väl-lŭm.)
Intervalle, Ger. pl. (ĭn-tĕr-väl-lĕ.) Intervals.
Intervalli vietati, It. pl. (ĕn-tĕr-väl-lē vē-ä-tä-tē.) Forbidden intervals.
Intervening subject. An intermediate subject of a fugue.
Intimíssimo, It. (ĕn-tē-mĕs-sē-mō.) Very expressive, with great feeling.
Intimo, It. (ĕn-tē-mō.) Inward feeling, expressive.
Intonare, It. (ĕn-tō-nä́-rĕ.) } To pitch the
Intonáre, It. (ĕn-twō-nä́-rĕ.) } voice, to sound the key note; to begin.
Intonation. A word referring to the proper emission of the voice so as to produce any required note in exact tune; the act of modulating the voice.
Intonation, false. A variation in pitch from what is understood to be the true tone.
Intonato, It. (ĕn-tō-nä́-tō.) Tuned, set to music.
Intonatóre, It. (ĕn-tō-nä-tō-rĕ.) } Male singer.
Intuonatóre, It. (ĕn-twō-nä-tō-rĕ.) }
Intonatrice, It. (ĕn-tō-nä-trē-tshĕ.) } Female singer.
Intuonatrice, It. (ĕn-twō-nä-trē-tshĕ.) }
Intonatúra, It. (ĕn-tō-nä-too-rä.) } Intona-
Intonazione, It. (ĕn-tō-nä-tsē-ō-nĕ.) } tion.
Intoniren, Ger. (ĕn-tō-nē-r'n.) To intone, to sound.
Intráda, It. (ĕn-trä-dä.) } A short prelude or
Intrade, Ger. (ĭn-trä-dĕ.) } introductory movement.
Intrepidaménte, It. (ĕn-trĕ-pē-dä-mĕn-tĕ.) Boldly, with intrepidity.
Intrepidezza, It. (ĕn-trĕ-pē-dĕt-sä.) Intrepidity, boldness.
Intrépido, It. (ĕn-trä-pĕ-dō.) Intrepid, bold.
In triplo, It. (ĕn-trĕp-lō.) An old term, signifying a composition in three parts.
Introduciménto, It. (ĕn-trō-doo-tshĕ-mĕn-tō.) An introduction.

ă ale, ă add, ä arm, ĕ eve, ĕ end, I ice, l ill, ō old, ŏ odd, ô dove, oo moon, ū lute, ŭ but, ü French sound.

INTR   ISTE

Introduction. That movement in a composition, the design of which is to prepare the ear for the movements which are to follow.
Introductorio, *It.* (ĕn-trŏ-dook-tŏ-rē-ō.) Introductory, preliminary.
Introductory, A term proper to those movements which are preparatory.
Introduzione, *It.* (ĕn-trŏ-doo-tsē-ō-nĕ.) An introduction.
Introduzione marziale, *It.* (ĕn-trŏ-doo-tsē-ō-nĕ mär-tsē-ä-lĕ.) An introduction in martial style.
Introit, *Eng.* (In-trŏ-It.)   ⎫ Entrance; a
Introit, *Fr.* (ănh-trwä.)   ⎬ hymn or anthem
Introïto, *It.* (ĕn-trŏ-ē-tō.)   ⎬ sung while the
Introïto, *Spa.* (ĕn-trŏ-ē-tō.)   ⎬ priest enters
Introïtus, *Lat.* (In-trŏ-ĭ-tŭs.) ⎭ within the rails at the communion table; also, the commencement of the mass.
Inventio, *Lat.* (In-vĕn-shĭ-ō.) A name sometimes given to a Tricinium.
Invention, *Fr.* (ănh-vänh-sĭ-ŏnh.) An old name for a species of prelude or short fantasia.
Invenzione, *It.* (ĕn-vĕn-tsē-ō-nĕ.) Invention, contrivance.
Inversio, *Lat.* (In-văr-sĭ-ō.) Inversion; see that word.
Inversio cancrizans, *Lat.* (In-văr-sĭ-ō kăn-krĭ-zăns.) Retrograde, or crab-like inversion, or imitation; because it goes backwards.
Inversio in octavam acutam, *Lat.* (In-văr-sĭ-ō In ŏk-tă-văm ă-kū-tăm.) Inversion in the octave above, the transposition of the lower part an octave above.
Inversio in octavam gravem, *Lat.* (In-văr-sĭ-ō In ŏk-tă-văm grā-vĕm.) Inversion in the octave below; the transposition of the upper part an octave below to form the bass, while the other part remains stationary.
Inversion. A change of position with respect to intervals and chords; the lower notes being placed above, and the upper notes below.
Inversion, first. A term given to a chord when the written bass takes the *third.*
Inversion, retrograde. An inversion made by commencing on the last note of the subject and writing it backwards to the first note.
Inversion, second. Where the bass note takes the fifth from the fundamental.
Inversion, simple. An inversion made by reversing the notes of a subject in its answer, so that the ascending notes of the original passage descend in the answer, and *vice versa.*
Inversion, strict. The same as simple inversion, yet requiring that whole tones should be answered by whole tones, semitones by semitones, etc.
Inversion, third. Name given to a chord when the bass takes the seventh.
Invert. To change the position either in a subject or chord.
Inverted. *Changed in position.*
Inverted chord. A chord whose fundamental tone is not its lowest.
Inverted counterpoint. Where the parts are not only reversed toward each other, but are also conducted, step by step, in an opposite direction.

Inverted turn. A turn which commences with the lowest note instead of the highest.
Invitatorio, *Spa.* (ĕn-vē-tä-tō-rĭ-ō.) Psalm or anthem sung at the beginning of the matins.
Invitatorium, *Lat.* (In-vĭ-tă-tō-rĭ-ŭm.) The name applied to the *antiphone,* or response, to the psalm "Venite Exultemus."
Invitatory. A part of the service sung in the Roman Catholic church; a psalm or anthem sung in the morning.
Invocatis, *Lat.* (In-vō-kă-tĭs.)   ⎫ An invo-
Invocáto, *It.* (ĕn-vō-kä-tō.)   ⎬ cation, or
Invocazióne, *It.* (Ĕn-vō-kă-tsē-ō-nĕ.) ⎭ prayer.
Io bacche, *Lat.* (yō băk-kĕ.) A burden used in the lyric poetry of the Romans.
Ionian, *Gr.* (I-ō-nĭ-ăn.)   ⎱ One of the ancient
Ionic, *Gr.* (I-ŏn-Ik.)   ⎰ Greek modes.
Ionic music. A light, airy style of music.
Io triumphe, *Lat.* (yō trĭ-ŭm-fĕ.) A phrase of exultation often found in the lyric poetry of the ancient Romans.
Ira, *It.* (ē-rä.) Anger, wrath.
Iráta, *It.* (ē-rä-tä.)   ⎱ Angrily,
Iráto, *It.* (ē-rä-tō.)   ⎬ passionately.
Iratamĕnte, *It.* (ē-rä-tä-mān-tĕ.) ⎭
Irish harp. An instrument having more strings than the lyre, yet for a long time only used for playing a simple melody or a single part.
Irish tunes. Tunes peculiar to the Hibernians, generally of a sweet, mellow character.
Irlandais, *Fr.* (ēr-länh-dā.)   ⎱ An air or dance
Irländisch, *Ger.* (ēr-län-dish.) ⎰ tune in the Irish style.
Ironicamĕnte, *It.* (ē-rōn-ē-kä-mān-tĕ.) Ironically.
Irónico, *It.* (ē-rōn-ē-kō.) Ironical.
Irregolare, *It.* (ēr-rĕ-gō-lä-rĕ.) Irregular.
Irregular cadence. An imperfect cadence.
Irregular period. A period in which a false cadence interrupts or suspends an expected final close.
Irregular phrase. Any variation of the melody by which three measures are used instead of two; an extended phrase.
Irrelative chords. Any two chords which do not contain some sound common to both.
Irrelative keys.   ⎱ Those which are remote
Irrelative scales. ⎰ from each other, having few tones in common.
Irresolúto, *It.* (ēr-rĕ-zō-loo-tō.) Irresolute, wavering.
Ischmophony, *Gr.* (Is-knŏf-ō-ny.) Weakness of the voice.
Isdegno, con, *It.* (ĕs-dān-yō kōn.) With indignation.
Ismania, con, *It.* (ĕs-mä-nē-ä.) With wildness, with madness.
Isochronal, *Gr.* ⎱ Uniform in time; performed
Isochronous.   ⎰ in equal time.
Isotonic system. A system of music consisting of intervals in which each concord is tempered alike, and in which there are twelve equal semitones.
Ison. The name by which the first note of every chant was formerly designated, and which note indicated the key or tone of the melody.
Istésso, *It.* (ĕs-tās-sō.) The same.

ā ate, ă add, ä arm, ē eve, ĕ end, ī ice, ĭ ill, ō old, ŏ odd, ô dove, oo moon, ū lute, ŭ but, ü French sound.

ISTE — JODE

Istésso tempo, *It.* (ĕs-tăs-sō tăm-pō.) The same time.
Istésso valóre ma un póco piu lénto, *It.* (ĕs-tăs-sō vä-lō-rĕ mä oon pō-kō pē-oo lăn-tō.) The notes to have the same value, but a little more slowly.
Istrepito, con, *It.* (ĕs-trĕ-pē-tō.) With noise and bluster.
Istrumentále, *It.* (ĕs-troo-mĕn-tä-lĕ.) Instrumental.
Istrumentazióne, *It.* (ĕs-troo-mĕn-tä-tsē-ō-nĕ.) Instrumentation.
Istruménto, *It.* (ĕs-troo-mĕn-tō.) An instrument.
Istriónica, *It.* (ĕs-trē-ŏn-ē-kä.) Histrionic; the theatrical art.

Italian mordent. A short shake, or trill, consisting of the alternation of a tone with the next tone above it.
Italian sixth. A name sometimes given to a chord composed of a major third and an augmented sixth.
Italiáno, *It.* (ē-tä-lē-ä-nō.)
Italienisch, *Ger.* (It-ä-lī-än-ĭsh.) } Italian.
Italienne, *Fr.* (ĕt-ä-lē-ĕn.)
Ita missa est, *Lat.* (ē-tä mĭs-sä ĕst.) The termination of the mass sung by the priest to Gregorian music.
Il trovatori, *It.* (ĕ trō-vä-tō rē.) The troubadours.

J.

Jack. The quill which strikes the strings of a harpsichord, or the upright lever in piano action.
Jaeger-chor, *Ger.* (yā-ghĕr-kōr.) Hunting chorus.
Jagd-ruf, *Ger.* (yăgd roof.) Sound of the bugle or hunting horn.
Jagd-horn, *Ger.* (yăgd hōrn.) } Hunting horn.
Jagd-zink, *Ger.* (yăgd tsĭnk.) } bugle horn.
Jagd-sinfonie, *Ger.* (yăgd sĭn-fō-nē.) Hunting symphony.
Jagd-sttlck, *Ger.* (yăgd stŭk.) A hunting piece.
Jäger-chor, *Ger.* (yä-ghĕr-kōr.) See Jaeger Chor.
Jäger-horn, *Ger.* (yä-ghĕr hōrn,) Hunting horn, bugle horn.
Jaltage. (yăl-tăj.) The only musical instrument of Tartary, consisting of a box of fir about four feet long, and three inches wide, the upper part of which is open, over which six wire strings are stretched. It is played on with both hands, but chiefly with the left, and produces both treble and bass.
Jaleme, *Gr.* (jă-lĕ-mĕ.) The song of lamentation; so called by the ancient Greeks.
Jaléo, *Spa.* (hä-lā-ō.) A national Spanish dance.
Jambe, *Ger.* (yăm-bĕ.) See Iambus.
Jambico, *It.* (ĕ-ăm-bē-kō.) } An iambic.
Jambo, *It.* (ĕ-ăm-bō.)
Jangle. To sound discordantly or inharmoniously.
Janitscharen-musik, *Ger.* (yä-nĭt-shä-r'n moo-zĭk.) Janizary music, Turkish music.
Jarábe, *Spa.* (hä-rä-bĕ.) A Spanish dance.
Jargon. The union of several discordant notes.
Jauchzend, *Ger.* (youkh-tsĕnd.) Shouting, joyful.

Jeu, *Fr.* (zhüh.) Play; the style of playing on an instrument; also a register in an organ or harmonium.
Jeu céleste, *Fr.* (zhüh sā-lĕst.) The name of a soft stop in an harmonium; also, an organ stop of French invention, formed of two dulciana pipes, the pitch of one being slightly raised, giving to the tone a waving undulating character.
Jeu d'anche, *Fr.* (zhüh d'änsh.) A reed stop in an organ.
Jeu d'anges, *Fr.* (zhüh d'änzh.) Soft stops.
Jeu d'échos, *Fr.* (zhüh d'ē-kō.) Echo stop.
Jeu de flutes, *Fr.* (zhüh düh floot.) Flute stop.
Jeu d'orgues, *Fr.* (zhüh d'ŏrg.) Register, or row of pipes, in an organ.
Jeu-parte, *Fr.* (zhüh pärt.) Songs written in the style of a dialogue.
Jeux, *Fr. pl.* (zhüh.) Stops or registers, in an organ, or harmonium.
Jeux forts, *Fr.* (zhüh fŏr.) Loud stops; *forte* stops.
Jew's-harp. A small instrument of brass or steel, and shaped somewhat like a *lyre* · when played, it is placed between the teeth, and struck with the forefinger.
Jewstrump. A term applied by old writers to the jews-harp.
Jig. A light, brisk movement; an old species of dance in 6-8 or 12-8 time; the name is supposed to have been derived from *Geig*, a fiddle.
Jingles. Loose pieces of metal placed around a tambourine to increase the sound.
Jocosus, *Lat.* (jŏ-kō-sŭs.) Jocose, merry, funny.
Jodeln, *Ger.* (yō-d'ln.) A style of singing peculiar to the Tyrolese peasants, the natural voice and the falsetto, being used alternately.

ā *ale,* ă *add,* ä *arm,* ē *eve,* ĕ *end,* ī *ice,* ĭ *ill,* ō *old,* ŏ *odd,* ô *dove,* oo *moon,* ū *lute,* ŭ *but,* ü *French sound.*

JOIE

Joie, *Fr.* (zhwä.) Joy, gladness.
Jongleurs, *Fr. pl.* (zhŏnh-gloor.) } An old
Jongleurs, *Fr. pl.* (zhŏnh-glŭr.) } term for the itinerant musicians of the tenth and following centuries.
Jóta, *Spa.* (hō-tä.) A Spanish national dance.
Jouer, *Fr.* (zhoo-ā.) To play upon an instrument.
Jouer de harpe, *Fr.* (zhoo-ā düh härp.) To play on the harp.
Jouer de la lyre, *Fr.* (zhoo-ā düh lä lēr.) To play the lyre.
Jouer de la vielle, *Fr.* (zhoo-ā düh lä vē-yŭh.) To play on a hurdy gurdy.
Jouer du chalumeau, *Fr.* (zhoo-ā dü shä-lü-mō.) To pipe.
Jouer du luth, *Fr.* (zhoo-ā dü lüt.) To play the lute.
Jouer du violin, *Fr.* (zhoo-ā dü vē-ō-lănh.) To play the violin.
Joueur de cornemuse, *Fr.* (zhoo-ŭr düh kŏr-nä-mūs.) A performer on the bagpipes.
Joueur de flute, *Fr.* (zhoo-ŭr düh floot.) A flutist.
Joueur de musette, *Fr.* (zhoo-ŭr düh mü-zĕt.) A bagpiper.
Joueur d'instrumens, *Fr.* (zhoo-ŭr d'ănh-strü-mănh.) A player upon musical instruments.
Jovialisch, *Ger.* (yō-fī-ä-lĭsh.) Jovial, joyous, merry.
Jube, *Gr.* (jū-bē.) A harvest hymn of the Greeks and Romans in honor of Ceres and Bacchus.
Jubel-flöte, *Ger.* (yoo-b'l-flō-tĕ.) An organ stop of the flute species.
Jubel-gesang, *Ger.* (yoo-b'l ghĕ-zăng.) } Song
Jubel-lied, *Ger.* (yoo-b'l lēd.) } of Jubilee.

JUST

Jubelnd, *Ger.* (yoo-bĕlnd.) Rejoicing.
Jubilant. Joyful, triumphant.
Jubilar, *Ger.* (yoo-bĭ-lăr.) The recipient of a jubilee; one in whose honor a public performance is given.
Jubilee. A season of great public joy and festivity. Among the Jews, every *fiftieth* year was a jubilee.
Jubiléso, *It.* (yoo-bē-lō-zō.) Jubilant, exulting.
Juglaresa, *Spa.* (hool-yä-rä-za.) A female buffoon.
Juguete, *Spa.* (hoo-yoo-ā-tē.) A carol; a song of joy and exultation.
Jugum, *Lat.* (jū-gŭm.) A contrivance affixed to the lyre of the ancients to stretch or slacken the strings.
Jule, *Gr.* (jū-lē.) See Jube.
Jurer, *Fr.* (zhü-rā) To jar, to render a discordant sound.
Just. A term applied to all consonant intervals, and to those voices, strings and pipes that give them with exactness.
Juste, *Fr.* (zhüst.) Accurate in time, tone, harmony and execution.
Justesse, *Fr.* (zhüs-tăss.) Exactness, correctness or purity of intonation.
Justesse de la voix, *Fr.* (zhüs-tăss düh lä vwä.) Purity of voice.
Justesse de l'oreille, *Fr.* (zhüs-tăss düh l'ō-rä-yŭh.) Correctness of ear.
Justiniána, *It.* (yoos-tē-nē-ä-nä.) } A rude
Justiniáne, *It. pl.* (yoos-tē-nē-ä-nē.) } and loose kind of song; now obsolete.
Justo, con, *It.* (yoos-tō, kŏn.) With exact precision.
Just relations. Relations whose extremities form consonant intervals.

ā *ale*, ă *add*, ä *arm*, ē *eve*, ĕ *end*, ī *ice*, ĭ *ill*, ō *old*, ŏ *odd*, ô *dove*, oo *moon*, ū *lute*, ŭ *but*, ü *French sound*.

KABA

Kabaro. (kä-*bä*-rō.) A small drum, used in Egypt and Abyssinia.
Kaba-suma, *Tur.* (kä-bä-soo-mä.) An oboe used by the Turkish soldiers.
Kachapi, *Jav.* (kä-kä-pē.) A Javanese instrument resembling a lute.
Kafo. An instrument used in Africa resembling a small horn.
Kalamaika. (käl-ä-*mä*-kä.) A lively Hungarian dance in 2-4 time.
Kalando. A species of tambourine used by the Africans.
Kallinikos. (käl-lĕ-nĭ-kōs.) A Grecian dance, accompanied with singing.
Kammer, *Ger.* (käm-měr.) Chamber.
Kammer-concert, *Ger.* (käm-měr kŏn-tsěrt.) Chamber concert.
Kammer-musik, *Ger.* (käm-měr moo-zĭk.) Chamber music; music for private performance.
Kammer-musikus, *Ger.* (käm-měr moo-zĭ-koos.) Chamber musician; member of a prince's private band.
Kammer-sängerin, *Ger.* (käm-měr säng-ĕr-ĭn.) Private singer to a prince or king.
Kammer-spiel, *Ger.* (käm-měr spēl.) See Kammer-Musik.
Kammer-styl, *Ger.* (käm-měr stēl.) Style of chamber music, as opposed to the ecclesiastical and theatrical styles.
Kammer-ton, *Ger.* (käm-měr tōn.) The *pitch*, or lower *tuning*, of the instruments in chamber music, opposed to the higher tuning of the organ in church music.
Kampoul. (käm-*pool*.) A gong of small dimensions used by the Maylays
Kandele. (kän-*dä*-lě.) A stringed instrument used in Finland.
Kanon, *Ger.* (kä-nōn.) A canon.
Kanoon. A species of dulcimer.
Kanzel-lied, *Ger.* (kän-tsěl lēd.) Hymn before the sermon.
Kappelle, *Ger.* (käp-*pěl*-lě.) Chapel.
Kappell-meister, *Ger.* (käp-*pěl* mīs-tŏr.) Chapel master; musical director.
Karfreitag, *Ger.* (kär-*frī*-täg.) Good Friday.
Karine, *Per.* (kä-rē-nĕ.) A Persian instrument in the form of the tuba; the ancient Roman horn eight feet in length.
Kassa, *It.* (käss.) A species of drum used by the negroes of Angola.
Kasside. *Per.* (käs-sēd.) An elegy of the Persians.
Katachresis, *Gr.* (kät-ä-*krā*-sĭs.) The use of a discord contrary to the old rules.
Kathedrale, *Ger.* (kăt-ĕ-*drä*-lĕ.)
Kathedral-kirche, *Ger.* (kăt-ĕ-*dräl* kĭr-khĕ.) } Cathedral.
Keck, *Ger.* (kěk.) Pert, fearless, bold.
Keckheit, *Ger.* (kĕk-hīt.) Boldness, vigor.
Keeners. Singers engaged by the Irish, to sing lamentations over the dead.
Kehle, *Ger.* (kā-lě.) The voice, the throat.
Kehl-laut, *Ger.* (kāl lout.) A guttural sound.
Kehraus, *Ger.* (kā-rous.) *Sweep dance;* a peculiar kind of dance, practiced at the conclusion of an entertainment.

KEYE

Keman. (kä-män.) A Turkish violin with three strings.
Kemangeh, *Tur.* (kĕ-män-gäh.) A stringed instrument of the Turks, played with a bow.
Kenet. (kĕn-ĕt.) An Abyssinian trumpet.
Kenner, *Ger.* (kĕn-něr.) A connoisseur; a professor.
Kenner in der musik, *Ger.* (kĕn-něr ĭn děr moo-zĭk.) Professor of music.
Kent bugle. A bugle having six keys, four of which are commanded by the right hand and two by the left.
Kerana, *Per.* (kĕ-rä-nä.) A wind instrument, forming a kind of long trumpet much used by the Persians.
Keranim. (kĕ-rä-nĭm.) The sacred trumpet of the ancient Hebrews.
Keras, *Gr.* (kĕr-äs.) The appellation given by Hedylus, and other writers, to the hydraulica or water organ of the ancients.
Keren, *Heb.* ·(kĕr-ĕn.) A horn; an instrument first used by the Hebrews, formed of a ram's horn and subsequently made of metal.
Keraulophon, *Ger.* (kĕ-rou-lō-fōn.) An 8 feet organ stop, of a reedy and pleasing quality of tone; its peculiar character being produced by a small round hole bored in the pipe near the top.
Kerklenorgelen, *Dut.* (kĕrk-lĕ-*nōr*-gĕln.) Church organ.
Kern, *Ger.* (kärn.) The languid, or langward, in organ pipes.
Kerna, *Gr.* (kĕr-nä.) A kind of trumpet used by Tamerlane, the sound of which it is said could be heard several miles.
Keron-jebel, *Heb.* (kĕr-ŏn yā-b'l.) Jubilee horn.
Kerrena, *It.* (kĕr-rä-nä.) An Indian trumpet.
Ketch. Name applied by old writers to a catch.
Ketten-triller, *Ger.* (kĕt-t'n trĭl-lĕr.) Chain of shakes.
Kettle-drum. A brass drum, of a cup-like shape, over which the parchment head is stretched; used in pairs, one of which is tuned to the keynote, the other to the fifth of the key.
Kettle-drummer. A performer upon the kettle drum.
Key. The lever by which the sounds of a pianoforte, organ or harmonium are produced. Also, an arrangement by which certain holes are opened and closed in flutes, hautboys and other wind instruments. A key also means, a scale or series of notes progressing diatonically, in a certain order of tones and semitones, the first note of the scale being called the *Key-note*.
Key-board. The rows of keys of a pianoforte, organ or similar instrument.
Key-board, chromatic. An attachment applied to the keys of a piano for the purpose of enabling players of moderate skill to execute chromatic scales and passages with facility and correctness.
Key bugle. A Kent bugle.
Keyed. Furnished with keys.
Keyed cithara. An oblong box holding a series of strings in triangular form, struck by plectra of quill affixed to the inner ends of the keys.
Keyed harmonica. An instrument with keys, the hammers striking upon plates of glass.

ă *ale,* ă *add,* ă *arm,* ē *eve,* ĕ *end,* ī *ice,* ĭ *ill,* ō *old,* ŏ *odd,* ô *dove,* oo *moon,* ū *lute,* ŭ *but,* ü *French sound.*

KEYE

Keyed instruments. All instruments whose tones are produced by the pressure of the fingers upon keys.

Keyed-stop violin. An arrangement which may be attached to a violin, consisting of a finger-board made of ebony, with thirty-three stops, called key stops, which stand above the strings and act upon them perpendicularly.

Keyed violin. An instrument having forty strings, arranged like those of a piano, and acted upon by horsehair bows, under the pressure of keys like those of an organ.

Key, fundamental. The original key.

Key, governing. The principal or original key.

Key harp. An instrument of recent invention, resembling a piano externally, with a similar arrangement of keys and pedals. It consists of an adjustment of tuning forks of various pitches, over cavities of sonorous metal.

Key, major. That scale or key in which the third from the tonic is major.

Key, minor. That scale or key in which the third from the tonic is minor.

Key, natural. That which has neither sharp nor flat at the signature.

Key note. The tonic, or first note of every scale.

Keys, authentic. Keys in the ancient system of the Greeks, whose tones extend from the tonic to the fifth and octave above.

Keys, chromatic. The black keys of a pianoforte; every key in whose scale one or more so called chromatic tones occur, and in which a chromatic signature is requisite.

Keys, parallel. The major and its relative minor.

Keys, pedal. That set of keys belonging to an organ which are acted upon by the feet.

Keys, plagal. In the ancient Greek system, those keys whose tones extended from the dominant or fifth upward to the octave and twelfth.

Keys relative. Keys which only differ by having in their scales one flat or sharp more or less, or which have the same signature.

Keys, remote. Those which are at a distance from each other as the keys of one sharp and six sharps.

Key stops. The stops on a keyed-stop violin.

Key tone. The key note.

Key, transposed. A key removed or changed from that in which a piece was originally written.

Key, tuning. An instrument for the purpose of tightening or loosening the strings of a piano or harp.

Khasan, *Heb.* (khă-zän.) The principal singer in a synagogue.

Khuruj, *Hin.* The first note in the Hindoo musical scale.

Kielen, *Ger.* (kē-l'n.) To *quill* the "jacks" of the harpsichord, etc.

Kin Chi, (kin kē.) A Chinese musical instrument possessing a body of thin wood, with five strings of silk of different sizes.

King Chi, (king kee.) A Chinese instrument consisting of a frame of wood with pendent stone, graduated through sixteen notes and struck with a hammer.

KLAR

Kink-horn, *Ger.* (kĭnk-hörn.) Cornet, clarion. See Zinke.

Kink-hörner, *Ger. pl.* (kĭnk hör-nĕr.) Cornets, clarions. See Zinken.

Kinnor, *Heb.* (kĭn-nōr.) A small harp held in the hand and played upon while dancing.

Kirchen-componist, *Ger.* (kĭr-kh'n-kŏm-pō-nĭst.) Composer of church music.

Kirchen-dienst, *Ger.* (kĭr-kh'n dēnst.) Church service; form of prayer.

Kirchen-fest, *Ger.* (kĭr-kh'n fĕst.) Church festival.

Kirchen-gesang, *Ger.* (kĭr-kh'n ghĕ-säng.) }
Kirchen-lied, *Ger.* (kĭr-kh'n lēd.) }
Spiritual song, canticle, psalm or hymn.

Kirchen-musik, *Ger.* (kĭr-kh'n moo-zĭk.) Church music.

Kirchen-sänger, *Ger.* (kĭr-kh'n säng-ĕr.) A chorister; a chanter.

Kirchen-stück, *Ger.* (kĭr-kh'n stük.) Church piece, or composition.

Kirchen-styl, *Ger.* (kĭr-kh'n stēl.) Church style, ecclesiastical style.

Kirchen-ton, *Ger.* (kĭr-kh'n tōn.) Church mode, or tone.

Kirchen-tonarten, *Ger. pl.* (kĭr-kh'n tōn-ärt'n.) The old church modes.

Kirchen-trio, *Ger.* (kĭr-kh'n trē-ō.) An obsolete species of composition for two violins and bass.

Kirchen-weise, *Ger.* (kĭr-kh'n vī-zĕ.) A church melody.

Kit. The name of a small pocket violin used by dancing masters. Its length is about sixteen inches, and that of the bow about seventeen.

Kitar, (kĭ-tär.) A musical instrument of the Arabs.

Kithara, *Gr.* (kĭth-ä-rä.) A cithara.

Klage, *Ger.* (klä-ghĕ.) Lamentation.

Klagend, *Ger.* (klä-g'nd.) Plaintive.

Klage-gedicht. (klä-ghĕ ghĕ-dĭkht.) } Elegy,
Klage-lied, *Ger.* (klä-ghĕ lēd.) } mournful song, lamentation.

Klage-ton, *Ger.* (klä-ghĕ tōn.) Plaintive tune, or melody.

Klang, *Ger.* (kläng.) Sound; tune; ringing.

Klang-boden, *Ger.* (kläng bō-d'n.) Sound board.

Klänge, *Ger. pl.* (kläng-ĕ.) Sounds, melodies.

Klangeschlecht, *Ger.* (klän-ghĕ-shlĕkht.) A genus, or mode.

Klanglehre, *Ger.* (kläng-lā-rĕ.) Acoustics.

Klanglos, *Ger.* (kläng-lōs.) Soundless.

Klangnachbildung, *Ger.* (kläng-näkh-bĭl-doong.) Imitation of a sound.

Klang-saal, *Ger.* (kläng-säl.) Concert room; music room.

Klang-stein, *Ger.* (kläng stīn.) Sonorous stone.

Klappe, *Ger.* (kläp-pĕ.) Key of any wind instrument; a valve.

Klappen-flügelhorn, *Ger.* (kläp-p'n flü-g'l-hörn.) The keyed bugle.

Klappen-horn, *Ger.* (kläp-p'n hörn.) A keyed horn.

Klapp-trompete, *Ger.* (kläp-tröm-pā-tĕ.) A keyed trumpet.

Klar, *Ger.* (klär.) Clear, bright.

ā ale, ă add, ä arm, ē eve, ĕ end, ī ice, ĭ ill, ō old, ŏ odd, ō dove, oo moon, ū lute, ŭ but, ü French sound.

KLAR — KURZ

Klarheit, *Ger.* (klär-hït.) Clearness, plainness.
Klärlich, *Ger.* (klär-lĭkh.) Clearly, distinctly.
Klausel, *Ger.* (klou-zĕl.) A close; a regular section of a movement.
Klavier, *Ger.* (klä-fēr.) Pianoforte, harpsichord; see *Clavier*.
Klavier-sonaten, *Ger.* (klä-fēr sō-nä-tĕn.) Pianoforte sonata.
Klavier-spieler, *Ger.* (klä-fēr spē-lĕr.) Pianoforte player.
Klein, *Ger.* (klīn.) Minor; speaking of intervals.
Klein-bass, *Ger.* (klīn bäss.)
Klein-bass-geige, *Ger.* (klīn bäss ghī-ghĕ.) } Violincello.
Kleine alt possaune, *Ger.* (klī-nĕ ält pössou-nĕ.) A small sackbut, the trombone piccolo of the Italians.
Kleine lieder, *Ger.* (klī-nĕ lē-dĕr.) Little songs.
Klein-gedacht, *Ger.* (klī-nĕ ghĕ-däkht.) A small covered stop in an organ; a stopped flute.
Kleinlaut, *Ger.* (klīn-lout.) Small or low in tone or voice.
Klingbar, *Ger.* (klĭng-bär.) Resonant, sonorous.
Klingel, *Ger.* (klĭng-ĕl.) A bell.
Klingeln, *Ger.* (klĭng-ĕln.) To ring or sound a small bell; to jingle.
Klingen, *Ger.* (klĭng-'n.) } Sonorous, resonant, ringing.
Klingend, *Ger.* (klĭng-ĕnd.) }
Kling-gedicht, *Ger.* (klĭng ghĕ-dĭkht.) Sonnet.
Kling klang, *Ger.* (klĭng kläng.) Tinkling, bad music.
Klingspiel, *Ger.* (klĭng-spĕl.) The sound or noise of instruments.
Klutter, *Ger.* (kloot-tĕr.) A bird call.
Knabenstimme, *Ger.* (knä-b'n-stĭm-mĕ.) A boy's voice; counter tenor.
Knell. The tolling of a bell at a death or funeral.
Knie-geige, *Ger.* (knē-ghī-ghĕ.) Viol da Gámba, violincello.
Knie-röhre, *Ger.* (knē rō-rĕ.) A pipe or tube, bent like a knee.
Knopf-regal, *Ger.* (knŏpf rē-gäl.) See *Apfel-Regal*.
Koan. One of the eight apieces of musical sounds of the Chinese system.
Kodha, *Cor.* (kō-dä.) Cadence.
Kollo, *Jap.* (kŏl-lō.) A Japanese instrument somewhat resembling a harp.
Komiker, *Ger.* (kŏm-ī-kĕr.) A writer of burlettas; also a comic performer.
Komisch, *Ger.* (kŏm-ĭsh.) Comical.
Komma, *Gr.* (kŏm-mä.) } Comma: a musical
Komma, *Ger.* (kŏm-mä.) } section or division.
Komödiant, *Ger.* (kō-mō-dĭ-änt.) Comedian, actor, player.
Komödiantinn, *Ger.* (kō-mō-dĭ-än-tĭn.) An actress.
Komödie, *Ger.* (kō-mō-dĭ-ē.) Comedy, play.
Komponiren, *Ger.* (kŏm-pō-nēr-'n.) To compose.
Komponist, *Ger.* (kŏm-pō-nĭst.) A composer.
Komposition, *Ger.* (kŏm-pō-zĭt-sĭ-ōn.) A composition.
Konzert-meister, *Ger.* (kŏn-tsĕrt-mīs-tĕr.) See *Concert-Meister*.

Koous. A Persian drum made of brass, two feet in circumference.
Kopf-stimme, *Ger.* (kŏpf stĭm-mĕ.) Falsetto, head voice.
Koppel, *Ger.* (kŏp-p'l.) Coupler; coupling stop in an organ.
Kor, *Ger.* (kŏr.) } Choir, chorus. See
Köre, *Ger. pl.* (kŏ-rĕ.) } *Chor*.
Koryphæus, *Gr.* (kō-rĭf-ĕ-ŭs.) Chief or leader of the dancers.
Kos, *Hun*, (kŏz.) An Hungarian dance.
Kosake. (kō-sä-kĕ.) A national dance of the Cossacks.
Krächzen, *Ger.* (kräkh-ts'n.) To sing with a croaking voice.
Kraft, *Ger.* (kräft.) Power, strength, energy.
Kräftig, *Ger.* (kräf-tĭg.) } Powerful, vig-
Kräftiglich, *Ger.* (kräf-tĭg-lĭkh.) } orous, full of energy.
Kräftig und kurz, *Ger.* (kräf-tĭg oond koorts.) Loud and detached.
Krakoviak. (krä-kō-vī-äk.) } The Cra-
Krakovienne, *Fr.* (krä-kō-vī-ĕn.) } covienne, a Polish dance in 2-4 time.
Kreisfuge, *Ger.* (krīs-foo-ghĕ.) Circulating fugue; a canon.
Kreistanz, *Ger.* (krīs-tänts.) Dance in a circle.
Kreuz, *Ger.* (kroits.) A *sharp*.
Kreuz-doppeltes, *Ger.* (kroits dŏp-pĕl-tĕs.) A double sharp, × or 𝄪.
Kriegerisch, *Ger.* (krē-ghĕr-ĭsh.) Warlike, martial.
Kriegs-gesang, *Ger.* (krēgs-ghĕ-säng.) } A war
Kriegs-lied, *Ger.* (krēgs-lēd.) } song, a soldier's song.
Kriegs-spieler, *Ger.* (krēgs-spē-lĕr.) A musician of a regiment.
Krome. See *Croma*.
Krousta, *Gr.* (kroua-tä.) A general name applied by the ancients to all pulsatile instruments.
Krumm, *Ger.* (kroom.) Crooked, curved, bent.
Krummhorn, *Ger.* (kroom-hŏrn.) *Crooked horn*. The name of a portable wind instrument formerly much in use, resembling a small cornet. Organ builders corrupt this word into *cremona*, and apply it to one of their organ stops.
Krustische instrumente, *Ger.* (kroos-tĭ-shĕ ĭn-atroo-mĕn-tĕ.) Instruments of percussion, as the drum, cymbals, etc.
Kuh-horn, *Ger.* (koo-hŏrn.) Cow horn, Swiss horn, Alpine horn.
Kühn, *Ger.* (kün.) Short.
Kuhreihen, *Ger.* (koo-rī-h'n.) Ranz des Vaches.
Kunst, *Ger.* (koonst.) Art; skill.
Kunstpfeifer, *Ger.* (koonst-pfī-fĕr.) Street musician.
Kunstwerk der zukunft, *Ger.* (koonst-värk dĕr tsoo-koonft.) *Art work of the future*. A term given by Richard Wagner to his peculiar theory of the music of the future; musical composition.
Kuppel, *Ger.* (koop-p'l.) See *Koppel*.
Kurz, *Ger.* (koorts.) Short, detached, staccato.
Kürzen, *Ger.* (kür-tsen.) To abridge.
Kurzer singesatz, *Ger.* (koort-sĕr sĭn-ghĕ-säts.) Cavatina.

8

ă ale, ă add, ä arm, ē eve, ŏ end, ĭ ice, ĭ ill, ō old, ŏ odd, ô dove, oo moon, ū lute, ŭ but, ü French sound.

KRUZ

Kurz und rein, *Ger.* (koorts oond rīn.) Distinct and clear.
Kürzung, *Ger.* (kŭr-tsoong.) Abbreviation.
Kürzungszeichen, *Ger.* (kŭr-tsoongs-tsī-kh'n.) Sign of abbreviation.
Kussir, *Fr.* (küs-sēr.) A Turkish musical instrument.

LAND

Kützial-flöte, *Ger.* (kŭt-sĭ-ăl flō-tě.) An organ stop of the flute species.
Kynnor, *Heb.* (kĭn-nŏr.) The harp of David.
Kyrie eleison, *Gr.* (kē-rē ä-lā-zōn.) Lord have mercy upon us. The first movement in a mass.
Kyrielle, *Fr.* (kē-rē-ĕl.) Litany.

L.

L. Left hand. Notes, to be played with the left hand or foot, are sometimes written with an L over them.
La. A syllable applied in *solfaing,* to the note A; the sixth sound in the scale of Guido.
La, *It.* (lä.)
La, *Fr.* (lä.) } The.
La bémol, *Fr.* (lä bā-mōl.) The note A flat.
La bémol majeur, *Fr.* (lä bā-mōl mä-zhŭr.) The key of A flat major.
La bémol mineur, *Fr.* (lä bā-mōl mē-nŭr.) The key of A flat minor.
Labial. Organ pipes with *lips,* called also *flue pipes.*
Labial-stimmen, *Ger.* (lä-bĭ-ăl stĭm-m'n.) Stops belonging to the *flue* work, not reed stops.
Labium, *Lat.* (lā-bĭ-ŭm.) The *lip* of an organ pipe.
La chasse, *Fr.* (lä shäss.) In the hunting style.
Lacrimándo, *It.* (lä-crē-män-dō.) } Sadly, in a
Lacrimóso, *It.* (lä-crē-mō-zō.) } mournful, pathetic style.
Lade, *Ger.* (lä-dě.) *Wind chest,* in an organ.
La déstra, *It.* (lä dās-trä.) The right hand.
La diese, *Fr.* (lä dī-äs.) The note A sharp.
La finale, *Fr.* (lä fĭ-näl.) The last figure of a quadrille.
La flute douce, *Fr.* (lä floot dooss.) The *flute* a *bec,* or common flute.
Lage der linken hand, *Ger.* (lä-ghě děr lĭn-k'n händ.) Position of the left hand.
Lagnoso, *It.* (län-yō-zō.) Plaintive, doleful.
Lagrimándo, *It.* (lä-grē-män-dō.) } Weeping,
Lagrimóso, *It.* (lä-grē-mō-zō.) } tearful, in a sad and mournful style.
Laeva, *Lat.* (lē-vä.) The left; the left hand.
Lai, *Fr.* (lä.) Lay, ditty, short plaintive song.
L'amiable vainqueur, *Fr.* (lä-mĭ-ābl vänh-kŭr.) A French air and dance; the louvre.
Laissant mourir le son peu a peu, *Fr.* (lās-sänh moo-rēr lŭh sōnh pŭh ă pŭh.) Diminishing the sound by degrees.
Lali. A very large drum, used by the natives of the Fiji Islands.

La majeur, *Fr.* (lä mä-zhŭr.) The key of A major.
L'ame, *Fr.* (l'äm.) Sound post of a violin, viola, etc.
Lament. An old name for harp music of the pathetic kind; applied also to the pathetic tunes of the Scotch.
Lamentábile, *It.* (lä-měn-tä-bē-lě.) Lamentable, mournful.
Lamentabilménte, *It.* (lä-měn-tä-bēl-měn-tě.) Lamentably, mournfully.
Lamentabondo, *It.* (lä-měn-tä-bŏn-dō.) Mournful, doleful.
Lamentándo, *It.* (lä-měn-län-dō.) Lamenting, mourning.
Lamentations. The funeral music of the ancient Jews was called by this name.
Lamentatrice, *It.* (lä-měn-tä-trē-tshě.) Female vocal performers, hired, to chant over the dead, and to sing dirges at funerals.
Lamentazione, *It.* (lä-měn-tä-tsē-ō-ně.) A lamentation.
Lamentévole, *It.* (lä-měn-tā-vō-lě.) Lamentable, mournful, plaintive.
Lamentevolménte, *It.* (lä-měn-tā-vōl-měn-tě.) Mournfully, plaintively.
Lamentóso, *It.* (lä-měn-tō-zō.) Lamentable, mournful.
La mineur, *Fr.* (lä mĭ-nŭr.) The key of A minor.
Lampadarius, *Gr.* (läm-pä-dä-rĭ-ŭa.) The two principal singers in the patriarchal church of Constantinople.
Lampons, *Fr.* (länh-pōnh.) Drinking songs.
Länderer, *Ger.* (län-dě-rěr.) } A country dance
Ländler, *Ger.* (länd-lěr.) } or air in a rustic and popular style, in 3-8 or 3-4 time.
Länderisch, *Ger.* (län-děr-ĭsh.) In the manner or measure of a country dance.
Ländlich, *Ger.* (länd-lĭkh.) Rural.
Land-lied, *Ger.* (länd lēd.) Rural song, rustic song.
Landu, *Por.* (län-doo.) A Portuguese dance in 2-4 or 2-2 time.

ā *ale,* ă *add,* ü *arm,* ē *eve,* ĕ *end,* Ī *ice,* Ĭ *ill,* Ō *old,* Ŏ *odd,* Ō *dove,* oo *moon,* ū *lute,* ŭ *but,* ü *French sound.*

LAND

Landums, *Por.* (lăn-dooms.) A class of Portuguese music, of a sentimental, melancholy nature.
Lăng, *Ger.* (lăng.) Long.
Langsam, *Ger.* (lăng-săm.) Slowly; equivalent to *Largo.*
Langsamer, *Ger.* (lăng-sä-měr.) Slower.
Language, melodic. An expression of feelings and ideas by the aid of melodic expressions.
Language. } In an organ flue pipe, this is, the
Languid.   } flat piece of metal or wood placed horizontally just inside of the mouth.
Langueménte, *It.* (lăn-guĕ-*măn*-tĕ.) Languishingly.
Languéndo, *It.* (lăn-*guăn*-dō.).) }
Languénte, *It.* (lăn-*guăn*-tĕ.)   } feeble; with
Lánguido, *It.* (*lăn*-guĕ-dō.)   } languor.
Languettes, *Fr.* (lănh-gătt.) The brass tongues, belonging to the reed pipes in an organ.
La parte di violino, *It.* (lä pär-tĕ dĕ vē-ō-lē-nō.) The part to be played by the violin.
La parte prima, *It.* (lä *pär*-tĕ *prē*-mä.) The first voice or part; the leading part.
La pastourelle, *Fr.* (lä păs-too-*răl.*) One of the five dance movements forming the quadrille.
La poule, *Fr.* (lä pool.) The second figure in a quadrille.
La prima intenzione, *It.* (lä prē-mä ĕn-tăn-tsē-ō-nĕ.) An expression applied by the Italians to the form of any composition, as originally designed by the composer, and distinguished from the improved or altered copy.
La prima vólta fórte, la secónda piáno, *It.* (lä *prē*-mä *vōl*-tä fōr-tĕ, lä sē-*kōn*-dä pē-*ä*-nō.) The first time loud, the second time soft.
Largamente, *It.* (lăr-gă-*măn*-tĕ.) } Largely,
Largaménto, *It.* (lăr-gă-*măn*-to.) } fully; in a full, free, broad style of performance.
Large. The longest note formerly in use, in ancient music. It is equal to eight semibreves or four breves.
Largement, *Fr.* (lärzh-mänh.) Full, free in style; see Largamente.
Larghetto, *It.* (lăr-*gĕt*-tō.) A word specifying a time not quite so slow as that denoted by *largo,* of which word it is the diminutive.
Larghezza, *It.* (lăr-*gĕt*-tsä.) Breadth, largeness, freedom.
Larghissimo, *It.* (lăr-ghēs-sĕ-mō.) Extremely slow; the superlative of *largo.*
Lárgo, *It.* (*lăr*-gō.) A slow and solemn degree of movement.
Lárgo andante, *It.* (lăr-gō ăn-*dăn*-tĕ.) Slow, distinct, exact.
Lárgo assai, *It.* (lăr-gō äs-sä-ē.)   } Very
Lárgo di mólto, *It.* (lăr-gō dē *mŏl*-tō.) } slow.
Lárgo ma non tróppo, *It.* (lăr-gō mä nōn trōp-pō.) Slow, but not too much so.
Lárgo un póco, *It.* (lăr-gō oon pō-kō.) Rather slow.
Larigot, *Fr.* (lăr-ĭ-gō.) Shepherd's flute or pipe; an organ stop tuned an octave above the twelfth; the former named the flageolet.
Laringe, *It.* (lä-rēn-ghĕ.) Larynx.
Larmoyant, *Fr.* (lăr-mwä-yänh.) Weeping, with a tearful expression.
Larynx. The upper part of the *trachea.* It is composed of five annular cartilages, placed above

LAVO

one another and united by elastic ligaments, by which it is so dilated and contracted, as to be capable of varying the tones of the voice.
Lastimosaménte, *Spa.* (läs-tē-mō-zä-*măn*-tĕ.) In a doleful manner.
La stretta, *It.* (lä strät-tä.) A term indicating that a passage is to be played in quicker time.
Last shift. On a violin, the shift on the twentieth line, or E.
La treuise, *Fr.* (lä trä-nēz.) The fourth figure in a quadrille, also called *pastorale.*
Laud. To praise with words alone, or with words and music.
Laud, *Spa.* (lä ood.) A lute.
Láuda, *It.* (lä-oo-dä.) Laud, praise; hymn of praise.
Laudamus te, *Lat.* (law-*dă*-mŭs tĕ.) *We praise Thee;* part of the Gloria.
Laudes, *Lat.* (law-dĕs.)   } Canticles, or hymns
Láudi, *It. pl.* (lä-oo-dē.)   } of praise, that follow the early Mass.
Laudeci, *Lat.* (law-*dă*-sē.) } The name applied
Laudisti, *Lat.* (law-*dēs*-tē.) } to the members of a society, instituted in Florence about the year 1310, for the performance of those spiritual songs, called *Laudi.*
Laudi spirituali, *Lat.* (*law*-dē spĭr-ĭt-ū-*ä*-lē.) Sacred songs and dialogues sung by the priests in the oratory.
Lauf, *Ger.* (louf.) That part of a violin, etc., into which the pegs are inserted; also, a rapid succession of notes; a trill.
Läufe, *Ger. pl.* (loi-fĕ.)   } Rapid divisions of
Läufer, *Ger.* (*loi*-fĕr.)   } notes; a flight or run of rapid notes; a roulade, a trill or shake.
Launenstück, *Ger.* (lou-něn-stük.) A voluntary.
Launig, *Ger.* (*lou*-nĭg.) Humorous.
Laus perennis, *Lat.* (laws pĕr-*ĕn*-nĭs.) Name given to the *Perpetual Psalmody* established in the early ages of Christianity at Antioch by an order of monks.
Laut, *Ger.* (lout.) Loud; also, sound.
Laute, *Ger.* (*lou*-tĕ.) The lute.
Läuten, *Ger.* (*loi*-t'n.) To ring, to toll, to sound.
Lautenbalken, *Ger.* (*lou*-t'n-*băl*-k'n.) The bridge of a lute.
Lautenblatt, *Ger.* (*lou*-t'n-blätt.) The table of a lute.
Lauten-futter, *Ger.* (*lou*-t'n *foot*-tĕr.) } Lute
Lauten-kasten, *Ger.* (*lou*-t'n *käs*-t'n.) } case.
Lautengriff, *Ger.* (*lou*-t'n-grĭff.) Touch of a lute.
Lautenist, *Ger.* (lou-t'n-*ĭst.*) Lute-player, lutanist.
Lauten-macher, *Ger.* (*lou*-t'n *mă*-kĕr.) Lutemaker.
Lauten-schläger, *Ger.* (*lou*-t'n *shlă*-ghĕr.) }
Lauten-spieler. *Ger.* (*lou*-t'n *spē*-lĕr.)   }
Lute-player, lutanist.
Lautenzug, *Ger.* (*lou*-t'n-tsoog.) Lute-register.
Lautlos, *Ger.* (*lout*-lōs.) Soundless, mute.
La vóce, *It.* (lä vō-tehĕ.) The voice.
La volta, *It.* (lä *vōl*-tä.) } A lively, animated
La volte, *It.* (lä *vōl*-tĕ.) } tune performed to an old dance, the action of which consisted chiefly of quick turns and high leaps.

116   PRONOUNCING MUSICAL DICTIONARY.

ă *ale*, ă *add*, ä *arm*, ē *eve*, ŏ *end*, ī *ice*, ĭ *ill*, ō *old*, ŏ *odd*, ô *dove*, oo *moon*, ū *lute*, ŭ *but*, ü *French sound*.

LAY

Lay. A song; a species of narrative poetry among the ancient minstrels.
Lay clerk. A vocal officiate in a cathedral, who takes part in the services and anthems but is not of the priesthood.
Lay, greater. One of the two classes of ancient lays, consisting of twelve couplets of verses in different measures.
Lay, lesser. One of the two classes of ancient lays comprising sixteen or twenty verses.
Laymen. Those vocal officiates in a cathedral who are not of the priesthood; the laity or people in distinction from the clergy.
Le, *Fr.* (lŭh.) } The.
Le, *It. pl.* (lě.) }
Leader. The first or principal violin in an orchestra; a director of a choir.
Leading chord. The dominant chord.
Leading melody. The principal melody in a composition of several parts.
Leading note. The major seventh of any scale; the semitone below the key note; the major third of the dominant.
Leaning note. See Appogiatura.
Leaps. A distance composed of several intermediate intervals.
Leben, *Ger.* (lā-b'n.) Life, vivacity.
Lebhaft, *Ger.* (lāb-häft.) Lively, vivacious, quick.
Lebhaftigkeit, *Ger.* (lāb-häf-tĭg-kīt.) Liveliness, vivacity.
Le bruit des tambours, *Fr.* (lŭh brū-ē dĕ tănh-boor.) The rattle of drums.
Le chant royal, *Fr.* (lŭh ĕ h ä n h r w ā-y ä l.) Verses chanted by pilgrims on their return from the Holy Land.
Le clavier broumer, *Fr.* (lŭh klä-vī-ā broomā.) An instrument invented in Paris for the purpose of strengthening the fingers of piano players.
Leçon, *Fr.* (lā-sônh.) A lesson, an exercise.
Ledger lines. } The short extra, or additional
Leger lines. } lines drawn above or below the staff, for the reception of such notes as are too high or too low to be placed on or within the staff.
Leera viola. A stringed instrument of the ancients.
Leero. A lyre.
Left beat. A movement to the left in beating time.
Legábile, *It.* (lĕ-gä-bē-lĕ.) } See Legato.
Legándo, *It.* (lĕ-gän-dō.) }
Legáre, *It.* (lĕ-gä-rĕ.) To slur, or bind.
Legáre le note, *It.* (lĕ-gä-rĕ lĕ nō-tĕ.) To join the notes closely; to play *legato*.
Legatissimo, *It.* (lĕ-gä-tĭs-sē-mō.) Exceedingly smooth and connected.
Legáto, *It.* (lĕ-gä-tō.) In a close, smooth, graceful manner; the opposite to *staccato*. It is often indicated by a sign called a tie, thus, ⌒.
Legato assai, *It.* (lĕ-gä-tō äs-sä-ē.) Very close and connected.
Legato touch. A sliding of the fingers on and off the keys, holding down one key until the finger is fairly on another. It is indicated by the word *legato*, or by a curved line, ⌒.
Legatúra, *It.* (lĕ-gä-too-rä.) A slur, a ligature.
Léger, *Fr.* (lā-zhā.) Light, nimble.

LEIE

Légerement, *Fr.* (lā-zhār-mänh.) Lightly, nimbly, gaily.
Léger et animé, *Fr.* (lā-zhārĕt än-ē-mā.) Light and animated.
Légereté, *Fr.* (lā-zhā-rĕ-tā.) Lightness, agility.
Leggatissimo, *It.* (lĕg-gä-tĭs-sē-mō.) See Legatissimo.
Leggénda, *It.* (lĕd-jăn-dä.) A legend, a tale.
Leggeramente, *It.* (lĕd-jĕr-ä-mān-tĕ.) Lightly, easily.
Leggeranza, *It.* (lĕd-jĕr-än-tsä.) } Lightness
Leggerezza, *It.* (lĕd-jĕr-ät-tsä.) } and agility.
Leggerissimamente, *It.* (lĕd-jĕr-ēs-sē-mä-män-tĕ.) Very light and sprightly.
Leggerissimo, *It.* (lĕd-jĕr-ēs-sē-mō.) Very light and sprightly.
Leggermente, *It.* (lĕd-jĕr-mān-tĕ.) A light and easy movement.
Leggiadra, *It.* (lĕd-jē-ä-drä.) Graceful, elegant.
Leggiadramente, *It.* (lĕd-jē-ä-drä-mān-tĕ.) Gracefully, elegantly.
Leggiárdo, *It.* (lĕd-jē-är-dō.) Lightly, delicately.
Leggieramente, *It.* (lĕd-jē-ār-ä-mān-tĕ.) }
Leggiére, *It.* (lĕd-jē-ā-rĕ.) }
Leggierménte, *It.* (lĕd-jē-ĕr-mān-tĕ.) }
Easily, lightly, delicately.
Leggierezza, *It.* (lĕd-jē-ā-rät-tsä.) Lightness, delicacy; in a light, elastic style.
Leggiéro, *It.* (lĕd-jē-ā-rō.) Light, swift, delicate.
Leggieruccolo, *It.* (lĕd-jē-ä-roo-kō-lō.) Rather light and delicate.
Leggio, *It.* (lĕd-jē-ō.) A chorister's desk, in a church choir.
Leggio di musica, *It.* (lĕd-jē-ō dō moo-zē-kä.) A music stand.
Légno, *It.* (lān-yō.) Wood; see *Col Légno*.
Lehrer, *Ger.* (lā-rĕr.) Teacher, master.
Lehrerin, *Ger.* (lā-rĕr-ĭn.) Instructress, mistress.
Lehr-gedicht, *Ger.* (lār-ghĕ-dĭkht.) Didactic poem.
Lehr-ode, *Ger.* (lār ō-dĕ.) Diadactic ode.
Leib-stückhen, *Ger.* (lĭb stŭk-kh'n.) Favorite air or tune.
Leichen-gedicht, *Ger.* (lī-kh'n ghĕ-dĭkht.) Funeral poem, elegy.
Leichen-gesang, *Ger.* (lī-kh'n ghĕ-säng.) Dirge, funeral song.
Leichen-musik, *Ger.* (lī-kh'n moo-zĭk.) Funeral music.
Leichenton, *Ger.* (lī-kh'n-tōn.) A lugubrious sound.
Leicht, *Ger.* (līkht.) Light, easy, facile.
Leichtheit, *Ger.* (līkht-hīt.) } Lightness,
Leichtigkeit, *Ger.* (līkht-tĭg-kīt.) } facility.
Leichtfertig, *Ger.* (līkht-fār-tĭg.) Lightly, carelessly.
Leid, *Sco.* (lēd.) A lay, a song, a ballad.
Leidenschaft, *Ger.* (lī-d'n-shäft.) Passion.
Leidenschaftlich, *Ger.* (lī-d'n-shäft-līkh.) Impassioned, passionate.
Leier, *Ger.* (lī-ĕr.) A lyre, a hurdy gurdy.
Leierer, *Ger.* (lī-ĕ-rĕr.) A player on the lyre.
Leiermädchen, *Ger.* (lī-ĕr-mād-kh'n.) A girl who plays on a hurdy gurdy.
Leiermann, *Ger.* (lī-ĕr-män.) A player on a hurdy gurdy.

ā ale, ă add, ä arm, ē eve, ĕ end, ī ice, ĭ ill, ō old, ŏ odd, ô dove, oo moon, ū lute, ŭ but, ü French sound.

LEIE

Leiern, *Ger.* (lī-ĕrn.) To play on the lyre or hurdy gurdy.
Leierorgel, *Ger.* (lī-ĕr-ŏr-g'l.) Hand organ; barrel organ.
Leierspieler, *Ger.* (lī-ĕr-spē-lĕr.) One who plays on a lyre.
Leicht, *Ger.* (līht.) Easy.
Leigla, *Spa.* (lĕl-yä.) A Moorish dance.
Leimma, *Spa.* (lā-ĕm-mä.) An interval.
Leine, *Ger.* (lī-nē.) A line of the staff.
Leise, *Ger.* (lī-zĕ.) Low, soft, gentle.
Leit-accord, *Ger.* līt äk-kōrd.) A chord or harmony leading instinctively to another, as the chord of the dominant leading to the tonic.
Leiter, *Ger.* (lī-tĕr.) Leader; also the scale of any key.
Leitereigen, *Ger.* (lī-tĕr-ī-g'n.) Such tones as belong to the scale of any key; the notes forming the scale.
Leiter-fremd, *Ger.* (lī-tĕr-frĕmd.) Accidental sharps or flats which do not belong to the key.
Leit-ton, *Ger.* (līt-tōn.) The leading note, the leading note.
Lene. An old term applied to a note sustained in one of the harmonic parts of a composition, whilst the other parts are in motion.
Lengua, *Spa.* (lăn-guä.) The tongue of a bell.
Lenguetas, *Spa.* (lăn-guē-täs.) Valves of wind instruments.
Lengueteria, *Spa.* (lăn-guē-tā-rē-ä.) A collection of tubes with valves as in an organ.
Leno, *It.* (lā-nō.) Weak, feeble, faint.
Lent, *Fr.* (länh.) Slow.
Lentamente, *It.* (lĕn-tä-män-tĕ.) Slowly.
Lentando, *It.* (lĕn-tän-dō.) With increased slowness.
Lentement, *Fr.* (länht-mänh.) } Slowly, leisurely.
Lentemente, *It.* (län-tĕ-män-tĕ.) }
Lentement, tres, *Fr.* (länht-mänh trä.) Very slow.
Lenteur, *Fr.* (länh-tŭr.) Slowness, delay.
Lenteur, avec, *Fr.* (länh-tŭr ä-vĕk.) } With
Lentezza, con, *It.* (lĕn-tät-tsa kōn.) } slowness and delay.
Lentissimamente, *It.* (lĕn-tĕs-sĕ-mä-män-tĕ.) }
Lentissimo, *It.* (lĕn-tĕs-sĕ-mō.) } Extremely slow.
Lento, *It.* (län-tō.) Slow.
Lento assai, *It.* (län-tō äs-sä-ē.) } Very
Lento di molto, *It.* (län-tō dĕ mōl-tō.) } slowly.
Lento lento, *It.* (län-tō län-tō.) }
Leonine verses. So called from Leo, the inventor. They are verses the end of which rhyme with the middle.
Le pantalon, *Fr.* (luh pänh-tä-lōnh.) The first figure of a quadrille.
Le plus lent de tous les mouvements, *Fr.* (luh plü länht düh too lĕ moov-mänht.) The slowest kind of time.
Lepsis, *Gr.* (lĕp-sĭs.) The ascending scale.
Les douze gammes majeures, *Fr.* (lĕ dooz găm mä-zhŭr.) The twelve major scales.
Les douze gammes mineures, *Fr.* (lĕ dooz găm mē-nŭr.) The twelve minor scales.
Lesser appoggiatura. The short appoggiatura.

LIBR

Lesser barbiton. A name formerly given to the kit, or small violin used by dancing masters.
Lesser comma. The difference between the comma and the enharmonic dieses; the *Diachisma*.
Lesser lay. One of the two classes among the ancients, comprising sixteen or twenty verses.
Lesser sixth. A minor sixth.
Lesser third. A minor third.
Lesson. Formerly applied to exercises or pieces consisting of two or three movements for the harpsichord or pianoforte.
Lessus, *Lat.* (lĕs-sŭs.) A word in the twelve tables of the Romans, supposed by some to mean a funeral song.
Lestaménte, *It.* (lĕs-tä-män-tĕ.) Quickly, lively.
Lestézza, *It.* (lĕs-tät-tsä.) Agility, quickness.
Lestissimamente, *It.* (lĕs-tĕs-sĕ-mä-män-tĕ.) Very quickly.
Lestissimo, *It.* (lĕs-tĕs-sĕ-mō.) Very quick.
Lésto, *It.* (lăs-tō.) Lively, nimble, quick.
Letane. See Litania.
L' été, *Fr.* (l'ā-tā.) One of the five dance movements in a quadrille.
Le ton d'ut, *Fr.* (luh tŏnh d'oot.) The key of C.
Letrilla, *Spa.* (lĕ-trēl-yä.) A song.
Letters. The first seven letters of the alphabet, A, B, C, D, E, F, G, are used to form the letters of the scale, and are repeated in every octave. These letters serve to distinguish the notes and determine their pitch.
Letters, doubled. Capital letters doubled, indicating that the tone is an octave lower than when the letters stand single.
Letterále, *It.* (lĕt-tĕ-rä-lĕ.) } Literally,
Letteralménte, *It.* (lĕt-tĕr-äl-män-tĕ.) } exactly as written.
Lettúra, *It.* (lĕt-too-rä.) A reading, lecture; an instruction given by a master to his scholars.
Lettúra di música, *It.* (lĕt-too-rä dē moo-zē-kä.) A musical lecture.
Leutéssa, *It.* (loo-tās-sä.) A bad lute.
Leúto, *It.* (loo-tō.) A lute.
Levé, *Fr.* (lĕ-vā.) The up-stroke of the bâton.
Levet. A blast of a trumpet; probably that by which soldiers are called in the morning, (obsolete.)
Levézza, *It.* (lĕ-vät-tsä.) Lightness.
Levier pneumatique, *Fr.* (lĕv-ī-ā noo-mä-tēk.) The pneumatic lever; a series of small bellows, or levers, placed on the wind chest of an organ, containing air at a high pressure; by means of this the touch of a large organ may be made very light.
Le viole sole, *It.* (lĕ vē-ō-lĕ sō-lĕ.) The viol alone.
Le voci, *It.* (lĕ vō-tshē.) The voices.
Lezzioni, *It. pl.* (lĕt-tsē-ō-nē.) Lessons.
L. H. Initials indicating the use of the left hand in pianoforte music.
Liaison, *Fr.* (lē-ā-zōnh.) Smoothness of connection; also, a *bind* or *tie*.
Liaison de chant, *Fr.* (lē-ā-zōnh dŭh shänht.) The *sostenuto* style of singing.
Liberaménte, *It.* (lē-bĕ-rä-män-tĕ.) } Freely,
Librement, *Fr.* (lēbr-mänh.) } easily, plainly.

ă *ale*, ă *add*, ă *arm*, ĕ *eve*, ĕ *end*, ī *ice*, ĭ *ill*, ō *old*, ŏ *odd*, ô *dove*, oo *moon*, ū *lute*, ŭ *but*, ü *French sound*.

LIBE

Libero, *It.* (lē-bĕ-rō.) Free, unrestrained.
Librétto, *It.* (lē-brăt-tō.) The text of an opera or other extended piece of music.
License. A deviation for the time being from the received rules which form the established system of harmony.
Licénza poética, *It.* (lē-tchăn-tsă pō-ā-tē-kă.) Poetic license; alterations or deviations from common rules.
Lié, *Fr.* (lī-ā.) Smoothly; the same as *Legáto*.
Liebes-lied, *Ger.* (lē-bĕs lēd.) Love-song.
Liebhaber, *Ger.* (lēb-hä-bĕr.) Amateur; a lover of music.
Lieblich, *Ger.* (lēb-līkh.) Lovely, charming.
Lieblich-gedacht, *Ger.* (lēb-līkh ghē-dǎkht.) A stopped-diapason organ register of sweet tone.
Lié, coulant, *Fr.* (lī-ā koo-länh.) Slurred, flowing.
Lied, *Ger.* (lēd.) A song, a ballad, a lay.
Liedchen, *Ger.* (lēd-kh'n.) A short song or melody.
Lieder, *Ger.* (lē-dĕr.) Songs.
Lieder-buch, *Ger.* (lē-dĕr bookh.) A song book, a hymn book.
Lieder-bund. *Ger.* (lē-dĕr boond.) A society of song singers.
Lieder-dichter, *Ger.* (lē-dĕr dīkh-tĕr.) A lyrical poet, a song writer.
Lieder-kranz, *Ger.* (lē-dĕr kränts.) Glee club.
Lieder ohne worte, *Ger.* (lē-dĕr ō-nĕ vōr-tĕ.) Songs without words.
Lieder-sammlung, *Ger.* (lē-dĕr säm-loong.) Collection of songs.
Lieder-sänger. *Ger.* (lē-dĕr säng-ĕr.) A song singer, a ballad singer.
Lieder-spiel, *Ger.* (lē-dĕr spēl.) An operetta, consisting of dialogue and music of a light, lively character.
Lieder-sprache, *Ger.* (lē-dĕr sprā-khē.) Words or language adapted to songs.
Lieder-tafel, *Ger.* (lē-dĕr tä-f'l.) Song-table; German glee club, generally consisting of male voices alone.
Lieder-täfler, *Ger.* (lē-dĕr tä-flĕr.) Glee singers.
Lieder-tanz, *Ger.* (lē-dĕr tänts.) A dance intermingled with songs.
Lieder-vers, *Ger.* (lē-dĕr fĕrs.) Verse of a song or hymn.
Lieder-form, *Ger.* (lē-dĕr form.) The form or subject of a song.
Lied ohne worte, *Ger.*) (lēd ō-nĕ vōr-tĕ.) See Lieder ohne Worte.
Lied singen, *Ger.* (lēd sĭng-'n.) To sing a song.
Lier, *Dut.* (lēr.) A lyre.
Ligare, *It.* (lē-gä-rĕ.) To bind, to tie, to join together.
Ligato, *It.* (lē-gä-tō.) See *Legáto*.
Ligatur, *Ger.* (lē-gä-toor.) See Ligature.
Ligatura, *It.* (lē-gä-too-rä.) See Legatura.
Ligature. An old name for a *tie* or *bind*.
Light. A general term applied to any thin, airy composition; also to the keys of any instrument when they make little resistance to the pressure of the fingers. Such an instrument is said to have a *light touch*.
Ligne, *Fr.* (lēnh.) A line of the staff.

LIRA

Ligneum psalterium, *Lat.* (līg-nē-ŭm săl-tā-rĭ-ŭm.) The wooden dulcimer, called in Germany the straw fiddle.
Lignes additionnelles, *Fr.* (lēnhs ăd-dē-sǐ-ŏn-nĕl.) Leger lines.
Lilt, *Sco.* (lĭlt.) To sing or play merrily.
Limma, *Gr.* (lĭm-mä.) An interval used in the ancient Greek music, less by a comma than a major semitone.
Linea, *It.* (lē-nĕ-ä.) A line of the staff.
Line, continuous horizontal. A line indicating that the different parts are to be played or sung in unison.
Lines. That portion of the staff on and between which the notes are placed. At their first invention, the spaces between them were not used.
Lines, added. Leger lines; lines added above and below the staff.
Lines, bar. Lines drawn perpendicularly across the staff, dividing it into measures.
Lines, horizontal. Lines placed after figures to signify that the same harmony is to be continued.
Lines, ledger.) Lines added above or below
Lines, leger.) the staff for the reception of such notes as are too high or too low to be placed upon or within it.
Linea, riga, *It.* (lē-nä-ä rē-gä.) The lines of the staff.
Lines, waving. A line which when placed perpendicularly upon the staff indicates that the notes of the chord are to be played successively one after another.
A waving horizontal line shows that the effect of the 8va sign is to be continued as far as the line extends.
Lingua, *It.* (lēn-guä.) The tongue in organ stop reeds.
Lingual. Pertaining to the tongue; a letter or sound pronounced chiefly by the tongue.
Lingulæ, *Gr.* (lĭn-gŭ-lē.) The tongues of Greek flutes.
Linie, *Ger.* (lĭn-ē.) A line of the staff.
Linien, *Ger. pl.* (lĭn-ī-ĕn.) Lines of the staff.
Linien-system, *Ger.* (lĭn-ī-ĕn sĭs-tām.) A scale; the lines of the staff.
Lining. A term applied to a practice of reading one or two lines of a hymn before singing them, alternating reading and singing.
Link, *Ger.* (lĭnk.) } Left.
Links, (lĭnks.) }
Linke hand, *Ger.* (lĭn-kĕ hănd.) The left hand.
Linon, *Gr.* (lē-nŏn.) A string.
Linos, *Gr.* (lē-nŏs.) A rustic air; also a dirge.
Linto. A small lute; the mandoline.
Liotna, *Rus.* (lĭot-nä.) A lute.
Liquid. An epithet applied to the smooth succession of the sweet and mellow sounds of any voice or wind instrument, also, to the tones themselves separately considered.
Lira, *It.* (lē-rä.) A lyre.
Lira da bráccio, *It.* (lē-rä dä brät-tshē-ō.) The Italian lyre, an obsolete instrument with seven strings.
Lira da gámba, *It.* (lē-rä dä gäm-bä.) An instrument similar to the *Lira da bráccio*, but held

ā ale, ă add, ä arm, ē eve, ĕ end, ī ice, ĭ ill, ō old, ŏ odd, ô dove, oo moon, ū lute, ŭ but, ü French sound.

LIRA

between the knees, and with twelve or sixteen strings.
Lira doppia, *It.* (lē-rä dŏp-pē-ä.) Double lyre.
Lira grande, *It.* (lē-rä grän-dē.) The viol di gamba, a viol with six strings, formerly much used in Germany.
Lira rústica, *It.* (lē-rä roos-tē-kä.) A species of lyre, formerly in use among the Italian peasants.
Lira tedesca, *It.* (lē-rä tā-dĕs-kä.) The German lyre.
Lire, *Fr.* (lēr.) To read.
Lire la musique, *Fr.* (lēr lä mü-zēk.) To read music.
Liréssa, *It.* (lē-rās-sä.) A bad lyre, or harp.
Lírica, *It.* (lē-rē-kä.) } Lyric, lyric poetry; poetry
Lírico, *It.* (lē-rē-kō.) } adapted for music.
Liróne, *It.* (lē-rō-nē.) A large lyre, or harp.
Liscio, *It.* (lē-shē-ō.) Simple, unadorned, smooth.
Lispelnd, *Ger.* (līs-pēlnd.) Lisping, whispering.
L'istésso, *It.* (l'ēs-tās-sō.) The same.
L'istésso moviménto, *It.* (l'ēs-tās-sō mō-vē-mĕn-tō.)
L'istésso tempo, *It.* (l'ēs-tās-sō tăm-pō.) In the same time as the previous movement.
L'istésso tempo poi a poi di nuovo vivénte, *It.* (l'ēs-tās-sō tăm-pō pō-ē ä pō-ē dē nwō-vō vē-vĕn-tĕ.) The same time, with gradually increasing animation.
Litanía, *Lat.* (lĭ-tā-nī-a.)
Litanie, *Fr.* (lĭ-tä-nē.) } A litany.
Litanei, *Ger.* (lĭt-ä-nī.)
Litany. A solemn form of supplication used in public worship.
Little sharp-sixth. A name given by French theorists to the second inversion of the dominant seventh formed on the second degree of the scale, and consisting of a bass note with its minor third, perfect fourth and major sixth.
Lituo, *Spa.* (lē-too-ō.) An ancient military instrument of music.
Liturgía, *It.* (lē-toor-jē-ä.) Liturgy.
Liturgy. The ritual for public worship in those churches which use written forms.
Lituus, *Lat.* (līt-ū-ŭs.) An instrument of martial music; a kind of trumpet making a shrill sound.
Liutájo, *It.* (lē-oo-tā-yō.) A lute maker.
Liutessa, *It.* (lē-oo-tĕs-sä.) A bad lute.
Liutiere, *It.* (lē-oo-tē-ĕ-rĕ.) A lute maker.
Liúto, *It.* (lē-oo-tō.) A lute.
Livre, *Fr.* (lĕvr.) A book.
Lob-gesang, *Ger.* (lŏb-ghĕ-zäng.) } A hymn
Lob-lied, *Ger.* (lŏb-lēd.) } or song of praise.
Lobpsalm, *Ger.* (lŏb-psälm.) A psalm of praise.
Lobsingen, *Ger.* (lŏb-sĭng-'n.) To sing praises.
Lobsinger, *Ger.* (lŏb-sĭng-ĕr.) One who sings praises.
Lóco, *It.* (lō-kō.) *Place;* a word used in opposition to *8va-alta,* signifying that the notes over which it is placed are not to be played an octave higher, but just as they are written.
Locrense, *Gr.* (lō-krĕn-sē.) One of the ancient tones or modes.
Locrian, *Gr.* (lō-krĭ-ăn.) } The hyper-Dorian
Locrico, *Gr.* (lō-krĭ-kō.) } mode of the ancient Greeks.

LOWB

Lodi, *It.* (lō-dē.) A name formerly given to certain sacred songs.
Loft, organ. That part of the gallery of a church where the organ is placed.
Logierian system. A system of musical instruction, introduced by John Bernard Logier, which, with instruction on the pianoforte, combines simultaneous performance in classes, and also, the study of harmony, modulation, etc. In connection with this system Logier invented and employed the *chiroplast.*
Lombárda, *It.* (lŏm-bär-dä.) A species of dance used in Lombardy.
Long. A note formerly in use, equal to four semibreves, or half the length of the large.
Longa, *Lat.* (lŏn-gä.) A long.
Long appoggiatura. An appoggiatura consisting of a single note forming a part of the melody. It borrows half the length of the next note and is accented.
Long, double. An old character equal in duration to four breves.
Long drum. The large drum used in military bands, carried horizontally before the performer and struck at both ends.
Long metre. A stanza of four lines in Iambic measure, each line containing eight syllables.
Long mordent. A mordent formed of four notes.

Long particular meter. A stanza of six lines in Iambic measure, each line containing eight syllables.
Long roll. A drum-beat calling the soldiers to arms.
Long spiel. An ancient Icelandic instrument, long and narrow, and played upon with a bow.
Longue pause, *Fr.* (lônh pōz.) Make a long rest, or pause.
Lontáno, *It.* (lŏn-tä-nō.) Distant, remote, a great way off.
Lontáno, da, *It.* (lŏn-tä-nō dä.) At a distance.
Lorgnette, *Fr.* (lôrn-yĕt.) An opera glass.
Lo stesso, *It.* (lō stĕs-sō.) The same.
Lo stretto, *It.* (lō strĕt-tō.) A general term applied to that part of a composition designed to be delivered in a quicker time than the rest.
Loure, *Fr.* (loor.) A dance of slow time and dignified character. It has sometimes three and sometimes four crotchets in a bar, with the peculiarity of the second crotchet of every bar being dotted.
Lourré, *Fr.* (loo-rā.) Smoothly, connectedly; the same meaning as *Legáto.*
Louvre, *Fr.* (loovr.) A name applied to a French air, called also "*L'Amiable Vainqueur,*" for which Louis XIV. had a remarkable predilection. This air has since formed a well known dance.
Love-song. A song the words and melody of which are expressive of love.
Low. A word of relative signification and applied to any part, passage or note situated beneath, or lower in pitch than some other part, passage or note; depressed in the scale of sounds; grave.
Low bass. Second bass.

ā ale, ă add, ä arm, ē eve, ĕ end, ī ice, ĭ ill, ō old, ŏ odd, ō dove, oo moon, ū lute, ŭ but, ü French sound.

LOWE

Lower changing note. That note which descends from the perfect or augmented fourth on to the minor or major seventh. Little used.
Low soprano. Second soprano, second treble.
Low tenor. A species of voice half way between bass and tenor; a baritone.
Luctuosamente, *Spa.* (look-too-ō-zä-mān-tē.) Mournfully.
Ludi, *Lat.* (ū-dī.) The name originally applied to what are now called oratorios.
Ludi magister, *Lat.* (lū-dī mäj-ĭs-tĕr.)
Ludi moderator, *Lat.* (lū-dī mŏd-ē-rä-tĕr.) } Theatrical manager or director.
Ludi spirituales, *Lat.* (lū-dī spīr-ĭt-ū-ă-lēs:) A species of ancient dramatic oratorio, acted or .he stage.
Ludus fidicinus, *Lat.* (lū-dūs fĭ-dĕ-sĭ-nūs.) A music school.
Lugubre, *It.* (loo-goo-brē.) Lugubrious, sad, mournful.
Luinig. A short, plaintive song much used in the Hebrides and on the western coasts of Scotland. It is generally sung by the women at their work and diversions.
Luit, *Dut.* (loit.) A lute.
Lullaby. A song to quiet infants; a soft, gentle song.
Lundu, *Por.* (loon-doo.) A Portuguese dance in 2-4 or 2-2 time.
Lunga pausa, *It.* (loon-gä pä-oo-zä.) A *long pause* or rest.
Luogo, *It.* (loo-ō-gō.) See *Loco*.
Luonator di liuto, *It.* (loo-ō-nä-tōr dē lē-oo-tō.) A player on the lute.
Lusing. An abbreviation of *Lusingáto*.
Lusingándo, *It.* (loo-zēn-gán-dō.) } Sooth-
Lusingánte, *It.* (loo-zēn-gán-tē.) } ing,
Lusingáto, *It.* (loo-zēn-gá-tē.) } coax-
Lusinghévole, *It.* (loo-zēn-gá-vō-lĕ.) } ing; persuasively, insinuatingly, in a playful, persuasive style.
Lusinghevolménte, *It.* (loo-zēn-gä-vōl-mān-tĕ.) Soothingly, persuasively.
Lusinghiére, *It.* (loo-zēn-ghĕ-ā-rĕ.) } Flatter-
Lusinghiéro, *It.* (loo-zēn-ghĕ-ā-rō.) } ing, fawning, coaxing.
Lustig, *Ger.* (loos-tĭg.) Merrily, cheerfully, gaily.
Lustlied, *Ger.* (loost-lēd.) A gay, merry song.
Lut, *Dan.* (loot.) } A lute.
Luta, *Swe.* (loo-tä.) }
Lutanist. A performer upon the lute.
L'ut de poitrine, *Fr.* (l'oot duh pwä-trēn.) C with chest tone.
Lute. A very ancient stringed instrument, formerly much used, and containing at first, only five rows of strings, but to which six or more were afterward added. The *lute* consists of four parts, viz., the table; the body which has nine or ten sides; the neck which has as many stops, or divisions; and the head or cross, in which the screws for tuning it are inserted. In playing this instrument, the performer strikes the strings with the fingers of the right hand, and regulates the sounds with those of the left.
Lut, *Fr.* (loot.) A lute.
Lute, arch. A stringed instrument resembling

LYRE

the theorbo, by some considered synonymous with it.
Lute, harp. An instrument having ten strings and resembling the lute.
Lutenist, } A performer on the lute.
Luter. }
Luth, *Fr.* (loot.) A lute.
Luthier, *Fr.* (lū-tĭ-ā.) Formerly a maker of lutes; at present a maker of stringed and wind instruments.
Lutina. A small lute, or mandolin.
Lutist. A player on the lute.
Luttuosaménte, *It.* (loot-too-ō-z ă-mān-tē.) Sadly, sorrowfully.
Luttuóso, *It.* (loot-too-ō-zō.) Sorrowful, mournful.
Lychanoides, *Gr.* (lĭ-kă-noi-dēs.) The name given by the ancients to the middle sounds called *spicsi*, by some of the Greek writers.
Lychanos, *Gr.* (lĭ-kă-nōs.) The third string of the ancient diapason or octave.
Lychanos hypaton, *Gr.* (lĭ-kă-nōs hī-pă-tŏn.) The name given by the ancients to the third sound of the lowest tetrachord in the diatonic genus.
Lychanos meson, *Gr.* (lĭ-kă-nōs mā-sŏn.) The name by which the ancients distinguished the third sound of the *meson* or middle tetrachord.
Lydian. See Greek modes.
Lydian chant. A chant of a sorrowful, melancholy style.
Lyidh, *Iri.* (lī-ēdh.) A lay; a species of narrative or description.
Lyra, *It.* (lē-rä.) } The lyre.
Lyra, *Ger.* (lēr-ä.) }
Lyra barbarina, *It.* (lē-rä bär-bä-rē-nä.) An old instrument, resembling in shape the Spanish guitar, having three double niches.
Lyra doppia, *It.* (lē-rä dŏp-pē-ä.) Double lyre, not at present used, but supposed to be a kind of *viol da gamba*.
Lyra hexachordis, *Gr.* (lēr-ä hĕx-ä-kōr-dĭs.) A lyre with six strings.
Lyra mendicorum, *Lat.* (lēr-ä mĕn-dĭ-kō-rŭm.) A hurdy gurdy.
Lyrasänger, *Ger.* (lēr-ä-sāng-ĕr.) } A performer
Lyraspieler, *Ger.* (lēr-ä-spē-lĕr.) } on the lyre.
Lyra-viol. An old instrument of the lyre or harp species; it had six strings and seven frets.
Lyre. One of the most ancient of stringed instruments, said to have been invented by Mercury about the year 2000 A. M., and formed of a tortoise shell; a species of harp.
Lyre Æolian. The Æolian harp.
Lyre, double. The *lyra doppia;* an instrument of the viol kind.
Lyre, Grecian. A lyre of the ancient Greeks, quite small and having but seven strings, and held in the hand while being played upon.
Lyre guitar. An instrument of six strings, in form resembling a lyre.
Lyre guitarre, *Fr.* (lĕr ghĭt-ār.) See *Lyre Guitar*.
Lyre, Mercurian. One of the earliest musical instruments, formed of the shell of a tortoise and having seven strings.

ă ale, ă add, ă arm, ē eve, ĕ end, ī ice, ĭ ill, ō old, ŏ odd, ô dove, oo moon, ū lute, ŭ but, ü French sound.

LYRI

Lyric. } Poetry adapted for singing. The
Lyrical. } word is borrowed from the lyre, and was originally confined to poetry meant to be accompanied by that instrument.
Lyric comedy. A comedy in which vocal music forms a principal part; comic opera.
Lyric drama. Opera; acting accompanied by singing.
Lyrichord. Name formerly given to an upright harpsichord.

MAES

Lyricism. A lyric composition.
Lyric tragedy. Tragic opera.
Lyricus, *Lat.* (lĭr-ĭ-kŭs.) Pertaining to the lyre.
Lyriker, *Ger.* (lĭr-ĭ-kĕr.) } Lyric, lyrical.
Lyrisch, *Ger.* (lĭr-ish.) }
Lyrist. One who plays upon the harp or lyre.
Lyrodi, *Gr.* (lĭr-ō-dē.) Ancient vocalists who accompanied themselves on the lyre.
Lytierse, *Gr.* (lĭt-ĭ-ăr-sē.) Song of the reapers.

M.

M. This letter is used as an abbreviation of Mezzo, also of various other words, as Metronome, Mano, Main, and also in connection with other letters; as, M. F. for Mezzo Forte; M. P., *Mezzo Piano;* M. V., *Mezzo Voce,* etc.
Ma, *It.* (mä.) But, as, *Allégro ma non tróppo,* quick, but not too much so.
Machalath, *Heb.* (mä-kä-läth.) A kind of lute or guitar used by the Hebrews.
Machicot, *Fr.* (mä-shē-kō.) A chorister; a bad singer.
Machul, *Heb.* (mä-kool.) Instruments used by the Hebrews. This name is supposed to have been given to two instruments, one of the string and the other of the pulsatile species.
Mach-werk, *Ger.* (mäkh värk.) *Made work;* music made up; merely the result of labor and study without any musical inspiration.
Madriále, *It.* (mä-drē-ä-lē.) A madrigal; the name formerly given by the Italians to the *intermezzi,* or pieces performed between the acts of a play or an opera.
Madrialétto, *It.* (mä-drē-ä-lăt-tō.) A short madrigal.
Madrigal. An elaborate vocal composition, in three, four, five or six parts, without accompaniment, in the strict or ancient style, with imitation and fugue; the parts or melodies moving in that conversational manner peculiar to the music of the sixteenth and seventeenth centuries. The madrigal is generally sung in chorus.
Madrigal, accompanied. A madrigal in which the voices are sustained by a pianoforte or organ.
Madrigále, *It.* (mä-drē-gä-lē.) A madrigal.
Madrigaleggiáre. *It.* (mä-drē-gä-lĕd-jē-ä-rē.) To compose madrigals.
Madrigalésco, *It.* (mä-drē-gä-lă-skō.) Of, or belonging to, a madrigal.
Madrigaléssa, *It.* (mä-drē-gä-lăs-sä.) A long madrigal.

Madrigalétto, *It.* (mä-drē-gä-lăt-tō.) } A short
Madrigalíno, *It.* (mä-drē-gä-lē-nō.) } madrigal.
Madrigali concertati, *It.* (mä-drē-gä-lē kōn-tshä-tä-tē.) Madrigals that have an accompaniment.
Madrigalist. A composer of madrigals.
Mæsa. A mass.
Mæsta, *It.* (mä-ĕs-tä.) } Majesty, dignity,
Mæstáde, *It.* (mä-ĕs-tä-dē.) } grandeur.
Mæstáte, *It.* (mä-ĕs-tä-tē.) }
Mæstévole, *It.* (mä-ĕs-tä-vō-lē.) Majestic, majestical.
Mæstevolíssimo, *It.* (mä-ĕs-tä-vō-lĕs-sē-mō.) Most majestically.
Maestevolménte, *It.* (mä-ĕs-tä-vōl-mān-tē.) }
Maestosaménte, *It.* (mä-ĕs-tō-zä-mān-tē.) }
Majestically, nobly.
Maestosíssimo, *It.* (mä-ĕs-tō-zĕs-sē-mō.) Exceedingly majestic.
Maestóso, *It.* (mä-ĕs-tō-zō.) Majestic, stately, dignified.
Maéstra, *It.* (mä-ăs-trä.) An *artiste,* female performer.
Maestrévole, *It.* (mä-ăs-trä-vō-lē.) Masterly, highly finished.
Maestri, *It.* (mä-ăs-trē.) Masters.
Maestría, *It.* (mä-ĕs-trē-ä.) Mastery, skill, art, ability.
Maestrína, *It.* (mä-ĕs-trē-nä.) A learned lady musician.
Maéstri secolári, *It.* (mä-äs-trē sä-kō-lä-rē.) Teachers of secular, or instrumental music, teachers of instruments at a *conservatorio.*
Maéstro, *It.* (mä-ăs-trō.) Master, composer, an experienced, skilful artist.
Maestro al cembele, *It.* (mä-ăs-trō äl tshĕm-bä-lē.) A skilful pianist; a master of the instrument.
Maestro del córo, *It.* (mä-ăs-trō dĕl kō-rō.) Master of the choir or chorus.

ă ate, ă add, ă arm, ĕ eve, ĕ end, ī ice, ĭ ill, ō old, ŏ odd, ô dove, oo moon, ū lute, ŭ but, ü French sound.

MAES

Maéstro di camera, *It.* (mä-ăs-trō dĕ kă-mĕ-rä.) Leader or conductor of chamber music.
Maéstro di canto, *It.* (mä-ăs-trō dĕ kăn-tō.) A singing master.
Maéstro di cappélla, *It.* (mä-ăs-trō dĕ käp-pāl-lä.) Chapel master; composer; director of the musical performances in a church or chapel.
Magadis, *Gr.* (mä-gä-dĭs.) The name of an ancient Greek treble instrument, furnished with double strings tuned in octaves, like those of a three stop harpsichord.
Magadizing. A term in the ancient Greek music, signifying a vocal performance in octaves, when men and women, or men and boys, joined in the same air.
Magas, *Gr.* (mä-gäs.) The bridge of stringed instruments.
Maggioláta, *It.* (mäd-jē-ō-lä-tä.) A hymn or song in praise of the mouth of May.
Maggióre, *It.* (mäd-jē-ō-rĕ.) Greater, in respect to scales and intervals; major; the major key.
Magiscóro, *It.* (mä-jēs-kō-rō.) The chief of a choir.
Magníficat, *Lat.* (măg-nĭf-ĭ-kăt.) A part of the vespers, or evening service of the Roman Catholic church.
Magodi, *Gr.* (mä-gō-dī.) Strolling musicians among the Greeks who perambulated the streets singing comic ballads.
Magodía, *Gr.* (mä-gō-dī-ä.) The lyric poems sung by the Magodi.
Magodis, *Gr.* (mä-gō-dīs.) An ancient instrument having two sets of strings.
Maidmarian. The lady of the May games in a morris dance; an old dance.
Main, *Fr.* (mănh.) The hand.
Main droite, *Fr.* (mănh drwăt.) Right hand.
Main gauche, *Fr.* (mănh gōsh.) The left hand.
Maitre, *Fr.* (mätr.) A master, a director.
Maitre de chapelle, *Fr.* (mätr dŭh shä-pĕll,) Chapel master; director of the choir.
Maitre de musique, *Fr.* (mätr dŭh mŭ-zĕk.) Musical director.
Maitre des menetriers, *Fr.* (mätr dĕ mănh-ä-trĭ-ăr.) Master of the minstrels.
Maitresse, *Fr.* (mä-trĕss.) Mistress, instructress.
Maitresse de chant, *Fr.* (mä-trĕss dŭh shänh.) A singing mistress.
Majesta, *It.* (mä-yĕs-tä.) } Majesty, dignity.
Majesté, *Fr.* (mä-zhĕs-tä.) }
Majestueux, *Fr.* (mä-zhĕs-tū-ŭr.) Majestic.
Majeur, *Fr.* (mä-zhŭr) Major; major key.
Major. Greater, in respect to intervals, scales, etc.
Major, bob. A full peal upon eight bells.
Major diatonic scale. That scale in which the semitones fall between the third and fourth and seventh and eighth tones, both in ascending and descending.
Major, drum. The chief drummer of a regiment.
Major, fife. An officer who superintends the fifers of a regiment.
Major fourth. Properly a *perfect* fourth; an interval containing two whole tones and one semitone.

MANI

Major intervals. Those intervals containing the greatest number of semitones under the same denomination.
Major key. } That mode or scale in which
Major mode. } the third from the tonic is major.
Major-modus, *Lat.* (mä-jōr mō-dŭs.) Major mode.
Major semitone. A semitone which *changes* its degree, or *letter* on the staff; thus, C-Db, A-Bb, etc. The distinction between major and minor semitones is not usually regarded by late theorists.
Major seventh. An interval consisting of five tones and a semitone.
Major sixth. A sixth composed of four tones and a semitone.
Major third. An interval containing two whole tones or steps.
Major tonic. A major scale.
Major triad. A union of any sound with its major third and perfect fifth.
Majosis. (mä-yō-sĭs.) A jovial dance of the Polish Jews.
Majuscule, *Lat.* (mä-jŭs-kū-lĕ.) A name given by the ancients to what is called now a semibreve.
Markirt, *Ger.* (mŭ-kĕrt.) Well marked.
Malanconía, *It.* (mä-län-kō-nē-ä.) } Melan-
Malencónico, *It.* (mä-lĕn-kō-nē-kō.) } choly, sadness.
Malimba, *Spa.* (mä-lăm-bä.) A curious musical instrument used by the Incas before the conquest of South America. It is formed of slats of wood from ten to fifteen inches in length, the pitch of the note varying with the length of the slat.
Malincólico, *It.* (mä-lĕn-kō-lē-kō.) } Melan-
Malinconía, *It.* (mä-lĕn-kō-nī-ä.) } choly.
Malinconicaménte, *It.* (mä-lĕn-kō-nē-kä-măn-tĕ.) In a melancholy style.
Malinconico, *It.* (mä-lĕn-kō-nē-kō.)
Malinconióso, *It.* (mä-lĕn-kō-nē-ō-zō.) }
Malinconóso, *It.* (mä-lĕn-kō-nō-zō.) }
In a melancholy style.
Malsonnant, *Fr.* (mäl-sŏn-nänh.) Ill sounding, bad toned.
Mama, *It.* (mä-mä.) In drum music, a term indicating the right hand.
Manca, *It.* (män-kä.) The left.
Mancándo, *It.* (män-kän-dō.) Decreasing, dying away.
Manche, *Fr.* (mänh-sh.) The neck of a violin or other instrument.
Mandola, *It.* (män-dō-lä.) A mandoline, or cithern, of the size of a large lute.
Mandoline. A Spanish instrument of the guitar species, with frets like a guitar and four strings, tuned like the violin, and put in vibration with a quill or plectrum.
Mandolino, *It.* (män-dō-lē-nō.) A mandolin.
Mandora. } A small kind of lute or guitar, with
Mandore. } frets and seven gut strings, three of which are duplicates.
Mandura, *It.* (män-doo-rä.) The name of a lesser kind of lute.
Manggang, *Jav.* (mänd-gäng.) The most simple and ancient kind of music among the Javanese.
Mánica, *It.* (mä-nē-kä.) Fingering.

ā ale, ă add, ä arm, ē eve, ĕ end, ī ice, ĭ ill, ō old, ŏ odd, ȯ dove, oo moon, ū lute, ŭ but, ü French sound.

MANI — MARS

Mánico, *It.* (mä-nē-kō.) The neck of the violin, guitar, etc.
Manichord. } Originally, an instrument
Manichordon. } with but one string; subsequently a stringed instrument resembling a spinet or harpsichord.
Manichordion, *Fr.* (mä-nĭ-kŏr-dĭ-ŏnh.) }
Manichordium, *Lat.* (män-ĭ-kŏr-dĭ-ŭm.) }
See Manichord.
Manicordieudraht, *Ger.* (mä-nĭ-kŏr-dĭ-ĕn-drãht.) Wire for the manichord or clarichord.
Maniéra, *It.* (mä-nē-ā-rā.) } Manner, style.
Maniere, *Fr.* (män-ē-ār.) }
Maniéra affettáta, *It.* (mä-nē-ā-rä äf-fĕt-tä-tä.) An affected style or delivery.
Maniéra lánguida, *It.* (mä-nē-ā-rä län-gŭā-dä.) A languid, sleepy style.
Maniere d'attaque, *Fr.* (män-ĭ-ār d'ät-täk.) Touch, manner, or style of playing the pianoforte.
Manieren, *Ger. pl.* (mä-nē-r'n.) Graces, embellishments, ornaments.
Manifold fugue. A fugue in which more than one theme is elaborated.
Männergesangs-verein, *Ger.* (män-nĕr-ghē-zängs fĕ-rīn.) Men's vocal society.
Mannerism. Adherence to the same manner; the constant use of an ever-recurring set of phases; adherence to the same style without freedom or variety.
Männliche stimme, *Ger.* (män-līkh-ĕ. stĭm-mĕ.) A manly voice.
Máno. *It.* (mä-nō.) The hand.
Máno destra, *It.* (mä-nō dăs-trä.) } The
Máno diritta, *It.* (mä-nō dē-rēt-tä.) } right
Máno dritta, *It.* (mä-nō drēt-tä.) } hand.
Máno manca, *It.* (mä-nō män-kä.) }
Máno sinistra, *It.* (mä-nō sē-nēs-trä.) }
The left hand.
Manual. The key board; in organ music it means that the passage is to be played by the hands alone without using the pedals.
Manual, *Ger.* (mă-noo-ăl.) }
Manuale, *Lat.* (mă-nū-ā-lĕ.) } Manual.
Manuále, *It.* (mă-noo-ā-lĕ.) }
Manualiter, *Ger.* (mă-noo-ä-lĭ-tĕr.) Organ pieces to be played by the fingers alone without the pedals.
Manualmente, *It.* (mă-noo-ăl-mān-tĕ.) Manually.
Manual-untersatz, *Ger.* (mă-noo-ăl oon-tĕr-sätz.) An organ stop of 32 feet tone, with stopped pipes; the *sub bourdon*.
Manúbrio, *It.* (mă-noo-brē-ō.) } The handle or knob
Manubrium, *Lat.* (mă-nū-brĭ-ŭm.) } by which a stop is drawn in an organ.
Manuductor. Name given by the ancients to one whose province it was to beat the time with his band at public performances.
Manuscriptum, *Lat.* (män-ū-skrĭp-tŭm.) Manuscript.
Marcándo, *It.* (mär-kăn-dō.) } Marked, ac-
Marcáto, *It.* (mär-kä-tō.) } cented, well pronounced.
Marcatissimo, *It.* (mär-kä-tēs-sē-mō.) Very strongly marked.
Marcáto il póllice, *It.* (mär-kä-tō ĭl pōl-lē-tshĕ.) Mark or accent strongly the note played by the thumb.

Marcáto la melodia ed accell, *It.* (mär-kä-tō lä mĕl-ō-dē-ä ĕd ät-tshĕl.) In a marked style and the time accelerated.
March. A military air or movement especially adapted to martial instruments; it is always written in common time, and an odd quaver or crotchet at the beginning is often used.
Marcha, *Spa.* (mär-kä.) Signal of the drum to march.
Marchand de musique, *Fr.* (mär-shänh dŭh mū-zēk.) A music seller.
March, dead. A funeral march.
Marche, *Fr.* (märsh.) A march; in harmony, a symmetrical sequence of chords.
Marche harmonique, *Fr.* (märsh här-mō-nēk.) Harmonic progression.
Marche redoublée, *Fr.* (märsh rĕ-doob-lā.) A double quick march.
Marche triomphale, *Fr.* (märsh trē-ŏnh-fäl.) A triumphal march.
March, funeral. A slow, measured march. adapted to the movement of a funeral procession.
Márcia, *It.* (mär-tshē-ä.) A march.
Márcia, con móto, *It.* (mär-tshē-ä kŏn mō-tō.) A spirited martial movement.
Márcia funebre, *It.* (mär-tshē-ä foo-nā-brĕ.) Funeral march.
Marcial, *Spa.* (mär-thĭ-äl.) In the style of a march.
Marciále, *It.* (mär-tshē-ä-lĕ.) See Marziále.
Marcia lugubre, *It.* (mär-tshē-ä loo goo-brĕ.) A slow, mournful march.
Marciáta, *It.* (mär-tshē-ä-tä.) A march.
Marine band. A band employed on vessels of war.
Mariona, *Spa.* (mä-rē-ō-nä.) A Spanish dance.
Marjunee, *Hin.* (mär-yoo-nā.) A portion of the Hindoo scale.
Mark, *Dut.* (märkh.) A march.
Marked. Accented.
Mark, harmonic. A sign (O) used in music for the violin, violincello, and harp, to indicate that the notes over which it is placed are to be produced on such parts of the open strings as will give the harmonic sounds.
Markiren, *Ger.* (mär-kē-r'n.) } To mark, to em
Marquer, *Fr.* (mär-kā.) } phasize.
Marks, abbreviation. Signs of abbreviation.
Marks, cadence. Short perpendicular lines which indicate the cadence notes in chanting.
Marks, division. Figures with a curved line above them showing the number of equal parts into which notes are divided, when instead of 2, 4, or 8, they are divided into 3, 5, 7, 9, etc., 3̃, 7̃, etc.
Marks, metronomic. Figures appended to music, referring to corresponding figures on a metronome. ♩=120 ♩=80
Marks, staccato. Dots or small dashes placed over notes to indicate that they are to be played short and detached.
Marquez un peu la mélodie, *Fr.* (mär-kā ŭnh pūh lä mā-lō-dē.) The melody to be slightly marked, or accented.
Marsch, *Ger.* (märsh.) A march.

ă *ale*, ă *add*, ă *arm*, ĕ *eve*, ĕ *end*, ī *ice*, ĭ *ill*, ō *old*, ŏ *odd*, ô *dove*, oo *moon*, ū *lute*, ŭ *but*, ü *French sound*.

MARS

Marschartig, *Ger.* (märsh-är-tĭg.) In the style of a march.
Märsche, *Ger. pl.* (mär-shĕ.) Marches.
Marseillaise, *Fr.* (mär-sāl-yāz.) The Marseilles hymn; a French national air.
Martelé, *Fr.* (mär-tĕ-lā.) } Hammer-
Martellándo, *It.* (mär-tĕl-län-dō.) } ing, strongly marking the notes as if hammered.
Martelláre, *It.* (mär-tĕl-lä-rĕ.) To *hammer*, to strike the notes forcibly like a hammer.
Martelláto, *It.* (mär-tĕl-lä-tō.) *Hammered*, strongly marked.
Martial music. Music adapted for war and warlike occasions. An expression applied to marches, dirges, songs of triumph and all compositions, intended to stimulate to battle, excite commiseration for the fallen, or celebrate heroic deeds.
Martillo, *Spa.* (mär-tĭl-yō.) A tuning hammer.
Martinete, *Spa.* (mär-tĭ-nä-tĕ.) A jack in a harpsichord.
Martráza, *It.* (mär-trä-tsa.) A Spanish dance.
Marziále, *It.* (mär-tsĕ-ä-lĕ.) Martial, in the style of a march.
Mascharáda, *It.* (mä-skä-rä-dä.) } Music com-
Mascheráta, *It.* (mä-skĕ-rä-tä.) } posed for grotesque characters; masquerade music.
Maschera, *It.* (mä-skĕ-rä.) A mask.
Mask. } A species of musical
Maske, *Ger.* (mäs-kĕ.) } drama, or operetta, in-
Masque, *Fr.* (mäsk.) } cluding singing and dancing, performed by characters in masks; also, an utensil used by the ancient Roman actors and singers for the purpose of augmenting the power of the voice.
Masrakitha. (mäs-rä-kē-thä.) A pneumatic instrument of the ancient Hebrews, consisting of pipes musically proportioned to each other, fitted into a wooden chest, into which the wind was conveyed from the lips by means of a pipe and the sounds were produced by stopping and unstopping with the fingers, the apertures at the upper extremity.
Mass. A vocal composition, performed during the celebration of High Mass, in the Roman Catholic church, and generally accompanied by instruments. It consists of five principal movements, the *Kyrie*, *Gloria*, *Credo*, *Sanctus*, and *Agnus Dei*.
Mass, *Ger.* (mäss.) Measure, time.
Mass bell. A small bell used in the service of the Roman Catholic church to direct attention to the more solemn parts of the mass.
Mass book. The Missal, or Roman Catholic service book.
Mass, canonical. A mass in which the various parts of the musical service of the church are followed in their regular course, or in strict canonical order.
Mass, high. The mass celebrated in the Catholic churches by the singing of the choristers; distinguished from the low mass, in which prayers are read without singing.
Mässig, *Ger.* (mäs-sĭg.) Moderate, moderately.
Mässig geschwind, *Ger.* (mäs-sĭg ghĕ-shvĭnd.) Moderately playful.

MAZU

Mässig langsam, *Ger.* (mäs-sĭg läng-säm.) Moderately slow.
Mässig schnell, *Ger.* (mäs-sĭg shnĕll.) Moderately fast and animated.
Mássima, *It.* (mäs-sē-mä.) A semibreve.
Master. One eminently skilled in music, a teacher.
Master, ballet. One who superintends the rehearsals and performances of the ballet.
Master, choir. A chorister, a choir leader.
Master of music. In the sixteenth century this appellation was given to eminent practical composers.
Master of song. The name given in the sixteenth century to the person appointed to teach the children of the Chapel Royal to sing and perform on the organ.
Master-singers. A class of poets who flourished in Germany during the fifteenth and part of the sixteenth centuries.
Masure, *Ger.* (mä-zoo-rĕ.) } A lively Pol-
Masureck, *Ger.* (mä-zoo-rĕk.) } ish dance, in
Masurek, *Ger.* (mä-zoo-rĕk.) } 3-8 or 3-4 time,
Masurka, *Ger.* (mä-zoor-kä.) } quicker than the Polonaise, and has an emphasis on one of the unaccented parts of the bar; the *Mazurka*.
Matachin, *Spa.* (mä-tä-kēn.) An old dance with swords and bucklers.
Matalan. A small Indian flute, used to accompany the Baysdere dances.
Matassins, *Fr.* (mä-täs-sēn.) A matachin dance; the dancers.
Matelotte, *Fr.* (mä-tĕ-lŏt.) A French sailor's dance in 3-4 time.
Matinare, *It.* (mä-tĕ-nä-rĕ.) To sing matins.
Matinata, *It.* (mä-tĕ-nä-tä.) A song for the morning; a serenade.
Matinatore, *It.* (mä-tĕ-nä-tō-rĕ.) A morning serenader.
Matinée, *Fr.* (mü-tĭ-nä.) An entertainment given in the early part of the day.
Matinée musicale, *Fr.* (mä-tĭ-nä mü-zē-käl.) A musical performance given in the daytime.
Matines, *Fr.* (mä-tĕn.) Matins, morning worship.
Matins. The name of the first morning service in the Roman Catholic church.
Mattutino delle tenebre, *It.* (mät-too-tē-nō dāl-lĕ tĕ-nä-brĕ.) The service of the Tenebrae.
Maul-trommel, *Ger.* (moul trŏm-mĕl.) A Jew's harp.
Maxima, *Lat.* (mäx-ĭ-mä.) The name of the longest note used in the fourteenth and fifteenth centuries; see *Large*.
Maximum immestatum, *Lat.* (mäx-ĭ-mŭm ĭm-mĕs-tä-tŭm.) The great system among the ancients, consisting of four tetrachords and the chord named proslambanomenos.
Maximus, bob. A full peal upon twelve bells, comprising 479,001,600 changes.
Mazourk, *Ger.* (mä-tsoork.) } A lively Pol-
Mazourka, *Ger.* (mä-tsoor-kä.) } ish dance of
Mazur, *Ger.* (mä-tsoor.) } a sentiment-
Mazurca, *Ger.* (mä-tsoor-kä.) } al character,
Mazurka, *Ger.* (mä-tsoor-kä.) } in 3-8 or 3-4
Mazurke, *Ger.* (mä-tsoor-kĕ.) } time, of a peculiar rythmic construction, quicker than the Polonaise or Polacca; see Masurka.

ă ale, ă add, ä arm, ē eve, ĕ end, I ice, ĭ ill, ō old, ŏ odd, ō dove, oo moon, ū lute, ŭ but, ü French sound.

M. D.

M. D. The initials of Main Droit, the right hand.
Mean. A term formerly applied to the tenor or medium part in compositions for several parts, male and female.
Mean clef. Tenor clef.
Mean, harmonical. The third in the harmonic triad.
Mean parts. Middle parts.
Measure. That division of time by which the air and movement of music are regulated; the space between two bar lines on the staff.
Measure accent. The regular alternation of strong and weak part in a measure.
Measure, common. A measure having an even number of parts in a bar.
Measure, four-eight. A measure of the value of four eighth notes, marked 4-8.
Measure, fourfold. A measure of four even parts.
Measure, four-half. A measure of the value of four half notes, marked 4-2.
Measure, four-quarter. A measure of the value of four quarter notes, marked 4-4.
Measure, nine-eighth. A measure containing nine eight notes or their equivalent, marked 9-8.
Measure, passy. An old stately kind of dance; a cinque pas.
Measure, six-eighth. A measure containing the value of six eighth notes, marked 6-8.
Measure, sixfold. A measure consisting of two musical feet, each formed of an accented and unaccented notes; a measure of six equal parts.
Measure, six-quarter. A measure of the value of six quarter notes, marked 6-4.
Measure, three-eighth. A measure containing the value of three eighth notes, marked 3-8.
Measure, threefold. A measure divided into three equal parts.
Measure, three-half. A measure containing the value of three half notes, and marked 3-2.
Measure, three-quarter. A measure containing the value of three quarter notes, marked 3-4.
Measure, twelve-eighth. A measure containing the value of twelve-eighth notes, marked 12-8.
Measure, two-eighth. A measure containing the value of two eighth notes, marked 2-8.
Measure, twofold. A measure of two equal parts.
Measure, two-half. A measure containing the value of two half notes, marked 2-2 or
Measure, two-quarter. A measure containing the value of two quarter notes, marked 2-4.
Mechanically. A word applied to spiritless styles of performance.
Medésimo, *It.* (mē-dā-zē-mō.) } The same.
Medésmo, *It.* (mē-dăs-mō.)
Medésmo móto, *It.* (mē-dăs-mō mō-tō.) }
Medésmo tempo, *It.* (mē-dăs-mō tĕm-pō.) }
In the same time or movement as before.
Mediant, *Lat.* (mā-dī-ănt.) } The third note
Médiante, *Fr.* (mā-dī-ănht.) } of the scale; the *middle note* between the tonic and the dominant.
Meditatio, *Lat.* (mĕd-I-tā-shī-ō.) A word formerly used to signify the middle of a chant, or

MELO

the sound which terminates the first part of the verse in the Psalms.
Medius harmonicus, *Lat.* (mā-dī-ŭs här-mŏn-I-kŭs.) The third or middle note of the fundamental common chord.
Medley. A mixture; an assemblage of detached parts or passages of well known songs or pieces so arranged that the end of one connects with the beginning of another.
Meer-trompete, *Ger.* (mār trŏm-pā-tĕ.) }
Meer-horn, *Ger.* (mār hŏrn.) }
Sea Trumpet.
Megalophonous, *Gr.* (mĕg-ā-lŏf-ō-nous.) Having a loud voice.
Mehr, *Ger.* (mār.) More.
Mehr-stimmig, *Ger.* (mār stĭm-mĭg.) For several voices.
Mehr stimmiger gesang, *Ger.* (mār stĭm-mĭ-ghĕr ghĕ-zăng.) A glee or part song.
Meister, *Ger.* (mīs-tĕr.) Master, teacher.
Meister-gesang, *Ger.* (mīs-tĕr ghĕ-zăng.) Master's song, minstrel's song.
Meister-sänger, *Ger.* (mīs-tĕr săng-ĕr.) Master singer, minstrel.
Meister-stück, *Ger.* (mīs-tĕr stŭk.) Master piece.
Mélancolie, *Fr.* (mā-länh-kō-lē.) Melancholy, in a mournful style.
Mélange, *Fr.* (mā-länzh.) A medley; a composition founded upon several popular airs.
Meleket, *Aby.*. An Abyssinian trumpet.
Melisma, *Gr.* (mē-lĭs-mā.) A vocal grace or embellishment; several notes sung to one syllable.
Melismatik, *Ger.* (mĕl-ĭs-mā-tĭk.) } Florid
Melismatisch, *Ger.* (mĕl-ĭs-mā-tĭsh.) } vocalization; see Melisma.
Mellifluous. (mĕl-lĭf-lū-ous.) Smoothly flowing, very melodious.
Mellow. Soft, melodious.
Melóde, *It.* (mā-lō-dĕ.) Melody, tune.
Melodeon. A reed instrument having a key board like the pianoforte. It is supplied with wind by a bellows worked with the feet of the performer.
Melodeon, double reed. A melodeon with two sets of reeds.
Melodeon, organ. A melodeon having a register of stops similar to those of an organ.
Melodistik, *Ger.* (mĕl-ō-dĭs-tĭk.) The rules or science of melody.
Melodie, *It.* (mā-lō-dē-ā.) Melody, tune.
Melodic. (mĕ-lŏd-ĭk.) Relating to melody.
Melodica. An instrument invented by Stein, at Augsburg, similar to the pianoforte.
Melodic language. The language of melody or song; ideas expressed by a melodious combination of sounds.
Melodic modulation. A change from one key into another.
Melodics. That department of vocal elementary instruction which relates to the *pitch* of tones.
Melodic step. The movement of a voice or part from one tone to the following one.
Melódico, *It.* (mā-lō-dē-kō.) Melodious, tuneful.
Melodicon. An instrument invented by Riffel, in Copenhagen, the tones of which are produced from bent metal bars.
Mélodie, *Fr.* (mā-lō-dē.) Melody, tune.

ā *ale,* ă *add,* ä *arm,* ē *eve,* ĕ *end,* ī *ice,* ĭ *ill,* ō *old,* ŏ *odd,* ŏ *dove,* oo *moon,* ū *tute,* ŭ *but,* ü *French sound.*

MELO

Melodies, authentic. Melodies written principally between the key note and its octave.
Melodies, Ethiopian. Negro melodies.
Melodies, Hibernian. Irish songs and melodies.
Melodies, plagal. Melodies whose tones lie between the fifth of the key and its octave or twelfth.
Mélodie bien sentie, *Fr.* (mā-lō-dē bĭ-änh sänh-tē.) The melody to be well expressed or accented.
Mélodieuse, *Fr.* (mā-lō-dĭ-ūz.) Melodious, smooth.
Mélodieusement, *Fr.* (mā-lō-dĭ-ŭs-mäuh.)
Melodiosaménte, *It.* (mā-lō-dē-ō-zä-*män*-tē.)
Melodiously, sweetly.
Melodieux, *Fr.* (mā-lō-dĭ-ūz.) ⎫ Melodious,
Melodik, *Ger.* (mĕ-*lō*-dĭk.) ⎬ tuneful.
Melodioso, *It.* (mā-lō-dē-ō-zō.) ⎫ Melodious,
Melodioso, *Spa.* (mĕ-lō-dē-ō-zō.) ⎬ musical, tuneful.
Melodisch, *Ger.* (mĕ-*lō*-dĭsh.) ⎭
Melodisissimo, *It.* (mā-lō-dē-ō-*sēs*-sē-mō.) Extremely melodious.
Melodious. Having melody, musical; a term applied to a succession of pleasing sounds.
Melodious bass. The "bass chantante;" the singing bass.
Melodiously. In a melodious, musical manner.
Melodist. A composer, or singer of melodies.
Melodista, *It.* (mā-lō-*dēs*-tä.)
Melodista, *Spa.* (mā-lō-*dēs*-tä.) ⎫ Melodist.
Melodiste, *Fr.* (mā-lō-*dēst*.) ⎭
Melodium. A variety of the harmonium.
Melodize. To make melodious; to form a succession of sounds which shall produce an agreeable effect.
Melodrama. ⎫ A modern species of drama of
Melodrame. ⎭ French origin, with music interspersed, both vocal and instrumental, the latter of a descriptive kind, serving to elucidate the action and heighten the passion of the piece.
Melodram, *Ger.* (mĕ-lō-*drăm*.)
Melodram, *Fr.* (mĕ-lō-*drăm*.) ⎫ Melodrama.
Melodrámma, *It.* (mā-lō-*drä*-mä.) ⎭
Melodrammático, *It.* (mā-lō-drä-*mä*-tē-kō.) Melodramatic.
Melody. A succession of simple sounds so arranged as to produce a pleasing effect upon the ear; distinguished from *harmony* by not necessarily including a combination of parts.
Melody, chromatic. A melody consisting of a series of tones moving by chromatic intervals.
Melody, diatonic. A melody whose tones move by diatonic intervals.
Melody, leading. The principal part of a composition containing several parts.
Melograph. A piano invented in 1827, connected with which was machinery which recorded in notes whatever was improvised on the piano. The invention was not a complete success.
Melologue. A combination of recitative and music.
Meloman, *Gr.* (mā-lō-măn.) ⎫ A passionate
Mélomane, *Fr.* (mā-lō-măn.) ⎬ lover of music.
Melomanie, *Fr.* (mā-lō-mä-nē.) ⎫ Excessive
Melomany. (mĕ-*lōm*-ă-ny.) ⎬ love of music;
music mania.

MERC

Melopéa, *It.* (mā-lō-pā-ä.) ⎫ Poetical, or rhetor-
Mélopée, *Fr.* (mā-lō-pā.) ⎬ ical melody; words
and music combined; the vocal declamation or chant of the drama.
Melophare. A lantern, inside of which music paper, previously soaked in oil is placed, so that the notes can be read when a light is placed inside; used for serenades, at night.
Melopiano. (mē-lō-pĭ-*ă*-nō.) A stringed instrument invented in 1870, combining tones resembling those of the pianoforte and organ.
Meloplaste. (*mĕl*-ō-plăst.) An instrument for teaching vocal music from a staff without either clefs or notes.
Melopœa, *Gr.* (mĕ-lō-*pē*-ă.) A term in ancient music signifying the art or rules of composition in melody; melody.
Melopomenos, *Gr.* (mĕl-ō-*pŏm*-ĕ-nŏs.) Vocal melody.
Melos, *Gr.* (mā-lŏs.) Tune, song, melody.
Melothesia, *Gr.* (mĕl-ō-*thā*-zĭ-ä.) The composition of a melody.
Melotheta, *Gr.* (mā-*lō*-thĕ-tä.) Composer, musician.
Melpomene, *Lat.* (mĕl-*pŏm*-ĕ-nē.) One of the nine Muses.
Même, *Fr.* (mām.) The same.
Même mouvement, *Fr.* (mām moov-mänh.) In the same movement.
Même mouvement que précédement, *Fr.* (mām moov-mänh küh prē-*sēd*-mänh.) In the same movement as the preceding.
Mén, *It.* (mān.) Less; an abbreviation of *méno.*
Mén allégro, *It.* (mān äl-*lā*-grō.) Less quick.
Mener le branle, *Fr.* (mē-*nā* läh brănh.) To lead the dance.
Ménéstrels, *Fr.* (mē-năs-trĕl.) Minstrels.
Ménétrier, *Fr.* (mē-nā-trĭ-ā.) A minstrel, a rustic musician.
Méno, *It.* (mā-nō.) Less.
Méno allégro, *It.* (mā-nō äl-*lā*-grō.) Less quick.
Méno fórte, *It.* (mā-nō *fōr*-tē.) Less loud.
Méno mósso, *It.* (mā-nō *mŏs*-sō.) Less movement, slower.
Méno piáno, *It.* (mā-nō pē-*ă*-nō.) Not so softly.
Méno presto, *It.* (mā-nō *prĕs*-tō.) Less rapid.
Méno vivo, *It.* (mā-nō vē-vō.) Not so fast.
Menschen-stimme, *Ger.* (mĕn-sh'n *stĭm*-mĕ.) Human voice.
Mensur, *Ger.* (mĕn-*soor*.) Time, tune, measurement of intervals; also, the diameter, or scale of organ pipes.
Mensural-gesang, *Ger.* (mĕn-soo-*răl* ghĕ-*säng*.) Florid vocalization.
Mensural-noten, *Ger.* (mĕn-soo-*răl* nō-t'n.) Musical notation.
Mensural members. Notes of less value than the mensural parts indicated at the beginning of a piece.
Mensural signature. Fractions placed at the beginning of a composition, indicating the time or measure.
Menuet, *Fr.* (mā-noo-ĕ.) ⎫ A minuet, a slow
Menuetto, *It.* (mā-noo-*ĕt*-tō.) ⎬ dance in 3-4 time.
Mén vivo, *It.* (mān vē-vō.) Less spirit.
Mercurian lyre. One of the earliest musical

ă ale, ă add, ă arm, ē eve, ĕ end, ī ice, ĭ ill, ō old, ŏ odd, ȯ dove, oo moon, ū lute, ŭ but, ü French sound.

MESA

instruments, formed of the shell of a tortoise and having seven strings.
Mesaulici, *Gr.* (mĕs-aw-lĭ-shī.) Pieces performed between the divisions of the Greek drama.
Mesaulion, *Gr.* (mĕ-saw-lĭ-ŏn.) Symphonies or ritornelli.
Mescal, *Tur.* (mĕs-kăl.) A Turkish instrument, composed of twenty-three cane pipes of unequal length, each of which gives three different sounds, from the manner of blowing it.
Mescolánza, *It.* (mĕs-kō-lăn-tsä.) A medley, a mixture of discordant sounds; bad harmony.
Mescolomento, *Gr.* (mĕs-kō-lō-mĕn-tō.) A term used by the ancient Greeks, signifying that branch of the *melopora* which gave the rules for so arranging the sounds of melody that the voice or instrument might be kept within a certain compass.
Mese, *Gr.* (mā-sĕ.) A term applied by the ancient Greeks to the sound that completed their second tetrachord, and which was the centre of their whole system. It was also the name given to the central string of the lyre.
Mesochori, *Gr. pl.* (mā-sō-kō-rē.) Musicians among the ancients, who presided at public performances, and by beating a desk in a regular manner directed the time of the music.
Mesoides, *Gr.* (mĕ-soi-dēs.) A kind of melopora in the ancient system of music, the sounds of which were chiefly confined to the middle chords.
Mesolabe, *Gr.* (mĕs-ŏ-lă-bĕ.) An instrument of the ancients, the use of which was to halve an interval.
Meson, *Gr.* (mĕ-sŏn.) The genitive plural of *mesis*, the middle. A term applied by the ancient Greeks to the second of their tetrachords.
Mesonyeticon, *Gr.* (mĕ-sŏn-ĭk-tĭ-kŏn.) Midnight singing of the early Christians.
Mesopycni, *Gr.* (mĕs-ŏ-pĭk-nē.) The second sound in each tetrachord of the ancient Greek system of music.
Méssa, *It.* (mās-sä.) A mass.
Méssa bássa, *It.* (mās-sä bäs-sä.) A silent mass whispered by the priest during a musical performance.
Méssa concertáta, *It.* (mās-sä kŏn-tshĕr-lä-tä.) A mass consisting of concerted music.
Méssa di vóce, *It.* The gradual swelling and diminishing of the voice.
Messánzo, *It.* (mĕs-sän-tsō.) See *Mescolánza.*
Messe, *Fr.* (mäss.) } A mass.
Messe, *Ger.* (mĕs-sĕ.) }
Messe brevi. *It.* (mās-sĕ brā-vē.) A short mass.
Messe concertati, *It.* (mās-sĕ kŏn-tshĕr-tä-tē.) Masses in which the recitation is intermixed with choruses.
Messa di cappella, *It.* (mās-sä dē kăp-pāl-lä.) Masses sung by the grand chorus.
Messe, haute, *Fr.* (mās-ō.) Grand mass, high mass.
Messe per gli desonti, *It.* (mās-sä pär l-yē dā-zŏn-tē.) A mass for the dead.
Mésto, *It.* (mās-tō.) Sad, mournful, melancholy.
Mestóso, *It.* (mās-tō-zō.) Sadly, mournfully.
Mesure, *Fr.* (mā-zür.) The bar or measure; the species of time.

METR

Mesure a deux temps, *Fr.* (mā-zür ä düh tänh.) Common time of *two* beats in a measure.
Mesure a trois temps, *Fr.* (mā-zür ä trwä tänh.) Triple time of *three* beats in a measure.
Mesure demi, *Fr.* (mā-zür dĕ-mē.) Half measure.
Mesymnicon, *Gr.* (mĕ-sĭm-nĭ-kŏn.) In ancient poetry, a repetition at the end of a stanza; a refrain.
Met. An abbreviation of *Metronome.*
Metal organ. The material of which some organ pipes are made, composed of a mixture of tin and lead in certain proportions.
Metal, *Spa.* (mĕ-tăl.) Strength; compass of the voice.
Metállico, *It.* (mā-tăl-lē-kō.) } Metallic, clear
Metállo, *It.* (mā-tăl-lō.) } in tone; *bel metállo di voce* means a voice clear, full and brilliant.
Meter. See Metre.
Method. A course of instruction; classification; system.
Méthode, *Fr.* (mā-tōd.) } A method, system,
Método, *It.* (mā-tō-dō.) } style; a treatise or book of instruction.
Metre. Measure; verse; arrangement of poetical feet, or of long and short syllables in verse.
Metre, common. A stanza of four lines in iambic measure, the syllables of each being in number and order as follows: 8, 6, 8, 6.
Metre, common hallelujah. A stanza of six lines in iambic measure, the syllables in each being in number and order as follows: 8, 8, 6, 8, 8, 6.
Metre, eights. A stanza of four lines in anapestic measure, each line containing eight syllables and marked thus, 8s.
Metre, eights and sevens. Consists of four lines in trochaic measure, designated thus, 8s and 7s, the syllables as follows: 8, 7, 8, 7.
Metre, eights, sevens and four. A metre designated thus, 8s, 7s, and 4s, containing six lines in trochaic measure, the syllables being in number and order as follows: 8, 7, 8, 7, 4, 7.
Metre, elevens. Designated thus, 11s, and consisting of a stanza of four lines in anapestic measure, each line containing eleven syllables.
Metre, hallelujah. A stanza of six lines in iambic measure, the syllables of each being in number and order as follows: 6, 6, 6, 6, 8, 8.
Metre, long. Four lines in iambic measure, each line containing eight syllables.
Metre, long particular. Six lines in iambic measure, each line containing eight syllables.
Metre, sevens. Consists of four lines in trochaic measure, each line containing seven syllables.
Metre, short. Consists of four lines in iambic measure, the syllables in number and order as follows: 6, 6, 8, 6.
Metre, short particular. Consists of six lines in iambic measure, the syllables in number and order as follows: 6, 6, 8, 6, 6, 8.
Metre, tens and elevens. A metre designated thus, 10s and 11s, consisting of a stanza of four lines in anapestic measure, the syllables in number and order thus: 10, 10, 11, 11; or of six lines in iambic measure, as follows: 10, 10, 10, 10, 11, 11.

ă ale, ă add, ä arm, ē eve, ĕ end, Ī ice, ĭ ill, ō old, ŏ odd, ô dove, oo moon, ū lute, ŭ but, ü French sound.

METR

Metre, twelves. A metre designated thus, 12s, consisting of a stanza of four lines in anapestic measure, each line containing twelve syllables.
Metrical. Pertaining to measure, or due arrangement and combination of long and short syllables.
Metrically. In a metrical manner; according to poetic measure.
Metrik, *Ger.* (mĕt-rĭk.) Metrical art.
Metrisch, *Ger.* (mĕt-rish.) Metrical.
Metro, *It.* (mă-trō.) } Metre, verse.
Metro, *Spa.* (mā-trō.) }
Metrometer, *Ger.* (mĕ-trŏm-ĕ-tĕr.) } A metronome.
Metrometro, *It.* (mā-trō-mā-trō.) }
Metronom, *Ger.* (mĕt-rō-nōm.) } A machine
Metronome, *Gr.* (mĕt-rō-nō-mĕ.) } invented by John Maelzel, for measuring the time or duration of notes by means of a graduated scale and pendulum, which may be shortened or lengthened at pleasure.
Metronome, bell. A metronome with the addition of a small bell, which strikes at the commencement of each bar.
Metronome, pocket. A metronome of the size and form of a watch, on one side of which is marked the number of vibrations, and on the other the principal Italian musical terms.
Metronomic marks. Figures appended to pieces of music, referring to corresponding figures on a metronome: ex., { ♩ = 120, ♩ = 80 }
Metronomy. (mĕ-trŏn-ŏ-my.) The measuring of time by an instrument.
Metrum, *Ger.* (mĕt-room.) Measure, time.
Mette, *Ger.* (mĕt-tĕ.) Matins.
Mettere in musica, *It.* (mĕt-tā-rĕ ēn moo-zē-kā.) To set to music.
Mettre d'accord, *Fr.* (mātr d'āk-kōr.) To tune.
Mettre en musique, *Fr.* (mātr ānh mü-zēk.) To set to music.
Mettre en repetition, *Fr.* (mātr ānh rā-pĕ-tā-sī-ōnh.) To put in rehearsal.
Mez. An abbreviation of Mezzo.
Mez. F. An abbreviation of Mezzo Forte.
Mez. Pia. An abbreviation of Mezzo Piano.
Mezza, *It.* (mĕt-tsā.) } Medium, in the middle,
Mezzo, *It.* (mĕt-tsō.) } half.
Mezza bravúra, *It.* (mĕt-tsā brā-voo-rā.) A moderately difficult song.
Mezza forza, *It.* (mĕt-tsā fōr-tsā.) Moderately loud.
Mezza mánica, *It.* (mĕt-tsā mā-nē-kā.) The *half-shift*, in playing the violin, etc.
Mezzána, *It.* (mĕt-tsā-nā.) The middle string of a lute.
Mezza orchéstra, *It.* (mĕt-tsā ōr-kĕs-trā.) Half the orchestra.
Mezza vóce, *It.* (mĕt-tsō vō-tshĕ.) Half the power of the voice; with moderate strength of tone.
Mezzo caráttere, *It.* (mĕt-tsō kā-rāt-tā-rĕ.) A moderate degree of expression and execution; music of a medium character.
Mezzo fórte, *It.* (mĕt-tsō fōr-tĕ.) Moderately loud.
Mezzo fórte piáno, *It.* (mĕt-tsō fōr-tĕ pē-ā-nō.) Rather loud, than soft.
Mezzo piáno, *It.* (mĕt-tsō pē-ā-nō.) Rather soft.

MINA

Mézzo sopráno, *It.* (mĕt-tsō sō-prā-nō.) A female voice of lower pitch than the soprano, or treble, but higher than the contralto. The general compass is from A under the lines to A above them.
Mézzo-sopráno clef. The C clef when placed on the second line of the staff, occurring in old church music or madrigals. The treble or soprano clef now supplies its place.
Mézzo staccáto, *It.* (mĕt-tsō stăk-kā-tō.) A little detached.
Mézzo tenóre, *It.* (mĕt-tsō tĕ-nō-rĕ.) A half tenor voice, nearly the same as a baritone.
Mézzo tuóno, *It.* (mĕt-tsō twō-nō.) A semitone, a half tone.
Mézzo vóce, *It.* (mĕt-tsō vō-tshĕ.) In a subdued voice.
M. F. The initials of Mezzo Forte.
M. G. The initials of Main Gauche.
Mi, *It.* (mē.) A syllable used in solfaing to designate E, or the third note of the major scale.
Mi bémol, *Fr.* (mē bā-mōl.) The note E flat.
Mi bémol majeur, *Fr.* (mē bā-mōl mā-zhŭr.) The key of E flat major.
Mi bémol mineur, *Fr.* (mē bā-mōl mī-nŭr.) The key of E flat minor.
Mi contra fa. *Lat.* (mē kŏn-trā fā.) An expression used by old theorists meaning a *false relation.*
Microcoustic. An instrument to increase the intensity of small sounds, and assist in hearing.
Microfono, *Spa.* (mē-krō-fō-nō.) } An instrument for the augmentation of small sounds; a *microcoustic.*
Microphone. (mī-krō-fōn.) }
Microphonics. The science or art of increasing the intensity of sounds.
Middle C. That C which is between the bass and treble staves.
Middle part. Any parts that lie between the outside voices.
Middle voices. Tenor and alto voices.
Mi dièse, *Fr.* (mē dī-āz.) The note E sharp.
Mignon, *Fr.* (mēn-yōnh.) Favorite.
Militairement, *Fr.* (mĭl-ē-tār-mānh.) }
Militáre, *It.* (mē-lē-tā-rĕ.) }
Militarménte, *It.* (mē-lē-tār-mān-tĕ.) }
Military; in a warlike, martial style.
Military music. Music intended for military bands, marches, quicksteps, etc.
Milote, *Spa.* (mē-lō-tĕ.) An Indian dance.
Mi majeur, *Fr.* (mē mā-zhŭr.) The key of E major.
Mi mineur, *Fr.* (mē mī-nŭr.) The key of E minor.
Mimes, (mī-mēs.) A kind of vocal, mimic actors, formerly very numerous in Europe.
Minaccevolménte, *It.* (mē-nāt-tshĕ-vōl-mān-tĕ.) In a threatening, menacing manner.
Minacciándo, *It.* (mē-nāt-tshē-ān-dō.) }
Minaccievóle, *It.* (mē-nāt-tshē-ā-vō-lĕ.) }
Threatening, menacing.
Minacciosaménte, *It.* (mē-nāt-tshē-ō-zā-mān-tĕ.) Threatening, menacing, in a menacing manner.
Minaccióso, *It.* (mē-nāt-tshē-ō-zō.) Threatening, menacing, in a menacing manner.

ă *ale*, ă *add*, ä *arm*, ĕ *eve*, ŭ *end*, ī *ice*, ĭ *ill*, ō *old*, ŏ *odd*, ô *dove*, oo *moon*, ū *lute*, ŭ *but*, ü *French sound*.

MINA

Minagnghinim, *Heb.* (mĭ-năngā́-ghĭ-nĭm.) A pulsatile instrument used by the Hebrews, consisting of a square table of wood furnished with a handle; over this table was stretched an iron chain and a hempen chord which passed through balls of wood or brass, and striking against the table when the instrument was in motion, produced a clear, ringing sound.
Minder, *Ger.* (mĭn-dĕr.) Minor, less, not so much.
Mineur, *Fr.* (mĭ-nŭr.) Minor.
Minim. A half note; a note equal to one-half of a semibreve.
Minima, *It.* (mē-nē-mā.) ⎫ A minim; literally, the *least*, because formerly the minim was the shortest note.
Minima, *Spa.* (mē-uē-mä.) ⎬
Minima, *Lat.* (mĭn-ī-mä.) ⎭
Minime, *Fr.* (mĭn-ēm.) A minim.
Minim rest. A mark of silence equal in duration to a minim; made thus, —.
Ministrellus, *Lat.* (mĭn-ĭs-trĕl-lūs.) Harpist.
Ministril, *Spa.* (mĭn-ĭs-trĕl.) A minstrel.
Ministriles, *Spa.* (mĭn-ĭs-trē-lĕs.) Wind instruments.
Minnedichter, *Ger.* (mĭn-nē-dĭkh-tĕr.)
Minnesinger, *Ger.* (mĭn-nē-sāng-ĕr.)
Minnesänger, *Ger.* (mĭn-nē-sĭng-ĕr.)
Minstrels of the twelfth and thirteenth centuries, who wandered from place to place singing a great variety of songs and melodies.
Minnim, *Heb.* (mĭn-nĭm.) The strings of an instrument.
Minor. Less, smaller, in speaking of intervals, etc.
Minor canons. Those clergymen of a cathedral or chapel, who occasionally assist at the performance of the service and anthem.
Minor diatonic scale. There are two kinds: one where the semitones fall between the second and third and seventh and eighth, both in ascending and descending; in the other the semitone falls between the second and third and seventh and eighth ascending, and descending, between the fifth and sixth and second and third. The former is the *harmonic*, the latter the *melodic* form.
Minóre, *It.* (mē-nō-rĕ.) Minor.
Minor key. ⎫ One of the modern modes, or
Minor mode. ⎬ scales, in which the third note is a minor third from the tonic.
Minor second. The smallest interval in practicable use, consisting of five commas.
Minor semibreve. A note among the ancients having the value of one-third of a breve.
Minor semitone. A semitone which *retains* its place or *letter* on the staff; thus, C, C♯; A, A♯, etc.
Minor seventh, An interval consisting of four tones and two semitones.
Minor sixth. An interval composed of three tones and two semitones.
Minor tactus. Among the ancients, the act of beating time; consisting of a semitone in a bar.
Minor third. A diatonic interval containing three semitones.
Minor threefold chord. A threefold chord having the interval of a small third between its fundamental tone and its third.
Minor triad. A union of any tone with its minor third and perfect fifth.

MISS

Minstrels. The wandering poets or musicians of the tenth and following centuries.
Minstrels, Ethiopian. Negro minstrels.
Minstrel, squire. A title formerly given to a professional minstrel, a character combining the offices of poet, singer and musician.
Minstrelsy. The art or profession of a minstrel.
Minue, *Spa.* (mē-nooā.) A minuet.
Minuet. An ancient slow and stately dance in two strains, in triple 3-4 time, and supposed to be of French origin; a movement of a quicker time formerly used as the conclusion of overtures, sonatas, etc.
Minuettina, *It.* (mēn-wĕt-tē-nä.) A little minuet.
Minuétto, *It.* (mē-noo-ăt-tō.) A minuet.
Minuétto, alternativo, *It.* (mē-noo-ăt-tō ăl-tĕr-nä-tē-vō.) Alternately perform the minuet and trio.
Minuge, *It.* (mē-nooā-jĕ.) Strings of instruments; catgut.
Minum. An old term for *minim*.
Minute bell. A bell sounded regularly at intervals of one minute.
Miring, *Jav.* (mē-rĭng.) Music of the Javanese for accompanying their theatrical performances.
Mirliton, *Fr.* (mĕr-lĭ-tōnh.) A small pan reed.
Misa, *Spa.* (mē-zä.) Mass.
Misa del gallo, *Spa.* (mē-zä dĕl gäl-yō.) Midnight mass.
Misch-masch, *Teu.* (mĭsh-mäsh.) A pot-pourri; a medley.
Mise de voix, *Fr.* (mēz düh vwä.) See *Mézza Vóce*.
Miserere, *Lat.* (mē-sĕ-rā-rĕ.) Have mercy; a psalm of supplication.
Misericordia, *Lat.* (mē-sĕ-rĭ-kŏr-dĭ-ä.) A small movable seat in the choir of a church; a miserere.
Mishrokitha, *Cha.* (mĭsh-rō-kĭ-thä.) A flute, a pipe.
Miskin. A little bagpipe.
Missa, *Lat.* (mĕs-sä.) A mass.
Missa brevis, *Lat.* (mĕs-sä brā-vĭs.) A short mass.
Missa canonica, *Lat.* (mĕs-sä kä-nŏn-ĭ-kä.) A canonical mass.
Missal. The Mass book.
Missa pro defunctis, *Lat.* (mĕs-sä prō dĕ-fŭnk-tĭs.) A Requiem; a Mass for departed souls.
Missa solennis, *Lat.* (mĕs-sä sō-lĕn-nĭs.) A solemn Mass, for high festivals.
Missel, *Fr.* (mĕs-sĕl.) Missal; the Mass book.
Misshällig, *Ger.* (mĭss-hăl-lĭg.) Dissonant, discordant.
Misshälligkeit, *Ger.* (mĭss-hăl-lĭg-kīt.) Dissonance, discordance.
Misshellig, *Ger.* (mĭss-hĕl-lĭg.) See *Misshällig*.
Missklang, *Ger.* (mĭss-kläng.) Dissonance, discordance.
Missklänge, *Ger. pl.* (mĭss-kläng-ĕ.) Discordant sounds.
Missklingen, *Ger.* (mĭss-klĭng-ĕn.) To sound discordant.
Misslaut. *Ger.* (mĭss-lout.) Unharmonious, discordant sound.
Misslauten, *Ger.* (mĭss-lou-t'n.) To sound inharmoniously.

130   PRONOUNCING MUSICAL DICTIONARY.

ă ale, ă add, ä arm, ē eve, ĕ end, īce, ĭ ill, ō old, ŏ odd, ô dove, oo moon, ū lute, ŭ but, ü French sound.

MISS

Misslautend, Ger. (mĭss-lou tĕnd.) Dissonant; discordant.
Miss-stimmen, Ger. (mĭss-stĭm-m'n.) To put out of tune.
Miss-stimmig, Ger. (mĭss-stĭm-mĭg.) Discordant, dissonant.
Miss-stimmung, Ger. (mĭss-stĭm-moong.) Dissonance, discord.
Miss-stimmung, Ger. (mĭss-stĭm-moong.) }
Miss-ton, Ger. (mĭss-tōr.)   } Discord, dissonance.
Miss-töne, Ger. pl. (mĭss-tŏ-nĕ.) Discords, dissonances.
Misteriosamente, It. (mĕs-tĕr-ē-ō-zä-män-tĕ,) }
Misterióso, It. (mĕs-tĕr-ē-ō-zō.)   }
Mysteriously; in a mysterious manner.
Mistero, con, It. (mĕs-tā-rō.) With an air of mystery.
Misto, Gr. (mēa-tō.) Mixed; a term given by the ancients to some of their modes.
Mistune. To tune incorrectly, to put out of tune.
Mistuned. Put out of tune.
Misúra, It. (mē-soo-rä.) A bar, a measure; time.
Misuráto, It. (mē-soo-rä-tō.) Measured, in strict, measured time.
Mit, Ger. (mĭt.) With, by.
Mit abwechselnden manualen, Ger. (mĭt äb-vĕkh-sĕl'n-dĕn mä-noo-ä-l'n.) Alternately, from the choir to the great organ.
Mit begleitung, Ger. (mĭt bē-glī-toong.) With an accompaniment.
Mit bewegung, Ger. (mĭt bē-vä-goong.) Synonymous with con móto.
Mit einhelliger stimme, Ger. (mĭt ĭn-hĕl-lĭ-gĕr stĭm-mĕ.) With one voice.
Mit ganz schwachen registern, Ger. (mĭt gänts shvä-kh'n rĕg-ĭs-tĕrn.) With very soft stops.
Mit gedämpfter stimme, Ger. (mĭt gĕ-dämpf-tĕr stĭm-mĕ.) With a voice moderately loud.
Mit gefühl, Ger. (mĭt ghē-fül.) With feeling and sentiment.
Mit keckheit, Ger. (mĭt kĕk-hīt.) With vigor and boldness; in the bravúra, or dashing style.
Mit keckheit vorgetragen, Ger. (mĭt kĕk-hīt fōr-ghē-trä-g'n.) In a bold and vigorous style of performance.
Mit klingendem spiele, Ger. (mĭt klĭng-ĕn-dĕm spē-lĕ.) With drums beating.
Mitlant, Ger. (mĭt-lout.)   } Concord, consonance.
Mitlauter, Ger. (mĭt-lou-tĕr.)   }
Mitlauten, Ger. (mĭt-lou-t'n.) To sound at the same time, or in common with.
Mitleidsvoll, Ger. (mĭt-lĭds-fōl.) Compassionate.
Mit sanften stimmen, Ger. (mĭt-sänf-t'n stĭm-m'n.) With soft stops.
Mit sang und klang, Ger. (mĭt säng oond kläng.) With song and instrumental music.
Mit starken stimmen, Ger. (mĭt stär-k'n stĭm-m'n.) With loud stops.
Mittel-cadenz, Ger. (mĭt-t'l kä-dĕnts.) A half, or imperfect cadence.
Mittel-laut, Ger. (mĭt-t'l lout.) Middle sound.
Mittel-mässig, Ger. (mĭt-t'l-mäs-sĭg.) Middling.

MODE

Mittel-stimme, Ger. (mĭt-t'l stĭm-mĕ.) The mean or middle voice, or part; the tenor.
Mittel-stimmen, Ger. pl. (mĭt-t'l stĭm-m'n.) The middle voices or parts.
Mittel-ton, Ger. (mĭt-t'l tōn.) The mediant; see that word.
Mit voller orgel, Ger. (mĭt fōl-lĕr ōr-g'l.) With full organ.
Mixed cadence. An old name for a cadence composed of the triad on the sub-dominant, followed by that upon the dominant.
Mixed canon. A canon of many parts, in which the parts begin at different intervals.
Mixolydian. See Greek modes.
Mixolydian sharp. The Hyper-Ionian of the ancient Greek system.
Mixture stop. An organ stop, of a shrill and piercing quality, consisting of two or more ranks of pipes.
M. M. The initials of Maelzel's Metronome.
Móbile, It. (mō-bĕ-lĕ.) Movable.
Mobile, Gr. (mō-bĭ-lĕ.) Name given by the Greeks to the two middle chords of each tetrachord, because they varied, while the two extreme chords, which they called stábile, never changed their tone or pitch.
Mobili, suoni, It. (mō-bĭ-lĕ awō-nĕ.) Movable sounds; the second and third sounds of every tetrachord of the ancient system.
Mociganga, Spa. (mō-thē-gän-gä.) A musical interlude common in Spain.
Mode. A particular system or constitution of sounds, by which the octave is divided into certain intervals, according to the genus.
Mode, doric. The first of the authentic modes in the system of the ancient Greeks, employed on martial and religious occasions.
Mode, major. That in which the third from the key note is major.
Mode, minor. That which in the third degree from the tonic forms the interval of a minor third.
Mode, orthian. One of the ancient Greek modes.
Moderaménte, It. (mōd-ĕ-rä-tä-män-tĕ.) }
Moderáto, It. (mōd-ĕ-rä-tō.)   }
Moderately, in moderate time.
Moderatissimo, It. (mōd-ĕ-rä-tĭs-sē-mō.) In very moderate time.
Moderáto assái con mólto sentimento, It. (mōd-ĕ-rä-tō äs-sä-ē kōn sĕn-tē-män-tō.) A very moderate degree of quickness with much expression.
Moderazióne, It. (mōd-ĕ-rä-tsē-ō-nĕ.) Moderation.
Modere, Fr. (mō-dār.) Moderate.
Mode, relative. A relative key.
Modern. Not in the ancient style.
Moderna, alla, It. (mō-dār-nä äl-lä.) In the modern style.
Modern music. Music composed within the last half century.
Modes, authentic. The modes or scales of the ancient Greeks and Romans.
Modes, authentic. Church modes, the melody of which was confined within the tonic and its octave.
Modes, church. The ancient modes called by the following names: Dorian, Phrygian, Lydian, Mixo-Lydian, Æolian, Ionian or Iastian.

PRONOUNCING MUSICAL DICTIONARY. 131

ă ale, ă add, ă arm, ĕ eve, ĕ end, ĭ ice, ĭ itt, ō old, ŏ odd, ō dove, oo moon, ū tute, ŭ but, ü French sound.

MODE

Modes, ecclesiastical. The ancient church modes.
Modes, irregular. Modes running many degrees both above and below their octaves.
Modes, plagal. Those modes in the Greek system whose tones lay between the dominant and octave and twelfth.
Modestamente, *It.* (mō-dĕs-tä-mănˈ-tĕ.)
Modésto, *It.* (mō-dĕsˈ-tō.)
Modestly, quietly, moderately.
Modification. A term applied to the temperament of the sounds of those instruments whose tones are fixed, which gives a greater degree of perfection to one key than to another; as in organs, pianofortes, and the like.
Modificazióni, *It.* pl. (mō-dē-fē-kä-tsĕ-ōˈ-nē.) Modifications, light and shade of intonation, slight alterations.
Modinha, *Por.* (mō-dĕnˈ-ä) A short Portuguese song.
Mod. An abbreviation of Moderato.
Mŏdo, *It.* (mōˈ-dō.) } A mode, a scale.
Modo, *Spa.* mō-dōˈ.) }
Módo maggióre, *It.* (mō-dō mäd-jĕ-ōˈ-rĕ.) The major mode.
Módo maggióre imperfetto, *It.* (mō-dō mäd-jĕ-ōˈ-rĕ ĕm-pĕr-fătˈ-tō.) In ancient music, two lines across two spaces, showing that the large contained eight semibreves.
Módo majóre perfetto, *It.* (mō-dō mä-jōˈ-rĕ pĕr-fătˈ-tō.) In ancient music, three lines across three spaces, and three others across two only, showing the large to contain three longs.
Módo minóre, *It.* (mō-dō mĕ-nōˈ-rĕ.) The minor mode.
Módo minóre imperfetto, *It.* (mō-dō mĕ-nōˈ-rĕ ĕm-pĕr-fĕtˈ-tō.) In ancient music, a line drawn across two spaces, fixing the value of the long to two breves.
Módo minóre perfetto, *It.* (mō-dō mĕ-nōˈ-rĕ pĕr-fĕtˈ-tō.) In ancient music, a line across three spaces, showing that the long contained three breves.
Modˈto. An abbreviation of Moderato.
Modoláre, *It.* (mō-dō-läˈ-rĕ.) } To modulate;
Moduláre, *It.* (mō-doo-läˈ-rĕ.) } to accommodate
Modular, *Spa.* (mō-doo-lärˈ.) } the voice or instrument to a certain intonation.
Modulacion, *Spa.* (mō-doo-lä-thī-ōnˈ.) Modulation.
Modulánte, *It.* (mō-doo-länˈ-tĕ.) Modulating.
Modulate. To move from one key to another in a manner agreeable to the ear.
Modulation. A transition of key; going from one key to another, by a certain succession of chords, either in a natural and flowing manner, or sometimes in a sudden and unexpected manner. As applied to the voice, modulation means to accommodate the tone to a certain degree of intensity, or light and shade.
Modulation, abrupt. Sudden modulation into keys which are not closely related to the original key.
Modulation, deceptive. Any modulation by which the ear is deceived and led to an unexpected harmony.

MOLO

Modulation, enharmonic. A modulation effected by altering the *notation* of one or more intervals belonging to some *characteristic* chord, and thus changing the key and the harmony into which it would naturally have resolved. The chords which admit of these alterations are, first, the diminished seventh and its inversions; secondly, the dominant seventh not inverted, and the chord of the superfluous sixth and perfect fifth.
Modulation, extraneous. A modulation into some other than the original key and its relatives.
Modulation, melodic. A change from one key to another, produced by the result of successive melodic intervals.
Modulation, note of. A note introducing a new key; usually the leading note or major seventh of the key introduced.
Modulation, passing. } A form of modula-
Modulation, transient. } tion which leaves a key nearly as soon as entered upon.
Modulatore, *It.* (mō-doo-lä-tōˈ-rĕ.) Singer, tuner.
Modulazióne, *It.* (mō-doo-lä-tsĕ-ōˈ-nĕ.) Modnlation.
Moduliren, *Ger.* (mō-doo-lēˈ-r'n.) To modulate.
Modulo, *Lat.* (mō-dŭˈ-lō.) To modulate, to compose.
Modus, *Lat.* (mōˈ-dŭs.) A key, mode, scale.
Modus Æolus, *Lat.* (mōˈ-dŭs ē-ōˈ-lŭs.) The Æolian mode.
Modus Dorius, *Lat.* (mōˈ-dŭs dō-rĭˈ-ŭs.) The Doric mode.
Modus Ionius, *Lat.* (mōˈ-dŭs ĭ-ō-nĭˈ-ŭs.) The Ionic mode.
Modus mixo-Lydius, *Lat.* (mōˈ-dŭs mix-o-lĭdˈ-ĭ-ŭs.) The Mixo-Lydian key.
Modus mixo-Phrygian, *Lat.* (mōˈ-dŭs mix-o-frĭgˈ-ĭ-ăn.) The Mixo-Phrygian mode.
Modus major, *Lat.* (mōˈ-dŭs mäˈ-jŏr.) Major mode.
Modus minor, *Lat.* (mōˈ-dŭs mĕˈ-nŏr.) Minor mode.
Modus Phrygius, *Lat.* (mōˈ-dŭs frĭgˈ-ĭ-ŭs.) The Phrygian mode.
Moerologists. Professional mourners, among the ancients, whose office it was to accompany funeral processions, singing dirges.
Mohinda. A short Portuguese love song.
Mohrentanz, *Ger.* (mō-r'n-tänts.) Morisco, morris dance.
Moins, *Fr.* (mwä.) Less.
Moins lent que largo, *Fr.* (mwä länh kŭh lär-gō.) Less slow than *Largo.*
Moll, *Ger.* (mŏll.) Minor.
Mólla, *It.* (mŏlˈ-lä.) A *key* of the flute, etc.: for raising, or lowering a note.
Molle, *Fr.* (mŏl.) Soft, mellow, delicate.
Molleménte, *It.* (mŏl-lĕ-mănˈ-tĕ.) Softly, gently, delicately.
Mollis, *Lat.* (mŏlˈ-lĭs.) Soft.
Moll-touart, *Ger.* (mŏl-tōn-ärtˈ.) Minor key, or scale.
Moloso, *Spa.* (mō-lōˈ-zō.) A foot of Latin verse, consisting of three long syllables.
Molossic rhythm. Three long, strongly accented syllables in succession.

ă *ale*, ă *add*, ä *arm*, ĕ *eve*, ĕ *end*, ĭ *ice*, ĭ *ill*, ō *old*, ŏ *odd*, ŏ *dove*, oo *moon*, ü *lute*, ŭ *but*, ü *French sound*.

MOLO

Molossus, *Gr*. (mō lŏs-sŭs.) In Greek and Latin verse, a foot of three long syllables.
Mólta, *It*. (mŏl-tä.) } Much, very much, extreme-
Mólto, *It*. (mŏl-tō.) } ly, a great deal.
Moltisonánte, *It*. (mŏl-tē-zō-nän-tĕ.) Resounding; very sonorous.
Mólto adágio, *It*. (mŏl-tō ä-dä-jē-ō.) Extremely slow.
Mólto allégro, *It*. (mŏl-tō ŭl-lā-grō.) Very quick.
Mólto carattere, con, *It*. (mŏl-tō kär-ăt-tā-rĕ, kŏn.) With chaaacter and emphasis.
Mólto mósso, *It*. (mŏl-tō mŏs-sō.) Much movement, much motion.
Mólto passione, con, *It*. (mŏl-tō pās-sĕ-ō-nĕ, kŏn.) With passionate expression.
Mólto sentimento, con, *It*. (mŏl-tō sĕn-tē-män-tō, kŏn.) With much feeling and sentiment.
Mólto slargándo, *It*. (mŏl-tō slär-gän-dō.) *Much extended*; much slower.
Mólto sostenúto, *It*. (mŏl-tō sŏs-tĕ-noo-tō.) Very sustained; very *legáto*.
Mólto staccato con grazia, *It*. (mŏl-tō stäk-kä-tō kŏn grä-tsē-ä.) In staccato style and with grace.
Mólto vibrato, *It*. (mŏl-tō vē-brä-tō.) Very violent or rapid.
Mólto vivace, *It*. (mŏl-tō vē-vä-tshĕ.) Very lively.
Momentulum, *Lat*. (mō-měn-tū-lŭm.) A semiquaver rest.
Momentum, *Lat*. (mō-měn-tŭm.) A quaver rest.
Monacordia, *Spa*. (mŏn-ä-kŏr-dĭ-ä.) Monochord.
Monanlos, *Gr*. (mŏn-ou-lŏs.) An ancient flute, played through the mouth-piece at the end like the flageolet.
Mondinhas, *Port*. (mŏn-dēn-äs.) Portuguese national songs.
Monferína, *It*. (mŏn-fĕ-rē-nä.) A lively Italian dance in 6-8 time.
Monacórdo, *It*. (mŏn-ä-kŏr-dō.) } An instru-
Monochord. (mŏn-ō-kŏrd.) } ment with one string for measuring musical intervals or sounds.
Monochord pedal. The one stringed pedal.
Monocorde, *Fr*. (mŏn-ō-kŏrd.) } On one string
Monocórdo, *It* (mŏn-ō-kŏr-dō.) } only; see also Monochord.
Monodía, *It*. (mō-nō-dē-ä.) } A composition for
Monodie, *Fr*. (mŏn-ō-dē.) } a single voice. The
Monody, *Eng*. (mŏn-ō-dy.) } term originally applied to church solos.
Monodic. For *one* voice; a solo.
Monodist. One who writes a monody.
Monodram, *Ger*. (mŏn-ō-drăm.) } A musical
Monodrama, *It*. (mŏn-ō-drä-mä.) } drama in which only one actor appears; a monodrame.
Monodrame, *Fr*. (mŏn-ō-drăm.) A drama performed by a single individual.
Monologue. A soliloquy; a poem, song, or scene written and composed for a single performer.
Monomometer, *Gr*. (mŏn-ō-mŏm-ĕ-tĕr.) A rythmical series consisting of but one meter.
Monophonic, *Gr*. (mŏn-ō-fō-nĭk.) In *one* part only.
Monophthong. A letter having but one sound.
Monophthongal. Consisting of or having a single sound.

MORM

Monopody, *Gr*. (mŏ-nŏp-ō-dy.) A measure consisting of a single foot.
Monorhyme, *Gr*. (mŏn-ō-rā-mĕ.) Where all the lines of a verse end in the same rhyme.
Monostich, *Gr*. (mŏn-ō-stĭk.) A composition consisting of one verse only.
Monostrophe, *Gr*. (mŏn-ō-strō-fĕ.) Having one strophe only; not varied in measure.
Monotone. Uniformity of sound; one and the same sound.
Monotonia, *Spa*. (mŏn-ō-tō-nī-ä.) } Monotony,
Monotonie, *Fr*. (mŏn-ō-tō-nē.) } sameness of
Monotonie, *Ger*. (mŏn-ō-tō-nē.) } sound.
Monotonous, *Eng*. (mō-nŏt-ō-nŭs.) A epithet applied to any instrument which produces but one tone or note; as the drum, tambourine, etc.
Monotony. A wearisome uniformity of sound; a continued repetition of the same tone or notes.
Monta, *Spa*. (mŏn-tä.) A trumpet signal for cavalry to mount.
Montant, *Fr*. (mŏnh-tänh.) Ascending.
Montant de cloche, *Fr*. (mŏnh-tänh dŭh klōsh.) A belfry.
Montré, *Fr*. (mŏnh-trā.) *Mounted; in front;* a term applied to the organ pipes which are placed in front of the case.
Montré d'orgue, *Fr*. (mŏnh-trā d'ŏrg.) The range of pipes in the front of an organ.
Moorish drum. A tambourine.
Morbidezza, con, *It*. (mŏr-bē-dat-sä.) With excessive delicacy.
Morceau, *Fr*. (mŏr-sō.) A choice and select musical piece or composition; a fine phrase or passage.
Morceau d'ensemble, *Fr*. (mŏr-sō d'änh-sänhbl.) A piece harmonized for several voices.
Mordante, *It*. (mŏr-dän-tĕ.) See *Mordénte*.
Mordénte, *It*. (mŏr-dĕn-tĕ.) Transient shake or beat; an embellishment formed by two or more notes, preceding the principal note.
Mordente, long. The short mordente repeated.
Mordente, short. An embellishment consisting of the note over which the sign is placed and the note below it; thus,
Mordenten und doppel-schläger, *Ger*. (mŏr-dän-těn oond dŏp-pěl shlā-ghěr.) Beats and turns.
Morendo, *It*. (mō-rän-dō.) } Dying away, ex-
Moriénte, *It*. (mō-rē-än-tĕ.) } piring ; gradually diminishing the tone and the time.
Morésca, *It*. (mō-rĕs-kä.) } Moorish; morris-
Moresque, *It*. (mō-rěsk.) } dance, in which bells are jingled at the ankles and swords clashed.
Morgen-gesang, *Ger*. (mŏr-g'n ghĕ-zäng.) }
Morgen-lied, *Ger*. (mŏr-g'n-lēd.) } Morning song or hymn.
Morgen-ständchen, *Ger*. (mŏr-g'n ständ-kh'n.) Morning serenade.
Morisco, *It*. (mō-rēs-kō.) In the Moorish style; see *Morésca*.
Morisk, (mō-rīsk.) The morris dance.
Mormoramento, *It*. (mŏr-mō-rä-män-tō.) A murmur, warbling, buzzing, purling.

ă ale, ă add, ă arm, ē eve, ĕ end, ī ice, ĭ ill, ō old, ŏ odd, ô dove, oo moon, ū lute, ŭ but, ü French sound.

MORM

Mormorándo, *It.* (mŏr-mō-răn-dō.)
Mormorévole, *It.* (mŏr-mō-rā-vō-lĕ.)
Mormoróso, *It.* (mŏr-mō-rō-zō.)
With a gentle, murmuring sound.
Morrice dance. A peculiar kind of dance
Morris dance. practiced in the middle ages.
Morriske dance. It is supposed to have been introduced into England by Edward III. In the morris dance bells were fastened to the feet of the performer.
Mort. A tune sounded at the death of game.
Mósso, *It.* (mŏs-sō.) Moved, movement, motion.
Mosso, molto, *It.* (mŏs-sō mŏl-tō.), Quick, with much motion.
Móstra, *It.* (mŏs-trā.) A direct, ⁓.
Mot, *Fr.* (mō.) Literally, a *word;* a note or brief strain on a bugle.
Motet. A sacred composition of the anthem
Motett. style, for several voices. The words are not taken from the sacred Scriptures.
Motette, *Ger.* (mō-tĕt.)
Motet, *Fr.* (mō-tā.) A motet.
Motétto, *It.* (mō-tăt-tō.)
Motetten, *Ger.* (mō-tĕt-t'n.)
Motetti, *It.* (mō-lĕt-tē.) Motets.
Motetto per voci solé, *It.* (mō-tĕt-tō pār rō-tshĕ sō-lĕ.) A motet for voices without accompaniment; a motet each part of which is for a single voice.
Motetus, *Lat.* (mō-tĕt-ŭs.) A motet.
Motif, *Fr.* (mō-tĕf.) Motive, theme, subject.
Motion. The movement of voices, or harmonic parts.
Motion, contrary. The movement of one part in an opposite direction to another.
Motion, direct. The movement of two or more parts in the same direction.
Motion oblique. When one part ascends or descends while the other remains stationary, it is called oblique motion.
Motion, similar. When two or more parts ascend or descend at the same time.
Motive. The characteristic and predominant passage of an air; the theme or subject of a composition.
Motivi, *It.* (mō-tē-vē.) The themes of a composition.
Motívo, *It.* (mō-tē-vō.) Motive; the theme or
Motivo, *Spa.* (mō-tē-vō.) subject of a musical composition.
Móto, *It.* (mō-tō.) Motion, movement; con *mōto*, with motion, rather quick.
Móto accelerato, *It.* (mō-tō ăt-tshā-lĕ-rā-tō.) Accelerated motion.
Móto contrário, *It.* (mō-tō kŏn-trā-rē-ō.) Contrary motion.
Móto obliquo, *It.* (mō-tō ōb-lē-quō.) Oblique motion.
Móto precidénte, *It.* (mō-tō prā-tshē-dān-tĕ.) The same time as the preceding movement.
Móto primo, *It.* (mō-tō prē-mō.) The same time as the first.
Móto rétto, *It.* (mō-tō rāt-tō.) Direct, or similar motion.
Motteggiándo, *It.* (mōt-tād-jē-ăn-dō.) Jeeringly, mockingly, jocosely.
Mottétto, *It.* (mōt-tāt-tō.) A motet.

MUSA

Motus, *Lat.* (mō-tŭs.) Motion, movement.
Motus contrarius, *Lat.* (mō-tŭs kōn-trā-rĭ-ŭs.) Contrary motion.
Motus obliquus, *Lat.* (mō-tŭs ōb-lē-quŭs.) Oblique motion.
Motus rectus, *Lat.* (mō-tŭs rĕk-tŭs.) Direct, or similar motion.
Mougik, *Russ.* (moo-jĕk.) Music.
Mounted cornet, An organ stop, usually consisting of five ranks of pipes, of large scale, and loudly voiced, placed upon a raised sound-board of their own (hence the name.) It is only to be met with in old organs.
Mouth-piece. That part of a trumpet, horn, etc., which is applied to the lips.
Mouvement, *Fr.* (moov-mănh.) Motion,
Movimento, *It.* (mō-vē-mān-tō.) movement, impulse; the time of a piece.
Mouvement de l'archet, *Fr.* (moov-mănh dŭh l'är-shā.) Bowing, the movement of the bow.
Movement. The name given to any portion of a composition comprehended under the same measure or time; a composition consists of as many *movements* as there are positive changes in time.
Movement, organ. A system of levers with their appendages, called trackers, rollers, etc., is an organ, which serves to transmit the action of the keys to the wind-chest, pallets, and sound-board.
Movimento contrario, *It.* (mō-vē-mān-tō kōn-trā-rē-ō.) Contrary movement.
M. P. The initials of *Mézzo Piáno.*
M. S. The initials of *Máno Sinéstra.*
Mu. A syllable applied to the fourth note of the Hebrew scale in solfaing.
Nuance, *Fr.* (nü-dnhs.) A change or variation of notes; a division.
Muddhum, *Hin.* (mood-hoom.) The name of the fourth note in the Hindoo musical scale.
Muet, *Fr.* (mū-ā.) Mute.
Muffled tones. Deadened tones.
Multisonous, *Lat.* (mŭt-tĭ-sō-nŭs.) Many sounding, loud sounding.
Mund, *Ger.* (moond.) The mouth.
Mund-harmonica, *Ger.* (moond här-mō-nĭ-kä.) The Jew's harp; or, a mouth harmonica.
Mund-stück, *Ger.* (moond stük.) Reed, mouthpiece.
Mundrica, *Hin.* (moon-drē-kä.) The third note of the srootis into which the first note of the Hindoo scale is divided.
Mundutee, *Hin.* The first of the srootis into which the sixth note of the Hindoo scale is divided.
Münster, *Ger.* (mŭn-stēr.) Minster, cathedral.
Munter, *Ger.* (moon-tēr.) Lively, sprightly.
Munterkeit, *Ger.* (moon-tēr-kĭt.) Liveliness, briskness, vivacity.
Murmeln, *Ger.* (moor-mĕln.) To murmur.
Murmelnd, *Ger.* (moor-mĕlnd.) Murmuring.
Murmugear, *Spa.* (moor-moo-hā-är.) To murmur, to utter a low sound.
Murmur. A low, indistinct sound.
Musa, *Lat.* (mū-sä.) A song.
Musars. Name given to itinerant musicians who performed on the musette, formerly much in vogue in Europe.

ā *ale,* ă *add,* ä *arm,* ē *eve,* ĕ *end,* ī *ice,* ĭ *ill,* ō *old,* ŏ *odd,* ô *dove,* oo *moon,* ū *lute,* ŭ *but,* ü *French sound.*

MUS B

Mus. Bac. An abbreviation of *Bachelor of Music.* (Little used.)
Mus. Doc. An abbreviation of *Doctor of Music.*
Muse. Name originally given to the muzzle or tube of the bagpipe. One of the nine fabled goddesses presiding over art, literature or music.
Muses. In mythology, the nine sister goddesses who presided over the fine arts.
Musetta, *It.* (moo-zĕt-tä.)
Musette, *Fr.* (mū-sĕt.) { A species of small bagpipes inflated by means of bellows placed under the arm of the performer; an air or dance composed for the musette.
Music. The science of harmonical sounds, which treats of the principles of harmony, or the properties, dependencies and relations of sounds to each other.
Música, *It.* (moo-zē-kä.) Music.
Música antiqua, *Lat.* (mŭ-sĭ-kä än-tī-quä.) Ancient music.
Música arithmetica, *Lat.* (mŭ-sĭ-kä ä-rĭth-mĕt-ĭ-kä.) That part of musical science which considers sounds by the help of numbers.
Música arrabbiáta, *It.* (mŭ-sĭ-kä är-räb-bē-ä-tä.) Burlesque music.
Música, ars, *Lat.* (mŭ-sĭ-kä ars.) The art of music.
Música di gátti, *It.* (mŭ-sē-kä dē gät-tē.)} Burlesque music; caterwauling.
Música choralis, *Lat.* (mŭ-sĭ-kä kō-rä-lĭs.) The music of a chorus or chant.
Música chromatica, *Lat.* (mŭ-sĭ-kä krō-mät-ĭ-kä.) Music in which there are many chromatic signs.
Música colorata, *Lat.* (mŭ-sĭ-kä kō-lō-rä-tä.)
Música fichta, *Lat.* (mŭ-sĭ-kä fēk-tä.) }
An old name for music which deviated from the church modes.
Música corcada, *Spa.* (moo-sĭ-kä kŏr-ŏ-ä-dä.) Chorus music; music for two or more parts.
Música da cámera, *It.* (moo-zē-kä dä kä-mä-rä.) Music for the chamber.
Música da chiésa, *It.* (moo-zē-kä dä kē-ē-zä.) Church music.
Música da gatta, *It.* (moo-zē-kä dä gät-tä.) Discordant music.
Música da teátro, *It.* (moo-zē-kä dä tē-ä-trō.) Dramatic music.
Música didactica, *Lat.* (mŭ-sĭ-kä dĭ-dăk-tĭ-kä.) That department of music which treats of the quantity, proportions and different qualities of sounds.
Música dramatica, *Lat.* (mŭ-sĭ-kä drä-mä-tĭ-kä.) Dramatic music.
Música ecclesiastica, *Lat.* (mŭ-sĭ-kä ĕk-klä-zĭ-ăs-tĭ-kä.) Church music.
Música enharmonica, *Lat.* (mŭ-sĭ-kä ĕn-här-mŏn-ĭ-kä.) That system of music wherein the enharmonic dieses was frequently used.
Música hyporchemata, *Lat.* (mŭ-sĭ-kä hī-pŏr-kē-mä-tä.) Music suitable for ballads and dancing.
Música instrumentalis, *Lat.* (mŭ-sĭ-kä īn-stroo-mĕn-tä-lĭs.) Instrumental music.
Musicále, *It.* (moo-zē-kä-lē.) Musical, belonging to music.

MUSI

Musical androides. Automatic figures so constructed as to play on musical instruments.
Musical brachygraphy. The art of writing musical notation in an abbreviated style by means of signs, characters, etc.
Musical clocks. Clocks containing an arrangement similar to a barrel organ, moved by weights and springs and producing various tunes.
Musical convention. A gathering of choristers and teachers for the study and practice of music.
Musical design. The invention and conduct of the subject; the disposition of every part; the general order of the whole; counterpoint.
Musical director. A conductor; one who has charge of public musical performances.
Musical drama. Opera, lyric drama.
Musical ear. The ability of determining by the sense of hearing the finest gradation of sound.
Musicalement, *Fr.* (mū-zē-kăl-mänh.) {
Musicalménte, *It.* (moo-zē-kăl-män-tē.) {
Musically, harmoniously.
Musical glasses. Drinking glasses so tuned in regard to each other, that a wet finger being passed round their brims, they produce the notes of the diatonic scale, and are capable of giving the successive sounds of regular tunes or melodies.
Musical grammar. The rules of musical composition.
Musical kaleidoscope. An arrangement of cards upon each of which a bar of an air is placed according to a certain key, from four packs of which, mingled together, cards are drawn, thus producing an original air.
Musically. In a musical, melodious manner.
Musical nomenclature. The vocabulary of names and technical terms in music.
Musical pandect. A treatise comprehending the entire harmonic science.
Musical pantomine. A dramatic performance, the ideas and sentiments of which are expressed by music and gestures.
Musical scale, Chinese. A scale consisting of five notes without semitones, the music being written on five lines in perpendicular columns, and the elevation and depression of tones indicated by distinctive names.
Musical science. The *theory* of music, in contradistinction from the *practice,* which is an *art;* the general principles and laws of harmonic relations.
Musical soirée. An evening musical entertainment, public or private.
Musical terms. Words or phrases appended to passages of music, indicating the manner in which they should be performed.
Musica melismatica, *Lat.* (mŭ-sĭ-kä mĕl-ĭs-mät-ĭ-kä.) Correct arrangement of music according to the rules of melody.
Musica melodica, *Lat.* (mŭ-sĭ-kä mĕ-lō-dĭ-kä.) Correct arrangement of music, according to the rules of melody.
Musica melopoetica, *Lat.* (mŭ-sĭ-kä mĕl-ō-pō-ĕt-ĭ-kä.) Correct arrangement of music, according to the rules of melody.

ă *ate,* ă *add,* ă *arm,* ĕ *eve,* ĕ *end,* ī *ice,* ĭ *ill,* ō *old,* ŏ *odd,* ō *dove,* oo *moon,* ū *lute,* ŭ *but,* ü *French sound.*

MUSI

Musica mensurabilis, *Lat.* (mū-sĭ-kă mĕn-sū-rā-bĭ-lĭs.) Music the notes of which, controlled by certain times, are unequal.
Musica mensurata, *Lat.* (mū-sĭ-kă mĕn-sū-rā-tă.) Music the notes of which, controlled by certain times, are equal.
Musica misurata, *Lat.* (mū-sĭ-kă mĭs-ū-rā-tă.) Music the notes of which, controlled by certain times, are unequal.
Musica moderna, *Lat.* (mū-sĭ-kă mō-dĕr-nă.) Modern music.
Musica odica, *Lat.* (mū-sĭ-kă ō-dĕ-kă.) Music suitable for dancing.
Musica pathetica, *Lat.* (mū-sĭ-kă pă-thĕt-ĭ-kă.) Pathetic music; a style of music of a moving and affecting kind.
Musica piana, *Lat.* (mū-sĭ-kă pĭă-nă.) Plain chant, or song.
Musica prattica, *It.* (moo-zō-kă prăt-tĭ-kă.) Practical music.
Musica profana, *Lat.* (mū-sĭ-kă prō-fā-nă) Secular music.
Musica ratonera, *Spa.* (moo-zō-kă ră-tō-nā-ră.) Harsh music.
Musicáre, *It.* (moo-zō-kă-rō.) To sing or to play, to perform music.
Musica recitativa, *Lat.* (mū-sĭ-kă rō-sĭ-tă-tē-vă.) Recitative music.
Musica scenica, *Lat.* (mū-sĭ-kă sĕn-ĭ-kă.)
Musica theatra, *Lat.* (mū-sĭ-kă thē-āt-ră.)
Musica theatralis, *Lat.* (mū-sĭ-kă thē-ă-trā-lĭs.)
Music suited to theatrical performance.
Musica theoretica, *Lat.* (mū-sĭ-kă thē-ō-rētĭcă.) The theory of music.
Musica tragica, *Lat.* (mū-sĭ-kă trā-jĭ-kă.) Tragic, mournful music.
Musica vocalis, *Lat.* (mū-sĭ-kă vō-kā-lĭs.) Vocal music.
Music, Bachelor of. The first music degree conferred at the universities.
Music box. A small box producing various tunes by the revolution of a cylinder.
Music, burlesque. A ludicrous representation of music, comic music.
Music, calathumpian. A combination of discordant sounds upon various instruments out of tune and non-musical.
Music, choral. Music written and performed in the style of a choral.
Music, church. Music suited to church service.
Music classical. Music of the highest order; constituting the best model or authority.
Music compositor. One who sets up music type.
Music, concerted. Instrumental music with various parts in which all the instruments are equally required.
Music, dance. A general name for all kinds of music suitable for dancing.
Music, didactic. Scales and exercises for instruction and practice.
Music, Doctor of. A degree conferred by the universities.
Music, elementary. The first principles or rudiments of music.

MUSI

Music, enharmonic. Music that proceeds by intervals smaller than the diatonic and chromatic.
Music, field. Martial music.
Music folio. A case for holding loose sheets of music; a wrapper used in a music store for the convenience of a classified arrangement of the stock.
Music, Gregorian. Those chants and melodies introduced into the Roman Catholic service by St. Gregory in the sixth century.
Music, hunting. Music suited to the chase.
Music, hypocritic. All music suited as an accompaniment to scenic performance.
Musichétto, *It.* (moo-zē-kăt-tō.) A little musician.
Musichévole, *It.* (moo-zē-kā-vō-lē.) Musical.
Musichéno, *It.* (moo-zē-kā-no.) A little musician.
Musician. One who understands the science of music, or who sings or performs on some instrument according to the rules of art.
Musician, practical. One whose regular business is to sing or perform on some musical instrument.
Musician, scientific. One who is versed in the theory or science of music.
Musicien, *Fr.* (mū-zē-sī-ănh.) Musician.
Musicienne, *Fr.* (mū-zē-sī-ĕnn.) A female musician.
Musiciens par excellence, *Fr.* (mū-zē-sĭ-ănh pār ĕx-sĕl-lănhs.) Musicians of great excellence; superior performers.
Music, Ionic. An airy, light species of music.
Music, martial. } Music composed for military bands; warlike music.
Music, military.
Music, Moravian. The music of the Moravian church, in which the congregation unite, the tune being some old German Choral.
Músico, *It.* (moo-zē-kō.) A musician; a professor or practitioner of music. The name was also applied to those male vocalists who formerly sang soprano parts.
Music of the future. A term applied to the music of Richard Wagner and others of his school.
Musicography, *Gr.* (mū-sĭ-kŏg-ră-fy.) The symbolical writing of music; the writing of the notes of music.
Musicomania, *It.* (moo-zē-kō-mā-nē-ā.) A monomania in which a passion for music absorbs every other feeling of the soul.
Musicône, *It.* (moo-zē-kō-nē.) A great musician or composer.
Musico pratico, *It.* (mōo-zē-kō prā-tē-kō.) A practical musician.
Music, passion. Music used during Passion week in the Catholic church.
Music, pastoral. Music in a simple and rural style.
Music, plaintive. Music expressive of sadness and grief.
Musicprobe, *Ger.* (moo-zĭk-prō-bē.) A musical rehearsal.
Music, profane. A general term formerly used for all music not adapted to the service of the church; secular music.

ă ale, ă add, ä arm, ē eve, ĕ end, ī ice, ĭ ill, ō old, ŏ odd, ô dove, oo moon, ū lute, ŭ but, ü French sound.

MUSI — MYST

Music recorder. An instrument to be attached to a pianoforte for the purpose of recording upon paper the notes that are played.
Music timekeeper. An English instrument designed to enable a performer to keep time in any measure in which a piece of music is written.
Music trade-mark. A mark adopted by the United States Board of Music Trade, being a star enclosing figures denoting the retail price of the work upon which it is printed, the figures representing the number of dimes at which it is sold.
Musicus, Ger. (moo-zī-koos.) A musician.
Musiker, Ger. (moo-zī-kĕr.) A musician.
Musikfest, Ger. (moo-zīk-fĕst.) A musical festival.
Musikino, Ger. (moo-zī-kē-nō.) A little musician.
Musik-lehrer, Ger. (moo-zīk lā-rĕr.) Teacher of music.
Musikkenner, Ger. (moo-zīk-kĕn-ner.)
Musikliebhaber, Ger. (moo zīk-lēb-hä-hĕr.) A lover of music, an amateur.
Musikmeister, Ger. (moo-zīk-mīs-tĕr.) A music master.
Musik-saal, Ger. (moo-zīk-säl.)
Musik-zimmer, Ger. (moo-zīk-tsĭm-mĕr.) Music hall, music room.
Musik stunde, Ger. (moo-zīk stoon-dĕ.) A music lesson.
Musikunterricht, Ger. (moo-zīk-oon-t'r-rĭkht.) Instruction in music.
Musik-verein, Ger. (moo-zīk fē-rīn.) A musical society.
Musik-zeitung, Ger. (moo-zīk tsī-toong.) A musical paper.
Musique, Fr. (mū-zēk.) Music.
Musique d'eglise, Fr. (mū-zēk d'ā-glēz.) Church music.
Musique de guitare, Fr. (mū-zēk dŭh ghī-tăr.) Guitar music.
Musique vocale, Fr. (mū-zēk vō-kăl.) Vocal music.

Musurgus, Lat. (mū-sŭr-gŭs.) A musician or composer.
Muta, It. (moo-tä.) Change; in horn and trumpet music it means to change the crooks: in drum parts it means that the tuning of the drum is to be altered.
Mutation. Change, transition; the transformation of the voice occurring at the age of puberty.
Mutation, Fr. (mū-tă-sĭ-ŏnh.)
Mutazióne, It. (moo-tä-tsē-ō-nĕ.) } Mutation.
Mutation, or *filling up Stops,* are those which do not give a sound corresponding to the key pressed down; such as the quint, tierce, twelfth, etc.
Mute. A small instrument of brass, ivory, or wood, sometimes placed on the bridge of a violin, viola, or violincello, to diminish the tone of the instrument by damping or checking its vibrations.
Mute, Æolian. A combination of the "A" Æolian pitch-pipe and the mute for the violin.
Mute, folding violin. An article imparting to a violin a soft, pure tone.
Muthig, Ger. (moo-tĭg.) Courageous, spirited.
Muthwillig, Ger. (moot-vĭl-lĭg.) Mischievous, lively.
Mutiren, Ger. (moo-tē-r'n.) To change the voice from soprano, to tenor baritone, or bass.
Mykterophonie, Gr. (mĭk-tĕr-ŏf-ō-nē.) } To
Mykterophonie, Ger. (mĭk-tĕr-ŏf-ō-nē.) } sing nasally, to sing through the nose.
Myriologist. (mĭr-ĭ-ŏl-ō-jĭst.) One who composes or sings a myriologue, usually a woman.
Myriologue. (mĭr-ĭ-ō-lŏg.) An extemporary funeral song composed for and sung at the funeral of a friend.
Mysteres, Fr. (mĭs-tăr.) } A species of sacred
Mysteries. } drama with music, which was practiced in many of the European churches before the Reformation.

ă ale, ă add, ă arm, ē eve, ŏ end, ī ice, ĭ ill, ō old, ŏ odd, ō dove, oo moon, ū tute, ŭ but, ü French sound.

NABL

Nabla, Heb. (nă-blä.) The nebel, a ten-stringed instrument of the ancient Hebrews; the harp of the Jews, sometimes written Nebel Nasar.
Nacaire, Fr. (nă-kär.) A brass drum with a loud metallic tone, formerly much used in France and Italy.
Nacara, It. (nă-kä-rä.)
Nacarre, It. pt. (nă-kä-rē.)
Nácchera, It. (näk-kä-rä.) Kettle drums.
Naccherétta, It. (näk-kĕ-rāt-tä.) A small kettle drum.
Naccheríno, It. (näk-kä-rē-nō.) A kettle drummer.
Naccheróne, It. (näk-kä-rō-nĕ.) A large pair of kettle drums.
Nachahmung, Ger. (nä-kä-moong.) Imitation.
Nach dem tact singen, Ger. (näkh dĕm täkt sĭng-ĕn.) To sing in time.
Nach dem tact spielen, Ger. (näkh dĕm täkt spē-l'n.) To play in time.
Nach der reihe, Ger. (näkh dĕr rī-ĕ.) In succession.
Nachdruck, Ger. (näkh-drook.) Emphasis, accent.
Nachdrücklich, Ger. (näkh-drük-līkh.)
Nachdrucksvoll, Ger. (näkh-drooks-fōl.) Energetic, emphatic, forcible.
Nachfolge, Ger. (näkh-fōl-ghĕ.) Imitation.
Nachklang, Ger. (näkh-kläng.) Resonance, echo.
Nachklingen, Ger. (näkh-klĭng-ĕn.) To ring,
Nachschallen, Ger. (näkh-shäl-l'n.) to echo, to resound.
Nach-hall, Ger. (näkh häll.) Reverberation, echo.
Nachmittagsgeläute, Ger. (näkh-mĭt-täg s-ghē-toi-tĕ.) Ringing for vespers.
Nach noten singen, Ger. (näkh nō-t'n sĭng-ĕn.) To sing by note.
Nachschlag, Ger. (näkh-shläg.) Additional, or after note.
Nachsingen, Ger. (näkh-sĭng-ĕn.) To repeat a song, to sing after.
Nachspiel, Ger. (näkh-spēl.) After play; a postlude or concluding piece.
Nächstverwandte töne, Ger. (näkhst-fĕr-vänd-tĕ tö-nĕ.) The nearest relative keys.
Nacht-glocke, Ger. (näkht glŏ-kĕ.) Night bell, curfew.
Nacht-horn, Ger. (näkht hōrn.) Night-horn; an organ stop of 8 feet tone, nearly identical with the Quintation but of larger scale and more hornlike tone.
Nacht-musik, Ger. (näkht moo-zĭk.) Night music, serenade.
Nacht-sänger, Ger. (näkht säng-ĕr.) A night singer, a serenader.
Nacht-schläger, Ger. (näkht shlä-gĕr.) Nightingale.
Nachtigall, Ger. (näkh-tĭ-gäll.)
Nachtständchen, Ger. (näkht-ständ-kh'n.) A serenade.
Nachstück, Ger. (näkht-stück.) A serenade, a nocturne.
Nach und nach, Ger. (näkh oond näkh.) By little and little, by degrees.
Nach und nach immer rascher, schneller, Ger. (näkh oond näkh ĭm-mĕr rä-shĕr, shnĕl-lĕr.) By degrees, continually increasing in rapidity.

NAY

Nafle. (nă-fĕ.) A Persian trumpet.
Nafiri. (nă-fē-rē.) An Indian trumpet.
Nagarah, Per. (nă-gä-rä.) The kettle drum of the Persians.
Naif, Fr. (nă-ēf.)
Naiv, Ger. (nä-ēf.) Simple, artless, natural.
Naive, Fr. (nă-ēv.)
Naivement, Fr. (nă-ēv-mänh.) Simply, naturally.
Naked. A term significantly applied by modern theorists to fourths, fifths and other chords when unaccompanied.
Nakokus. (nă-kŏ-kŭs.) The name of an instrument much used by the Egyptians in their Coptic churches, and in their religious processions and consisting of two brass plates suspended by strings, and struck together by way of beating time.
Nänien, Ger. (nä-nĭ-ĕn.) A dirge, an elegy.
Narránte, It. (när-rän-tä.) In a narrative style.
Narrator. A name formerly given to the chief performer in an oratorio.
Narrentanz, Ger. (när-r'n-tänts.) A foolish dance; a fool's dance.
Nasallaut, Ger. (nă-zäl-lout.) Nasal sound, or tone.
Nasal tone. That reedy unpleasant tone produced by the voice when it issues in too great a degree through the nostrils.
Nasard.
Nasat. An old name for an organ stop,
Nassat. tuned a twelfth above the diapasons.
Nazard.
Nasardo, Spa. (nă-zär-dō.) One of the registers of an organ.
Nasenhauch, Ger. (nä-z'n-houkh.) Nasal
Nasenton, Ger. (nä-z'n-tōn.) sound, or tone.
Nason. A very quiet, and sweet toned flute stop, of 4 feet scale, sometimes found in old organs.
Nasutus, Lat. (nă-sū-tŭs.) A wind instrument formerly in use, so called on account of its thick, reedy or nasal tone.
National-lied, Ger. (nă-tsĭ-ō-näl lēd.) National song.
National music. Music identified with the
National song. history of a nation, or the manners and customs of its people, either by means of the sentiment it expresses or by long use.
Natural. A character marked ♮, used to contradict a sharp or flat.
Naturále, It. (nă-too-rä-lĕ.) Natural, easy, free.
Natural harmony. The harmony of the triad or common chord.
Naturali suoni, It. (nă-too-rä-lē swŏ-nē.) Sounds within the compass of the human voice; natural sounds.
Natural keys. Those which have no sharp or flat at the signature as, C major, and A minor.
Naturalménte, It. (nă-too-räl-mān-tĕ.) Naturally.
Natural modulation. That which is confined to the key of the piece and its relatives.
Naublum, Heb. (naw-bloom.) See Nabla.
Nautical songs. Songs relating to the sea.
Nay Tur. (nă.) A Turkish flute; the Nei.

138   PRONOUNCING MUSICAL DICTIONARY.

ă *ale*, ă *add*, ä *arm*, ĕ *eve*, ĕ *end*, ĭ *ice*, ĭ *ill*, ō *old*, ŏ *odd*, ō *dove*, oo *moon*, ū *lute*, ŭ *out*, ü *French sound*.

NEAN

Neanes, *Gr.* (nĕ-ä-nĕs.) One of the eight modes used by the modern Greeks in their intonations of church modes.
Neapolitan sixth. A chord composed of a minor third and minor sixth, and occurring on the sub-dominant, or fourth degree of the scale. In the key of C (major or minor) this chord is really the same as the first inversion of the triad of D♭.
Nebel, *Heb.* (nā-bĕl.)
Nebel nassor, *Heb.* (nā-bĕl nās-sōr.) } The name given by the ancient Jews to their ten stringed harp, supposed to have been triangular in form and used in religious worship.
Neben-gedanken, *Ger.* (nā-b'n ghĕ-dänk-'n.) Accessory and subordinate ideas.
Neben-note, *Ger.* (nā-b'n nō-tĕ.) Auxiliary note.
Neben-register, *Ger.* (nā-b'n rĕ-ghĭs-tĕr.) }
Neben-züge, *Ger.* (nā-b'n tsü-ghĕ.) }
Secondary, or accessory stops in an organ, such as *couplers, tremulant, bells.* etc.
Neben-stimmen, *Ger.* (nā-b'n stĭm-mĕn.) Subordinate harmonic parts; also, secondary or mutation stops, such as the quint, twelfths, etc.
Necessario, *It.* (nā-tchĕs-sä-rē-ō.) A term indicating that the passage referred to must not be omitted.
Nechiloth, *Heb.* (nĕk-ĭ-lōth.) A wind instrument of the Hebrews, formed of a double set of pipes.
Neck. That part of a violin, guitar, or similar instrument, extending from the head to the body, and on which the finger-board is fixed.
Neghinoth, *Heb.* (nā-ghī-nōth.) } A word fixed
Neginoth, *Heb.* (nā-ghī-nōth.) } at the head of certain of the psalms, and supposed to announce the particular tune to which they were to be sung; answering to the modern *giving out*. Neginoth was also the name given to ancient stringed instruments.
Negligénte, *It.* (nāl-yē-jän-tĕ.) Negligent; unconstrained.
Negligenteménte, *It.* (nāl-yē-jĕn-tĕ-mān-tĕ.) Negligently.
Negligénza, *It.* (nāl-yē-jän-tsä.) Negligence, carelessness.
Negli, *It. pl.* (nāl-yē.) } In the, at the.
Nel, *It. pl.* (nā-ē.) }
Nel, *Tur.* (nā-ē) A fashionable musical instrument of the Turks, being a flute made of cane.
Nehiloth, *Heb.* (nā-hī-lōth.) Ancient wind instruments.
Nekeb, *Heb.* (nā-kĕb.) A wind instrument of the ancient Hebrews, formed of a single tube.
Nei, *It.* (nā.)
Nella, *It.* (nāl-lä.)
Nelle, *It. pl.* (nāl-lĕ.) } In the, at the.
Nello, *It.* (nāl-lō.)
Nell', *It.* (nāl'l.)
Nel battere, *It.* (nāl bät-tā-rĕ.) In the *down beat* of the measure.
Nelle parte di sopra, *It.* (nāl-lĕ pär-tĕ dē sō-prä.) In the higher or upper part.
Nello stesso tempo, *It.* (nāl-lō stĕs-sō tām-pō.) In the same time.
Nel stilo antico, *It.* (nāl stē-lō än-tē-kō.) In the ancient style.

NINA

Nel tempo, *It.* (nāl tām-pō.) In time, in the previous time.
Nenia, *Lat.* (nĕn-ĭ-ä.) } A funeral song, an
Nenien, *Ger.* (nĕn-ĭ-ĕn.) } elegy.
Nervio, *Spa.* (när-vĭ-ō.) String of an instrument.
Nesso, *Lat.* (nĕs-sō.) One of the fourth parts into which Euclid divided the Melopœa.
Nete, *Gr.* (nā-tĕ.) The last or most acute string of the lyre; the name given by the ancient Greeks to the fourth, or most acute chord of each of the three tetrachords which followed the first two or deepest two.
Nete diczeugmenon, *Gr.* (nā-tĕ dē-*zoog*-mĕ-nŏn.) The final or highest sound of the fourth tetrachord, and the first or gravest of the fifth.
Nete hyperbolæon, *Gr.* (nā-tĕ hē-pĕr-bō-lē-ōn.) The last sound of the *hyperbolæon*, or highest tetrachord, and of the great system or diagram of the Greeks.
Nete synemmenon, *Gr.* (nā-tĕ sĭ-*nĕm*-mĕ-nŏn.) The fourth or most acute sound of the third tetrachord, when conjoint with the second.
Netoides, *Gr.* (nā-toi-dĕs.) Name given by the ancients to the sounds forming the higher portion of their scale or system.
Net, *Fr.* (nā.)
Nett, *Ger.* (nĕt.) } Neatly,
Nettaménte, *It.* (nĕt-tä-*män*-tĕ.) } clearly,
Nette, *Fr.* (nāt.) } plainly.
Nettete, *Fr.* (nāt-tā.) } Neatness, clear-
Nettheit, *Ger.* (nĕt-hīt.) } ness, plainness.
Nettigkeit, *Ger.* (nĕt-tĭg-kīt.) }
Nétto, *It.* (nāt-tō.) Neat, clear; quick, nimble.
Neu, *Ger.* (noi.) New.
Neumæ, *Lat.* (nŭ-mē.) An old name for *divisions:* which see.
Neun, *Ger.* (noin.) Nine.
Neun-achtel takt, *Ger.* (noin äkh't'l täkt.) Measure in nine-eighth time.
Neunte, *Ger.* (noin-tĕ.) A ninth.
Neunzehnte, *Ger.* (noin-tsĕn-tĕ.) Nineteenth.
Neutralizing sign. The sign of a natural, ♮.
Neuvième, *Fr.* (nŭh-vĭ-ām.) The interval of a ninth.
Nexus, *Gr.* (nĕx-ŭs.) An old term for a phrase or a sequence.
Nexus, anacamptos, *Gr.* (nĕx-ŭs än-ä-kämp-tōs.) Descending.
Nexus, circumstans, *Gr.* (nĕx-ŭs sĕr-kŭm-stäns.) Descending and ascending.
Nexus, rectus, *Gr.* (nĕx-ŭs rĕk-tŭs.) Ascending.
Ni, (nē.) A syllable applied to the seventh note of the Hindoo scale in solfaing.
Nicht, *Ger.* (nĭkht.) Not.
Nicht schreiende stimmen, *Ger.* (nĭkht shrī-ĕn-dĕ stĭm-m'n.) *Not shrill stops*, in organ playing.
Nicht zu geschwind, *Ger.* (nĭkht tsoo ghĕsh-vĭnd.) Not too quick.
Nieder-schlag, *Ger.* (nē-dĕr shläg.) The down beat or accented part of the bar.
Niedrig, *Ger.* (nē-drĭg.) Low or deep in voice.
Niggeritore, *It.* (nĕd-jĕ-rē-tō-rĕ.) The prompter.
Nikhad, *Hin.* (nĕk-äd.) The name of the seventh note in the Hindoo musical scale.
Nina, *It.* (nē-nä.) A lullaby.

ā ale, ă add, ä arm, ē eve, ĕ end, ī ice, ˑĭ ill, ō old, ŏ odd, ȯ dove, oo moon, ū lute, ŭ but, ü French sound.

NINE

Nine-eighth measure. A measure containing nine eighth notes or their equivalent, marked 9-8.
Nineteenth. An interval comprising two octaves and a fifth; also, an organ stop, tuned a nineteenth above the diapasons; see *Larigot*.
Niunare, *It.* (nĕn-nä-rĕ.) To sing children to sleep.
Ninth. An interval consisting of an octave and a second.
Nóbile, *It.* (nō-bē-lĕ.) Noble, grand, impressive.
Nobilita, con, *It.* (cō-bē-lē-tä kōn.) With nobility; dignified.
Nobilménte. *It.* (nō-bēl-*män*-tĕ.) } **Nobly,**
Noblement, *Fr.* (nō-bl-mänh.) } grandly.
Nobilménte ed animato, *It.* (nō-bēl-*män*-tĕ ĕd än-ä-*mä*-tō.) With grandeur and spirit.
Noctúrn. } A composition of a light and elegant character suitable for evening recreation; also, a piece resembling a serenade to be played at night in the open air.
Nocturne, *Fr.* (nŏk-tūrn.) } A nocturne.
Nocturno, *It.* (nŏk-toor-nō.) }
Nodal points. } In *music*, the fixed points of a
Nodes. } sonorous chord, at which it divides itself, when it vibrates by aliqnot parts and produces the harmonic sounds; as the strings of the Æolian harp.
Noël, *Fr.* (nō-ĕl.) A Christmas Carol, or hymn.
Noire, *Fr.* (nwär.) *Black note;* a crotchet.
Noire pointée, *Fr.* (nwär pwänh-tā.) A dotted crotchet.
Nomenclature, musical. A vocabulary of names and technical terms employed in music.
Nomes, *Gr.* (nō-mēs.) Certain airs in the ancient music sung to Cybele, the mother of the gods, to Bacchus, to Pan and other divinities. The name *nome* was also given to every air, the composition of which was regulated by certain determined and inviolable rules.
Nomion, *Gr.* (nō-mĭ-ŏn.) Among the ancient Greeks, a species of love song.
Nomo, *It.* (nō-mō.) Nome. (See Nomes.)
Nomodictai, *Lat.* (nō-mō-dĭk-tä-ē.) The umpires at the sacred games and musical contests of the ancient Romans.
Nomos, *Gr.* (nō-mŏs.) } A tune, melody; a me-
Nomus, *Lat.* (nō-mŭs.) } lodic sequence.
Non, *It.* (nŏn.) Not, no.
Nona, *It.* (nō-nä.) The interval of a ninth.
Nona chord. The dominant chord with a third added to it.
Nouétto. *It.* (nō-nät-tō.) A composition for nine voices or instruments.
Non mólto, *It.* (nōn mōl-tō.) Not much.
Non mólto allégro, *It.* (nōn mōl-tō äl-*lā*-grō.) Not very quick.
Non raccourcir, *Fr.* (nŏnh räb-koor-sēr.) Unabridged.
Non tánto, *It.* (nōn-*tän*-tō.) Not so much, not too much.
Non tánto allégro, *It.* (nōn *tän*-tō äl-*lā*-grō.) Not so quick, not too quick.
Non troppó, *It.* (ōōn trŏp-pō.) Not too much, moderately.
Non troppo allégro, *It.* (nōn trŏp-pō äl-*lā*-grō.) }
Non troppo présto, *It.* (nōn trŏp-pō *prās*-tō.) } Not too quick.

NOTA

Nonupla, *Lat.* (nŏn-ū-plä.) A quick species of time, consisting of nine crotchets, or nine quavers in a bar.
Nonupla di crome, *It.* (nō-noo-plä dē krō-mē.) A species of time wherein nine quavers make a bar, instead of eight as in common time.
Nonupla di semi-crome, *It.* (nō-noo-plä dē sĕm-ē-*krō*-mē.) Where nine semiquavers make a bar, instead of sixteen as required in common time.
Nonupla di semi-minime, *It.* (nō-noo-plä dē sĕm-ē mē-nē-mē.) A species of time in which nine crotchets are in the bar, of which four make a semibreve in common time.
Normal musical Institute. A school, the object of which is to afford instruction to persons desirous of becoming qualified to teach music.
Normal-ton. *Ger.* (nōr-mäl-tōn.) The normal tone, the note A, the sound to which instruments are tuned in an orchestra.
Normal-tonleiter. *Ger.* (nōr-mäl tōn-lī-tĕr.) The natural scale, the scale of C, the open key.
Nóta, *It.* (nō-tä.) } A note.
Nota, *Lat.* (nō-tä.) }
Nota abbiétta, *It.* (nō-tä äb-bē-ät-tä.) } A use-
Nota abjecta, *Lat.* (nō-tä äb-jĕk-tä.) } less cancelled note.
Nota anticipata, *It.* (nō-tä än-tē-tshē-pä-tä.) A note in anticipation, or a note that is sounded in a chord previous to that to which it belongs.
Nota buóna, *It.* (nō-tä boo-ō-nä.) A strong, or accented note.
Nota cambiáta, *It.* (nō-tä käm-bē-ä-tä.) A changed, or irregularly transient note, a passing note.
Nota caratterística, *It.* (nō-tä kär-ät-tĕr-es-tē-kä.) A characteristic, or leading note.
Nota cattiva, *It.* (nō-tä kät-tē-vä.) A weak, or unaccented note.
Nota contra notam, *Lat.* (nō-tä kŏn-trä nō-täm.) Note against note; see Counterpoint.
Nota coronáta, *It.* (nō-tä kō-rō-nä-tä.) A note marked with a hold.
Nota d'abbelliménto, *It.* (nō-tä d'äb-bĕl-lē-*män*-tō.) A note of embellishment, an ornamental note.
Nota di passággio. *It.* (nō-tä dē päs-*säd*-jē-ō.) A passing note, a note of regular transition.
Nota di piacére, *It.* (nō-tä dē pē-ä-*tshā*-rē.) An optional grace note, an *ad libitum* embellishment.
Nota intiera, *It.* (nō-tä ĕn-tē-ā-rä.) A whole note.
Nota sensíbile, *It.* (nō-tä sĕn-sē-bē-lē.) }
Nota sensíbilis, *Lat.* (nō-tä sĕn-sē-bĭl-ĭs.) } The *sensibile*, or leading note of the scale.
Nota signáta, *Lat.* (nō-tä sĭg-nä-tä.) A note marked with a sign.
Nota sostenúta, *It.* (nō-tä sōs-tĕ-*noo*-tä.) A sustained note.
Notation. The art of representing by notes, characters, etc., all the different musical sounds.
Notation, numerical. A system of notation first introduced by Rousseau, in which the first eight of the numerals are substituted for the eight notes, and points, cyphers, etc., for such characters as represent pauses, time, etc.

ā ale, ă add, ä arm, ē eve, ĕ end, ī ice, ĭ ill, ō old, ŏ odd, ô dove, oo moon, ū lute, ŭ but, ü French sound.

NOTA

Notazione musicàle, *It.* (nō-tä-tsē-ō-nĕ moo-zē-kä-lĕ.) Musical notation.
Note. A character, which by its formation indicates the duration of a tone, and by its situation upon the staff its proper pitch.
Note, characteristic. A leading note.
Note, clef. The note upon which the clef is placed.
Note, connecting. A note held in common by two chords.
Note, crowned. A note marked with a hold.
Note d'agrement, *Fr.* (nŏt d'ä-grä-mänh.) An ornamental note.
Note de passage, *Fr.* (nŏt düh päs-sähz.) A passing note; a note of regular transition.
Note diésée, *Fr.* (nŏt dī-ā-zā.) Note marked with a sharp.
Note, double. The ancient breve.
Note, double dotted. A note whose length is increased three-fourths of its original value, by the dots placed after it.
Note, double stemmed. A note having two stems, one upward and the other downward, the one showing the length of its duration and the other its relative value towards other notes in the measure.
Note, eighth. A quaver.
Note, fore. An appoggiatura.
Note, fundamental. The lowest note of a fundamental chord.
Note, grace. A note of embellishment.
Note, half. A minim.
Note, key. A note to which all the other notes of a piece bear a distinct and subordinate relation, which usually commences a composition and with which it generally closes.
Note, leading. The major seventh of any scale; the semitone below the key note; the major third of the dominant.
Note, leaning. An appoggiatura, or fore note.
Noten auf den 5'linien, *Ger.* (nō-t'n ouf dĕn 5'lēn-ĭ-ĕn.) Notes upon the five lines.
Noten-blatt, *Ger.* (nō-t'n blät.) A sheet of music.
Noten-drucker, *Ger.* (nō-t'n drook-ĕr.) A music printer.
Noten-buch, *Ger.* (nō-t'n hookh.) Music book, note book.
Noten-druck, *Ger.* (nō-t'n drook.) The art of printing music; printed music.
Noten-gestell, *Ger.* (nō-t'n ghĕs-tĕl.) Music stand.
Noten-händler, *Ger.* (nō-t'n hănd-lĕr.) A music seller.
Noten-handlung, *Ger.* (nō-t'n hănd-loong.) Music store.
Noten in den 4 zwischenr, *Ger.* (nō-t'n in dĕn 4 tsvĭsh-ĕnr.) Notes between the four spaces.
Noten-kopf, *Ger.* (nō-t'n köpf.) Head of a note.
Noten-linien, *Ger.* (nō-t'n lē-nĭ-ĕn.) Music lines.
Noten-papier, *Ger.* (nō-t'n pä-pēr.) Music paper.
Noten-plan, *Ger.* (nō-t'n plän.) The staff, the scale.

NOTE

Noten-pult. *Ger.* (nō-t'n poolt.) A music desk.
Noten-schreiber, *Ger.* (nō-t'n shrī-bĕr.) Music copyist.
Noten-schwanz, *Ger.* (nō-t'n shvänts.) The stem of a note.
Noten-stecher, *Ger.* (nō-t'n stĕkh-ĕr.) An engraver of music.
Noten-stossen, *Ger.* (nō-t'n stō-s'n.) To play or sing staccato.
Noten-stück, *Ger.* (nō-t'n stück.) A piece of music.
Noten-system, *Ger.* (nō-t'n sĭs-tām.) The staff.
Note of modulation. A note which introduces a new key, usually applied to the leading note or sharp seventh.
Note of prolation. A note, the original and nominal duration of which is extended by the addition of a dot or hold.
Note, open. A note produced on the strings of a violin, guitar, etc., when not pressed by the finger.
Note, pedal. A note held by the pedal while the harmony forming the remaining parts is allowed to proceed.
Note, quarter. A crotchet.
Noter, *Fr.* (nō-tā.) To write out a tune or air.
Note raddoppiate, *It.* (nō-tĕ räd-dŏp-pē-ä-tĕ.) Repeated notes.
Note, radical. The fundamental note.
Note, reciting. The note in a chord upon which the voice dwells until it comes to a cadence.
Notes, accented. Notes upon which emphasis is placed; in common time the first and third notes, and in triple time the first note.
Notes, accessory. Notes situated one degree above and one degree below the principal note of a turn.
Notes, accidental. Chromatic tones that do not belong to the harmony; passing tones.
Notes, added. Notes written upon ledger or added lines.
Note, scolte, *It.* (nō-tĕ skŏl-tĕ.) Staccato note.
Notes coulees, *Fr.* (nŏt koo-lā.) Slurred notes.
Notes dans les interlignes, *Fr.* (nŏt dänh lā sänh-tär-lēn-yĕ.) Notes in the spaces.
Notes de gout, *Fr.* (nŏt düh goo.) Notes of embellishment.
Notes, passing. When one or more notes of a harmonic chord move to a tone foreign to the harmony, the chord otherwise remaining unchanged, these notes are called *Passing Notes.*
Note sensible, *Fr.* (nŏt sänh-sēbl.) The leading note of the scale; the seventh of the scale.
Notes, essential. The notes of a chord which constitute its real component parts in distinction from accidental and ornamental notes.
Note, sixteenth. A semiquaver.
Note, sixty-fourth. A hemidemisemiquaver.
Notes liees, *Fr.* (nŏt lē-ā.) Tied notes.
Notes, ornamental. Appoggiaturas, grace notes, all notes of embellishment, not forming an essential part of the harmony.
Notes, stopped. In music for the violin, violincello, and similar instruments, those notes that are sounded while the string is pressed.
Notes, subsidiary. Accessory notes.

ā ale, ă add, ä arm, ē eve, ĕ end, ī ice, ĭ ill, ō old, ŏ odd, ō dove, oo moon, ū lute, ŭ but, ü French sound.

NOTE

Notes sur les lignes, *Fr.* (nŏt sūr lă lēn-yŭh.) Notes on the lines. [copated notes.
Notes syncopees, *Fr.* (nŏt sēn-kŏ-pā.) Syn-
Notes, tied. Notes having a tie over them denoting they are to be slured. If on the same degree of the staff the tone must be sustained throughout.
Note, thirty-second. A demisemiquaver, 𝄿
Note, tonic. The first note of any scale, the key note.
Note, triple dotted. A note whose value is increased seven-eighths, by three dots after it.
Noteur, *Fr.* (nō-tŭr.) Music copyist.
Note, whole. A semibreve, 𝅝
Nothus, *Gr.* (nō-thŭs.) A name applied by the ancient Greeks to the Hyper-Æolian and Hyper-Phrygian modes.
Notte bianche o nere, *It.* (nō-tĕ bē-ăn-kĕ ō nā-rĕ.) White and black notes.
Notte oscurate, *It.* (nō-tĕ ŏa-koo-rā-tĕ.)
Notte piene, *It.* (nō-tĕ pē-ā-nĕ.)
Black notes.
Notte vacue, *It.* (nō-tĕ vă-koo-ĕ.) White notes.
Notturni, *It.* (nŏt-toor-nē.) Nocturnes.
Notturno, *It.* (nŏt-toor-nō.) A nocturne; a light elegant composition suitable for an evening performance; a serenade.
Nourrir le son, *Fr.* (noo-rēr lŭh sŏnh.) To commence or attack a note in singing, forcibly, and sustain it.

OBOE

Nourrissons, *Fr.* (noor-rēs-sōnh.) Bards, poets.
Nova, *It.* (nō-vă.) A species of small flute or pipe.
Nouvelle methode, *Fr.* (noo-vĕl mă-tōd.) A new method.
Novemole. A group of nine notes, to be performed in the same time as *six* of equal value.
Novice. (nŏv-ĭs.) A beginner, one unskilled.
Nrit-udhyay, *Hin.* (nrĕt-ood-yā.) The fourth division of Hindoostanee music, comprising the music of the dance.
Nuances, *Fr. pl.* (nū-änh-s.) Lights and shades of expression, variety of intonation.
Numerical notation. A system of notation first introduced by Rousseau, in which the first eight of the numerals are substituted for the eight notes, and points, cyphers, etc., for such other characters as represent pauses, time, etc.
Numero, *It.* (noo-mā-rō.) } *Number*, used to
Numerus, *Lat.* (nū-mĕ-rŭs.) } denotes musical time, rhythm, harmony.
Nunnia, *Gr.* (nŭn-nī-ă.) The name given by the Greeks to a song peculiar to the nurses.
Nuóvo, *It.* (noo-ō-vō.) New; *di nuóvo*, newly, again.
Nuptial songs. Wedding songs, marriage songs.
Nut. The small bridge at the upper end of the finger board of a guitar, over which the strings pass to the pegs or screws.

O.

O. This letter, forming a circle or double C, was used by the ancients as the sign of triple time from the idea that the *ternary* or number *three*, being the most perfect of all numbers, would be best expressed by a circle the most perfect of all figures. The imperfect, or common time was designated by a C, or semicircle.
O, before a consonant, *It.* (ō.) } Or, as, either.
Od, before a vowel, *It.* (ōd.)
Obbligáto, *It.* (ŏb-blē-gä-tō.)
Obbligáti, *It. pl.* (ŏb-blē-gä-tē.) } Indispensable, necessary; a part, or
Obligé, *Fr.* (ŏb-lĭ-zhā.)
Obligat, *Ger.* (ŏb-lĭ-gät.)
parts which cannot be omitted, being indispensably necessary to a proper performance.
Ober, *Ger.* (ō-bĕr.) Upper, higher.
Ober manual, *Ger.* (ō-bĕr mă-noo-ăl.) The upper manual.
Ober-stimme, *Ger.* (ō-bĕr stĭm-mĕ.) Treble, upper voice part.
Ober-tasten, *Ger.* (ō-bĕr täs-t'n.) The black keys.
Ober-theil, *Ger.* (ō-bĕr tīl.) The upper part.
Obertura, *Spa.* (ō-bĕr-too-rä.) Overture.
Ober-werk, *Ger.* (ō-bĕr vărk.) Upper work, highest row of keys.
Obligato accompaniment. An accompaniment that must be used.
Oblique motion. When one part ascends or descends, whilst the others remain stationary.
Obliquo, *It.* (ŏb-lē-quō.) Oblique.
Oboe, *Ger.* (ō-bō-ĕ.) } A hautboy; also, the
Oboé, *It.* (ō-bō-ā.) } name of an organ stop.
Oboé d'amóre, *It.* (ō-bō-ā d'ä mō-rĕ.) } A species of
Oboé lúngo, *It.* (ō-bō-ā toon-gō.) } oboe, longer than the ordinary *oboe*, with a thinner bore and lower pitch.
Oboé da caccia, *It.* (ō-bō-ā dä kät-tshē-ă.) A larger species of *oboe* with the music written in the alto clef,

OBOE

Oboé lúnghi, *It.* (ō-bō-ă loon-ghă.) See *Oboe Lúngo.*
Oboen, *Ger. pl.* (ō-bō-ĕn.) Hautboys.
Oboe-flute. An organ stop of small 4 feet scale; the tone is very delicate and reedy.
Oboé osia clarinetto, *It.* (ō-bō-ă ō-zē-ă klăr-ĕ-nĕt-to.) The oboe or clarionet.
Oboé tacente, *It.* (ō-bō-ă tă-tshĕn-tĕ.) The oboe is silent.
Oboi, *It.* (ō-bō-ē.) Hautboys.
Oboi all'unisono del violini, *It.* (ō-bō-ē äl-l'oo-nē-zō-nō vē-ō-lē-nē.) The oboes in unison with the violins.
Oboist. A performer on the oboe or hautboy.
Oboísta, *It.* (ō-bō-ēs-tä.) An oboist.
Obsistente, *Spa.* (ōb-sĭs-tăn-tĕ.) Resonant, resounding.
Obue, *Spa.* (ō-boo-ĕ.) Hautboy; a player on the hautboy.
Ocio, *Spa.* (ō-thē-ō.) } Adagio, slowly; with
Ocio, *Port.* (ō-thē-ō.) } ease and grace.
Octachord. An instrument or system comprising eight sounds or seven degrees.
Octachorde, *Fr.* (ŏk-tă-kōrd.) An octachord.
Octachordum Pythagoræ, *Lat.* (ŏk-tă-kōr-dŭm pĭ-thăg-ō-rē.) The ancient Pythagorean lyre, a stringed instrument tuned to the eight degrees of the diatonic scale.
Octaphonic. Composed of eight voices.
Octava, *Lat.* (ŏk-tă-vă.) Octave; applied to 4 feet organ stops.
Octava acuta, *Lat.* (ŏk-tă-vă ă-kū-tă.) The octave raised by transposition.
Octava alta, *It.* (ŏk-tă-vă äl-tă.) Play the passage an octave higher.
Octava grave, *Sp.* (ŏk-tă-vă grä-vă.) Octave below.
Octava gravis, *Lat.* (ŏk-tă-vă grä-vĭs.) The octave lowered by transposition.
Octavar, *Spa.* (ŏk-tă-vär.) To form octaves on stringed instruments.
Octave. An interval of eight diatonic sounds, or degrees; also the name of an organ stop.
Octave, augmented. An interval consisting of thirteen half steps or semitones.
Octave clarion. A two feet reed stop in an organ.
Octave, diminished. An interval consisting of eleven half steps or semitones.
Octave, double. An interval of two octaves, or fifteen notes in diatonic progression.
Octave fifteenth. An organ stop of bright, sharp tone, sounding an octave above the fifteenth.
Octave flute. A small flute an octave higher than the German or ordinary flute; a piccolo.
Octave-gang, *Ger.* (ŏk-tăf gäng.) See *Rule of the Octave.*
Octave hautboy. A 4 feet organ reed stop; the pipes are of the hautboy species.
Octave, large. The third octave, indicated in the German tablature by capital letters.
Octave, large, once-marked. The second octave, indicated by capital letters having a single line below.
Octave, large, twice-marked. The first octave, indicated by capital letters having two lines below them.

OCTE

Octave, perfect. An interval of twelve half-steps or semitones.
Octaves, consecutive. Two parts moving in unison or octaves with each other.
Octaves, covered. Certain apparent consecutive octaves which occur in harmony, in passing by similar motion to a perfect concord.
Octaves, disallowed. } Progressions of two
Octaves, false. } parts in similar motion by octaves.
Octave, small. The fourth octave, so-called because indicated by small letters in the German tablature.
Octave, small, five times marked. The ninth octave, represented by small letters with four lines above them.
Octave, small, four times marked. The eighth octave, represented by small letters with four lines above them.
Octave, small, once-marked. The fifth octave, indicated by small letters with one line above them.
Octave, small, six times marked. The tenth octave, indicated by small letters with six lines above them.
Octave, small, thrice-marked. The seventh octave, indicated by small letters with three lines above them.
Octave, small, twice-marked. The sixth octave, indicated by small letters with two lines above them.
Octaves, short. Those lower octaves of an organ the extreme keys of which, on account of the omission of some of the intermediate notes, lie nearer to each other than those of the full octave.
Octave staff. A system of notation introduced by a Mr. Adams of New Jersey, which consists of three groups of lines combined, comprising three octaves of ordinary vocal music, dispensing with flats and sharps, and giving to each tone its own position.
Octave stop. An organ stop an octave above corresponding stops.
Octave, triple. The tri-diapason of the Greeks; a twenty-second.
Octave trumpet stop. An organ stop an octave higher than the ordinary trumpet stop.
Octave twelfth stop. An organ stop the scale of which is an octave above the twelfth.
Octavflötchen, *Ger.* (ŏk-tăf-flŏt-kh'n.) An octave flute; a flageolet.
Octavflöte, *Ger.* (ŏk-tăf-flŏ-tĕ.) Octave flute, flageolet; also an organ stop of four feet scale.
Octavflötlein, *Ger.* (ŏk-tăf-flŏt-līn.) An octave flute.
Octavilla, *Spa.* (ŏk-tă-vĕl-yä.) An octave.
Octavin, *Fr.* (ŏk-tă-vănh.) An organ stop of 2 feet scale.
Octavina, *Lat.* (ŏk-tă-vē-nă.) An old stringed instrument resembling a spinet, about three octaves in compass and tuned an octave higher than the spinet and harpsichord.
Octavine, *Fr.* (ŏk-tă-vēn.) The small spinet.
Octavilla supra, *Sp.* (ŏk-tă-vĕl-yä.) An octave higher.
Octet. } A composition for eight parts, or for
Octett. } eight voices.

PRONOUNCING MUSICAL DICTIONARY. 143

ă *als*, ă *add*, ă *arm*, ĕ *eve*, ĕ *end*, ī *ice*, ĭ *ill*, ō *old*, ŏ *odd*, ô *dove*, oo *moon*, ū *lute*, ŭ *but*, ü *French sound*.

OCTE

Octétto, *It.* (ŏk-tăt-tō.) An octet.
Octiphonium, *Lat.* (ŏk-tĭ-fō-nĭ-ŭm.) A vocal composition in eight parts.
Octo-bass. A stringed instrument invented by M. Vuillaume, of Paris,—the low octave of the violincello. It is of colossal size, with three strings, and for the left hand there are moveable keys, by which the string is pressed on the frets placed on the finger-board, with seven other pedal keys for the foot of the player. The sounds are full and strong, of great power without roughness.
Octochord, *Lat.* (ŏk-tō-kŏrd.) An instrument like a lute, with eight strings.
Octogenary. (ŏk-tō-jĕ-nā-ry.) An instrument of eight strings.
Octosilabico, *Spa.* (ŏk-tō-sĭ-lä-bĭ-kō.) Consisting of eight syllables.
Octuor, *Fr.* (ŏk-twŏr.) A piece in eight parts, or for eight voices or instruments.
Ode. A Greek word signifying an air or song; a lyrical composition, of greater length and variety than a song, resembling the cantata.
Odelet. A short ode.
Odem, *Ger.* (ō-dĕm.) The breath; see *Athem*.
Odéon, *Ger.* (ō-dā-ōn.) ⎫ A circular building in
Odeum, *Lat.* (ō-dē-ŭm.) ⎭ which the ancient Greeks and Romans held their festivals; a concert room or hall for musical performance.
Oder, *Ger.* (ō-dĕr.) Or, or else; *für ein oder zwei Claviere*, for one or two manuals.
Odicum, *Gr.* (ō-dĭ-kŭm.) Name given by the ancient Greeks to that part of practical music which concerned vocal performance.
Odische musik, *Ger.* (ō-dĭ-shē moo-zĭk.) Vocal music.
Œuvre, *Fr.* (ŭvr.) Work, composition, piece—a term used in numbering a composer's published works in the order of their publication.
Œuvre premier, *Fr.* (ŭvr prĕ-mĭ-ā.) The first work.
Offen-flöte, *Ger.* (ŏf-f'n flō-tĕ.) An open flute, organ stop; see also *Clarabella*.
Ofertorio, *Spa.* (Ō-fĕr-tō-rĭ-ō.) Offertory.
Offertoire, *Fr.* (ŏf-fĕr-twär.) ⎫ A hymn,
Offertório, *It.* (ŏf-fĕr-tō-rē-ō.) ⎬ prayer,
Offertorium, *Lat.* (ŏf-fĕr-tō-rĭ-ŭm.) ⎪ anthem,
Offertory, *Eng.* (ŏf-fĕr-tō-ry.) ⎭ or instrumental piece sung or played during the collection of the offertory.
Officium, *Lat.* (ŏf-fĭ-shĭ-ŭm.) The mass.
Officium defunctorum, *Lat.* (ŏf-fĭ-shĭ-um dĕ-fŭnk-tō-rŭm.) A requiem or mass for the dead.
Officium diurnum, *Lat.* (ŏf-fĭ-shĭ-um dī-ŭr-nŭm.) The *horæ*, the day service in the Catholic church.
Officium divinum, *Lat.* (ŏf-fĭ-shĭ-um dĭ-vē-nŭm.) High mass.
Officium matutinum, *Lat.* (ŏf-fĭ-shĭ-um mă-tŭ-tĭ-nŭm.) Early mass.
Officium nocturnum, *Lat.* (ŏf-fĭ-shĭ-um nŏk-tŭr-nŭm.) The *Hora* sung at night.
Officium vespertinum, *Lat.* (ŏf-fĭ-shĭ-um vĕs-pĕr-tĭ-nŭm.) Vespers, evening service.
Oficleida, *It.* (o-fē-klā-dă.) ⎫ The ophicleide; a
Oficleide, *It.* (o-fē-klā-dĕ.) ⎭ French bass horn
Ogdoastich, *Ger.* (ŏg-dō-ăs-tĭkh.) A poem of eight lines.

OPER

Ohne, *Ger.* (ō-nĕ.) Without.
Ohne begletiungen, *Ger.* (ō-nĕ bĕ-glā-toong-g'n.) Without accompaniments.
Ohne pedale, *Ger.* (ō-nĕ pĕ-dä-lĕ.) Without the pedals.
Oktave, *Ger.* (ŏk-lä-fĕ.) Octave, eighth.
Olio. A miscellaneous collection of musical pieces.
Olivettes, *Fr.* (Ō-lĭ-rĕt.) The dances of the peasants in Province after the olives are gathered.
Ollapodrida, *Spa.* (ol-lä-pō-drē-dă.) An olio.
Olmos, *Gr.* (ŏl-mōs.) The mouth of the bombix, an ancient wind instrument.
Omerti, *Hin.* (ō-mĕr-tē.) One of the earliest bowed instruments.
Omnes, *Lat.* (ŏm-nĕs.) ⎫ All; see *Tutti*.
Omnia, *Lat.* (ŏm-nĭ-ä.) ⎭
Once marked octave. The name given in Germany to the notes between and inclusive; these notes are expressed by small letters with one short stroke.
Ondeggiaménto, *It.* (ŏn-dăd-jĕ-ă-măn-tō.) Waving; an undulating or tremulous motion of the sound; also a *close shake* on the violin.
Ondeggiánte, *It.* (ŏn-dăd-jĕ-ăn-tĕ.) Waving, undulating, trembling.
Ondeggiare, *It.* (ŏn-dăd-jĕ-ă-rĕ.) Wave the voice.
Ondeggiare la máno, *It.* (ŏn-dăd-jĕ-ă-rĕ lă mă-nō.) An expression signifying that the hand in beating time must be waived to mark the last part of the measure.
Ondulé, *Fr.* (ŏnh-dū-lă.) Waiving, trembling.
Onduliren, *Ger.* (ŏn-doo-lē-r'n.) A tremulous tone in singing or in playing the violin, etc.
Ongarese, *It.* (ŏn-gă-rā-zĕ.) ⎫ Hungarian.
Ongherese, *It.* (ŏn-ghĕ-rā-zĕ.) ⎭
Ongleur, *Fr.* (ŏnh-glŭr.) An old term for a performer on the lyre, harp, etc.
Onzieme, *Fr.* (ŏnh-zhĭ-ām.) Eleventh.
Open diapason. An organ stop, generally made of metal, and thus called because the pipes are open at the top. It commands the whole scale, and is the most important stop of the instrument.
Open harmony. See Dispersed Harmony.
Open note. A note on the open string of a violin, etc.
Open pedal. The right hand pedal of a pianoforte; that which raises the dampers and allows the vibrations of the strings to continue.
Open stop. That which regulates the open pipes.
Open string. The string of a violin, etc., when not pressed by the finger.
Open tone. A tone produced on an open string.
Open unison stop. The open diapason stop.
Oper, *Ger.* (ō-pĕr.) ⎫ A drama set to music, for
Opera, *It.* (ō-pĕ-rä.) ⎭ voices and instruments, airs, choruses, etc., and with scenery, decorations and action. The term is also applied to any *work*, or publication of a composer; see also *Opus*.
Opera buffe, *It.* (ō-pĕ-rä boof-fĕ.) Comic opera.
Opera, comic. An opera interspersed with light songs, amusing incidents, dances, etc.
Opera di cámera, *It.* (ō-pĕ-rä dĕ kă-mĕ-rä.) A short opera to be performed in a room.

ā ale, ä add, ă arm, ē eve, ĕ end, ī ice, ĭ ill, ō old, ŏ odd, ô dove, oo moon, ū lute, ŭ but, ü French sound.

Oper-dichter, *Ger.* (ō-pĕ-rä dĭkh-tĕr.) An operatic poet; writer of operatic librettos.

Opera glass. An optical instrument of low magnifying power designed to enable a person to see with more distinctness at the opera, theatre, etc.

Opera, grand. An opera consisting of a deep and intricate plot and a great variety of incidental events.

Opern-gucker, *Ger.* ŏp-ĕrn goŏk-ĕr.) An opera glass.

Opern-haus, *Ger.* (ŏp-ĕrn hous.) Opera house.

Opera house. A building erected with special regard to musical effects with all the scenes and appliances required for operatic performances.

Opéra héroïque, *Fr.* (ō-pä-rä hā-rō-ēk.) An heroic opera.

Opera libretto. The text of an opera; a small book containing the words of an opera.

Opera prima, *It.* (ō-pā-rä prē-mä.) First production.

Opern-saal, *Ger.* (ō-pĕrn säl.) An opera saloon.

Opern-sängerin, *Ger.* (ō-pern sän-ghĕ-rĭn.) An opera singer.

Opera season. The period during which operatic performances take place.

Opera seconda, *It.* (ō-pā-rä sĕ-kōn-dä.) Second production.

Opera sémi séria, *It.* (ō-pā-rä sā-mē sĕ-rē-ä.) A semi-serious opera of a romantic cast, neither comic nor tragic.

Opera séria, *It.* (ō-pā-rä sĕ-rē-ä.) } A serious
Opéra sérieux, *Fr.* (ō-pä-rä sĕ-rĭ-ŭh.) } rious, or tragic opera.

Operatic. In the style of an opera.

Operatic concert. A performance of music selected from the opera.

Opera troupe. A company of singers associated together for the purpose of giving operas.

Opern-zettel, *Ger.* ō-pĕrn tsĕt-t'l.) A play bill of an opera.

Operétta, *It.* (ō-pĕ-rät-tä.) } A short opera,
Operette, *Ger.* (ō-pĕ-rĕt-tĕ.) } sometimes interspersed with dialogue.

Operist, *Ger.* (ō-pĕ-rĭst.) An opera singer.

Oper-mädchen, *Ger.* (ō-pĕr mäd-khĕn.) Opera girl, opera singer.

Opern-haus, *Ger.* (ō-pĕrn hous.) Opera house.

Opern-sänger, *Ger.* (ō-pĕrn säng-ĕr.) Opera singer.

Ophicleide, (ŏf-ĭ-klīd.) A large bass wind instrument of brass, of modern invention, sometimes used in large orchestras, but chiefly in military music. It has a compass of three octaves and the tone is loud and of deep pitch.

Ophicleide stop. The most powerful manual reed stop known, in an organ, of 8 or 4 feet scale and is usually placed upon a separate soundboard, with a great pressure of wind.

Ophicleidist. A performer on the ophicleide.

Opus, *Lat.* (ō-pŭs.) } Work; composition: as,
Opus, *Ger.* (ō-poos.) } Op. 1, the first work or publication of a composer.

Opusculum, *Lat.* (ō-pŭs-kū-lŭm.) A short, or little work.

Opus postumum, *Lat.* (ō-pŭs pŏs-tŭ-mŭm.) A posthumous work, published after the death of a composer.

Oracion, *Spa.* (ō-rä-thē-ōn.) Oration: a part of the mass.

Orage, *Fr.* (ō-rash.) A *storm;* the name of an organ stop intended to imitate the noise of a storm.

Oratoire, *Fr.* (ŏr-ä-twär.) Oratorio.

Oratorio. A species of musical drama consisting of airs, recitatives, trios, choruses, etc. It is founded upon some Scriptural narrative, and performed without the aid of scenery and action.

Oratório, *It.* (ō-rä-tō-rĭ-ō.) }
Oratorium, *Lat.* (ō-rä-tō-rĭ-ŭm.) } Oratorio.
Oratorium, *Ger.* (ō-rä-tō-rĭ-oom.) }

Orchestra. That portion of a theatre or concert room where the musicians play; the term is also applied to the performers themselves, collectively.

Orchester, *Ger.* (ŏr-khĕs-tĕr.) }
Orchéstra, *It.* (ōr-kĕs-trä.) } The orchestra.
Orchestre, *Fr.* (ŏr-kĕstr.) }

Orchester-verein, *Ger.* (ōr-kĕs-tĕr vĕr-rĭn.) An orchestral society; instrumental association.

Orchéographie, *Fr.* (rō-kā-ŏ-gräf-ē.) }
Orchestrik, *Ger.* (ōr-kĕs-trĭk.) } art of scientific dancing for the ballet.

Orchestique, *Fr.* (ŏr-kĕs-tēk.) An old term, meaning the art of dancing; belonging to dancing.

Orchestra, full. A general combination of stringed and wind instruments.

Orchestral. Belonging to the orchestra.

Orchestral concert. A performance of miscellaneous music by an orchestra.

Orchestral music. Music composed for a number of instruments.

Orchestra, stringed. An orchestra formed exclusively of stringed instruments.

Orchestration. The performance of an orchestra; the arranging of music for an orchestra; scoring; instrumentation.

Orchestrer, *Fr.* (ŏr-kĕs-trä.) To score.

Orchestrina. (ŏr-kĕs-trē-nä.) } An instrument
Orchestrion. (ŏr-kĕs-trĭ-ōn.) } combining the power and variety of a full orchestra with crescendo and diminuendo.

Orden de epistola, *Spa.* (ōr-dĕn dĕ ĕ-pĕs-tō-lä.) The office of singing the epistles at the mass.

Ordinário, *It.* (ōr-dē-nä-rē-ō.) Ordinary, usual, common; *a tempo ordinário,* in the usual time.

Ordine, *It.* (ōr-dē-nĕ.) The arrangement of many parts to make a whole.

Ordine di quatro corde, *It.* (ōr-dē-nĕ dē quä-trō kōr-dĕ.) A term in ancient music applied to a tetrachord, and signifying a whole one, composed of, and divisible by, four chords.

Ordines, *Lat.* (ōr-dī-nĕs.) The register, or stop, in an organ.

Orécchia, *It.* (ō-ra-kĕ-ä.) } The ear.
Orécchio, *It.* (ō-ra-kĕ-ō.) }

Orecchia musicale, *It.* (ō-rät-kĕ-ä moo-zĕ-kä-lĕ.) A musical ear.

Orecchiante, *It.* (ō-rät-kĕ-äu-tĕ.) Singing by ear.

Orécchi, *It. pl.* (ō-rät-kĕ.) }
Orécchie, *It. pl.* (ō-rät-kĕ-ĕ.) } The ears.

ă *ale,* ă *add,* ă *arm,* ē *eve,* ĕ *end,* ĭ *ice,* ĭ *ill,* ō *old,* ŏ *odd,* ċ *dove,* oo *moon,* ū *lute,* ŭ *but,* ü *French sound.*

OREI

Oreille musicale, *Fr.* (ō-rā-yüh mū-zĭ-kăl.) A musical ear.
Oreja, *Spa.* (ō-rā-hā.) The ear.
Orfidigh, *Iri.* (ŏr-fē-dĕh.) Musicians of the orchestra.
Organ. The largest and most harmonious of wind instruments of music, of very ancient origin, used in churches and large concert halls. It contains numerous pipes of various kinds and dimensions and of multifarious tones and powers; in solemnity, grandeur, and rich volume of tone it stands preëminent over every other instrument.
Organarii, *Lat.* (ŏr-găn-ā-rĭ-ē.) Among the ancients, those who performed on the hydraulic organ, and controlled it by means of keys and stops.
Organ, barrel. A hand organ.
Organ bellows. A machine for supplying the pipes of an organ with wind.
Organ blower. One who works the bellows of an organ.
Organ, buffet. A very small organ.
Organ, cabinet. An improvement on the reed organ, designed for the parlor and for small churches.
Organ, choir. In an organ with three rows of keys, the first or lower row, used to accompany the choir, solos, duets, etc.
Organe, *Fr.* (ŏr-găn.) An organ.
Organ, enharmonic. | An instrument of
Organ, enharmonic. | American origin, containing three or four times the usual number of distinct sounds within the compass of an octave, furnishing the precise intervals for every key, the tones comprising the scale of each key being produced by pressing a pedal corresponding to its key note.
Organétto, *It.* (ŏr-găn-ăt-tō.) A small organ.
Organ, full. An organ performance with all the registers or stops in use.
Organ, great. In an organ with three rows of keys, usually the middle row, so called because it contains the greatest number of stops, and the pipes are voiced louder than those in the swell or choir organ.
Organ, hand. A common wind instrument carried about the street, consisting of a cylinder, turned by hand, the revolution of which causing the machinery to act upon the keys, produces a number of well-known airs and tunes.
Organ, harmonium. A reed instrument, the reeds of which are voiced to imitate organ stops.
Organ, hydraulic. An invention of Ctesibius, of Alexandria. Its construction is unknown.
Organic. Epithet applied by the ancients to that part of practical music which concerned instrumental performance.
Organical. Relating to the organ.
Organillo, *Spa.* (ŏr-găn-ăl-yō.) A chamber organ, a parlor organ.
Organique, *Fr.* (ŏr-găn-ăk.) Relating to the organ.
Orgel musik, *Ger.* (ŏr-gh'l moo-zĭk.) Organ music.
Organist. A player on the organ.
Organista. *It.* (ŏr-găn-ăs-tā.) } An organist.
Organista, *Spa.* (ŏr-găn-ĕs-tā.) }

ORGA

Organistic. An epithet applied to music composed for the organ.
Organi vocáli, *It. pl.* (ŏr-gă-nē vō-kā-lē.) The vocal organs.
Organizar, *Spa.* (ŏr-găn-ĭ-thăr.) To tune an organ.
Organizare, *Lat.* (ŏr-găn-ĭ-zā-rē.) To organize, to sing in parts.
Organized lyre. An instrument by which the performer can imitate the lyre, harp, pianoforte, etc., the instrument being fingered like the guitar lyre.
Organized pianoforte. An instrument consisting of an organ and pianoforte, so conjoined that the same set of keys serve for both, or for either singly, at the pleasure of the performer.
Organizing. Arranging in parts.
Organ loft. That part of the gallery of a church where the organ is placed.
Organ melodeon. A melodeon having a register of stops similar to those of an organ.
Organ, mouth. The shepherd's pipe; Pandean pipes.
Organ movement. The complex machinery of the interior of an organ.
Organ music. Voluntaries, anthems, chants, etc., composed for the organ, or which require the organ to accompany them.
Organo, *It.* (ŏr-gă-nō.) } An organ.
Organo, *Spa.* (ŏr-gă-nō.) }
Organo-chordium, *Lat.* (ŏr-gă-nō kŏr-dĭ-ŭm.) An instrument invented by Vogler, at Stockholm, in 1797.
Organo-lyricon, *It.* (ŏr-gă-nō lĭr-ē-kŏn.) A French instrument similar to an organ but more complex, and giving the tones of a greater number of instruments.
Organo di campána, *It.* (ŏr-gă-nō dē kăm-pā-nā.) An organ with bells.
Organographie, *Lat.* (ŏr-găn-ō-grăf-ē.) A description of an organ and all its various stops.
Organologie. *Lat.* (ŏr-găn-ō-lō-jē.) Instructions for using all the various organ stops.
Organo picciolo, *It.* (ŏr-gă-nō pĕt-tshē-ō-lō.) A small or chamber organ.
Organo pléno, *It.* (ŏr-gă-nō pē-ā-nō.) } The
Organo pléno, *Lat.* (ŏr-gă-nō plā-no.) } full organ with all the stops drawn.
Organo portátile, *It.* (ŏr-gă-nō pŏr-tā-tē-lē.) A portable organ.
Organo simplex. *Lat.* (ŏr-gă-nō sĭm-plĕx.) A term occurring frequently in the writings of the musical monks, and seems to mean the unisonous accompaniment of a single voice in the versicles of the service.
Organorum intabulaturæ, *Lat.* (ŏr-gă-nō-rŭm ĭn-tă-bū-lă-tū-rē.) The general name formerly given to voluntaries, preludes and all compositions for the organ.
Organ, parlor. An organ adapted by its size and tone to a parlor.
Organ, partial. A series of pipes collected in one group and forming a part, though complete in itself, of the entire organ.
Organ point. A long pedal note, or stationary bass, upon which is formed a series of chords, or harmonic progressions.

ă *ale*, ă *add*, ä *arm*, ĕ *eve*, ĕ *end*, ī *ice*, ĭ *ill*, ō *old*, ŏ *odd*, ô *dove*, oo *moon*, ū *lute*, ŭ *but*, ü *French sound*.

ORGA

Organ, pneumatic. An organ moved by wind, so called by the ancients to distinguish it from the hydraulic organ, which is moved by water.
Organ, reed. An organ of small size, the keys of which open valves that allow the wind from the bellows to act upon reeds.
Organ stop. A collection of pipes of like tone and quality, passing through the whole or a greater part of the compass of an organ; a register.
Organ, swell. In an organ with three rows of keys, usually the upper row, controlling one or more sets of pipes enclosed by a set of sliding shutters, the opening or closing of which by the swell pedal increases or diminishes the tone by degrees, at the pleasure of the performer.
Organ-tone. A tone that commences, continues, and closes with an uniform degree of power.
Organum. A word used in various senses by the ancient composers. Sometimes it meant the organ itself; at other times it meant that kind of choral accompaniment which comprehended the whole harmony then known, also, a brazen vessel forming a principal part of the hydraulic organ.
Organuto, *It.* (ōr-gä-noo-tō.) Organical.
Orgel, *Ger.* (ōr-ghĕl.) An organ.
Orgel-bälge, *Ger.* (ōr-ghĕl bäl-ghĕ.) Organ bellows.
Orgel-bank, *Ger.* (ōr-ghĕl bänk.) Organist's seat.
Orgel-bauer, *Ger.* (ōr-ghĕl bou-ĕr.) Organ builder.
Orgel-bühne, *Ger.* (ōr-ghĕl bü-nĕ.) ⎱ Organ
Orgel-chor, *Ger.* (ōr-ghĕl kōr.) ⎰ loft.
Orgel-gehäuse, *Ger.* (ōr-ghĕl ghĕ-hoy-ze.) Organ case.
Orgel-kasten, *Ger.* (ōr-ghĕl käs-t'n.) A cabinet organ; organ case.
Orgel-klang, *Ger.* (ōr-ghĕl kläng.) Sound or tone of an organ.
Orgel-kunst, *Ger.* (ōr-ghĕl koonst.) The art of organ playing; art of constructing an organ.
Orgeln, *Ger.* (ōr-gĕln.) To play on the organ.
Orgel-pfeife, *Ger.* (ōr-gĕl pfī-fĕ.) Organ pipe.
Orgel-platz, *Ger.* (ōr-ghĕl pläts.) Organ loft.
Orgel-punkt, *Ger.* (ōr-g'l poonkt.) Organ point.
Orgel-schule, *Ger.* (ōr-g'l shoo-lĕ.) School or method for the organ.
Orgel-spiel, *Ger.* (ōr-g'l spēl.) Playing on an organ; piece played on an organ.
Orgel-spieler, *Ger.* (ōr-g'l spē-lĕr.) An organ player.
Orgel-stein, *Ger.* (ōr-g'l stīn.) Pan's pipes.
Orgel-stimme, *Ger.* (ōr-g'l stĭm-mĕ.) Row of pipes in an organ.
Orgel-stücke, *Ger.* (ōr-g'l stü-kĕ.) Organ pieces.
Orgel-treter, *Ger.* (ōr-g'l trĕt-ĕr.) Organ treader, bellows tender, or bellows blower.
Orgel-virtuose, *Ger.* (ōr-g'l vĭr-too-ō-zĕ.) An accomplished organ player.
Orgel-zug, *Ger.* (ōr-g'l tsoog.) Organ stop, or row of pipes.
Orgue, *Fr.* (ōrg.) An organ.
Orgue à touches, *Fr.* (ōrg ä too-shā.) Finger organ.

ORQU

Orgue de salon, *Fr.* (ōrg düh sä-lōnh.) ⎱
Orgue expressif, *Fr.* (ōrg ĕgz-prā-sēf.) ⎰ The harmonium.
Orgue hydraulique, *Fr.* (ōrg hī-drō-lēk.) Hydraulic organ; water organ.
Orgue plein, *Fr.* (ōrg plănh.) Full organ; all the stops drawn.
Orgue portatif, *Fr.* (ōrg pōr-tä-tēf.)
Orgue portatif de barbarie, *Fr.* (ōrg pōr- ⎱ tä-tēf düh bär-bä-rē.)
A portable organ, a barrel organ, a street organ.
Orgue positif, *Fr.* (ōrg pō-zĭ-tēf.) The choir organ in a large organ; also a small *fixed* organ, thus named in opposition to a *portative* organ.
Orgues a eau, *Fr.* (ōrg sä ō.) Water organs.
Orgues de barbarie, *Fr.* (ōrg düh bär-bä-rē.) Barbarian organs — an epithet applied by the French to street organs.
Oricalco, *It.* (ō-rē-käl-kō.) Trumpet.
Orificio, *It.* (ō-rē-fē-tshē-ō.) ⎱ The orifice of organ
Orifizio, *It.* (ō-rē-fē-tsē-ō.) ⎰ gan pipes, in front and at the top.
Originalität, *Ger.* (ō-rĭg-ĭ-näl-ĭ-tät.) Originality in composition.
Original key. The key in which a composition is written.
Originell, *Ger.* (ō-rĭg-ĭ-nĕll.) Original.
Orieus. The name of one of the ten tones used in the middle ages.
Orlo, *Spa.* (ōr-lō.) A wind instrument.
Ornamental counterpoint. A kind of counterpoint admitting the use and mixture of every kind of note.
Ornamental notes. Appoggiaturas, grace notes; all notes not forming an essential part of the harmony, but introduced as embellishments.
Ornaménti, *It. pl.* (ōr-nä-mān-tē.) Ornaments, graces, embellishments, as the *appoggiatúra*, turn, shake, etc.
Ornataménte, *It.* (ōr-nä-tä-mān-tĕ.) ⎱ Orna-
Ornáto, *It.* (ōr-nä-tō.) ⎰ mented, adorned, embellished.
Ornate. (ōr-nāt.) A style of music, or musical execution, highly ornamental.
Ornements, *Fr.* (ōrn-mänh.) Graces, embellishments.
Orotund. A mode of intonation directly from the larynx, which has a fullness, clearness, smoothness, and ringing quality which form the highest perfection of the human voice.
Orpharion. (ōr-fā-rĭ-ōn.) An old instrument of the lute species, with more strings and frets than the lute; the strings were of wire.
Orphéon, *Fr.* (ōr-fā-ōnh.) ⎱ Species of
Orphéoron, *Fr.* (ōr-fā-ō-rōnh.) ⎰ musical instruments, of which nothing is now known.
Orpheus. (ōr-fē-ŭs.) A poet in Greek mythology, said to have the power of moving inanimate bodies by the music of his lyre.
Orpheus-harmonic. An instrument of the piano and harpsichord class.
Orphica. Certain mystic poems, incorrectly ascribed to Orpheus.
Orphic hymns. Hymns pertaining to Orpheus.
Orquesta, *Spa.* (ōr-kĕs-tä.) ⎱
Orquestra, *Spa.* (ōr-kĕs-trä.) ⎰ An orchestra.

PRONOUNCING MUSICAL DICTIONARY. 147

ă *ale,* ă *add,* ă *arm,* ĕ *eve,* ŏ *end,* ī *ice,* ĭ *ill,* ō *old,* ŏ *odd,* ō *dove,* oo *moon,* ū *lute,* ŭ *but,* ü *French sound.*

ORRI

Orrisonante, *It.* (ŏr-rē-zō-nän-tĕ.) Horrid sounding.
Orthian, *Gr.* (ŏr-thī-än.) A term applied by the ancients to a dactylic nome or song.
Orthian mode. In the Orthian style; one of the Greek musical modes.
Orthisch, *Gr.* (ŏr-thish.) } High, acute.
Orthisch, *Ger.* (ŏr-tish.) }
Orthoëpik, *Gr.* (ŏr-tho-ă-pīk.) } The art of cor-
Orthoëpik, *Ger.* (ŏr-tō-ă-pik.) } rect verbal declamation in singing.
Orthophony. (ŏr-thŏf-ō-ny.) A systematic cultivation of the voice.
Orthotonie, *Gr.* (ŏr-thō-tō-nē.) } Correct ac-
Orthotonie, *Ger.* (ŏr-tō-tō-nē.) } centuation in singing.
Osanna, *It.* (ō-zän-nä.) Hosanna.
Osannare, *It.* (ō-zän-nä-rē.) Tosing hosannas.
Oscillation. The vibration of tones in organ tuning, etc.
Oscuro, *It.* (ōs-koo-rō.) Obscure; a term applied to black notes.
Osservánza, *It.* (ōs-sĕr-vän-tsä.) Observation, attention, strictness in keeping time.
Osia, *It.* (ō-zē-ä.) } Or, otherwise, or else.
Ossia, *It.* (ōs-sē-ä.) }
Ossia piu fácile, *It.* (ōs-sē-ä pē-oo fä-tchē-lē.) Or else in this more easy manner.
Ostináto, *It.* (ōs-tē-nä-tō.) Obstinate, continuous, unceasing; adhering to some peculiar melodial figure, or group of notes.
Otacoustic. Assisting the sense of hearing.
Oter ce qui assourdit, *Fr.* (ō-tä sŭh kĕ äs-soor-dē.) To unmuffle a bell.
Otez les anches, *Fr.* (ō-tä lĕ sänhsh.) Remove, or push in the reeds.
Othem, *Ger.* (ō-tĕm.) The breath.
Otium, *Lat.* (ō-shĭ-ŭm.) Adagio, slowly, with grace and ease.
Ottardo, *It.* (ŏt-tär-dō.) Octachord; a system of eight sounds.
Ottáva, *It.* (ŏt-tä-vä.) An octave, an eighth.
Ottáva álta, *It.* (ŏt-tä-vä äl-tä.) The octave above, an octave higher; marked thus, 8va.
Ottáva bássa, *It.* (ŏt-tä-vä bäs-sä.) The octave below, marked thus, 8va bássa.

OXYT

Ottavarima, *It.* (ŏt-tä-vä-rē-mä.) Italian stanzas of eight-rhymed verses.
Ottava supra, *It.* (ŏt-tä-vä soo-prä.) The octave above.
Ottavina, *It.* (ŏt-tä-vē-nä.) The higher octave.
Ottavino, *It.* (ŏt-tä-vē-nō.) The *flauto piccolo,* or small octave flute.
Ottemole. A group of eight notes, marked with the figure 8.
Ottétto, *It.* (ŏt-tĕt-tō.) A composition in eight parts, or for eight voices or instruments.
Ottupia, *It.* (ŏt-too-pē-ä.) An expression implying common time, or a measure of four times, marked with a C, or semicircle placed at the beginning of the movement.
Ou, *Fr.* (oo.) Or.
Ougab, *Heb.* (oo-gäb.) An ancient instrument formed of reeds of unequal lengths bound together.
Ouie, *Fr.* (oo-ē.) The hearing; *l'ouie d'un instrument;* the sound-hole of an instrument.
Outer voices. The highest and lowest voices.
Out of tune. Want of tune; discord.
Ouvert, *Fr.* (oo-vär.) Open.
Ouverture, *Fr.* (oo-vär-tūr.) } An introduc-
Overtúra, *It.* (ō-vĕr-too-rä.) } tory symphony
Overtüre, *Ger.* (ō-fĕr-too-rĕ.) } to an oratorio,
Overture, *Eng.* (ō-vĕr-tshŭr.) } opera, etc., generally consisting of three or four different movements; also an independent piece for a full band or orchestra, in which case it is called a *concert overture.*
Overtúra di bállo, *It.* (ō-vĕr-too-rä dē bäl-lō.) An overture composed upon or introducing dance melodies.
Overstrung pianoforte. Where the strings of at least two of the lowest octaves are raised, running diagonally in respect to the other strings above them.
Ovraggio, *It.* (ō-vrăd-jē-ō.) Opus, work.
Oxipyeni, *Gr.* (ŏx-ĭ-pĭk-nē.) Name given by the ancient Greeks to high sounds.
Oxyphones, *Gr.* (ŏx-ĭ-fō-nōs.) The person who sung a high part.
Oxyphony. Acuteness or shrillness of voice.
Oxytone. An acute sound.

ă *ale*, ă *add*, ä *arm*, ĕ *eve*, ŏ *end*, ī *ice*, ĭ *ill*, ō *old*, ŏ *odd*, ô *dove*, oo *moon*, ū *lute*, ŭ *but*, ü *French sound*.

PACA

Pacaménte, *It.* (pä-kä-tä-*män*-tĕ.) Placidly, quietly, calmly.

Pæan. ⎱ Among the *ancients* a song of rejoicing
Pean. ⎰ in honor of Apollo; a loud and joyous song; a song of triumph.

Pages, dancing. Boys who take part in the services of the cathedral at Seville, dancing with castanets in their hands and singing with the orchestra.

Pagina, *It.* (*pä*-jē-nä.) A page or folio.

Paisana, *Spa.* (pä-ī-*zä*-nä.) A Spanish country dance.

Palco, *It.* (päl-kō.) The stage of a theatre.

Palillo, *Spa.* (pä-*lĕl*-yō.) A drumstick.

Pallet. A spring valve in the wind chest of an organ covering a channel leading to a pipe or pipes.

Palmadilla, *Spa.* (päl-mä-*dĕl*-yä.) A Spanish dance.

Palmelodicon. An instrument similar to the harmonica, played upon by the friction of the fingers of the performer.

Palmula, *Lat.* (päl-*mū*-lä.) The keys of an instrument.

Palote, *Spa.* (pä-*lō*-tĕ.) A drumstick.

Paloteado, *Spa.* (pä-lō-tĕ-*ä*-dō.) Rustic dance performed with sticks.

Pambe. A small Indian drum.

Pamula, *Lat.* (pä-*mū*-lä.) An old name for the manual keys of an organ, etc.

Pan. One of the deities in Grecian mythology, so called because he exhilirated the minds of all the gods with the music of his *pipe* which he invented, and with the *cithern*, which he played skilfully as soon as he was born.

Panarmion, *Gr.* (pä-*när*-mī-ŏn.) A wind instrument used by the ancient Greeks, consisting, as far as known, of an assemblage of pipes, each hole being capable of emitting *three* and sometimes more sounds.

Panathenae, *Gr.* (pä-nä-*thä*-nē.) An Athenian festival at which contests in singing and playing on the flute and cithera were held.

Panaylon, *Gr.* (pä-*nā*-lŏn.) The G flute, a new species of flute invented by Prof. Bayr, which has fifteen keys and five whole tones below added to its compass; the inventor produced from it double notes, as thirds, fourths, sixths, etc., which in the softer keys sound like musical glasses.

Pandean. An epithet formed from the name of *Pan*, and applied to any music adapted to the *Fistulæ Panis*, or Pipes of Pan.

Pandean pipes. ⎱ One of the most ancient
Pan's pipes. ⎰ and simple of musical instruments; it was made of reeds or tubes of different lengths, fastened together and tuned to each other, stopped at the bottom and blown into by the mouth at the top.

Pandect, musical. A treatise comprising the entire harmonic science.

Panderada, *Spa.* (pän-dä-*rä*-dä.) A number of timbrels joined in concert.

Panderetear, *Spa.* (pän-dĕ-rä-tĕ-*är*.) To play on the timbrel.

Pandero, *Spa.* (pän-dä-rō.) A timbrel.

PARA

Pandoran, *Gr.* (pän-*dō*-rän.) ⎫ An ancient
Pandóra, *It.* (pän-*dō*-rä.) ⎪ stringed instru-
Pandore. *Ger.* (pän-*dō*-rĕ.) ⎬ ment resem-
Pandúra, *It.* (pän-*doo*-rä.) ⎪ bling a lute, a
Pandure, *Fr.* (pänh-*dūr*.) ⎭ small Polish lute, a Bandore; see Bandora.

Panharmonicon. An automatic instrument invented by Maelzel, which produced the sounds of a variety of instruments.

Pantaleone. (*pän*-tä-lĕ-ō-nĕ.) An old instrument invented by Hebenstreit, and much celebrated in the beginning of the eighteenth century. It was more than nine feet long, nearly four feet wide and had one hundred and eighty-six strings of gut, which were played on with two small sticks like the dulcimer.

Pantalon, *Fr.* (pänh-tä-lŏnh.) One of the movements of the quadrille; also, the name of an old instrument of the dulcimer species, but larger: see *Pantaleone.*

Pantalonnade, *Fr.* (pänh-tä-lŏnh-*nād*.) A pantaloon dance; a merry dance of buffoons.

Pantomima, *It.* (*pän*-tō-mē-mä.) Pantomime.

Pantomime. An entertainment in which not a word is spoken or sung, but the sentiments are expressed by mimicry and gesticulation accompanied by instrumental music.

Pantomimist. One who acts in a pantomime.

Pantomimo, *It.* (*pän*-tō-mē-mō.) A pantomime player.

Pantomimus, *Lat.* (*pän*-tō-*mĭ*-mŭs.) Pantomime.

Papageno-flüte, *Ger.* (pä-pä-ghēn-ō flōt.) Pan's pipe, mouth organ.

Para, *Gr.* (*pä*-rä.) Near.

Paracontacion. (*pä*-rä-kŏn-*tä*-sī-ōn.) Alternating singing, formerly much in vogue in the Greek church.

Paracrostic. A poetical composition, in which the first verse contains in order, all the letters which commence the remaining verses of the poem.

Parademarsch, *Ger.* (pä-*rä*-dĕ-*märsh*.) Grand march.

Paradetas, *Spa.* (pä-rä-dĕ-*läs*.) A kind of Spanish dance.

Paradiazeuxis, *Gr.* (pä-*rä*-dī-ä-*zūx*-ĭs.) The name given by the ancients to an interval between two tetrachords consisting of one tone.

Paradiddle. A drum beat.

Paradis, *Fr.* (pär-ä-dē.) The upper gallery of a play house.

Paradoxus, *Gr.* (pär-ä-*dŏx*-ŭs.) The winner of the prize in the musical Olympic games of the ancients.

Parafoni suoni, *It.* (pär-ä-*fō*-nē swō-nä.) Sounds having between them the interval of a fourth or fifth, or their double, and therefore concordant.

Para hypate, *Gr.* (*pä*-rä hī-*pä*-tĕ.) The next sound above the gravest of the lowest of the ancient diapason or octave.

Parallel intervals. Intervals passing in two parallel parts in the same direction; consecutive intervals.

Parallel keys. The major and its relative minor.

ă *ale,* ă *add,* ă *arm,* ā *eve,* ĕ *end,* ī *ice,* ĭ *ill,* ō *old,* ŏ *odd,* ô *dove,* oo *moon,* ū *lute,* ŭ *but,* ü *French sound.*

PARA

Parallel motion. When the parts continue on the same degree, and only repeat the same sounds; also, two parts continuing their course and still remaining at exactly the same distance from each other.

Paramese, *Gr.* (pär-ă-mā-zē.) The fifth string of the lyre; see *Hypate.*

Paranete, *Gr.* (păr-ă-nā-tē.) The sixth string of the lyre; see *Hypate.*

Paraphonoi, *Gr.* (pă-rā-fō-noi.) Certain combinations in ancient music, which were neither concords nor discords, but between both.

Paraphrase. An explanation of some text or passage in a more clear and ample manner than is expressed in the words of the author.

Parat, *Wel.* (pă-rät.) To sing.

Paratretos, *Gr.* (pă-rä-trā-tōs.) A kind of flute for playing mournful airs.

Paratripemata, *Gr.* (pă-rä-trē-pē-mā-tä.) Name given by the ancients to the side apertures of their flutes.

Pardessus de viole, *Fr.* (pär-dăs-sū dūh vē-ŏl.) The treble viol.

Parfait, *Fr.* (pär-fā.) Perfect, as to intervals, etc.

Parhypate, *Gr.* (pär-hī-pā-te.) The second string of the lyre; see *Hypate.*

Parisienne, *Fr.* (pă-rē-zī-ĕn.) A patriotic song of the French revolution of 1830.

Parlándo, *It.* (pär-län-dō.) ⎫ Accented; in a
Parlánte, *It.* (pär-län-tē.) ⎬ declamatory style; in a recitative or speaking style.

Parlor organ. A small organ suited to a private dwelling.

Parnassus. A mountain in Greece, celebrated in mythology as sacred to Apollo and the Muses, and famous, also, for the Castilian spring and the temple of Apollo.

Parodía, *It.* (pă-rō-dē-ä.) A parody; music or words slightly altered, and adapted to some new purpose.

Parodiare, *It.* (pă-rō-dē-ä-rē.) To parody, to burlesque.

Parodiste, *Fr.* (pă-rō-dēst.) Author of a parody.

Parodos. (pär-ō-dōs.) The commencement of an ancient Greek chorus, in which the whole chorus used to join.

Parody. Music or words slightly altered and adapted to some new purpose.

Paroles, *Fr.* (pă-rōl.) Words for setting to music.

Part. The music for each separate voice or instrument.

Parte, clarino, *It.* (klä-rē-nō.) The highest or first trumpet part.

Parte, complimentary. That part of a fugue additional to the subject and counter subject.

Párte, *It.* (pär-tē.) A part or portion of a composition; a part or rôle in an opera.

Párte cantánte, *It.* (pär-tē kän-tän-tē.) The singing or vocal part; the principal vocal part, having the melody.

Párte con. parte senza violíni, *It.* (pär-tē kōn, pär-tē sän-tsä vē-ō-lē-nē.) Part with and part without violins.

Parthenia, *Gr.* (pär-thĕn-ĭ-ä.) Songs by a chorus of virgins at festivals among the ancient Greeks.

Parterre, *Fr.* (pär-tărr.) The pit of a theatre.

PASS

Partie, *Fr.* (pär-tē.) See *Párte.*

Partial turn. A turn consisting of the chief note and three small notes, the leading note of which may be either a large or small second above the principal.

Participating tones. Accessory tones.

Particular systems. Among the ancient Greeks, those systems which were composed of at least two intervals.

Parti d'accompagnaménto, *It.* (pär-tē d'äk-kōm-pän-yă-mān-tō.) Accompanying voices.

Parti di ripieno, *It.* (pär-tē dē rē-pē-ā-nō.) Parts not obligato; supplementary parts.

Partie du violon, *Fr.* (pär-tē dū vē-ō-lōnh.) A violin part.

Partien, *Ger.* (pär-tī-ĕn.) Instrumental pieces designed to be performed by viols, lutes, etc.

Parties de remplissage, *Fr.* (pär-tē dŭh ränh-plē-säzh.) Parts which fill up the middle harmony between the bass and upper part.

Partiménti, *It. pl.* (pär-tē-mān-tē.) Exercises for the study of harmony and accompaniment.

Partiménto, *It.* (pär-tē-mān-tō.) An exercise, figured bass; see *Partimenti.*

Partíta, *It.* (pär-tē-tä.) An old term synonymous with *variation.*

Partition, *Fr.* (pär-tē-sī-ōnh) ⎫ A *score,* a
Partitur, *Ger.* (pär-tī-toor.) ⎬ *full score,*
Partitúra, *It.* (pär-tē-too-rä.) ⎪ or entire
Partiziōne, *It.* (pär-tē-tsē-ō-nē.) ⎭ draft of a composition for voices or instruments, or both.

Partito, *It.* (pär-tē-tō.) Scored, divided into parts.

Partitur-spiel, *Ger.* (pär-tē-toor spēl.) Playing from the score.

Part songs. Songs for voices in parts, introduced in Germany in the present century.

Pas, *Fr.* (pă.) A step, a dance.

Passage, *Spa.* (pä-sä-hē.) A transition or change of voice; a passage.

Pas courant, *Fr.* (pă koo-ränh.) The courant step.

Pas de bourrée, *Fr.* (pă dŭh boo-rā.) The bouree step.

Pas de danse, *Fr.* (pă dŭh dänh.) A step, in dancing.

Pas de deux, *Fr.* (pă dŭh dŭh.) A dance by two performers.

Pas de gaillarde, *Fr.* (pă dŭh gä-yärd.) The galliard step.

Pas de hache, *Fr.* (pă dŭh häsh.) Axe or hatchet step; a warlike dance.

Pas de menuet, *Fr.* (pă dŭh mĕ-noo-ā.) The minuet step.

Pas de quatre, *Fr.* (pă dŭh kătr.) A dance by four performers.

Pas de trois, *Fr.* (pă dŭh trwä.) A dance by three performers.

Pas grave, *Fr.* (pă gräv.) The courant step.

Paspie, *Spa.* (päs-pī-ā.) A kind of dance.

Paspy. See *Passepied.*

Pasionero, *Spa.* (pä-sī-ō-nā-rō.) One who sings the passion.

Paso de gargante, *Spa.* (pä-sō dē gär-gän-tā.) Trill of the voice; to quaver.

ā *ate,* ă *add,* ä *arm,* ē *eve,* ĕ *end,* ī *ice,* ĭ *ill,* ō *old,* ŏ *odd,* ô *dove,* oo *moon,* ū *lute,* ŭ *but,* ü *French sound.*

PASR

Pas redoublé, *Fr.* (pä rĕ-doo-blă.) A quick-step; an increased, redoubled step.
Passacáglio, *It.* (päs-sä-käl-yē-ō.) } A species
Passacaille, *Fr.* (päs-sä-käl.) } of chacone, a slow dance with divisions on a ground bass in 3-4 time and always in a minor key.
Passage. Any phrase, or short portion of an air, or other composition. Every member of a strain or movement is a *passage*.
Passages, pedal. Those parts of a composition in which the pedals are used.
Passággio, *It.* (päs-säd-jē-ō.) A passage or series of notes.
Passaggi vietati, *It.* (päs-säd-jē vē-ä-tä-tē.) Forbidden passages.
Passamézzo, *It.* (päs-sä-mät-sō.) An old slow dance, little differing from the action of walking.
Passepied, *Fr.* (päs-pĭ-ā.) A sort of jig; a lively old French dance in 3-4, 3-8, or 6-8 time; a kind of quick minuet, with three or more strains or reprisas, the first consisting of eight bars.
Pas seul, *Fr.* (pā sŭl.) A dance by one performer.
Passing modulation. A transient modulation.
Passing notes. Notes which do not belong to the harmony, but which serve to connect those which are essential, and carry the ear more smoothly from one harmony to another.
Passing tone. Passing note.
Passionáta, *It.* (päs-sē-ō-nä-tä.)
Passionataménte, *It.* (päs-sē-ō-nä-tä-män-tē.)
Passionáte, *It.* (päs-sē-ō-nä-tē.)
Passionáto, *It.* (päs-sē-ō-nä-tō.)
Passionate, impassioned, with fervor and pathos.
Passióne, *It.* (päs-sē-ō-nĕ.) Passion, feeling.
Passióne, *It.* (päs-sē-ō-nē.) The Passion, or seven last words of the Savior on the cross, set to solemn and devotional music.
Passiones, *Lat.* (päs-sī-ō-nĕs.) Passion music.
Passion music. Music composed in Roman Catholic countries, expressly for Passion week.
Passions-musik, *Ger.* (päs-sī-ōns moo-zīk.) Passion music.
Passo innanzi passo, *It* (päs-sō ēn-nän-tsē päs-sō.) By degrees, gently.
Passo-mezzo, *It.* (päs-sō mĕt-sō.) See *Passamézzo*.
Passy measure. An old, stately kind of music; a cinque pace.
Pasticio, *It.* (päs-tĭ-tshe-ō.) } A medley, an
Pastiche, *Fr.* (päs-tăsh.) } opera made up of songs, etc., by various composers; the poetry being written to the music, instead of the music to the poetry.
Pastoral. A musical drama, the personages and scenery of which are chiefly rural. A *pastoral* is also any lyrical production, the subject of which is taken from rural life; and the Italians give the same name to an instrumental composition written in the pastoral style.
Pastorále, *It.* (päs-tō-rä-lĕ.) } Pastoral, rural.
Pastorelle, *Fr.* (päs-tō-rĕl.) } belonging to a shepherd, a soft movement in a pastoral and rural style.
Pastoral flute. Shepherd's flute.

PAVA

Pastoral music. Music the style of which is rustic or rural.
Pastorello, *It.* (päs-tō-rĕl-lō.) A pastoral.
Pastourelle, *Fr.* (päs-too-rĕll.) One of the movements of a quadrille.
Fataletilla, *Spa.* (pä-tä-lĕ-tăl-yä.) A kind of dance.
Patética, *It.* (pä-tā-tē-kä.) Pathetic.
Pateticaménte, *It.* (pä-tä-tē-kä-män-tē.) Pathetically.
Patético, *It.* (pä-tā-tē-kō.)
Pathétique, *Fr.* (pä-tā-tēk.) } Pathetic.
Pathetisch, *Ger.* (pä-tĕt-ĭsh.)
Pathetic. Applied to music when it excites emotions of sorrow, pity, sympathy, etc.
Pathetica, *Lat.* (pä-thĕt-ĭ-kä.) Pathetic.
Patiménto. *It.* (pä-tē-män-tō.) Affliction, grief, suffering.
Patriotic. Songs having for their theme love of country.
Pauan. A peculiar species of old Spanish dance; also, a tune adapted to the movements of the dance.
Pauke, *Ger.* (*pou*-kĕ.) A kettle drum.
Pauken, *Ger. pl.* (*pou*-k'n.) Kettle drums.
Pauken-fell, *Ger.* (*pou*-k'n fĕll.) The leather or skin of the kettle drum.
Pauken-klang, *Ger.* (*pou*-k'n kläng.) The clang of kettle drums.
Pauken-klöpfel, *Ger.* (*pou*-k'n klŏp-fĕl.)
Pauken-schlägel, *Ger.* (*pou*-k'n shlā-g'l.)
Pauken-stock, *Ger.* (*pou*-k'n stŏk.)
Kettle drum stick.
Pauken-schläger, *Ger.* (*pou*-k'n shlā-gĕr.)
Pauker, *Ger.* (*pou*-kĕr.)
Kettle drummer.
Paulatinaménte, *It.* (pou-lä-tē-nä-män-tē.) Gently, slowly.
Pausa, *It.* (pou-zä.)
Pausa, *Spa.* (pon-zä.) } A pause.
Pausa, *Lat.* (paw-zä.)
Páusa generále, *It.* (pou-zä jä-nĕ-rä-lĕ.)
Pause générale, *Fr.* (pōz zhā-nä-rä-lĕ.)
A pause or rest for *all* the performers.
Pause, *Fr.* (pōz.) A semibreve rest; also, a whole bar's rest in any species of time.
Pause, *Ger.* (*pou*-zĕ.) A rest.
Pause, *Eng.* A character (⌢) which lengthens the duration of a note or rest over which it is placed, beyond its natural value, or at the pleasure of the performer. When placed over a double bar, it shows the termination of the movement or piece.
Pause, demi, *Fr.* (pōz dĕ-mē.) A minim rest.
Pause, general. A general cessation or silence of all the parts.
Pause, initial. A character of silence, so called when placed at the beginning of a piece.
Pausen, *Ger.* (*pou*-z'n.) } To pause, to
Pauser, *Fr.* (pō-zä.) } rest, to keep silence.
Pausiren, *Ger.* (pou-zä-rĕn.)
Pavan, *Eng.* } A grave, stately dance,
Paváne, *It.* (pä-vä-nĕ.) } which took its name
Pavane, *Fr.* (pä-vänh.) } from *pavo*, a peacock. It was danced by princes in their mantles and ladies in gowns with long trains, whose motions resembled those of a peacock's tail. It was in

ā ale, ă add, ä arm, ē eve, ĕ end, Ī ice, Ĭ ill, ō old, ŏ odd, Ȯ dove, oo moon, ū lute, ŭ but, ū French sound.

PAVE

3-4 time and generally in three strains, each of which was repeated.
Paventáto, *It.* (pä-vĕn-tä-tō.) } Fearful, tim-
Paventóso, *It.* (pä-vĕn-tō-zō.) } orous, with anxiety and embarrassment.
Pavillon, *Fr.* (pä-vē-yônh.) The bole of a horn or other wind instrument.
Pavillon chinois, *Fr.* (pä-vē-yônh shē-nwä.) An instrument with numerous little bells, which impart brilliancy to lively pieces, and pompous military marches.
Peal. A set of bells tuned to each other; the changes rung upon a set of bells.
Peen. A pæsn; a song of praise.
Peana, *It.* (pē-ä-nä.) A pean, a hymn, or song of praise.
Pectis, *Gr.* (pĕk-tĭs.) An ancient stringed instrument resembling a harp, used by the Greeks.
Ped. An abbreviation of pedal.
Pedal. An appliance for the foot, under a pianoforte, by the use of which the dampers are raised from the strings, thus allowing them their full vibration. On the organ see *Pedale.*
Pedal, damper. See *Pedal.*
Pedal-claves. *Ger.* (pĕd-äl klä-fĕa.) }
Pedal-claviatur, *Ger.* (pĕd-äl klä-vĭ-ä-toor.) }
The pedal key board, in an organ.
Pedále, *It.* (pĕ-dä-lē.) A pedal bass, or a stationary bass; See Pedal.
Pedal point. In pianoforte music this word means that the pedal which takes off the dampers must be pressed down.
Pedale, *Ger. pt.* (pĕ-dä-lĕ.) The pedals, or that set of keys in an organ, which are played by the feet; in organ music, it means that the notes or passage must be played by the feet.
Pedále a ógni battúta, *It.* (pĕ-dä-lē ä ōn-yē bä-too-tä.) Use the pedal at each beat or division of time.
Pedále doppelt, *Ger.* (pĕ-dä-lĕ dōp-pĕlt.) }
Pedále dóppio, *It.* (pä-dä-lē dōp-pē-ō.) }
Double pedals, in organ playing; playing the pedals with both feet at once.
Pedále d'órgano, *It.* (pä-dä-lē 'd'ōr-gä-nō.) The pedals of an organ.
Pédales, *Fr. pl.* (pā-dál.) The pedals.
Pédales de combinaison, *Fr.* Combination of pedals.
Pedal extension. The loud pedal of a pianoforte; that by which the sound is increased and extended.
Pedal harmonies. The chords formed by placing the dominant seventh, diminished seventh, or seventh of a leading note, on the tonic or on the dominant treated as a temporary key note.
Pedal-harfe, *Ger.* (pĕd-äl här-fĕ.) } A harp
Pedal-harp, *Eng.* (pĕd-äl härp.) } with pedals, to produce the semitones.
Pedáli, *It. pt.* The pedals.
Pedaliéra, *It.* (pĕ-dä-lē-ä-rä.) The pedal keys of an organ.
Pedal keys. That set of keys belonging to an organ, or similar instrument, which is played by the feet.
Pedal monochord. The one stringed pedal.

PERC

Pedal note. A note held by the pedal while the harmony formed by the other parts proceeds independently.
Pedal open. Loud pedal; that which raises the dampers and allows the full vibration of the strings to continue.
Pedal passages. Passages in which the pedals are employed.
Pedal pianoforte. A pianoforte having pedals suitable for organ practice, the pedal strings of which are in the rear and extend lengthwise of the instrument.
Pedal pipes. Pipes in an organ which sound only when the pedals are pressed.
Pedal point. A sustained bass, or pedal note, held on or sustained for several bars, while a variety of chords are introduced.
Peiteagh, *Iri.* (pī-tĕ-äh.) A general name for the tunes of the ancient poems and songs of Ireland.
Pelak. A Javanese musical instrument of limited scale.
Penaylon, *Gr.* (pĕ-nä-lōn.) See Panaylon.
Penorçon, *Fr.* (pĕ-nōr-sônh.) } An ancient in-
Penorkon, *Ger.* (pĕ-nōr-kōn.) } strument resembling a *Ghittern.*
Pensóso, *It.* (pĕn-sō-zō.) Pensively, mournfully.
Pentachonium, *Gr.* (pĕn-tä-kō-nĭ-ŭm.) A composition in five parts.
Pentachord. An instrument with five strings; a scale or system of five diatonic sounds.
Pentachordus, *Lat.* (pĕn-tä-kōr-dŭs.) Five-stringed; a general name for all instruments of five strings.
Pentacrostic. A set of verses so disposed as to have five acrostics of the same name in five divisions of each verse.
Pentameter. In ancient poetry, a verse of five feet, the first two of which may be either dactyls or spondees, the third always a spondee, and the last two anapests.
Pentametro, *It.* (pĕn-tä-mä-trō.) Pentameter; verse of five feet.
Pentastich, *Gr.* (pĕn-tăs-tĭk.) A composition in poetry of five verses.
Pentatonon, *Gr.* (pĕn-tä-tō-nŏn.) The name of that interval in the ancient music which corresponds with our superfluous sixth, consisting of five tones, hence it receives the name of Pentatonon, or *five tones.*
Pentatonic scale. A scale of five notes, sometimes called the Scotch scale, and similar to the modern diatonic major scale, with the fourth and seventh degrees omitted.
Penultieme, *Fr.* (pĕ-nŭl-tĭ-ām.) Penultimate.
Penultimate. (pĕ-nŭl-tĭ-māt.) The last syllable but one.
Per, *It.* (pĕr.) For, by, through, in.
Per biscantum, *Lat.* (pĕr bĭs-kăn-tŭm.) An old term for music in two parts.
Perçant, *Fr.* (pĕr-sänh.) Piercing, shrill.
Percés, *Fr.* (pĕr-sā.) Holes of musical instruments.
Percotiménto, *It.* (pär-kō-tē-mĕn-tō.) Percussion.

ă *ate*, ă *add*, ă *arm*, ĕ *eve*, ĕ *end*, ĭ *ice*, ĭ *ill*, ō *old*, ŏ *odd*, ô *dove*, oo *moon*, ū *lute*, ŭ *but*, ü *French sound*.

PERC

Percussion, *Eng.* (pĕr-kŭsh-ŏn.) ⎱ Striking;
Percussiŏne, *It.* (pĕr-koos-sĕ-ō-nĕ.) ⎰ as applied to instruments, notes or chords; or the *touch* on the pianoforte.
Percussional. A general name for all instruments that are struck, as a gong, drum, bell, tabor, etc.
Perdas, *Per.* (pĕr-däs.) The musical modes or systems of the Persians.
Perdéndo, *It.* (pĕr-dăn-dō.) ⎱ Gradnally
Perdendósi. *It.* (pĕr-dăn-dō-zē.) ⎰ decreasing the tone and the time; dying away, becoming extinct.
Perfect. A term applied to certain intervals and chords.
Perfect cadence. Dominant harmony followed by that of the tonic; a close upon the key-note preceded by the dominant.
Perfect close. A perfect cadence.
Perfect concords. ⎱ These are, the uni-
Perfect consonances. ⎰ son, the perfect fourth, perfect fifth, and the octave.
Perfect fifth. An interval containing three whole tones and one semitone.
Perfect fourth. An interval containing two whole tones and one semitone.
Perfect octave. An interval containing five whole tones and two semitones.
Perfect period. A complete termination satisfactory and agreeable to the ear.
Perfect prolation. In the music of the ancients, that prolation comprising three minims in a semibreve.
Perfect time. Among the ancients a measure consisting of three beats in a measure and designated by the letter O.
Perfect triad. A fundamental note with its major third and perfect fifth.
Perfétto, *It.* (pĕr-făt-tō.) Perfect, complete.
Performer. A practical instrumental or vocal musician.
Pergolo, *It.* (pĕr-gō-lō.) A box in a theatre; a stage for operatic performance.
Perielsis, *Lat.* (pĕr-ĭ-ĕl-sĭs.) A term formerly used in church music, signifying the interposition of one or more notes in the intonation, to indicate the approach of the *finale* and to apprise the choir that they were to take up the point.
Per il violino, *It.* (păr ĕl vē-ō-lē-nō.) For the violin.
Perigourdine. (pĕr-ĭ-goor-dĕn.) A French dance in 3-8 time.
Period, *Eng.* ⎱ A complete and per-
Période, *Fr.* (pă-rī-ōd.) ⎰ fect musical sentence,
Periode, *It.* (pă-rē-ō-dĕ.) ⎰ containing several phrases and bringing the ear to a perfect conclusion or state of rest.
Période musicale, *Fr.* (pă-rī-ōd mū-zē-kăl.) A musical period.
Periodenban, *Ger.* (pĕ-rī-ō-d'n-bou.) Composition; the construction of musical periods.
Period, imperfect. A close not satisfactory to the ear.
Period, irregular. Where an imperfect cadence interrupts or suspends an expected final close.

PEU

Period, perfect. A termination agreeable to the ear.
Perlé, *Fr.* (pĕr-lā.) Pearled, brilliant; *cadence perlée*, brilliant cadence.
Per ogni tempi, *It.* (păr ōn-yē tăm-pē.) A term sometimes introduced in a motet, signifying that it is suited to any time and occasion.
Perpetual fugue. A canon so constructed that its termination leads to its beginning, and hence may be perpetually repeated.
Perpetual psalmody. See *Laus Perennis*.
Perpetui suoni, *It.* (pĕr-pā-too-ē swō-nē.) Perpetual sounds; the highest and lowest in the tetrachords of the ancient Greek system.
Per recte et retro, *Lat.* (pĕr rĕk-tē ĕt rā-trō.) Forward, then backward; the melody or subject reversed, note for note.
Personæ dramatis, *Lat.* (pĕr-sō-nē drăm-ă-tĭs.) The characters of an opera or play.
Personaggio, *It.* (pĕr-sōn-ăd-jē-ō.) One of the characters of a play.
Pes, *Lat.* (pĕs.) Foot, measure, species of verse; rhythm, time; also, a kind of ground, or burden, the basis for the harmony in old English music.
Pesánte, *It.* (pĕ-zăn-tē.) Heavy, ponderous; with importance and weight, impressively.
Pesantemĕnte, *It.* (pĕ-zăn-tĕ-măn-tĕ.) Heavily, forcibly, impressively.
Pestalozzian system. A system of *induction*, presenting the rudiments of music in their natural progressive order. It was first applied to music by a wealthy Swiss gentleman by the name of Pestalozzi.
Petit, *Fr.* (pĕ-tē.) Little, small.
Petit chœur, *Fr.* (pĕ-tē kūr.) Little choir; a sacred composition in three parts.
Petite flute-a-bec, *Fr.* (pĕ-tēt flūt ă bĕk.) A flageolet.
Petite mesure a deux temps, *Fr.* (pĕ-tēt mē-zūr ă dū tănh.) Two-crotchet time, marked 2-4.
Petites flutes, *Fr.* (pĕ-tēt flūt.) The small flutes; the octave or piccolo flutes.
Petites notes breves, *Fr.* (pĕ-tēt nōt brăv.) Short small notes.
Petites notes doubles, *Fr.* (pĕ-tēt nōt doo-bl.) Double small notes.
Petites notes longues, *Fr.* (pĕ-tēt nōt lŏnh-gūh.) Long small notes.
Petites notes vives, *Fr.* (pĕ-tēt nōt vēv.) Short grace notes.
Petit piano droit, *Fr.* (pĕ-tē pĭ-ă-nō drwă.) Semi-cabinet piano.
Petits morceaux, *Fr.* (pĕ-tē mōr-sō.) Short pieces.
Petits pièces, *Fr.* (pĕ-tē pĭ-ās.) Little pieces, short and easy compositions.
Petits riens, *Fr.* (pĕ-tē rĭ-ănh.) Light; trifling compositions.
Petits violins, *Fr.* (pĕ-tē vē-ō-lănh.) Small violins.
Petteia, *Gr.* (pĕ-tī-ă.) Among the ancients the art of ascertaining the sounds which ought, or ought not to be used.
Pétto, *It.* (păt-tō.) The chest, the breast; *vóce di petto*, the chest voice.
Peu, *Fr.* (pūh.) Little, a little.

PRONOUNCING MUSICAL DICTIONARY. 153

ā *ale*, ă *add*, ä *arm*, ē *eve*, ĕ *end*, ī *ice*, ĭ *ill*, ō *old*, ŏ *odd*, ȯ *dove*, oo *moon*, ū *lute*, ŭ *but*, ü *French sound*

PEUA

Peu a peu, *Fr.* (pŭh ă pŭh.) Little by little, by degrees.
Pézze, *It. pl.* (păt-sĕ.) Fragments, scraps; select, detached pieces.
Pézzi concertanti, *It. pl.* (păt-sē kŏn-tshĕr-tăn-tē.) Concertante pieces, in which each instrument has occasional solos.
Pézzi di bravura, *It.* (păt-sē dē brä-*voo*-rä.) Compositions for the display of dexterity or rapid execution.
Pezzo, *It.* (păt-sō.) A fragment; a detached piece of music.
Pfeife, *Ger.* (pfī-fĕ.) Pipe, fife, flute.
Pfeifen, *Ger.* (pfī-f'n.) To play on a fife or flute.
Pfeifen-deckel, *Ger.* (pfī-f'n dĕk-ĕl.) The stopper, or covering of an organ pipe.
Pfeifer, *Ger.* (pfī-fĕr.) A fifer, a piper.
Phantasie, *Ger.* (făn-tä-zē.) See *Fantasia*.
Phantasiren, *Ger.* (făn-tä-zē-r'n.) Improvising.
Phantasirte, *Ger.* (făn-tä-zĭr-tĕ.) Improvised.
Phantasy. A fantasia.
Pheateah. See *Peiteagh*.
Philharmonic, *Gr.* (fĭl-här-*mŏn*-ĭk.) Music-loving.
Philomelia, *Gr.* (fĭl-ō-*mā*-lĭ-ä.) A style of hymn sung by the ancient Greeks in honor of Apollo.
Philomousos, *Gr.* (fĭ-lō-*mou*-sŏs.) A lover of music.
Philomusical. Loving music. (Not used.)
Phisharmonica. (fĭs-bär-*mŏn*-ĭ-kä) A kind of octagonal accordeon.
Phonascos, *Gr.* (fō-*năs*-kŏs.) The name given by the ancients to one who taught the management of the voice.
Phonascetics, *Gr.* (fō-năs-*sĕt*-ĭks.) The art or method of restoring the voice.
Phonagogos, *Gr.* (fō-nă-gŏ-gŏs.) The leading voice or subject in a fugue.
Phonaskia. *Gr.* (fō-năs-kī-ă.) Practice in vocalization.
Phonaskos, *Gr.* (fō-*năs*-kŏs.) } Teacher of
Phonaskus, *Lat.* (fō-*năs*-kŭs.) } singing and declamation
Phone. *Gr.* (fō-nē.) The voice; a sound or tone.
Phonetic. Vocal, representing sounds.
Phonetik, *Ger.* (fō-*nĕt*-ĭk.) System of singing, or of notation and harmony.
Phonetics. } The doctrine or science of sounds,
Phonics. } especially those of the human voice.
Phonocamptic, (fō-nō-kămp-tĭk.) Having the power to inflect sound, or turn it from its direction and thus alter it.
Phonology. The theory or doctrine of the elementary sounds of the human voice.
Phonometer. A monochord with its wire stretched by a weight capable of very accurate apportionment, designed as an aid in tuning.
Phonomimo, *Gr.* (fō-*nŏm*-ĭ-nō.) To imitate the human voice.
Phonomine. An instrument invented in Vienna, the tones of which, produced by means of pipes, are similar to those of the human voice.
Phonoscope, electro-magnetic. An instrument of recent English invention, the motive power of which is produced by a Voltaic battery, and which upon being put in communication with

PIAN

a piano, organ, etc., prints the music as it is played.
Phorbeia, *Gr.* (fŏr-bī-ä.) A bandage used by vocal performers; called also a *Capistrum*.
Phorminx, *Ger.* (fŏr-mĭnx.) A stringed instrument of remote antiquity, resembling the lyre.
Photinx, *Gr.* (fō-tĭnx.) Name given by the ancients to their crooked flute.
Phrase. A short musical sentence; a musical thought or idea.
Phrase, extended. } Any variation of a mel-
Phrase, irregular. } ody by which three measures are used instead of two.
Phrases manquées, *Fr.* (träz- mänh-kä.) Certain imperfect and unsymmetrical passages or phrases, sometimes introduced by injudicious composers, by which the melody is maimed, and the expression destroyed or weakened.
Phraser, *Fr.* (frä-zĕ.) To form phrases, to mark the phrases.
Phrasing. Dividing the musical sentences into rhythmical sections.
Phrygian. One of the ancient Greek modes.
Phrygische tonart. *Ger.* (frĭg-ĭ-shĕ tō-närt.) The Phrygian mode.
Phthongometer, *Gr.* (fthŏn-gō-mä-tĕr.) An instrument with which to measure vocal sounds.
Phthoggos, *Gr.* (fthŏn-gŏs.) A tone, or sound.
Physharmonica, *Gr.* (fĭs-bär-*mŏn*-ĭ-kä.) An instrument, the tone of which resembles that of the reed pipes in an organ, and is produced by the vibration of thin metal tongues, of a similar construction to those of the harmonium; the name is also applied to a stop in the organ with *free reeds*, and with tubes of half the usual length.
Piacére, *It.* (pē-ä-tshā-vō-lĕ.) Pleasure, inclination, fancy; *a piacére*, at pleasure.
Piacévole, *It.* (pē-ä-tshā-vō-lĕ.) Pleasing, graceful, agreeable.
Piacevolézza, *It.* (pē-ä-tsbā-vō-lăt-zä.). Gracefulness, sweetness.
Piacevolménte, *It.* (pē-ä-tshē-vŏl-*măn*-tĕ.) Gracefully, delicately.
Piaciménto, *It.* (pē-ä-tshē-*măn*-tō.) See *Piacére*.
Piagnévole, *It.* (pē-än-yā-vō-lĕ.) Mournful, doleful, lamentable.
Pianaménte, *It.* (pē-ä-nä-*măn*-tĕ.) Softly, gently, quietly.
Pianétto, *It.* (pē-ä-*năt*-tō.) Very low, very soft.
Piagéndo, *It.* (pē-ä-găn-dō.) Plaintively, sorrowfully.
Piangévole, *It.* (pē-än-gā-vō-lĕ.) Lamentable, doleful.
Piangevolménte, *It.* (pē-än-gä-vŏl-*măn*-tĕ.) Lamentably, dolefully.
Pianino, *It.* (pē-ä-nē-nō.) A small pianoforte.
Pianíssimo, *It.* (pē-än-ēs-sē-mō.) Extremely soft.
Pianissimo quánto possíbile, *It.* (pē-än-ēs-sē-mō quäu-tō pōs-sē-bĭ-lĕ.) As soft as possible.
Pianist. An amateur or professional player on the pianoforte.
Pianíste, *Fr.* (pē-än-ēst.) Pianist.
Piano, *It.* (pē-ä-nō.) Soft, gentle.
Piano a queue, *Fr.* (pē-ä-nō ä kŭh.) A grand pianoforte.

ă ale, ă add, ă arm, ĕ eve, ĕ end, ĭ ice, ĭ ill, ŏ old, ŏ odd, ŏ dove, oo moon, ũ lute, ũ but, ũ French sound.

PIAN

Piano assai. *It.* (pē-ä-nō ä́-sä́-ḗ.) As soft as possible.
Piano carré, *Fr.* (pē-ä-nō kär-rā.) A square pianoforte.
Piano droit, *Fr.* (pē-ä-nō drwä.) An upright pianoforte.
Pianoforte. A stringed and keyed instrument of German origin, so called from its equal command both of softness and strength. It was invented about 1746 by Christopher Gottlieb Schröter, and is a great improvement upon the spinet and harpsichord, which instruments it has entirely superseded; improvements are constantly being made in it and it is the most agreeable and popular instrument now in use.
Pian-piáno, *It.* (pē-än pē-ä-nō.) Very softly, with a low voice. (See *Piano-piano*.)
Pian-pianissimo, *It.* (pē-än pē-än-ĕs-sē-mō.) Exceedingly soft and gentle.
Pianoforte action. The mechanism of a pianoforte.
Pianoforte action, double. That in which two hammers are employed, the second or under one multiplying the velocity of the first.
Pianoforte, Æolian. A pianoforte so united with a reed instrument that the same set of keys serve for both, or for either singly at the pleasure of the player.
Pianoforte, compensating. An English piano so made as to allow of the use of heavy strings, by which the full power of a grand is obtained from a cottage or small piano.
Pianoforte, concert grand. The largest sized grand pianoforte.
Pianoforte, cottage. An upright pianoforte.
Pianoforte, dumb. A key-board arranged for the practice of pupils without producing sound.
Pianoforte, electric. A pianoforte invented in 1851, the wires of which are vibrated by electro-magnetism.
Pianoforte, grand. A pianoforte in which most of the octaves have for each note, three strings tuned in unison and struck at once by the same hammer.
Pianoforte hammer. That part of the mechanism of a pianoforte which strikes the wires.
Pianoforte, melographic. A piano connected with which was a clock movement, by which the improvisation of a composer was recorded.
Pianoforte, overstrung. An arrangement by which the strings of at least two of the lowest octaves are raised, running in respect to the other strings, diagonally above them.
Pianoforte, parlor grand. A grand pianoforte of the smallest size.
Pianoforte, piccolo. A small upright pianoforte.
Pianoforte school. A book of instruction for the pianoforte.
Pianoforte score. A score in which every part has been so arranged that it may be played on a pianoforte.
Pianoforte, upright. A pianoforte whose strings run obliquely or vertically upward.
Pianographe. An ingenious machine, invented by M. Guérin, which, on being attached to the

PIFF

pianoforte, indicates on paper prepared for the purpose, any thing played by the pianist.
Piano, mezzo, *It.* (pē-ä-nō mät-zō.) Moderately soft.
Piano-piano, *It.* pē-ä-nō pē-ä-nō.) Very soft.
Piano, sempre staccato e marcato il basso, *It.* (pē-ä-nō sĕm-prĕ stäk-kä-tō mär-kä-tō ĕl bäs-sō.) Soft, with the bass always well marked and detached.
Piano solo. For the pianoforte only.
Piano-violino. *It.* (pē-ä-nō vē-ō-lē-nō.) A new and curious instrument invented in 1837. It is a common piano containing a violin arrangement inside of it, which is set in motion by a pedal. When this instrument is played upon it gives the sound of both violin and piano.
Piátti, *It. pl.* (pē-ät-tē.) Cymbals.
Pib, *Wel.* (pĕb.) A pipe, a fife.
Pibcorn, or **hornpipe.** The name given by the Welsh to a wind instrument consisting of a wooden pipe with holes at the sides and a horn at each end, the one to collect the wind blown into it by the mouth and the other to carry off the sounds as modulated by the performer.
Pibe, *Dan.* (pē-bĕ.) A pipe.
Pibroch. (pē-brŏk.) A wild, irregular species of music, peculiar to the Highlands of Scotland; performed on the bagpipe.
Picchiettáto. *It* (pē-kē-ĕt-tä-tō.) Scattered, detached: in violin playing it means, that sort of staccato indicated by dots under a slur.
Picciolo, *It.* (pĕt-tshē-ō-lō.)
Piccolino, *It.* (pē-kō-lē-nō.) } Small, little.
Piccolo, *It.* (pē-kō-lō.)
Piccolo. A 2 feet organ stop, of wood pipes, producing a bright and clear tone in unison with the fifteenth.
Piccolo flute. A small flute.
Piccolo pianoforte. A small upright pianoforte.
Pischettáto, *It.* (pē-kĕt-tä-tō.) See *Picchiettáto*.
Pièce, *Fr.* (pī-äs.) A composition or piece of music; an opera or drama.
Pieces, fugitive. Short compositions of no permanent value.
Pieds, *Fr. pl.* (pī-ä.) The foot; *avec les pieds,* with the feet, in organ playing.
Piéna, *It.* (pē-ä-nä.) } Full.
Piéno, *It.* (pē-ä-nō.)
Pienaménte, *It.* (pē-ä-nä-mán-tĕ.) Fully.
Piéno córo, *It.* (pē-ä-nō kō-rō.) A full chorus.
Piéno organo, *It.* (pē-ä-nō ōr-gä-nō.) With the full organ.
Pierced gamba. An organ stop of the gamba species.
Pieta, *It.* (pē-ä-tä.)
Pietosaménte, *It.* (pē-ä-tō-zä-mán-tĕ.) }
Pietóso, *It.* (pē-ä-tō-zō.)
Compassionately, tenderly; implying also a rather slow and sustained movement.
Pifano, *Spa.* (pē-fä-nō.)
Pifaro, *Spa.* (pē-fä-rō.) } A fife, a fifer.
Pifara, *It.* (pē-fä-rä.)
Pifferáre, *It.* (pĕf-fē-rä-rē.) To play upon the fife; also a piper, such as, in Italy, play pastoral airs in the streets at Christmas. One of these

ā ale, ă add, ä arm, ē eve, ĕ end, ī ice, ĭ ill, ō old, ŏ odd, ô dove, oo moon, ū lute, ŭ but, ü French sound.

PIFF

airs forms the basis of Handel's Pastoral Symphony, in the " Messiah."
Pifferári, *It. pl.* (pĕf-fĕ-rä-rē.) Pipers; see Pifferáre.
Pifferína, *It.* (pĕf-fĕ-rē-nä.) A little fife.
Píffero, *It.* (pĕf-fĕ-rō.) A fife or small flute; also an organ stop of 4 feet.
Pifferóne, *It.* (pĕf-fĕ-rō-nĕ.) A large fife.
Pincé, *Fr.* (pănh-sā.) Pinched; see *Pizzicáto*.
Pincer, *Fr.* (pănh-sā.) To play upon a musical instrument.
Pincés, *Fr.* (pănh-a.) A general name for stringed instruments.
Pinching. A practice by which bagpipers gain one or two notes by half covering the thumb hole.
Pindaric. An ode in imitation of Pindar; an irregular ode.
Piob, *Gae.* (pī-ōb.) A pipe.
Piobaireachd, *Gae.* Pipe music.
Piobamala, *Iri.* (pī-ō-bä-mä-lä.) The harp of the ancient inhabitants of Ireland.
Pip. A pipe.
Pipa, *Spa.* (pē-pä.) A pipe.
Pipe. Any tube formed of a reed, or of metal, or of wood, which, being inflated at one end, produces a musical sound. The *pipe*, which was originally no more than a simple oaten straw, was one of the earliest instruments by which musical sounds were attempted.
Pipeau, *Fr.* (pē-pō.) A pipe.
Piper. A performer on the pipe; pipers were formerly one of the class of itinerant musicians, and performed in a variety of wind instruments, as the bagpipe, musette, etc.
Pipes of pan. A wind instrument consisting of a range of pipes bound together, side by side, and gradually lessening with respect to each other in length and diameter: Pandean pipes.
Pipes, organ. Square and cylindrical tubes in an organ, from which proceed the sound of the instrument.
Pipes, pandean. Pan's pipes.
Papitana, *Spa.* (pä-pē-tä-nä.) Flute made by boys of green cane.
Piqué, *Fr.* (pī-kā.) | To play on the violin,
Piquer, *Fr.* (pī-kā.) | etc., a series of notes a little staccáto, and with a light pressure of the bow to each note.
Pitancero, *Spa.* (pē-tän-thā-rō.) Superintendent of a choir in a cathedral.
Pitar, *Spa.* (pē-tär.) To play on a pipe.
Pitch. The acuteness or gravity of any particular sound, or of the tuning of any instrument.
Pitch, concert. The pitch generally adopted for some one given note and by which every other note is governed.
Pitch-pipe. An instrument formerly used to sound the key note of any vocal composition.
Pitillo, *Spa.* (pī-tĭl-yō.) } A pipe, a flute.
Pito, *Spa.* (pē-tō.) }
Pitofero, *Spa.* (pē-tō-fā-rō.) Piper, flutist.
Pittorico, *It.* (pĕt-tō-rē-kō.) Embellished, pictorial or figured.
Piu, *It.* (pē-oo.) More.
Piu allégro, *It.* (pē-oo äl-lā-grō.) A little quicker, more lively.

PLAN

Piu che lento, *It.* (pē-oo kĕ lăn-tō.) Slower than lento.
Piu fórte, *It.* (pē-oo fōr-tĕ.) Louder.
Piu lénto, *It.* (pē-oo lăn-tō.) More slowly.
Piu mósso, *It.* (pē-oo mōs-sō.) | More motion.
Piu móto, *It.* (pē-oo mō-tō.) | quicker.
Piu piáno, *It.* (pē-oo pē-ä-nō.) Softer.
Piu piú, *It.* (pē-oo pē-oo.) Somewhat more.
Piu présto, *It.* (pē-oo prăs-tō.) Quicker, more rapidly.
Piu pósto, *It.* (pē-oo pōs-tō.) Rather, inclined to; it also means quicker.
Piu pósto allégro, *It.* (pē-oo pōs-tō äl-lā-grō.) Rather quicker.
Piu pósto lénto, *It.* (pē-oo pōs-tō lăn-tō.) Rather slower.
Piu vívo, *It.* (pē-oo vē-vō.) More lively, more animated.
Píva, *It.* (pē-vä.) A pipe, a bagpipe.
Pizzicándo, *It.* (pĕt-sē-kăn-dō.) | Pinched;
Pizzicáto, *It.* (pĕt-sē-kä-tō.) | meaning that the strings of the violin, violincello, etc., are not to be played with the bow, but pinched, or snapped with the fingers, producing a *staccáto* effect.
Placebo, *Lat.* (plā-sē-bō.) In the Roman Catholic church, the vesper hymn for the dead, commencing, "Placebo Domino."
Placenteraménte, *It.* (plä-tshĕn-tĕr-ä-män-tĕ.) Joyfully.
Placidaménte, *It.* (plä-tshĕ-dä-män-tĕ.) Calmly, placidly, quietly.
Plácido, *It.* (plä-tshĕ-dō.) Placid, tranquil, calm.
Plagal. Those ancient modes, in which the melody was confined within the limits of the dominant and its octave.
Plagal cadence. A cadence in which the final chord on the tonic is preceded by the harmony of the sub-dominant.
Plagalisch, *Ger.* (plä-gä-lĭsh.) Plagal.
Plagiário, *It.* (plä-jē-ä-rē-ō.) } A plagiarism;
Plagiat, *Ger.* (plä-ghĭ-ät.) } ideas borrowed or imitated from the works of another composer.
Plagiarist, musical. A composer who purloins or borrows from the productions of others.
Plain chant, *Fr.* (plănh shănh.) The plain song: see *Cánto Férmo*.
Plain counterpoint. } Simple counterpoint.
Plain descant. } Written. Played.
Plain shake. A shake ending without a turn.

Plain song. The name given to the old ecclesiastical chant when in its most simple state and without those harmonic appendages with which it has since been enriched.
Plainte, *Fr.* (plănht.) A complaint, a lament.
Plaintif, *Fr.* (plănh-tēf.) Plaintive, doleful.
Plaintive music. A style of music expressive of grief.
Plaisant, *Fr.* (plā-zănh.) Pleasing.
Plaisanteries, *Fr.* (plā-zănh-t'rē.) Amusing, light compositions.
Planxty. Old harp music of a lively, tuneful kind.

ă *ale*, ă *add*, ä *arm*, e *eve*, ĕ *end*, ī *ice*, ĭ *ill*, ō *old*, ŏ *odd*, ô *dove*, oo *moon*, ū *lute*, ŭ *but*, ū *French sound*.

PLAQ

Plaqué, *Fr.* (plă-kā́.) *Struck at once,* without any arpéggio, or embellishment.
Plaquer, *Fr.* (plă-kā̄.) To strike at once, speaking of chords.
Plärren, *Ger.* (plăr-r'n.) To sing monotonously; to sing with a hoarse or cracked voice.
Plasma, *Gr.* (plăs-mä.) A term used by the ancients, meaning sometimes a florid, and at other times a soft and delicate modulation of the voice.
Platéa, *It.* (plä-tā̄-ä.) The pit, in a theatre.
Plates, music. Quadrilateral sheets of copper, or pewter, on which music is stamped or engraved in order to be printed.
Plauso, *It.* (plou-zō.) Applause.
Play. To perform on a musical instrument; to take a part in an operatic performance.
Players on high and low instruments. A title assumed by the French minstrels of the fourteenth century when the laws of counterpoint were forming and began to give exercise to bass and treble instruments in concert.
Playhouse tunes. The general name by which, in the seventeenth century all melodies first introduced to the public by the theatres were designated.
Plectrum, *Lat.* (plĕk-trŭm.) A quill, or piece of ivory or hard wood used to twitch the strings of the *mandolins*, lyre, etc.
Plegaria, *Spa.* (plä-gä-rī-ä.) Bell rung at noon for prayers.
Plein jeu, *Fr.* (plănh zhŭ.) Full organ; the term is also applied to a mixture stop of several ranks of pipes.
Plein jeu harmonique, *Fr.* (plănh zhŭ hăr-mōnhū-ēk.) A mixture stop in an organ.
Pieno organo, *Lat.* (plä-nō ōr-gä-nō.) Full organ.
Plettro, *It.* (plĕt-trō.) A bow, a fiddlestick; also, a plectrum.
Plice, *Lat.* (plä-kō.) A kind of ligature used in the old music, as a sign of hesitation or pause.
Plus, *Fr.* (plū.)
Plus animé, *Fr.* (plū să-nē-mä.) With more animation.
Plus lentement, *Fr.* (plū lănht-mănh.) Slower, more slowly.
Pneumatic, (nū-măt-ĭk.) Relating to the air or wind: a term applied to all *wind* instruments collectively.
Pneumatic action. Mechanism intended to lighten the touch, etc., in large organs: see *Levier Pneumatique*.
Pneumatic lever.
Pneumatic organ. An organ moved by wind, so named by the ancients to distinguish it from the hydraulic organ, moved by water.
Pocetta, *It.* (pō-tshăt-tä.) A kit, a small violin used by dancing masters.
Poche, *Fr.* (pŏsh.)
Pochette, *Fr.* (pō-shĕt.)
Pochettino, *It.* (pō-kĕt-tē-nō.) A little; as, *retard un pochettros*, a little slower.
Pochétto, *It.* (pō-kăt-tō.)
Pochino, *It.* (pō-kē-nō.)
Pochéssimo, *It.* (pō-kĕs-sē-mō.) A very little, as little as possible.
Pocket metronome. An English metronome of the size and form of a small watch, on one side of which is marked the number of vibrations, and on the other the principal Italian musical terms.

POET

Póco, *It.* (pō-kō.) Little.
Póco adágio, *It.* (pō-kō ä-dä-jē-ō.) A little slower.
Póco allégro, *It.* (pō-kō äl-lā-grō.) A little faster.
Póco animáto, *It.* (pō-kō än-ē-mä-tō.) A little more animated.
Póco a póco, *It.* (pō-kō ä pō-kō) By degrees, little by little.
Póco a póco crescéndo, *It.* (pō-kō ä pō-kō krĕ-shän-dō.) Gradually louder and louder.
Póco a póco diminuéndo, *It.* (pō-kō ä pō-kō dē-mē-noo-än-dō.) Gradually diminishing.
Póco a póco, piu di fuoco, *It.* (pō-kō ä pō-kō pē-oo dē foo-ō-kō.) With gradually increasing fire and animation.
Póco a póco, piu lénto, *It.* (pō-kō ä pō-kō pē-oo län-tō.) Gradually slower and slower.
Póco a póco, piu móto, *It.* (pō-kō ä pō-kō pē-oo mō-tō.) Gradually increasing the time.
Póco a póco rallentando, *It.* (pō-kō ä pō-kō räl-lĕn-tän-dō.) Gradually diminishing.
Póco fórte, *It.* (pō-kō fōr-tĕ.) Moderately loud, a little loud.
Póco lárgo, *It.* (pō-kō lär-gō.) Moderately slow.
Póco lénto, *It.* (pō-kō lĕn-tō.)
Póco méno, *It.* (pō-kō mä-nō.) A little less, somewhat less.
Póco piáno, *It.* (pō-kō pē-ä-nō.) Somewhat soft.
Póco piu, *It.* (pō-kō pē-oo.) A little more, somewhat more.
Póco piu allégro, *It.* (pō-kō pē-oo äl-lā-grō.) A little quicker.
Póco piu che allegrétto, *It.* (pō-kō pē-oo kĕ äl-lĕ-grāt-tō.) A little quicker than allegrétto.
Póco piu che andánte, *It.* (pō-kō pē-oo kĕ än-dän-tĕ.) A little slower than andánte.
Póco piu forte, *It.* (pō-kō pē-oo fōr-tĕ.) A little louder.
Póco piu lárgo, *It.* (pō-kō pē-oo lär-gō.) A little slower.
Póco piu lénto, *It.* (pō-kō pē-oo tän-tō.)
Póco piu mósso, *It.* (pō-kō pē-oo mōs-sō.) A little faster.
Póco piu piáno, *It.* (pō-kō pē-oo pē-ä-nō.) A little softer.
Póco présto, *It.* (pō-kō präs-tō.) Rather quick.
Póco présto accelerándo, *It.* (pō-kō präs-tō ät-tshĕl-ä-rän-dō.) Gradually accelerate the time.
Poemetto, *It.* (pō-ē-măt-tō.) A short poem.
Poesia, *It.* (pō-ē-zē-ä.) Poetry.
Poesie legere, *Fr.* (pō-ē-zē lĕ-zhăr.) Light poetry.
Poesie sacrée, *Fr.* (pō-ē-zē sä-krā.) Sacred poetry.
Poesies diverses, *Fr.* (pō-ē-zē dē-vărs) Fugitive poems; minor poems.
Poeta. *It.* (pō-ē-tä.) A playwright.
Poetare, *It.* (pō-ē-tä-rĕ.) To write poetry.
Poete lyrique, *Fr.* (pō-ĕt līr-ēk.) A lyric poet, a song writer.
Poetessa, *It.* (pō-ē-tăs-sä.) A poetess.
Poetic. A term applied by the ancients to the art of accommodating melody to verse.

PRONOUNCING MUSICAL DICTIONARY. 157

ā ale, ă add, ä arm, ē eve, ĕ end, ī ice, ĭ ill, ō old, ŏ odd, ō dove, oo moon, ū lute, ŭ but, ü French sound

POET

Poetical overture. A descriptive species of overture.
Poetino, It. (pō-ĕ-tē-nō.) A little poet.
Poetique, Fr. (pō-ĕt-ĕk.) Poetic.
Poet musicians. Bards and lyrists of former times who sang their poetry to melodies of their own composing.
Poggiáto, It. (pŏd-jē-ä-tō.) Dwelt upon, leaned upon.
Pói, It. (pō-ē.) Then, after, afterwards: piáno pói fórte, soft, then loud.
Pói a pói, It. (pō-ē ä pō-ē.) By degrees.
Pói a pói tútte le córde, It. (pō-ē ä pō too-tē lē kōr-dĕ.) All the strings one after another.
Point, Fr. (pwänh.) A dot.
Point de repos, Fr. (pwänh dŭh rĕ-pō.) A pause.
Point d'orgue, Fr. (pwänh d'ōrg.) See *Organ point.*
Pointée, Fr. (pwänh-tā.) Dotted: *blanche pointée,* a dotted minim.
Point final, Fr. (pwänh fĭ-näl.) A final or concluding cadence.
Point of repose. A pause; a cadence.
Point, organ. A long or stationary bass note, upon which various passages of melody and harmony are introduced.
Pól ségne, It. (pō-ē sā-gwĕ.) ⎫ Then
Pól seguénte, It. (pō-ē sā-guän-tĕ.) ⎬ follows, here follows.
Pól ségue il rondo, It. (pō-ē sā-gwĕ ĕl rōn-dō.) After this the rondo.
Poláeca, It. (pō-lăk-kä.) A Polish national dance in 3-4 time; a dance tune in which an emphasis is placed on the first unaccented part of the measure.
Poláeca alla, It. (pō-lăk-kä äl-lä.) In the style of a Polácca.
Poliphant. An instrument supposed to be a species of lute, or cither, strung with wire. Queen Elizabeth is said to have been a good performer upon it.
Polka. A lively Bohemian or Polish dance in 2-4 time, the first three quavers in each bar being accented, and the fourth quaver unaccented.
Polka mazurka. (pŏl-kä mä-zŭr-kä.) A dance in triple time, played slow, and having its accent on the last part of the measure.
Polka redowa. (pŏl-kä rĕd-ō-ä.) A dance tune in triple time, played faster than the polka mazurka, and having its accent on the first part of the measure.
Póllice, It. (pŏl-lē-tshĕ.) The thumb.
Polonaise. (pŏl-ō-nāz.) ⎫ A movement of three
Polonese. ⎬ crotchets in a measure, the rhythmical pause coming on the last crotchet of the bar.
Polonoise. A *polácca.*
Polnischer bock, Ger. (pōl-nĭ-shĕr bōk.) The bagpipe.
Polyacoustic. (pŏl-ĭ-ä-koos-tĭk.) An instrument to multiply sounds.
Polycephale. A kind of air in the ancient Greek music performed by flutes in honor of Apollo.

PORT

Polychord, Gr. (pŏl-ĭ-kŏrd.) Having many strings; an instrument with a great number of strings.
Polyhymnia, Gr. (pŏl-ĭ-hĭm-nĭ-ä.) The muse of song or of vocal music.
Polymnastic, Gr. (pŏl-ĭm-năs-tĭk.) The epithet by which the ancients distinguished certain flutes, invented, some authors say, by Polymneste.
Polymorphous, Gr. (pŏl-ĭ-mŏr-foos.) Of many forms, a term generally used in reference to canons.
Polyodia, Gr. (pŏl-ĭ-ō-dĭ-ä.) A term applied by the Greeks to any conjunction or combination of sounds, whether rude or dissonant, unisonous or in octaves.
Polyphonia, Gr. (pŏl-ĭ-fō-nĭ-ä.) A combination of many sounds; a composition for many voices.
Polyphony. (pō-lĭf-ō-ny.) ⎫ Multiplicity
Polyphonism. (pō-lĭf-ō-nĭsm.) ⎬ of sounds, as in the reverberation of an echo.
Polyphonic. (pŏl-ĭ-fŏn-ĭk.) ⎫ Full voiced, for
Polyphonous. (pō-lĭf-ō-nŭs.) ⎬ many voices.
Polyplectrum, Gr. (pŏl-ĭ-plĕk-trŭm.) A kind of ancient spinet, said to have been invented by Guido; so called from its strings being agitated by a number of quills.
Polythongum, Lat. (pŏl-ĭ-thŏn-gŭm.) An instrument used by the ancients and so named from its containing many strings.
Pompös, Ger. (pŏm-pōs.) Pompous, majestic.
Pomposaménte, It. (pŏm-pō-zä-män-tĕ.) Pompously, stately.
Pompóso, It. (pŏm-pō-zō.) Pompous, stately, grand.
Ponderóso, It. (pŏn-dĕ-rō-zō.) Ponderously, massively, heavily.
Ponticéllo, It. (pŏn-tē-tshăl-lō.) The bridge of the violin, guitar, etc.
Pont-neuf, Fr. (pŏnh-nŭf.) A street ballad, a vulgar song.
Porréctus, Lat. (pŏr-rĕk-tŭs.) The name of one of the ten notes used in the middle ages.
Portaménto, It. (pŏr-tä-mān-tō.) A term applied by the Italians to the manner or habit of sustaining and conducting the voice. A singer who is easy, and yet firm and steady in the execution of passages and phrases, is said to have a good *portaménto.* It is also used to connect two notes separated by an interval, by gliding the voice from one to the other, and by this means anticipating the latter in regard to intonation.
Portaménto di vóce, It. (pŏr-tä-män-tō dē rō-tshĕ.) Carrying the voice; the blending of one tone into another.
Portándo la vóce, It. (pŏr-tän-dō lä vō-tshĕ.) Carrying the voice, holding it firmly on the notes.
Portár la battúta, It. (pŏr-tär lä bät-too-tä.) To beat the time.
Portáre la vóce, It. (pŏr-tä-rĕ lä vō-tshĕ.) To sustain the voice.
Portative. A portable organ.
Portáto, It. (pŏr-tä-tō.) Sustained, drawn out.
Porte de voix, Fr. (pŏrt dŭh vwä.) An appoggiatura, or beat.
Portée, Fr. (pŏr-tā.) The staff.

ă ale, ă add, ă arm, ē eve, ĕ end, Ī ice, Ĭ ill, ō old, ŏ odd, ō dove, oo moon, ū lute, ŭ but, ü French sound.

PORT

Porter la voix, *Fr.* (pōr-tā lă vwă.) To carry the voice.
Porte-vent, *Fr.* (pōrt-vănh.) The pipe which conveys the wind from the bellows into the sound board of an organ.
Porte-voix, *Fr.* (pōr-vwă.) A speaking trumpet.
Portez la voix, *Fr.* (pōr-tā lă vwă.) See Portándo la Voce.
Portunal-flaut, *Ger.* (pōr-too-näl.) An organ stop of the clarabella species, the pipes of which are larger at the top than at the bottom and produce a tone of clarionet quality.
Posa, *Spa.* (pō-zā.) The passing bell; pauses made by the clergyman at a funeral to sing a responsary.
Posáto, *It.* (pō-zā-tō.) Quietly, steadily.
Posanne, *Ger.* (pō-zou-nĕ.) A trumpet; also, a trombone, a sackbut; also, an organ stop; see *Trombóne*.
Posaunen, *Ger.* (pō-zŏu-nĕn.) To sound on the trombone.
Posaunen-bläser, *Ger.* (pō-zŏu-nĕn blā-zăr.)
Posauner, *Ger.* (pō-zŏu-nĕr.)
A trombone player, a trumpet player.
Posaunenzug, *Ger.* (pō-zŏu-nĕn-tsoog.) A sackbut.
Posément, *Fr.* (pō-zā-mănh.) Without hurry, moderately, gravely, slowly.
Positif, *Fr.* (pō-zē-fĕf.)
Positiv, *Ger.* (pō-zi-ĭf.)
The choir organ, or lowest row of keys with soft toned stops in a large organ; also, a small *fixed* organ, thus named in opposition to a *portative* organ.
Position. A shift on the violin, tenor, or violincello; the arrangement or order of the several members of a chord.
Position, close. A term given to a chord when its tones are near together.
Position, dispersed. A term given to a chord when its tones are remote from each other.
Position, fundamental. A term applied to an uninverted chord, its root forming the lowest note of the chord.
Positive. An appellation formerly given to the little organ placed in front of the full or great organ.
Possíbile, *It.* (pōs-sē-bē-lĕ.) Possible; *il piu forte possibile*, as loud as possible.
Post-horn, *Ger.* (pōst-hŏrn.) A species of bugle.
Postlude, *Lat.* (pōst-lūde.)
Postludium, *Lat.* (pōst-lū-dĭ-ŭm.)
After-piece, concluding voluntary.
Post position. The putting a discord upon the accented part of a bar, followed by a concord upon the next unaccented part, but not prepared and resolved according to the rules for discords.
Post, sound. A small post within a violin, nearly under the bridge.
Potenza, *It.* (pō-tĕnt-sā.) A name applied by the ancients to the notes and signs of music; any sound produced by an instrument.
Pot-pourri, (pōt-poor-rĕ.) A medley: a *capriccio*, or *fantasia* in which favorite airs and fragments of musical pieces are strung together and contrasted.

PREC

Pouce, *Fr.* (pooss.) The thumb; a term used in guitar music, indicating that the thumb of the right hand must be passed lightly over all the strings.
Poule, *Fr.* (pool.) One of the movements of a quadrille.
Pour, *Fr.* (poor.) For.
Pour faire passer dessous le pouce, *Fr.* (poor făr păs-sā dĕs-soo lŭh pooss.) To pass the thumb under the fingers.
Pour finir, *Fr.* (poor fĭ-nĕr.) To finish; indicating a chord or bar which is to terminate the piece.
Pour la harpe, *Fr.* (poor lă hărp.)
Pour la premiere fois, *Fr.* (poor lă prŏm-I-ăr fwă.) For the first time, meaning that on the repetition of the strain this passage is to be omitted.
Pour reprendre au commencement. *Fr.* (poor rĕ-prănhdr ō kŏm-mănhs-mănh.) To go back to the beginning.
Poussé, *Fr.* (pooss-ā.) *Pushed*; meaning the up-bow.
Poyn, *Russ.* To sing.
Practice. The frequent repetition of a performance for the purpose of improvement; the actual performance of music, as distinguished from a mere theoretical knowledge.
Præambulam, *Lat.* (prē-ăm-bū-lăm.)
Præcentio, *Lat.* (prē-sĕn-shĭ-ō.)
A prelude.
Præcentor, *Lat.* (prē-sĕn-tŏr.) Precentor, leader of the choir.
Præfectus, *Lat.* (prē-fĕk-tŭs.) A president.
Præfectus chori, *Lat.* (prē-fĕk-tŭs kō-rē.) Master of the choristers.
Præsciæ, *Lat.* (prēs-sē-ē.) Females hired by the ancients to sing over the dead at funerals.
Prält-triller, *Ger.* (prălt trĭl-lĕr.) A transient or passing shake.
Präludien, *Ger. pl.* (prā-loo-dĭ-ĕn.) Preludes.
Präludiren, *Ger.* (drā-loo-dē-r'n.) To prelude, to play a prelude.
Präludium, *Ger.* (prā-loo-dĭ-oom.)
Präludium, *Lat.* (prā-lū-dĭ-ŭm.)
A prelude, an introduction.
Prästanten, *Ger.* (prā-stăn-t'n.) Pipes belonging to the *Prestant*, or open diapason, placed in the front of an organ case.
Prático, *It.* (prā-tē-kō.) Practical, skillful, experienced.
Precenteur, *Fr.* (prē-sănh-tŭr.) A precentor.
Precentor. The appellation given formerly to the master of the choir.
Precentore, *It.* (prā-tshĕn-tō-rĕ.) A precentor.
Precettóre di música, *It.* (prā-tshĕt-tō-rĕ dē moo-zē-kā.) A teacher of music.
Precipitaménte, *It.* (prā-tshē-pē-tă-mān-tĕ.)
Precipitáto, *It.* (prā-tshē-pē-tā-tō.)
In a precipitate manner, hurriedly.
Precipitándo, *It.* (prā-tshē-pē-tăn-dō.) Hurrying.
Precipitazióne, *It.* (prā-tshē-pē-tāt-sē-ō-nĕ.) Precipitation, haste, hurry.
Précipité, *Fr.* (prā-sē-pĭ-tā.) Hurried, accelerated.
Precipitóso, *It.* (prā-tshē-pē-tō-zō.) Hurrying, precipitous.

ā ale, ă add, ä arm, ē eve, ĕ end, ī ice, ĭ ill, ō old, ŏ odd, ô dove, oo moon, ū lute, ŭ but, ü French sound

PREC

Precisióne, *It.* (prā-tshē-zē-ō-nĕ.) Precision, exactness.
Preciso, *It.* (prā-tshē-zō.) Precise, exact, exactly.
Preetee, *Hin.* (prā-tā.) The third of the srovtis into which the fourth note of the Hindoo scale is divided.
Prefacion, *Spa.* (prā-fā-thē-ōn.) } Preface, introduction.
Prefazióne, *It.* (prā-fā-tsē-ō-nĕ.) } troduction.
Preghiéra, *It.* (prā-ghē-ā-rā.) Prayer, supplication.
Prelude. A short introductory composition, or extempore performance, to prepare the ear for the succeeding movements.
Preludiare, *It.* (prē-loo-dē-ā-rē.) To perform a prelude.
Preludio, *Spa.* (prē-loo-dē-ō.) } A prelude,
Preludio, *It.* (prē-loo-dē-ō.) } or introduction.
Preludium, *Lat.* (prē-lū-dī-ŭm) } tion.
Premier, *Fr.* (prĕm-ī-ă.) } First.
Premiere, *Fr.* (prĕm-ī-ār.) }
Premiére dessus, *Fr.* (prĕm-ī-ār dās-sū.) First treble, first soprano.
Premiére fois, *Fr.* (prĕm-ī-ār fwā.) First time.
Premiére partie, *Fr.* (prĕm-ī-ār pār-tē.) First part.
Preparation. That disposition of the harmony by which discords are lawfully introduced. A discord is said to be prepared, when the discordant note is heard in the preceding chord and in the same part as a consonance.
Preparative notes. Appoggiaturae or leaning notes.
Ppreparazione, *It.* (prē-pā-rā-tsē-ō-nĕ.) Preparation.
Prepared. Arranged in conformity to the rules of preparation.
Prepared discord. That discord the discordant notes of which have been heard in a concord.
Prepared intervals. Intervals changed from large to small, and from small to large, by the aid of intermediate tones.
Prepared shake. A shake preceded by two or more introductory notes. Prepared shake or trill.
Prés de la table, *Fr.* (prā dūh lā tābl.) Near the sound board.
Pressante, *Fr.* (prĕs-sänht.) Pressing on, hurrying.
Pressure tone. A sudden crescendo, ex.
Prestaménte, *It.* (prĕs-tā-mān-tĕ.) Hurriedly, rapidly.
Prestant, *Fr.* (prĕs-tänh.) The open diapason stop in an organ, of either 32, 16, 8, or 4 feet scale; see *Prästanien.*
Prestézza, *It.* (prĕs-tēt-sā.) Quickness, rapidity.
Prestissimaménte, *It.* (prĕs-tēs-sē-mä-mān-tĕ.) }
Prestíssimo, *It.* (prĕs-tēs-sē-mō.) } Very quickly, as fast as possible.
Présto, *It.* (prās-tō.) Quickly, rapidly.

PRIN

Présto assái, *It.* (prās-tō äs-sāī-ē.) Very quick, with the utmost rapidity.
Présto, ma non tróppo, *It.* (prās-tō mä nōn trōp-pō.) Quick, but not too much so.
Priére, *Fr.* (prē-ār.) A prayer, supplication.
Priests, chantry. Stipendiary priests whose particular object it was to sing mass in the chantries.
Prima, *It.* (prē-mā.) First, chief, principal.
Prima búffa, *It.* (prē-mā boof-fā.) The principal female singer in a comic opera.
Prima dónna, *It.* (prē-mā dŏn-nā.) Principal female singer in a serious opera.
Prima dónna assolúta, *It.* First female singer in an operatic establishment: the only one who can claim that title.
Prima opera, *It.* (prē-mā ōp-ē-rā.) First productions.
Prima párte, *It.* (prē-mā pär-tĕ.) First part.
Prima párte repetíta, *It.* (prē-mā pär-tĕ rā-pē-tē-tā.) Repeat the first part.
Primarii, *Lat.* (prē-mā-rī-ē.) Of the first rank—a term applied to the first and second tones by old writers.
Primary chord. The common chord; the first chord.
Prima vísta, *It.* (prē-mā vēs-tā.) At first sight.
Prima vólta, *It.* (prē-mā vōl-tā.) The first time.
Prime, *Ger.* (prēm.) First note, or tone of a scale.
Prime donne, *It. pl.* (prē-mē dŏn-nĕ.) The plural of prima donna.
Primes. Two notes placed on the same degree of the staff, and having the same pitch of sound.
Primes, perfect. Primes uninfluenced in their tones by sharps or flats.
Prime, superfluous. An interval arising from the flatting or sharping of one of the two notes denominated primes.
Primicerio, *Spa.* (prē-mē-thā-rī-ō.) Precentor.
Primitive chord. That chord the lowest note of which is of the same literal denomination as the fundamental bass of the harmony.
Primo, *It.* (prē-mō.) Principal, first.
Primo búffo, *It.* (prē-mō boof-fō.) First male singer in a comic opera.
Primo músico, *It.* (prē-mō moo-zē-kō.) Principal male singer.
Primo témpo, *It.* (prē-mō tăm-pō.) The first, or original time.
Primo tenóre, *It.* (prē-mō tĕ-nō-rĕ.) } The first
Primo uómo, *It.* (prē-mō wō-mō.) } tenor singer.
Primo violíno, *It.* (prē-mō vē-ō-lē-nō.) The first violin.
Prim-tône. *Ger. pl.* (prĭm-tō-nĕ.) Fundamental tones, or notes.
Principal, or octave. An important organ stop, tuned an octave above the diapasons, and therefore of four feet pitch on the manual, and eight feet on the pedals. In German organs the term *Principal* is also applied to all the open diapasons of 32, 16, 8 and 4 feet.
Principal bass. An organ stop of the open diapason species on the pedals.
Principal close. The usual cadence in the principal key, so called because generally occuring at the close of a piece.

ă *ale*, ă *add*, ä *arm*, ō *eve*, ŏ *end*, ī *ice*, ĭ *ill*, ō *old*, ŏ *odd*, ō *dove*, oo *moon*, ū *lute*, ŭ *but*, ü *French sound*.

PRIN

Principále, *It.* (prēn-tshē-pä-lĕ.) Principal, chief: *violíno principále*, the principal violin.
Principalménte, *It.* (prēn-tshē-päl-mān-tĕ.) Principally, chiefly.
Principal octave. An organ stop: see Principal.
Principal violin. The first or leading violin in a performance.
Principal voices. The highest and lowest; the soprano and bass.
Principiante, *It.* (prēn-tshe-pē-än-tĕ.) A beginner.
Principien, *Ger.* (prĭn-tsĭp-ĭ-ĕn.) Rudiments; elements.
Probe, *Ger.* (prō-bĕ.) Proof, trial, rehearsal.
Proceleusmatic, *Gr.* (prō-sĕl-oos-măt-ĭk.) A metrical foot in poetry consisting of four short syllables.
Procélla, *It.* (prō-tshäl-lä.) A storm, musical delineation of a storm.
Producente, *It.* (prō-doo-tshĕn-tĕ.) Fifth tone of the scale.
Profane music. A term formerly applied to all music not adapted to church service; secular music.
Professeur de chant, *Fr.* (prō-fĕa-sŭr dŭh shänh.) A professor of vocal music; a singing master.
Professeur de musique, *Fr.* (prō-fĕa-sŭr dŭh mü-zēk.)
Professóre di música, *It.* (prō-fĕa-sō-rĕ dē moo-zĕ-kä.) Professor of music. In the universities, the professor of music enjoys academical rank, confers musical degrees, lectures on harmonic science, etc.
Prográmme, *It.* (prō-gräm-mĕ.) A programme.
Programme. An order of exercises for musical or other entertainments.
Pregressio harmonica, *Lat.* (prō-grĕs-sī-ō här-mŏn-ē-kä.) A mixture stop in German organs, commencing with two ranks at the bottom, and increasing to three, four, or five ranks, in the upper part of the manual.
Progression. A succession of triads or perfect chords, which are confined to the tonic.
Progressióne, *It.* (prō-grĕs-sē-ō-nĕ.) Progression.
Progressive. A term applied to exercises, or lessons, arranged especially for practical performance, commencing with the elementary and rising by slow grades to the most difficult style of performance.
Progression, triple. In old music, a series of fifths.
Progressive notes. Those notes which succeed each other, either in ascent or descent, by those degrees, the settled order of which constitutes the key of the composition or of the passage in which they are found.
Prolatio, *Lat.* (prō-lă-shĭ-ō.) Adding a dot, to increase, or lengthen, the value of a note.
Prolation. A method used in old music of determining the value of semibreves and minims.
Prolazióne, *It.* (prō-lä-tsē-ō-nĕ.) Prolation.
Prologhétto, *It.* (prō-lō-gĕt-tō.) A short prologue.

PROV

Prólogo, *Spa.* (prō-lō-gō.) A prologue.
Prologue, musical. The preface or introduction to a musical composition or performance; a prelude.
Prolonged shake. A shake which can be opened or closed at pleasure.
Proloquium, *Lat.* (prō-lō-quī-ŭm.) An introductory excess of words or syllables which preceeds the first bar of a chant.
Promenade concert. A vocal or instrumental concert during which the audience promenade the hall instead of being seated.
Promptement, *Fr.* (prŏnht-mänh.) } Readily,
Prontaménte, *It.* (prōn-tä-män-tĕ.) } quickly, promptly.
Prónto, *It.* (prōn-tō.) Ready, quick.
Pronunziáre, *It.* (prō-noon-tsē-ä-rĕ.) To pronounce, to enunciate. [nounced.
Pronunziato, *It.* (prō-noon-tsē-ä-tō.) Pro-
Prophet. Name given in remote times to bards and rhapsodists.
Proportion, rhythmical. The proportion in relation to time or measure between the notes representing duration.
Propósta, *It.* (prō-pōs-tä.) Subject or theme of a fugue.
Prosæ sequentiæ, *Lat.* (prō-sē sĕ-quĕn-shĭ-ē.) Hymns sung at the festivals of Easter and Pentecost.
Proscenio, *It.* (prōs-shä-nē-ō.) } Proscenium.
Proscenio, *Spa.* (prōs-thä-nī-ō.) }
Proscenium. (prōs-sĕn-ī-ŭm.) The front part of the stage where the drop scene separates the stage from the audience.
Proscorda, *Gr.* (prōs-kŏr-dä.) An instrumental and varied accompaniment to the ancient vocal music, invented by the Greek musician Crexus, before whose time the accompaniment was in unison, or *note for note*.
Proslambanomenos, *Gr.* (prōs-läm-bä-nŏm-ĕ-nōs.) The lowest note in the Greek system, equivalent to A on the first space in the base of the modern.
Prosodia, *Gr.* (prō-sō-dĭ-ä.) A sacred song, or hymn, sung by the ancients in honor of the gods.
Prosodiac. (prō-sō-dĭ-ăk.) An epithet by which the ancient Greeks distinguished a species of *nome* or air sung in honor of Mars.
Prosody. A term, partly grammatical and partly musical, relating to the accent and metrical quantity of syllables, in lyrical composition.
Protagonísta, *It.* (prō-tä-gō-nēs-tä.) The principal character of a drama.
Protesis, *Gr.* (prŏt-ĕ-sĭs.) A certain pause in ancient Greek music.
Prothalamion, *Gr.* (prō-thă-lă-mĭ-ŏn.) A nuptial song.
Protopsaltes, (prō-tō-psăl-tĕs.) The name of that one of the two principal singers in the patriarchal church of Constantinople who is stationed on the right side of the choir.
Próva, *It.* (prō-vä.) Proof, trial, rehearsal.
Próva generale, *It.* (prō-vä jĕn-ĕ-rä-lĕ.) The last rehearsal previous to a public performance.
Provençales, (prō-vĕn-sä-lĕs.) Poets, or troubadours, in the eleventh century.

ā *ale*, ă *add*, ä *arm*, ē *eve*, ĕ *end*, I *ice*, Ĭ *ill*, ō *old*, ŏ *odd*, O *dove*, oo *moon*, ū *lute*, ŭ *but*, ü *French sound*.

PROV

Provvisatóre, *It.* (prōv-vē-sä-*tō*-rĕ.) See Improvvisatore.
Prusarunee, *Hin.* (proo-sä-roo-nä.) The second of the Srootis into which the Mnddhum or fourth note of the Hindoo scales is divided.
Psallette, *Fr.* (psäl-lĕt.) Singing-place, choir.
Psallo, *Gr.* (săl-lō.) To play on, or to sing to, a stringed instrument.
Psalm. A sacred song or hymn.
Psalm-buch, *Ger.* (*psălm* bookh.) A psalter, a book of psalms.
Psalmen, *Ger.* (psăl-mĕn.) To sing, to chant psalms.
Psalm-gesang, *Ger.* (psălm ghĕ-zăng.) Psalmody.
Psalmist. A composer, writer, or singer of psalms or sacred songs.
Psalmistæ, *Lat.* (săl-mĭs-tē.) Certain canonical singers in the primitive church.
Psalm-lied, *Ger.* (psălm lĕd.) Psalm, sacred song or hymn.
Psalmodie, *Fr.* (psăl-mō-dē.) Psalmody.
Psalmodier, *Fr.* (psăl-mō-dĭ-ā.) To chant psalms.
Psalmodist. One who sings sacred songs or psalms.
Psalmody. The practice or art of singing psalms; a style or collection of music designed for church service.
Psalmody Island. An island, formerly in the diocese of Nismes, France, which had its name from a monastery founded there about the end of the fourteenth century, the constitution of which enjoined the preserving of a perpetual psalmody, called by the monkish writers *Laus Perennis*.
Psalmody, perpetual. The *Laus Perennis*.
Psalmographist. A writer of psalms, or divine songs and hymns.
Psalmography. (săl-mō-grăf-y.) The art of writing, or composing psalms or hymns.
Psalmsammlung, *Ger.* (sălm-säm-loong.) Collection of psalms.
Psalm-sänger, *Ger.* (psălm säng-ĕr.) Psalmodist, psalm singer.
Psalm-singen, *Ger.* (psălm sĭng-ĕn.) Psalmody.
Psalter. The book of Psalms.
Psalter, *Ger.* (*psăl*-tĕr.) Psaltery.
Psalter-spiel, *Ger.* (psăl-tĕr spēl.) Playing on the psaltery.
Psalterion, *Fr.* (psăl-tā-rĭ-ŏnh.) } A stringed
Psalterium, *Lat.* (săl-tā-rĭ-ŭm.) } instrument
Psaltery, *Eng.* } much used by the Hebrews, supposed to be a species of lyre, harp, or dulcimer.
Psaltes, *Gr.* (săl-tēs.) A player on, or singer to, a stringed instrument.
Psaltriæ, *Lat.* (săl-trĭ-ē.) Female singers and players on the *psalterium*, who entertained the ancient Romans at their banquets.
Psaume, *Fr.* (psŏm.) A psalm.
Psaume des morts, *Fr.* (psŏm dĕ mŏr.) Death psalm, funeral hymn.

PYTH

Pseautier, *Fr.* (psō-tĭ-ā.) A Psalter, or book of psalms.
Pu. A syllable applied to the fifth note of the Hindoo scale in solfaing.
Puente, *Spa.* (poo-ăn-tĕ.) The bridge of a stringed instrument.
Pulcha, *Rus.* (pool-kä.) A Russian dance, the original of the polka.
Pulcher, *Lat.* (pŭl-kĕr.) Beautiful, gay.
Pulsatile. (*pŭl*-să-tĕl.) *Striking;* instruments of percussion, as the drum. tambourine, etc.
Pulsatilia, *Lat.* (pŭl-să-*tĭl*-ĭ-ă) Pulsatile instruments.
Punchum. The name of the fifth note in the Hindoo musical scale.
Punctum contra punctum, *Lat.* (*pŭnk*-tŭm *kŏn*-trä *pŭnk*-tŭm.) Point against point; see *Counterpoint*.
Punctus, *Lat.* (*pŭnk*-tŭs.) A dot, a point.
Punctus caudatus, *Lat.* (*pŭnk*-tŭs kaw-*dä*-tŭs.) In ancient music, a character otherwise called point of alteration or division.
Punkt, *Ger.* (poonkt.) A dot.
Punkte, *Ger.* (*poonk*-tĕ.) Dots.
Punktirt, *Ger.* (poonk-*tĭrt*.) Dotted.
Punktirte noten, *Ger.* (poonk-tĭr-tĕ nō-t'n.) Dotted notes.
Punta, *It.* (poon-tä.) The point, the top; also, a thrust, or push.
Púnta d'arco, *It.* (*poon*-tä d'är-kō.) }
Púnta del'arco, *It.* (*poon*-tä dĕl är-kō.) }
The point or tip of the bow.
Puntáto, *It.* (poon-*tä*-tō.) Pointed, detached, marked.
Puntear, *Spa.* (poon-tĕ-är.) To pinch the strings of a guitar.
Púnto, *It.* (poon-tō.) A dot, a point.
Púnto d'organo, *It.* (poon-tō d'ŏr-gä-nō.) Organ point.
Púnto d'accressimento, *It.* (poon-tō d'ăk-krĕs-sĕ-*măn*-tō.) The point of augmentation.
Púnto di divisione, *It.* (poon-tō dĕ dĕ-vĕ-zĕ-ō-nĕ.) Point of division.
Púnto per púnto, *It.* (poon-to pĕr poon-tō.) Note for note.
Pupitre, *Fr.* (pū-pĕtr.) A music desk.
Pycnos, *Gr.* (pĭk-nŏs.) A name given by the ancient Greeks to two of their genera of music, the chromatic and enharmonic.
Pyp, *Dut.* (pĭp.) A pipe.
Pyramidal flute. An 8 feet organ stop of wood.
Pyramidon, *Gr.* (pĭ-*răm*-ĭ-dŏn.) An organ stop of 16 or 32 feet tone, on the pedals, invented by the Rev. F. A. G. Ouseley. The pipes are four times larger at the top than at the mouth, and the tone of remarkable gravity, resembling that of a stopped pipe in quality.
Pyrrhica, *Gr.* (*pĭr*-hĭks.) Ancient military dances in which the dancers are armed.
Pyrrhique, *Fr.* (pĭr-hĕk.) A military dance.
Pythagorian lyre. An instrument said to have been invented by Pythagoras.

ă *ale*, ă *add*, ă *arm*, ŏ *eve*, ĕ *end*, 1 *ice*, ĭ *ill*, ō *old*, ŏ *odd*, ȯ *dove*, oo *moon*, ū *lute*, ŭ *but*, ü *French sound*.

QUAD

Quadrat, *Ger.* (quăd-*rät.*) The marked called a natural, ♮.
Quadráto, *It.* (quăd-*rä*-tō.) The note B in the natural or diatonic scale.
Quadricinium, *Lat.* (quăd-rĭ-sĭn-ĭ-ŭm.)
Quadripartite, *Fr.* (kăd-rĭ-păr-tĕt.)
A quartet, a composition in four parts.
Quadriglio, *It.* (quăd-*rēl*-yē-ō.) Quadrille.
Quadrille, *Fr.* (kă-*drēl*.) A French dance, or set of five consecutive dance movements, called La Pantalon, La Poule, L'Ete, La Trenise (or La Pastourelle), and La Finale.
Quadrillen, *Ger.* (quăd-rĭl-l'n.) Quadrilles.
Quadripartire, *It.* (quăd-rē-păr-tē-rē.) To divide into four parts.
Quadriplicato, *It.* (quăd-rē-plē-*kä*-tō.) Quadruple.
Quadrivium, *Lat.* (quăd-*rĭv*-ĭ-ŭm.) The general term in the ninth and tenth centuries for the four sciences, music, arithmetic, geometry and astronomy.
Quadro, *It.* (quă-drō.) The mark called a natural, ♮.
Quadruple. Fourfold.
Quadruple counterpoint. Counterpoint in four parts, all of which may be inverted, and each of them taken as a bass, middle, or high part.
Quadruple croche, *Fr.* (kăd-rüpl krŏsh.)
Quadruple quaver, *Eng.* (*kwăd*-rŭ-pl quă-vĕr.)
Four-hooked; a half-demisemiquaver, or semidemisemiquaver.
Quádruplo, *It.* (quăd-roo-plō.) } In four
Quadruplo, *Lat.* (quăd-roo-plō.) } parts.
Quantity. The relative duration of notes or syllables.
Quárta, *It.* (quăr-tă.) } A fourth; also the fourth
Quarto, *It.* (quăr-tō.) } voice, or instrumental part.
Quárta módi, *It.* (quăr-tă mō-dē.) } The sub-
Quárta tóni, *It.* (quăr-tă tō-nē.) } dominant, or fourth note of the scale.
Quart de son, *Fr.* (kăr dŭh sŏnh.) } A quarter
Quart de ton, *Fr.* (kăr dŭh tŏnh.) } tone.
Quart de soupir, *Fr.* (kăr dŭh soo-pēr.) A semiquaver rest.
Quarte, *Fr.* (kărt.) } A fourth.
Quarte, *Ger.* (quăr-tĕ.) }
Quarte augmentee, *Fr.* (kărt ōg-mănh-*tă*.) Sharp fourth.
Quarte diminuee, *Fr.* (kărt dĭ-mē-noo-*ă*.) Minor fourth.
Quarte de nazard, *Fr.* (kărt dŭh nă-*zărd*.) Fourth above the *nazard*, an organ stop identical with the fifteenth.
Quarte du ton, *Fr.* (kărt dŭ tŏnh.) The fourth note of the scale.
Quarter note. A crotchet.
Quarter rest. A pause equal in duration to a quarter note.
Quarter tone. A small interval, or deviation in pitch, which, in the mathematical theory of music is found to exist, approximately, between D♯ and E♭, G♯ and A♭, etc.
Quartet, stringed. A quartet, or composition arranged for four stringed instruments, consisting of first and second violins, viola and violincello.

QUIE

Quartes, *Fr.* (kărt.) Fourths.
Quartet, *Eng.* (quăr-*tĕt*.) } A composition
Quartett, *Ger.* (quăr-*tĕtt*.) } for four voices or
Quartétto, *It.* (quăr-tĕt-tō.) } instruments.
Quartettíno, *It.* (qnăr-tĕt-tē-nō.) A short quartet.
Quartet, wood. A quartet consisting of the flute, oboe, clarionet and bassoon.
Quart-fagott, *Ger.* (quărt fä-*gŏt*.) } An old
Quart-fagótto, *It.* (quărt fä-*gŏt*-tō.) } sort of bassoon, formerly used as a tenor to the hautboy; called also, *Dulcino* and *Dulzain*.
Quart-flöte, *Ger.* (quărt *flö*-tĕ.) A flute sounding a fourth above.
Quárto, *It.* (quăr-tō.) The fourth; the quarter note.
Quárto d'aspétto, *It.* (quăr-tō d'ăs-*păt*-tō.) A semiquaver rest.
Quárto di tuóno, *It.* (quăr-tō dĕ *twō*-nō.) Quarter tone.
Quárto violíno, *It.* (quăr-tō vē-ō-*lē*-nō.) The fourth violin.
Quási, *It.* (quă-zē.) In the manner of, in the style of.
Quási allegrétto, *It.* (quă-zē äl-lĕ-*grĕt*-tō.) Like an *Allegrétto*.
Quási andánte, *It.* (quă-zē än-*dăn*-tĕ.) In the style of an *Andánte*.
Quási présto, *It.* (quă-zē *präs*-tō.) Like a *Prèsto*.
Quási recitativo, *It.* (quă-zē rĕ-tshĕ-tä-*tē*-vō.) Resembling a recitative.
Quási una fantasía, *It.* (quă-ze oo-nă făn-tă-*zē*-ă.) As if it were a fantasia.
Quatrain. A stanza of four lines rhyming alternately.
Quatre, *Fr.* (kătr.) } Four: *a quatre mains,*
Quáttro, *It.* (quăt-trō.) } or, *a quáttro máni,* for four hands; a pianoforte duet.
Quatricinium, *Lat.* (quăt-rē-sĭn-ĭ-ŭm.) A short piece for four horns or trumpets.
Quattricóma, *It.* (quăt-trē-*kō*-mä.) A demisemiquaver.
Quátuor, *Lat.* (quă-tŭ-ŏr.) A quartet.
Quaver. A note equal to half a crotchet.
Quaver rest. A mark of silence equal in value to a quaver.
Quedo, *Spa.* (*kā*-dō.) Softly, gently, in a low voice.
Querstriche, *Ger.* (quăr-strĭ-khĕ.) Ledger lines.
Quer-flöte, *Ger.* (quăr *flö*-tĕ.) German flute; see *Flaúto Travérso*.
Querimonia, *Lat.* (quĕr-ĭ-*mō*-nĭ-ă.) A religious cantata of a dolorous cast; in the manner of the *Lachrimæ*.
Quer-pfeife, *Ger.* (quăr *pfī*-fĕ.) A fife.
Quer-stand, *Ger.* (quăr stănd.) False relation; in harmony.
Quésta, *It.* (quĕs-tă.) } This, or that.
Quésto, *It.* (quĕs-tō.) }
Queue, *Fr.* (küh.) The tail, or stem, of a note; also, the tail-piece of a violin, etc.
Quickstep. A lively march, generally in 3-4 time.
Quiebro, *Spa.* (kē-ĕ-brō.) A shake, or trill.
Quiéto, *It.* (quē-ĕ-tō.) Quiet, calm, serene.

ă ale, ă add, ä arm, ĕ eve, ĕ end, ī ice, ĭ ill, ō old, ŏ odd, ô dove, oo moon, ū lute, ŭ but, ü French sound.

QUIL

Quilisma, *Lat.* (quĭ-lĭs-mä.) The name of one of the ten notes used in the middle ages.
Quills. The plectrums, or instruments formerly used instead of the fingers in playing upon the harp, guitar, etc.
Quinque, *Lat.* (quĭn-quĕ.) Five.
Quint, *Lat.* (quĭnt.) ⎫ A fifth: also, the
Quinta, *It.* (quĕn-tä.) ⎬ name of an organ stop
Quinte, *Fr.* (kănht.) ⎬ sounding a fifth (or
Quinte, *Ger.* (quĭn-tĕ.) ⎭ twelfth) above the foundation stops.
Quinta acuta, *Lat.* (quĭn-tä ä-kū-tä.) Fifth above.
Quinta décima, *It* (quĕn-tä dā-tshē-mä,) ⎫
Quintus decimus, *Lat.* (quĭn-tŭs dĕs-ĭ-mŭs.) ⎬
The *fifth above the tenth*, an organ stop identical with the fifteenth.
Quintadena. ⎫ An organ stop: see *Quinta-*
Quinta-ed-una. ⎬ *tion.*
Quinta módi, *It.* (quĕn-tä mŏ-dē.) ⎫ The dom-
Quinta tóni, *It.* (quĕn-tä tō-nē.) ⎬ inaut or fifth from the tonic.
Quinta pars, *Lat.* (quĭn-tä pärs.) An expression applied by the ecclesiastical musicians of the fourteenth century to the fifth or additional part of the choral service. The established number was four; the *cantus*, or treble; altus, or counter tenor; the tenor and the bass. When an additional part was employed it was called the *Quinta Pars*.
Quintaton, *Ger.* (quĭn-tä-tōn.) A manual organ stop of eight feet tone; a stopped diapason of rather small scale producing the twelfth, as well as the ground tone; it also occurs as a pedal stop of thirty-two and sixteen feet tone.
Quint-bass. An organ pedal stop; see *Quint.*
Quinte, *Fr.* (kănht.) Interval of a fifth.
Quinte cachee, *Fr.* (kănht kä-shā.) Hidden fifth.

QUON

Quinte de viole, *Fr.* (kănht dŭh vē-ŏl.) The viola.
Quinte octaviante, *Fr.* (kănht ŏk-tä-vĭ-änht.) Octave quint, the twelfth.
Quinterne. An obsolete Italian instrument, resembling a lute.
Quintes, *Fr.* (kănht.) Fifths.
Quintet. A composition for five voices or instruments.
Quintétto, *It.* (quĕn-tăt-tō.) ⎫ A quintet.
Quintette, *Fr.* (kănh-tĕt.) ⎬
Quint-fagott, *It.* (quĕnt fä-gŏt.) The small bassoon, or *fagottina*, sounding a fifth higher than the common bassoon.
Quint-gedacht, *Ger.* (quĭnt ghĕ-däkht.) An organ stop of the stopped diapason species, sounding the fifth above.
Quintilla, *Spa.* (kĕn-tēl-yä.) A metrical composition of five feet in each line.
Quinto, *It.* (quĕn-tō.) A fifth.
Quintoire, *Fr.* (kănh-twăr.) An old French term applied to a species of descant consisting chiefly of fifths.
Quintole, *Lat.* (quĭn-tō-lĕ.) A group of five notes, having the same value as four of the same species.
Quint-saite, *Ger.* (quĭnt sī-tĕ.) Treble string.
Quintuple. A species of time now seldom used, containing five parts in a bar.
Quire. A choir, a body of singers; that part of a church where the choristers sit; see *Choir.*
Quirister. A chorister (little used).
Qui tollis, *Lat.* (qoē tŏl-lĭs.) A part of the *Gloria.*
Quodlibet. *Lat.* (quŏd-lĭ-bĕt.) A medley of airs, etc., out of different works, or by various composers; a musical pot-pourri.
Quoniam tu solus, *Lat.* (quō-nĭ-ăm tū sō-lŭs.) Part of the Gloria.

PRONOUNCING MUSICAL DICTIONARY.

ā ale, ă add, ä arm, ē eve, ĕ end, ī ice, ĭ ill, ō old, ŏ odd, ô dove, oo moon, ū lute, ŭ but, ü French sound.

R

R, or R H, indicates the right hand in pianoforte playing.
Rabani. (rä-*bä*-nē.)) A species of tambourine
Rabbana. (rä-*bä*-nä.) ∫ used by the negroes.
Rábbia, *It.* (rab-bē-ä.) Rage, fury, madness.
Rabel, *Spa.* (rä-*bäl*.) An ancient musical instrument of three strings played with a bow.
Raccourcir, *Fr.* (rä-coor-sēr.) To abridge.
Racleur, *Fr.* (rä-klŭr.) A poor player.
Raddolcéndo, *It.* (räd-dōl-*tshăn*-dō.)) With
Raddolcénte, *It.* (räd-dōl-*tshăn*-tē.) ∫ increasing softness; becoming softer by degrees.
Raddoppiaménto, *It.* (räd-dōp-pē-ä-*măn*-tō.) Augmentation; reduplication; the doubling of an interval.
Raddoppiáte nóte, *It.* (räd-dōp-pē-ä-tĕ nō-tĕ.) Repeated, or reiterated notes.
Raddoppiáto, *It.* (räd-dōp-pē-ä-tō.) Doubled, increased, augmented.
Radical bass. The fundamental bass, the roots of the various chords.
Raggióne, *It.* (räd-jē-ō-nĕ.) Ratio; proportion.
Ragoke. A small Russian horn.
Rallentaménto, *It.* (räl-lĕn-tä-*măn*-tō.))
Rallentándo, *It.* (räl-lĕn-*tăn*-dō.))
Rallentáto, *It.* (räl-lĕn-*tä*-tō.))
The time gradually slower and the sound gradually softer.
Rallentándo assai, *It.* (räl-lĕn-*tăn*-dō äs-sä-ē.) A slackening of the time.
Rans des vaches, *Fr.* (ränh dĕ väsh.) Pastoral airs played by the Swiss herdsmen, to assemble their cattle together for the return home.
Rapidaménte, *It.* (rä-pē-dä-*măn*-tē.) Rapidly.
Rapidaménte e brillánte, *It.* (rä-pē-dä-*măn*-tē ā brēl-*lăn*-tē.) Rapidly and brilliantly.
Rapidita, *It.* (rä-pē-dē-*tä*.) Rapidity.
Rápido, *It.* (*räd*-pē-dō.) Rapid.
Rappel. A noisy Egyptian instrument, something like a drum.
Rapsodie, *Fr.* (rāp-sō-dē.)) A *capriccio*, a
Rapsody, *Eng.* (răp-sō-dy.) ∫ fragmentary piece, a wild, unconnected composition.
Rasch, *Ger.* (räsh.) Swift, spirited.
Rase-gesang, *Ger.* (rä-zĕ ghē-zăng.)) A wild
Rase-lied, *Ger.* (rä-zĕ lēd.) ∫ song, a dithyrambic.
Rasgádo, *Spa.* (rüs-gä-dō.) Drawing the thumb over the strings of a guitar, so as produce an *arpéggio* effect.
Rastral, *Lat.* (räs-trāl.)) A little instru-
Rastrum, *Lat.* (räs-trŭm.) ∫ ment for drawing music lines on staves.
Ratenéndo, *It.* (rät tĕ-*năn*-dō.)) Holding
Rattenúto, *It.* (rät-tĕ-*noo*-tō.) ∫ back, restraining the time.
Rattézza, *It.* (rät-*tăt*-sä.) Swiftness, rapidity.
Raucedíne, *It.* (rä-oo-tshē-dē-nĕ.) Hoarseness.
Rauco, *It.* (rä-oo-kō.) Hoarse, harsh.
Rauh, *Ger.* (*rä*-ooh.)) Rough.
Rauque, *Fr.* (rōk.) ∫
Rausch-pfeife, *Ger.* (ronsh-pfī-fĕ.)) *Rustling*
Rausch-quint, *Ger.* (roush quĭnt.) ∫ *Afth*; a mixture stop in German organs, the 12th and 15th on one slide.
Ravanastron. A very simple form of bow instrument among the Hindoos of ancient origin.

RECI

Ravvivándo, *It.* (räv-vē-*văn*-dō.) Reviving, quickening, accelerating.
Ravvivándo il témpo, *It.* (räv-vē-*văn*-dō ēl *tăm*-pō.) Accelerating the time.
Re. (rā.) A syllable applied in solfaing, to the note D.
Reading music. The act of singing or playing music at sight.
Realejo, *Spa.* (rā-ä-*lā*-hō.) A chamber organ.
Rebec.) A Moorish word signifying an instru-
Rebecca. ∫ ment with two strings played on with a bow. The Moors brought the Rebec into Spain, whence it passed into Italy, and after the addition of a third string obtained the name of *Rebecca*, whence the old English Rebec, or fiddle with three strings.
Rebecchíno, *It.* (rā-bĕt-*kē*-nō.) Small rebec guitar.
Re bémol, *Fr.* (rā bā-mōl.) The note D-flat.
Re bémol majeur, *Fr.* (rā bā-mōl mä-zhŭr.) The key of D-flat major.
Rechanter, *Fr.* (rē-shänb-*tā*.) To sing again.
Recheat. An old term for a series of notes which huntsmen sound on a horn to recall the dogs from a false scent.
Rebab.) A *rebec*.
Rebeb. ∫
Recherche, *Fr.* (rē-*shärsh*.) Research; name formerly given by the French to an extemporaneous prelude introducing a piece.
Recherché, *Fr.* (rē-shēr-*shā*.) Rare, affected, formal.
Recht, *Ger.* (rĕkht.) Right.
Rechte hand, *Ger.* (rĕkht *händ*.) Right hand.
Recitado, *Spa.* (rā-tshē-tä-dō.) Recitative.
Recitánti, *It.* (rā-tshē-*tăn*-dō.)) Declamatory,
Recitánte, *It.* (rā-tshē-*tăn*-tē.) ∫ in the style of a recitative.
Recitative. (rĕ-sĭ-tä-*tēv*.) A species of musical declamation in which the performer rejects the rigorous rules of time and endeavors to imitate the inflections, accent and emphasis of natural speech.
Recitatif, *Fr.* (rē-sē-tä-*tēf*.))
Recitativ, *Ger.* (rĕt-sĭ-tĭl-tĭf.)) Recitative.
Recitatívo, *It.* (rē-tshē-tä-*tē*-vō.))
Recitative accompanied. A recitative is said to be accompanied when, besides the bass, there are *parts* for other instruments, as violins, flutes, hautboys, etc.
Recitativo instromentáto, *It.* (rē-tshē-tä-tō-vō ēn-strō-mĕn-tä-tō.) Accompanied recitative.
Recitativo parlánte, *It.* (rē-tshē-tä-tē-vō pär-*lăn*-tē.)
Recitativo sécco, *It.* (rē-tshē-tä-tē-vō *săk*-kō,) Unaccompanied recitative; also, when accompanied only by the violoncello and double bass, or the pianoforte or organ.
Recitativo stromentáto. (rē-tshē-tä-tē-vō strō-mĕn-*tä*-tō.) Recitative accompanied by the orchestra: see Recitativo Instromentáto.
Recitativzug, *Ger.* (rĕt-sĭ-tä-tĭf-tsoog.) Recitative stop.
Recitatore, *It.* (rē-tshē-tä-*tō*-rĕ.) One who recites.
Recitazione, *It.* (rē-tshē-tä-tsē-ō-nĕ.) Recitation.

ă ale, ă add, ä arm, ō eve, ĕ end, ī ice, ĭ ill, ō old, ŏ odd, ô dove, oo moon, ū lute, ŭ but, ü French sound

RECI

Réciter, *Fr.* (rā-sī-tā.) To recite.
Reciting note. The note in a chord upon which the voice dwells until it comes to a cadence.
Réclame, *Fr.* (rā-klām.) The song of a bird.
Réclamer, *Fr.* (rā-klā-mā.) To sing in imitation of a bird.
Recomposed. Composed again; reset.
Record. Among bird fanciers this verb is used to signify the first essays of a bird in singing.
Recorder. An old wind instrument somewhat resembling a flute, but of smaller bore and shriller tone.
Recorder. An instrument which, when attached to a pianoforte, will record upon paper the notes that are played.
Recreation. A composition of attractive style, designed to relieve the tediousness of practice; an amusement.
Récréations musicales, *Fr.* (rĕk-rā-ä-sī-ŏnh mū-zǐ-kăl.) Musical recreations.
Recte, *Lat.* (rĕk-tē.) Right, straight, forward.
Recte et retro, *Lat.* (rĕk-tē ĕt rā-trō.) Forward, then backward; the subject, or melody, reversed, note for note.
Rector chori, *Lat.* (rĕk-tŏr kō-rī.) The leader of choral performances.
Recueil d'hymnes, *Fr.* (rē-kŭ-ĕ d'ēmn.) Hymn book.
Reddita, *It.* (rĕd-dē-tä.) } Return to the subject;
Redita, *It.* (rē-dē-tä.) } repetition of a melody.
Redoble, *Spa.* (rē-dō-blĕ.) A repetition, a double beat on a drum.
Redondilla, *Spa.* (rē-dŏn-dēl-yä.) A roundelay; a stanza of four lines of eight syllables each.
Redoubled. An epithet applied to any simple interval carried into its octave; as the thirteenth, composed of a sixth and octave, is a redoubled sixth.
Redoublement, *Fr.* (rē-doobl-mänh.) See *Raddoppiamento.*
Redowa. (rĕd-ō-wä.) } A Bohemian
Rédowak. (rĕd-ō-wäk.) } dance, in 2-4
Redowazka. (rĕd-ō-wäts-kä.) } and 3-4 time alternately.
Redublicánte, *It.* (rē-doob-lē-kän-tē.) Redoubling.
Redublicáto, *It.* (rē-doob-lē-kä-tō.) Redoubled.
Redneiren, *Ger.* (rē-doo-tsīr-ĕn.) To reduce, or arrange, a full instrumental score, for a smaller band, or for the pianoforte or organ.
Reductio, *Lat.* (rē-dŭk-shī-ō.) Reducing, or bringing back augmented intervals to their original value; see, also, *Reduciren.*
Redundant chord. A chord which contains a greater number of tones or half tones than it has in its natural state, as from C to sharp G.
Redundant fourth. An augmented fourth.
Redundant intervals. See *Augmented Intervals.*
Reed. The flat piece of cane placed on the beak or mouthpiece of the clarinet and and bassethorn; this is called a *single reed.* The *double* reed is the mouthpiece of the hautboy, English horn and bassoon, formed of two pieces of cane joined together. The term *reed* is also applied to the small metal tube through which the wind passes, in some organ pipes.

REGU

Reed fifth. } A *stopped quint* register in an
Reed Nasat. } organ, the stopper of which has a hole or tube in it.
Reed, free. When, in an organ reed pipe, the tongue vibrates in the middle of the tube, without striking against its sides, it is called a *free* reed.
Reed instruments. Instruments whose sounds are produced by the action of air upon reeds formed of metal or wood.
Reed organ. An organ of small size in which the keys open valves and allow the wind from the bellows to act upon reeds.
Reed pipe. A pipe formed of reed, used singly or in numbers, as the pipes of Pan, in ancient times, or in connection with other kinds of pipes, as in the organ.
Reed stops. Those stops in an organ, the peculiar tone of which is produced by the wind having to pass through a reed placed at the bottom of the pipe and putting the *tongue* into vibration.
Reed, striking. When in an organ reed pipe, the wind passing through causes the tongue to strike against the tube, it is called a *striking* reed.
Reed trumpet. An instrument invented in 1822, consisting of a trumpet enclosing thirty-six small pipes, each having a brass tongue or reed, arranged in a circle and pointing toward the centre so that by turning the circle each pipe could be brought in succession between the mouthpiece and the bell of the instrument.
Reedy-toned. Partaking somewhat of the tone of the reed.
Reel. A lively Scotch dance. Originally the term *Rhay,* or *Reel,* was applied to a very ancient English dance, called "the Hay"; see *Rhay.*
Réfléchir, *Fr.* (rā-flā-shēr.) To throw back, to reverberate.
Reforzada, *Spa.* (rā-fŏr-thä-dä.) The base chord of a stringed instrument.
Refrain. The *burden* of a song, a ritornel; a repeat; see *Burden.*
Regal. A portable organ, used in former times in religious processions.
Regalia, *Spa.* (rä-gä-lī-ä.) In an organ a pipe whose tones resemble the human voice.
Regens chori, *Lat.* (rā-jĕns kō-rī.) The choir master in German churches.
Regimental band. A company of musicians attached to a regiment; a military band.
Regina coeli, *Lat.* (rā-jē-nä sē-lī.) *Queen of Heaven;* a hymn to the Virgin.
Register. The stops, or rows of pipes in an organ; also applied to the high, low, or middle parts, or divisions, of the voice; also the compass of a voice or instrument.
Registering. The proper management of the stops in an organ.
Registerstimme, *Ger.* (rē-ghĭs-tĕr-stĭm-mē.) Tone produced by a register or stop on the organ.
Registre, *Fr.* (rĕg-ĭstr.) } Register, draw
Registro, *It.* (rĕ-jēs-trō.) } stop.
Regle, *Fr.* (rägl.) } Rule, or precept, for
Regola, *It.* (rā-gō-lä.) } composition or performance.
Regle de l'octave, *Fr.* (rägl dŭh l'ŏk-täv.) See Rule of the Octave.
Regula, *Lat.* (rĕg-ū-la.) A rule.

REGU

Regulæ, *Lat.* (rĕg-ū-lĕ.) The registers or stops in an organ.
Regular. Alike applicable to any clef, motion, phrase or section.
Regular motion. Similar motion.
Rehabeh. A viol with one string, used by the Arabians.
Rehearsal. (rĕ-hĕr-sŭl.) A trial, or practice, previous to a public performance.
Reihen, *Ger.* (rī-ĕn.) Song, dance.
Reihen-tanz, *Ger.* (rī-ĕn tănts.) Circular dance.
Rein, *Ger.* (rīn.) Pure, clear, perfect; *kurz und rein*, distinct and clear.
Reine stimme, *Ger.* (rī-nĕ stĭm-mĕ.) Clear voice.
Reiselied, *Ger.* (rī-zĕ-lĕd.) A traveling song; a pilgrim's hymn or song.
Reiteracion, *Spa.* (rā-ĕ-tĕr-ă-thĕ-ōn.) Repetition, reiteration.
Relacion, *Spa.* (rĕ-lă-thĕ-ŏn.) A ballad.
Relacionero, *Spa.* (rĕ-lă-thĕ-ō-nă-ro.) A ballad singer.
Related. A term applied to those chords, modes, or keys, which, by reason of their affinity and close relation of some of their component sounds, admit of an easy and natural transition from one to the other.
Relation. That connection which any two sounds have with one another in respect of the interval which they form.
Relatio non harmonica, *Lat.* (rĕ-lă-shī-ō nŏn hăr-mŏn-ī-kă.) False relation.
Relation, false. That connection which any two sounds have with one another when the interval which they form is either superfluous or diminished. See *false relation*.
Relative keys. Keys which only differ by one sharp or flat, or which have the same signatures.
Religiosaménte, *It.* (rĕ-lē-jē-ō-ză-mān-tĕ.) }
Religióso, *It.* (rĕ-lē-jē-ō-zō.) }
Religiously, solemnly, in a devout manner.
Relish, double. One of the old English graces.
Re majeur, *Fr.* (rā mă-zhūr.) D major.
Re mineur, *Fr.* (rā mē-nūr.) D minor.
Remissio, *Lat.* (rĕ-mĭs-sī-ō.) The passage of the voice from the acute to the grave; the reverse of *intentio.*
Reminiscenz, *Ger.* (rĕ-mī-nīs-tsĕnts.) Reminiscence; see *Plagiat.*
Remote keys. Those keys whose scales have few tones in common, as the key of C and the key of D♭.
Remplissage, *Fr.* (rănh-plī-săzh.) Filling up; the middle parts; also, a term applied to the decorative flourishes introduced in concertos and bravura airs.
Rendre un ton, *Fr.* (rănhdr ûnh tōnh.) To yield or give a sound.
Rentrée, *Fr.* (rănh-trā.) *Return;* re-entry of the subject or theme.
Renverdie, *Fr.* (rănh-vĕr-dē.) Songs celebrating the return of verdure and spring time.
Renversement, *Fr.* (rănh-věrs-mănh.) An inversion.
Renverser, *Fr.* (rănh-věr-sā.) To invert.

REQU

Renvoi, *Fr.* (rănh-vwā.) A repeat; the mark of repetition.
Reol, *Dan.* (rā-ōl.) A Danish peasant dance very similar to the reel.
Repeat. A character indicating that certain measures or passages are to be sung or played twice. [Sign of Repetition]
Repeat 8va. Repeat an octave higher.
Repercotiménto, *It.* (rĕ-pĕr-kō-tĕ-mān-tō.) }
Repercussio, *Lat.* (rĕp-ĕr-kŭs-sī-ō.) }
Repercussion; the answer, in a fugue.
Repercussion. A frequent repetition of the same sound. This happens in the harmonic triad, the essential sounds of whose three chords are repeated oftener than the others; *i. e.,* the *final* and the *dominant*, which are properly the *repercussions* of each mode.
Répercuter, *Fr.* (rā-pěr-kŭ-tā.) To repercuss, to reverberate.
Repetatur, *Lat.* (rĕp-ĕ-tă-tūr.) Let it be repeated.
Repetent, *Ger.* (rĕp-ĕ-tĕnt.) A teacher who conducts the rehearsals.
Répéter, *Fr.* (rā-pā-tā.) To repeat.
Repetiménto, *It.* (rĕ-pā-tĕ-mān-tō.) } Repetizione,
Repetizione, *It.* (rĕ-pā-tĕ-tsē-ō-nĕ.) } tion.
Répétateúr, *Fr.* (rā-pā-tă-tūr.) Private music teacher.
Répétition, *Fr.* (rā-pā-tē-sī-ŏnh.) Rehearsal; repetition.
Repetitious. Containing repetitions.
Repetitóre, *It.* (rĕp-ă-tĕ-tō-rĕ.) The director of a rehearsal.
Répertoire de l'opera, *Fr.* (rā-pěr-twăr dŭh l'ŏp-ĕ-rā.) A collection of pieces from an opera.
Repicar, *Spa.* (rā-pī-kăr.) To chime; to ring a merry peal.
Repique, *Spa.* (rā-pē-kĕ.) A merry peal rung on festive occasions.
Repitatore, *It.* (rĕp-ē-tă-tō-rĕ.) A private teacher; the director of a rehearsal.
Réplica, *It.* (rā-plē-kă.) Reply, repetition; see, also, *Repercussio.*
Replicate. (rĕp-lī kăt.) A repetition.
Replication. A return or repercussion of sound. (Seldom used.)
Replicáto, *It.* (rĕp-lē-kă-tō.) Repeated.
Replicazióne, *It.* (rĕp-lē-kă-tsĕ-ō-nĕ.) Repetition.
Répondre, *Fr.* (rā-pōnhdr.) To respond, to answer.
Réponse, *Fr.* (rā-pōnhs.) The answer, in a fugue.
Repos, *Fr.* (rā-pō.) A pause.
Reprise, *Fr.* (rā-prēz.) The burden of a song; a repetition, or return, to some previous part; in old music, when a strain was repeated, it was called a *reprise.*
Reprise d'un opéra, *Fr.* (rā-prēz d'ûnh n'ō-pĕ-ră.) The reproduction or revival of an opera.
Requarta, *Spa.* (rĕ-kăr-tă.) One of the chords of a guitar.
Requiebro, *Spa.* (rĕ-kĕ-ā-brō.) A trill of the voice.
Requiem, *Lat.* (rā-quī-ĕm.) A Mass, or musical service for the dead.

ă *ale*, ă *add*, ă *arm*, ĕ *eve*, ŏ *end*, ĭ *ice*, ĭ *ill*, ō *old*, ŏ *odd*, ô *dove*, oo *moon*, ū *lute*, ŭ *but*, ŭ *French sound*

REQU

Requintar, *Spa.* (rĕ-kĕn-*tär.*) To raise or lower the tone.
Resilience. (rĕ-sĭl-ĭ-ĕns.) The return or rebound of a sound.
Ressina, *It.* (rä-sē-nä.) Resin, rosin.
Resolutio, *Lat.* (rĕz-ō-*tū*-shĭ-ō.) Resolution.
Resolution. Resolving a discord into a concord according to the rules of harmony.
Resoluzione, *It.* (rĕs-ō-loo-tsē-ō-nĕ.) Resolution, decision, firmness; also, the progression from a discord to a concord.
Resolved canon. Formerly a *canon* was said to be *resolved*, or written in resolution, when, instead of being comprised in a single staff, all the *parts* were given in separate staves.
Resolving a discord. Passing a dissonance into a concord, usually after it has been heard in the preceding harmony.
Resonacion, *Spa.* (rĕs-ō-nä-thē-*ōn.*) Resounding.
Resonance. Sound, reverberation, echo.
Resonancia, *Spa.* (rĕa-ō-*nän*-thĭ-ä.) Resonance, consonance, harmony.
Resonant. Resounding, returning sound.
Resonanz-boden. *Ger.* (rĕ-sō-*nänts*-bō-d'n.) The sounding board, of a pianoforte, etc.
Résonnement, *Fr.* (rā-sŏnh-mänh.) Resonance.
Résonner, *Fr.* (rä-sŏnh-nä.) To resound, to echo.
Respiration, *Eng.* (rĕa-pĭ-*rā*-shŭn.) } Taking
Respirazione, *It.* (rĕs-pē-rä-tsē-ō-nĕ.) } breath
Respiro, *It.* (rĕs-pē-rō.) } in singing.
Respiro, *It.* (rĕa-pē-rō.) A semiquaver rest.
Response. } Response or
Responsióne, *It.* (rĕ-spŏn-sē-ō-nĕ } answer of the
Respónso. (rĕ-*spŏn*-sō.) } choir.
The name of a kind of anthem sung in the Roman Catholic church after the morning lesson, and which concludes in the form of a rondo. In a fugue the *response* is the repetition of the given subject by another part.
Responsorien, *Lat.* (rĕ-spŏn-*sō*-rĭ-ĕn.) }
Responsorium, *Lat.* (rĕ-spŏn-sō-rĭ-ŭm.) }
Responsum, *Lat.* (rĕ-*spŏn*-sŭm.) }
See response.
Responsivo, *It.* (rĕ-spŏn-sē-vō.) Responsive.
Resserrement, *Fr.* (rĕs-sĕr-mänh.) See Strétto.
Rest. A character indicating silence.
Rest, crotchet. A rest equal in duration to the length of a crotchet or quarter note.
Rest, demisemiquaver. A rest equal in duration to a demisemiquaver or thirty-second note.
Rest, dotted. A rest having a dot affixed, by which its value is increased one-half.
Rest, double dotted. A rest with two dots after it, which increase its value by three-fourths.
Rest, eighth. See *Quaver Rest.*
Rest, half. See Minim Rest.
Rest, hemidemisemiquaver. A rest equal in value to a hemidemisemiquaver.
Rest, minim. A rest equal in length to a minim.
Restoration. The restoring a note made flat or sharp to its primitive sound.

RH

Rest, quarter note. See Crotchet Rest.
Rest, quaver. A rest equalling in length a *quaver.*
Rest, semibreve. A rest equal in duration to a semibreve.
Rest, semiquaver. A rest equal in duration to a semiquaver.
Rest, sixteenth. See Semiquaver rest.
Rest, sixty-fourth. See Hemidemisemiquaver rest.
Rest, thirty-second. See Demiaemiquaver rest.
Rest, whole. See Semibreve rest.
Retard. To hold back, to diminish the time.
Retardándo, *It.* (rĕ-tär-*dän*-dō.) A retarding of the movement.
Retardation. Slackening, or retarding the time; also, a suspension, in harmony, prolonging some note of a previous chord into the succeeding one.
Retentir, *Fr.* (rā-tänh-tēr.) To resound.
Retentissement, *Fr.* (rā-tänh-tĕss-mänh.) Peal, loud sound, re-echoing.
Retinte, *Spa.* (rā-*tän*-tĕ.) A tinkling sound.
Retintin, *Spa.* (rä-*tĕn*-tĕn.) An affected tone of the voice, a tinkling sound.
Retraite, *Fr.* (rĕ-*trāt.*) Retreat; tattoo, in military music.
Retro, *Lat.* (rā-trō.) Backward, the melody reversed, note for note.
Retrograde. (*rĕt*-rō-grāde.) Going backward.
Retrograde imitation. Where the answer, or imitating part, takes the subject backward.
Retrograde inversion. An inversion made by commencing on the last note of the subject, and writing it backward to the first note.
Retrográdo, *It.* (rā-trō-*grā*-dō.) Retrograde, going backward.
Retto, *It.* (*rāt*-tō.) Right, straight, direct.
Retumbante, *Spa.* (rā-toom-*bän*-tĕ.) Resonant, sonorous.
Retumbo, *Spa.* (rā-*toom*-bō.) Resonance, echo.
Return. A repetition.
Retusa, *Lat.* (rĕ-*tū*-sä.) An old term for a stopped organ pipes.
Réveille, *Fr.* (rĕ-*vä*-yĕ.) Awaking, a military morning signal; also horn music played early in the morning, to awake the hunter.
Reverberate. (rĕ-*vĕr*-bĕ-rāt.) To throw back a sound; to echo.
Reverberiren, *Ger.* (rĕf-ĕr-bĕ-rē-r'n.) To reverberate.
Reversed C. A sign in old music signifying a diminution of one-half of the value of the notes.
Reversed retrograde imitation. A form of imitation in which the subject is commenced backward in the answer, and in contrary motion.
Reversed motion. Imitation by contrary motion, in which the ascending intervals are changed into descending and *vice versa.*
Re-voice. To repair an organ pipe so as to restore its proper quality of tone.
Rey, *Spa.* (rā.) A Spanish dance.
R. H. In pianoforte music used to indicate the right hand.

168 PRONOUNCING MUSICAL DICTIONARY.

ā *ate*, ă *add*, ä *arm*, ē *eve*, ĕ *end*, Ī *ice*, Ĭ *ill*, ō *old*, ŏ *odd*, ô *dove*, oo *moon*, ū *lute*, ŭ *but*, ü *French sound*.

RHAP

Rhapsodie, *Ger.* (răp-sō-dē.) } See Rapsodia.
Rhapsody, *Eng.* (răp-sō-dy.) }
Rhapsodi, *Gr.* (răp-sō-dē.) Persons among the ancients whose profession it was to sing or recite the verses of Homer and other celebrated poets.
Rhay. An old Anglo-Saxon name for the dance called "the Hay"; see *Reel.*
Rhythm, *Eng.* (rĭthm.) ⎫ The division
Rhythmus, *Gr.* (rĭth-mŭs.) ⎪ of musical
Rhythmus, *Lat.* (rĭth-mŭs.) ⎬ ideas or sen-
Rhythmus, *Ger.* (rĭth-moos.) ⎭ tences into regular metrical portions; musical accent and cadence as applied to melody.
Rhythme, *Fr.* (rĭthm.) Rhythm.
Rhythmical. Conformable to rhythm.
Rhythmically. In a rhythmical manner.
Rhythmique, *Fr.* (rĭth-mēk.) } Rhythmical.
Rhythmisch, *Ger.* (rĭt-mĭsh.) }
Ribattere, *It.* (rē-băt-tā-rē.) To reverberate.
Ribattiménto, *It.* (rē-băt-tē-măn-tō.) Repercussion, reverberation.
Ribattúta, *It.* (rē-băt-too-tä.) A beat, a passing note.
Ribéba, *It.* (rē-bā-bä.) A Jew's harp.
Ribéca, *It.* (rē-bā-kä.) See *Rebec.*
Ribecchíno, *It.* (rē-běk-kē-nō.) A small *Rebec.*
Ribible. An old instrument supposed to be of the ghittern, or riddle species; see Rebec.
Ricantare, *It.* (rē-kän-tä-rē.) To sing again.
Ricercáre, *It.* (rē-tshĕr-kä-rē.) ⎫ Sought
Ricercári, *It. pl.* (rē-tshĕr-kä-rē.) ⎪ after; this
Ricercáta, *It.* (rē-tshĕr-kä-tä.) ⎬ term is ap-
Ricercáto, *It.* (rē-tshĕr-kä-tō.) ⎭ plied to every kind of composition wherein researches of musical design are employed. It is suitable to certain figures replete with contrapuntal artifices, also to madrigals, and the term was formerly applied to solfeggi, and also to instrumental exercises, when of considerable difficulty.
Rich. An epithet applied to those compositions, the parts of which are elaborately and ingeniously combined, and which in performance produce an elegance and fullness of effect.
Richiamáre, *It.* (rē-kē-ä-mä-rē.) To sing with a shrill tone of voice; to warble, or whistle, in imitation of a bird.
Richtig singen, *Ger.* (rĭkh-tĭg sĭng-ĕn.) To sing in tune.
Ricominciamo, *It.* (rē-kō-mĕn-tshē-ä-mō.) Let us commence again.
Ricordánza, *It.* (rē-kōr-dän-tsä.) Remembrance, recollection.
Riddone, *It.* (rēd-dō-nē.) A roundelay, a village dance.
Rideau d'entr'acte, *Fr.* (rē-dō d'änh-tr'äkt.) Drop scene.
Ridevolménte, *It.* (rē-dĕ-vōl-măn-tā.) Ludicrously, pleasantly.
Ridiciménto, *It.* (rē-dē-tshē-măn-tō.) Repetition, repeating.
Ridicolosaménte, *It.* (rē-dē-kō-lō-zä-măn-tā.) Ridiculonsly.
Ridótto, *It.* (rē-dōt-tō.) *Reduced; arranged* or *adapted* from a full score; also, an entertainment consisting of singing and dancing; a species of opera.

RIPR

Riesen-harfe, *Ger.* (rē-z'n här-fē.) Æolian harp.
Riesen-stimme, *Ger.* (rē-z'n stĭm-mē.) Stentorian voice.
Rifaciménto, *It.* (rē-fä-tshē-măn-tō.) Reconstruction of a work in order to improve it.
Rifiormenti, *It. pl.* (rē-fē-ōr-măn-tē.) Ornaments, embellishments.
Rigadoon. A lively old French or Provencal dance in triple time.
Rigodon. *Fr.* (rē-gō-dōnh.) A *rigadoon.*
Rigolétto, *It.* (rē-gō-lăt-tō.) A round dance.
Rigoll. An old instrument consisting of several sticks placed by the side of each other, but separated by beads. It was played by being struck with a ball at the end of a stick.
Rigóre, *It.* (rē-gō-rē.) Rigor, strictness: *al rigóre di tĕmpo,* with strictness as to time.
Rigoróso, *It.* (rē-gō-rō-zō.) Rigorous, exact, strict.
Rilasciándo, *It.* (rē-lä-shē-än-dō.) Relaxing the time, giving way a little.
Rilch. A Russian lute.
Rima, *It.* (rē-mä.) Verse, poem, song.
Rimailleur, *Fr.* (rē-mä-yŭr.) A rhymster.
Rimbombamento, *It.* (rēm-bōm-bä-măn-tō.) Resounding, booming.
Rindermagen, *Ger.* (rĭn-dĕr-mä-ghĕn.) Psalter; psalm book.
Rinforzándo, *It.* rĕn-fōr-tsän-dō.) ⎫ Strength-
Rinsorzáre, *It.* (rĕn-fōr-tsä-rē.) ⎪ ened rein-
Rinforzáto, *It.* (rĕn-fōr-tsä-tō.) ⎬ forced; a
Rinfórzo, *It.* (rĕn-fōr-tsō.) ⎭ repeated reinforcement of tone or expression; indicating that *several* notes are to be played with energy and emphasis.
Ringelstück, *Ger.* (rĭn-g'l-stŭk.) Rondeau, roundelay.
Ringen, *Ger.* (rĭng-ĕn.) To ring or sound.
Rintoccáre, *It.* (rĕn-tōk-kä-rē.) To toll a bell.
Rintócco. *It.* (rĕn-tōk-kō.) Tolling; a knell.
Rintronáto, *It.* (rĕn-trō-nä-tō.) Resounded; reechoed.
Ripetitúra, *It.* (rē-pĕ-tē-too-rä.) } Repeti-
Ripetizióne, *It.* (rē-pĕ-tē-tsē-ō-nē.) } tion; the burden of a song; a refrain.
Ripienist, A player of the *ripiéno* or tutti parts, in an orchestra.
Ripiéni, *It, pl.* (rē-pē-ä-nē.) } The *tŭtti,* or full
Ripiéno, *It.* (rē-pē-ä-nō.) } parts which fill up and augment the effect of the full chorus of voices and instruments. In a large orchestra all the violins, violas, and basses, except the principals, are sometimes called *Ripiéni.*
Ripiéno di cínque, *It.* (rē-pē-ä-nō dē tshēn-quē.) }
Riplèur de cínque, *Fr.* (rĭp-ĭ-ŭhr dŭh sänhk.) }
Mixture stop of five ranks in Italian organs.
Ripiéno di due, *It.* (rē-pē-ä-nō dē doo-ē.) Mixture stop of two ranks.
Ripiéno di quáttro, *It.* (rē-pē-ä-nō dē quăt-trō.) Mixture stop of four ranks.
Ripiéno di tre, *It.* (rē-pē-ä-nō dē trä.) Mixstop of three ranks.
Ripòsta, *It.* (rē-pōs-tä.) Repeat.
Riprésa, *It.* (rē-prä-zä.) } Repetition, reitera-
Riprése, *It.* (rē-prä-zē.) } tion.

ā *ate*, ă *add*, ä *arm*, ĕ *eve*, ĕ *end*, ī *ice*, ĭ *ill*, ō *old*, ŏ *odd*, ô *dove*, oo *moon*, ū *lute*, ŭ *but*, ü *French sound*.

RISE

Risentitaménte, *It.* (rē-sĕn-tē-tä-*măn*-tĕ.) }
Risentíto, *It.* (rē-sĕn-*tē*-tō.) }
Marked, distinct, forcibly, firmly.
Risolutaménte, *It.* (rē-zō-loo-tä-*măn*-tĕ.) Resolutely, boldly.
Risolutézza, *It.* (rē-zō-loo-*tăt*-sä.) Resolution, boldness.
Risolutíssimo, *It.* rē-zō-loo-*tĭs*-sē-mō.) Very resolutely, as boldly as possible.
Risolúto, *It.* (rē-zō-*loo*-tō.) Resolved, resolute, bold.
Risoluzióne, *It.* (rē-zō-loo-tsē-ō-nĕ.) Resolution, determination; also, the resolution of a discord.
Risonánte, *It.* (rē-zō-*năn*-tĕ.) Resounding, ringing, sounding.
Rissonánza, *It.* (rē-zō-*năn*-tsä.) Resonance.
Risonáre, *It.* (rē-zō-nä-rĕ.) To resound, to ring, or echo.
Rispósta, *It.* (rēs-*pōs*-tä.) The answer, in a fugue.
Ristrétto, *It.* (rē-*străt*-tō.) The *Stretto*, the restriction, or contraction, of the subject, in a fugue.
Risvegliáre, *It.* (rēs-vāl-yā-ä-rĕ.) To wake up, to revive, to reanimate.
Risvegliáto, *It.* (rēs-vāl-yē-ä-tō.) Awakened, reanimated.
Rit. }
Ritard. } Abbreviations of *Ritardándo*.
Ritartándo, *It.* (rē-tär-*dăn*-dō.) Retarding, delaying the time gradually.
Ritardáto, *It.* (rē-tär-*dä*-tō.) Retarded, delayed.
Ritárdo, *It.* (rē-*tär*-dō.) Retardation, gradual delay; in harmony, prolonging some note of a previous chord into the succeeding one.
Ritárdo un pochettíno, *It.* (rē-*tär*-dō oon pō-kĕt-*tē*-nō.) Slacken the time a little.
Riten. An abbreviation of *Ritenúto*.
Ritenéndo, *It.* (rē-tĕ-*năn*-dō.) } Detaining, holding back the
Ritenénte, *It.* (rē-tĕ-*năn*-tĕ.) } time.
Ritenénto, *It.* (rē-tĕ-*năn*-tō.) } Detained, slowing**Ritenúto**, *It.* (rē-tĕ-noo-tō.) } er, kept back; the effect differs from *Ritardándo*, by being done at once, while the other is effected by degrees.
Ritmo, *It.* (rēt-mō.) } Rhythm, cadence, measure.
Ritmo, *Spa.* (rēt-mō.) } ure.
Ritmo a tre battute, *It.* (rēt-mō ä trä bät-*too*-tĕ.) Rhythm in three beats.
Ritornél, *It.* (rē-tōr-*năl*.) } The burden of
Ritornéllo, *It.* (rē-tōr-*năl*-lō.) } a song; also, a
Ritournelle, *Fr.* (rē-toor-*năl*.) } short symphony or introduction to an air; and the symphony which follows an air: it is also applied to *tutti* parts, introductory to, and between, or after, the solo passages in a concerto.
Riverberaménto, *It.* (rē-vĕr-bĕ-rä-*măn*-tō.) Reverberation.
Rivérso, *It.* (rē-*vär*-sō.) } See Rovéscio.
Rivérscio, *It.* (rē-*văr*-shē-ō.) }
Rivolgiménto, *It.* (rē-vōl-yē-*măn*-tō.) Inversion of the parts, in double counterpoint.
Rivoltáre, *It.* (rē-vōl-*tä*-rĕ.) To change.
Rivoltáto, *It.* (rē-vōl-*tä*-tō.) } Inverted, in coun**Rivólto**, *It.* (rē-*vōl*-tō.) } terpoint.
Robáto, *It.* (rō-*bä*-tō.) Robbed, borrowed.
Róche, *It.* (*rō*-kĕ.) } Hoarse, rough sounding,
Róco, *It.* (*rō*-kō.) } jarring.
Rochézza, *It.* (rō-*kăt*-sä.) Hoarseness.

RONZ

Rococo. (rō-kō-kō.) } Old fashioned, odd.
Rococo. (rō-kō-kō.) }
Roehr-quint, *Ger.* (rŏh'r-quĭnt.) } Reed-fifth;
Rohr-quint, *Ger.* (rŏr-quĭnt.) } an organ stop, sounding the fifth above the diapasons.
Rohr, *Ger.* (rŏr.) Reed, pipe.
Röhre, *Ger. pl.* (*rō*-rĕ.) Reeds.
Rohr-flöte, *Ger.* (rŏr-*flō*-tĕ.) Reed-flute, a stopped diapason in an organ.
Rohr-nasat, *Ger.* (rŏr nä-*sät*.) See Reed-Nasat.
Rohr-pfeife, *Ger.* (rŏr pfī-*fŏ*.) Reed-pipe.
Rohr-werk, *Ger.* (rŏr värk.) Reed-work; the reed stops in an organ.
Roi des violons, *Fr.* (rwä dĕ vī-ō-lŏnh.) King of the violins.
Role, *Fr.* (rōll.) A part or character performed by an actor in a play or opera.
Rollándo, *It.* (rōl-*tän*-dō.) Rolling on the drum and tambourine.
Rolling. A term applied to that rapid pulsation of the drum by which the sounds so closely succeed each other as to beat upon the ear with a rumbling continuity of effect.
Roll. long. A prolonged roll of drums signalizing an attack by the enemy, and for the troops to place themselves in line of battle.
Róllo, *It.* (*rōl*-lō.) The roll on the drum and tambourine.
Romaíka. A dance tune of the modern Greeks to accompany a dance of the same name.
Romance, *Fr.* (rō-minha.) } Formerly the
Románza, *It.* (rō-*măn*-tsä.) } name given to the
Romanze, *Ger.* (rō-*măn*-tsĕ.) } long lyric tales sung by the minstrels; now a term applied to an irregular, though delicate and refined composition.
Romanésca, *It.* (rō-mä-*năs*-kä.) } A favorite
Romanesque, *Fr.* (rō-mäu-*ĕsk*.) } Roman, or Italian, dance of the sixteenth century, resembling the *Galliard*.
Romantique, *Fr.* (rō-mänh-tĕk.) } Romantic,
Romanzesco, *It.* (rō-män-taĕs-kō.) } imaginative, fairy-like.
Römischer gesang, *Ger.* (*rō*-mĭ-ahĕr ghĕ-*säng*.) Gregorian plain chant.
Roncon, *Spa.* (rōn-kōn.) The drone of a bagpipe.
Ronde, *Fr.* (rōnd.) A semibreve.
Rondeau, *Fr.* (rŏnh-*dō*.) } A composition, vocal,
Rondo, *It.* (*rōn*-dō.) } or instrumental, generally consisting of three strains, the first of which terminates in a cadence on the tonic and is repeated several times during the movement.
Rondeau mignon, *Fr.* (rŏnh-dō mē-yŏnh.) A favorite rondo.
Rondeaux, *Fr.* (rŏnh-dō.) Rondos.
Ronde pointee, *Fr.* (rŏnhd pwĕnh-tä.) Dotted semibreve.
Rondilétta, *It.* (rōn-dē-*lăt*-tä.) } A short
Rondinétto, *It.* (rōn-dē-*năt*-tō.) } and easy
Rondíno, *It.* (rōn-*dē*-nō.) } rondo.
Rondolétto, *It.* (rōn-dō-*lăt*-tō.) }
Rondo form. In the style of a rondo.
Ronquedad, *Spa.* (rōn-kĕ-*däd*.) Hoarseness, roughness of voice.
Ronzaménto, *It.* (rōn-tsä-*măn*-tō.) Humming, buzzing.

ā ale, ă add, ä arm, ē eve, ĕ end, ī ice, ĭ ill, ō old, ŏ odd, ō dove, oo moon, ū lute, ŭ but, ü French sound.

ROOT

Root. The fundamental note of any chord.
Rosalia, *Lat,* (rō-sā́l-yä.) The repetition of a passage several times over, each time on a different degree of the staff.
Rossignoler, *Fr.* (rō-sēn-yō-lā.) To imitate the song of the nightingale.
Rostral, *Ger.* (rōs-trä́l.) A music pen.
Róta, *It.* (rō-tä.) A wheel; applied to a canon, or a round.
Rote. Name formerly applied to the hurdy-gurdy.
Rote, singing by. The act of singing, not from a knowledge of music, but from listening to the singing of others.
Rotóndo, *It.* (rō-lŏ́n-do.) Round, full.
Rotruenges. (rō-trū-ĕn-jĕs.) Songs, resembling catches, of the ancient minstrels or troubadours.
Rótte, *It.* (rōt-tĕ.) Broken, interrupted.
Rotulæ, *Lat.* (rō-tū-lē.) Christmas roundelays.
Roulade, *Fr.* (roo-lä́d.) A florid vocal passage; a division, or rapid series of notes, using only one syllable.
Roucouler, *Fr.* (roo-koo-lā́.) To coo, to trill, to quaver.
Roulades aux frais de l'auteur, *Fr.* (roo-lä́d-a'ō frä düh l'ō-tür.) Roulades in bad taste, such as injure the melody of the composer.
Roulement, *Fr.* (rool-mänh.) A roll, or shake, upon the drum or tambourine; prolonged reiterations of one note, upon the guitar, etc.
Round. A species of canon in the unison or octave; also a vocal composition in three or more parts, all written in the same clef, the performers singing each part in succession. They are called *rounds* because the performers follow one another in a circulatory motion.
Roundel. } From the French word *rondelet;*
Roundelay. } a species of antique rustic song or ballad, common in the fourteenth century, and so called on account of form, by which it constantly returned to the first verse and thus went *round.*
Rovérscio, *It.* (rō-vä́r-shĕ-ō.) } See *Roiscio.*
Rovésio, *It.* (rō-vä-sĕ-ō.) }

RYTH

Rovesclaménto, *It.* (rō-vä-shĕ-ä-män-tō.) }
Rovéscio, *It.* (rō-vä́-shĕ-ō.) }
Reverse motion, the subject backward, in double counterpoint.
Rubáto, *It.* (roo-bä́-tō.) *Robbed, stolen;* taking a portion of the duration from one note and giving it to another; see *Témpo Rubáto.*
Rückung, *Ger.* (rük-oong.) Syncopation.
Rudiments. The first elements or principles of music.
Ruf, *Ger.*. (roof.) Call, cry, voice; to wind a horn; to sound a trumpet call.
Ruhepunct, *Ger.* (roo-hĕ-poonkt.) } P a u s e,
Ruhepunkt, *Ger.* (roo-hĕ-poonkt.) } point of rest or repose; a cadence.
Ruhestelle, *Ger.* (roo-hĕ-stĕ́l-lĕ.) } A pause,
Ruhezeichen, *Ger.* (roo-hĕ-tsī-k'n.) } a rest.
Rule of the octave. The art of accompanying the scale, either ascending or descending, when taken in the bass, with the proper chords or harmony.
Rullándo, *It.* (rool-lä́n-dō.) } Rolling on the
Rullánte, *It.* (rool-lä́n-tĕ.) } drum or tambourine.
Run. A rapid flight of notes introduced as an embellishment; a roulade.
Rundgedicht, *Ger.* (roond-ghĕ-dīkht.) } Roun-
Rundgesang, *Ger.* (rond-ghĕ-sä́ng.) } delay, roundelay, a convivial song.
Running passages. Divisions; series of notes appropriated to a single syllable.
Russe, *Fr.* (rüss.) Russian; *a la Russe,* in the Russian style.
Russian bassoon. A deep-toned instrument of the serpent species, sometimes used in military bands.
Rústico, *It.* (roos-tĕ-kō.) Rural, rustic.
Rutscher. (roots-kĕr.) The dance called a *Galopade.*
Rythmus, *Ger.* (rĭt-moos.) See *Rhythmus.*

ă ale, ă add, ä arm, ē eve, ĕ end, ī ice, ĭ ill, ō old, ŏ odd, ȯ dove, oo moon, ü tute, ü but, ü French sound

SABE

Sabeca. (să-bĭ-kă.) Sackbut.
Sacabuche, *Spa.* (să-kă-*boo*-kĕ.) A sackbut.
Saccade, *Fr.* (săk-*kăd*.) A firm pressure of the violin bow against the strings, enabling the player to produce two, three, or four notes at one stroke.
Sackbut. An old bass wind instrument, resembling a trombone.
Sack-geige, *Ger.* (*săk* ghī-ghĕ.) A pocket fiddle, a *kit*.
Sack-pfeife, *Ger.* (*säk pfī-*fĕ.) A bagpipe; see *Cornamúsa*.
Sack-pfeifer, *Ger.* (*săk pfī-*fĕr.) Player on the bagpipe.
Sack-pipe. A bagpipe; see *Cornamúsa*.
Sacquebuxe, *Por.* (săk-boo-shō.) A sackbut.
Sacred music. Music composed for public religious worship or private devotion; oratorios, psalmody, etc.
Sacrist. A person employed in a cathedral, whose office it is to copy out the music for the use of the choir, and take care of the books.
Saengerfest, *Ger.* (*săng-ĕr-fĕst*.) A festival among the Germans of a musical and social character.
Sàggio, *It.* (*săd*-jē-ō.) An essay, a trial.
Saison, *Fr.* (să-sōnh.) The musical season.
Saite, *Ger.* (sī-tĕ.) A string of a musical instrument.
Saiten, *Ger.* (sī-t'n.) Timbrel; strings of a violin.
Saiten-bändiger, *Ger.* (sī-t'n băn-dĭ-ghĕr.) A musician.
Saiten-bezug, *Ger.* (sī-t'n bĕ-tsoog.) Set of strings.
Saiten-draht, *Ger.* (sī-t'n drăt.) Wire string.
Saiten-halter, *Ger.* (sī-t'n hăl-tĕr.) The tailpiece of a violin, etc.
Saiten-instrument, *Ger.* (sī-t'n in-stroo-mĕnt.) A stringed instrument.
Saiten-klang, *Ger.* (sī-t'n klăng.) The sound or vibration of a string.
Saiten-spiel, *Ger.* (sī-t'n spēl.) Stringed instrument, music of a stringed instrument.
Saiten-spieler, *Ger.* (sī-t'n spē-lĕr.) Player on a stringed instrument.
Saiten-spielerinn, *Ger.* (sī-t'n spē-lĕ-rinn.) Female performer on a stringed instrument.
Saiten-ton, *Ger.* (sī-t'n tōn.) The tone of a stringed instrument.
Saitig, *Ger.* (sī-tĭg.) Stringed.
Salamanie. An Oriental flute.
Salcional, *Fr.* (săl-sĭ-ō-năl.) } An eight or
Salicet, *Fr.* (să-lĭ-sā.) } sixteen feet or-
Salicional, *Fr.* (să-lĕ-sĭ-ō-năl.) } gan stop of small scale and reedy tone.
Salii, *Lat. pl.* (să-lĭ-ī.) The name given by the Romans to the young men, twelve in number, appointed out of the patricians, as dancers and singers of hymns in praise of the god of war.
Salle de concert, *Fr.* (săll dŭh kŏnh-sărt.) A concert room.
Salle de musique, *Fr.* (săll dŭh mŭ-sĭk.) A music room.
Salm, *Ger.* (săm.) }
Sálme, *It.* (săl-mŏ.) } A psalm.
Salmo, *Spa.* (săl-mō.) }
Salmear, *Spa.* (săl-mĕ-ăr.) To sing psalms.

SANF

Salmeggiamènto, *It.* (săl-măd-jē-ă-*mĕn*-tō.) Psalmody.
Salmeggiáre, *It.* (săl-măd-jē-ă-rĕ.) To sing psalms.
Salmeggiatòre, *It.* (săl-măd-jē-ă-tō-rĕ.) Psalmist, singer.
Salmi concertati, *It. pl.* (săl-mē cŏn-tshĕr-tă-tē.) Psalms accompanied with instrumental music.
Salmi di terza, *It. pl.* (săl-mē dē tăr-tsă.) Psalms in three parts.
Salmista, *Spa.* (săl-mĕs-tă.) } A writer of
Salmista, *It.* (săl-mēs-tă.) } psalms, a chanter of psalms, a psalm book.
Salmodia, *It.* (săl-mō-dē-ă.) Psalmody.
Salmografo, *Spa.* (săl-mō-*gră*-fō.) A writer of psalms.
Salpinx. The ancient Greek trumpet.
Saltándo, *It.* (săl-*tăn*-dō.) Leaping, proceeding by skips, or jumps.
Saltarèlla, *It.* (săl-tă-*rĕl*-lă.) } A Roman or
Salterèlla, *It.* (săl-tĕ-*rĕl*-lă.) } Italian dance, very quick, and in 2-4 time.
Saltatóri, *It. pl.* (săl-tă-tō-rē.) Jumpers, or dancers of very great agility.
Salter, *Ger.* (săl-tĕr.) Psalter, book of psalms.
Salterètto. *It.* (săl-tĕ-*răt*-tō.) A musical figure in 6-8 time, the first and fourth quavers being dotted; very usual in movements *alla Siciliana*.
Salterio, *It.* (săl-tă-rē-ō.) } Psalter, book of
Saltéro, *It.* (săl-tă-rō.) }
Saltéro, *It.* (săl-tă-rō.) Psaltery, instrument with ten strings.
Sálto, *It.* (săl-tō.) A leap, or skip, from one note to a distant one; also, a dance.
Salve Regina, *Lat.* (săl-vĕ rā-jē-nă.) Hail Queen! a hymn to the Virgin Mary.
Sambúca, *It.* (săm-*boo*-kă.) An ancient stringed instrument used by the Greeks, the peculiar structure of which is unknown.
Sambucistria, *Lat.* (săm-bŭ-sĭs-trĭ-ă.) A player on the *Sambúca*.
Sambucus. An ancient wind instrument resembling a flute; supposed to be so called from its being made of elder wood, the Latin name for which is *sambucus*.
Sambuque, *Heb.* (săm-book.) An old Hebrew instrument of the harp kind.
Samlung, *Ger.* (săm-loong.) A collection of airs, etc.
Sampógna, *It.* (săm-*pŏn*-yă.) A species of pipe, see *Zampógna*.
Sampunia. A pneumatic instrument used by the ancient Hebrews, resembling the modern bagpipe.
Sanctus, *Lat.* (*sănk*-tŭs.) Holy; a principal movement of the Mass.
Sanft, *Ger.* (sănft.) Soft, mild, smooth; *mit sanften stimmen*, with soft stops.
Sanft-flöte, *Ger.* (sănft flō-tĕ.) Soft-toned flute.
Sanftheit, *Ger.* (*sănft*-hīt.) Softness, smoothness, gentleness.
Sänftig, *Ger.* (*sănft*-tĭg.) Soft, gentle.
Sanftmuth, *Ger.* (*sănft*-moot.) }
Sauftmüthigkeit, *Ger.* (*sănft*-mŭ-tĭg-kīt.) } Softness, gentleness.
Sanftmüthig, *Ger.* (*sănft*-mŭ-tĭg.) Softly, gently.

ă *ale,* ă *add,* ä *arm,* ē *eve,* ĕ *end,* ī *ice,* ĭ *ill,* ō *old,* ŏ *odd,* ô *dove,* oo *moon,* ū *lute,* ŭ *but,* ü *French sound.*

SANG

Sang, *Ger.* (säng.) Song.
Sänger, *Ger.* (säng-ĕr.) A singer.
Sängerbund, *Ger.* (säng-ĕr-boond.) A league, or brotherhood of singers; a convention of singing societies.
Sängerinn, *Ger.* (säng-ĕr-Inn.) A female singer, a songstress.
Sängerverein, *Ger.* (säng-ĕr-fē-rīn.) Singers' union.
Sang-meister, *Ger.* (säng-mīs-tĕr.) Singing master.
Sans, *Fr.* (sänh.) Without.
Sans frappé, *Fr.* (sänh fräp-pā.) *Without striking;* play the notes without striking them hard or forcibly.
Sans pédales, *Fr.* (sänh pā-dăl.) Without the pedals.
Saquebute, *Fr.* (săk-büt.) The sackbut.
Santoral, *Spa.* (sän-tō-rāl.) A church choir book.
Santur, *Tur.* (sän-toor.) A Turkish stringed instrument; the psaltery.
Saraband, *Eng.* (sär-ă-bănd.) ⎫ A dance
Sarabánda, *It.* (sär-ă-bän-dā.) ⎬ said to be
Sarabande, *Fr.* (sär-ă-bänd.) ⎨ originally
Sarabande, *Ger.* (sär-ă-bän-dĕ.) ⎭ derived from the Saracens, and danced with castanets; it is in slow 3-4 or 3-2 time, and characterized by the second note of the measure being lengthened which gives gravity and majesty to the movement.
Sartarélla, *It.* (sär-tă-rāl-lă.) ⎱ A Neapolitan
Sartarello, *It.* (sär-tă-rāl-lō.) ⎰ dance; see *Saltarélla.*
S'attácca, *It.* (s'ät-täk-kă.) See *Attácca.*
Sattel, *Ger.* (sät-t'l.) The nut of the fingerboard of the violin, etc.
Satz, *Ger.* (sätz.) Musical passage, composition, theme.
Saut, *Fr.* (sō.) See *Sálto.*
Sautereau, *Fr.* (sō-tĕ-rō.) The jack of the spinet.
Savoyarde, *Fr.* (să-vwă-yärd.) See *A la Savoyarde.*
Sawtry. A term used in olden time for psaltery.
Sax-horn. A brass instrument introduced by M. Sax, with a wide mouthpiece and 3, 4, or 5 cylinders, and much used in military bands; the tone is round, pure and full.
Saxophones. A new family of brass wind-instruments invented by M. Sax. The body of these instruments is a parabolic cone of brass, provided with a set of keys; their tones are soft and penetrating in the higher part and full and rich in the lower part of their compass. The Saxophones are six in number, the high, the soprano, the alto, the tenor, the baritone and the bass; they are played with a single reed and a clarinet mouthpiece.
Saxotromba. A brass instrument introduced by M. Sax, with a wide mouthpiece and 3, 4, or 5 cylinders; the tone is of a shrill character, partaking of the quality both of the trumpet and the bugle.
Sax-tuba. A brass instrument introduced by M. Sax, with a wide mouthpiece and 3 cylinders; the tone is very sonorous.
Sbálzo, *It.* (sbăl-tsō.) Skip, or leap, in melody.
Sbárra dóppia, *It.* (sbär-rä dōp-pē-ă.) A double bar

SCAL

Scagnéllo, *It.* (skän-yāl-lō.) The bridge of the violin, etc.
Scála, *It.* (skä-lă.) A scale, or gamut.
Scála cromática, *It.* (skä-lă krō-mă-tē-kă.) The chromatic scale.
Scald. The name given by the ancient Scandinavians to their bards, whose employment it was to compose odes and songs which were chanted at their public festivals.
Scale. From the Latin word *scata.* The denomination first given to the arrangement made by Guido, of the six syllables, *ut, re, mi fa, sol, la;* also called the *gamut.* A series of lines and spaces on which notes are placed; the regular gradations of sound limited to an octave, or extended to the compass of any voice or instrument; compass.
Scale, accompaniment of the. The harmony assigned to the series of notes forming the diatonic scale, ascending and descending.
Scale, bell. A scale employed to determine the size, weight, and tone of bells.
Scale, Chinese. A scale consisting of five notes without semitones, the music being written on five lines in perpendicular columns, and the rising and falling of tones indicated by distinctive names.
Scale, chromatic. A scale consisting entirely of semitones, there being twelve in an octave.
Scale, diatonic. A melodic representation of the seven gradations of tone arranged in conformity with some particular key.
Scale, enharmonic. A scale proceeding by intervals less than the diatonic and chromatic.
Scale, German. A scale of the natural notes formed of A, H, C, D, E, F, G, the B being reserved to express B flat.
Scale, Guido's. The syllables *ut, re, mi, fa, sol, la,* used by Guido d'Arezzo, called also the Aretinian scale; the syllable *si* was introduced afterward.
Scale, major diatonic. A scale in which the semitones fall between the third and fourth and seventh and eighth notes, both in ascending and descending.
Scale, minor diatonic. A scale in which the semitones fall between the second and third and seventh and eighth in ascending and between the fifth and sixth and second and third in descending.
Scale, natural. The scale of C, called *natural* because it does not require the aid of flats or sharps.
Scalen-schule, *Ger.* (skä-l'n shoo-lĕ.) School for scale playing; exercises on the scales.
Scále rótte, *It. pl.* (skä-lĕ rŏt-tĕ.) Broken scales, imperfect, or unequal scales.
Scale of A flat major. A scale having for its key note A flat, and for its signature A, B, D, and E flat.
Scale of A major. A scale having D for its key note, and for its signature F, C, and G sharp.
Scale of B-flat major. A scale having B-flat for its key note, and for its signature B and E flat.
Scale of B major. A scale having F, C, G, D, and A sharp for its key note, and for its signature F, C, G, D, and A sharp.
Scale of C major. The natural scale, having no flats or sharps in its signature.

ă ale, ă add, ä arm, ĕ eve, ĕ end, ī ice, ĭ ill, ō old, ŏ odd, ô dove, oo moon, ū lute, u but, ü French sound.

SCAL

Scale of D-flat major. A scale having for its key note D-flat, and for its signature G, A, B, D, and E-flat.
Scale of D major. A scale in which D is the key note, having for its signature F, and C sharp.
Scale of E-flat major. A scale having for its key note E-flat and for its signature E, A, and B flat.
Scale of E major. A scale having E for its key note, and for its signature F, G, C, and D sharp.
Scale of F major. A scale having F for its key note, and for its signature B-flat.
Scale of G-flat major. A scale having G flat for its key note, and for its signature G, A, B, C, D, and E flat.
Scale of G major. A scale in which G is the key note, having for its signature F sharp.
Scale of A minor. A scale having its key note a minor third below its relative major C, and having the same signature.
Scale of B minor. The relative of D Major, having the same signature and its key note a minor third below.
Scale of B-flat minor. The relative of D-flat major.
Scale of C minor. The relative of E-flat major.
Scale of C-sharp minor. The relative of E major.
Scale of D minor. The relative of F major.
Scale of E minor. The relative of G major.
Scale of E flat minor. The relative of G-flat major.
Scale of F minor. The relative of A-flat major.
Scale of F sharp minor. The relative of A major.
Scale of G minor. The relative of B-flat major.
Scale of G-sharp minor. The relative of B major.
Scale of nature. The scale from which our modern scales arise. It is a gradual succession of fixed sounds, which nature produces from a string when divided into equal parts. Theorists have made three grand divisions, viz., the *diatonic*, the *chromatic*, and the *enharmonic*.
Scales, relative. A major and minor scale having the same signature; as C major and A minor.
Scampanare, *It.* (skäm-pä-nä-rĕ.) To chime bells.
Scampanio, *It.* (skäm-pä-nē-ō.) Christmas chimes; chimes.
Scannello, *It.* (skän-nĕl-lō.) } The bridge of a
Scannetto, *It.* (skän-nĕt-to.) } violin, violincello, etc.
Scarabillare un violino, *It.* (skär-ă-bŏl-lä-rĕ oon vē-ō-lē-nō.) To scrape a fiddle.
Scavezze, *It.* (skä-vĕt-sĕ.) Divisions within the compass of the sixth, so called because, never extending to the octave, the compass becomes broken or cut short.
Scemándo, *It.* (shĕ-män-dō.) Diminishing, decreasing in force.
Scéna, *It.* (shā-nä.) A scene or portion of an opera or play.

SCHE

Seéna da camera, *It.* (shā-nä dä kä-mĕ-rä.) Chamber music; compositions not designed for the church or theatre.
Scenario, *It.* (shĕ-nä rē-ō.) Actor's guide-book, a programme; scenes, decorations.
Scene. Part of an act, portion of an opera; an act generally comprises several scenes.
Scenic music. Music adapted to dramatic performances.
Schäfer-gedicht, *Ger.* (shä-fĕr-ghĕ-dĭkht.) Idyl, eclogue, pastoral.
Schäfer-lied, *Ger.* (shä-fĕr-lēd.) Pastoral song, shepherd song.
Schäfer-pfeife, *Ger.* (shä-fĕr pfī-fĕ.) Shepherd's pipe.
Schall, *Ger.* (shäll.) Sound.
Schälle, *Ger. pl.* (shäl-lĕ.) Sounds.
Schallen. *Ger.* (shäl-l'n.) To sound, to echo.
Schall-becken, *Ger.* (shäll-bĕk-ĕn.) Cymbal.
Schall-bret, *Ger.* (shäll-brĕt.) Sound-board.
Schall-horn, *Ger.* (shäll-hŏrn.) Horn, cornet, trumpet.
Schall-loch, *Ger.* (shäll lŏkh.) Sound-hole.
Schall-rohr, *Ger.* (shäll rōr.) Speaking trumpet.
Schall-stück, *Ger.* (shäll stük.) The bell of a trumpet, bugle, horn, etc.
Schalmay, *Ger.* (shäll-mī.) } A shawm; also,
Schalmei, *Ger.* (shäll-mī.) } an eight feet reed organ stop; the tone resembles that of the cremona, or clarinet.
Schalmeier, *Ger.* (shäll-mī-ĕr.) A player on the pipe; a hautboy player.
Scharf, *Ger.* (shärf.) *Sharp, acute;* a shrill mixture stop, of several ranks of pipes.
Schauspiel, *Ger.* (shou-spēl.) Drama, dramatic piece.
Schauspieler, *Ger.* (shou-spē-lĕr.) Actor, player.
Schauspielerinn, *Ger.* (shou-spē-lĕ-rĭnn.) Actress.
Schauspielhaus, *Ger.* (shou-spēl-hou-s.) A theatre.
Schelle, *Ger.* (shĕl-lĕ.) A bell; a jingle.
Schellen, *Ger.* (shĕl-l'n.) To ring.
Schellentrommel, *Ger.* (shĕll-l'n-trŏm-mĕl.) A tambourine, a timbrel.
Scheme. A term used in ancient music to express the varieties arising from the different positions of tones and semitones in a consonance.
Scherzandíssimo, *It.* (skĕr-tsän-dĕs-sē-mō.) Exceedingly playful and lively.
Scherzándo, *It.* (skĕr-tsän-dō.) } Playful,
Scherzánte, *It.* (skĕr-tsän-tĕ.) } lively,
Scherzévole, *It.* (skĕr-tsĕ-vō-lĕ.) } sportive,
Scherzhaft, *Ger.* (shĕrts-häft.) } merry.
Scherzevolménte, *It.* (skĕr-tsĕ-vōl-mān-tĕ.) Playfully, merrily.
Scherzhaftigkeit, *Ger.* (shĕrts-häf-tĭg-kīt.) Playfulness, sportiveness.
Scherz, *Ger.* (shĕrts.) } Play, sport, a jest; a
Scherzo, *It.* (skĕr-tsō.) } piece of a lively, sportive character, and marked, animated rhythm; also one of the movements in a symphony.
Scherzlich, *Ger.* (shĕrts-līkh.)
Scherzosaménte, *It.* (skĕr-tsō-zä-män-tĕ.) } Merrily, playfully, sportively.

ā ale, ă add, ä arm, ē eve, ĕ end, ī ice, ĭ ill, ō old, ŏ odd, ō dove, oo moon, ū lute, ŭ but, ü French sound.

SCHE

Scherzóso, *It.* (skĕr-tsō-zō.) Merry, playful, jocose.
Schiettaménte, *It.* (skē-ăt-tă-măn-tĕ-) Simply, unadorned.
Schiétto, *It.* (skē.ăt-tō.) Simple, plain, neat.
Schisma, *Ger.* (shĭs-mă.) A very minute difference between the sound of intervals. In ancient music, a small interval equal to the half of a comma, or the eighteenth part of a tone.
Schlacht-gesang, *Ger.* (shlăkht ghĕ-săng.)
Schlacht-lied, *Ger.* (shlăkht lēd.) } War song.
Schlag, *Ger.* (shlăg.) Stroke, blow; a beat, as regards time.
Schlagen, *Ger.* (shlă-g'n.) To strike, to beat; to warble or trill.
Schleifen, *Ger.* (shlī-f'n.) To slide, to glide.
Schleifer, *Ger.* (shlī-fĕr.) Slurred note, gliding note.
Schleife-zeichen, *Ger.* (shlī-fĕ tsī-khĕn.) A slur, a mark of the *legato* style.
Schleppend, *Ger.* (shlĕp-pĕnd.) Dragging, drawling.
Schluss, *Ger.* (shlooss.) The end, conclusion.
Schlüssel, *Ger.* (shlüs-s'l.) A clef.
Schluss-fall, *Ger.* (shloos făll.) A cadence.
Schluss-reim, *Ger.* (shloos rīm.) The burden, or refrain, of a song.
Schluss-stück, *Ger.* (shloos stük.) Concluding piece, finale.
Schmachtend, *Ger.* (shmăkh-tĕnd.) Languishing.
Schmelzend, *Ger.* (shmĕl-tsĕnd.) Diminishing, dying away.
Schmelzkessel, *Ger.* (shmĕlts-kĕs-s'l.) A pit employed by organ builders in which to smelt tin and lead for pipes.
Schmerz, *Ger.* (shmĕrts.) Grief, sorrow.
Schmerzhaft, *Ger.* (shmĕrts-hăft.) Dolorous, sorrowful.
Schmerzhaftigkeit, *Ger.* (shmĕrts-hăf-tĭg-kĭt.)
Schmerzlich, *Ger.* (shmĕrts-lĭkh.) } In a dolorous style.
Schnarr-bass, *Ger.* (shnărr-băss.) The drone bass.
Schnarr-pfeifen, *Ger.* (shnărr-pfī-f'n.)
Schnarr-werk, *Ger.* (shnărr-vĕrk.) } Reed pipes, reed work, or stops, in an organ.
Schnell, *Ger.* (shnĕll.) Quickly, rapidly; *etwas bewegter schnell,* a little quicker.
Schnelle, *Ger.* (shnĕl-lĕ.)
Schnelligkeit, *Ger.* (shnĕl-lĭg-kĭt.) } Quickness, swiftness, rapidity.
Schneller, *Ger.* (shnĕl-lĕr.) Quicker, faster.
Schnell-waltzer, *Ger.* (shnĕl vălt-tsĕr.) Quick waltzes.
Schoenion, *Gr.* (skē-nī-ōn.) A term used in ancient music signifying a kind of *nome,* or scientific air, composed for flutes.
Schola cantorum, *Lat.* (skō-lă kăn,tō-rŭm.) Name given by St. Gregory to a body of chanters.
Schollrohr, *Ger.* (shōll-rōr.) Trumpets, bugles, brass wind instruments.
Schottisch, *Ger.* (shŏt-tĭsh.) A modern dance, rather slow, in 2-4 time.

SCOL

Schreibart, *Ger.* (shrīb-ărt.) Style, manner of composing.
Schreiber, *Ger.* (shrī-bĕr.) A music copyist.
Schreiend, *Ger.* (shrī-ĕnd.) Acute, shrill, screaming.
Schreiwerk, *Ger.* (shrī-vărk.) *Shrill-work;* acute, or mixture stops.
Schrittmässig, *Ger.* (shrĭt-mäs-sĭg.) Slow time, andante.
Schuif-tromppet, *Dut.* (shwĭf-trōm-pĕt.) A sackbut.
Schule, *Ger.* (shoo-lĕ.) A school, or method for learning any instrument; also, a peculiar style of composition, the manner or method, of an eminent composer, performer, or teacher.
Schulsänger, *Ger.* (shool-săng-ĕr.) A *school singer;* a chorister.
Schulgerecht, *Ger.* (shool-ghĕ-rĕkht.) Regular, in due form; written correctly, in accordance with the rules and principles of musical art.
Schusterfleck, *Ger.* (shoos-tĕr-flĕk.) See *Rosalia.*
Schwach, *Ger.* (shvăkh.) *Piāno.* soft, weak.
Schwächer, *Ger.* (shvă-kĕr.) Fainter, softer, more *piăno.*
Schwache stimme, *Ger.* (shvăkh-ĕ stĭm-mĕ.) A weak voice.
Schwebung, *Ger.* (shvē-boong.) *Waving;* a lighter species of *tremulant,* for the more delicate stops, such as the vox humana, etc.
Schweige, *Ger.* (shvī-ghĕ.) A rest.
Schweigen, *Ger.* (shvī-ghĕn.) Silence, being silent.
Schweizer-flüte, *Ger.* (shvī-tsĕr flō-tĕ.)
Schweizer-pfeife, *Ger.* (shvī-tsĕr pfī-fĕ.) } Swiss flute or pipe.
Schwer, *Ger.* (shvĕr.) Heavily, ponderously.
Schwermüthig, *Ger.* (shvĕr-mü-tĭg.) In a pensive, melancholy style.
Schwiegel, *Ger.* (shvē-g'l.) An organ stop of the flute species, of metal, pointed at the top.
Schwingung, *Ger.* (shvĭng-oong.) Vibration of a string, etc.
Scialumo, *Fr.* (sē-ă-lū-mō.) A word employed in clarionet music, signifying that the notes are to be played an octave lower than written.
Science of music. The *theory* of music, in distinction from its *practice,* the latter being the art of music.
Scientific musician. One who is thoroughly acquainted with music in theory, without regard to the practice.
Scilla, *Lat.* (sĭl-lă.) Small bells, formerly used to hang upon the tail of the ermine, upon royal ermine robes; an heraldic term.
Sciolist. One who professes to understand and teach, or perform upon, many different instruments, but who is not a thorough master of any.
Scioltaménte, *It.* (shē-ōl-tă-măn-tĕ.) With freedom, agility; easily, the notes being rather detached than *legāto.*
Scioltézza, *It.* (shē-ōl-tăt-să.) Freedom, ease, lightness.
Sciólto, *It.* (shē-ōl-tō.) Free, light; see *Scioltaménte.*
Scoccobrino, *It.* (skŏk-kō-brē-nō.) A buffoon.
Scoláro, *It.* (skō-lă-rō.) A scholar.

ă ale, ă add, ă arm, ĕ eve, ĕ end, ī ice, ĭ ill, ō old, ŏ odd, ô dove, oo moon, ū tute, ŭ but, ü French sound.

SCOL

Scolia, *Gr.* (skō-lī-ā.) Among the ancients, songs in general, but more especially those of a festive kind.
Scordáre, *It.* (skŏr-dā-rĕ.) To be out of tune; to grate upon the ear with discordant notes.
Scordáto, *It.* (skŏr-dā-tō.) Out of tune, false, untuned.
Scordatúra, *It.* (skŏr-dä-too-rä.) Tuning a violin differently, for the more easily performing certain peculiar passages.
Score. The whole instrumental and vocal parts of a composition, written on separate staves, placed under each other.
Score, full. A complete score of all the parts of a composition, either vocal or instrumental, or both.
Score, instrumental. A score in which the instrumental parts are given in full.
Score, piano. A score in which the orchestral accompaniments are compressed into a pianoforte part; an arrangement of music for the piano.
Score, vocal. The notes of all the voice parts placed in their proper order under each other for the use of the conductor.
Scoring. The forming of a score, by collecting and properly arranging the detached parts of a composition.
Scorréndo, *It.* (skŏr-rĕn-dō.) Gliding from one sound into another.
Scotch scale. A scale differing from that of the other nations of Europe by its omission of the fourth and seventh; see *Pentatonic Scale*.
Scotch snap. A peculiarity in Scotch tunes, and those written in imitation of the Scotch character; it is the lengthening the time of a second note at the expense of the one before it, placing a semiquaver before a dotted quaver; it gives emphasis and spirit to dance tunes, and, when well applied, has a lively effect.
Scozzése, *It.* (skŏt-sā-zĕ.) In the Scotch style.
Scrape. To make a harsh noise; to play awkwardly and harshly on a violin or similar instrument.
Scriva, *It.* (skrē-vä.) *Written; si scriva*, as it is written, without any alteration or embellishment.
Scuóla, *It.* (skoo-ō-lä.) A school; a course of study.
Scuóla dicánto, *It.* (skoo-ō-lä dē-kän-tō.) A singing school.
Sdegnánte, *It.* (sdān-yän-tĕ.) Angry, passionate.
Sdégno, *It.* (sdān-yō.) Anger, wrath, passion.
Sdegnosaménte, *It.* (sdān-yō-zā-mān-tĕ.) Scornfully, disdainfully.
Sdegnóso, *It.* (sdān-yō-zō.) Furious, passionate, fiery.
Sdrucciolándo, *It.* (sdroot-tshē-ō-län-dō.) Sliding, slipping.
Sdrucciolare, *It.* (sdroot-tshē-ō-lā-rĕ.) To slide the hand, by turning the finger nails toward the keys of the pianoforte, and drawing the hand lightly, and rapidly, up or down.
Sdrucciolaménto, *It.* (sdroot-tshē-ō-lā-män-tō.)
Sdrucciolato, *It.* (sdroot-tshē-ō-lā-tō.)
Sliding the fingers along the strings, or the keys of an instrument.

SECT

Se, *It.* (sā.) If, in case, provided, as, so, etc.
Sea trumpet. A marine trumpet formerly much used on ship board.
Se bisógna, *It.* (sā be-sōn-yä.) If necessary, if required.
Sec, *Fr.* (sĕk.) } Dry, unornamented, cold-
Sécco, *It.* (sĕk-kō.) } ly; the note, or chord, to be struck plainly, without ornament or *arpéggio*.
Seccarára, *It.* (sĕk-kä-rā-rä.) A Neapolitan dance.
Sechs, *Ger.* (sĕkhs.) Six.
Sechs-achteltact, *Ger.* (sĕkhs äkh-t'l-täkt.) Measure in 6-8 time.
Sechs-saitig, *Ger.* (sĕkhs sī-tĭg.) Instrument with six strings.
Sechs-theilig, *Ger.* (sĕkhs tī-lĭg.) In six parts.
Sechste, *Ger.* (sĕkhs-tĕ.) A sixth.
Sechzehn, *Ger.* (sĕkh-tsēn.) Sixteen.
Sechzehnte, *Ger.* (sĕkh-tsēn-tĕ.) Sixteenth.
Sechzehntel, *Ger.* (sĕkh-tsēn-t'l.) Semiquavers.
Sechzehntelpause, *Ger.* (sĕkh-tsēn-t'l-pou-zĕ.) A semiquaver rest.
Sechzehntheil-note, *Ger.* (sĕkh-tsēn-tīl-nō-tĕ.) A semiquaver.
Second. An interval of one degree, as from A to B, B to C, etc.
Secónda, *It.* (sā-kōn-dä.) Second, a second.
Secónda dónna, *It.* (sā-kōn-dä dōn-nä.) Second female singer.
Secondary tones. Tones introduced between the principal tones wherever large seconds occur denoted by adding to the letters sharps or flats.
Second, augmented. An interval containing three half steps.
Secónda vólta, *It.* (sā-kōn-dä vōl-tä.) The second time.
Secónda vólta molto crescendo, *It.* (sā-kōn-dä vōl-tä mōl-tō krā-shĕn-dō.) Much louder the second time.
Second-dessus, *Fr.* (sā-kōnhd dĕs-sū.) The second treble.
Seconde, *Fr.* (sā-kōnhd.) Second.
Seconde fois, *Fr.* (sā-kōnhd fwä.) Second time.
Second inversion. A term applied to a chord when its fifth is the lowest tone.
Second, major. An interval consisting of two half steps.
Second, minor. An interval measured by one half step.
Secóndo, *It.* (sā-kōn-dō.) Second, a second.
Secóndo partíto, *It.* (sā-kōn-dō pär-tē-tō.) The second part, or voice.
Second soprano. The low soprano.
Second subject. The counter subject of a fugue when it remains unchanged in all the parts.
Second tenor. Low tenor.
Second treble. Low treble.
Sectio canonis, *Lat.* (sĕk-shī-ō kä-nō-nĭs.) The name given to that celebrated division of a chord, by which the portions of its several sounds are precisely ascertained. It was invented by Euclid.
Section. A complete, but not an independent musical idea; a part of a musical period, composed of one or more phrases.
Section, cadence. A section concluding with a perfect cadence,

ă *ale*, ă *add*, ă *arm*, ĕ *eve*, ĕ *end*, ī *ice*, ĭ *ill*, ō *old*, ŏ *odd*, ô *dove*, oo *moon*, ū *lute*, ŭ *but*, ü *French sound*.

SECT

Section, contracted. A section containing not over three bars.
Section, dominant. A section ending on the chord of the dominant.
Section, extended. A section containing from five to eight bars.
Section, tonic. A section terminating on the common chord of the tonic.
Secular music. Music which is composed for the theatre or chamber; an expression used in opposition to *sacred* music, which is for the church or worship.
Seculars. Unordained officiates of any cathedral or chapel, whose functions are confined to the vocal department of the choir.
Secunde, *Ger.* (sĕ-*koon*-dĕ.) Second.
Secundiren, *Ger.* (sĕ-koon-dĭr-ĕn.) To play the second part.
Secundum artem, *Lat.* (sĕ-*kŭn*-dŭm är-tĕm.) According to art or professional rule; with skill and accuracy.
Seelen-amt, *Ger.* (sā-l'n-ämt.) } Requiem,
Seelen-messe, *Ger.* (sā-l'n-mĕs-sĕ.) } or mass for departed souls.
Seer. The ancient name for a bard or rhapsodist.
Segnáre, *It.* (sān-yä-rĕ.) To beat time.
Ségno, *It.* (sān-yō.) A *sign*, 𝄋: *at ségno*, return to the sign; *dal ségno*, repeat from the sign.
Segue, *It.* (sĕ-gwĕ.) } Follows, now follows,
Seguíto, *It.* (sā-gwē-tō.) } as follows; it also means, go on, in a similar, *or like manner*, showing that a passage is to be played like that which precedes it.
Segue córo, *It.* (sā-guĕ kō-rō.) } The cho-
Segue il córo, *It.* (sā-guĕ ĕl kō-rō.) } rus follows, go on to the chorus.
Segue il duétto, *It.* (sā-guĕ ĕl doo-ät-tō.) The duet follows.
Segue il menuétto, *It.* (sā-guĕ ĕl mĕ-noo-ät-tō.) The minuet follows.
Segue la finále, *It.* (sā-guĕ lä fē-nä-lĕ.) The finále now follows.
Seguéndo, *It.* (sĕ-guän-dō.) } Following, next.
Seguénte, *It.* (sĕ-guän-tĕ.) }
Seguénza, *It.* (sĕ-guän-tsä.) A sequence.
Segue sénza interruzióne, *It.* (sā-guĕ sän-tsä ĕn-tĕr-roo-tsē-ō-nĕ.) Go on without stopping.
Segue subito sénza cambiare il tempo, *It.* (sā-guĕ soo-bē-tō sän-tsä käm-bē-ä-rĕ ĕl tämpō.) Proceed directly, and without changing the time.
Seguidilla, *Spa.* (sā-guĕ-dĕl-yä.) A favorite Spanish dance in 3-4 time.
Seguidillera, *Spa.* (sā-guĕ-dĕl-yĕ-rä.) A person who sings and dances seguidillas.
Seguíto, *It.* (sā-guĕ-tō.) Followed, imitated.
Segundilla. *Spa.* (sā-goon-dĕl-yä.) A small bell used for certain acts of devotion.
Segundo, *Spa.* (sā-*goon*-dō.) } Second.
Segundo, *Por.* (sā-*goon*-dō.) }
Sehnsucht, *Ger.* (sān-sookht.) Desire, longing; ardor, fervor.
Sehnsüchtig, *Ger.* (sān-sükh-tĭg.) Longingly.
Sehr, *Ger.* (sār.) Very, much, extremely.
Sehr lebhaft. *Ger.* (sār lāb-häft.) Very lively; extremely animated and vivacious.
Séi, *It.* (sā-ē.) Six.

SEME

Seis, *Spa.* (sā-ēs.) Six; sixth; a boy who sings in a choir of a cathedral.
Seisillo, *Spa.* (sā-ē-sĕl-yō.) Union of six equal notes.
Seintenbart, *Ger.* (sī-t'n-bärt.) The ear or mouth of an organ pipe.
Seiten-bewegung, *Ger.* (sī-t'n-bĕ-vĕ-goong.) Oblique motion.
Seizieme de supir, *Fr.* (sĕ-zē-äm düh soo-pĕr.) Semidemisemiquaver rest.
Sekunde, *Ger.* (sĕ-*koon*-dĕ.) Second.
Selah, *Heb.* (sĕ-lä.) A term anciently used to indicate the interlude, in which the priests should blow the trumpets, to carry up the sentiments expressed for a memorial before God.
S'élever, *Fr.* (s'äl-ĕ-vä.) To ascend in tone.
Semeiotechnie, *Fr.* (sĕ-mä-ō-tĕk-nē.) A system of musical characters.
Se mettre à l'unísson de, *Fr.* (süh mätr ä l'ū-nē-sŏnh düh.) To be in unison with.
Semi, *Lat.* (sĕm-ī.) Half.
Semibreve, *Eng.* (sĕm-ī-brĕv.) }
Semibréve, *It.* (sĕm-ē-brā-vĕ.) }
Semibrevis, *Lat.* (sĕm-ī-brĕ-vĭs.) }
Half a breve; the longest note now in general use.
Semibreve rest. A rest equal in duration to a semibreve.
Semicadenza, *It.* (sĕm-ē-kä-*dän*-tsä.) Semicadence.
Semi-chorus. A chorus to be sung by half or only a few of the voices.
Semicon. An instrument used by the ancients, of which, at present, little more is known than that it resembled the harp, and contained thirty-five strings.
Semicorchea, *Spa.* (sĕm-ē-kŏr-kĕ-ä.) A semiquaver.
Semi-croma, *Gr.* (sĕm-ī-krō-mä.) } A semi-
Semi-cróma, *It.* (sĕm-ē-krō-mä.) } quaver.
Semi-demisemiquaver. A half demisemiquaver; sixty-four of them being equal to a semibreve.
Semi-demisemiquaver rest. A rest equal in duration to a semi-demisemiquaver.
Semi-diapason, *Gr.* (sĕm-ī-dī-ä-*pā*-sŏn.) An octave diminished by a semitone.
Semi-diapente, *Lat.* (sĕm-ī dī-ä-*pän*-tĕ.) Diminished, or imperfect fifth.
Semi-diatessaron, *Lat.* (sĕm-ī dī-ä-*tās*-sä-rŏn.) Diminished fourth.
Semi-ditone, *Lat.* (sĕm-ī dī-tō-nĕ.) }
Semi-ditóno, *It.* (sĕm-ē dē-tō-nō.) }
A minor third.
Semi-fredon, *Fr.* (sĕm-ī frä-dŏnh.) A demiquaver.
Semi-fusa, *Lat.* (sĕm-ī fū-sä.) A semiquaver.
Semi-minim, *Lat.* (sĕm-ī mĭn-ĭm.) } A half
Semi-mínima, *It.* (sĕm-ē mē-nē-mä.) } minim,
a crotchet, a quarter note.
Seminima, *Spa.* (sĕm-ē-nē-mä.) A crotchet, a quarter note.
Semioctava, *Spa.* (sĕm-ī-ŏk-tä-vä.) A poetical composition of four verses in alternate rhymes.
Semiographie, *Gr.* (sĕm-ī-o-grä-fē.) } The art
Semeiographie, *Gr.* (sĕm-ē-o-grä-fē.) } of notation, or writing music in notes.

PRONOUNCING MUSICAL DICTIONARY. 177

ă *ale,* ă *add,* ă *arm,* ē *eve,* ĕ *end,* ī *ice,* ĭ *ill,* ō *old,* ŏ *odd,* ō *dove,* oo *moon,* ū *lute,* ŭ *but,* û *French sound.*

SEMI

Semiped, *Lat.* (sĕm-ĭ-pĕd.) In poetry, half a foot.
Semiquaver. A note equal to half a quaver; a sixteenth note.
Semiquaver rest. A rest equal in duration to a semiquaver.
Semisospiro, *It.* (sā-mē-sōs-pē-rō.) A pause equal to an eighth of a bar in common time.
Semitone, *Eng.* (sĕm-ĭ-tōn.) } A half-
Semitonium, *Lat.* (sĕm-ĭ-tō-nĭ-ŭm.) } tone.
Semitone, major. A semitone produced by ascending a degree, as from G to A flat. (This distinction of major and minor semitones is uncalled for, and not usually accepted.)
Semitone, minor. A semitone produced by passing from a note to its sharp or flat.
Semitonium modi, *Lat.* (sĕm-ĭ-tō-nĭ-ŭm mō dī.) The leading note or major seventh.
Semituōno, *It.* (sā-mē-*two*-nō.) A semitone.
Semper contrarius esto, *Lat.* (sĕm-pĕr kŏn-trā-rī-ŭs ĕs-tō.) A term in enigmatical canons of the seventeenth century, indicating that the consequent should imitate the antecedent by a retrograde movement.
Semplice, *It.* (sām-plē-tshĕ.) Simple, pure, plain.
Semplicemente, *It.* (sām-plē-tshĕ-*mān*-tō.) Simply, plainly, without ornament.
Semplicissimo, *It.* (sām-plē-tshē-sē-mō.) With the utmost simplicity.
Semplicita, *It.* (sām-plē-tshē-tā.) Simplicity, plainness.
Sempre, *It.* (sām-prē.) Always, evermore, continually.
Sempre forte, *It.* (sām-prē *fōr*-tĕ.) Always loud.
Sempre legáto, *It.* (sām-prē lē-gā-tō.) Always smooth.
Sempre piáno, *It.* (sām-prē pē-ā-nō.) Always soft.
Sempre piu affrettándo il tempo, *It.* (sām-prē pē-oo äf-frĕt-*tān*-dō ĭl tām-pō.) Continually increasing the time.
Sempre piu fòrte, *It.* Continually increasing in power.
Sempre piu presto, *It.* (sām-prē pē-oo *prās*-tō.) Continually quicker.
Sempre ritardándo, *It.* (sām-prē rē-tār-*dān*-dō.) Always slower, slower and slower.
Sempre staccáto, *It.* (sām-prē stāk-kā-tō.) Always detached, *staccáto* throughout.
Sena, *Spa.* (sā-nā.) A sign.
Senario, *Spa.* (sā-nā-rī-ō.) A verse of six iambic feet.
Sensibile, *It.* (sĕn-sē-bē-lĕ.) Sensible, expressive, with feeling.
Sensibilita, *It.* (sĕn-sē-bē-lē-tā.) Sensibility, expression, feeling.
Sensibilmente, *It.* (sĕn-sē-bēl-*mān*-tō.) Sensibly, expressively, in a feeling manner.
Sensible, *Fr.* (sänh-sēbl.) The leading note, or major seventh of the scale.
Sentences. Certain interlude strains sometimes introduced into the service of the established church, especially of particular chapels; short anthems.
Sentie, *Fr.* (sänh-tē.) Felt, expressed; *mélodie bien sentie,* the melody well expressed or accented.

SERE

Sentimentále, *It.* (sĕn-tē-mĕn-*tā*-lĕ.) } Feel-
Sentiménto, *It.* (sĕn-tē-*mān*-tō.) } ing, sentiment, delicate expression.
Senza, *It.* (sān-tsā.) Without.
Senza accompagnaménto, *It.* (sān-tsā ăk-kōm-pān-yā-*mān*-tō.) Without accompaniment.
Senza battúta, *It.* (sān-tsā bā-too-tā.) At the pleasure of the performer as regards the beat or time.
Senza fióri, *It.* (sān-tsā fē-ō-rē.) }
Senza ornaménti, *It.* (sān-tsā ōr-nā-*mān*-tē.) } Without ornaments, without embellishments.
Senza interruzióne, *It.* (sān-tsā ĭn-tĕr-roo-tsē-ō-nĕ.) Without interruption.
Senza oboé, *It.* (sān-tsā ō-bō-ā.) Without the hautboy.
Senza órgano, *It.* (sān-tsā ōr-gā-nō.) Without the organ.
Senza pedále, *It.* (sān-tsā pĕ-dā-lĕ.) Without the pedals.
Senza piáno, *It.* (sān-tsā pē-ā-nō.) Without the piano.
Senza repetizióne, *It.* (sān-tsā rā-pĕ-tē-tsē-ō-nĕ.) }
Senza réplica, *It.* (sān-tsā rā-plē-kā.) } Without repetition.
Senza rigóre, *It.* (sān-tsā rē-gō-rē.) Without regard to exact time.
Senza sordíni, *It. pl.* (sān-tsā sōr-dē-nē.) Without the dampers, in pianoforte playing, meaning that the dampers are to be raised from the strings.
Senza sordíno, *It.* (sān-tsā sōr-dē-nō.) Without the mute, in violin playing, etc.
Senza stroménti, *It. pl.* (sān-tsā strō-*mān*-tē.) Without instruments.
Senza tempo, *It.* (sān-tsā *tām*-pō.) Without regard to the time; in no definite time.
Se piáce, *It.* (sā pē-ā-tshĕ.) A will, at pleasure.
Septet, *Eng.* (sĕp-tĕt.) } A composition for
Septétto, *It.* (sĕp-*tāt*-tō.) } seven voices or instruments.
Septieme, *Fr.* (sĕt-ĭ-ām.) The interval of a
Septime, *Ger.* (sĕp-tē-mĕ.) } seventh.
Septimen-accord, *Ger.* (sĕp-tĭ-mĕn ăk-kōrd.) A chord in which the seventh is an important sound; the chord of the seventh, comprising the root, the third, fifth and seventh.
Septimole, *Lat.* (sĕp-tĭ-mō-le.) } A group of
Septiole, *Lat.* (sĕp-tĭ-ō-lē.) } seven notes, having the value, and to be played in the time of four, of the same species.
Séquence, *Eng.* (sē-quĕns.) } A series, or
Séquence, *Fr.* (sā-*känhss*.) } progression, of
Sequenz, *Ger.* (sē-*quĕnts*.) } similar chords,
Sequénza, *It.* (sĕ-*quān*-tsā.) } or intervals, in succession.
Seraphine. (sĕr-ā-fēn.) A species of harmonium.
Serbáno, *It.* (sĕr-bā-nō.) The serpent, a bass wind instrument.
Serēnáde, *Fr.* (sĕr-ē-*nād*.) Night music; an
Serenáta, *It.* (sĕr-ē-nā-tā.) } evening concert in the open air and under the window of the person to be entertained. Also, a musical composition on an amorous subject; also, any light, pleasing instrumental composition comprising several movements.

12

ā *ale,* ă *add,* ä *arm,* ē *eve,* ĕ *end,* ī *ice,* ĭ *ill,* ō *old,* ŏ *odd,* ô *dove,* oo *moon,* ū *lute,* ŭ *but,* ü *French sound.*

SERE

Seréno, *It.* (sĕ-rā́-nō.) Serene, calm, tranquil, cheerful.
Séria, *It.* (sā-rē-ä.) } Serious, grave, in a
Seriŏso, *It.* (sā-rē-ō-zō.) } serious, sedate style.
Séria, opera, *It.* (sā-rē-ä ō-pĕ-rä.) Serious, or tragic opera.
Sérieusement, *Fr.* (sā-rĭ-ŭs-mänh.) Seriously, gravely.
Serinette, *Fr.* (sĕr-ĕ-nĕt.) A bird organ.
Seringhi, *Hin.* (sĕ-rĕn-ghē.) A Hindoo instrument of the violin class.
Sério. *It.* (sā-rē-ō.) } Serious, grave.
Serio, *Spa.* (sā-rĭ-ō.) } Serious, grave.
Serio-comic. A song combining the grave with the ludicrous, or humorous.
Serpeggiándo, *It.* (sĕr-pĕd-jĕ-än-dō.) Gently winding, sliding, creeping.
Serpent, *Eng.* (sĕr-pĕnt.) } A bass wind
Serpénte, *It.* (sĕr-pän-tĕ.) } instrument,
Serpentóno, *It.* (sĕr-pĕn-tō-nō.) } of deep, coarse tone, resembling a serpent in form. It is chiefly used in military bands, though nearly superseded by the ophicleide; the name is sometimes given to a reed stop in an organ.
Serpent bläser, *Ger.* (sĕr-pĕnt blä-zĕr.) A player on the serpent.
Serráta, *It.* (sĕr-rä-tä.) A concluding performance.
Service. A musical composition adapted to the services of religious worship.
Service book. A Missal; a book containing the musical service of the church.
Service, choral. A form of religious service in which the priest sings in response to the choir.
Servi symphoniaci. *Lat. pl.* (sĕr-vē sĭm-fō-nĭ-ä-sē.) Among the Romans, a band of musicians kept by a person of rank for his own amusement, or that of his guests.
Sesqui, *Lat.* (sĕs-quī.) A Latin particle, signifying a whole and a half, and which, when joined with *altera, terza, quarta,* etc., expresses a kind of ratio.
Sesquialtera, *Lat.* (sĕs-quī-ăl-tĕ-rā.) The name given by the ancients to that ratio which includes one and a half to one. An organ stop, comprising two or more ranks of pipes, of acute pitch.
Sesqui-alterate. *The greater Perfect.* A triple in the old music, in which the breve is three measures, or semibreves, and that without having any point, or dot, annexed to it.
Sesqui-alterate. *Lesser Perfect.* That in which the semibreve contains three measures, or minims, independent of any dot.
Sesqui-alterate. *The greater Imperfect.* Where the breve, when dotted, contains three measures, or semibreves, and when without a dot, two.
Sesqui-alterate. *Lesser Imperfect.* Where the semibreve, when dotted, contains three measures, or minims, and when without a dot, two.
Sesquitertia, *Lat.* (sĕs-quō-tĕr-shĭ-ä.) A musical ratio is said to be *sesquitertia* when it is as four to three.
Sesquitone, *Lat.* (sĕs-quō-tō-nĕ.) A minor third, or interval consisting of three semitones.
Sésta, *It.* (sās-tä.) } The interval of a sixth; see
Sésto, *It.* (sās-tō.) } also *Sexte.*

SEXT

Sestet, *Eng.* (sĕs-tĕt.) } A composition for
Sestétto, *It.* (sĕs-tāt-tō.) } six voices or instruments.
Sestína, *It.* (sĕs-tē-nä.) } A sextole.
Sestóla. *It.* (sĕs-tō-lä.) } A sextole.
Set to music. An expression applied to any language to which music is adapted. Such a composition is said to be *set to* music.
Sétte, *It.* (sāt-tĕ.) Seven.
Séttima, *It.* (sāt-tē-mä.) } The interval of a
Séttimo, *It.* (sāt-tē-mō.) } seventh.
Séttima maggióre, *It.* (sāt-tē-mä mäd-jē-ō-rĕ.) Major seventh.
Séttima minóre, *It.* (sāt-tē-mä mē-nō-rĕ.) Minor seventh.
Settimóla, *It.* (sĕt-tē-mō-lä.) A septimole.
Setz-art, *Ger.* (sāts-ärt.) Style, or manner of composition.
Setzen, *Ger.* (sāt-tsēn.) To compose.
Setzer, *Ger.* (sāt-tsĕr.) A composer.
Setz-kunst, *Ger.* (sāts koonst.) The art of musical composition.
Seventeenth. An organ stop: see *Tierce.*
Seventh. An interval containing six diatonic degrees.
Sevens and eights metre. A metre consisting of a stanza of eight lines in trochaic measure and designated thus, 7s and 8s.
Sevens and fives metre. Consists of a stanza of four lines in trochaic measure and designated, 7s and 5s.
Sevens and sixes metre. A metre designated thus, 7s and 6s, consisting of a stanza of eight lines in trochaic and iambic measure.
Sevens, eights, and sevens metre. A metre designated thus, 7s, 8s, and 7s, consisting of a stanza of eight lines in iambic measure.
Sevens metre. A stanza of four lines in trochaic measure, each line containing seven syllables.
Sevens, sixes, and eights metre. A metre designated thus, 7s, 6s, and 8s, consisting of eight lines in trochaic and iambic measure.
Seventh, diminished. An interval measured by nine half-steps.
Seventh, major. An interval measured by eleven half-steps.
Seventh, minor. An interval measured by ten half-steps.
Severaménte, *It.* (sĕ-vĕr-ä-män-tĕ.) Severely, strictly, rigorously.
Severita, *It.* (sĕ-vĕ-rē-tä.) Severity, strictness.
Sexta, *Lat.* (sĕx-tä.) Sixth.
Sextain. A stanza of six lines.
Sexta pars. *Lat.* (sĕx-tä pärs.) When two parts were added to the four parts to which church music was usually limited in the fifteenth century, the second part was denominated *sexta pars.*
Sexta toni, *Lat.* (sĕx-tä tō-nē.) The sixth interval from the tonic.
Sexte, *Ger.* (sĕx-tĕ.) A sixth; also, the name of an organ stop with two ranks of pipes, sounding the interval of a major sixth, a twelfth and tierce on one slide.
Sextetto. See *Sestetto.*
Sextilla, *Spa.* (sĕx-tĕl-yä.) A Spanish metrical composition of six feet.

ă *ale*, ă *add*, ä *arm*, ē *eve*, ĕ *end*, ī *ice*, ĭ *ill*, ō *old*, ŏ *odd*, ô *dove*, oo *moon*, ū *lute*, ŭ *but*, ü *French sound*.

SEXT

Sexto, *Spa.* (sĕx-tō.) A sixth.
Sextole, *Lat.* (sĕx-tō-lĕ.) } A group of six
Sextuplet, *Lat.* (sĕx-tū-plĕt.) } notes, having the value, and to be played in the time, of four.
Sextuple measure. The name formerly given to measures of two parts, composed of six equal notes, three for each part. This is more generally called, now, *compound common time*.
Sfogato, *It.* (sfō-gä-tō.) A very high soprano.
Sforza, *It.* (sfōr-tsä.) Forced, with force and energy.
Sforzándo, *It.* (sfōr-tsän-dō.) } *Forced*, one
Sforzáto, *It.* (sfōr-tsä-tō.) } particular chord, or note, to be played with force and emphasis.
Sforzáre la voce, *It.* (sfōr-tsä-rĕ lä vō-tshĕ.) To overstrain the voice.
Sforzataménte, *It.* (sfōr-tsä-tä-mān-tĕ.) Impetuously, energetically.
Sfuggito, *It.* (sfood-jē-tō.) Avoided, shunned; rambling; see *Cadénza Sfuggita*.
Sgallinacciáre, *It.* (sgäl-lē-nät-tshē-ä-rĕ.) To crow; a bad method of singing.
Shake. An ornament produced by the rapid alternation of two successive notes, comprehending an interval not greater than a whole tone, nor less than a semitone.
Plain shake or trill.
Shake, double. Two simultaneous shakes on notes which are either sixths or thirds to each other.
Double shake.
Shake, passing. A short trill made in flowing passages of quavers or semiquavers without breaking the time, or interfering with the natural course of the melody.

Shake, prepared. A shake preceded by two or more introductory notes.
Shalishim. A triangle, invented by the Syrians. Triangular rods were used, of metal, charged with rings.
Shalm. A shawm.
Sharp. A character which raises a note one semitone, ♯.
Sharp, accidental. An occasional sharp placed before a note in the course of a piece, but not the same letter found sharp in the signature.
Sharpen. To make higher; to render more acute; to sharp, or to make sharp.
Sharp, double. A double sharp is equivalent to two sharps, raising a note a whole tone instead of a semitone; expressed thus, ♯♯, or ×.
Sharp sixth. In the first inversion of the minor chord of the seventh; by sharping the fundamental tone we obtain the chord of the *Sharp Sixth*, or, as some writers call it, the *German Sixth*.
Shawm. A wind instrument of the ancient Hebrews, supposed to be of the reed or hautboy species.

SICC

Shell. An ancient musical instrument consisting of the shell of a tortoise, over which strings were drawn, forming the lyre of early times.
Sheminith, *Heb.* (shĕm-ĭ-nĭth.) A stringed instrument. It was also sometimes used to denote a species of music, and also a particular part of a composition.
Shepherd's flute. A pastoral flute, shorter than the transverse flute, and blown through a lip-piece at the extremity.
Shift A change of position of the left hand, in playing the violin, etc. See *violin shifts*.
Shift, double. A shift on the violin to D in alt.
Shift, first. A violin shift on the fifth line, also called the half shift.
Shift, half. See *First Shift*.
Shift, last. In violin playing, the shift nearest the bridge.
Shift, second. } A violin shift on the eighth
Shift, whole. } line, or A.
Shiginoth, *Heb.* (shĕ-ghĭ-ō-nŏth.) *According to variable tunes.*
Shophar, *Heb.* (shō-fär.) A trumpet, or bent horn, so called because it gave a brilliant, clear, ringing sound.
Short appoggiatura. An appoggiatura consisting of one or more notes played without regard to the value of the next note, though governed somewhat by the character of the piece; the lesser appoggiatura.
Short hallelujah metre. A stanza of six lines in iambic measure.
Short metre. A stanza of four lines in iambic measure.
Short mordent. A Mordent consisting of two notes, viz., that having the sign over it and that below or above it, before the principal note.
Short octaves, A term applied to the lower notes in old organs, where some of the notes were omitted.
Short particular metre. A stanza of six lines in iambic measure.
Short shake. An embellishment formed by two or more notes preceding the principal note.
Shrill. An epithet applied to those acute sounds which form the upper part of the scale of soprano voices and treble instruments.
Shur, *Heb.* (shŭr.) To sing.
Shushanednth, *Heb.* (shū-shăn-ĕ-douth.) }
Shoshannim, *Heb.* (shō-shăn-nĭm.) }
A musical instrument somewhat resembling the lily. It is possible the cymbal is meant as that instrument resembles the lily.
Si, *Fr.* (sē.) Applied in *solfäing* to the note B.
Si bémol, *Fr.* (sē bā-mŏl.) } The note B-flat.
Si bemolle, *It.* (sē bā-mŏl-lĕ.) }
Si bémol majeur, *Fr.* (sē bā-mŏl mä-zhŭr.) The key of B-flat major.
Si bémol mineur, *Fr.* (sē bā-mŏl mē-nŭr.) The key of B-flat minor.
Sibilate. (sĭb-ĭ-lāte.) To sing with a hissing sound.
Sibilio, *It.* (sē-bē-lē-ō.) A hiss; a hissing sound.
Sibilus, *Lat.* (sĭb-ĭ-lŭs.) A little flute or flageolet used to teach birds to sing.
Siccama flute. A diatonic flute.

180   PRONOUNCING MUSICAL DICTIONARY.

ă *ale*, ă *add*, ă *arm*, ĕ *eve*, ĕ *end*, ī *ice*, ĭ *ill*, ō *old*, ŏ *odd*, ö *dove*, oo *moon*, ū *lute*, ŭ *but*, ü *French sound*.

SICI

Siciliána, *It.* (sē-tshē-lē-*ä*-nä.) } A dance of the
Siciliáno, *It.* (sē-tshē-lē-*ä*-nō.) } Sicilian peasants, a graceful movement of a slow, soothing pastoral character, in 6-8 or 12-8 time.
Side-drum. The common military drum, so called from its hanging at the side of the drummer when played upon.
Si diese, *Fr.* (sē di-āz.) The note B sharp.
Sieben, *Ger.* (sē-b'n.) Seven.
Sieben-klang, *Ger.* (sē-b'n *kläng*.) Heptachord, a scale of seven notes.
Siebente, *Ger.* (sē-bĕn-tĕ.) Seventh.
Siebenzehnte, *Ger.* (sē-bĕn-tsēn-tĕ.) Seventeenth.
Siegesgesang, *Ger.* (sē-ghĕs-ghĕ-*säng*.) }
Siegeslied, *Ger.* (sē-ghĕs-*lēd*.) }
A triumphal song.
Siegesmarsch, *Ger.* (sē-ghĕs-*märsh*.) A triumphal march.
Siegue. See *Segue*.
Siegue il córo, *It.* (sē-*ä*-gwē ēl *kō*-rō.) The chorus follows.
Siegue il menuétto, *It.* (sē-*ä*-gwē ēl mē-noo-ĕt-tō.) The minuet follows.
Siegue l'ária, *It.* (sē-*ä*-gwē l'*ä*-rē-ä.) The air follows.
Siegue súbito l'allégro, *It.* (sē-*ä*-gwē soo-bē-tō l'äl-*lä*-grō.) The allegro follows immediately.
Siff-nöte, *Ger.* (sĭff *flō*-tĕ.) An organ stop of 2 or 1 foot scale, of the *hohl-flute* species.
Siffler, *Fr.* (sĭf-flā.) To make a hissing noise.
Siffler un air, *Fr.* (sĭf-flā ŭnh n'ăr.) To whistle a tune.
Sifflet, *Fr.* (sēf-flā.) A cat-call, a squeaking instrument used in play-houses to condemn a performance.
Signalist, *Ger.* (sĭg-näl-ĭst.) A military trumpet player.
Signatur, *Ger.* (sĭg-nä-*toor*.) } Name given
Signatura, *Spa.* (sēn-yä-*too*-rä.) } to the sharps
Signature, *Eng.* (sĭg-nā-tshūr.) } or flats placed at the beginning of a piece, and at the commencement of each staff, to indicate the key in which it is written.
Signature, time. Figures, in the form of a fraction, placed at the beginning of a piece to indicate the time.
Sign, canceling. A natural.
Sign, da capo. A mark placed before a bar, indicating that the piece or movement is to be repeated from that point.
Signe, *Fr.* (sēn.) The sign, 𝄋; see *Segno*.
Signes accidentels, *Fr.* (sēn ăk-sĭ-*dänh*-t'l.) Accidental sharps, flats, or naturals.
Signes de silences, *Fr.* (sēn dŏ sĭ-*länhs*.) Rests.
Sign, neutralizing. A cancelling sign; a natural.
Signs. A general name for all the different characters used in music, such as flats, sharps, dots, etc.
Signs of abbreviation. Strokes, waving lines, dots, and figures, employed to denote a repetition of notes, continuation of rests, etc.
Signs of sforzándo. Certain characters showing that a tone is to be emphasized stronger than its rhythmical accent requires, > ∨ ∧.

SINC

Signs of the organ tone. Two parallel lines indicating that the tone is to commence, continue, and close with a uniform degree of power, ═══.
Signs of the pressure tone. Signs indicating a very sudden increase of the tone, > >.
Siguidilla, *Spa.* (sē-gwē-*dēl*-yä.) See *Seguidilla*.
Silbador, *Spa.* (sēl-bä-*thōr*.) One who whistles.
Silbar, *Spa.* (sēl-*bär*.) To whistle.
Silbern, *Ger.* (sĭl-bĕrn.) Of a silvery tone.
Silberton, *Ger.* (sĭl-bĕr-*tōn*.) Silvery tone, silvery sound.
Silboso, *Spa.* (sēl-bō-zō.) Whistling, hissing.
Silence, *Fr.* (sē-länhs.) }
Silencio, *Spa.* (sī-*lĕn*-thī-ō.) } A rest.
Silénzio, *It.* (sē-*län*-tsē-ō.) }
Silences pointes, *Fr. pl.* (sē-länhs pwänh-tā.) Dotted rests.
Silenciosamente, *Spa.* (sē-lĕn-thē-ō-zä-*män*-tē.) Quietly, softly.
Si lentándo, *It.* (sē lĕn-*tän*-dō.) A term denoting a slackening of the time.
Silénzio perfétto, *It.* (sē-*län*-tsē-ō pĕr-*fät*-tō.) Perfect silence, general rest.
Si leva il sordíno, *It.* (sē *lā*-vä ēl sōr-*dē*-nō.) Take off the mute.
Si leváno i sordíno, *It.* (sē lē-*vä*-nō ē sōr-*dē*-nō.) Raise the dampers.
Silver trumpet. The *chatsoteroth* of the ancient Hebrews, straight, a cubit long, with a bell-shaped mouth.
Si majeur, *Fr.* (sē mä-zhūr.) The key of B major.
Similar motion. Where two or more parts ascend or descend at the same time.
Simile, *It.* (sē-mē-lē.) Similarly; in like manner.
Si mineur, *Fr.* (sē mi-nūr.) The key of B mineur.
Simple counterpoint. That counterpoint in which note is set against note, and which is called *simple*, in opposition to more elaborate counterpoint which is known as *figurative*.
Simple fugue. } That style of composition in which a single subject is employed.
Simple imitation. }
Simple intervals. Those which do not exceed an octave.
Simple inversion. An inversion made by reversing the notes of fugal, or other subject in its answer, so that the ascending notes of the original passage descend in the answer, and *vice versa*.
Simple recitative. A recitative with the accompaniment of a bass part only; a plain recitative.
Simple times. Those which contain but one principal accent in a bar; as 2-4, 3-4, 3-8, etc.
Simplicity. In composition, a natural, unadorned melody; or a natural, simple, arrangement of *parts*. In performance, a chaste, unaffected style.
Simplified. Rendered free from difficult passages.
Sin 'al fine, *It.* (sēn äl fē-nē.) To the end, as far as the end.
Sincopa, *It.* (sēn-kō-pä.) } See *Syncopáio*.
Sincope, *It.* (sēn-kō-pē.) }

ä ale, ă add, ä arm, ē eve, ĕ end, ī ice, ĭ ill, ō old, ŏ odd, ō dove, oo moon, ū lute, ŭ but, ü French sound.

SINF

Sinfonía, *It.* (sĕn-fō-nē-ä.) \ An orchestral com-
Sinfonie, *Fr.* (sănh-fō-nē.) / position in many parts; a symphony.
Sinfonía a pittorica. *It.* (sĕn-fō-nē-ä ä pĕt-tō-rē-kä.) A symphony descriptive of scenes and events.
Sinfonía concertánte. *It.* (sĕn-fō-nē-ä kŏn-tshĕr-tän-tĕ.)
Sinfonía concertáta, *It.* (sĕu-fō-nē-ä kŏn-tshĕr-tä-tä.)
Sinfonía concertáte, *It.* (sĕn-fō-nē-ä kŏn-tshĕr-tä-tĕ.)
A concerto for many instruments; a concerto symphony.
Sinfonía da cámera, *It.* (sĕn-fō-nē-ä dä kä-mē-rä.) Symphonies composed for chamber use, as quartets, trios, etc.
Sinfonía eróica, *It.* (sĕn-fō-nē-ä ä-rō-ē-kä.) A symphony in the heroic style.
Sinfonía fugáta, *It.* (sĕn-fō-nē-ä foo-gä-tä.) In the style of a fugue.
Sinfonie, *Ger.* (sĭn-fō-nē.) A symphony.
Sing. To utter sounds with various inflections or modulations of the voice as fancy may dictate, or according to the notes of a song or tune.
Sing-akadamie, *Ger.* (sĭng äk-ä-dä-mē.) Vocal academy.
Sing-anstalt, *Ger.* (sĭng än-stält.) Singing club.
Sing-art, *Ger.* (sĭng ärt.) Manner, or style of singing.
Singbar, *Ger.* (sĭng-bär.) That may be sung.
Sing-bass, *Ger.* (sĭng bäss.) A vocal bass.
Sing-chor, *Ger.* (sĭng kōr.) Singing choir, a chorus.
Singen, *Ger.* (sĭng-ĕn.) To sing, to chant; singing, chanting.
Singend, *Ger.* (sĭng-ĕnd.) See *Cantábile*.
Sing-gedicht, *Ger.* (sĭng ghĕ-dĭkht.) Hymn, poem intended to be sung.
Singhiozzándo, *It.* (sĕn-ghē-ōt-sän-dō.) Sobbingly.
Sing-kunst, *Ger.* (sĭng-koonst.) The art of singing.
Single-action harp. A harp with pedals, by which each string can be raised one semitone.
Single chant. A simple harmonized melody, extending only to one verse of a psalm, as sung in cathedrals, etc.
Sing-mährchen, *Ger.* (sĭng-mär-k h'n.) A ballad.
Sing-meister. *Ger.* (sĭng-mīs-tĕr.) Singing master.
Sing-pult, *Ger.* (sĭng-poolt.) Singing desk.
Sing-sang, *Ger.* (sĭng-säng.) Sing-song.
Sing-schauspiel, *Ger.* (sĭng-shous-pēl.) Singing-drama, a drama with songs, etc. interspersed.
Sing-schule, *Ger.* (sĭng-shoo-lĕ.) Singing school; a school, or method, for the voice.
Sing-schüler. *Ger.* (sĭng-shü-ler.) Singing-pupil.
Sing-spiel, *Ger.* (sĭng-spēl.) An opera, melodrama, a piece interspersed with songs.
Sing-stimme, *Ger.* (sĭng-stĭm-mĕ.) Singing voice; a vocal part.
Sing-stimmen, *Ger. pl.* (sĭng-stĭm-mĕn.) The voices; the vocal parts.
Sing-stück, *Ger.* (sĭng-stük.) Air, melody.

SIXE

Sing-stunde, *Ger.* (sĭng-stoon-dĕ.) Singing lesson.
Sing-tanz, *Ger.* (sĭng-tänts.) Dance, accompanied by singing.
Sing-verein, *Ger.* (sĭng-vĕ-rīn.) A choral society.
Sing-weise, *Ger.* (sĭng-vī-sĕ.) Melody, tune.
Siniestra, *Spa.* (sē-nī-ĕs-trä.) \ The left hand.
Sinistra, *Lat.* (sĭn-ĭs-trä.) /
Sinistræ, *Lat.* (sĭn-ĭs-trē.) Left-handed flutes; see *Dextræ*.
Sinístra máno, *It.* (sē-nĕs-trä mä-nō.) \ The
Sinístra manu, *Lat.* (sĭn-ĭs-trä mä-nū.) / left hand.
Síno, *It.* (sē-nō.) \ To, as far as, until; *confuóco*
Sin, *It.* (sēn.) / sĭn *al fine*, with spirit to the end.
Sino al fine pianíssimo, *It.* (sē-nō äl fē nō pē-än-ĭs-sē-mō.) *Pianissimo* to the end.
Sino al ségno, *It.* (sē-nō äl sān-yō.) As far as the sign.
Slöng, *Swe.* (sl-ōng.) Song.
Sipario, *It.* (sē-pä-rē-ō.) The curtain of a theatre.
Si piáce, *It.* (sē pē-ä-tshĕ.) At pleasure, as you please.
Si raddóppia il témpo, *It.* (sē räd-dŏp-pē-ä äl täm-pō.) Redouble the time; as fast again.
Siren. In ancient mythology, a goddess who enticed men into her power by the charms of music, and devoured them.
Sirene. An instrument used for ascertaining the velocity of aërial vibration, corresponding to the different pitches of musical sounds.
Sirenion. (sī-rĕn-ī-ŏn.) An instrument of the piano and harpsichord class.
Siren song. A song of a bewitching, fascinating style.
Sirenen-gesang, *Ger.* (sīr-ē-nĕn ghĕ-säng.) Siren-song; a soft, luscious, seductive melody.
Si réplica, *It.* (sē rä-plē-kä.) A repeat; to be repeated.
Si réplica una vólta, *It.* (sē rä-plē-kä oo-nä vŏl-tä.) Play the part over again.
Si scriva, *It.* (sē scrē-vä.) As written, without any alteration or embellishment.
Si segue, *It.* (sē sā-guĕ.) Go on.
Sistema, *It.* (sĕs-tē-mä.) System.
Sistrum, *Lat.* (sĭs-trŭm.) An instrument of percussion of very great antiquity, supposed to have been invented by the Egyptians, and was much used by the priests of Iris and Osiris in sacrifice. It consisted of a rod of iron, bent into an oval or oblong shape, or square at two corners and curved at the others, and furnished with a number of movable rings, so that, when shaken, or struck with another rod of iron, it emitted the sound desired.
Si táce, *It.* (sē tä-tshĕ.) Be silent.
Si vólta, *It.* (sē vŏl-gä.) Turn over the leaf.
Sixain, *Fr.* (sēz-änh.) Stanza; strophe of six verses.
Six-eighth measure. A measure having the value of six eighth notes, marked 6-8.
Sixes and fives metre. A metre consisting of a stanza of eight lines in iambic or trochaic measure, designated thus, 6s & 5s.

ă *ale*, ă *add*, ă *arm*, ĕ *eve*, ĕ *end*, 1 *ice*, ĭ *ill*, ō *old*, ŏ *odd*, ô *dove*, oo *moon*, ū *lute*, ŭ *but*, ü *French sound*.

SIXE

Sixes and four. A metre designated thus, 6s & 4, consisting of a stanza of four lines in iambic measure.
Sixes and tens. A metre designated thus, 6s & 10s, consisting of a stanza of six lines in iambic measure.
Sixes metre. A metre designated thus, 6s, consisting of a stanza of eight lines of six syllables each, in iambic measure.
Sixes and sevens, and eights metre. A metre designated thus, 6s, 7s, & 8s, consisting of a stanza of eight lines in iambic measure.
Sixfold measure. A measure consisting of two trochees, or musical feet, each formed of a long and a short note, or of an accented and unaccented one; a measure of six equal parts.
Sixieme, *Fr.* (sĕz-ĭ-ăm.) A sixth.
Six pour quatre, *Fr.* (sĕz poor kătr.) A double triplet, or sextuplet; six notes to be played in the time of four.
Six quarter measure. A measure having the amount of six quarter notes, marked 6-4.
Six semibreve rest. A rest having the duration of six semibreves:
Sixte, *Fr.* (sĕkst.) A sixth.
Sixteenth note. A semiquaver.
Sxteenth rest. A pause equal in duration to a sixteenth note.
Sixtes, *Fr.* (sēkst.) Sixths.
Sixth. An interval comprising six sounds, or five diatonic degrees.
Sixth augmented. An interval measured by ten half-steps.
Sixth diminished. An interval measured by seven half-steps.
Sixth sharp. An interval obtained from the first inversion of the minor chord of the seventh, by sharping the fundamental tone.
Sixth German. See *Sharp Sixth.*
Sixth Italian. An interval obtained by suppressing the original seventh in the chord of the sharp sixth.
Sixth major. An interval measured by nine half-steps.
Sixth minor. An interval measured by eight half-steps.
Sixty-fourth note. A hemidemisemiquaver.
Sixty-fourth rest. A pause equal in point of duration to a sixty-fourth note.
Skalde, *Ger.* (skȧl-dĕ.) A scald; ancient Scandinavian bard.
Skene manuscript. This manuscript existed during the reign of James VI., and is supposed to have been noted in great part between 1615 and 1620. It contained in all one hundred and five tunes, most of them Scottish, and some of them familiar, a number of dancing tunes, etc.; it belonged to John Skene, of Hallyards.
Skip. A term applied to any transition exceeding that of a whole tone step.
Skizzen, *Ger. pl.* (skĭts-tsĕn.) *Sketches;* short pieces.
Skolien, *Swe.* (skō-lĕn.) Drinking song.
Slargándo, *It.* (slär-găn-dō.) } Extend-
Slargandósi, *It.* (slär-găn-dō-zē.) } ing, enlarging, widening; the time to become gradually slower.

SOLB

Sientándo, *It.* (slĕn-tăn-dō.) Relaxing the time, becoming gradually slower.
Slide. See *Glisser.*
Slide, tuning. An English instrument producing thirteen semitones, and used for pitching the key note.
Slogan. The war-cry or gathering word of a Highland clan in Scotland.
Slur. A curved line over two or more notes, to show that they must be played smoothly.
Slurred. Notes or passages performed in a smooth and gliding manner, are said to be *slurred.*
Slurring. Performing in a smooth, gliding style.
Small octave. The name given in Germany to the notes included between C on the second space of the bass staff and the B above, these notes being expressed by small letters, as a, b, c, d, etc.
Smanicáre, *It.* (smän-ē-kä-rē.) To shift, or change the position of the hand in playing the violin, guitar, etc.
Smaniánte, *It.* (smän-ē-än-tē.) } Furious, ve-
Smaniáto, *It.* (smä-nē-ä-tō.) } hement, fran-
Smanióso, *It.* (smä-nē-ō-zō.) } tic; with rage.
Smiunéndo, *It.* (smē-noo-ăn-dō.) } Diminish-
Sminuíto, *It.* (smē-noo-ē-tō.) } ing, decreas-
Smorendo, *It.* (smo-rän-dō.) } ing, gradually softer.
Smorfióso, *It.* (smor-fē-ō-zō.) Affected, coquettish, full of grimaces.
Smorz. An abbreviation of *Smorzándo.*
Smorzándo, *It.* (smŏr-tsăn-dō.) } Extinguish-
Smorzáto. *It.* (smŏr-tsä-tō.) } ed, put out, gradually dying away.
Snare drum. The commonly used small drum, so named on account of strings of raw hide drawn over its lower head, and to distinguish it from the large or bass drum.
Soáve, *It.* (sō-ä-vĕ.) A word implying that a movement is to be played in a gentle, soft and engaging style.
Soavemēnte, *It.* (sō-ä-vĕ-män-tĕ.) Sweetly, agreeably, delicately.
Sochantre, *Spa.* (sō-kăn-trĕ.) Subchanter.
Société chantante, *Fr.*(sō-sĭ-ā-tā shänh-tänht.) Singing society.
Sock-pipe. The appellation given by the ancient northern poets to the bagpipe.
Soggétto, *It.* (sŏd-jăt-tō.) Subject, theme, motive.
Soggétto di fúga, *It.* (sŏd-jăt-tō dē foo-gä.) Subject of the fugue.
Soggétto invariato, *It.* (sŏd-jăt-tō ēn-vä-rē-ä-tō.) The invariable subject—a term applied to the subject of counterpoint when it does not change the figure or situation of the notes.
Soggétto variato, *It.* (sŏd-jăt-tō vä-rē-ä-tō.) Variable subject—a term applied to the subject of a counterpoint when it changes the figure or situation of the notes.
Soirée musicále, *Fr.* (swä-rā mū-zē-kăl.) A musical evening.
Sol. (sŏl.) A syllable applied by the Italians to G, the fifth sound of the diatonic scale or octave of C.
Sóla, *It.* (sō-lä.) Alone; see *Sólo.*
Sol bémol, *Lat.* (sŏl bā-mŏl.) The note G-flat.

ā ale, ă add, ä arm, ē eve, ĕ end, ī ice, ĭ ill, ō old, ŏ odd, ô dove, oo moon, ū lute, ŭ but, ü French sound.

| SOLB | SONN |

Sol bémol majeur, *Fr.* (sŏl bā-mōl mă-zhŭr.) The key of G-flat major.
Sol bémol mineur, *Fr.* (sŏl-bā-mōl mē-nŭr.) The key of G-flat minor. (Not in use.)
Sol diese, *Fr.* (sŏl dī-āz.) The note G-sharp.
Sol diese mineur, *Fr.* (sŏl-dī-āz mē-nŭr.) The key of G-sharp minor.
Solénne, *It.* (sō-lān-nē.) Solemn.
Solennemēnte, *It.* (sō-lĕn-n ē-m ā n-tē.) Solemnly.
Solfaing. Singing the notes of the scale to the monosyllables applied to them by Guido.
Solfeador, *Spa.* (sŏl-fē-ä-dōr.) A singer; a music master.
Solfege, *Fr.* (sŏl-*fāsh*.) } Exercises for the
Solféggi, *It. pl.* (sŏl-*fäd*-jē.) } v o i c e according
Solféggio, *It.* (sŏl-*fäd*-jē-ō.) } to the rules of solmization.
Solfeggiaménti, *It.* (sŏl-fäd-jē-ă-mān-tē.) Solféggi.
Solfeggiáre, *It.* (sŏl-fäd-jē-ä-rē.) To practice Solféggi.
Solfeggiren, *Ger.* (sŏl-fĕg-gbī-r'n.) } To solfa.
Solfier, *Fr.* (sŏl-fē-ā.) }
Solfista, *Spa.* (sŏl-*fēs*-tä.) Musician; a person skilled in music.
Soli, *It.* (sō-lē.) A particular passage played by principals only, one performer to each part.
Sólito, *It.* (sō-lē-tō.) Accustomed; in the usual manner.
Sollécito, *It.* (sō-lā-tahē-tō.) · C a r e f u l, solicitous; meaning an attentive and careful style of execution.
Sol majeur, *Fr.* (sŏl mä-zhŭr.) The key of G major.
Sol mineur, *Fr.* (sŏl mē-nŭr.) The key of G minor.
Solmisáre, *It.* (sŏl-mē-zä-rē.) } The prac-
Solmizáre, *It.* (sŏl-mē-*tsä*-rē.) } tice of the
Solmisiren, *Ger.* (sŏl-mī-sĭr-ĕn.) } s c a l e s, applying to the different tones their respective syllables, *do, re, mi, fa, sol, la, si*; to this kind of vocal exercise the practice of Solféggi is added.
Solmisation. See *Solféggi* and *Solmisáre*.
Solmization a la Grec, *Fr.* (ă lä grĕk.) A s p e c i e s of solmization formerly practiced, in which the old Greek system of tetrachords was adhered to, so far as to use but four characters, which were repeated from tetrachord to tetrachord as we now repeat from scale to scale.
Sólo, *It.* (sō-lō.) } A composition for a single
Solo, *Fr.* (sō-lō.) } voice or instrument.
Solo, *Ger.* (sō-lō.) }
Solomanie, *Tur.* (sō-lō-mä-nē.) The Turkish flute, entirely open and without any reed.
Solo, piano. A solo for the pianoforte.
Solo-sänger, *Ger.* (sō-lō-*säng*-ĕr.) A solo-singer, principal singer.
Solo-spieler, *Ger.* (sō-lō-spē-lĕr.) Solo player.
Sólo-sopráno, *It.* (sō-lō sō-prä-nō.) For soprano only.
Sol post vesperas declinat, *Lat.* (sŏl pŏst vĕs-pē-räs dē-*klī*-nät.) In old enigmatical canons, a term implying that at each repeat the canon should be lowered ŏne tone.
Sómma, *It.* (sŏm-mä.) Extreme, exceeding great.

Sómma espressióne. *It.* (sŏm-mä ĕs-prĕs-sē-ō-nē.) Very great expression.
Sommeils. (sŏm-māl.) The name by which the French distinguished the airs in their old serious operas, because they were calculated to tranquilize the feelings and induce drowsiness.
Sommerlied, *Ger.* (sŏm-mĕr-lēd.) A song in praise of summer.
Sommier, *Fr.* (sŏ-mī-ä.) The sound board.
Sommier d'orgue, *Fr.* (sŏ-mī-ä d'ōrg.) Sound board of an organ.
Son, *Fr.* (sŏnh.) } Sound.
Son, *Spa.* (sŏn.) }
Sonábile, *It.* (sō-nä-bē-lē.) } Sonorous, resonant.
Sonable, *Spa.* (sō-nä-blē.) }
Sonagliáre, *It.* (sō-näl-yē-ä-rē.) To jingle, to ring a small bell.
Sonáglio, *It.* (sō-näl-yē-ō.) A small bell.
Son aigu, *Fr.* (sŏnh ä-gü.) A sharp, acute sound.
Sonajero, *Spa.* (sō-nä-*hä*-rō.) } A small tabor
Sonajica, *Spa.* (sō-nä-hē-kä.) } or timbrel.
Sonajor, *Spa.* (sō-nä-hōr.) A timbrel.
Sonaménto, *It.* (sō-nä-*män*-tō.) Sounding, ringing, playing.
Sonante, *Spa.* (sō-nän-tē.) Sounding, sonorous.
Sonáre, *It.* (sō-nä-rē.) To sound, to have a sound, to ring, to play upon.
Sonáre álla ménte, *It.* (sō-nä-rē ät-lä män-tē.) To play extempore, to improvise.
Sonáre il violíno, *It.* (sō-nä-rē ēl vē-ō-lē-nō.) To play upon the violin.
Sonáta, *It.* (sō-nä-tä.) } An instrumental com-
Sonate, *It.* (sō-nät.) } position, usually of three or four distinct movements, each with a unity of its own, yet all related so as to form a perfect whole. It commonly begins with an allegro, sometimes preceded by a slow introduction. Then come the andante, adagio, or largo; then the minuet and trio, or scherzo; and lastly the finale in quick time.
Sonata da cámera, *It.* (sō-nä-tä dä kä-mō-rä.) A sonata designed for the chamber or parlor.
Sonata da chiésa, *It.* (sō-nä-tä dä kē-ä-zä.) A church sonata, an organ sonata.
Sonata di bravúra, *It.* (sō-nä-tä dē brä-voo-rä.) A brave, bold style of sonata.
Sonata form. In the style of a sonata.
Sonata, grand. A massive and extended sonata, consisting usually of four movements.
Sonata per il cémbalo sólo. *It.* (sō-nä-tä pär ēl *tshäm*-hä-lō sō-lō.) A sonata for the harpsichord without accompaniment.
Sonata per il violíno. *It.* (sō-nä-tä pär ēl vē-ō-lē-nō.) A sonata for the violin.
Sonate, *Ger.* (sō-nä-tē.) A sonata.
Sonatina, *It.* (sō-nä-tē-nä.) } A short, easy
Sonatine, *Fr.* (sō-nä-tēn.) } sonata.
Sonatójo, *It.* (sō-nä-tō-hō.) A sounding board.
Sonatór di violíno, *It.* (sō-nä-tōr dē vē-ō-lē-nō.) A fiddler, violin player.
Sonatóre, *It.* (sō-nä-tō-rē.) An instrumental performer.
Sonatríce, *It.* (sō-nä-trē-tahē.) A female performer.
Son doux, *Fr.* (sŏnh doo.) Soft sound.
Sonnecillo, *Spa.* (sŏn-nē-*thēl*-lō.) A short tune; a slight sound.

ă ale, ă add, ä arm, ĕ eve, ĕ end, ī ice, ĭ ill, ō old, ŏ odd, ô dove, oo moon, ū lute, ŭ but, ü French sound.

SONE

Sonetazo, *Spa.* (sō-nĕ-tä-thō.) A loud sound.
Sonettánte, *It.* (sō-nĕt-tän-tĕ.) A singer of sonnets.
Sonétto, *It.* (sō-nät-tō.) A sonnet.
Sonévole, *It.* (sō-nä-vŏ-lĕ.) Sonorous, ringing, sounding.
Song. A short lyric poem set to music; a short musical composition, either with or without words; a hymn; poetry.
Song, Bacchanalian. A song which either in sentiment or style relates to scenes of revelry.
Song, boat. A song sung by the rowers; gondolier song.
Song, erotic. A love song.
Song, florid. A term applied by musicians of the 14th century to figured descant, in order to distinguish it from the old chant or plain song.
Song form. In the style of a song.
Song, four-part. A song arranged for four voices.
Song, gondolier. A song sung by the Venetian gondoliers; a barcarolle.
Song, hunting. A melody set to words in praise of the chase.
Song, martial. A song, the subject and style of which are warlike.
Song, national. A song identified with the history of a nation, on account of the sentiments it expresses, or from long use.
Song, nautical. A song relating to the sea.
Song, nuptial. A song celebrating marriage.
Song, patriotic. A song intended to inspire a love of country.
Song, plain. The old ecclesiastical chant, without any of the harmony which now enriches it.
Song, rustic. A plain, simple melody, suitable to rural themes.
Song, sacred. A devotional song, a hymn.
Song, secular. A song not designed for religious worship.
Songs of the wells. The fountain hymns of the ancients, and still common in the Greek isles.
Songs without words. Pianoforte pieces, consisting of a melody with an accompaniment.
Songs, table. Songs for male voices, formerly much in vogue among German glee clubs.
Sonido, *Spa.* (sō-nē-thŏ.) Sound.
Sonido agudo, *Spa.* (sō-nē-thō ä-goo-thō.) An acute sound.
Soniferous. Producing sound.
Soni mobiles, *Gr.* (sō-nē mō-bĭ-lĕs.) The name by which the ancients distinguished the intermediary sounds of their tetrachords.
Soni stabiles, *Gr.* (sō-nē stä-bĭ-lĕs.) } The extremes of the Greek tetrachords.
Soni stantes, *Gr.* (sō-nē stän-tēs.) }
Sonnant, *Fr.* (soo-nänh.) Sounding.
Sonner, *Fr.* (sŏnh-nä.) To sound, to ring, to blow.
Sonner a toute voix, *Fr.* (sŏnh-nä ä toot vwä.) To ring a full peal.
Sonner de la trompette, *Fr.* (sŏnh-nä dŭh lä trŏnh-pät.) To sound the trumpet.
Sonner du cornet, *Fr.* (sŏnh-nä dŭ kŏr-nä.) To sound a horn.
Sonner la cloche, *Fr.* (sŏnh-nä lä klōeh.) To ring a bell.

SOPR

Sonnet. A short poem of fourteen lines, two stanzas of four verses each and two of three each, the rhymes being adjusted by a particular rule.
Sonneteer. A composer of sonnets or small poems; usually a term of contempt.
Sonnettier, *Fr.* (sŏnh-nĕt-tĭ-ä.) Bell-maker or seller.
Sonnettucciaccio, *It.* (sŏn-nĕt-toot-tshē-ät-tshō-ō.) A poor sonnet.
Sonneur, *Fr.* (sŏnh-nūr.) A bell ringer.
Sonometer. (sō-nŏm-ĕ-tĕr.) An instrument for measuring intervals or the vibrations of sounds.
Sonoraménte, *It.* (sō-nō-rä-män-tĕ.) Sonorously, harmoniously.
Sonora, *Spa.* (sō-nō-rä.) A cithern.
Sonore, *Fr.* (sō-nōr.) } Sonorous, harmonious,
Sonóro, *It.* (sō-nō-rō.) } resonant.
Sonoridad, *Spa.* (sō-nō-rĭ-däd.) Sonorousness.
Sonorific. (sō-nō-rĭf-ĭk.) Producing sound.
Sonorita, *It.* (sō-nō-rē-tä.)
Sonorité, *Fr.* (sō-nō-rē-tä.) } Harmony, sound,
Sonorite. *Spa.* (sō-nō-rē-tĕ.) } sonorousness.
Sonoroso, *Spa.* (sō-nō-rō-zō.) Sonorous, pleasing.
Sonorous. (sō-nō-rous.) An epithet applied to whatever is capable of yielding sound; full or loud in sound; rich-toned, musical.
Son perçant. *Fr.* (sŏnh pär-sänh.) A shrill, piercing sound.
Sons étouffés, *Fr. pl.* (sŏnhs'ä toof-fä.) Stifled, or muffled tones.
Sons harmoniques, *Fr. pl.* (sŏnhs' här-mŏnh-ēk.) Harmonic sounds.
Sons pleins, *Fr. pl.* (sŏnhs' plänh.) In flute music, this means that the notes must be blown with a very full, round tone.
Sonus, *Lat.* (sō-nŭs.) Sound, tone.
Sonus exclusus, *Lat.* (sō-nŭs ĕx-clū-sŭs.) Excluded sound; one of the three radical sounds composing the harmonic triad; the fifth.
Sópra, *It.* (sō-prä.) Above, upon, over, before.
Sópra domimánte, *It.* (sō-prä dō-mē-nän-tĕ.) The fifth or upper dominant.
Soprání, *It. pl.* (sō-prä-nē.) Treble voices.
Sopran, *Ger.* (sō-prän.) } The treble, the high-
Sopráno, *It.* (sō-prä-nō.) } est kind of female voice; a treble, or soprano singer.
Sopráno acúto, *It.* (sō-prä-nō ä-koo-tō.) High soprano.
Soprano clef. The treble or G clef.
Soprano clef. The C clef on the first line of the staff for soprano, instead of using the G clef on the second line for that part.
Soprano clef, mezzo. The C clef when placed on the second line of the staff, formerly used for the second treble voice, and for which the soprano clef is now substituted.
Sopráno concertáto, *It.* (sō-prä-nō kŏn-tshĕr-tä-tō.) The soprano solo part, the part for a solo treble voice in a chorus.
Soprano concertina. A concertina having the compass of a violin.
Sopráno córda, *It.* (sō-prä-nō kŏr-dä.) The E string of a violin.
Sopráno mézzo, *It.* (sō-prä-nō mät-sō.) A species of female voice between soprano and alto.

ä *ale*, ă *add*, ä *arm*, ē *eve*, ĕ *end*, I *ice*, ĭ *ill*, ō *old*, ŏ *odd*, ô *dove*, oo *moon*, ū *lute*, ŭ *but*, ü *French sound*.

SOPR

Soprano, second. Low soprano.
Sopráno secúndo od álto, *It.* (sō-prä-nō sā-koon-dō ŏd äl-tō.) The second soprano or alto.
Sopran-stimme, *Ger.* (sō-prän stĭm-mĕ.) A soprano voice.
Sópra quínta, *It.* (sō-prä quēn-tä.) Upper dominant.
Sópra úna córda, *It.* (sō-prä oo-nä kōr-dä.) On one string.
Sórda, *It.* (sōr-dä.) Muffled, veiled tone.
Sordaménte, *It.* (sōr-dä-mǎn-tĕ.) Softly, gently; also, damped, muffled.
Sordellína, *It.* (sōr-dĕl-lē-nä.) A species of bagpipe.
Sordína, *It.* (sōr-dē-nä.) } A sordine.
Sordína, *Spa.* (sōr-dē-nä.) }
Sordet. } A small instrument or damper in the
Sordine. } mouth of a trumpet, or on the bridge of a violin or violincello, to make the sound more faint and subdued.
Sordini, *It. pl.* (sōr-dē-nē.) *Mutes* in violin playing; and the *Dampers* in pianoforte music; see *Con Sordini*, and *Senza Sordini*.
Sordini levati, *It.* (sōr-dē-nē lē-vä-tē.) The dampers removed.
Sordino, *It.* (sōr-dē-nō.) A sordine.
Sórdo, *It.* (sōr-dō.) Muffled, veiled tone.
Sorgfältig, *Ger.* (sōrg-fäl-tĭgh.) Carefully.
Sorgfältig gebunden, *Ger.* (sōrg-fäl-tĭgh ghĕ-boon-d'n.) Very smoothly.
Sortíta, *It.* (sōr-tē-tä.) The opening air in an operatic part, the entrance *ária*.
Sospensióne, *It.* (sōs-pĕn-sē-ō-nĕ.) A suspension.
Sospensivaménte, *It.* (sōs-pĕn-sē-vä-mǎn-tĕ.) Irresolutely, waveringly.
Sospirándo, *It.* (sōs-pē-rän-dō.) } Sighing.
Sospiránte, *It.* (sōs-pē-rän-tĕ.) } very subdued,
Sospirévole, *It.* (sōs-pē-rä-vō-lĕ.) } doleful.
Sospiróso, *It.* (sōs-pē-rō-zō.) }
Sospíro, *It.* (sōs-pē-rō.) A crotchet rest.
Sosteněndo, *It.* (sōs-tĕ-nǎn-dō.) } Sustaining
Sostenúto, *It.* (sōs-tĕ-noo-tō.) } the tone, keeping the notes down their full duration.
Sostenúto mólto, *It.* (sōs-tĕ-noo-tō mōl-tō.) In a highly sustained manner.
Sótto, *It.* (sōt-tō.) Under, below.
Sótto bóce, *It.* (sōt-tō bō-tshĕ.) } Softly, in a
Sótto vóce, *It.* (sōt-tō vō-tshĕ.) } low voice in an undertone.
Soubrette, *Fr.* (soo-brĕtt.) A female singer for a subordinate part in a comic opera.
Sou-chantre, *Fr.* (soo-shäntr.) A sub-chanter.
Soufflerie, *Fr.* (soof-flĕ-rē.) The machinery belonging to the bellows in an organ.
Souffler l'orgue, *Fr.* (soof-flä l'ōrg.) To blow the bellows of an organ.
Souffleur, *Fr.* (soof-flūr.) } Bellows-blower;
Souffleuse, *Fr.* (soof-flūs.) } also a prompter in a theatre.
Souffleur d'orgues, *Fr.* (soof-flūr d'ōrgh.) Bellows-blower of an organ.
Sound-board. } The thin board over which
Sounding-board. } the strings of the pianoforte and similar instruments are distended.
Sound post. A small post or prop within a violin, nearly under the bridge.

SPIE

Sound register. An apparatus invented in Paris in 1858, by means of which sounds are made to record themselves, whether those of musical instruments or of the voice in singing or speaking.
Sounds, accessory. } Those sounds which
Sounds, concomitant. } in a secondary manner assist in producing an effect.
Sounds, harmonical. Those sounds produced by the higher parts of the chords, which vibrate a certain number of times while the lowest fundamental tone of the chord vibrates but once.
Soupir, *Fr.* (soo-pēr.) A crotchet rest.
Soupir de croche, *Fr.* (soo-pēr duh krŏsh.) See *Demi-soupir*.
Soupir de double croche, *Fr.* (soo-pēr duh doobl krŏsh.) See *Quart de soupir*.
Soupir de triple croche, *Fr.* (soo-pēr duh trĕpl krŏsh.) See *Demi-quart de soupir*.
Sourdeline, *Fr.* (soor-dĭ-lĕn.) An Italian bagpipe, or *musette*.
Sourdement, *Fr.* (soord-mänh.) In a subdued manner.
Sourdet, *Fr.* (soor-dä.) The little pipe of a trumpet; a sordine.
Sourdine, *Fr.* (soor-dēn.) The name of a harmonium stop; see also *Sordino*.
Sous, *Fr.* (soo.) Under, below.
Sous-chantre, *Fr.* (soo shänhtr.) A sub-chanter.
Sous-dominante, *Fr.* (soo dō-mĭ-nänht.) The sub-dominante, or fourth of the scale.
Sous-médiante, *Fr.* (soo mā-dĭ-änht.) The sub-mediant, or sixth of the scale.
Sous-tonique, *Fr.* (soo tōn-ēk.) The seventh of the scale, or sub-tonic.
Soutenir, *Fr.* (soo-tĕ-nēr.) To sustain a sound.
Souvenir, *Fr.* (soo-vĕ-nēr.) Recollection, reminiscence.
Spaces. The intervals between the lines of the staff.
Spanisch, *Ger.* (spän-ĭsh.) } In the
Spagnolésco, *It.* (spän-yō-lǎs-kō.) } Spanish style.
Spagnolétta, *It.* (spän-yō-lǎt-tä.) A Spanish dance, a species of minuet.
Spagnuola, *It.* (spän-yoo-ō-lä.) The guitar.
Spassapensiére, *It.* (späs-sä-pĕn-sē-ā-rĕ.) The Jew's harp.
Spasshaft, *Ger.* (apdäs-häft.) Sportively, playfully, merrily.
Spasshaftigkeit, *Ger.* (spdäs-häf-tĭg-kĭt.) Sportiveness, playfulness.
Spasshaftlich, *Ger.* (spdäs-häft-lĭkh.) Sportively, merrily, playfully.
Spatium, *Lat.* (spē-shĭ-ŭm.) } A space between
Spázio, *It.* (spä-tsē-ō.) } the lines where music is written; a distance, an interval.
Spianáto, *It.* (spē-ä-nä-tō.) Smooth, even; *legáto*.
Spiccataménte, *It.* (spĕk-kä-tä-mǎn-tĕ.) Brilliantly.
Spiccáto, *It.* (spĕk-kä-tō.) Separated, pointed, distinct, detached; in violin music it means that the notes are to be played with the point of the bow.
Spiel, *Ger.* (spēl.) Play, performance.

ă ale, ă add, ä arm, ĕ eve, ĕ end, 1 ice, ĭ ill, ō old, ŏ odd, ô dove, oo moon, ū lute, ŭ but, ü French sound.

SPIE

Spiel-art, *Ger.* (spēl ärt.) Manner of playing, style of performance.
Spielen, *Ger.* (spē-l'n.) To play on an instrument.
Spieler, *Ger.* (spē-lĕr.) Performer.
Spiel-leute, *Ger. pl.* (spēl loi-tĕ.) Musicians.
Spiel-mann, *Ger.* (spēl män.) A musician.
Spinæ, *Lat.* (spē-nē.) *Horns;* a name formerly applied to the quills of the spinet.
Spinet, *Eng.* (spĭn-ĕt.) ⎫ A stringed instru-
Spinett, *Ger.* (spĭ-nĕt.) ⎬ ment formerly much
Spinétta, *It.* (spē-nāt-tä.) ⎭ in use, somewhat similar to the harpsichord, and, like that, consisting of a case, sounding board, keys, jacks, and a bridge. It was evidently derived from the harp, and was originally called the *couched harp*, though since denominated *spinet*, from its quills, which resemble *thorns*, called in Latin *spinæ*.
Spinett-draht, *Ger.* (spĭn-ĕt drät.) Virginal, or spinet wire.
Spírito, *It.* (spē-rē-tō.) Spirit, life, energy.
Spiritosaménte, *It.* (spē-rē-tō-zä-mān-tĕ.) ⎫
Spiritóso, *It.* (spē-rē-tō-zō.) ⎬
Lively, animated, brisk, spirited.
Spirituále, *It.* (spē-rē-too-ä-lĕ.) ⎫ Sacred, spir-
Spirituel, *Fr.* (spĭr-ē-too-ĕl.) ⎬ itual.
Spirituóso, *It.* (spē-rē-too-ō-zō.) See *Spiritóso*.
Spissi gravissimi, *Lat.* (spĭs-sē grä-vĭs-sĭ-mē.) Hypatoïdes — the deep or bass sounds of the ancient Greek system.
Spissus, *Lat.* (spĭs-sŭs.) Thick; full, referring to intervals.
Spitz, *Ger.* (spĭtz.) Pointed.
Spitz-flöte, *Ger.* (spĭtz flō-tĕ.) ⎫ Pointed-
Spitz-flute, *Ger.* (spĭtz floo-tĕ.) ⎬ flute; an organ stop of a soft, pleasing tone, the pipes of which are conical, and pointed at the top.
Spitz-quinte, *Ger.* (spĭtz quĭn-tĕ.) An organ stop with pointed pipes, sounding a fifth above the foundation stops.
Spondaula, *Gr.* (spŏn-daw-lä.) Name given by the ancients to a performer on the flute, or some similar instrument, who, while the sacrifice was offering, played to the priest some suitable air, to prevent him from listening to anything that might interfere with his duty.
Spondee, *Lat.* (spŏn-dē.) A musical foot consisting of two long notes or syllables, ——.
Spondiasm. An alteration in the harmonic genus, by which a chord was elevated three dieses above its ordinary pitch, so that the *spondiasm* was precisely the opposite of the *eclysis*.
Spondeo, *It.* (spŏn-dē-ō.) A spondee.
Spottlied, *Ger.* (spŏt-lēd.) A satirical song.
Spring. An embellishment. The German spring consists of two small notes before a principal, similar to the Italian mordente, but very distinct; thus:

Spruchgesang. *Ger.* (sprookh-ghĕ-săng.) An anthem.
Square B. Name formerly given to B natural on account of the shape of its signature.

STAN

Squilla, *It.* (squĕl-lä.) A little bell; a shrill-sounding bell; the clang of a trumpet.
Squillánte, *It.* (squĕl-län-tĕ.) Clear, plain, sounding, ringing.
Squillanteménte, *It.* (squĕl-län-tĕ-mān-tĕ.) Clearly, loudly, shrilly.
Squilláre, *It.* (squĕl-lä-rĕ.) To sound loud and shrill.
Srootis. A general name for the twenty-two minor subdivisions of the octave of the Hindoo scale.
Sta, *It.* (stä.) This, as it stands; to be played as written.
Stabat mater, *Lat.* (stä-bät mä-tĕr.) The Mother stood — a hymn on the crucifixion.
Stábile, *It.* (stä-bē-lĕ.) Firm.
Stabili suóni, *It. pl.* (stä-bē-lē swō-nē.) The highest and lowest sounds of every tetrachord, so named because their places could not be changed.
Stac. An abbreviation of *Staccáto*.
Staccatíssimo, *It.* (stäk-kä-tĭs-sē-mō.) Very much detached, as *staccáto* as possible.
Staccáto, *It.* (stäk-kä-tō.) Detached; distinct, separated from each other.
Staccáto delicataménte, *It.* (stäk-kä-tō dĕl-ē-kä-tä-mān-tĕ.) In staccato style, lightly and delicately.
Staccato marks. Small dots or dashes placed over or under the notes, thus:
Staccato touch. A sudden lifting up of the fingers from the keys, giving to the music a light, detached, airy effect.
Staccáre, *It.* (stäk-kä-rĕ.) To detach, to separate each from.
Stadt-musikus, *Ger.* (städt moo-sĭ-kŭs.) ⎫
Stadt-pfeifer, *Ger.* (städt pfī-fĕr.) ⎬
Town musician.
Staff. The five horizontal and parallel lines on, and between which, the notes are written.
Staff of four lines. In the earlier ages of the Christian church, the monks frequently used music written on four lines with treble and bass clefs. It was entirely for the voice, and consisted of loose themes without any attempt whatever at artistic effect.
Staff, bass. The staff marked with the bass clef.
Staff, tenor. The staff marked with the tenor clef.
Staff, treble. The staff marked with the treble clef.
Stagióne, *It.* (stä-jē-ō-nĕ.) The season, the musical season.
Stagióne di cartéllo, *It.* (stä-jē-ō-nĕ dē kär-tĕl-lō.) The operatic season.
Stambuzáre, *It.* (stäm-boo-tsä-rĕ.) To beat the drum.
Stamm-accord, *Ger.* (stäm äk-kŏrd.) A radical, or fundamental chord from which others are derived.
Stammentin-pipe. An organ stop: see *Schwiegel*.
Stampíta, *It.* (stäm-pē-tä.) An air, a tune, a song.
Stance, *Fr.* (stänhts.) A stanza.
Ständchen, *Ger.* (stănd-khĕn.) A serenade.

ă *ale,* ă *add,* ä *arm,* ĕ *eve,* ĕ *end,* ī *ice,* ĭ *ill,* ō *old,* ŏ *odd,* ō *dove,* oo *moon,* ū *lute,* ŭ *but,* ü *French sound.*

STAN

Standhaft, *Ger.* (*stănd*-häft.) Steadily, firmly, resolutely.
Standhaftigkeit, *Ger.* (*s t ă n d*-häft-tĭg-kĭt.) Firmness, resolution.
Stand, music. A light frame designed for holding sheets or books for the convenience of performers.
Stanghétta, *It.* (stăn-gāt-tä.) A bar line. The fine line drawn across and perpendicular to the staff.
Stanza, *It.* (stăn-tsä.) A verse of a song or hymn.
Stark, *Ger.* (stärk.) Strong, loud, vigorous.
Stärke, *Ger.* (stăr-kě.) Vigor, force, energy.
Starke stimmen, *Ger.* (stăr-ke stĭm-měn.) Loud stops; *Mit Starken Stimmen*, with loud stops.
Stat, *Lat.* (stăt.) This, as it stands.
Station. This word is sometimes used by ancient musical authors for any fixed pitch or degree of sound, whether produced by intension or remission.
Stave. Name formerly given to the staff.
Steg, *Ger.* (stěgh.) The bridge of a violin, etc.
Stegreif spielen, *Ger.* (stěgh-rīf spē-l'n.) To play at sight.
Stem. The thin stroke which is drawn from the head of a note.
Stem, double. A stem drawn both upward and downward from a note, indicating that the note belongs to two parts, in one of which it has its natural and appropriate length, while in the other it is shorter, corresponding to the notes that follow it.
Stentándo, *It.* (stĕn-tăn-dō.) Delaying, retarding.
Stentáto, *It.* (stĕn-tă-tō.) Hard, forced, loud.
Stenteréllo, *It.* (stĕn-tĕ-rĕl-lō.) A buffoon.
Stentor. A herald, in Homer, having a very loud voice—hence, any person having a powerful voice.
Stentorian. Extremely loud.
Stentorophonic. Speaking or sounding very loud, from Stentor, a herald in Homer, whose voice was said to be as loud as that of fifty other men.
Stentorophonic tube. A speaking trumpet, so called from Stentor. The stentorophonic horn of Alexander the Great is famous; it was so powerful that he could give orders at a distance of one hundred stadia, which is about twenty English miles.
Step. A degree upon the staff. Americans use the terms *step* and half-step in place of *tone* and semitone.
Step, half. A semitone.
Sterbe-gesang, *Ger.* (stěr-bě ghě-săng.) }
Sterbe-lied. *Ger.* (stĕr-bĕ lēd.) }
Funeral hymn.
Sterbe-ton. *Ger.* (stĕr-bĕ tōn.) A tone diminishing, dying away insensibly.
Stéso, *It.* (stā-zō.) Extended, diffused, large.
Stéso móto, *It.* (stā-zō mō-tō.) A slow movement.
Stésso, *It.* (stăs-sō.) The same: *l'istésso tempo*, in the same time.
Sthénochire. A machine for strengthening and imparting flexibility to the fingers; being a compound of the *dactylion* and the *hand guide.*

STOP

Stibacchiáto, *It.* (stē-bäk-kē-ä-tō.) Relaxing, retarding the time.
Sticcádo, *It.* (stĕk-kä-dō.) } An instrument
Siccáto, *It.* (stĕk-kä-tō.) } consisting of little bars of wood rounded at the top and resting on the edges of a kind of open box. They gradually increase in length and thickness, are tuned to the notes of the diatonic scale and are struck with a little ball at the end of a stick.
Stich, *Gr.* (stĭkh.) A dot or point.
Sticker. A portion of the connection, in an organ, between the keys or pedals and the valve; a short link attached to a key or pedal, and acting on the backfall.
Stile, *It.* (stē-lĕ.) Style.
Stile a cappélla, *It.* (stē-lĕ ä kăp-pāl-lä.) In the chapel style.
Stile grandióso, *It.* (stē-lĕ grän-dē-ō-zō.) In a grand style of composition or performance.
Stile rigoróso, *It.* (stē-lĕ rē-gō-rō-zō.) In a rigid, strict style.
Stift, *Ger.* (stĭft.) The jack of a spinet, etc.
Still, *Ger.* (stĭll.) Calmly, quietly.
Still-gedacht, *Ger.* (stĭll ghĕ-däkt.) A stopped diapason, of a quiet tone.
Stilo, *It.* (stē-lō.) Style, manner of composition or performance.
Stilo alla cappélla, *It.* (stē-lō äl-lä kä-pāl-lä.) In the church or chapel style.
Stilo di recitativo, *It.* (stē-lō dē rā-tshē-tä-tē-vō.) A tedious, monotonous style of composition, in the manner of recitative, formerly much adopted in Italy, and sometimes extending through a whole narrative or drama, without the least change of measure or mixture of air, except now and then a formal close.
Stimm-deckel. *Ger.* (stĭm dĕk-ĕl.) Sound-board.
Stimme, *Ger.* (stĭm-mě.) The voice, sound; also, the sound-post in a violin, etc.; also a part in vocal or instrumental music; also an organ stop or register.
Stimmen, *Ger. pl.* (stĭm-m'n.) Parts, or voices; also organ stops.
Stimmer. *Ger.* (stĭm-měr.) Tuner; also a tuning hammer.
Stimm-gabel, *Ger.* (stĭm gä-b'l.) Tuning fork.
Stimm-hammer, *Ger.* (stĭm häm-měr.) Tuning key, tuning hammer.
Stimmig, *Ger.* (stĭm-mĭg.) Having a sound.
Stimm-pfeife, *Ger.* (stĭm pfī-fě.) Wooden fife, pitch-pipe.
Stimm-stock, *Ger.* (stĭm stōk.) The sound-post of a violin, etc.
Stimmung, *Ger.* (stĭm-moong.) Tuning, tune, tone.
Stinguéndo, *It.* (sten-gwĕn-dō.) Dying away, becoming extinct.
Stiracchiáto, *It.* (stē-räk-kē-ä-tō.) } Stretched,
Stiráto, *It.* (stē-rä-tō.) } forced, retarded; see *Allargándo.*
Stonánte, *It.* (stō-nän-tě.) Discordant, out of tune.
Stop. A register, or row of pipes, in an organ; on the violin, etc., it means the pressure of the finger upon the string.

ā ale, ă add, ä arm, ē eve, ĕ end, ī ice, ĭ ilt, ō old, ŏ odd, ō dove, oo moon, ū lute, ŭ but, ū French sound.

STOP

Stop, bassoon. A reed stop in an organ resembling the bassoon in quality of tone.
Stop, claribel. A stop similar to the clarinet stop.
Stop, clarion or octave trumpet. A stop resembling the tone of a trumpet, but an octave higher than the trumpet stop.
Stop, cornet. A stop consisting of five pipes to each note.
Stop, cremona. A reed stop in unison with the diapasons.
Stop, double diapason. An open set of pipes tuned an octave below the diapasons.
Stop, double trumpet. The most powerful reed stop in the organ, the pipes being of the same length as the double diapason, to which it is tuned in unison.
Stop, duleiana. A stop of peculiar sweetness of tone, which it chiefly derives from the bodies of its pipes being longer and smaller than those of the pipes of other stops.
Stop, fagotto. The bassoon stop.
Stop, fifteenth. A stop which derives its name from its pitch, or scale, being fifteen notes above that of the diapason.
Stop, flute. An organ stop resembling in tone a flute or flageolet.
Stops, foundation. The diapasons and principal, to which the other stops, be they few or many, are tuned, and which are absolutely required in an organ.
Stop, hautboy. A reed stop having a tone in imitation of the hautboy.
Stop, larigot, or octave twelfth. A stop the scale of which is an octave above the twelfth. It is only used in the *full organ*.
Stop, mixture, or furniture. A stop comprising two or more ranks of pipes, shriller than those of the *sesquialtera*, and only calculated to be used together with that and other pipes.
Stop, nazard. Twelfth stop.
Stop, open diapason. A metallic stop which commands the whole scale of the organ, and which is called *open* in contradistinction to the *stop* diapason, the pipes of which are closed at the top.
Stop, organ. A collection of pipes similar in tone and quality, running through the whole, or a great part, of the compass of the organ; a register.
Stop, stopped diapason. A stop the pipes of which are generally made of wood, and its bass, up to middle C, *always* of wood. They are only half as long as those of the open diapason, and are stopped at the upper end with wooden *stoppers*, or plugs, which render the tone more soft and mellow than that of the open diapason.
Stopples. Certain plugs with which the ancients stopped or opened the holes of a flute, before the performance began, in order to accommodate its scale, or range of sounds, to some particular mode or genus.
Stop, principal. A metallic stop, originally distinguished by that name, because holding, in point of pitch, the middle station between the diapason and the fifteenth, it forms the standard for tuning the other *stops*.

STRA

Stop, salcional. The dulcima stop.
Stops, compound. An assemblage of several pipes in an organ, three, four, five, or more to each key, all answering at once to the touch of the performer.
Stops, draw. Stops in an organ placed on each side of the rows of keys in front of the instrument, by moving which the player opens or closes the stops within the organ.
Stop, sesquialtera. A stop resembling the mixture, running through the scale of the instrument, and consisting of three, four, and sometimes five ranks of pipes, tuned in thirds, fifths, and eighths.
Stops, mutation. In an organ, the twelfth, tierce, and their octaves.
Stop, solo. A stop which may be drawn alone, or with one of the diapasons.
Stops, reed. Stops consisting of pipes upon the end of which are fixed thin, narrow plates of brass, which, being vibrated by the wind from the bellows, produce a reedy thickness of tone.
Stop, stopped unison. The stopped diapason stop.
Stop, tierce. A stop tuned a major third higher than the fifteenth, and only employed in the full organ.
Stop, treble forte. A stop applied to a melodeon, or reed organ, by means of which the treble part of the instrument may be increased in power, while the bass remains subdued.
Stop, tremolo. A contrivance, by means of which a fine, tremulous effect is given to some of the registers of an organ.
Stop, trumpet. A stop so called, because its tone is imitative of a trumpet. In large organs it generally extends through the whole compass.
Stop, twelfth. A metallic stop so denominated from its being tuned twelve notes above the diapason. This stop on account of its pitch, or tuning, can never be used alone; the open diapason, stopped diapason, principal and fifteenth are the best qualified to accommodate it to the ear.
Stop, vox-humana. A stop, the tone of which resembles the human voice.
Stórta, *It.* (stōr-tā.) A *serpent:* see that word.
Stortína, *It.* (stōr-tē-nä.) A small serpent.
Straccináto, *It.* (strä-tshē-nä-tō.) See Strascináto.
Stradivari. The name of a very superior make of violin, so called from their makers, Stradivarius (father and son), who made them at Cremona, Italy, about A. D. 1650.
Strain. A portion of music divided off by a double bar.
Strascicándo, *It.* (strä-shē-kän-dō.) *Dragging* the time, *trailing*, playing slowly.
Strasciáto, *It.* (strä-she-kä-tō.) *Dragged*, *trailed*, played slowly.
Strascinándo, *It.* (strä-shē-nän-dō.) *Dragging* the time, playing slowly.
Strascinándo l'árco. (strä-shē-nän-dō l'är-kō.) Keeping the bow of the violin close to the strings, as in executing the tremolándo, so as to slur or bind the notes closely.
Strascináto, *It.* (strä-shē-nä-tō.) *Dragged* along, played slowly.

ă *ale*, ă *add*, ă *arm*, ĕ *eve*, ĕ *end*, ī *ice*, ĭ *ill*, ō *old*, ŏ *odd*, ô *dove*, oo *moon*, ū *lute*, ŭ *but*, ü *French sound*.

STRA

Strascinío, *It.* (strä-shē-nē-ō.) *Dragging*, playing slowly.
Strascino, *It.* (strä-shē-nō.) A *drag.* This grace, or embellishment is chiefly confined to vocal music and only used in slow passages. It consists of an unequal and descending motion, and generally includes from eight to twelve notes and requires to be introduced and executed with great taste and judgment.
Strathspey. A lively Scotch dance, in common time.
Stravagánte, *It.* (strä-vä-gän-tě.) Extravagant, odd, fantastic.
Stravagánza, *It.* (strä-vä-gän-tsä.) Extravagance, eccentricity.
Street organ. Hand organ.
Streng, *Ger.* (strěng.) Strict, severe, rigid.
Strenge gebunden, *Ger.* (strěn-ghĕ ghĕ-boond'n.) Strictly legáto, exceedingly smooth.
Streng im tempo, *Ger.* (strěng im těm-pō.) Strictly in time.
Strépito, *It.* (strä-pě-tō.) Noise.
Strepitosaménte, *It.* (strä-pě-tō-sä-män-tě.) With a great noise.
Strepitóso, *It.* (strä-pě-tō-zō.) Noisy, boisterous.
Strétta, *It.* (strät-tä.) A concluding passage, coda, or finale, in an opera, taken in quicker time to enhance the effect.
Strétto, *It.* (strä-tō.) *Pressed, close*, contracted; formerly used to denote that the movement indicated was to be performed in a quick, concise style. In fugue writing, that part where the subject and answer succeed one another.
Striscíándo, *It.* (strět-tshē-än-dō.) See *Strascíándo*.
Strich, *Ger.* (strĭkh.) *Stroke*, the manner of bowing.
Strich-arten, *Ger.* (strĭkh är-t'n.) Different ways of bowing.
Strict canon. A canon in which the rules of this form of composition are closely followed.
Strict composition. A composition in which voices alone are employed; that which rigidly adheres to the rules of art.
Strict fugue. Where the fugal form and its laws are rigidly observed.
Strict inversion. The same as simple inversion, but requiring that whole tones should be answered by whole tones, and semitones by semitones.
Strictly inverted imitation. A form of imitation in which half and whole tones must be precisely answered in contrary motion.
Strict style. A style in which a rigid 'adherance to the rules of the art is observed.
Strident, *Fr.* (stre-dänh.) } Sharp, shrill,
Stridente, *It.* (strē-dän-tě.) } acute.
Stridevole, *It.* (strē-dě-vō-lě.)
Striking reed. That kind of reed pipe in an organ, in which the tongue strikes against the tube in producing the tone.
Strillare, *It.* (strēl-lä-rě.) To scream, shriek, screech.
Strillo, *It.* (strēl-lō.) A loud scream, shrill cry, shriek.
String band. A band of stringed instruments only.

STRO

Stringed instruments. Instruments whose sounds are produced by striking or drawing strings, or by the friction of a bow drawn across them.
Stringéndo, *It.* (strěn-gän-dō.) Pressing, accelerating the time.
String quartet. A composition for four instruments of the violin species, as, two violins, a viola, and violincello.
String pendulum. A Weber chronometer.
Strings. Wires or chords used in musical instruments, which, upon being struck or drawn upon, produce tones; the stringed instruments in a band or orchestra.
Strings, latten. Wires made of a composition consisting of copper and zinc.
Strings, open. The strings of an instrument when not pressed.
Strisciándo, *It.* (strē-shē-än-dō.) Gliding, slurring, sliding smoothly from one note to another.
Strófa, *It.* (strō-fä.) } A strophe, stanza.
Strófe, *It.* (strō-fě.) }
Strofaccia, *It.* (strō-fät-tshē-ä.) A bad strophe or stanza.
Strofetta, *It.* (strō-fät-tä.) A little couplet.
Stroke. A dash.
Stroke, diagonal. A transverse heavy stroke having a dot each side of it, denoting that the previous measure or the previous group of notes in the same measure is to be repeated.
Stroke, double. Two strokes or dashes drawn over or under a semibreve or through the stem of a minim or crotchet, implying that such note must be divided into as many semiquavers as are equivalent to it in duration.
Stroke, single. A stroke or dash drawn over or under a semibreve, or through the stem of a minim or crotchet, implying that such a note must be divided into as many quavers as are equivalent to it in duration.
Stroke, transverse. A heavy stroke placed above a fundamental note to indicate the intervals of changing notes, and also used for anticipation in an upper part.
Stroke, triple. Three strokes or dashes placed over or under a semibreve, or through the stem of a minim or crotchet, implying that such note must be divided into as many demisemiquavers as are equivalent to it in duration.
Strombazzáta, *It.* (strŏm-bät-tsä-tä.) } The
Strombettáta, *It.* (strŏm-bět-tä-tä.) } sound of a trumpet.
Strombettáre, *It.* (strŏm-bět-tä-rě.) To sound, or play on the trumpet.
Strombettiére, *It.* (strŏm-bět-tē-ä-rě.) A trumpeter.
Stromentáto, *It.* (strō-měn-tä-tō.) Instrumented, scored for an orchestra.
Stroménti, *It. pl.* (strō-män-tě.) Musical instruments.
Stroménti d'arco, *It. pl.* (strō-män-tě d'är-kō.) Instruments played with the bow.
Stroménti da fiáto, *It. pl.* (strō-män-tě dä fē-ä-tō.) }
Stroménts di vénto, *It. pl.* (strō-män-tě dě věn-tō.) } Wind instruments.

ă ale, ă̆ add, ä arm, ē eve, ĕ end, ī ice, ĭ ill, ō old, ŏ odd, ô dove, oo moon, ū lute, ŭ but, ü French sound.

STRO   SUBT

Stroménti di rinfórzo, *It. pl.* (strō-mĕn-tē dē rēn-fōr-tsō.) Instruments employed to support or strengthen a performance.

Strométo, *It.* (atrō-mĕn-tō.) An instrument.

Strophe. In the ancient theatre, that part of a song or dance around the altar which was performed by turning from the right to the left. It was succeeded by the antistrophe, in a contrary direction. Hence, in ancient lyric poetry, the former of two stanzas was called the *strophe* and the latter the *antistrophe.*

Strophicus, *Gr.* (strŏf-ĭ-kŭs.) One of the ten notes forming the musical system in the middle ages.

Strosciáre, *It.* (strō-shē-ä-rĕ.) To sound like the dash of waters; to murmur, to purl, to boom.

Strumentájo, *It.* (stroo-mĕn-tä-yō.) A musical instrument maker.

Strumentále, *It.* (stroo-mĕn-tä-lĕ.) Instrumental.

Strumentáre, *It.* (stroo-mĕn-tä-rĕ.) To perform on an instrument.

Strumentazióne, *It.* (stroo-mĕn-tä-tsē-ō-nĕ.) Instrumentation.

Strumenti, con, *It. pl.* (stroo-mĕn-tē.) With instruments.

Strumentíno, *It.* (stroo-mĕn-tē-nō.) A small instrument.

Struménto, *It.* (stroo-mĕn-tō.) See *Stroménto.*

Strung, high. Strung to a full tone or high pitch.

Stuben-orgel, *Ger.* (stoo-b'n ōr-g'l.) Small portable organ.

Stück, *Ger.* (stük.) Piece, air, tune; musical entertainment.

Stücken, *Ger.* (stük-ĕn.) Little airs or tunes.

Studien, *Ger. pl.* (stoo-dĭ-ĕn.) Studies.

Stúdio, *It.* (stoo-dē-ō.) A study, an exercise intended for the practice of some particular difficulty.

Studium, *Ger.* (stoŏ-dĭ-ŭm.) } A study, an exercise intended for the practice of some particular difficulty.

Stufe, *Ger.* (stoo-fĕ.) Step, degree.

Stufe der tonleiter, *Ger.* (stoo-fĕ dĕr tōn-lī-tĕr.) A degree of the scale.

Stufen, *Ger. pl.* (stoo-f'n.) Steps or degrees.

Stufenweise, *Ger.* (stoo-f'n-vī-sĕ.) By degrees.

Stuonánte, *It.* (stoo-ō-nän-tĕ.) } Dissonant, out of tune.

Stuonáto, *It.* (stoo-ō-nä-tō.) }

Stuonáre, *It.* (stoo-ō-nä-rĕ.) To sing out of tune.

Sturm-drommete, *Ger.* (stoom drōm-mĕ-tĕ.) The alarum trumpet.

Sturm-glocke, *Ger.* (stoom glo-kĕ.) The tocsin; the alarm bell.

Stürmisch, *Ger.* (stürm-ĭsh.) Impetuously, boisterously, furiously.

Style. That manner of composition or performance on which the effect chiefly, if not wholly, depends.

Style, ballad. In the manner of a ballad.

Style décousu, *Fr.* (still dā-koo-sü.) Loose, unconnected style.

Style, free. A style deviating somewhat from the rules of music.

Style, legato. A close, connected, gliding manner of performance.

Style, staccato. A manner of execution in which the notes are played distinct, short, and detached from one another.

Style, strict. A style in which a rigid adherence to the rules of music is observed.

Stylo, *It.* (stē-lō.) Style.

Stylo choraico, *It.* (stē-lō kō-rä-ē-kō.) A style suitable for dances.

Stylo dramatico, *It.* (stē-lō drä-mä-tē-kō.) In dramatic style.

Stylo ecclesiastico, *It.* (stē-lō ĕk-klä-zē-äs-tē-kō.) In church style.

Stylo fantastico, *It.* (stē-lō fän-täs-tē-kō.) An easy, humorous style; free from all restraint.

Stylo rappresentativo, *It.* (stē-lō räp-rä-zĕn-tä-tē-vō.) A term applied to recitative music, because almost exclusively adapted to the drama.

Stylo recitativo, *It.* (stē-lō rä-tshē-tä-tē-vō.) In the style of a recitative.

Su, *It.* (soo.) Above, upon.

Suabe-flute. An organ stop of clear, liquid tone, not so loud as the *wald-flute;* it was invented by William Hill, of London.

Suáve, *It.* (swä-vē.) } Sweet, mild, agreeable, pleasant.

Suave, *Spa.* (swä-vē.) }

Suave, *Fr.* (swäv.) }

Suavemente, *Spa.* (swä-vē-mān-tē.) } Sauvity,

Suavemēnte, *It.* (swä-vē-mān-tĕ.) } sweetness, del-

Suavita, *It.* (swä-vē-tä.) } icacy.

Sub, *Lat.* (sŭb.) Under, below, beneath.

Sub-bass, *Ger.* (soob bäss.) *Under-bass;* an organ register in the pedals, usually a double-stopped bass of 32 or 16 feet tone, though sometimes open wood pipes of 16 feet, as at Haarlem; the ground bass.

Sub-bourdon. An organ stop of 32 feet tone, with stopped pipes.

Sub-cantor, *Spa.* (soob kän-tōr.) Sub-chanter.

Sub-chanter. The percentor's deputy in a cathedral choir.

Sub-diapente, *Lat.* (sŭb dī-ä-pĕn-tē.) Subdominant.

Sub-dominant. The fourth note of any scale or key.

Subitaménte, *It.* (soo-bē-tä-mān-tĕ.) } Suddenly, imme-

Súbito, *It.* (soo-bē-tō.) } diately, at once.

Subject. A melody, or theme; a leading text or *motivo.*

Subject, counter. The first part of a fugue when continued along with the subject.

Sub-mediant. The sixth tone of the scale.

Sub-octave. An organ coupler producing the octave below.

Sub-principal. *Under principal;* that is, below the pedal diapason pitch; in German organs this is a double open bass stop of thirty-two feet scale.

Sub-semifusa, *Lat.* (sŭb-sĕm-ĭ-fū-sä.) A demisemiquaver.

Sub-semitone. The semitone below the key note, the sharp seventh of any key.

Sub-semitonium modi, *Lat.* (sŭb-sĕm-ĭ-tō-nĭ-ŭm mō-dī.) The leading note.

Subsidiary notes. Notes situated one degree above and one degree below the principal note of a turn.

Sub-tonic. Under the tonic; the semitone immediately below the tonic.

ā *ale*, ă *add*, ä *arm*, ĕ *eve*, ĕ *end*, ī *ice*, ĭ *ill*, ō *old*, ŏ *odd*, ô *dove*, oo *moon*, ū *lute*, ŭ *but*, ü *French sound*.

SUCC

Succession. A word applied to the notes of a melody, in contradistinction to those of harmony, which are given in *combination*.
Succession, conjunct. A succession of sounds proceeding regularly upward or downward, through the several intervening degrees.
Succession, disjunct. Where the sounds pass from one degree to another without touching the intermediate degrees.
Sudden modulation. Modulation to a distant key, without any intermediate chord to prepare the ear.
Suffolamento, *It.* (soof-fō-lä-män-t'ō.) Hiss, whistle, murmur.
Suffolo, *It.* (soof-fō-lō.) A little flute or flageolet used to teach birds to sing certain tunes.
Suggeritore di teatro, *It.* (sood-jä-rē-tō-rĕ dĕ tä-ä-trō.) The prompter of a theatre.
Suggetto, *It.* (sood-jĕt-tō.) The subject or theme of a composition.
Suite, *Fr.* (swēt.) A series, a snccession; *une suite de piéces*, a series of lessons, or pieces.
Suivez, *Fr.* (swē-vä.) Follow, attend, pursue; the accompaniment must be accommodated to the singer or solo player.
Sujet, *Fr.* (sü-zhā.) A subject, melody, or theme.
Sul, *It.* (sool.)
Sull', *It.* (sool.)
Sulla, *It.* (sool-lä.)
Sul A. On the A string.
Sul D. On the D string.
Sulla mezza corda, *It.* (sool-lä mät-sä kōr-dä.) On the middle of the string.
Sulla tastiéra, *It.* (sool-lä täs-tē-ä-rä.) Upon the keys, upon the finger board.
Sul ponticello, *It.* (sool pōn-tē-tshĕl-lō.) On, or near, the bridge.
Sumara. A species of flute having two pipes, common in Turkey; the shorter pipe is used for playing airs, and the longer for a continued base.
Sumpunjah, *Heb.* (soom-poon-yäh.) The dulcimer of the ancients. It was a wind instrument made of reeds; by the Syrians called *samboujah*, and by the Italians *zampogna*.
Sumsen, *Ger.* (soom-s'n.) To hum.
Súo loco, *It.* (soo-ō lō-kō.) In its own, or usual place.
Suonantina, *It.* (swō-nän-tē-nä.) A short, easy sonata.
Suonáre, *It.* (swō-nä-re.) To play upon an instrument.
Suonáre il córno, *It.* (swō-nä-re ĕl kōr-nō.) To wind the horn.
Suonár sordaménte, *It.* (swō-när sōr-dä-män-tĕ.) To play softly.
Suonáre le campáne, *It.* (swō-nä-rē lĕ käm-pä-nĕ.) To ring the bells.
Suonáta, *It.* (swō-nä-tä.) A sonata.
Suonáte di chiésa, *It.* (swō-nä-tĕ dĕ kē-ā-zä.) See *Sonéta da Chiésa*.
Suonatóre, *It.* (swō-nä-tō-rĕ.) A musical performer.
Suonatóre di violino, *It.* (swō-nä-tō-rĕ dĕ vē-ō-lē-nō.) A violin player.
Suonatóre di flauto, *It.* (swō-nä-tō-rĕ dĕ floo-tō.) A performer on the flute.
Suóni, *It. pl.* (swō-nē.) Sounds.

SUPE

Suóni alteráti, *It. pl.* (swō-nē äl-tĕ-rä-tē.) Notes raised or lowered by flats or sharps.
Suóni armónichi, *It. pl.* (swō-nē är-mō-nē-kē.) Harmonic sounds.
Suóni baripieni, *It. pl.* (swō-nē bä-rē-pē-ä-nē.) Fixed sounds.
Suóni chromatici, *It. pl.* (swō-nē krō-mä-tē-tshē.) Chromatic tones.
Suóni consoni, *It. pl.* (swō-nē kōn-sō-nē.) Concords.
Suóni diafoni, *It. pl.* (swō-nē dē-ä-fō-nē.)
Suóni dissoni, *It. pl.* (swō-nē dēs-sō-nē.)
Discords.
Suóni diatonici, *It. pl.* (swō-nē dē-ä-tō-nē-tshē.) Sounds within the compass of the human voice.
Suóni ecmeli, *It. pl.* (swō-nē ĕk-mä-lē.) Unmelodious sounds.
Suóni emmeli, *It. pl.* (swō-nē ĕm-mä-lē.) Melodious sounds.
Suóni enarmonici, *It. pl.* (swō-nē ĕn-är-mō-nē-tshē.) Sounds raised above their natural pitch by means of the enharmonic diesis.
Suóni equi, *It. pl.* (swō-nē ā-quē.) Equal sounds.
Suóni mobili, *It. pl.* (swō-nē mō-bē-lē.) Movable sounds; the second and third sounds of every tetrachord of the ancient system.
Suóni musicáli, *It. pl.* (swō-nē moo-sē-kä-lē.) Musical sounds.
Suóni naturáli, *It. pl.* (swō-nē nä-too-rä-lē.) Natural sounds.
Suóni parafoni, *It. pl.* (swō-nē pär-ä-fō-nē.) Sounds having between them the interval of a fourth or fifth, or their double, and therefore concordant.
Suóni perpetui, *It. pl.* (swō-nē pĕr-pä-too-ē.) Perpetual sounds; the highest and lowest sounds of every tetrachord in the ancient system.
Suóni stabili, *It. pl.* (swō-nē stä-hē-lē.) See *Suóni Perpetui*.
Suóni unisoni, *It. pl.* (swō-nē oo-nē-sō-nē.) Unisons.
Suóni vaganti, *It. pl.* (swō-nē vä-gän-tē.) See *Suóni Mobiles*.
Suóno, *It.* (swō-nō.) Sound, tone, music; a song.
Suóno argentino, *It.* (swō-nō är-jĕn-tē-nō.) Silver tone; soft, clear tone.
Suóno armonióso, *It.* (swō-nō är-mō-nē-ō-zō.) Harmonious sounds.
Suóno délle campáne, *It.* (swō-nō dāl-lĕ käm-pä-nĕ.) The sound of bells.
Super, *Lat.* (sü-pĕr.) Above, over.
Superano, *Spa.* (soo-pĕr-ä-nō.) Soprano.
Super-dominant. The note in the scale, next above the dominant.
Superfluous intervals. Those which are one semitone more than the *perfect*, or *major*, intervals; see *Augmented Intervals*.
Superius, *Lat.* (sü-pä-rī-ŭs.) The name by which the contrapuntists of the 15th and 16th centuries distinguished the upper part of any composition.
Supernumerary. The last chord added to the ancient Greek system.
Super-octave. An organ stop tuned two octaves, or a fifteenth, above the diapason; also, a coupler producing the octave above.

PRONOUNCING MUSICAL DICTIONARY.

ā ale, ă add, ä arm, ē eve, ĕ end, ī ice, ĭ ill, ō old, ŏ odd, ō dove, oo moon, ū lute, ŭ but, ü French sound.

SUPE

Supersus, *Lat.* (sū-pĕr-sŭs.) Name formerly given to trebles when their station was very high in the scale.
Super-tonic.
Supertonique, *Fr.* (sū-pĕr-tŏnh-ēk.) }
The note next above the tonic, or key note; the second note of the scale.
Supplichévole, *It.* (soo-plē-kā-vō-lē.)
Supplichevolménte, *It.* (soop-plē-kā-vōl-mān-tē.)
In a supplicatory manner.
Supposed bass. A term applied to any bass note when it is not the fundamental note of the chord.
Supposition. The use of two successive notes of equal value as to time, one of which being a discord supposes the other to be a concord.
Sûr, *It.* (soor.) } On, upon, over.
Sur, *Fr.* (sūr.) }
Surdeline. The old Italian bagpipe, a large and rather complicated instrument, consisting of many pipes and conduits for the conveyance of the wind, with keys for the opening of the holes by the pressure of the fingers, and inflated by means of bellows which the performer blows with his arm, at the same time that he fingers the pipe.
Surgum, *Hin,* (soor-gŭm.) The gamut.
Surigx, *Gr.* (sū-riga.) The pipes of Pan.
Sur la quatrieme corde, *Fr.* (sūr lä kāt-rī-ām kŏrd.) On the fourth string.
Sur la seconde corde, *Fr.* (sūr lä sā-kŏnhd kŏrd.) Upon the second string.
Sur-sharp. The fifth tetrachord above, added by Guido, was called the tetrachord of the *sur.sharp*.
Sur úna córda, *It.* (soor oo-nā kŏr-dā.) }
Sur une corde, *Fr.* (sūr ūnh kŏrd.) }
Upon one string.
Suspended cadence. See Interrupted Cadence.
Suspension. A theoretical expression applied to the retaining in any chord some note or notes of the preceeding chord.
Suspension, double. A suspension retaining two notes and requiring a double preparation and resolution.
Suspension, single. A suspension retaining but one note and requiring only a single preparation and resolution.
Suspension, triple. A suspension formed by suspending a dominant or diminished seventh on the tonic, mediant, or dominant of the key.
Süss, *Ger.* (süss.) Sweetly.
Süssflöte, *Ger.* (süss-flō-tĕ.) In organs, the soft flute.
Sussurándo, *It.* (soos-soo-rän-dō.) } Whisper-
Sussuránte, *It.* (soos-soo-rän-tĕ.) } ing, murmuring.
Susurra, *Spa.* (soo-soor-rä.) To purl, as a stream.
Susurration. A whispering; a soft, murmuring sound.
Susurro, *Spa.* (soo-soo-rō.) Humming.
Sutonique, *Fr.* (sū-tŏnh-ēk.) Supertonic.
Sustained. Notes are said to be sustained when their sound is continued through their whole time or length; see *Sostenáto*.
Svegliáto, *It.* (svāl-yē-ā-tō.) Brisk, lively, sprightly.

SYMP

Svegliatojo, *It.* (svāl-yē-ā-tō-yō.) An alarm bell.
Svélto, *It.* (svāl-tō.) Free, light, easy.
Swell. A gradual increase of sound.
Swell organ. In organs having three rows of keys, the third, or upper row, controlling a number of pipes enclosed in a box, which may be gradually opened or shut, and thus the tone increased or diminished by degrees.
Swell pedal. That which raises the dampers from the strings.
Swiss flute. An organ stop, of agreeable tone, something like that of the *gámba*.
Sword dance. An ancient Spanish melody, played on solemn occasions.
Syllable, fixed. Syllables which do not change with change of key.
Syllables, Guidonian. The syllables ut, re, mi, fa, sol, la, used by Guido for his system of tetrachords.
Syllabic song. A melody in which every syllable has its distinct note; the recitative belongs to this species.
Symbal. See Cymbal.
Symbols. The musical name given by the Greeks to the twenty-four letters of their alphabet, all of which they employed as characters indicative of sounds.
Sympathetic strings. Strings which were formerly fastened under the finger-board of the viola d'amore, beneath the bridge, and, being tuned to the strings above, vibrated with them and strengthened the tone.
Symphonia, *Gr.* (sim-fō-nī-ā.) A pulsatile instrument of the ancients, made of a hollow tree, closed at each end with leather, and struck with sticks, producing tones of varied pitch.
Symphoniæ, *Gr.* (sĭm-fō-nī-ē.) An epithet applied to music in parts or *counterpoint*; see that word.
Symphonial. Said of tones agreeing in quality. The tones of the violin and violincello, or of the hautboy and bassoon, are *symphonial*.
Symphoniale. A word frequently prefixed to the old canons or perpetual fugues, to indicate that they are in unison; *i. e.*, that the second part is to follow the first in the same intervals, and the third to observe the same rule in regard to the second.
Symphonic. In the style or manner of a symphony; harmonious; agreeing in sound.
Symphonic poem. A style of composition of recent invention, partaking of the character both of the opera and symphony, but more elevated in its style and character than the former.
Symphonie, *Fr.* (sänh-fō-nē.) } A grand com-
Symphonie, *Ger.* (sĭm-fō-nē.) } position of sev-
Symphony, *Eng.* } eral movements, for a full orchestra. The symphony, in its present form, was introduced by Haydn, and generally consists of an *adagio*, allégro, andánte, minuétto (or *schérzo*), trio, and finále. The term is also applied to the introductory and concluding instrumental parts of a song, or other vocal composition.
Symphoniesesser, *Ger.* (sĭm-fō-nī-ĕn-sĕ-sĕr.) Symphonist; a composer of symphonies.

ă ale, ă add, ă arm, ĕ eve, ŏ end, ĭ ice, ĭ ill, ō old, ŏ odd, ō dove, oo moon, ū lute, ŭ but, ŭ French sound.

SYMP

Symphonion. An instrument invented by Fr. Kaufmann, resembling the orchestrion, and combining the tone of a pianoforte with that of the flute, clarinet, etc.

Symphonious. Harmonious, agreeing in sound.

Symphonische dichtung, *Ger.* (sĭm-fŌ-nĭ-shĕ dĭkh-toong.) Symphonic poem.

Symphonist. A composer of symphonics. In France the term *symphonist* is also applied to a composer of church music.

Symphonoi, *Gr.* (sĭm-fō-noy.) A name given by the ancients to concords and those sounds which so mix and unite that the tone of the lower is scarcely distinguishable from the upper.

Symposia. An epithet generally applicable to cheerful and convivial compositions, as catches, glees, rounds, etc.

Synaphe, *Gr.* (sĭ-nā-fĕ.) A term applied by the ancients to the conjunction of two tetrachords; or, more properly, it is the resonance of the homologous chords of two conjoint tetrachords.

Synaulia, *Gr.* (sĭ-nau-lĭ-ā.) In the ancient music, a concert of flute who answered each other alternately without any unison of the voice.

Syncopáta, *It.* (sēn-kō-pā-tā.) } Contracted,
Syncopáte, *It.* (sēn-kō-pā-tĕ.) } bound to-
Syncopáto, *It.* (sēn-kō-pā-tō.) } gether; con-
Syncopated, *Eng.* } traction of a note by cutting off part of its value and giving it to the following note.

Syncopation, *Eng.* } An un-
Syncopatio, *Lat.* (sĭn-kō-pā-shĭ-ō.) } equal division of the

Syncope, *Fr.* (sănh-kōp.) time or notes; irregular accent; binding the last note of one bar to the first note of the next; accented notes occuring on the unaccented part of a bar.

Syncope. The division of a note, introduced when two or more notes of one part answer to a single note of another, as when the semibreve of the one corresponds with two or three notes of the other.

Syncoper, *Fr.* (sănh-kō-pā.) } To synco-
Syncopiren, *Ger.* (sĭn-kō-pē-r'n.) } pate.

Synnemnon, *Gr.* (sĭn-nĕm-nōn.) The united, or conjunct. The appellation given by the ancients to their third tetrachord, from its beginning with the last note of the second tetrachord.

Synnemnon diatonos, *Gr.* (sĭn-nĕm-nōn dī-ā-tō-nōs.) This was, in the music of the ancients, the third chord of the *tetrachord* synnemnon in *diatonic genus.*

SYZY

Syntonic. The epithet by which Aristoxenus and other ancient musical writers distinguish a species of the diatonic genus, which was nearly the same with our natural diatonic.

Syntono-Lydian. One of the modes in the ancient music.

Syren. Siren.

Syringa, *Lat.* (sĭ-rĭn-gā.) Pandean pipes.

Syringe. A kind of fistula, or pipe, used by the ancient Romans to regulate the voice in oratory and singing.

Sysigia. (sĭ-sĭ-ghĭ-ā.) A Greek term signifying any combination of sounds so proportioned to each other as to affect the ear with pleasure.

Systaltic. An epithet applied by the ancients to that of the subdivisions of their *meloposa* which constituted the mournful and pathetic.

System. An interval compounded, or supposed to be compounded, of several lesser ones, as the fourth, the fifth, the sixth, the octave, etc ; a method of calculation to determine the relations of sounds, or an order of signs established to express them; the code of harmonic rules drawn from those common principles by which they are computed.

Systema participato, *It.* (sĭs-tĕ-mā pār-tĕ-tshĕ-pā-tō.)
Systema participatum, *Lat.* (sĭs-tĕ-mā pār-tĭs-ĭ-pā-tŭm.)
A division of the octave or diapason into twelve semitones.

Systema temperatum, *Lat.* (sĭs-tĕ-mā tĕm-pĕ-rā-tŭm.) The attempered system.

System, cipher. An old system of music, in which the notes were represented by numerals.

Systeme, *Fr.* (sĭs-tăm.) A system.

System, isotonic. A system consisting of intervals in which each concord is alike tempered, and in which there are twelve equal semibreves.

System, logieran. See Logieran System.

System, pestalozzian. See Pestalozzian System.

Syzygia, *Gr.* (sĭ-zĕ-jĭ-ā.) A pleasing combination of sounds.

Syzygia, compound. A combination of sounds in which one or more of those of the harmonical triad are doubled, or raised one or more octaves.

Syzygia, simple. A combination of sounds in which two concords at least are heard together.

PRONOUNCING MUSICAL DICTIONARY.

ă ale, ă add, ă arm, ĕ eve, ŏ end, ĭ ice, ĭ ill, ō old, ŏ odd, ô dove, oo moon, ū lute, ŭ but, ü French sound.

TA

Ta, *Gr.* (tă.) One of the four syllables used by the ancient Greeks in *solfaing* their music, answering to the *hyphate*, or first sound of their tetrachord.
Tabal, *Spa.* (tă-băl.) A tambour; a tabor.
Tabállo, *It.* (tŭ-băl-lō.) A kettle-drum.
Tabar, *It.* (tă-băr.) A small drum; a tabor.
Tablatūra, *It.* (tăb-lă-too-ră.) ⎫ A term for-
Tablature, *Fr.* (tŭ-blă-tür.) ⎬ merly ap-
Tablature, *Eng.* (tăb-lă-tehŭr.) ⎪ plied to the
Tabulatur, *Ger.*(tă-boo-lŭ-toor.) ⎭ totality or general assemblage of the signs used in music; so that to understand the notes, clefs, and other necessary marks, and to be able to sing at sight, was to be skilled in the *tablature*. The method of notation for the lute, and other similar instruments, was also distinguished by this appellation.
Table. A portion of the lute, also of the violin.
Table d'harmonie, *Fr.* (tăbl d'ăr-mō-nĕ.) A table, or diagram of chords, intervals, etc.
Table d'instrument, *Fr.* (tăbl d'ănh-strŭ-mănh.) The belly of an instrument.
Table songs. Songs for male voices formerly much in vogue in German glee clubs.
Table, time. A representation of the several notes in music, showing their relative lengths or or durations.
Tabor. A small drum, generally used to accompany the pipe or fife in dances.
Taborèt. A small tabor.
Tabourin, *Fr.* (tă-boo-rănh.) A tabor or tambourine—a shallow drum with but one head.
Tabret. A kind of drum used by the ancient Hebrews.
Tacet, *Lat.* (tă-sĕt.) ⎫ Be silent; mean-
Tāce, *It.* (tă-tshĕ.) ⎬ ing that certain in-
Tácĭ, *It.* (tă-tshē.) ⎪ struments are not
Taciăsĭ, *It.* (tă-tshē-ă-zē.) ⎭ to play; as, *violino tacet*, the violin is not to play; *oboe tacet*, let the oboe be silent.
Tact, *Ger.* (tăkt.) Time, measure.
Tact-art, *Ger.* (tăkt ărt.) Species of time; common, or triple.
Tactfest, *Ger.* (tăkt-fĕst.) Steadiness in keeping time.
Tact-fūhrer, *Ger.* (tăkt-füh-rĕr.) A conductor; leader.
Tact-linie, *Ger.* (tăkt lĭn-ĕ-ĕ.) ⎫ A bar-line,
Tact-strich, *Ger.* (tăkt strĭkh.) ⎬ the lines which mark the bars.
Tactmässig, *Ger.* (tăkt-mă-sĭg.) Conformable to the time.
Tactmesser, *Ger.* (tăkt-mĕs-sĕr.) A metronome.
Tact-note, *Ger.* (tăkt nō-tĕ.) A semibreve.
Tact-pause, *Ger.* (tăkt pou-zĕ.) Bar rest.
Tact-schläger, *Ger.* (tăkt shlă-ghĕr.) Time-beater.
Tact-stock. (tăkt stŏck.) A *bâton*, for beating time.
Tactus, *Lat.* (tăk-tŭs.) In the ancient music, the stroke of the hand by which the time was measured or beaten.
Tactus major. When the time consisted of a breve in a bar, the *time stroke* was called *tactus major*.

TANZ

Tactus minor. When the time consisted of a semibreve in a bar, the time stroke was called *tactus minor*.
Tact-zeichen, *Ger.* (tăkt tsī-kh'n.) The figures, or signs, at the beginning of a piece, to show the time.
Tafel-musik, *Ger.* (tă-f'l moo-zĭk.) Table music, music sung at the table; as, part-songs, glees, etc.
Tagliáto, *It.* (tăl-yē-ă-tō.) Clef.
Taille, *Fr.* (tă-üh.) The tenor part; the viola.
Taille de violon, *Fr.* (tă-üh dŭh vē-ŏ-lŏnh.) The viola, or tenor violin.
Tail-piece. That piece of ebony to which the strings of the violin, viola, etc., are fastened.
Takt, *Ger.* (tăkt.) See *Tact*.
Talabalácco, *It.* (tă-lă-bă-lăk-kō.) A species of Moorish drum.
Talon, *Fr.* (tă-lŏnh.) The *heel* of the bow; that part nearest the nut.
Tambor, *Spa.* (tăm-bŏr.) A tambour.
Tamborilero, *Spa.* (tăm-bō-rē-lă-ro.) One who beats the tabor, taboret, or tambourine.
Tambour, *Fr.* (tănh-boor.) Drum; the great drum; also, a drummer.
Tambour de basque, *Fr.* (tănh-boor dŭh băsk.) A tabour or tabor; a tambourine.
Tambouret, *Fr.* (tănh-boo-ră.) ⎫ A timbrel, a
Tambourine, *Eng.* ⎬ small instrument of percussion, like the head of a drum, with little bells placed round its rim to increase the noise.
Tambourine, *Fr.* (tănh-boo-rēn.) A species of dance, accompanied by the tambourine; also, a tambourine.
Tambourineur, *Fr.* (tănh-boo-rē-nŭr.) Drummer, tambourine player.
Tambour major, See *Drum-Major*.
Tamburáccio, *It.* (tăm-boo-răt-tshē-ō.) A large old drum; a tabor.
Tamburéllo, *It.* (tăm-boo-răl-lō.) ⎫ A tambour-
Tamburétto, *It.* (tăm-boo-răt-tō.) ⎬ ine; a little drum.
Tamburino, *It.* (tăm-boo-rē-nō.) A little drum; also, a drummer.
Tambúro, *It.* (tăm-*boo*-rō.) A drum.
Tamburóne, *It.* (tăm-boo-rō-nĕ.) The great drum.
Tam-tam. An Indian instrument of percussion, a species of drum, or tambourine.
Tändelud, *Ger.* (tăn-dĕlnd.) In a playful manner.
Tañedor, *Spa.* (tă-nĕ-thŏr.) Player on a musical instrument.
Tangent, *Ger.* (tăn-ghĕnt.) The *jack* of a harpsichord.
Tanido, *Spa.* (tă-nē-dō.) Played, touched; tune, sound.
Tánto, *It.* (tăn-tō.) So much, as much; *allégro non tánto*, not so quick, not too quick.
Tantum ergo, *Lat.* (tăn-tŭm ĕr-gō.) A hymn sung at the benediction in the Roman Catholic service.
Tanz, *Ger.* (tănts.) A dance.
Tänze, *Ger. pl.* (tăn-tsĕ.) Dances.
Tänzer, *Ger.* (tăn-tsĕr.) A dancer.
Tänzerinn, *Ger.* (tăn-tsĕr-ĭn.) A female dancer.

ă *ale*, ā *add*, ä *arm*, ē *eve*, ĕ *end*, I *ice*, ĭ *ill*, ō *old*, ŏ *odd*, ö *dove*, oo *moon*, ū *lute*, ŭ *but*, ü *French sound*

TANZ

Tanz-kunst, *Ger.* (tänts koonst.) The art of dancing.
Tanz-stück, *Ger.* (tänts stook.) A dance tune.
Tap. A drum beat of a single note.
Tapatan, *Spa.* (tă-pā-tän.) The sound of a drum.
Tarabouk. A musical instrument used by the Turks, formed by drawing a parchment over the bottom of a large earthern vessel.
Tarantélla, *It.* (tär-rŭn-tĕl-lä.) A swift, delirious sort of Italian dance in 6-8 time. The form has been adopted by many of the modern composers, as Lietz, Chopin, etc.
Tarantula dance. A peculiar tune, so called from its reputed power in curing the effects of the poisonous bite of the *tarantula*.
Tardaménte, *It.* (tär-dä-män-tĕ.) Slowly.
Tardándo, *It.* (tär-dän-dō.) Lingering, retarding the time.
Tárdo, *It.* (tär-dō.) Tardy, slow.
Tarrenas, *Spa.* (tär-rä-nds.) Small castanets.
Tastáme, *It.* (täs-tä-mĕ.) ⎫ The keys, or
Tastatur, *Ger.* (täs-tä-toor.) ⎬ key-board of
Tastatúra, *Ger.* (täs-tä-too-rä.) ⎭ a pianoforte,
Tastiéra, *It.* (täs-tē-ä-rä.) organ, etc.
Taste, *Ger.* (täs-tĕ.) ⎱ The touch of any instru-
Tásto, *It.* (täs-tō.) ⎰ ment; hence, also, a key or thing touched.
Tasten-brett, *Ger.* (täs-t'n brĕt.) Key-board of a pianoforte, etc.
Tásto sólo, *It.* (täs-tō sō-lō.) *One key alone;* in organ or pianoforte music, this means a note without harmony, the base notes over or under which it is written are not to be accompanied with chords.
Tátto, *It.* (tä-tō.) The touch.
Tattoo. ⎱ The beat of a drum at night calling the
Tapto. ⎰ soldiers to their quarters.
Tautology. A tiresome repetition of the same passage or passages.
Te, *Gr.* (tā.) One of the syllables used by the ancient Greeks in solfaing their music.
Teatrino, *It.* (tā-ä-trē-nō.) A little theatre.
Teátro, *It.* (tā-ä-trō.) A theatre, play house.
Teátro di gran cartéllo, *It.* (tā-ä-trō dē grän kär-tĕl-lō.) Lyric theatre of the first rank.
Teátro diúrno, *It.* (tā-ä-trō dē-oor-nō.) A theatre in which performances take place by day.
Technik, *Ger.* (tĕkh-nĭk.) Technical terms.
Technisch, *Ger.* (tĕkh-nish.) Technical; this word is also used to indicate mechanical proficiency, as regards execution.
Tecla, *Spa.* (tĕk-lä.) The key of a pianoforte or harpsichord.
Teddéo, *It.* (tĕd-dā-ō.) Te Deum.
Tedésca, *It.* (tĕ-däs-kä.) ⎱ German: álla tedésca,
Tedésco, *It.* (tĕ-däs-kō.) ⎰ in the German style.
Te Deum laudamus, *Lat.* (tĕ dā-ŭm law-dä-mŭs.) *We praise Thee;* a canticle, or hymn of praise.
Telemann's curve. A curve indicating a diminished triad and distinguishing it from the minor third.
Telephonic. Far sounding; that which propels sound a great distance.
Tell-tale. A movable piece of metal, bone, or ivory, attached to an organ, indicating by its position the amount of wind supplied by the bellows.

TEMP

Téma, *It.* (tā-mä.) A theme, or subject; a melody.
Temperament. The accommodation or adjustment of the imperfect sounds of the scale, by transferring a part of the defects to the more perfect ones, in order to remedy, in some degree, the false intervals of the organ, pianoforte, and similar instruments, whose sounds are fixed; that equalization of the intervals, in tuning, which brings their whole system as near as possible to that of the diatonic scale.
Temperament, equal. That equalization or tempering of the twelve sounds included in an octave, which renders all the scales equally in tune; the imperfection being divided equally amongst the whole.
Temperament, unequal. That method of tuning the twelve sounds included in an octave, which renders some of the scales more in tune than the others.
Temperatur, *Ger.* (tĕm-pĕ-rä-toor.) Temperament.
Tempered. Having a perfect adjustment of sounds; tuned.
Tempestosaménte, *It.* (tĕm-pĕs-tō-zä-män-tĕ.) Furiously, impetuously.
Tempestóso, *It.* (tĕm-pĕs-tō-zō.) Tempestuous, stormy, boisterous.
Tempéte, *Fr.* (tänh-pät.) A boisterous dance in 2-4 time.
Templador, *Spa.* (tĕm-plä-dōr.) Key for tuning; a tuner.
Templar, *Spa.* (tĕm-plär.) To temper; to tune an instrument.
Témpo, *It.* (tăm-pō.) Time; the degree of movement; *a tempo,* in time.
Témpo alla bréve, *It.* (tăm-pō äl-lä brä-vĕ.) In a quick species of common time.
Témpo a piacére, *It.* (tăm-pō ä pē-ä-tshä-rĕ.) The time at pleasure.
Témpo assimilándo al moviménto seguénte, *It.* (tăm-pō äs-sē-mē-län-dō äl mō-vē-män-tō sĕ-quän-tĕ.) Assimilating in time to the following movement.
Témpo buóno, *It.* (tăm-pō bwō-nō.) Good time.
Témpo cómodo, *It.* (tăm-pō kō-mō-dō.) Convenient time; an easy, moderate degree of movement.
Témpo di bállo, *It.* (tăm-pō dĕ bäl-lō.) In dance time; rather quick.
Témpo di cappélla, *It.* (tăm-pō dĕ käp-pĕl-lä.) In the Church-time; see Alla Bréve.
Témpo di gavótta, *It.* (tăm-pō dĕ gä-vŏt-tä.) In the time of a gavot.
Témpo di márcia, *It.* (tăm-pō dĕ-mär-tshē-ä.) In the time of a march.
Témpo di menuétto, *It.* (tăm-pō dĕ mĕ-noo-ĕt-tō.) In the time of a minuet.
Témpo di polácca, *It.* (tăm-pō dĕ pō-läk-kä.) In the time of a polacca.
Témpo di prima párte, *It.* (tăm-pō dĕ prē-mä pär-tĕ.) In the same time as the first part.
Témpo di valse, *It.* (tăm-pō dĕ väl-sĕ.) In waltz time.
Témpo frettévole, *It.* (tăm-pō frĕt-tä-vō-lĕ.) ⎱
Témpo frettolóso, *It.* (tăm-pō frĕt-tō-lō-zō.) ⎰
In quicker time, hurrying, hastily.

ă ale, ă add, ă arm, ĕ eve, ĕ end, ī ice, ĭ ill, ō old, ŏ odd, ō dove, oo moon, ū lute, ŭ but, ü French sound.

TEMP

Témpo giústo. *It.* (tăm-pō jē-oos-tō.) In just, exact, strict time.
Témpo maggióre, *It.* (tăm-pō mäd jē-ō-rē.) In a quick species of common time.
Témpo ordinário, *It.* (tăm-pō ōr-dē-nä-rē-ō.) Ordinary, or moderate time.
Témpo perdúto, *It.* (tăm-pō pār-doo-tō.) Lost, interrupted, irregular time.
Témpo prímo, *It.* (tăm-pō prē-mō.) First, or original time.
Temporeggiáto, *It.* (tăm-pō-rĕd-jē-ä-tō.) The time is to be accommodated to the solo singer or player.
Témpo rubáto, *It.* (tăm-pō roo-bä-tō.) *Robbed,* or *stolen* time; irregular time; meaning a slight deviation to give more expression, by retarding one note, and quickening another, but so that the time of each bar is not altered in the whole.
Témpo wie vorher, *Ger.* (těm-pō vē fō-rěr.) The time as before.
Temps, *Fr.* (tänh.) Time; also, the various parts or divisions of a bar.
Tems, *Fr.* (tänh.)
Temps foible, *Fr.* (tänh fwäbl.) The weak, or unaccented parts of a bar.
Temps fort, *Fr.* (tänh fōr.) The strong, or accented parts of a bar.
Temps trappé, *Fr.* (tänh trăp-pā.) The downbeats, or accented parts.
Temps levé, *Fr.* (tänh lĕ-vā.) The up-beats, or unaccented parts.
Tempus imperfectum, *Lat.* (tăm-pŭs im-pĕr-fĕk-tŭm.) *Imperfect time;* a term used by old writers, meaning common time of *two* in a bar.
Tempus perfectum, *Lat.* (tăm-pŭs pĕr-fĕk-tŭm.) *Perfect time;* a term used by old writers, meaning time of three in a bar.
Tendada scéna, *It.* (těn-dä-dä shā-nä.) Curtain of a theatre.
Tendre, *Fr.* (tänhdr.) Tender.
Tendrement, *Fr.* (tänhdr-mänh.) Tenderly, affectionately.
Tenebræ, *Lat.* (těn-ĕ-brā.) *Darkness;* a name given to the Roman Catholic evening service, during Holy Week, in commemoration of the darkness which attended the crucifixion.
Tenéndo il cánto, *It.* (tĕ-nän-dō ēl kän-tō.) Sustain the melody.
Teneraménte, *It.* (těn-ĕ-rä-män-tĕ.) Tenderly, delicately.
Tenerézza, *It.* (těn-ĕ-rāt-tsä.) Tenderness, softness, delicacy.
Ténero, *It.* (lā-nĕ-rō.) Tenderly, softly, delicately.
Tenéte sino álla fíne del suóno, *It.* (tĕ-nā-tĕ sē-nō äl-lä fē-nĕ däl swō-nō.) Keep down the keys as long as the sound continues.
Tenir, *Fr.* (tĕ-nēr.) To hold, a violin bow, etc.
Tenir l'accord, *Fr.* (tĕ-nēr l'äk-kōr.) To keep in tune.
Tenor. That species of male voice next above the barytone, and extending from the C upon the second space in the bass, to G on the second line in the treble.
Tenor C. The lowest C in the tenor voice; the lowest string of the viola, or tenor violin.
Tenor clef. The C clef, when placed upon the fourth line.

TERC

Tenor cornet. A style of cornet in use about a century ago, formed of a curved tube three feet in length, its diameter increasing from the mouthpiece to its end.
Tenóre, *It.* (tĕ-nō-rĕ.) Tenor voice; a tenor singer; see, also, *Vióla.*
Tenóre búffo, *It.* (tĕ-nō-rĕ boof-fō.) The second tenor singer of an opera company for comic parts.
Tenóre di grázia, *It.* (tĕ-nō-rĕ dē grä-tsē-ä.) A delicate and graceful tenor.
Tenóre leggiéro, *It.* (tĕ-nō-rĕ lĕd-jē-ā-rō.) A tenor voice of a light quality of tone.
Tenóre prímo, *It.* (tĕ-nō-rĕ prē-mō.) First tenor.
Tenóre ripiéno, *It.* (tĕ-nō-rĕ rē-pē-ā-nō.) Tenor of the grand chorus.
Tenóre robústo, *It.* (tĕ-nō-rĕ rō-boos-tō.) A strong tenor voice.
Tenóre secóndo, *It.* (tĕ-nō-rĕ sĕ-kŏn-dō.) Second tenor.
Tenóre vióla, *It.* (tĕ-nō-rĕ vē-ō-lä.) Tenor viol.
Tenorist, *Ger.* (tĕn-ō-rīst.) A tenor singer.
Tenorista, *It.* (tĕn-ō-rēs-tä.)
Tenoroon. The old tenor hautboy, the compass of which extended downward to tenor C. The name is sometimes applied to an organ stop.
Tenor-possaune, *Ger.* (tĕn-ōr pō-zou-nĕ.) The tenor trombone.
Tenor-schlüssel, *Ger.* (tĕn-ōr shlŭs-s'l.) The tenor clef.
Tenór, second. Low tenor.
Tenor-stimme, *Ger.* (tĕn-ōr stĭm-mĕ.) Tenor voice; a tenor.
Tenor trombone. A trombone having a compass from the small c to the one-lined g, and noted in the tenor clef.
Tenor-viole, *Ger.* (tĕn-ōr-vī-ō-lĕ.) The viola.
Tenor-violin, *Eng.*
Tenor voice, counter. The male voice next above the tenor voice; the lowest of the female voices.
Tenor-zeichen, *Ger.* (tĕn-ōr tsī-kh'n.) The tenor clef.
Tensile. A term applied to all stringed instruments on account of the tension of their strings.
Tentellare, *It.* (tĕn-tĕl-lä-rĕ.) To jingle.
Tenth. An interval comprising an octave and a third; also, an organ stop tuned a tenth above the diapasons, called, also, decima and double tierce.
Tenue, *Fr.* (tă-nū.) See *Tenúto.*
Tenúte, *It.* (tă-noo-tĕ.) Held on, sustained, or kept down the full time.
Tenúto, *It.* (tă-noo-tō.)
Teodía, *It.* (tă-ō-dē-ä.) A song in praise of the Deity.
Téorbe, *Fr.* (tă-ōrb.) See Theorbo.
Teorético, *It.* (tă-ō-rā-tē-kō.) Theoretical.
Teoría, *It.* (tă-ō-rē-ä.) Theory.
Teoría del cánto, *It.* (tă-ō-rē-ä dĕl kän-tō.) The theory, or art, of singing.
Tepidaménte, *It.* (tă-pē-dä-män-tĕ.) Coldly, with indifference.
Tepiditá, *It.* (tă-pē-dē-tä.) Coldness, indifference.
Ter. *Lat.* (tĕr.) Thrice, three times.
Tercero, *Spa.* (tĕr-thā-rō.) Third.

ă ale, ă add, ă arm, ē eve, ĕ end, ī ice, ĭ ill, ō old, ŏ odd, ô dove, oo moon, ū lute, ŭ bur, ȧ French sound.

TERC

Tercet, *Fr.* (tĕr-sā.) A triplet.
Terceto, *Spa.* (tĕr-thā-tō.) A triplet.
Termini technici. *Lat.* (tĕr-mĭ-nē tĕk-nĭ-sē.) Techoical terms.
Terms, musical. Words and sentences applied to passages of music for the purpose of indicating the style in which they should be performed.
Ternario témpo, *It.* (tĕr-nä-rē-ō tăm-pō.) Triple time.
Ternary measure. Threefold measure; triple time.
Terpodion. An instrument invented by Buschmann, of Hamburg, resembling the harmonium in appearance, the tone being produced from sticks of wood; the name is also given to an organ stop of eight feet tone.
Terpsichore. In classical mythology, the muse of choral dance and song.
Terpsichorean. Relating to Terpsichore, the muse who presided over dancing.
Tertia, *Lat.* (tĕr-shĭ-ä.)   } Third, tierce; also an
Tertzia, *Ger.* (tĕr-tsĭ-ē.) } organ stop, sounding a third, or tenth, above the foundation stops.
Tertian, *Lat.* (tĕr-shĭ-ăn.) An organ stop composed of two pipes, tierce and larigot, on one slide, sounding the interval of a minor third.
Ter unca, *Lat.* (tĕr ŭn-kä.) *Three-hooked;* the old name of the demisemiquaver.
Terz, *Ger.* (tĕrts.)   } A third, the interval
Térza, *It.* (tĕr-tsä.)   } of a third; also, an
Terze, *Ger.* (tĕr-tsĕ.)   } organ stop sounding
Terzie, *Ger.* (tĕr-tsĭ-ĕ.) } a third above the fif-
Térzo, *It.* (tĕr-tsō.)   } teenth: see *Tierce.*
Terz decimole, *Ger.* (tĕrts d ā-t sĭ-m ō-lĕ.) A group of thirteen notes having the value of eight similar ones.
Térza maggióre, *It.* (tĕr-tsä mäd-jē-ō-rĕ.) Major third.
Térza minóre, *It.* (tĕr-tsä mē-nō-rĕ.) Minor third.
Terzen, *Ger.* (tĕr-ts'n.) Thirds.
Terzétto. *It.* (tĕr-tsĕt-tō.) A short piece or trio for three voices.
Terz-flöte, *Ger.* (tĕrts flŏ-tĕ.) A flute sounding a minor third above; also, an organ stop.
Terzina, *It.* (tĕr-tsē-nä) A triplet.
Tésto, *It.* (tĕs-tō.) The text, subject, or theme of any composition. A word applied by the Italians to the poetry of a song; when the words are well written, the song is said to have a good *tésto*.
Testudo, *Lat.* (tĕs-tū-dō.) Name given by the Romans, in imitation of the Greeks, to the lyre of Mercury, because it was made of the back or hollow of a sea tortoise.
Tetartos. *Gr.* (tĕ-tär-tŏs.) Fourth; the epithet applied by the ancients to the one of their authentic modes called the Mixolydian.
Tetrachord, *Gr.* (tĕt-rä-kŏrd.)   } A fourth; also,
Tetracorde, *Fr.* (tĕt-rä-kŏrd.)   } a system of four
Tetracórdo, *It.* (tĕt-rä-kŏr-dō.)   } sounds among the ancients, the extremes of which were fixed, but the middle sounds were varied according to the *mode.*
Tetrachords, conjoint. Two tetrachords, or fourths, where the same note is the highest of one and the lowest of the other.
Tetrachordio, *Spa.* (tĕt-rä-kŏr-dē-ō.) Tetrachord.

THIR

Tetradiapason. The Greek appellation of the quadruple octave, which we also call the *twentyninth.*
Tetratonon. The Greek name for an interval of four tones, called at present, the superfluous fifth.
The, *Gr.* (thā.) One of the four words used by the ancient Greeks in solfaing, answering to the lychanos, or third sound of the tetrachord.
Theatre. A house for the exhibition of dramatic performances, as operas, tragedies, comedies, farces, etc.
Théâtre de la nation, *Fr.* (tä-ätr dŭh lä nä-sĭ-ŏnh.) The Grand Opera House.
Théâtre de la république, *Fr.* (tä-ätr dŭh lä rā-pŭb-lēk.) Théâtre Français.
Théâtre de la montansier. *Fr.* (tä-ätr dŭh lä mänh-tänh-sēr.) Formerly the Palais Royal.
Theatrical music. Compositions designed for the orchestra of a theatre; dramatic music.
Theile, *Ger. pl.* (tī-lĕ.) Parts, divisions of the bar; also, strains, or component parts of a movement or piece.
Thema, *Gr.* (thā-mä.)   }
Thema, *Lat.* (thā-mä.) } A theme, or subject.
Thema, *Ger.* (tā-mä.)   }
Theme, *Fr.* (tăm.)   }
Theme. The subject of a composition.
Theorbe, *Ger.* (tĕ-ŏr-bĕ.)   } An ancient instru-
Theorbo, *Eng.* (thē-ŏr-bō.) } ment of the lute species; see Arch-lute.
Theoretical musician. One who is acquainted with the essence, nature, and properties of sound as connected with the laws of harmony, melody, and modulation.
Theoretiker, *Ger.* (tĕ-ō-rĕt-ĭ-kĕr.) } A theoret-
Théoricien. *Fr.* (tā-ō-rē-sĭ-änh.)   } ical musician, a theorist.
Theoria, *Lat.* (thē-ō-rī-ä.) } The science of mu-
Théorie, *Fr.* (tā-ō-rē.)   } sic; the principles of
Theory, *Eng.* (thē-ō-ry.)   } sound, as regards concords and discords; the system of harmonical and melodial arrangement.
Thep, *Heb.* (thăp.) An instrument resembling the flute or hautboy, but having fewer holes, and possessing a more limited range of notes.
Thesis, *Gr.* (thā-sĭs.) Down-beat, the accented part of the bar.
Theurgic hymns. Songs of incantation, such as those ascribed to Orpheus, performed in the mysteries upon the most solemn occasions. These hymns were the first of which we have any account in Greece.
Thin. An epithet applied to harmony which is meagre and scanty. All tones, both of voices and instruments, that are not round and full are called *thin.*
Third. An interval comprising three diatonic degrees.
Third, diminished. An interval measured by two half-steps.
Third inversion. A name given to an inverted chord of the seventh when its seventh is the lowest.
Third, major. An interval measured by four half-steps.
Third, minor. An interval measured by three half-steps.

ă *ale,* ă *add,* ă *arm,* ā *eve,* ĕ *end,* ī *ice,* ĭ *ill,* ō *old,* ŏ *odd,* ô *dove,* oo *moon,* ū *lute,* ŭ *but,* ū *French sound.*

THIR

Third shift. The double shift in violin playing.
Thirteenth. An interval comprising an octave and a sixth. It contains twelve diatonic degrees, *i. e.,* thirteen sounds.
Thirty-second note. A demisemiquaver,
Thirty-second rest. A rest or pause equal to the length of a thirty-second note,
Tho, or to. One of the four words used by the ancient Greeks in solfaing, answering to the fourth sound of the tetrachord.
Thorough bass. Figured bass; a system of harmony which is indicated by a figured bass.
Three-eighth measure. A measure having the value of three eighth notes, marked 3-8.
Three fold. A chord consisting of three tones, comprising a tone combined with its third and fifth.
Threnodia, *Lat.* (thrĕ-*nō-*dī-ä.) ⎫ An e l e g y, a
Threnodie, *Gr.* (thrĕ-*nō-*dĕ.) ⎭ funeral song.
Threnody. Lamentation, a song of lamentation.
Thrice marked octave. The name given in Germany to the notes between the C on the second added line above the treble staff and the next B above, inclusive; these notes are expressed by small letters, with three short strokes.
Thumb rattles. A term applied by Germans to castanets.
Thurmgeläute, *Ger.* (*toorm-*ghĕ-*loi-*tĕ.) Set or peal of bells in a tower; ringing of the bells.
Thürner, *Ger.* (*tūr-*nĕr.) Town musician.
Tibia, *Lat.* (*tĭb-*ĭ-ä.) The ancient name of all wind instruments with holes, such as the flute, pipe, and fife; originally the term was applied to the human leg-bone made into a flute.
Tibia major, *Lat.* (*tĭb-*ĭ-ä mä-jŏr.) An organ stop of sixteen feet tone, the pipes of which are stopped or covered.
Tibiæ pares, *Lat. pl.* (*tĭb-*ĭ-ē *pä-*rēs.) Two flutes, one for the right hand, and the other for the left, which were played on by the same performer.
Tibia utricularia, *Lat.* (*tĭb-*ĭ-ä ŭt-rĭ-kū-*lā-*rĭ-ä.) Name by which the bagpipe was known among the ancient Romans.
Tibicen, *Lat.* (*tĭb-*ĭ-sĕn.) The ancient flute player, or piper.
Tibicina, *Lat.* (tĭb-ĭ-sē-nä.) A female flute player, or piper.
Tibicene, *It.* (tĕ-bē-tshĕ-nĕ.) A flute player, piper, minstrel.
Tie. A slur; a curved line placed over notes on same degree of staff requiring a connected tone.
Tief, *Ger.* (tēf.) Deep, low, profound.
Tiefer, *Ger.* (*tē-*fĕr.) Deeper, lower: 8va *tiefer,* octave below.
Tieftönend, *Ger.* (*tĕf-*tŏ-nĕnd.) Deep toned.
Tierce, *Fr.* (tērs.) A third; also, the name of an organ stop tuned a major third higher than the fifteenth.
Tierce de picardie, *Fr.* (tērs dŭh pī-*kăr-*dē.) *Tierce of Picardy;* a term applied to a *major third,* when introduced in the last chord of a composition in a minor mode; the custom was supposed to have originated in Picardy, and formerly was quite common.

TINT

Tierce maxime. *Fr.* (tērs măx-ēm.) *Augmented third,* containing five semitones; as, from F to A♯.
Tiercet, *Gr.* (tēr-sĕt.) A triplet.
Timbal, *Spa.* (tĭm-*bäl.*)
Timbale, *Fr.* (tănh-*bäl.*) ⎱ A kettle drum.
Timbállo, *It.* (tĕm-*bäl-*lō.)
Timbalear, *Spa.* (tĭm-bä-lĕ-*är.*) To beat the kettle drum.
Timbalero, *Spa.* (tĭm-bä-lä-rō.) ⎱ A kettle drum-
Timbalier, *Fr.* (tănh-bä-lī-ā.) ⎰ mer.
Timballes, *Fr. pl.* (tănh-bäl.) Kettle drums.
Timbre, *Fr.* (tănhbr.) *Quality* of tone, or sound.
Timbrel. An ancient Hebrew instrument, supposed to have been like a tambourine.
Time. The measure of sounds in regard to their continuance or duration.
Time, common. A time having an even number of parts in a measure.
Time, compound. Measures containing two or three principal accents.
Time, compound common. Measures of two times, composed of six equal notes, three for each time; sextuple measure.
Time, compound triple. A time having nine quarter or eighth notes in a measure.
Time, double. A time having two parts or motions in each and every measure.
Time, ottupla, *It.* (ŏt-too-plä.) Common time.
Time, simple. Measures containing but one principal accent.
Time table. A representation of the several notes in music, showing their relative lengths or durations.
Time, triple. A time in which each bar contains three measures of equal parts, the first two of which are indicated by a downward beat, the third by an upward; or, *down, left, up.*
Timidezza, con, *It.* (tē-mē-*dät-*sä.) With timidity.
Timist. A performer who preserves a just and steady time.
Timoresaménte, *It.* (tē-mō-rō-zä-*män-*tĕ. Timidly, with fear.
Timeróse, *It.* (tē-mō-rō-zo.) Timorous, with hesitation.
Timpanétto, *It.* (tĕm-pä-*nät-*tō.) A small drum, or timbrel.
Tímpani, *It. pl.* (tĕm-*pä-*nē.) ⎱ T h e kettle-
Timpani, *Spa. pl.* (tĕm-*pä-*nē.) ⎰ drums.
Tímpani scerdati, *It.* (tĕm-*pä-*nē skŏr-*dä-*tē.) Kettle drums out of tune.
Tímpani sordi, *It.* (tĕm-*pä-*nē sŏr-dē.) Drums having dampers.
Timpanísta, *It.* (tĕm-pä-*nēs-*tä.) A performer on the kettle drums.
Tímpano, *It.* (ĭm-pä-nō.) ⎱ Drum, timbrel,
Tímpane, *Spa.* (tĕm-pä-nō.) ⎰ labor.
Tintement, *Fr.* (tănh-t-mănh.) Tingling of a bell; vibration, or ringing sound.
Tinter, *Fr.* (tănh-tā.) To toll a bell; to jingle.
Tintermeil. An old dance.
Tintinnábulum, *Lat.* (ĭn-tĭn-*năb-*ū-lŭm.) ⎱
Tintinnábolo, *It.* (tĕn-tēn-*nä-*bō-lō.) ⎰
Tintinnábule, *It.* (tĕn-tēn-*nä-*boo-lō.) ⎰
A little bell.

ā ate, ă add, ä arm, ē eve, ĕ end, ī ice, ĭ ill, ō old, ŏ odd, ō dove, oo moon, ū lute, ŭ but, ü *French sound.*

TINT

Tintinnabulary. Having or making the sound of a bell.
Tintinnalogia, *Lat.* (tĭn-tĭn-nä-lō-jĭ-ä.) The art of ringing bells.
Tintinnaménto, *It.* (tēn-tēn-nä-mān-tō.) Tinkling of small bells.
Tintinnire, *It.* (tēn-tēn-nē-rē.) To tinkle; to resound.
Tintínno, *It.* (tēn-tēn-nō.) Vibration, ringing of a bell.
Tiórba, *It.* (tē-ōr-bä.)
Tiorba, *Spa.* (tē-ōr-bä.) } Theorbo.
Tiorbísta, *It.* (tē-ōr-bēs-tä.) A player on the theorbo.
Tiple, *Spa.* (tē-plē.) Treble; one who sings treble; a species of small guitar.
Tipping. A distinct articulation given to the tones of a flute by placing the end of the tongue on the roof of the mouth; see *Double-tongueing.*
Tiramantici. *It.* (tē-rä-män-tē-tshē.) An organ bellows blower.
Tiránna, *It.* (tē-rän-nä.) A Spanish national air or song accompanied by the guitar.
Tirant, *Fr.* (tē-ränh.)
Tirante, *Spa.* (tē-rän-tē.) } Brace of a drum.
Tirasse. *Fr.* (tĭ-räss.) The pedals of an organ which act on the manual keys, by pulling, or drawing them down.
Tiráta, *It.* (tē-rä-tä.) A term formerly applied to any number of notes of equal value or length, and moving in conjoint degrees.
Tiráta di semiminime, *It.* (tē-rä-tä dē sēm-ē-me-nē-mē.) When many crotchets follow one another, moving upward or downward in conjoint degrees.
Tiráta legatura, *It.* (tē-rä-tä lē-gä-too-rä.) When among many notes of the same value, the last of one bar and the first of the next are tied.
Tiráto, *It.* (tē-rä-tō.) Drawn, pulled, stretched out; a down-bow; see, also, *Tirasse.*
Tira tútto, *It.* (tē-rä toot-tō.) A pedal or mechanism in an organ, which, acting upon all the stops, enables the performer to obtain at once the full power of the instrument.
Tiré, *Fr.* (tē-rā.) *Drawn, pulled;* a down-bow.
Tiré-lirer, *Fr.* (tē-rā lē-rā.) To sing like a lark.
Tirolese, *It.* (tē-rō-lā-zē.) A kind of dance.
Tirotear, *Spa.* (tē-rō-tē-är.) To blow wind instruments.
Tiroteo, *Spa.* (tē-rō-tā-ō.) Blast or sound of a wind instrument.
To, *Gr.* (tō.) One of the four words used by the ancient Greeks in solfaing, answering to the fourth sound of the tetrachord.
Tobend, *Ger.* (tō-běnd.) Blusteringly, violently.
Tocador, *Spa.* (tō-kä-thōr.) A tuning key.
Tocar la retirada, *Spa.* (tō-kär lä rē-tē-rä-dä.) To sound a retreat.
Toccáta, *It.* (tō-kä-tä.) An obsolete form of composition for the organ or pianoforte, something like our capriccio or fantasia; a piece requiring brilliant execution.
Toccatína, *It.* (tōk-kä-tē-nä.) A short *toccáta.*
Tocsin. An alarm bell; ringing of a bell for the purpose of alarm.

TONE

Todesgesang, *Ger.* (tō-děs-ghě-säng.) } A dirge,
Todeslied, *Ger.* (tō-děs-lēd.) } a funeral song.
Todtenglöckchen, *Ger.* (tōd-t'n-glők-kb'n.) Funeral bell.
Todtenlied, *Ger.* (tōd-t'n-lēd.) Funeral song or anthem.
Todten-marsch, *Ger.* (tōd-t'n märsh.) Funeral march.
Todten-musik, *Ger.* (tōd-t'n moo-zĭk.) Funeral music.
Toeten, *Dut.* (tō-tēn.) To play upon a horn.
Toet-horn, *Dut.* (tōt-hōrn.) A bugle-horn.
Tolling. The act of ringing a church bell in a slow, measured manner.
Tome, *Fr.* (tōm.) Volume, book.
Tom-tom. A sort of drum used by the natives in the East Indies.
Ton, *Fr.* (tōnh.) ⎫ Tone, sound, voice.
Ton, *Ger.* (tōn.) ⎪ melody; also, accent,
Töne, *Ger. pl.* (tō-nē.) ⎬ stress; also, the pitch
Tono, *Spa.* (tō-nō.) ⎪ of any note as to its
Tons, *Fr. pl.* (tōnh.) ⎭ acuteness or gravity;
also, the key or mode; *le ton d'ut,* the key of C; see also *Tone.*
Ton-abstaud, *Ger.* (tōn-äb-ständ.) An interval.
Ton-achte, *Ger.* (tōn äkh-tě.) A quaver.
Tonada, *Spa.* (tō-nä-thä.) A tune.
Tonadica, *Spa.* (tō-nä-dē-kä.) ⎫ A song of a
Tonadilla, *Spa.* (tō-nä-dēl-yä.) ⎬ lively and cheerful character, generally with guitar accompaniment.
Tonart, *Ger.* (tō-närt.) Mode, scale, key.
Tonatilla, *Sp.* (tō-nä-tēl-yä.) ⎫ Spanish na-
Tonatillas, *Sp.* (tō-nä-tēl-yäs.) ⎬ tional airs, or dances; see *Tonadilla.*
Ton-ausweichung, *Ger.* (tōn ons-vī-khoong.) Modulation.
Ton bas, *Fr.* (tōnh bä.) A low, deep tone.
Ton, demi, *Fr.* (tōnh dě-mē.) A semitone.
Ton de voix, *Fr.* (tōnh düh vwä.) Tone of voice.
Ton-dichter, *Ger.* (tōn dĭkh-těr.) Poet of sound, a composer of music.
Ton-dichtung, *Ger.* (tōn dĭkh-toong.) Musical composition of a high character.
Tóndo, *It.* (tōn-dō.) Round or full, as regards tone.
Ton doux, *Fr.* (tōnh doo.) Soft, sweet tone.
Tone. A given, fixed sound, of certain pitch: it is used to signify a certain degree of distance or interval between two sounds, as in the Major tone and Minor tone; also, the particular quality of the sound of any voice or instrument.
Tone-art. A name given by the Germans to musical art.
Tone artist. A practical musician.
Tone, explosive. A tone produced by striking a note suddenly and with great force, and as suddenly causing it to cease, >V
Tone master. A composer of music.
Tone measurer. A monochord; an instrument used by the Greeks for determining the relations of tones and intervals.
Tönen, *Ger.* (tō-něn.) To sound; to resound.
Tönend, *Ger.* (tō-něnd.) Sounding.
Tönen des erz, *Ger.* (tō-něn děs ěrts.) Sounding brass.

ă ale, ă add, ă arm, ĕ eve, ĕ end, ĭ ice, ĭ ill, ŏ old, ŏ odd, ŏ dove, oo moon, ŭ lute, ŭ but, ŭ French sound.

TONE

Tone, open. A tone produced on an open string.
Tone piece. A name applied by the Germans to a musical composition.
Tone, pressure. A very sudden crescendo.
Tone, quarter. A small interval, which, in the mathematical theory of music, is found to exist between D♯ and E♭, G♯ and A♭, etc.
Tones, accessory. Harmonics; tones faintly heard in the higher octaves, as the principal tone dies away.
Tones, chest. The lowest register of the human voice.
Tones, Gregorian. The chants used for the Psalms in the Roman Catholic service; the ancient modes or tones on which the Gregorian chants are based.
Tones, head. The upper tones of the human voice.
Tones, passing. Whenever one or more of the parts constituting an harmonic chord moves to a tone foreign to the harmony, the chord otherwise remaining unchanged, such movements are called *Passing Tones.*
Tone, whole. An interval consisting of two half-tones.
Ton-fall, *Ger.* (tŏn făll.) A cadence.
Ton-farbe, *Ger.* (tŏn făr-hĕ.) Character of tone.
Ton-folge, *Ger.* (tŏn fŏl-ghĕ.) Tune, melody.
Ton-führung, *Ger.* (tŏn fü-roong.) Modulation; also, succession of melody or harmony.
Ton-fuss, *Ger.* (tŏn foos.) Metre.
Ton-gang, *Ger.* (tŏn gäng.) Tune, melody.
Ton-gattung, *Ger.* (tŏn gät-toong.)
Ton-geschlecht, *Ger.* (tŏn ghĕ-shlĕkht.)
The individuality of the two modes, the major and minor; Ton-*geschlecht* is the more correct term.
Ton-générateur, *Fr.* (tŏnh zhă-nă-ră-tūr.) The ruling, or principal key in which a piece is written.
Tongue. In the reed pipe of an organ, a thin elastic slip of metal, somewhat bent and placed near the reed.
Tonguing, double. A mode of articulating quick notes, used by flutists.
Ton haut, *Fr.* (tŏnh n'ō.) A high, acute tone.
Tonisæum, *Gr.* (tŏ-nĭ-ā-ŭm.) In the ancient music, one of the divisions of the chromatic genus.
Tonic. The key-note of any scale; the chief, fundamental ground-tone, or first note, of the scale.
Tónica, *It.* (tō-nē-kä.)
Tonica, *Ger.* (tō-nĕ-kä.) } : Tonic.
Tonique, *Fr.* (tŏnh-ēk.)
Tonic pedal. A continued bass note on which chords foreign to its harmony are given.
Tonic section. A section closing on the common chord of the tonic.
Tonic sol fa. A system of writing and teaching music, in which the letters of the alphabet, and other signs, are used, instead of the usual notation on the staff. In this system *do* is always applied to the tonic.
Ton-kunst, *Ger.* (tŏn-koonst.) Music; the art and science of music.
Ton-künstler, *Ger.* (tŏn künst-lĕr.) Musician.
Ton-künstlich, *Ger.* (tŏn künst-lĭkh.) Musical.

TOQU

Ton-kunstschule, *Ger.* (tŏn koonst-shoo-lĕ.) School of music.
Ton-lehre, *Ger.* (tŏn lā-rĕ.) Acoustics; tones.
Ton-leiter, *Ger.* (tŏn lī-tĕr.) Scale, gamut.
Ton-majeur, *Fr.* (tŏnh mä-zhūr.) Major key.
Ton-mass, *Ger.* (tŏn mäss.) Measure, time.
Ton-meisterinn, *Ger.* (tŏn mīs-tĕr-inn.) A virtuoso.
Ton-messer, *Ger.* (tŏn mĕs-sĕr.) A monochord.
Ton mineur, *Fr.* (tŏnh mē-nŭr.) Minor key.
Tono, *Spa.* (tō-nō.) Tone.
Tonorium, *Lat.* (tŏ-nō-rĭ-ŭm.) A kind of pitch-pipe used by the ancient Romans to regulate the voices of orators, actors, and singers.
Tonos, *Gr.* (tŏ-nōs.) Tone.
Tonotechnie, *Fr.* (tŏ-nō-tĕk-nē.) The art of marking the notes on the cylinder of a barrel organ.
Ton pathetique, *Fr.* (tŏnh pä-tĕt-ēk.) A plaintive, or pathetic tone.
Ton perçant, *Fr.* (tŏnh pĕr-säuh.) Shrill tone.
Ton relatif, *Fr.* (tŏnh rĕl-ä-tĭf.) A relative tone.
Ton relatif mineur, *Fr.* (tŏnh rĕl-ä-tĭf mē-nŭr.) Relative minor key.
Ton-satz, *Ger.* (tŏn sätz.) A musical composition.
Ton-schluss, *Ger.* (tŏn shlooss.) A cadence.
Ton-schlüssel, *Ger.* (tŏn shlüs-s'l.) The key; key-note.
Ton-schrift, *Ger.* (tŏn shrift.) Musical notes.
Tons de l'eglise, *Fr.* (tŏnh dŭh l'ä-glēz.) Church modes or tones.
Tons de la trompette, *Fr.* (tŏnh dŭh lä trŏm-pĕt.)
Tons du cor, *Fr.* (tŏnh dŭ kŏr.)
The additional crooks of the trumpet and horn, for raising or lowering the pitch.
Ton-setzer, *Ger.* (tŏn sĕt-tsĕr.) A composer; a less flattering term than *ton-dichter.*
Ton-setzer-kunst, *Ger.* (tŏn sĕt-tsĕr koonst.) The art of musical composition.
Ton-setzung, *Ger.* (tŏn sĕt-tsoong.) } A musical
Ton-stück, *Ger.* (tŏn-stŭk.) } piece or composition.
Ton-silbe, *Ger.* (tŏn sĭl-bĕ.) Accented.
Ton-spiel, *Ger.* (tŏn spēl.) Music, a concert.
Ton-spieler, *Ger.* (tŏn spē-lĕr.) Musical performer.
Ton-stufe, *Ger.* (tŏn stoo-fĕ.) A degree of the staff.
Ton-sylbe, *Ger.* (tŏn sĭl-bĕ.) Accented syllable.
Ton-system, *Ger.* (tŏn sĭs-tĕm.) System of tones or sounds; the science of harmony; the systematic arrangement to musical tones or sounds in their regular order.
Ton-veränderung, *Ger.* (tŏn fĕ-rän-dĕ-roong.) Modulation.
Ton-verhalt, *Ger.* (tŏn fĕr-hält.) Rhythm.
Ton-werk, *Ger.* (tŏn värk.) A musical composition.
Ton-wissenschaft, *Ger.* (tŏn-vĭs-s'n-shäft.) The science of music.
Ton-zeichen, *Ger.* (tŏn tsī-kh'n.) Accent.
Toph, *Heb.* (tŏf.) An instrument like the tambourine, which was known to the Jews before they left Syria.
Toque, *Spa.* (tō-kĕ.) Ringing of bells.

TOQU

Toque a muerto, *Spa.* (tŏ-kĕ ă moo-ā́r-tō.) Passing bell.
Torch dance. A dance of former times in which the dancers carried torches.
Torloroto, *Spa.* (tör-lō-rō-tō.) A shepherd's pipe or flute.
Torrente, *Spa.* (tör-rän-tē.) A strong, coarse voice.
Tostaménte, *It.* (tōs-tä-män-tĕ.) Quickly, rapidly.
Tostissimaménte, *It.* (tōs-tēs-sē-mä-män-tĕ.)
Tostissimo, *It.* (tōs-tĕs-sē-mō.)
Extremely quick, with great rapidity.
Tósto, *It.* (tōs-tō.) Quick, swift, rapid: see, also, *Piu Tósto*.
Touch. Style of striking or pressing the keys of an organ, pianoforte, or similar instrument; the resistance made to the fingers by the keys of any instrument, as, when the keys are put down with difficulty, an instrument is said to have a *hard* or *heavy touch;* when there is little resistance the *touch* is said to be *soft* or *light*.
Touch, demi legato. A touch indicated by dots under a slur, and played by gently raising the hand, with a motion from the wrist, and pressing the keys, carefully detaching the notes.
Touch, demi staccato. The striking the key and raising the hand quickly, retaining the note not more than half its full value.
Touche, *Fr.* (toosh.) The *touch;* also, a key of the pianoforte, etc.
Touche d'orgue, *Fr.* (toosh d'örg.) Key of an organ.
Toucher, *Fr.* (too-shā.) To play upon an instrument.
Toucher la guitare, *Fr.* (too-shā lä ghĭ-tär.) To play on the guitar.
Touches, *Fr. pl.* (toosh.) The keys of a pianoforte, organ, etc.
Touch, legato. A sliding of the fingers on and off the keys; holding down one key until the finger is fairly on to another. It is indicated by a curved line over or under the note,
Touch, organ. The manner of pressing the keys of an organ; playing passages of single notes as well as of chords in such a smooth, legato style that one note follows the other without any interruption of sound.
Touch, piano. The manner of striking the keys of the pianoforte.
Touch, staccato. A short and sudden striking of the keys with the ends of the fingers, making the notes very detached.
Touquet, *Fr.* (too-kā.) A term formerly given to the lowest trumpet part.
Tourne boute. *Fr.* (toorn boot.) A musical instrument similar to the flute.
Tours de force, *Fr.* (toor düh fōrs.) *Bravúra* passages, roulades, divisions, etc.
Tout ensemble, *Fr.* (too t'änh-sänhbl.) The whole together; the general effect.
Town pipers. Certain performers on the pipe, one of whom was formerly retained by most of the principal towns in Scotland, to assist in the celebration of particular holidays, festivals, etc.

TRAN

Toys. A name formerly given to little trifling airs or dance tunes.
Trabajar. *Spa.* (trä-bä-här.) A professional singer; one who performs in an opera.
Trabattere, *It.* (trä-bät-tā-rē.) To beat.
Trachea. *Lat.* (trā-kē-ä.) The wind-pipe.
Tracto, *Spa.* (träk-tō.) Versicles sung at mass between the Epistle and the Gospel.
Tradolce, *It.* (trä-dōl-tahĕ.) Very soft; sweet.
Tradótto, *It.* (trä-dō-tō.) Translated, arranged, adapted, fitted to.
Tragédie en musique, *Fr.* (trä-zhā-dē änh mü-zēk.) A serious, or tragic opera.
Tragedy. A dramatic poem representing some signal action performed by illustrious persons, and generally having a fatal issue.
Tragedy, lyric. A tragedy accompanied by singing; tragic opera.
Trainé, *Fr.* (trä-nā.) Slurred, bound; lingering, drawn along.
Trait, *Fr.* (trā.) Passage, run; a phrase.
Trait de chant, *Fr.* (trä düh shänh.) A melodic passage, or phrase.
Trait d'harmonie, *Fr.* (trä d'är-mō-nē.) Succession of chords, a sequence.
Trait d'octave, *Fr.* (trä d'ōk-täv.) See Rule of the Octave.
Traité, *Fr.* (trä-tā.) A treatise on the practice, or the theory of music.
Trällern, *Ger.* (trāl-lĕrn.) To trill, to hum a tune.
Tramoya, *Spa.* (trä-moi-ä.) Scene; operatic decoration.
Tranquillaménte, *It.* (trän-quēl-lä-män-tĕ.) Quietly, calmly, tranquilly.
Tranquillézza, *It.* (trän-quēl-lĕt-sä.)
Tranquillita, *It.* (trän-quēl-lē-tä.)
Tranquillo, *It.* (trän-quēl-lō.)
Tranquility, calmness, quietness.
Transcription. An arrangement for the pianoforte, of a song or other composition, not originally designed for that instrument; an adaptation.
Transient. An epithet applied to those chords of whose harmony no account is meant to be taken, but which are used as passing chords.
Transitio, *Lat.* (trän-sē-ahī-o.)
Transition, *Eng.*
Passing suddenly out of one key into another, without preparation for, or hinting at another key; or without making use of chords common to both keys.
Transitus, *Lat.* (trän-sī-tŭs.) A passing note.
Transitus irregularis, *Lat.* (trän-sī-tŭs ĭr-rĕg-ü-lä-rĭs.) Irregular passing notes; see *Changing notes*.
Transitus regularis, *Lat.* (trän-sī-tŭs rĕg-ü-lä-rĭs.) Passing notes placed on the *unaccented* parts of the bar.
Transportar, *Spa.* (träns-pōr-tär.) To change the key; to transpose.
Transposed. Removed, or changed into another key.
Transposer, *Fr.* (tranhs-pō-zā.)
Transponiren, *Ger.* (träns-pō-nē-rĕn.)
Change of key; removing a piece into another key.

ā ale, ă add, ä arm, ē eve, ĕ end, ī ice, ĭ ill, ō old, ŏ odd, ō dove, oo moon, ū lute, ŭ but, ü French sound.

TRAN

Transverse flute. The German flute; the flauto traverso.
Traquenard, *Fr.* (trä-kĕ-närd.) A brisk sort of dance.
Trascinándo, *It.* (trä-shē-*nän*-dō.) Dragging the time.
Trascrítto, *It.* (trä-*shrēt*-tō.) Copied, transcribed.
Traste, *Spa.* (träs-tē.) A fret.
Trattáto, *It.* (trät-*tä*-tō.) See *Traité.*
Trauer-gesang, *Ger.* (*trou-ĕr-ghĕ-zäng*.) Mourning song, dirge.
Trauer-laut, *Ger.* (*trou-ĕr-lout*.) A mournful sound.
Trauer-marsch, *Ger.* (*trou-ĕr märsh*.) Funeral march.
Trauer-musik, *Ger.* (*trou-ĕr moo-zik.*) Funeral music.
Trauer-stimme, *Ger.* (*trou-ĕr stim-mĕ.*) A sad, doleful strain.
Trauer-ton, *Ger.* (trou-ĕr tōn.) A doleful tone.
Traurig, *Ger.* (*trou-rig.*) Heavily, sadly, mournfully.
Traversiere, *Fr.* (trä-vĕr-sē-*är*.) Cross, across;
Travérso, *It.* (trä-*vär*-sō.) } applied to the *transverse,* or German flute, to distinguish it from the *flûte à bec.*
Travestie, *Ger.* (trä-fēs-tē.) Parody.
Travestiren, *Ger.* (trä-fēs-tīr-ĕn.) To parody.
Tre, *It.* (trā.) Three; *à tre,* for three voices or instruments.
Treadle, harp. The pedal of a harp, by the use of which the tone of the instrument is elevated a small second.
Treble. The upper part, the highest voice, the soprano, that which generally contains the melody.
Treble clef. The G clef, the soprano clef.
Treble note. That note which in the treble staff is placed on the line with the clef; *i. e.,* the second line.
Treble, cornet. An old style of cornet, consisting of a curvilineal tube about three feet in length, gradually increasing in diameter from the mouth-piece to the lower end.
Treble, first. The highest treble, or soprano.
Treble forte stop. A stop recently applied to cabinet organs, by means of which the treble part of the instrument may be increased in power, while the bass remains subdued.
Treble, second. Low soprano.
Treble staff. The staff upon which the treble clef is placed.
Treble viol. An instrument invented before the modern viol, furnished with six strings tuned chiefly by *fourths.*
Treble voice. The highest species of the female voice.
Tre córde, *It.* (trā kŏr-dĕ.) *Three strings;* in pianoforte music this means that the pedal which moves the keys, or action, must no longer be pressed down.
Tremándo, *It.* (trā-män-dō.) See *Tremolándo.*
Tremblant, *Fr.* (tränh-blänh.) *Shaking;* see *Tremulant.*
Tremblement, *Fr.* (tränbbl-mänh.) A trill or shake.

TRIA

Trembler, *Fr.* (tränh-blā.) To tremble, to shake.
Tremblotant, *Fr.* (tränh-blō-tänh.) Quivering.
Trembloter, *Fr.* (tränh-blō-tā.) To quiver, to shake.
Treméndo, *It.* (trĕ-*män*-dō.) Terrible, dreadful.
Tremolándo, *It.* (trĕm-ō-*län*-dō.) } *Trembling,*
Tremoláte, *It.* (trĕm-ō-*lä*-tĕ.) } *quivering;*
Trémolo, *It.* (trā-mō-lō.) } a *note,* or
Trémulo, *It.* (trā-moo-lō.) } chord, reiterated with great rapidity, producing a tremulous kind of effect.
Tremolant. } An organ stop which gives to the
Tremulant. } tone a waving, trembling, or undulating effect, resembling the *vibráto* in singing, and the *tremolándo* in violin playing; also, a harmonium stop of the same kind.
Tremóre, *It.* (trā-mō-rĕ.) } *Tremor,* trem-
Tremoróso, *It.* (trā-mō-rō-zō.) } bling; see also, *Tremolándo.*
Trenchmore. An old dance, supposed to have been of a lively species.
Trenise, *Fr.* (trä-nēz.) One of the movements of a quadrille.
Trenodia, *It.* (trā-nō-dē-ä.) A funeral dirge.
Trental. An office for the dead in the Roman Catholic church, consisting of thirty masses.
Tres, *Fr.* (trā.) Very, most.
Très-animé, *Fr.* (trä sän-ē-mā.) Very animated, very lively.
Trésca, *It.* (trās-kä.) A country dance.
Trescherélla, *It.* (trās-kĕ-*räl*-lä.) A little dance.
Trescóne, *It.* (tre-*kō*-nĕ.) A species of dance.
Très fort, *Fr.* (trä fōr.) Very loud.
Très lentement, *Fr.* (trä länht-mänh.) Very slow.
Très piano, *Fr.* (trä pē-ä nō.) Very soft.
Très vif, *Fr.* (trä vēf.) Very lively, very brisk.
Tres vite et impetneux, *Fr.* (trä vēt ä änh-pĕt-oo-tiz.) Very quick and impetuous.
Treter, *Ger.* (trē-tĕr.) *Treader,* of the bellows, in German organs.
Tre vólte, *It. pl.* (trā vōl-tĕ.) Three times.
Triad. The common chord, consisting of a note sounded together with its third and fifth.
Triad, extreme. A triad consisting of a fundamental tone, a major third, and an extreme fifth.
Triad, imperfect. The chord of the third, fifth, and eighth, taken on the seventh of the key, consisting of two minor thirds.
Triad, major. A union of any sound with its major third and perfect fifth.
Triad, minor. A union of any sound with its minor third and perfect fifth.
Triad of the dominant. A triad on the dominant or major fifth.
Triad, perfect. The harmonic division of the fifth into two thirds, of which the greater third is lowest.
Triad, tonic. A triad on the tonic, in major or minor.
Triangle. A small three-sided steel frame, which is played upon by being struck with a rod.
Triángolo, *It.* (trē-än-gō-lō.) }
Triangulo, *Spa.* (trē-än-goo-lō.) } A triangle.
Triagulus, *Lat.* (trī-än-gū-lŭs.) }
Trias deficiens, *Lat.* (trē-äs dĕ-fē-sī-ĕns.) The imperfect chord, or triad.

ă *ale*, ă *add*, ä *arm*, ē *eve*, ĕ *end*, I *ice*, ĭ *ill*, ō *old*, ŏ *odd*, ö *dove*, oo *moon*, ü *lute*, ŭ *but*, ü *French sound*.

TRIA

Trias harmonica, *Lat.* (trē-äs här-mŏn-ĭ-kä.) See *Triad*.
Tribon, *Spa.* (trē-bōn.) A triangular musical instrument.
Tribrach, *Lat.* (trē-bräk.) A trisyllabic musical foot, comprising three short notes or syllables, ‿‿‿.
Tribune d'orgué, *Fr.* (trē-bün d'örg.) An organ loft.
Trichord. The name given to the three stringed lyre, supposed to have been the invention of Mercury.
Trichordis, *Lat.* (trĭ-kŏr-dĭs.) Three stringed.
Trichordon, *Lat.* (trĭ-kŏr-dōn.) A *colachon* with three strings.
Tricórde, *It.* (trē-kŏr-dē.) With three strings.
Tricinium, *Lat.* (trē-sĭn-ĭ-ŭm.) A composition in three parts.
Tri-diapason. *Gr.* (trē dī-ä-pā-son.) A triple octave, or twenty-second.
Trigon. A three-stringed instrument, resembling the lyre used by the ancient Greeks.
Trigonum or triangular harp. An instrument supposed to have been of Phrygian invention, resembling the Theban harp.
Trihemitone. *Gr.* (trĭ-hĕm-ĭ-tō-nē.) A minor third.
Trill. A shake.
Trillándo, *It.* (trĕl-län-dō.) A succession or chain of shakes on different notes.
Trilláre, *It.* (trĕl-lä-rē.) To shake, to trill.
Trille, *Fr.* (trĕll.)
Triller, *Ger.* (trĭl-lĕr.) } A shake, a trill.
Trillo, *It.* (trĕl-lō.)
Triller-kette, *Ger.* (trĭl-lĕr kĕt-tĕ.) A chain or succession of shakes.
Trillern, *Ger.* (trĭl-lĕrn.) To trill, to shake.
Trillette, *Fr.* (trĭl-lĕtt.) } A short trill, or
Trilletta, *It.* (trĕl-lä-tä.) } shake.
Trilletto, *It.* (trĕl-lät-tō.)
Trillettino, *It.* (trĕl-lĕt-tē-nō.) A soft shake, a soft trilling.
Trill, imperfect. A trill, or shake without a turn at the close.
Trillo caprino, *It.* (trĕl-lō kä-prē-nō.) A false shake.
Trilli, *It.* (trĕl-lē.) Trills, shakes.
Trill, perfect. A quick alternation of two notes ending with a turn.
Trimeles. A kind of nome in the ancient music performed on flutes.
Trimeres. A nome of the ancient Greeks which was executed in three consecutive modes, viz., the Phrygian, the Doric, and the Lydian.
Trimeters. Ancient lyrical verses of a six-feet measure.
Trinado, *Spa.* (trē-nä-dō.) A trill, a shake, a tremulous sound.
Trinar, *Spa.* (trē-när.) To trill, to quaver.
Trink-gesang, *Ger.* (trĭnk ghĕ-säng.) } A Bacchanalian, or drinking song.
Trink-lied, *Ger.* (trĭnk lēd.) }
Trino, *Spa.* (trē-nō.) A trill.
Trinona. An organ stop, of open eight feet small scale, and pleasant, gamba-like tone.
Trio, *It.* (trē-ō.) A piece for three instruments: in England the word is also applied to a piece for three voices, but incorrectly, *tersétto* being the

TRIT

proper appellation. A *trio* is also the second movement to a *menuétto*, march, waltz, etc., and always leads back to a repetition of the first or principal movement.
Triole, *Ger.* (trĭ-ō-lĕ.) } A triplet, a group of
Triolet, *Fr.* (trĭ-ō-lĕ.) } three notes to be played in the time of two.
Triomphale, *Fr.* (trē-ōnh-fäl.) } Triumphal.
Trionfále, *It.* (trē-ōn-fä-lē.) }
Triomphant, *Fr.* (trē-ōnh-fänh.) } Triumphant.
Trionfánte, *It.* (trē-ōn-fän-tē.) }
Tripartite. Divided into three parts; scores in three parts are said to be *tripartite*.
Triphony. Three sounds heard together.
Triple. Three-fold, treble.
Triple counterpoint. Counterpoint in three parts, invertible; that is, so contrived that each part will serve indifferently for either bass middle, or upper part.
Triple croche, *Fr.* (krō-shä.) A demisemiquaver.
Triple dotted note. A note whose length is increased seven-eighths of its original value by three dots placed after it.
Triple dotted rest. A rest whose value is increased seven-eighths by three dots placed after it.
Triple octave. See Tri-diapason.
Triple progression. An expression in old music, implying a series of perfect fifths.
Triple suspension. A suspension formed by suspending a dominant, or diminished seventh, on the tonic, mediant, and dominant of the key.
Triplet. A group of three notes, played in the usual time of two similar ones.
Triplet, double. A sextole.
Triple time. Such as has an odd, or uneven number of parts in a bar, as *three*, *nine*.
Triplice, *It.* (trē-plē-tshē.) Triple, treble, three-fold.
Triplum, *Lat.* (trĭp-lŭm.) Formerly the name of the treble or highest part.
Tripodian, *Gr.* (trĭ-pō-dĭ-än.) An ancient stringed instrument, said to have been invented by Pythagoras.
Trisagion, *Gr.* (trĭ-sä-ghĕ-ŏn.) } A hymn in
Trisagium, *Lat.* (trĭ-sä-ghĕ-ŭm.) } which the word Holy is repeated three times in succession.
Trisemitonium, *Lat.* (trē-sĕm-ĭ-tō-nĭ-ŭm.) The lesser or minor third.
Tristézza, *It.* (trĭs-tät-sä.) Sadness, heaviness, pensiveness.
Trite. A Greek term signifying three, or third.
Trite-diezeugmenon, *Gr.* (trē-tē-dē-tsoog-mĕn-ŏn.) The third string of the diezeugmenon, or fourth tetrachord of the ancients, reckoning from the top, the sound of which corresponds with our C above the bass clef.
Trite-hyperbolæon, *Gr.* (trē-tē hĭ-pĕr-bō-lē-ŏn.) The third string of the hyperbolæon, or fifth tetrachord, answering to our G on the second line of the treble.
Trite-synemmenon, *Gr.* (trē-tē sĭ-nĕm-mē-nŏn) The third string, reckoning from the top of the third, or synemmenon, tetrachord, corresponding with our B-flat above the fifth line in the bass.
Trito-dactylo-gymnast. An instrument designed to render the third finger equal in power and pliancy to the others in piano playing.

ă *ale,* ă *add,* ä *arm,* ē *eve,* ĕ *end,* ī *ice,* ĭ *ill,* ō *old,* ŏ *odd,* ô *dove,* oo *moon,* ū *lute,* ŭ *but,* ū *French sound.*

TRIT

Triton, *Lat.* (trē-tŏn.) Of the third rank; a term given by old writers to the fifth and sixth modes or tones of their plain song.
Triton, *Fr.* (trē-tônh.) ⎱ A superfluous,
Tritone, *Eng.* (trī-tōn.) ⎰ or augmented,
Tritóno, *It.* (trē-tō-nō.) ⎱ fourth, containing three whole tones.
Tritonus, *Lat.* (trē-tō-nŭs.) ⎰
Triton avis, *Lat.* (trē-tŏn-ā-vĭs.) The name of a West Indian bird, remarkable for its musical powers, having three distinct notes, its tonic, or lower note, and the twelfth and seventeenth of that note, and capable of sounding them all at the same time.
Tritos, *Gr.* (trē-tōs.) Third; one of the four authentic modes of the ancients called the Æolian.
Tritt, *Ger.* (tritt.) Step, tread, treadle.
Tritt-brett, *Ger.* (tritt brĕtt.) ⎱ The board upon
Tritt-holtz, *Ger.* (tritt holts.) ⎰ which the bellows-treader steps, in blowing an organ.
Triumphirend, *Ger.* (trĭ-oom-fē-rĕnd.) Triumphant.
Triumphlied, *Ger.* (trĭ-oomf-lēd.) Song of triumph.
Trivagium. A hymn of the early Christians, likewise called the cherubical hymn.
Trochäisch, *Ger.* (trō-kā-ĭsh.) Trochaic.
Trocháus, *Ger.* (trō-kā-ŭs.) Trochee.
Trochee, *Lat.* (trō-kē.) A dissyllabic musical foot, containing one long and one short syllable. – ◡.
Trómba, *It.* (trŏm-bā.) A trumpet; also an eight feet reed organ stop.
Trombacelloclyde. A B-flat ophicleide.
Trómba cromática, *It.* (trŏm-bā krō-mā-tē-kā.) The modern valve trumpet, upon which semitones can be produced.
Trómba di básso, *It.* (trŏm-bā dē bās-sō.) The bass trumpet.
Trombadóre, *It.* (trŏm-bā-dō-rē.) A trumpeter.
Trómba marina, *It.* (trŏm-bā mā-rē-nā.) See *Trumpet Marine.*
Trómba príma, *It.* (trŏm-bā prē-mā.) First trumpet.
Trombare, *It.* (trŏm-bā-rē.) To sound the trumpet.
Trómba secónda, *It.* (trŏm-bā sā-kōn-dā.) Second trumpet.
Trómbe sórde, *It. pl.* (trŏm-bē sōr-dē.) Trumpets having dampers.
Trómba spezzáto, *It.* (trŏm-bā spĕt-sā-tā.) An obsolete name for the bass trombone.
Trombatóre, *It.* (trŏm-bā-tō-rē.) A trumpeter.
Trómba ventíle, *It.* (trŏm-bā vĕn-tē-lē.) See *Trómba Cromática.*
Trombétta, *It.* (trŏm-bāt-tā.) A small trumpet.
Trombettíno, *It.* (trŏm-bĕt-tē-nō.) A trumpeter.
Trombóne, *It.* (trŏm-bō-ně.) A very powerful and full-toned instrument of the trumpet species, but much larger, and with a sliding tube; also, a very powerful, and full-toned reed stop in an organ, of eight feet scale on the manual, and sixteen, or thirty-two feet on the pedal.
Trombone, *Fr.* (trŏnh-hōn.)
Trombone, alto. A trombone having a compass from the small c, or e, to the one-lined a, or two-lined c, and noted in the alto clef.

TROM

Trombone, bass. A trombone with a compass from the great C to the one-lined c and noted in the F clef.
Trombone, tenor. A trombone having a compass from the small c to the one-lined g, and noted in the tenor clef.
Tromboni, *It.* (trŏm-bō-nē.) Trombones.
Trombono piccolo, *It.* (trŏm-bō-nō pē-kō-lō.) A small sackbut.
Tromlo, *It.* (trŏm-lō.) Trumpet.
Trommel, *Ger.* (trŏm-m'l.) The military drum.
Trommel-boden, *Ger.* (trŏm-m'l bō-d'n.) Bottom of a drum.
Trommler, *Ger.* (trŏm-lĕr.) A drummer.
Trommel-kasten, *Ger.* (trŏm-m'l kās-t'n.) The body of a drum.
Trommel-klöpfel, *Ger.* (trŏm-m'l klōp-fĕl.) ⎱
Trommel-schlägel, *Ger.* (trŏm-m'l shlā-g'l.) ⎰ Drumstick.
Trommel-schläger, *Ger.* (trŏm-m'l shlā-gher.) Drummer.
Trommel-stück, *Ger.* (trŏm-m'l stŭk.) A tambourine; a tabor.
Trommeln, *Ger.* (trŏm-mĕln.) To drum; drumming, beating the drum.
Trompa, *Lat.* (trŏm-pā.) ⎱
Trompa, *Spa.* (trŏm-pā.) ⎰ A trumpet.
Trompe, *Fr.* (trŏnhp.)
Trompe de béarn, *Fr.* (trŏmhp dŭh bā-ārn.) The Jew's harp.
Trompeta, *Spa.* (trŏm-pĕ-tā.) A small trumpet.
Trompete, *Ger.* (trŏm-pā-tē.) A trumpet; also, a reed stop in an organ.
Trompetear, *Spa.* (trŏm-pĕ-tā-ār.) To sound a trumpet.
Trompeten, *Ger.* (trŏm-pā-t'n.) To play upon the trumpet.
Trompeten-bläser, *Ger.* (trŏm-pā-t'n blā-zĕr.) A trumpeter.
Trompeten-pfeife, *Ger.* (trŏm-pā-t'n pfī-fĕ.) Trumpet stop.
Trompeten-register, *Ger.* (trŏm-pā-t'n rā-ghĭs-tĕr.) ⎱
Trompeten-zug, *Ger.* (trŏm-pā-t'n tsūg.) ⎰ Trumpet stop or register in an organ.
Trompeten-schall, *Ger.* (trŏm-pā-t'n shāll.) Sound of the trumpet.
Trompeten-stück, *Ger.* (trŏm-pā-t'n stŭk.) A piece of music for the trumpet.
Trompeten-ton, *Ger.* (trŏm-pā-t'n tōn.)
Trompeter, *Ger.* (trŏm-pā-tĕr.) ⎱ A trumpeter
Trompeteur, *Fr.* (trŏnh-pā-tūr.) ⎰
Trompeter-stückchen, *Ger.* (trŏm-pā-tĕr stŭk-kh'n.) Flourish of a trumpet; a short piece of music played on the trumpet.
Trompetilla, *Spa.* (trŏm-pā-tēl-yā.) A small trumpet.
Trompette, *Fr.* (trŏnh-pāt.) A trumpet; also, a trumpeter; also, a reed stop in an organ.
Trompette a clefs, *Fr.* (trŏnh-pāt ā klā.) The keyed trumpet.
Trompette a pistons, *Fr.* (trŏnh-pāt ā pēs-tōnh.) The valve trumpet.
Trompette harmonique, *Fr.* (trŏnh-pāt hār-mōnh-ēk.) Harmonic trumpet, a reed stop in an organ of eight or sixteen feet: see Harmonic Flute.

ă ale, ă add, ă arm, ē eve, ĕ end, ī ice, ĭ ill, ō old, ŏ odd, ô dove, oo moon, ū lute, ŭ but, ü French sound.

TROM

Trompette marine, *Fr.* (trŏnh-pĕt mă-rēn.) See Trumpet Marine.
Trompette parlante, *Fr.* (trŏnh-pĕt pär-länht.) A speaking trumpet.
Tronco, *It.* (trŏn-kō.) An intimation that the sounds are to be cut short.
Tronco per grazia, *It.* (trŏn-kō pär grä-tsē-ä.) A term indicating that the voices as well as instruments, are not to draw out the sound to its natural length.
Troop. A quick march, a march in quick time.
Troper. A book formerly used in the church, containing the sequences or chants sung after the recital of the epistle.
Tróppo, *It.* (trŏp-pō.) Too much: *non tróppo allegro*, not too quick.
Tróppo caricáta, *It.* (trŏp-pō kä-rē-kä-tä.) Too much loaded. or overburdened; as, a melody with too much or too heavy accompaniment.
Troqueo, *Spa.* (trō-kā-ō.) A trochee.
Troubadours, *Fr. pl.* (troo-bä-door.) } The
Trouveres, *Fr. pl.* (troo-vār.) } bards,
Trouveurs, *Fr. pl.* (troo-vūr.) } and poet-musicians, of Provence, about the tenth century.
Troupe, opera. A company of musicians associated for the purpose of giving operas, generally traveling from place to place.
Trovatore, *It.* (trō-vä-tō-rĕ.) A minstrel.
Trug-schluss, *Ger.* (troog-shloos.) Interrupted, or deceptive cadence; an unexpected, or interrupted resolution of a discord.
Trumma, *Swe.* (troom-mä.) A drum.
Trum-marsch, *Swe.* (troom marsh.) A drum march.
Trummscheit, *Ger.* (troom-shīt.) A rude musical instrument, with one or more chords.
Trump. A trumpet; to blow a trumpet.
Trumpet. The loudest of all portable wind instruments, consisting of a folded tube, generally made of brass, but sometimes of silver; it is used chiefly in martial and orchestral music.
Trumpeter. One who sounds or plays the trumpet.
Trumpet, harmonical. An instrument, the sounds of which resemble those of a trumpet, differing from that instrument only in being longer and having more branches; the sackbut.
Trumpet marine. An ancient species of monochord, played with a bow, and producing a sound resembling that of a trumpet.
Trumpet, reed. An instrument consisting of a trumpet, within which were enclosed thirty-six brass-reeded pipes, arranged in a circle, so that in turning the circle each pipe could, in turn, be brought between the mouth-piece and the bell of the instrument.
Trumpet stop. A stop in an organ having a tone similar to that of a trumpet.
Trumpet stop, octave. A stop in an organ sounding an octave higher than the trumpet stop.
Trumpet, valve. A trumpet the tones of which are changed by the use of valves.
T. S. The initials of *Tasto Solo*.
Tseltsel, *Heb.* An ancient instrument, consisting of broad and large plates of brass of a convex form, like cymbals.

TURB

Tuba, *Lat.* (tū-bä.) A trumpet; also the name of a powerful reed stop in an organ: see Ophicleide.
Tuba clarion, *Lat.* (tū-bä klā-rĭ-ŏn.) A four feet reed stop of the *tuba* species.
Tuba communis, *Lat.* (tū-bä kŏm-mū-nĭs.) An ancient instrument of the trumpet kind; so called in contradistinction to the *tuba ductilis*.
Tuba ductilis, *Lat.* (tū-bä dŭk-tĭl-ĭs.) An ancient trumpet of a curvilinear form.
Tubare, *Lat.* (tū-bä-rĕ.) To blow the trumpet.
Tuba major, *Lat.* (tū-bä mā-jŏr.) }
Tuba mirabilis, *Lat.* (tū-bä mĭ-rā-bĭ-lĭs.) } An eight feet reed stop, on a high pressure of wind, first introduced into the Birmingham Town Hall organ, and invented by William Hill; see Ophicleide.
Tuba stentorofonica, *It.*(too-bä stĕn-tŏr-ō-fōn-ē-kä.) The name given by Sir Samuel Morehead and other writers to his invention of the Speaking Trumpet.
Tubatore, *It.* (too-bä-tō-rĕ.) A trumpeter.
Tubicen, *Lat.* (tū-bĭ-sĕn.) A trumpeter; one who plays on a trumpet.
Tubular instruments. Instruments formed of tubes, straight, or curved, of wood or metal.
Tudel, *Spa.* (too-dĕl.) A metal pipe with a reed, put into a bassoon.
Tuian d'orgue, *Fr.* (twē-ŏ d'ŏrg.) See *Tuyau d'orgue*.
Tumultuóso, *It.* (too-mool-too-ō-zō.) Tumultuous, agitated.
Tunable. An epithet given to those pipes, strings, and other sonorous bodies which, from the equal density of their parts, are capable of being perfectly tuned.
Tune. An air, a melody; a succession of measured sounds, agreeable to the ear, and possessing a distinct and striking character; to bring into harmony.
Tuned. Put in tune.
Tuneful. Harmonious, melodious, musical; as *tuneful* notes, tuneful birds.
Tuneless. Unmelodious, unmusical.
Tune, psalm. A melody adapted to a psalm or hymn.
Tuner. One whose occupation is to tune musical instruments.
Tuning. Putting in tune; rendering the tones of an instrument accordant.
Tuning fork. A small steel instrument, having two prongs, which upon being struck, gives a certain fixed tone, used for tuning instruments, and for ascertaining or indicating the pitch of tunes.
Tuning hammer. A steel or iron utensil used by harpsichord and pianoforte tuners.
Tuning key A *tuning hammer*.
Tuning slide. An English instrument for pitching the key note, producing thirteen semitones—from C to C.
Tuóni ecclesiástici, *It. pl.* (twō-nē ĕk-klā-zā-äs-tē-tshē.) Ecclesiastical modes or tones.
Tuóno, *It.* (twō-nō.) A tone, a sound; a tune.
Tuóno, mézzo, *It.* (twō-nō mät-sō.) A semitone.
Taorbe, *Fr.* (twōrb.) See Theorbo.
Turbo, *Gr.* (tūr-bō.) A sea shell anciently employed as a trumpet.

ā ale, ă add, ä arm, ĕ eve, ĕ end, ī ice, ĭ ill, ō old, ŏ odd, ō dove, oo moon, ū lute, ŭ but, ü French sound.

TURC

Túrca, *It.* (toor-kä.) } Turkish ; *álla*
Turchésco, *It.* (toor-käs-kō.) } *Túrca*, in the
Túrco, *It.* (toor-kō.) } style of Turkish music.
Türkisch, *Ger.* (tür-kĭsh.) See **Türka**.
Turkish music. See Janitscharen-musik.
Turdion, *Spa.* (toor-dĭ-ōn.) An ancient Spanish dance.
Turn. An embellishment formed of appoggiaturas, consisting of the note on which the turn is made, the note above, and the semitone below it.
Turn, back. A turn commencing on the semitone below the note on which the turn is made.
Turn, common. A turn commencing on the note above the note on which the turn is made.
Turn, inverted. An embellishment formed by prefixing three notes to a principal note; viz., the semitone below the principal note, the principal note, and the note above it.
Turn, regular. A turn consisting of the note above the principal note, the principal note and the semitone below it.
Tusch, *Ger.* (toosh.) A flourish of trumpets and kettle drums.
Tute, *Ger.* (too-tĕ.) A cornet.
Tuten, *Ger.* (too-t'n.) To blow the cornet.
Tuter, *Ger.* (too-tĕr.) A cornet player; a cowherd blowing his horn.
Tuthorn, *Ger.* (toot-hōrn.) The horn of a cowherd.
Tutrice, música, *It.* (too-trē-tshē moo-zē-kä.) A female music teacher.
Tútta, *It.* (too-tä.) } All, the whole; entirely,
Tútto, *It.* (too-tō.) } quite.
Tútta fórza, *It.* (too-tä fōr-tsä.) } The
Tútta la fórza, *It.* (too-tä lä fōr-tsä.) } whole power, as loud as possible, with the utmost force and vehemence.

TYRO

Tútte, *It.* (too-tĕ.) } All, the entire band or cho-
Tútti, *It.* (toot-tē.) } rus; In a solo, or concerto it means, that the full orchestra is to come in.
Tútte córde, *It.* (too-tĕ kōr-dĕ.) *All the strings;* in pianoforte music this means that the pedal which shifts the action, or movement, must no longer be pressed down.
Tútti unísoni, *It. pl.* (toot-tē oo-nē-zō-nē.) All in unison.
Tútto árco, *It.* (toot-tō är-kō.) With the whole length of the bow.
Tuyau d'orgue, *Fr.* (tü-yō d'ōrg.) An organ pipe.
Twelfth. An interval comprising eleven conjunct degrees or twelve sounds; also, an organ stop tuned twelve notes above the diapasons.
Twelfth-stop, octave. A stop of an organ sounding an octave higher than the twelfth stop.
Twenty-second. See *Octave-fifteenth*.
Twice-marked octave. The name given in Germany, to the notes between inclusive; these are expressed by small letters with two short strokes.
Twitter. To make a succession of small, tremulous, intermitted tones.
Tye. See *Tie.*
Tymbale. See *Timbale.*
Tymbres. Little bells used to hang upon royal ermine robes: see *Scilla.*
Tympani, *It. pl.* (tăm-pä-nē.) Kettle drums.
Tympanísta. See *Timpanista.*
Tympaníze. To act the part of a drummer.
Tympano, *It.* See *Timpano.*
Tympanon, *Fr.* (tănh-pä-nōnh.) Dulcimer.
Tympanum, *Lat.* (tăm-pä-nŭm.) Timbrel, tabor; old name for the drum.
Type, music. Notes of music cast in metal, or cut in wood, for the purpose of printing.
Tyrolienne, *Fr.* (tĭ-rō-lĭ-ĕn.) Songs, or dances, peculiar to the Tyrolese.

ā *ale*, ă *add*, ä *arm*, ē *eve*, ĕ *end*, ī *ice*, ĭ *ill*, ō *old*, ŏ *odd*, ô *dove*, oo *moon*, ū *tute*, ŭ *but*, ü *French sound*

UEBE — UNME

Uebel-klang, *Ger.* (*ü-bĕl-klăng.*) ⎱ Cacophony,
Uebel-laut, *Ger.* (*ü-bĕl-lout.*) ⎰ dissonance, a discord.
Uebereinstimmung, *Ger.* (*ü-bĕr-īn-stĭm-moong.*) Consonance, harmony, accordance.
Uebergang, *Ger.* (*ü-bĕr-gäng.*) Transition, change of key.
Uebermässig, *Ger.* (*ü-bĕr-mäs-sĭg.*) Augmented, superfluous.
Uebung, *Ger.* (*ü-*boong.) An exercise; a study for the practice of some peculiar difficulty.
Uebungen, *Ger. pl.* (*ü-*boon-ghĕn.) Exercises.
Udita, *It.* (oo-dē-tä.) ⎱ Heard; the sense of hear-
Udito, *It.* (oo-dē-tō.) ⎰ ing.
Uditore, *It.* (oo-dē-tō-rā.) An auditor, listener, hearer.
Ugab, *Heb.* (oo-gäb.) An organ.
Uguále, *It.* (oo-gwä-lē.) Equal, like, similar.
Ugualménte, *It.* (oo-gwäl-mān-tē.) Equally, alike.
Umána, *It.* (oo-*mä*-nä.) ⎱ Human; *vóce umána*,
Umáno, *It.* (oo-*mä*-nō.) ⎰ the human voice.
Umfang, *Ger.* (oom-fǎng.) Compass, extent.
Umfang der stimme, *Ger.* (oom-fǎng dĕr stĭm-mĕ.) Compass of the voice.
Umkehrung, *Ger.* (oom-kā-roong.) Inversion.
Umschreibung, *Ger.* (oom-shrī-boong.) Circumscription, limitation.
Un, *It.* (oon.)
Una, *It.* (oo-nä.) ⎱ A, an, one.
Uno, *It.* (oo-nō.) ⎰
Una altera vólta, *It.* (oo-nä ǎl-tā-rä vōl-tä.) Play it over again.
Unaccented. A term applied to those parts of a measure which have no accent.
Unaccompanied. A song or other vocal composition without instrumental accompaniment.
Unaccordant. Inharmonious.
Unacknowledged note. A passing note, a note foreign to the chord in which it occurs.
Una córda, *It.* (oo-nä kŏr-dä.) One string, on one string only; in pianoforte music it means that the soft pedal is to be used.
Unbezogen, *Ger.* (oon-bĕ-tsō-ghĕn.) Unstrung, not furnished with strings.
Unca, *Lat.* (ŭn-kä.) The old name for a quaver.
Un cánto spianato, *It.* (oon kǎn-tō spē-ä-nä-tō.) A vocal composition, the notes of which are peculiarly distinct from one another.
Und, *Ger.* (oond.) And; *Aria und Chor*, air and chorus.
Unda maris, *Lat.* (ŭn-dä mä-rĭs.) *Wave of the sea;* an organ stop tuned rather sharper than the others, and producing an undulating or waving effect, when drawn in conjunction with another stop; this effect is sometimes produced by means of a pipe with two mouths, the one a little higher than the other.
Undecima, *Lat.* (ŭn-dĕs-i-mä.) The eleventh.
Under part. That part beneath, or subordinate to the other part or parts.
Under song. In very old English music this was a kind of ground, or drone accompaniment to a song, and which was sustained by another singer; called also *burden* and *foot*.
Undulation. That agitation in the air caused by the vibration of any sonorous body. So called because it resembles the motion of waves.
Undulazióne, *It.* (oon-doo-lä-tsē-ō-nē.) Undulation, the expressive, tremulous tone produced by a peculiar pressure of the finger upon the strings of the violin.
Unequal counterpoint. Compositions in notes of unequal duration.
Unequal temperament. That method of tuning the twelve sounds included in an octave, which renders some of the scales more in tune than the others; see *Equal Temperament*.
Unequal voices. Male and female voices both employed in the same piece.
Unessential notes. Those which do not form an essential part of the harmony; passing, auxiliary, or ornamental notes.
Une suite de pièces, *Fr.* (ünh swēt düh pī-ăss.) A series of lessons.
Ungar, *Ger.* (oon-gär.) ⎱ Hungarian; in
Ungarisch, *Ger.* (oon-gä-rĭsh.) ⎰ the Hungarian style.
Ungerade takt-art, *Ger.* (oon-ghĕ-rä-dĕ täkt-ärt.) Triple time; uneven time.
Ungestüm, *Ger.* (oon-ghĕs-tüm.) Impetuous.
Ungezwungen, *Ger.* (oon-ghĕts-voon-g'n.) Easy, natural.
Unharmonious. Dissonant, discordant.
Unharmonischer querstand, *Ger.* (oon-hăr-mō-nĭsh-ĕr quĕr-stǎnd.)
Unharmonischer umstand, *Ger.* (oon-hăr-mō-nĭsh-ĕr oom-stǎnd.)
A false relation.
Unison. An accordance or coincidence of sounds proceeding from an equality in the number of vibrations made in a given time by a sonorous body; a string that has the same sound with another.
Unisonance. Accordance of sounds.
Unisonant. ⎱ Being in unison; having the same
Unisonous. ⎰ degree of gravity or acuteness.
Unisonancia, *Spa.* (oo-nē-zō-nän-*thē*-ä.) Uniformity of sound.
Unison, augmented. A semitone on same degree of staff.
Unisoni, *It. pl.* (oo-nē-zō-nē.) *Unisons;* two, three, or more parts are to play, or sing, in unison with each other; or, if this be not practicable, in octaves.
Unisono, *It.* (oo-nē-zō-nō.) ⎱ A unison, in
Unisonus, *Lat.* (ü-nĭ-sō-nŭs.) ⎰ unison, two or more sounds having the same pitch.
Unitaménte, *It.* (oo-nĭ-tä-mǎn-tē.) Together, jointly, unitedly.
Unite, *Fr.* (ü-nēt.) Unity.
Unity. Such a combination of parts as to constitute a whole, or a kind of symmetry of style and character.
Univalvo, *It.* (oo-nē-*väl*-vō.) Of one value.
Univocal. The epithet applied by Ptolemy to the octave and its replicates.
Univoco, *It.* (oo-nē-vō-kō.) Consisting of one voice or sound.
Unmeasured recitatives. Recitatives without definite measure.
Unmelodious. Wanting melody.

208   PRONOUNCING MUSICAL DICTIONARY.

ă *ale,* ă *add,* ă *arm,* ĕ *eve,* ĕ *end,* ī *ice,* ĭ *ill,* ō *old,* ŏ *odd,* ȯ *dove,* oo *moon,* ū *lute,* ŭ *but,* ü *French sound.*

UNMU . UTSU

Unmusical. Not musical, not harmonious, or agreeable to the ear. Unmusical sounds are those produced by irregular vibrations.
Uno a úno, *It.* (oo-nō ä oo-nō.) One by one, one after another.
Un pen, *Fr.* (ŭnh pŭh.) A little.
Un peu lent, *Fr.* (ŭnh pŭh länh.) Rather slow.
Un peu plus vite qu 'andante, *Fr.* (ŭnh pŭh plü vēt k'änh-dänht.) A little quicker than andante.
Un pochettíno, *It.* (oon pō-kĕt-*tē*-nō.) } A lit-
Un pochína, *It.* (oon pō-*kē*-nä.) } tle, a very little.
Un pochína piu mósso, *It.* (oon pō-*kē*-nä pē-oo-mōs-sō.) A very little more lively.
Un póco, *It.* (oon *pō*-kō.) A little.
Un póco allégro, *It.* (oon *pō*-kō äl-*lā*-grō.) A little quick, rather quick.
Un póco piu, *It.* (oon *pō*-kō pē-oo.) A little more.
Un póco piu présto, *It.* (oon *pō*-kō pē-oo präs-tō.) A little quicker.
Un póco ritenúto, *It.* (oon *pō*-kō rē-tĕ-*noo*-tō.) Gradually slower.
Un recitatívo spianáto, *It.* (oon rä-tshē-tä-*tē*-vō spē-ä-*nä*-tō.) A recitative having notes distinct from each other.
Unsingbar, *Ger.* (oon-*sĭng*-bär.) Impossible to be sung.
Unstrung. Relaxed in tension; an instrument from which the strings have been taken.
Un style aisé, *Fr.* (ŭnh stēl ā-zā.) A free, easy style.
Unter, *Ger.* (oon-tĕr.) Under, below.
Unter-bass, *Ger.* (oon-tĕr bäss.) The double bass.
Unterbrechung, *Ger.* (oon-tĕr-*brĕ*-khoong.) Interruption.
Unterhaltungs-stück, *Ger.* (oon-tĕr-*häl*-toongs stük.) Entertainment, short play, short piece of music.
Untertasten, *Ger.* (oon-tĕr-*täs*-t'n.) The white keys.
Unterricht, *Ger.* (oon-tĕr-*rĭkht*.) Instruction, information.
Untersatz, *Ger.* (oon-tĕr-*sätz*.) Supporter, stay; a pedal register, double stopped bass of thirty-two feet tone, in German organs; see *Sub-Bourdon.*
Un térzo di battúta, *It.* (oon tĕr-tsō dē bät-too-tä.) A third part of the bar.
Untönend, *Ger.* (oon-*tō*-nĕnd.) Not sonorous; void of tone.
Untunable. Incapable of being tuned.
Untune. To put out of tune; to make discordant.
Untuned. Not tuned; discordant.
Up beat. The raising of the hand, or baton, in beating or marking time.
Up bow sign. A mark used in violin music, showing that the bow is to be carried up, ∧.
Upinge, *Ger.* (ū-pĭn-ghē.) The name of a song consecrated by the ancient Greeks to Diana.
Upper voice. A designation applied to the person who sings the higher part.
Upright pianoforte. A pianoforte, the strings of which are placed obliquely or vertically upward.
Uranion. An instrument in make similar to a harpsichord or pianoforte.
Uscir di tuóno, *It.* (oos-tshēr dē *twō*-nō.) To get out of tune.
Usus, *Gr.* (ū-sūs.) That branch of the ancient meloposia which comprehended the rules for so regulating the order or succession of the sounds as to produce an agreeable melody.
Ut, *Fr.* (oot.) The note C; the syllable originally applied by Guido to the note C, or *do*.
Ut bémol, *Fr.* (oot bā-mōl.) The note C-flat.
Ut diese, *Fr.* (oot dī-āz.) The note C-sharp.
Ut diese mineur, *Fr.* (oot dī-āz mē-nŭr.) The key of C-sharp minor.
Ut mineur, *Fr.* (oot mē-nŭr.) C minor.
Ut queant laxis, *Lat.* (ūt *quä*-änt *läx*-ĭs.) The commencing words of the hymn to St. John the Baptist, from which Guido is said to have taken the syllables, *ut, re, mi, fa, sol, la,* for his system of solmisation. It was composed about the year 770.
Utricularis tibia, *Lat.* (ū-*trĭk*-ū-*lā*-rĭs *tĭb*-ĭ-ä.) The name given by the Romans to the bagpipe. See that word.
Ut supra, *Lat.* (ūt sū-prä.) As above, as before; see Come Sopra.

PRONOUNCING MUSICAL DICTIONARY. 209

ă *ale*, ă *'add*, ä *arm*, ĕ *eve*, ĕ *end*, ī *ice*, ĭ *ill*, ō *old*, ŏ *odd*, ô *dove*, oo *moon*, ū *lute*, ŭ *but*, ü *French sound*

VA

Va, *It.* (vä.) Go on.
Vaceto. (vä-tahā-tō.) Quick.
Vaccilándo, *It.* (vät-tshē-*lăn*-dō.) Wavering, uncertain, irregular in the time.
Va con spirito, *It.* (vä kōn *spē*-rē-tō.) Continue in a spirited style.
Va crescéndo, *It.* (vä krē-*shăn*-dō.) Go on increasing the tone.
Vaganti suóni, *It.* (vä-*găn*-tē *swō*-nē.) Movable sounds; the second and third sounds of every tetrachord in the ancient system.
Vágo, *It.* (*vä*-gō.) Vague, rambling, uncertain, as to the time or expression.
Válce, *It.* (*văl*-tshē.) ⎫ A waltz, a dance in 3-4
Valse, *Fr.* (väls.) ⎭ time.
Valeur, *Fr.* (vä-lūr.) ⎫ The value, length, or
Valóre, *It.* (vä-*lō*-rē.) ⎭ duration of a note.
Valse a deux temps, *Fr.* (väls ä dū tänh.) A modern quick waltz, in which the dancers make two steps in each measure.
Valse de l'oiseau, *Fr.* (väla dŭh l'*wä*-sō.) A waltz in imitation of the warbling of a bird.
Valve. A close lid or other contrivance designed to retard or modify the sound of an organ pipe or any wind instrument.
Valve horn. A horn in which a portion of the tube is opened or closed by the use of valves, whereby a higher or lower pitch is obtained.
Valve trumpets, whose tones are varied by the use of valves.
Va rallentándo, *It.* (vä räl-lĕn-*tăn*-dō.) Go on dragging the time, continue to drag the time.
Variaménte, *It.* (vä-rē-ä-*măn*-tē.) ⎫ In a varied,
Variaménto, *It.* (vä-rē-ä-*măn*-tō.) ⎭ free style of performance, or execution.
Variations. Repetitions of a theme or subject in new and varied aspects, the form or outline of the composition being preserved while the different passages are ornamented and amplified.
Variationen, *Ger. pl.* (fä-rē-ä-tē-ō-nĕn.) ⎫ Vari-
Variazióni. *It. pl.* (vä-rē-ä-tsē-ō-nē.) ⎭ ations.
Variazióne, *It.* (vä-rē-ä-tsē-ō-nē.) Variation.
Variáto, *It.* (vä-rē-*ä*-tō.) ⎫ Varied, diversified,
Varié, *Fr.* (vä-rē-*ä*.) ⎭ with variations.
Vaudevil. A ballad, a song, a vaudeville.
Vaudeville, *Fr.* (vō-dĕ-*vēl*.) A country ballad or song, a roundelay: also, a simple form of operétta; a comedy, or short drama, interspersed with songs.
Vedel, *Dut.* (fä-dĕl.) A fiddle.
Veeménte, *It.* (vä-*măn*-tē.) Vehement, forcible.
Veeménza, *It.* (vä-*măn*-tsä.) Vehemence, force.
Veláta, *It.* (vä-*lä*-tä.) ⎫ *Veiled;* a voice sound-
Veláto, *It.* (vä-*lä*-tō.) ⎭ ing as if it were covered with a veil.
Vellutáta. (vĕl-loo-*tä*-tä.) ⎫ In a velvety manner;
Vellutáto. (vĕl-loo-*tä*-tō.) ⎭ in a soft, smooth, and velvety style.
Velóce, *It.* (vē-*lō*-tshē.) ⎫ Swiftly,
Velocemente. (vē-lō-tshĕ-*măn*-tē.) ⎭ quickly, in a rapid time.
Velocissimaménte, *It.* (vē-lō-tshēs-sē-mä-*măn*-tē.)
Velocissimo, *It.* (vē-lō-*tshēs*-sē-mō.) Very swiftly, with extreme rapidity.
Velocita, *It.* (vē-lō-*tshē*-tä.) Swiftness, rapidity.

VERS

Veneziána, *It.* (vĕ-nä-tsē-*ä*-nä.) Venetian, the Venetian style.
Ventil, *Ger.* (*fĕn*-tĭl.) ⎫ Valve, in modern
Ventile, *It.* (vĕn-*tē*-lē.) ⎭ wind-instruments, for producing the semitones; also, a valve for shutting off the wind in an organ.
Venústo, *It.* (vē-*noos*-tō.) Beautiful; sweetly, gracefully.
Vêpres, *Fr.* (väpr.) Vespers, evening prayers.
Veränderungen, *Gr. pl.* (fĕ-rän-dĕ-roong-ĕn.) Variations.
Verbindung, *Ger.* (fĕr-*bĭn*-doong.) Combination, union, connexion.
Vergeilen, *Ger.* (fĕr-*ghīl*-l'n.) To diminish gradually.
Verger. The chief officer of a cathedral; a pew opener or attendant at a church.
Vergette, *It.* (vĕr-*gät*-tē.) ⎫ The tail or stem
Verghetta, *It.* (vĕr-*gät*-tä.) ⎭ of a note.
Vergliedern, *Ger.* (fĕr-*glē*-dĕrn.) To articulate.
Verhallen, *Ger.* (fĕr-*häl*-l'n.) To diminish gradually.
Verhallend, *Ger.* (fĕr-*häl*-lĕnd.) Dying away.
Verilay. Rustic ballad, a roundelay: see Vaudeville, and also, Freemen's songs.
Verlagsrecht, *Ger.* (fĕr-*lägs*-rĕkht.) Copyright.
Verlöschend, *Ger.* (fĕr-*lō*-shĕnd.) Extinguishing.
Vermindert, *Ger.* (fĕr-*mĭn*-dĕrt.) Diminished; diminished interval.
Vers, *Ger.* (fĕrs.) Verse, atrophe, stanza.
Verschen, *Ger.* (*fĕrs*-chĕn.) A small verse.
Verschiebung, *Ger.* (fĕr-*shē*-boong.) Delay; *mit Verschiebung*, with delay, lingering, retardation.
Verse. That portion of an anthem, or service, intended to be sung by one singer to each part, and not by the full choir in chorus. In secular music, as a song or ballad, each stanza of the words is a verse.
Verse, acatalectic. A verse having the complete number of syllables, without defect or excess.
Verse, adonic. A verse consisting of one long and two short and two long syllables.
Verse, alcaic. A form of verse employed by the poet Alcæus, consisting of two dactyls and two trochees.
Verse, alexandrian. A form of verse consisting of twelve syllables, or twelve and thirteen alternately, first introduced in a poem entitled the Alexandriad.
Verse, anapestic. A verse each metrical foot of which contains two short syllables and one long one.
Verse and chorus anthem. An anthem composed of verse and chorus, but commencing with chorus.
Verse anthem. An anthem which contains a solo, duet, etc., or one or more *verses:* see *Verse,* and *Full Anthem.*
Verse bringen, *Ger.* (fĕr-sĕ bring-ĕn.) To versify.
Verse, catalectic. Verse wanting a syllable at the end; terminating with an imperfect foot.
Verse, dactylic. A verse ending with a dactyl instead of a spondee.

14

ă ale, ă add, ä arm, ĕ eve, ĕ end, ī ice, ĭ ill, ō old, ŏ odd, ō dove, oo moon, ū lute, ŭ but, ü French sound.

VERS

Verse, epic. Hexameter verse used in the epic poetry of the Greeks and Romans.
Verse, heroic. That in which acts of heroism are commemorated; in Greek and Latin, the hexameter; in Italian, German, and English, the iambic of ten syllables; in French, the iambic of twelve syllables.
Verse, hexameter. A verse having six feet, of which the first four may be either dactyls or spondees, the fifth must be a dactyl, and the sixth a spondee.
Verse, iambic. A verse consisting of a short syllable followed by a long one, or of an unaccented syllable followed by an accented one.
Verse, lyric. Verse designed to be sung; among the ancients, verse sung to an accompaniment of the lyre.
Verse service. A service in which *verses* are introduced: see *Full Services*.
Verse, spondaic. A verse formed of spondees, that is, of feet consisting of two long syllables.
Versétta, *It.* (věr-sĕt-tä.) ⎫ A short, or little
Versétto, *It.* (věr-sĕt-tō.) ⎭ verse, a strophe.
Versette, *Ger.* (fěr-sĕt-tĕ.) ⎫ Short pieces for
Versetten, *Ger.* (fěr-sĕt-t'n.) ⎭ the organ, intended as preludes, interludes, or poetludes.
Versetzen, *Ger.* (fěr-sĕt-tsěn.) To transpose.
Versetzung, *Ger.* (fěr-sĕt-tsoong.) Transposition.
Versetzungs-zeichen, *Ger.* (fěr-sĕt-tsoongs tsī-kh'n.) The marks of transposition, the *sharp*, the *flat*, and the *natural*.
Versicle. A little verse.
Versikel, *Ger.* (fěr-sĭk'l.) ⎫ A versicle.
Versillo, *Spa.* (věr-sĕl-yō.) ⎭
Vérsi sciólti, *It.* (vär-sē shē-ōl-tē.) The name given by the Italians to their blank verse. The recitative portions of their operas are generally written in *vérsi sciólti*.
Versmass, *Ger.* (fěre-mäss.) The measure of the verse; the metre.
Vérso, *It.* (vär-sō.) Verse.
Vérso eróico, *It.* (vär-sō ā-rō-ē-kō.) Heroic verse.
Vérso obligáto, *It.* (vär-sō ŏb-lē-gä-tō.) A style of improvisation in which a set rhyme and theme are proscribed.
Vérso sciólto, *It.* (vär-sō shē-ōl-tō.) Blank verse.
Verspätung, *Ger.* (fěr-spä-toong.) Retardation, delay.
Verstimmt, *Ger.* (fěr-stĭmt.) Out of tune.
Versus Fescennini. Nuptial songs, so called because they were first used by the people of Fescennia, a city of Etruria.
Vertatur, *Lat.* (věr-tä-tür.) ⎫ Turn over.
Verte, *Lat.* (věr-tĕ.) ⎭
Verte subito, *Lat.* (věr-tĕ sŭb-ī-tō.) Turn the leaf quickly.
Vertical slur. A perpendicular slur, or curved line, denoting that the chord before which it stands is to be performed in imitation of harp music, or in arpeggio style.

VIEL

Vertönen, *Ger.* (fěr-tō-nĕn.) To cease sounding, to die away.
Verwandt, *Ger.* (fěr-vändt.) Related, relative keys, etc.
Verwechselung, *Ger.* (fěr-vĕk h-sĕl-oong.) Changing, mutation, as to key, tone, etc.
Verweilend, *Ger.* (fěr-vī-lĕnd.) Delaying, retarding the time.
Verwerfung, *Ger.* (fěr-věrf-oong.) Transposing.
Verziert, *Ger.* (fěr-tsērt.) Embellished, decorated.
Verzierung, *Ger.* (fěr-tsē-roong.) Embellishment, ornament.
Verzögerung, *Ger.* (fěr-tsō-ghē-roong.) Retardation.
Vesperæ, *Lat.* (věs-pě-rē.) Vespers, or the evening service in the Roman Catholic church.
Vesper, *Ger.* (fěs-pěr.)
Véspero, *It.* (vās-pĕ-rō.) ⎫ Vespers.
Véspro, *It.* (vās-prō.) ⎭
Vespers. Name of the last evening-service in the Roman Catholic church, consisting chiefly of singing.
Vesper bell. The sounding of a bell about half an hour after sunset in Roman Catholic countries, calling to vespers.
Vesper hymn. A hymn sung in the evening service of the Roman Catholic church.
Vespertini psalmi, *It. pl.* (věs-pěr-tē-nē peälmē.) Evening psalms or hymns.
Vezzosaménte, *It.* (vāt-tsō-zä-mān-tě.) Tenderly, softly, gracefully.
Vezzóso, *It.* (vāt-tsō-zō.) Graceful, sweet, tender.
Vibránte, *It.* (vē-brän-tě.) Vibrating, a tremulous, quivering touch, full resonance of tone.
Vibráte, *It.* (vē-brä-tě.) ⎫ A strong, vibrating,
Vibráto, *It.* (vē-brä-tō.) ⎭ full quality of tone; resonant.
Vibration. The tremulous or undulatory motion of any sonorous body by which the sound is produced, the sound being grave or acute as the vibrations are fewer or more numerous in a given time.
Vibratíssimo, *It.* (vē-brä-tēs-sē-mō.) Extremely vibrating and tremulous.
Vibrazióne, *It.* (vē-b rä-tsē-ō-n ě.) Vibration, tremulousness.
Vibráto mólto, *It.* (vē-brä-tō mōl-tō.) Extremely rapid.
Vicénda, *It.* (vē-tshān-dä.) Alternation, change.
Vicendévole, *It.* (vē-tshēn-dā-vō-lě.)
Vicendevoleménte, *It.* (vē-tshēn-dā-vō-lāmān-tě.) ⎭ Alternately, by turns.
Vide, *Fr.* (věd.) ⎫ See Vuide.
Vido, *It.* (vē-dō.) ⎭
Videl, *Ger.* (fīd-ĕl.) A fiddle.
Viel. An old name for instruments of the violin species.
Viel, *Ger.* (fēl.) Much, a great deal; *mit vielem Tone*, with much tone.
Vielle, *Fr.* (vēl.) The hurdy-gurdy.
Vielleur, *Fr.* (vē-yūr.) Hurdy-gurdy player.
Viel-stimmig, *Ger.* (fēl-stĭm-mĭg.) For many voices.

ă ale, ă add, ä arm, ē eve, ĕ end, ī ice, ĭ ill, ō old, ŏ odd, ō dove, oo moon, ū lute, ŭ but, ü French sound.

VIEL

Viel-stimmiges tonstück, Ger. (fēl stĭm-mĭ-ghĕs tōn-stŭk.) A piece for several voices, a choral piece, a glee.
Viel-tönig, Ger. (fēl tō-nĭg.) Multisonous, many sounding.
Vier, Ger. (fēr.) Four.
Viergestrichene note, Ger. (fēr-ghĕ-strī-khĕn-ĕ nō-tĕ.) A demisemiquaver.
Vier-fach, Ger. (fēr fäkh.) Four-fold, of four ranks of pipes, etc.
Vier-gesang, Ger. (fēr ghĕ-säng.) Song for four voices.
Vier-händig, Ger. (fēr hän-dĭg.) For four hands.
Vier-händiges tonstück, Ger. (fēr hän-dĭ-ghĕs tōn-stŭk.) A piece for four hands.
Vier-massig, Ger. (fēr mäs-sĭg.) Containing four measures.
Vier-saitig, Ger. (fēr sī-tĭg.) Four stringed.
Vier-saitige leier, Ger. (fēr sī-tĭ-ghĕ lī-ēr.) A four stringed lyre, a tetrachord.
Vier-spiel, Ger. (fēr spēl.) Quartet; for four performers.
Vier-stimmig, Ger. (fēr stĭm-mĭg.) Four voiced, in four parts, for four voices or instruments.
Vier-stimmiges tonstück, Ger. (fēr stĭm-mĭ-ghĕs tōn-stŭk.) A quartet.
Vier-stück, Ger. (fēr stŭk.) Quartet; for four performers.
Vierte, Ger. (fēr-tĕ.) Fourth.
Viertel-note, Ger. (fēr-t'l nō-tĕ.) Quarter-note; a crotchet, the fourth part of a semibreve.
Viertel-ton, Ger. (fēr-t'l tōn.) A quarter-tone.
Vierundsechzigstel, Ger. (fēr-oond-sěkh-tsĭg-stĕl.) Hemidemisemiquavers.
Vier-viertel-tact, Ger. (fēr fēr-t'l täkt.) Common time of four crotchets.
Vier-zweitel-tact, Ger. (fēr tsvī-t'l tä kt.) Time of four minims.
Vierzehn, Ger. (fēr-tsān.) Fourteen.
Vierzehnte, Ger. (fēr-tsĕn-tĕ.) Fourteenth.
Vietáto, It. (vē-ä-tä-tō.) Forbidden, prohibited; a term applied to such intervals and modulations as are not allowed by the laws of harmony.
Vif, Fr. (vēf) Lively, brisk, quick, sprightly.
Vigorosaménte, It. (vē-gō-rō-zä-mĕn-tĕ.) Vigorously, with energy.
Vigoróso, It. (vē-gō-rō-zō.) Vigorous, bold, energetic.
Vigüéla, Spa. (vē-goo-ā-lä.) A species of lute or guitar.
Vihuela, Spa. (vē-hoo-ā-lä.) Guitar.
Vihuelista, Spa. (vē-hwā-lēs-tä.) A guitar player.
Villageois, Fr. (vēl-lä-zhwä.) Rustic; à la villageoise, in a rustic style.
Villáncico, Sp. (vēl-yän-thē-kō.) } A species of
Villáncio, Sp. (vēl-yän-thī-ō.) } pastoral poem or song.
Villanélla, It. (vēl-lä-nĕl-lä.) } An old rustic
Villanélle, Fr. (vē-ä-nĕl.) } Italian dance, accompanied with singing.
Villánicos. See Villancico.
Villótte, It. (vēl-lŏt-tĕ.) An old name for secular music in parts.
Vináte, It. (vē-nä-tĕ.) Drinking songs.
Vinettes. See Vinate.

VIOL

Viol. An old instrument somewhat resembling the violin, of which it was the origin: it had six strings, with frets, and was played with a bow.
Vióla. A tenor violin; an instrument similar in tone and formation to the violin, but larger in size and having a compass a fifth lower.
Vióla da bráccio, It. (vē-ō-lä dä brät-tshē-ō.) The vióla; thus named because it rested on the arm.
Vióla d'amóre, It. (vē-ō-lä d'ä-mō-rĕ.) } An instrument
Viole d'amour, Fr. (vē-ōl d'ä-moor.) } a little larger than the vióla, furnished with frets, and a greater number of strings, some above the finger-board and some below. The name is also given to an organ stop of similar quality to the gamba, or salcional.
Vióla pompósa, It. (vē-ō-lä pōm-pō-zä.) An enlarged viol or vióla of the same compass as the violoncéllo, but with the addition of a fifth string. It is said to have been invented by J. S. Bach. It is no longer used.
Violars. Players on the viol, about the tenth and following centuries. Their office was to accompany the Troubadours, or bards, when they recited their poetry.
Viol da bráccio, It. (vē-ōl dä brät-tshē-ō.) See Vióla da Bráccio.
Viol da gámba, It. (vē-ōl dä gäm-bä.) } Leg-
Viol di gámba, It. (vē-ōl dē gäm-bä.) } viol; an instrument formerly much used in Germany, but nearly obsolete. It was a little smaller than the violincello, furnished with frets and five or six strings and held between the legs in playing, hence its name.
Viol, bass. The violoncello; a stringed instrument in the form of a violin, but much larger, having four strings, and is performed on with a bow.
Viol, double-bass. The largest and deepest-toned of stringed instruments.
Viole, Ger. (fē-ō-lĕ.) } The vióla.
Viole, Fr. (vē-ōl.) }
Viole alt. Ger. (fī-ō-lĕ ält.) The tenor violin.
Violentemĕnte, It. (vē-ō-lĕn-tĕ-mĕn-tĕ.) Violently, with force.
Violĕnto, It. (vē-ō-lĕn-tō.) Violent, vehement, boisterous.
Violĕnza, It. (vē-ō-lĕn-tsä.) Violence, force, vehemence.
Violet. A species of viole d'amour, with only six strings; the name is also applied to a gamba stop of four feet.
Violétta, It. (vē-ō-lĕt-tä.) Small alto viol.
Violétta marína, It. (vē-ō-lĕt-tä mä-rē-nä.) A stringed instrument not now in use, supposed to have been similar in shape and tone to the viole d'amour; the marine trumpet.
Viol, harpsichord. An instrument invented in Paris in 1717, resembling a viol, placed upon a table, and played with a wheel instead of a bow, producing a sound resembling that of a viol.
Violicembalo. A pianoforte played with a bow, invented in 1823.
Violin. A well known stringed instrument having four strings, and played with a bow. It is the most perfect musical instrument known, of brilliant tone and capable of every variety of ex-

ă *ate,* ă *add,* ä *arm,* ĕ *eve,* ĕ *end,* ī *ice,* ĭ *ill,* ō *old,* ŏ *odd,* ô *dove,* oo *moon,* ū *tute,* ŭ *but,* ü *French sound.*

VIOL

pression. When, or by what nation, this important instrument was first invented is not at present known.

Violinbogen, *Ger.* (fĭ-ō-lĭn-bō-g'n.) A violin bow.
Violine, *Ger.* (fĭ-ō-lĭn-ĕ.) The violin; also, an organ stop of eight, four or two feet.
Violinete, *Spa.* (vē-ō-lē-nā-tĕ.) A kit; pocket violin.
Violinier, *Fr.* (vē-ō-lĭ-nĕr.) A violinist.
Violinist. A performer on the violin.
Violinista, *It.* (vē-ō-lēn-ĕs-tä.) } A violinist.
Violinista, *Spa.* (vē-ō-lēn-ĕs-tä.) }
Violini unisoni, *It.* (vē-ō-lē-nē oo-nē-zō-nē.) The violins in unison.
Violin mute, folding. An article designed to increase the softness and purity of the tone of a violin.
Violino, *It.* (vē-ō-lē-nō.) The violin; it attained its present shape, with four strings, in the sixteenth century.
Violino, alto, *It.* (vē-ō-lē-nō äl-tō.) Counter tenor viol, or small tenor viol, on which the alto may be played.
Violin oder G, schlüssel, *Ger.* (fĭ-ō-lĭn ō-dĕr G shlüs-s'l.) The treble or G clef.
Vionlino picciolo, *It.* (vē-ō-lē-nō pāt-tshē-ō-lō.)
Violino piccolo, *It.* (vē-ō-lē-nō pĕk-kō-lō.)
Violino pochetto, *It.* (vē-ō-lē-nō pō-khāt-tō.) A small violin.
Violino primo, *It.* (vē-ō-lē-nō prē-mō.)
Violino principále, *It.* (vē-ō-lē-nō prĕn-tshē-pä-lĕ.)
The first, or principal violin part; the leading violin, or *chef d'attaque.*
Violin-principal. An eight or four feet organ stop, with an agreeable and violin-like tone.
Violin-saite, *Ger.* (fĭ-ō-lĭn sī-tĕ.) Violin string.
Violin-schlüssel, *Ger.* (fĭ-ō-lĭn shlüs-s'l.) }
Violin-zeichen, *Ger.* (fĭ-ō-lĭn tsī-kh'n.) }
The treble clef used for the violin.
Violin-steg. *Ger.* (fĭ-ō-lĭn stĕgh.) Violin bridge.
Violin-schule, *Ger.* (fĭ-ō-lĭn shoo-lĕ.) School for the violin.
Violin-spieler, *Ger.* (fĭ-ō-lĭn spē-lĕr.) A violin player.
Violin-stimme, *Ger.* (fĭ-ō-lĭn stĭm-mĕ.) Part for the violin.
Violin, tenor. A violin of low tone.
Violin-virtuosinn, *Ger.* (fĭ-ō-lĭn fĭr-too-ō-zĭnn.) A first class violinist; a virtuoso on the violin.
Viol, leg. The viola di gamba; the bass viol.
Violon, *Fr.* (vī-ō-lônh.) The French name for the violin.
Violon, *Ger.* (fĭ-ō-lŏn.) The double bass; see also. *Violóne.*
Violoncell, *Ger.* (fĭ-ō-lŏn-tsĕll.) } The large,
Violoncelle, *Fr.* (vĭ-ō-lŏnh-sĕll.) } or bass violoncello.
Violoncéllo, *It.* (vē-ō-lŏn-tshĕl-lō.) } lin; the name is also applied to an organ stop of small scale, and crisp tone.
Violoncellist. A player on the violoncello.
Violoncellista, *It.* (vē-ō-lŏn-tshēl-ēs-tä.) A violoncellist.
Violoncello, double-toned. A violoncello having steel wires within it drawn to a high degree of tension.

VIVI

Violonchelo, *Spa.* (vē-ō-lŏn-kā-lō.) Violoncello.
Violóne, *It.* (vē-ō-lō-nĕ.) } The name originally
Violóno, *It.* (vē-ō-lō-nō.) } given to the violoncello but afterward transferred to the double bass. Its pitch is an octave below that of the violoncello and its true use is to sustain the harmony; the name is also applied to an open wood stop, of much smaller scale than the diapason, on the pedals of an organ.
Viols, chest of. An expression formerly applied to a set of viols, consisting of six, the particular use of which was to play fantasias in six parts, generally two each of bass. tenor and treble.
Virelay. A rustic song or ballad, in the fourteenth century; nearly the same as the roundel, but with this difference, the roundel begins and ends with the same sentence, or strain, but the virelay is under no such restriction.
Virginal. A small keyed instrument, much used about the time of Queen Elizabeth, and placed upon a table when played upon. It is supposed to have been the origin of the spinet as the latter was of the harpsichord.
Vírgula, *Lat.* (vĕr-gū-lä.) The name of one of the ten notes used in the middle ages.
Virgulum, *Lat.* (vĕr-gū-lŭm.) The term formerly applied to that part of a note now called the tail or stem.
Virtu, *It.* (vĕr-too.) } Taste and
Virtuosita, *It.* (vĕr-too-ō-zē-tä.) } skill in performance.
Virtnose, *Ger.* (fĭr-too-ō-zĕ.) } A skillful performer
Virtúoso, *It.* (vĕr-too-ō-zō.) } former upon some instrument.
Virtuosität, *Ger.* (fĭr-too-ō-zĭ-tät.) Remarkable proficiency, fine execution; applied both to singers and players.
Vista. *It.* (vēs-tä.) Sight; *à prima vista,* at first sight.
Vistaménte, *It.* (vēs-tä-mān-tĕ.) } Quickly,
Vitaménte. *It.* (vē-tä-mān-tĕ.) } swiftly, briskly, immediately.
Vite, *Fr.* (vēt.) } Quickly, swiftly;
Vitement, *Fr.* (vēt-mänh.) } *un peu plus vite,* a little more quickly.
Vitesse, *Fr.* (vē-tĕss.) Swiftness, quickness.
Vitten, *Dut.* (fĭt-t'n.) To sing.
Viula. Name given, in the twelfth century, to the viol.
Vivaće, *It.* (vē-vä-tshĕ.) } Lively,
Vivaceménte, *It.* (vē-vä-tshē-mān-tĕ.) } briskly, quickly.
Vivaće, ma non tróppo présto. *It.* (vē-vä-tshĕ, mä nōn trŏp-pō prĕs-tō.) Lively, but not too quick.
Vivacétto, *It.* (vē-vä-tshĕt-tō.) A little lively, somewhat quick.
Vivacézza, *It.* (vē-vä-tshĕt-sä.) } Vivacity, live
Vivacita. *It.* (vē-vä-tshē-tä.) } liness.
Vivacíssimo, *It.* (vē-vä-tshēs-sē-mō.) Very lively, extreme vivacity.
Vivaménte, *It.* (vē-vä-mān-tĕ.) In a lively, brisk manner.
Vive, *Fr.* (vēv.) Lively, brisk, quick, sprightly.
Vivénte, *It.* (vē-vĕn-tĕ.) Animated, lively.
Vivézza, *It.* (vē-vĕt-tsä.) Vivacity, liveliness.
Vívido, *It.* (vē-vē-dō.) Lively, brisk.

ă *ale*, ă *add*, ä *arm*, ē *eve*, ĕ *end*, ī *ice*, ĭ *ill*, ō *old*, ŏ *odd*, ô *dove*, oo *moon*, ū *lute*, ŭ *but*, ü *French sound*.

VIVO

Vivo, *It.* (vē-vō.) Animated, lively, brisk.
Vivóla, *It.* (vē-vō-lä.) A viol, common in the fourteenth century.
Vocal. Belonging or relating to the human voice.
Vocále, *It.* (vō-kä-lĕ.) Vocal, belonging to the voice.
Vocalézzo, *It.* (vō-kä-lät-tsō.) A vocal exercise.
Vocalist. A singer.
Vocality. Quality of being utterable by the voice.
Vocalization. Command of the voice, vocal execution; also, vocal writing or composition.
Vocalize. To practice vocal exercises, using the vowels and the letter A sounded in the Italian manner, for the purpose of developing the voice and of acquiring skill and flexibility.
Vocalizes. Solfeggios; exercises for the voice.
Vocalizzare, *It.* (vō-kä-lĕt-tsä-rĕ.) To vocalize; to sing exercises for the voice.
Vocalizzi, *It. pl.* (vō-kä-lĕt-tsē.) Vocal exercises, to be sung on the vowels.
Vocal apparatus. The various organs which are employed in the formation and production of vocal sounds.
Vocal music. Music composed for the voice.
Vocal score. An arrangement of all the separate voice parts, placed in their proper order under each other, and used by the conductor of a vocal performance.
Vóce, *It.* (vō-tshĕ.) The voice.
Vóce di cámera, *It.* (vō-tshĕ dĕ kä-mä-rä.) Voice for the chamber; one suited for private, rather than public, singing.
Vóce di góla, *It.* (vō-tshĕ dĕ gō-lä.) The throat voice; also, a gutteral voice.
Vóce di pétto, *It.* (vō-tshĕ dĕ pät-tō.) The chest voice, the lowest register of the voice.
Vóce di tésta, *It.* (vō-tshĕ dĕ tās-tä.) The head voice, the *falsetto* or feigned voice; the upper register of the voice.
Vóce fiébile, *It.* (vō-tshĕ flā-bē-lĕ.) A doleful voice.
Vóce graníta, *It.* (vō-tshĕ grä-nē-tä.) A firm, massive voice, round and full.
Vóce intonáta, *It.* (vō-tshĕ ēn-tō-nä-tä.) A pure-toned voice.
Vóce mézza, *It.* (vō-tshĕ mät-tsä.) Half the power of the voice; a moderate, subdued tone, rather soft than loud.
Vóce musicále, *It.* (vō-tshĕ moo-zē-kä-lĕ.) The appellation by which the Italians formerly distinguished the tonic, or major key note; in solmization called *do*.
Vóce pastósa, *It.* (vō-tshĕ päs-tō-zä.) A soft flexible voice.
Vóce piacente, *It.* (vō-tshĕ pē-ä-tshän-tĕ.) A pleasing voice.
Vóce ráuca, *It.* (vō-tshĕ rä-oo-kä.) A hoarse, rough voice.
Vocerellína, *It.* (vō-tshĕ räl-lē-nä.) A pretty little voice.
Vóce sóla, *It.* (vō-tshĕ sō-lä.) The voice alone.
Vóce spianáta, *It.* (vō-tshĕ spē-ä-nä-tä.) *Drawn out;* an even, smooth, sustained voice.
Vóce spiccáta, *It.* (vō-tshĕ spĕk-kä-tä.) A clear, distinct voice, well articulated.
Vóce umána, *It.* (vō-tshĕ oo-mä-nä.) The human voice.

VOIX

Vociáccia, *It.* (vō-tshĕ-ät-tshĕ-ä.) A bad, disagreeable voice.
Vocína, *It.* (vō-tshē-nä.) A little, thin voice.
Vocíno, *It.* (vō-tshē-nō.) A pleasing little voice.
Vociolína, *It.* (vō-tshē-ō-lē-nä.) A small, thin voice.
Vocióne, *It.* (vō-tshē-ō-nĕ.) A strong, loud voice.
Vogel-flöte. *Ger.* (fō-g'l flō-tĕ.) Bird-flute.
Vogel-pfeife, *Ger.* (fō-g'l pfī-fĕ.) Bird-call, flageolet.
Vogel-gesang, *Ger.* (fō-g'l ghĕ-säng.) *Singing of birds;* an accessory stop in some very old German organs, producing a chirping effect, by some little pipes standing in a vessel with water, through which the wind passes to them.
Vóglia, *It.* (vōl-yĕ-ä.) Desire, longing, ardor, fervor.
Voice. The sound or sounds produced by the vocal organs in singing; applied also to the tuning, and quality of tone, of organ pipes, the *voicing* being a most important part of the organ-builder's work. To voice, also means, writing the voice parts, regard being had to the nature and capabilities of each kind of voice.
Voice, alto. The lowest female voice.
Voice, baritone. A male voice, intermediate in respect to pitch, between the bass and tenor, the compass usually extending from B flat to G.
Voice, bass. The gravest or deepest of the male voices.
Voice, chamber. A voice suited to the performance of parlor music.
Voice, chest. The register of the chest tones.
Voice, falsetto. *Head voice; feigned voice;* certain notes in a man's voice which are above its natural compass, and which can only be produced in an artificial, or feigned tone.
Voice, first. The soprano.
Voice, fourth. The bass.
Voice, guttural. A voice produced by a contracted pharynx.
Voice, head. The highest register of the female voice; the falsetto in male voices.
Voice, nasal. A voice unduly affected by the nose.
Voice, pure. A voice proceeding freely, and not affected by nasal, labial, guttural, or other tones.
Voices accessory. Accompanying voices.
Voice, second. The alto.
Voice, soprano. The highest female voice.
Voices, principal. The bass and soprano; the highest and lowest.
Voice, tenor. The highest male voice.
Voice, third. The tenor voice.
Voice, treble. The soprano.
Voice parts. The vocal parts, chorus parts.
Voicing. The adjustment of the parts of an organ pipe for the purpose of giving it its proper pitch and its peculiar character of sound.
Voix, *Fr.* (vwä.) The voice.
Voix aigre, *Fr.* (vwäsägr.) Harsh voice.
Voix argentine, *Fr.* (vwäsär-zhänh-tēn.) A clear-toned voice, a silvery voice.
Voix célestes, *Fr.* (vwä sä-lĕst.) *Celestial voices;* an organ stop of French invention, formed of two dulcianas, one of which has the pitch slightly raised, which gives to the stop a waving,

214   PRONOUNCING MUSICAL DICTIONARY.

ă *ale*, ă *add*, ă *arm*, ē *eve*, ĕ *end*, ī *ice*, ĭ *ill*, ō *old*, ŏ *odd*, ö *dove*, oo *moon*, ū *lute*, ŭ *but*, ü *French sound*.

VIOX

undulating character; also, a soft stop on the harmonium.
Voix de poitrine, *Fr.* (vwä düh pwä-trĕnn.) Chest voice, natural voice.
Voix de tete, *Fr.* (vwä düh tāt.) Head voice, falsetto voice.
Voix éclatante, *Fr.* (vwä'ä-klä-tänht.) Loud, piercing voice.
Voix glapissante, *Fr.* (vwä glä-pē-sänht.) A shrill voice.
Voix grele, *Fr.* (vwä grāl.) A sharp, thin voice.
Voix humaine, *Fr.* (vwä hü-mänh.) See *Vox Humana*.
Voix perçante, *Fr.* (vwä pēr-sänh t.) Shrill voice.
Voix perlée, *Fr.* (vwä pĕr-lā.) A pearly voice.
Voix ronde, *Fr.* (vwä rönhd.) A round, full voice.
Voix trainante, *Fr.* (vwä trä-nänht.) A drawling voice.
Volánte, *It.* (vō-län-tĕ.) *Flying;* a light and rapid series of notes.
Voláta, *It.* (vō-lä-tä.) A flight, run, rapid series of notes, a *roulade*, or *division*.
Voláte, *It. pl.* (vō-lä-tĕ.) See *Voláta*.
Volatína, *It.* (vō-lä-tē-nä.) A little flight, etc.: see *Voláta*.
Volatine, *It. pl.* (vō-lä-tē-nĕ.) Short runs: see *Voláta*.
Volée, *Fr.* (vō-lā.) A rapid flight of notes.
Volks-gesang, *Ger.* (fŏlks ghĕ-säng.)
Volks-lied, *Ger.* (fŏlks lēd.)
Volks-stückchen, *Ger.* (fŏlks stük-kh'n.) National song, popular air, tune, or ballad.
Voll, *Ger.* (fŏll.) Full; *mit vollem werke*, with the full organ.
Volle orgel, *Ger.* (fŏl-lĕ ōr-g'l.) Full organ.
Volle werk, *Ger.* (fŏl-lĕ värk.) See Volles Werk.
Völler, *Ger.* (fŏl-lĕr.) Fuller, louder.
Volles werk, *Ger.* (fŏl-lĕs värk.) The full organ.
Voll-gesang, *Ger.* (fŏll ghĕ-säng.) Chorus.
Vollkommen, *Ger.* (fŏll-kŏm-mĕn.) Perfect, complete.
Voll-stinmig, *Ger.* (fŏll stĭm-mĭg.) Full-toned, full-voiced.
Voll-stimmigkeit, *Ger.* (fŏll stĭm-mĭg-kīt.) Fullness of tone.
Voll-tönend, *Ger.* (fŏll tö-nĕnd.) Full sounding, sonorous.
Voll-tönige stimme, *Ger.* (fŏll tö-nĭ-ghĕ stĭm-mĕ.) Full-toned, sonorous voice.
Volonté, *Fr.* (vō-lönh-tā.) Will, pleasure: *à volonté*, at will.
Vólta, *It.* (vōl-tä.) Time; also, an old, three-timed air, peculiar to an Italian dance of the same name, and forming a kind of galliard.
Vólta prima, *It.* (vōl-tä prē-mä.) First time.
Voltáre, *It.* (vōl-tä-rĕ.) To turn, to turn over.
Vólta seconda, *It.* (vōl-tä sĕ-kōn-dä.) The second time.
Vólte, *It.* (vōl-tĕ.)) An obsolete dance in 3-4
Volte, *Fr.* (vŏlt.)) time, resembling the *galliard*, and with a rising and leaping kind of motion.
Volteggiándo, *It.* (vōl-tĕd-jĕ-än-dō.) Crossing the hands, on the pianoforte.

VOXN

Volteggiáre, *It.* (vōl-tĕd-jĕ-ä-rĕ.) To cross the hands, in playing.
Vólti, *It.* (vōl-tē.) Turn over.
Vólti, segue la secónda párte, *It.* (vōl-tē sĕ-guĕ lä sĕ-kōn-dä pär-tĕ.) Turn over, the second part follows.
Vólti súbito, *It.* (vōl-tē soo-bē-tō.) Turn over quickly.
Volubilita, *It.* (vō-loo-bē-lē-tä.)) Volubility,
Volubilménte, *It.* (vō-loo-bĕl-män-tĕ.)) freedom of performance, fluency in delivery.
Volume. The quantity of fullness of the tone of a voice or instrument.
Voluntary. An introductory performance upon the organ, either extemporaneous, or otherwise; also, a species of *toccáta*, generally in two or three movements, calculated to display the capabilities of the instrument, and the skill of the performer.
Volver a la misma cancion, *Spa.* (vōl-vär ä lä mēs-mä kän-thĕ-ōn.) To return to the old tune.
Von, *Ger.* (fŏn.) By, of, from, on.
Vorausnahme, *Ger.* (fō-rous-nä-mĕ.) Anticipation.
Vorbereituung, *Ger.* (fōr-bĕ-rī-toong.) Preparation, of discords, etc.
Vorbereitungsunterricht, *Ger.* (fōr-bĕ-rī-toongs-oon-tĕr-rĭkh t.) Preparatory lesson; elementary instruction.
Vorgreifung, *Ger.* (fōr-grī-foong.)) Anticipation.
Vorgriff, *Ger.* (fōr-grĭff.))
Vorhalt, *Ger.* (fōr-hält.) A suspension, or syncopation.
Vorher, *Ger.* (fōr-hĕr.) Before; *tempo wie vorher*, the time as before.
Vorsang, *Ger.* (fōr-säng.) Leading off in the song; act of beginning the tune.
Vorsänger, *Ger.* (fōr-säng-ĕr.) The leading ginger in a choir; a precentor.
Vorschlag, *Ger.* (fōr-shläg.) Appoggiatura, beat.
Vorspiel, *Ger.* (fōr-spēl.) Prelude, introductory movement.
Vorspieler, *Ger.* (fōr-spē-lĕr.) Leader of the band; the principal, *primo* performer upon any orchestral instrument.
Vorsteller, *Ger.* (fōr-stĕl-lĕr.) Performer, player.
Vortrag, *Ger.* (fōr-träg.) Execution, mode of executing a piece; delivery, elocution, diction; the act of uttering or pronouncing.
Vorzeichnung, *Ger.* (fōr-tsīkh-noong.) The signature; also, a sketch, or outline of a composition.
Vox, *Lat.* (vŏx.) Voice.
Vox acuta, *Lat.* (vŏx ä-kū-tä.) A shrill or high voice. In the ancient music, the highest note in the bisdiapason, or double octave.
Vox angelica, *Lat.* (vŏx än-jĕl-ĭ-kä.) Angelic voice; see *Vox Célestes*.
Vox gravis, *Lat.* (vŏx grä-vĭs.) A grave or low voice.
Vox humana, *Lat.* (vŏx hū-mä-nä.) *Human voice;* an organ reed stop of eight feet tone, intended to imitate the human voice, which it sometimes does, though very imperfectly.
Vox nasalis, *Lat.* (vŏx nä-sä-lĭs.) A nasal voice.

ā ale, ă add, ä arm, ē eve, ĕ end, ī ice, ĭ ill, ō old, ŏ odd, ō dove, oo moon, ū lule, ŭ but, ü French sound.

VOX — WHOL

Vox retusa, *Lat.* (vŏx rĕ-tū-să.) An eight feet organ stop.
Voz, *Spa.* (vōth.) Voice, sound in general, vocal music.
Voz argentada, *Spa.* (vōth är-jĕn-tä-dä.) A clear, sonorous voice.
Voz cascarrona, *Spa.* (vōth käs-kä-rō-nä.) A harsh, unpleasant tone of voice.

Voz de carretero, *Spa.* (vōth dĕ kär-rĕ-tā-rō.) A harsh, loud, unpleasant voice.
Vozes, *Spa.* (vō-thĕs.) Voices.
Vuide, *Fr.* (vwĕd.) *Open;* the note is to be played on the open string.

W.

Waits. An old word, meaning hautboys; also, players on the hautboys; see, also, *Wayghtes.*
Wald-flöte, *Ger.* (väld flö-tĕ.) *Forest-flute,* shepherd's flute; an organ stop with a full and powerful tone.
Wald-horn, *Ger.* (väld hŏrn.) *Forest-horn;* also, winding-horn.
Wals, *Dut.* (väls.) A waltz.
Walz, *Ger.* (välts.) } The name of a modern
Waltz, } dance originally used in Suabia. The measure of its music is triple, usually in 3-4 or 3-8 time, and performed moderately slow, or, at the quickest in allegretto.
Walzer, *Ger.* (väl-tsĕr.) Waltz, national German dance.
Warble. To quaver the sound; to sing in a manner imitating that of birds.
Wassail. An old term signifying a merry or convivial song.
Wasserorgel, *Ger.* (väs-sĕr-ŏr-g'l.) Hydraulic organ.
Water music. A term applied by Handel to certain airs composed by him and performed on the water by the first band of wind instruments instituted in England.
Water organ. The *hydrauticon.*
Waving line. When a waving line is placed vertically before the chord the notes are played successively, from the lowest ascending to the highest, and retained down the full time of the chord.
Wayghtes. Persons who play hymn tunes, etc., in the streets, during the night, about Christmas; see, also, *Waits.*
Way, One of the two modes of notation in the ancient Greek system.
Weber chronometer. An instrument similar to a metronome, but simpler in its construction, invented by Weber. It consists of a piece of twine, about five feet in length, on which are fifty-five inch spaces, and a small weight at the lower end, the degree of motion being determined by the length of string swinging with the weight. Web. Chron. ♩=38″ Rh., (39½ Eng.)
Wechselchor, *Ger.* (vĕkh-s'l-khŏr.) Alternate chorus or choir.

Wechsel-gesang, *Ger.* (vĕkh-s'l ghĕ-säng.) Alternative, or antiphonal, song.
Wechsel-noten, *Ger. pl.* (vĕkh-s'l nō-t'n.) *Changing notes:* passing notes, notes of irregular transition, appoggiaturas.
Wehmuth, *Ger.* (vā-muot.) Sadness.
Wehmüthig, *Ger.* (vā-moo-tig.) Sad, sorrowful.
Weiber-stimme, *Ger.* (vī-bĕr-stĭm-mĕ.) A female voice, a treble voice.
Weihnachtslied, *Ger.* (vīn-äkhts-lēd.) Canticle at Christmas; Christmas hymn or carol.
Weich, *Ger.* (vīkh.) Minor, in respect to keys and mode.
Weise, *Ger.* (vī-zĕ.) Melody, air, song.
Weisse-note, *Ger.* (vī-zĕ nō-tĕ.) *White note;* minim.
Weite harmonie, *Ger.* (wī-tĕ här-mō-nē.) Dispersed, or open harmony.
Welsh harp. See Harp.
Welsh singing. A mode of singing in which the harper plays the melody, and the singer chants an accompanying part, chiefly on the dominant; both contriving to finish together.
Weltliche, *Ger.* (vĕlt-lĭkh-ĕ.) Secular.
Weltliche lieder, *Ger.* (vĕlt-lĭkh-ĕ lē-dĕr.) Secular songs.
Wenig, *Ger.* (vā-nĭg.) Little; *ein venig stark,* a little strong, rather loud.
Werk, *Ger.* (värk.) *Work,* movement, action; see Hauptwerk, and Oberwerk.
Wesentlich, *Ger.* (vā-sĕnt-lĭkh.) Essential.
Wesentliche septime, *Ger.* (vā-sĕnt-lĭk-ĕ sĕp-tä-mĕ.) Dominant seventh.
Wettgesang, *Ger.* (vĕt-ghĕ-säng.) A singing match.
Whaightes. See Wayghtes.
Whiffle. Anciently, a fife or small flute.
Whistle. A small, shrill wind instrument, in tone resembling a fife, but blown at the end like an old English flute.
Whole note. A semibreve,
Whole rest. A pause equal in length to a whole note,
Whole shift. A violin shift on the eighth line, or A. See *violin shift.*

216   PRONOUNCING MUSICAL DICTIONARY.

ā ale, ă add, ä arm, ē eve, ĕ end, ī ice, ĭ ill, ō old, ŏ odd, ô dove, oo moon, ū lute, ŭ but, ü French sound.

WHOL

Whole tone. A tone; a large second; a whole step.
Wieder-anfangen, Ger. (vē-dĕr än-fäng'n.) To begin again, to recommence.
Wieder-holung, Ger. (vē-dĕr hō-loong.) Repeating, repetition.
Wieder-holungszeichen, Ger. (vē-dĕr hō-loongs-tsī-khĕn.) Signs of repetition.
Wieder-klang, Ger. (vē-dĕr kläng.) ⎫ Echo, resounding.
Wieder-schall, Ger. (vē-dĕr shäll.) ⎭
Wind. To give a prolonged and varied sound, as, to wind a horn.
Wind chest. An air-tight box under the sound-of an organ, into which the wind passes from the bellows, and from which it passes to the pipes.
Wind coupler. A valve in the wind trunk of an organ, to shut off, or on, the wind.
Wind instruments. A general name for all instruments the sounds of which are produced by the breath or by the wind of bellows.
Wind-harfe, Ger. (vīnd här-fē.) Æolian harp.
Wind-lade, Ger. (vīnd lä-dē.) Wind-chest in an organ.
Wind-messer, Ger. (vīnd mĕs-sĕr.) Anemometer, wind-gauge.
Wind-stock, Ger. (vīnd stŏk.) Cover of organ pipes.
Wind trunk. A large passage in an organ through which air is conveyed from the bellows to the wind-chest.
Windzunge, Ger. (vīnd-tsoon-ghē.) Tongue of an organ pipe.
Winselig, Ger. (vīn-sē-lĭg.) Plaintive.
Winselstimme, Ger. (vīn-s'l-stĭm-mē.) A plaintive voice.

YONI

Wirbel, Ger. (vĭr-b'l.) Peg of a violin, viola, etc.; the stopper in an organ pipe.
Wirbel einer geige, Ger. (vĭr-b'l ī-nĕr ghī-ghē.) Peg or screw of a violin.
Wirbel-kasten, Ger. (vĭr-b'l käs-t'n.) That part of the neck of a violin, etc., which contains the pegs.
Wirbel-stock, Ger. (vĭr-b'l stŏk.) A sound board.
Wogend, Ger. (vō-ghĕnd.) Waving.
Wohlklang, Ger. (vōlk-läng.) Agreeable sound, harmony.
Wohlklingend, Ger. (vōlk-lĭng-ĕnd.) Harmonious, sonorous.
Wohl-laut, Ger. (vōl lont.) Euphony, harmony.
Wohl-lauten, Ger. (vōl lou-t'n.) To sound agreeably.
Wolf. An old name applied to an impure fifth, which occurs in pianofortes, or organs, tuned in unequal temperament.
Wortklang, Ger. (vŏrt-kläng.) Accent; tone.
Wrest. An old name for a tuning key.
Wrest pins. Movable pins in a piano, about which one end of the string is wound, and by turning which the instrument is tuned.
Wrist-guide. A part of the chiroplast, invented by Logier, to assist young pianoforte players in keeping the wrist in proper position.
Wunderlich, Ger. (voon-d'r-lĭkh.) Odd, capricious.
Wunderstimme, Ger. (voon-d'r-stĭm-mē.) A wonderful, extraordinary voice.
Würde, Ger. (vür-dē.) Dignity.
Würdig, Ger. (vür-dĭg.) Dignified.
Wuth, Ger. (voot.) Madness, rage.

X.

Xabardillo, Spa. (ksä-bär-dĭl-yō.) A company of strolling players.
Xabega, Spa. (ksä-bā-gä.) ⎫ A Moorish wind instrument.
Xabeba, Spa. (ksä-bā-hä.) ⎭
Xacara, Spa. (ksä-kä-rä.) A rustic tune for singing or dancing; a dance.
Xacarero, Spa. (ksä-kä-rā-rō.) To sing xacaras.
Xanorphica. A keyed violin.
Xanorphika, Ger. (ksän-ŏr-fē-kä.) A German instrument having a violin bow and keys; a keyed violin.

Xenorphica. An instrument of the harpsichord and pianoforte class.
Xylharmonicon, Gr. (ksĭl-bär-mŏn-ĭ-kŏn.) The wooden harmonica, invented in 1810 by Uthe, an organ-builder at Sangerhausen.
Xylorgand, Fr. (ksĭ-lŏr-gänh.) A species of musical instrument.
Xylorganon, Ger. (ksĭ-lŏr-gä-nŏn.) An instrument composed of dry staves of wood united with straw and struck in the same manner as a dulcimer.

Y.

Yabal, Heb. (yä-bäl.) The blast of a trumpet.
Yambico, Spa. (jäm-bē-kō.) An iambic.
Yastlo, Gr. (yäs-tĭ-ō.) One of the ancient Greek modes or tones.

Yo. The Indian flute.
Yonico, Gr. (yō-nĭ-kō.) The Ionic mode of the Greeks.

ă ale, ă add, ä arm, ē eve, ĕ end, ī ice, ĭ ill, ō old, ŏ odd, ô dove, oo moon, ū lute, ŭ but, ü French sound.

ZA

Za. A syllable formerly applied by the French, in their church music, to B flat, to distinguish it from B natural, called *Si*.
Zamacuca. The national dance of the Chilians.
Zambacucca. A favorite dance of the Peruvians.
Zambapalo, *Spa.* (thäm-bä-pä-lō.) An ancient dance.
Zambomba, *Spa.* (thän-bŏm-bä.) A kind of rustic drum.
Zambra, *Spa.* (thäm-brä.) A festival attended with dancing and music.
Zampogino, *It.* (tsäm-pō-jē-nō.) A small flageolet or bagpipe.
Zampógna, *It.* (tsäm-pōn-yä.) } An ancient
Zampúgna, *It.* (tsäm-poon-yä.) } pipe, or bagpipe, now nearly extinct, with a reedy tone, resembling, but much inferior to the clarinet; see *Cornamusa,* and *Chalumeau.*
Zampognare, *It.* (tsäm-pōn-yä-rĕ.) To play on the pipes.
Zampognatore, *It.* (tsäm-pōn-yä-tō-rĕ.) A piper.
Zampognétta, *It.* (tsäm-pōn-yĕt-tä.) } A small
Zampogníno, *It.* (tsäm-pōn-yē-nō.) } bagpipe.
Zampona, *Spa.* (thäm-pō-nä.) A rustic instrument; a kind of bagpipe.
Zamponear, *Spa.* (thäm pō-nē-är.) To play the bagpipe.
Zang, *Dut.* (tsäng.) A song.
Zangl, *Per.* (tsän-gl.) A little bell.
Zapateádo, *Spa.* (thä-pä-tĕ-ä-dō.) A Spanish national dance in which a noise is made with the shoe.
Zapatear, *Spa.* (thä-pä-tĕ-är.) To beat time with the foot.
Zapfen-streich, *Ger.* (tsäpf-'n strīkh.) The tattoo.
Zarabánda, *Sp.* (thär-ä-bän-dä.) See *Sarabánde*.
Zarambeque, *Sp.* (thär-äm-bā-quě.) A kind of merry tune and noisy dance.
Zarge, *Ger.* (tsär-ghĕ.) The *sides* of a violin, guitar, etc.
Zart, *Ger.* (tsärt.) } Tenderly, softly,
Zärtlich, *Ger.* (tsärt-līkh.) } delicately.
Zarte stimmen, *Ger. pl.* (tsär-tĕ stĭm-m'n.) Delicate stops; *mit zarten.*
Zart-flüte, *Ger.* (tsärt flö-tĕ.) *Soft-flute;* an organ stop of the flute species.
Zarzuéla, *Spa.* (thär-thoo-ā-lä.) A short drama, with incidental music, something similar to the *vaudeville.*
Zauber-lied, *Ger.* (tsou-bĕr lēd.) A charming song.
Zauber-stimme, *Ger.* (tsou-bĕr stĭm-mĕ.) A charming voice.
Zehn, *Ger.* (tsān.) Ten.
Zehnte, *Ger.* (tsān-tĕ.) Tenth.
Zeichen, alt. *Ger.* (tsī-khĕn ält.) The C clef on the third line.
Zeit-mass, *Ger.* (tsīt mäss.) Time, measure.
Zel. A Moorish instrument of music, similar to the cymbals.
Zele, *Fr.* (zhāl.) } Zeal, ardor, energy.
Zélo, *It.* (tsā-lō.) }
Zelosaménte, *It.* (tsā-lō-zä-mān-tĕ.) Zealously, ardently.
Zelóso, *It.* (tsā-lō-zō.) Zealous, ardent, earnest.

ZU

Zeng, *Per.* (tsĕng.) The Persian cymbals.
Zerstreut, *Ger.* (tsĕr-stroit.) Dispersed, scattered, with respect to the notes of arpeggios or chords, the situation of the different parts of a composition, etc.
Zeze. An African instrument similar to a guitar.
Ziemlich, *Ger.* (tsēm-līkh.) Tolerably, moderately.
Ziemlich langsam, *Ger.* (tsēm-līkh läng-säm.) Tolerably slow.
Zierliches singen, *Ger.* (tsēr-līkh-ĕs sĭng-ĕn.) Modulation.
Zil. A Turkish musical instrument.
Zillo, *It.* (tsēl-lō.) Chirp, chirping.
Zinbel, *Ger.* (tsēm-bĕl.) Cymbal.
Zincke, *Ger.* (tsĭnk-ĕ.) See *Zinke.*
Zinfonia, *It.* (tsēn-fō-nē-ä.) A symphony.
Zingana, *It.* (tsēn-gä-nä.) Ballad; Bohemian song.
Zingarésa, *It.* (tsēn-gä-rā-zä.) In the style of gypsy music.
Zingarésca, *It.* (tsēn-gä-rĕs-kä.) A song or dance in the style of the gypsies.
Zingaro, *It.* (tsēn-gä-rō.) Gypsy, in the gypsy style.
Zingen, *Dut.* (tsīn-g'n.) To sing; singing.
Zink-bläser, *Ger.* (tsĭnk blā-zĕr.) Cornet player.
Zinke, *Ger.* (tsĭnk-ĕ.) } Small cornet, spe-
Zinken, *Ger. pl.* (tsĭn-k'n.) } cies of horn or trumpet of very ancient date, now almost obsolete. It was made either of wood, or the small branches on the head of the deer. Also, the name of a treble stop, in German organs, which is sometimes a reed, and at others a mixture stop.
Zinkenist, *Ger.* (tsĭn-k'n-ĭst.) Cornet player.
Zinzulare, *It.* (tsēn-tsoo-lä-rĕ.) To make a succession of tremulous sounds, to twitter.
Ziraleet, *Gr.* (zē-rä-lēt.) A species of chorus sung by the women of Eastern countries upon occasions of joy.
Zirlare, *It.* (tsēr-lä-rĕ.) To whistle like a thrush.
Zisch, *Ger.* (tsish.) A hiss.
Zischlaut, *Ger.* (tsish-lout.) A hissing sound.
Zither, *Ger.* (tsĭt-ĕr.) The guitar, or cithern.
Zithern. An instrument which may be called a compound of the harp and guitar. The harmonies of the first named instrument are produced from it, and it possesses the sweetest notes pertaining to both, but not great compass.
Zither-spieler, *Ger.* (tsĭt-ĕr spē-lĕr.) } Guitar
Zither-schläger, *Ger.* (tsĭt-ĕr shlä-gĕr.) } player.
Zittern de stimme, *Ger.* (tsĭt-tĕrn dĕ stĭm-mĕ.) A trembling voice.
Zittino, *It.* (tsēt-tē-nō.) Silence.
Zögernd, *Ger.* (tsö-ghĕrnd.) A continual retarding of the time.
Zólfa, *It.* (tsōl-fä.) See *Sólfa.*
Zólfa dégli arméni, *It.* (tsōl-fä dĕl-yē är-mā-nē.) The church music used by the Armenians.
Zóppa, *It.* (tsŏp-pä.) }
Zóppe, *It.* (tsŏp-pĕ.) } Lame, halting; see Syn-
Zóppo, *It.* (tsŏp-pō.) } copation.
Zornig, *Ger.* (tsŏr-nig.) Angry, wrathful.
Zourna, *Per.* (tsoor-nä.) A hautboy used by the Persians.
Zu, *Ger.* (tsoo.) At, by, in, to, unto.

ă *ale,* ă *add,* ă *arm,* ĕ *eve,* ĕ *end,* ī *ice,* ĭ *ill,* ō *old,* ŏ *odd,* ō *dove,* oo *moon,* ū *lute,* ŭ *but,* ü *French sound.*

ZUFA

Zufällig, *Ger.* (tsoo-fäl-lĭg.) Accidental sharp, flat, etc.
Zufolare, *It.* (tsoo-fō-lä-rĕ.) To whistle, to hiss.
Zufoletto, *It.* (tsoo-fō-lăt-tō.) A little whistle or flageolet.
Zufolo, *It.* (tsoo-fō-lō.) Flageolet, small flute, or whistle.
Zufolóne, *It.* (tsoo-fō-lō-nĕ.) A flute, large whistle.
Zug, *Ger.* (tsoog) Draw-stop, or register, in an organ.
Züge, *Ger. pl.* (tsü-ghĕ.) See *Zug.*
Zügeglöckchen, *Ger.* (tsü-ghĕ-glŏk-khĕn.) The passing bell; a knell.
Zuklang, *Ger.* (tsook-läng.) Unison, harmony, concord.
Zumbar, *Spa.* (thoom-bär.) To resound; to emit a continuous harsh sound; to hum.
Zum Klavier singen, *Ger.* (tsoom kl ä-fēr sĭng-ĕn.) To sing with pianoforte accompaniment.
Zummarah. An Egyptian musical instrument, very harsh and discordant in its tone, formed of reeds.
Zunehmend, *Ger.* (tsoo-nä-mĕnd.) Increasing.
Zunge, *Ger.* (tsoon-ghĕ.) The tongue of a reed pipe.
Zurna, *Tur.* (tsoor-nä.) A military instrument used by the Turks.
Zurück-blasen, *Ger.* (tsoo-rük b l ä-zĕn.) To blow a retreat.
Zurück-haltung, *Ger.* (tsoo-rük häl-toong.) Retardation, keeping back.
Zurück-tönen, *Ger.* (tsoo-rük tö-nĕn.)
Zurück-treiben, *Ger.* (tsoo-rük trī-b'n.) } To resound, to reverberate.
Zusammen, *Ger.* (tsoo-zäm-m'n.) Together.
Zusammen-blasen, *Ger.* (tsoo-zäm-m'n blä-z'n.) To play together on wind instruments.
Zusammen-gesetzt, *Ger.* (tsoo-zäm-m'n ghĕ-setst.) Compound, condensed, compound time.
Zusammen-klang, *Ger.* (tsoo-zäm-m'n kläng.) Harmony, consonance.
Zusammen-laut, *Ger.* (tsoo-z ä m-m'n lout.) Harmony, consonance.
Zusammen-schlag, *Ger.* (tsoo-zäm-m'n shläg.) A broken or abrupt manner of striking a chord.
Zusammen-singen, *Ger.* (tsoo-zäm-m'n sĭng-ĕn.) To sing together.
Zusammen-stimmig, *Ger.* (tsoo-z ä m-m'n stĭm-mĭg.) Harmonious, concordant.
Zusammen-stimmung, *Ger.* (tsoo-zäm-m'n stĭm-moong.) Harmony, concord, consonance.
Zutranlich, *Ger.* (tsoo-trou-lĭkh.) Confidently.
Zuversicht, *Ger.* (tsoo-fēr-sĭkht.) Confidence.
Zwazig, *Ger.* (tsvän-tsĭg.) Twenty.
Zwanzigste, *Ger.* (tsvän-tsĭgs-tĕ,) Twentieth.
Zwei, *Ger.* (tsvī.) Two.
Zwei-fach, *Ger.* (tsvī-fäkh.) } Two-fold, of
Zwei-fältig, *Ger.* (tsvī-fäl-tĭg.) } two ranks, in organ pipes; *compound,* speaking of intervals, such as exceed the octave; as, the 9th, 16th, etc.
Zwei-gesang. *Ger.* (tsvī ghĕ-säng.) For two voices, a duet.
Zwei-gestrichen, *Ger.* (ts vī ghĕs-trĭkh-ĕn.)

ZYMB

With two strokes; applied to C on the third space in the treble and the six notes above; see *Twice Marked Octave.*
Zweig-lied, *Ger.* (tsvīg lēd.) A sequence of two links or chords.
Zwei-händige übungsstücke, *Ger.* (tsvī-hän-dĭ-ghĕ ü-boongs-stük-ĕ.) Exercises for two hands.
Zwei-klang, *Ger.* (tsvī kläng.) A chord of two sounds.
Zwei-mal, *Ger.* (tsvī mäl.) Twice.
Zwei-mannale, *Ger. pl.* (tsvī mä-noo-ä-lĕ.) Two manuals.
Zwei-sang, *Ger.* (tsvī säng.) } For two
Zwei-stimmig, *Ger.* (tsvī stĭm-mĭg.) } voices or parts, a duet.
Zwei-spiel, *Ger.* (tsvī spēl.) A duet.
Zweite, *Ger.* (tsvī-tĕ.) Second.
Zweite-mal, *Ger.* (tsvī-tĕ mäl.) Second time.
Zweites manual, *Ger.* (tsvī-tĕs mä-noo-äl.) The second manual.
Zwei-und-dreissigstel-note, *Ger.* (tsvī oond drī-sĭg-stĕl nō-tĕ.) A demisemiquaver.
Zwei-und-dreissigstelspause, *Ger.* (tsvī oond drī-sĭgs-tĕls-pow-zĕ.) A demisemiquaver rest.
Zwei-viertelanote, *Ger.* (tsvī fēr-tĕls-nō-tĕ.) A minim.
Zwei-viertelspause, *Ger.* (tsvī fēr-tĕls-pou-zĕ.) A minim rest.
Zwei-viertel-takt, *Ger.* (tsvī fēr-tĕl täkt.) Time of two crotchets, 2-4.
Zwei-zweitel-takt, *Ger.* (tsvī tsvī-t'l täkt.) Time of two minims, 2-2.
Zwerch-flöte. *Ger.* (tsvĕrkh flö-tĕ.) Transverse flute, the German flute.
Zwerch-pfeife, *Ger.* (tsvĕrkh pfī-fĕ.) Transverse pipe, the fife.
Zwey, *Ger.* (tsvī.) See Zwei.
Zwey-fache intervallen, *Ger.* (tsvī fä-khĕ ĭn-tĕr-fäl-l'n.) Compound intervals.
Zwey-klang, *Ger.* (tsvī kläng.) See Zwei-klang.
Zwischen-gesang, *Ger.* (tsvī-shĕn ghĕ-zäng.)
Zwischen-handlung, *Ger.* (tsvī-shĕn händ-loong.) } An episode.
Zwischen-harmonie, *Ger.* (tsvī-shĕn här-mō-nē.) Between harmony; the connecting harmony in a fugue.
Zwischen-räume, *Ger. pl.* (tsvī-shĕn roy-mĕ.) The spaces between the lines of the staff.
Zwischen-satz, *Ger.* (tsvī-shĕn sätz.) Intermezzo, parenthesis, episode.
Zwischen-spiel, *Ger.* (tsvī-shĕn spēl.) Interlude played between the verses of a hymn.
Zwischen-stille, *Ger.* (tsvī-shĕn stĭl-lĕ.) A pause.
Zwischen-stimme, *Ger.* (tsvī-shĕn stĭm-mĕ.) High tenor or alto.
Zwischen-ton, *Ger.* (tsvī-shĕn tōn.) Intermediate tone.
Zwölf, *Ger.* (tsvölf.) Twelve.
Zymbel, *Ger.* (tsĭm-b'l.) Cymbal.

ADDITIONAL WORDS.

ă *ale*, ă *add*, ä *arm*, ē *eve*, ĕ *end*, ī *ice*, ĭ *ill*, ō *old*, ŏ *odd*, ô *dove*, oo *moon*, ū *lute*, ŭ *but*, ü *French sound*.

A

Abbandonarsi, *It.* (äb-bän-dō-när-sē.) To abandon oneself to the influence of music.
Abcidiren, *Ger.* (äb-sī-dīr-'n.) A series of exercises in which the names of the notes are used instead of words.
Abellare, *It.* (ä-běl-lä-rě.) To decorate, ornament or embellish.
Abellimento, *It.* (ä-běl-lē-män-tō.) A decoration, ornament or embellishment.
Abenteurlich, *Ger.* (ä-běu-toir-lĭkh.) Strange and uncouth.
Abgeleiteter akkord, *Ger.* (äb-ghě-lī-tĕ-tĕr äk-kŏrd) An inversion of a chord.
Abschnitt, *Ger.* (äb-shnit.) Section.
Accentuare, *It.* (ät-tshän-too-ä-rě.) To accent.
Action. The mechanism of an organ, pianoforte or other compound instruments.
Adagiosissimo, *It.* (ä-dä-jē-ō-sĭs-sē-mō.) Extremely slow.
Ad placitum, *Lat.* (äd plä-sī-tŭm.) At pleasure; a free part.
Ad vivendum, *Lat.* (äd vī-věn-dŭm.) A species of counterpoint which was written down, as opposed to that which was *alta mente* or improvised.
Agilité, *Fr.* (ä-zhě-lī-tä.) Lightness and freedom in playing or singing.
Agitazione, con, *It.* (ä-jē-tä-tsē-ō-ně kŏn.) With agitation.
Alcuna licenza, con, *It.* (äl-koo-nä lē-tshän-tsä kŏn.) With a little license; that is, the power of altering the time at will.
Al riverso, *It.* (äl rē-věr-sō.) } By contrary
Al rovescio, *It.* (äl rō-vě-shē-o.) } motion, that is, answering an ascending interval by one descending a like distance.
Ambira, *Afr.* (äm-bē-rä.) A kind of drum or pulsatile instrument made of wood, used by the negroes of Senegambia and Guinea.
Ambrosian hymn. The Te Deum, so-called because it was credited to Bishop Ambrose.
Amor-schall. A horn of peculiar construction, invented in the year 1760, by Kölbel, one of the musicians of the Emperor of Russia.
Anabathmi, *Gr.* (än-ä-bäth-mī.) The name given to certain antiphons in the Greek church.
Anaploke, *Gr.* (än-ä-plō-kě.) A combination of notes ascending the scale.

BASS

Antispastus. A foot consisting of two long between two short syllables.
Antode, *Gr.* (än-tō-dě.) Responsive singing.
Aoidoi, *Gr. pl.* Minstrels, bards.
Apolutikion, *Gr.* (äp-ō-lū-tĭ-kī-ŏn.) A hymn sung at the close of vespers in certain seasons of the Greek church.
Arched viall. An instrument somewhat like a hurdy-gurdy, invented about A. D. 1664.
Artist. One capable of appreciating and interpeting the refined and beautiful in art.
Asamentata, *Lat.* (ä-sĕl-měn-tä-tä.) } The songs
Assamenta, *Lat.* (äs-sä-měn-tä.) } or hymns
Axamenta, *Lat.* (äx-ä-měn-tä.) } sung by the Salii.
Ashantee trumpet. An instrument formed of the tusk of an elephant.
Ascaules, *Gr.* (äs-kou-lēs.) A player on the ascaulos.
Ascaulos, *Gr.* (äs-kou-lŏs.) A bagpipe.
A tempo primo, *It.* (ä täm-pō prē-mō.) In the time first given.
A tre stromente, *It.* (ä trā strō-měn-tě.) For three instruments.
Auletrides, *Gr.* (ou-lět-rĭ-děs.) Female players on the aulos or flute.
Ave regina, *Lat.* (ä-vě rě-jē-nä.) Vesper hymn to the Virgin, sung from the Purification till Easter.

B

Baar-pyp. The name of a stop in some of the Dutch organs.
Backfall. A turn in lute or harpsichord music.
Balafo. A musical instrument popular among the negroes of Senegambia.
Balg, *Ger.* (bälg.) Bellows, wind-chest.
Balgentreter, *Ger.* (bäl-g'n-trět-ěr.) The bellows-treader. In old organs the blower worked the bellows by standing on them in turns.
Band, *Ger.* (bänd.) A part, a volume, anything sewn together.
Basse de cremone, *Fr.* (bäss dŭh krě-mŏn.) The bassoon.
Basse de hautboys, *Fr.* (bäss dŭh ō-bwä.) Corno inglese.

ADDITIONAL WORDS.

ă ale, ă add, ä arm, ĕ eve, ĕ end, ī ice, ĭ ill, ō old, ŏ odd, ô dove, oo moon, ū lute, ŭ but, ü French sound.

BASS

Basse d'harmonie, *Fr.* (bäss d'är-mō-nē.) The ophicleide.
Basse de viole, *Fr.* (bäss düh vē-ōl.) The violincello.
Basse de violon, *Fr.* (bäss düh vē-ō-lônh.) Double-bass.
Basslaute, *Ger.* (bäss-lou-tĕ.) Bass lute.
Basspommer, *Ger.* (bäss-pŏm-měr.) A deep-toned instrument of the oboe family, precursor of the bassoon.
Battuta, *It.* (bät-too-tä.) (1) In correct time. (2) A bar.
Bauernleyer, *Ger.* (bou-ĕrn-lī-ĕr.) Hurdy-gurdy.
Bauernpfeife, *Ger.* (bou-ĕrn-pfī-fĕ.) An organ stop of 8 feet length, of a small scale.
Bebisation. A series of syllables, viz.: la, be, ce, de, mi, fe, gi, introduced by Daniel Hitsler, in place of ut, re, mi, fa, sol, la, si, already in use.
Bell diapason. An organ pipe consisting of open metal pipes with bell mouths.
Bemes. } Saxon trumpets or bugles.
Beemes. }
Berceuse, *Fr.* (běr-süss.) A cradle song.
Bilancojel. An Indian flute with seven holes, played by a mouthpiece.
Bina or Vina. An Indian guitar with a long finger board and a gaurd attached to each end. Its scale consists of a series of small intervals lying between a note and its octave, in the bass staff.
Binary form. The form of a movement which is founded on two principal themes or subjects.
Bit. A small piece of tube used for supplementing the crook of a trumpet, cornet-a-piston, etc., so as to adapt the instrument to a slight difference of pitch.
Bombaulius, *Gr.* (bŏm-bou-lī-ŭs.) A facetious name for a bagpiper.
Boulon. A harp used by the negroes of Senegambia and Guinea.
Bourdon, *Fr.* (boor-dônh.) (1) A drone bass, a burden such as that produced by the bagpipe or hurdy-gurdy. (2) An organ stop, consisting of stopped wooden pipes generally of 16 feet tone.
Brindisi, *It.* (brĕn-dē-zē.) A melody so arranged as to exhibit the change from the chest to the head voice in rapid succession, something similar to the German *jodl.*

C

C. A capital letter C signifies the note in the second space of the bass staff. A small c signifies the note on octave above this, *middle* C.
Calandrone, *It.* (kä-län-drō-nĕ.) A small reed instrument of the clarinet species, with two holes, much used by the Italian peasantry.
Cantici, *It.* (kän-tē-sē.) Another name for the *laudes spirituali.*
Canto a cappella, *It.* (kän-tō ä käp-pāl-lä.) Sacred music.
Carnyx, *Gr.* (kär-nĭx.) An ancient Greek trumpet of a shrill tone.
Cheng. The Chinese organ, consisting of a series of tubes and free reeds.

ENTR

Chiuso, *It.* (kē-oo-zō.) Close, hidden, concealed.
Claque, *Fr.* (kläk.) A body of men hired to applaud in theatres and opera houses.
Comus, *Gr.* (kō-mŭs.) A revel, carousal, merry making with music and dancing.
Comus, *Gr.* (kō-mŭs.) A mournful song sung in alternate verses by an actor and chorus in the Attic drama.
Contours, *Fr.* (kônh-toor.) } Troubadours.
Conteurs, *Fr.* (kônh-tür.) }
Cordax, *Lat.* (kōr-däx.) A Greek dance of a loose character in the ancient comedy.
Couronne, *Fr.* (koo-rônh.) The name for the sign of a pause ⌢.
Court capellmeister. Court musical director.
Covered strings. Strings of silk, wire or gut covered with a fine wire by means of a machine, and used for pianofortes, violins, guitars, etc.
Cremona. A violin made in the town of Cremona. A reed stop in the organ.
Crescendo-zug, *Ger.* (krĕ-shĕn-dō-tsoog.) The swell box in the organ.
Creticus, *Lat.* (krĕt-ī-kŭs.) A metrical foot, consisting of one short syllable between two long.
Cymbalista. A cymbal player.
Czakan. A flute made of cane or bamboo.
Czimken, *Pol.* (tsĭm-k'n.) A dance similar to the country dance.

D

D. The scale having two sharps in its signature.
D. The name given to a string tuned to D, e. g., the third string of the violin, the second of the viola and violincello.
Dach, *Ger.* (däkh.) Sounding board of an instrument.
Diaulion, *Gr.* (dī-ou-lī-ŏn.) An air played upon the aulos or flute during an interval in the choral song.
Diecetto, *It.* (dē-ā-tshät-tō.) A composition for ten instruments.
Diretta, alla, *It.* (dē-rät-tä.) In direct motion.
Discant-schlüssel, *Ger.* (dĭs-känt schlüs-s'l.) The soprano clef.
Division viol. A violin with frets upon the finger-board.
Dolzflöte, *Ger.* (dŏlts-flō-tĕ.) The old German flute.
Double bourdon. A organ stop of 32 feet tone.
Double-stopping. The stopping of two strings simultaneously with the fingers, in violin playing.
Doxologia magna, *Lat.* (dŏx-ō-lō-jĭ-ä mäg-nä.) The version of the "Gloria in Excelsio" sung at the celebration of the Holy Eucharist. The greater doxology.
Druckbalg, *Ger.* (drook-bälg.) A reservoir of wind, as in an organ, etc.

E

Emmelela, *Gr.* (ĕm-mĕ-lĭ-ä.) Consonance, concord in musical sounds. (2) A tragic dance accompanied by music.
Entrata, *It.* (än-trä-tä.) Entry, introduction or prelude.

ADDITIONAL WORDS. 221

ă *ale*, ă *add*, ä *arm*, ĕ *eve*, ĕ *end*, I *ice*, ĭ *ill*, ō *old*, ŏ *odd*, ô *dove*, oo *moon*, ū *lute*, ŭ *but*, ü *French sound*.

EPIT

Epitasis, *Gr.* (ĕp-ĭ-tā-sĭa.) The raising of the voice from a low to a higher pitch. (2) The tightening of the strings of an instrument.
Espirando, *It.* (ĕs-pĭ-rän-dō.) Dying away, gasping.
Etouffoirs, *Fr.* (ā-too-fwär.) Dampers.

F

False string. A badly woven string, which produces an uncertain and untrue tone.
Federclavier, *Ger.* (fā-dĕr-klä-fĭ-ĕr.) Spinnet.
Feld, *Ger.* (fĕld.) The distribution of pipes in an organ.
Ferial. Non-festal.
Ferial use. Music for use on ordinary days.
Five-eight time. } Irregular movements
Five-quarter time. } which are rarely employed.
Fling. A dance performed by Scottish Highlanders to a tune in common time.
Flutina, *It.* (floo-tē-nä.) A sweet-toned accordeon.
Flute-lining. The inside metallic tube of the first joint of the flute, forming a slide into the second joint, by means of which the pitch of the instrument is regulated.
Flügel-horn, *Ger.* (flü-g'l.) A bugle, a valve-horn.
Fourniture, *Fr.* (foor-nĭ-tūr.) A mixture stop in an organ.
Füllstimmen, *Ger.* (fŭl-stĭm-m'n.) Additional chorus parts.

G

Gabel, *Ger.* (gä-b'l.) A fork.
Gegensatz, *Ger.* (ghĕg-ĕn-sätz.) Counter-subject.
Geist, *Ger.* (ghīst.) Spirit, genius, soul.
Giocondato, *It.* (jō-ō-kŏn-dä-tō.) Happy, joyful.
Gloria Patri, *Lat.* (glō-rĭ-ä pä-trĭ.) Glory be to the Father, etc. Sung at the conclusion of a psalm.
Gosba. An Arabian flute.

H

Hadan, *Egypt.* (hä-d'n.) The call to prayer sung by the mueddins from the towers or minarets of the mosques.
Hey de guise. A country dance.
Hissing. A manner of showing dissatisfaction at a public performance.
Hyporchema, *Gr.* (hip-ŏr-kā-mä.) A religious hymn or dance connected with the worship of Apollo.

K

Khalil, *Heb.* The Hebrew flute.
Klangfarbe, *Ger.* (kläng-fär-bĕ.) Quality of sound, timbre.
Klangleiter, *Ger.* (kläng-lī-tĕr.) A scale.
Kroamatic. Instrumental.

L

Lacrimosa, *Lat.* (lăk-rĭ-mō-sä.) A part of the Dies Irae in the Requiem mass.

OCAR

Lancers. The name of one of the arrangements of sets of country dances; a military quadrille in five movements or figures.
Lantum. An instrument similar in form to the hurdy-gurdy, and partaking of the character of the accordion or harmonium.
Lauftanz, *Ger.* (louf-tänts.) A running dance.
Leichen-messe, *Ger.* (lī-k'n mĕs-sĕ.) Requiem mass.
Lu-lu, *Chi.* (loo-loo.) The Chinese official collection of treatises on the art of music.
Lures. Ancient Scandinavian trumpets.

M

Machine-head. An arrangement for the tightening and keeping in tension the strings of the double-bass, guitar, etc.
Maggot. A name given to fancies, airs and pieces of an impromptu character.
Magrepha. An organ of the second century, mentioned in the Talmud.
Malakat. Ashantee trumpet.
Mammets. Puppet shows.
Marionette, *Fr.* (mä-rē-ō-nĕt.) A puppet.
Mediation. Part of a chant between the reciting note and the next close.
Meisterfuge, *Ger.* (mīs-tĕr-foo-ghĕ.) A fugue without episodes, one in which the subject or answer is constantly heard.
Menaaneim, *Heb.* (mĕ-nä-nĭm.) See *Sistrum*.
Metzilloth, *Heb.* (mĕt-zĭl-lōth.) Small cymbals used by the Hebrews.
Miscella. A mixture stop in an organ.
Missa de angelis, *Lat.* (mĭs-sä dĕ än-jā-lĭs.) A requiem for young children.
Mitos, *Gr.* (mē-tŏs.) A thread, a term sometimes used for the string of a lyre.
Mouthpiece. That part of a wind instrument which is put into the mouth of the performer.

N

Naenia, *Lat.* (nă-nĭ-ä.) A funeral song of the Romans.
Naguar. An Indian drum with one head only.
Naker. A drum.
Nanga. A negro harp.
Natural harmonics. The sounds given off by any vibrating body over and above its original sound. Overtones.
Nefer. } An Egyptian guitar.
Nofer. }
Ninna, *It.* (nē-nä.) } A cradle song.
Nanna, *It.* (nä-nä.) }
Nodus, *Lat.* (nŏ-dŭs.) Literally a knot. A canon; so-called because compositions of this class were sometimes given as enigmas, the meaning of which had to be unravelled.
Noursingh. An Indian horn or trumpet.

O

Oaten-pipe. The simplest form of a reed pipe, a straw with a strip cut to form the reed, being closed at the end by the knot.
Obligé, *Fr.* (ōb-lĭ-zhā.) See *Obligáto*.
Ocarine, *It.* (Ōk-ä-rē-nā.) A series of seven mu-

222　ADDITIONAL WORDS.

ä ale, ă add, ä arm, ē eve, ĕ end, I ice, ĭ ill, ō old, ŏ odd, O dove, oo moon, ū lute, ŭ but, ü French sound.

OIOU

sical instruments, made of terra cotta pierced with small holes, invented by a company of performers calling themselves the Mountaineers of the Apennines.

Oioueae. The vowels of "World without end, amen," an imitation of Evovae, which see.

Oliphant. The name of an obsolete species of horn, so-called because it was made of ivory.

Ombi. A harp used by negroes in Western Africa.

Omqnäd. The name of the refrain of some old Danish ballads, called the "Kämpe Viser."

Orchesis, *Gr.* (ŏr-kā-sĭs.) The art of rhythmical dancing, as it existed in the Greek theatre.

Oton. An Indian wind instrument producing only a single sound.

P

P. An abbreviation of piano.

Pæon. A foot consisting of one long syllable and three short.

Palilia. Rustic dance at the festival of Pales.

Pastorita. A shepherd's pipe.

Pedal coupler. A stop in an organ, by means of which the pedal keys connect with the corresponding manual keys.

Pedal flügel, *Ger.* (pĕd'l flü-g'l.) A pianoforte to which a set of pedal keys is attached.

Poogye. The nose-flute of the Hindoos.

Pralltriller, *Ger.* (präl-trēl-lĕr.) A transient shake signified by ⁓.

Prefectus chori. Director of the choir, precentor.

Proasma. An introduction, or a short symphony.

Prosa, *Lat.* (prō-sä.) } A hymn sung after the
Prose, *Fr.* (prōz.) } gradual and before the gospel in the Roman church.

Q

Quintaton, *Ger.* (quĭn-tä-tŏn.) An organ stop of closed metal pipes, so voiced that the twelfth is heard with the ground tone.

R

Rackett. } An obsolete wind instrument of the
Rankett. } double bassoon kind, having ventages but not keys. (2) An organ stop now obsolete.

Rant. An old dance; a sort of country dance.

Rauscher. A passage of repeated notes.

Rebibe. } A small rebec or three-stringed viol.
Rebible. }

Re diese, *Fr.* (rä dī-āz.) The note D♯.

Resin or rosin. A gum used to rub over the hair of a bow, thereby making it rough and enabling it to "grip" the string.

Rikk. A small tambourine of modern Egypt.

Rinf. Abbreviation of Rinforzando.

Rolle, *Ger.* (rōl-lĕ.) A run, a group or series of groups of short notes.

Ruana. A Hindoo instrument of the violin class.

Ruollo, *It.* (roo-ōl-lō.) A roll, an Italian dance or waltz.

Rymour, *Old Eng.* A bard or minstrel.

S

Sancho. A negro instrument of the guitar species.

TETR

Saroh. Indian instrument played with a bow.

Scenici. *Lat.* (sä-nĭ-sē.) Games; they were the germ of the Roman play.

Schnabel, *Ger.* (schnä-b'l.) Mouth-piece of the clarinet, flute à bec, and other similar instruments.

School. A method or system of teaching.

Schultergeige, *Ger.* (shool-tĕr-gbī-ghē.) The shoulder-fiddle or common violin.

Schweigezeichen, *Ger.* (shvī-ghē-tsī-k'n.) A rest.

Scorrevole, *It.* (skŏr-rē-vō-lē.) Running, flowing, gliding.

Serena, *It.* (sē-rā-nä.) An evening song; an Abendlied.

Sfz. An abbreviation of sforzato, sforzando.

Shift. See *violin shift*.

Simicon, *Gr.* (sĭm-ĭ-kŏn.) A harp with thirty-five strings, sometimes used by the Greeks.

Sister, *Ger.* (sĭs-tĕr.) An old German guitar.

Sistro, *It.* (sĭs-trō.) A triangle.

Slancio, con, *It.* (slän-tshē-ō kŏn.) With eagerness, impetuosity.

Solennita, *It.* (sō-lĕn-nē-tä.) Solemnity, pomp.

Soloist. One who sings or performs alone, with or without the aid of accompaniment.

Sordun, *It.* (sŏr-doon.) } (1) An old form of
Sordono, *It.* (sŏr-dō-nō.) } wind instruments. (2) A sort of mute for a trumpet. (3) An organ reed stop of 16 feet pitch.

Soubasse, *Fr.* (soo-bäss.) Sub-bass. A stop in the organ of 32 feet pitch.

Souffarah, *Per.* (soof-fä-rä.) General name among the Persians and Arabs for wind instruments without reeds.

Soum. A Burmese harp.

Spanisches-kreuz, *Ger.* (spä-nĭ-shĕs-kroits.) The Spanish cross, the sign of a double sharp, ✕.

Spielmanieren, *Ger.* (spēl-mä-nē-r'n.) Ornaments, graces.

Streichinstrument, *Ger.* (strīk-ĭn-stroo-mĕnt.) A stringed instrument played with the *stroke* of a bow.

String-gauge. A small instrument for measuring the thickness of strings for violins, guitars, etc.

Subsemifusa, *Lat.* (sŭb-sĕm-ĭ-fū-zä.) A demisemiquaver.

Sultana. A violin with strings in pairs, like the cither or cittern.

Szopelka, *Russ.* A kind of oboe made of elder wood, and much used in Southern Russia.

T

Tabl el musahhir. A drum used by Egyptian criers during the Ramadan or annual fast.

Table shamee. An Egyptian drum, suspended from the neck and beaten with two small sticks.

Takigoti. A species of dulcimer used among the Japanese.

Technique, *Fr.* (tĕk-nēk.) That which pertains to the practical (or mechanical) part of an art or accomplishment.

Ten. An abbreviation of *tenuto*.

Terts-gnitarre, *Ger.* (tĕrts-ghĭt-är-rē.) A small guitar tuned a third higher than the regular size.

Tetrachordon. An instrument similar in ap-

ADDITIONAL WORDS.

ă ale, ă add, ă arm, ō eve, ĕ end, ī ice, ĭ ill, ō old, ŏ odd, ô dove, oo moon, ū lute, ŭ but, ū French sound.

THRU

pearance to a cottage pianoforte, but the tone is obtained by means of a cylinder charged with rosin, kept in motion by a pedal.

Thrum. To play without skill on an instrument.

Ton-gemälde, *Ger.* (tōn-ghĕ-mäl-dĕ.) Tone-picture.

Toomourah. An Indian tambourine.

Toorooree. A trumpet used by the Brahmins in their religious processions.

Tonmessung, *Ger.* (tōn-mĕs-soong.) Tone-measuring, metre, rhythm.

Tripeltakt, *Ger.* (trĭp'l-täkt.) Triple time.

Turr. A Burmese violin with three strings.

Tyro. A learner or beginner in music or another science.

Tzetze. An Abyssinian instrument of the guitar species.

U

Untersetzen, *Ger.* (oon-tĕr-sĕt-ts'n.) Passing under, as in passing the thumb under the fingers in playing scales upon the piano.

Urh-heen. The Chinese fiddle.

Uvula. The soft palate; or rather that portion which is pendant from the centre of it.

V

Vamp. To improvise an accompaniment.

Varsoviana. A dance in 3-4 time.

Vergnügt, *Ger.* (fĕr-gnügt.) Pleasantly.

Verilay, *Fr.* (vā-rī-lā.) See Vaudeville.

Violin clef. The G clef placed upon the second line of the staff.

Violin-shift. A change in the position of the hand in violin playing, by which the first finger of

ZEVO

the player has temporarily to become the nut. Shifts are complete changes of four tones or steps; thus, the first shift on the violin is when the first finger is on A of the first string; the second shift is when the first finger is on D above. The intermediate points on which the first finger can be placed, are called *positions*; thus, the *first position* (it is also called the *half-shift*) is when the first finger is on F; the *second position* is when the first finger makes G on the E string; the *third position* is the same as the first shift; the first finger making A on the E string; the *fourth position* is when the first finger takes B., etc., etc.

Voicing. The regulation of the tone and power of an organ pipe.

Vorgeiger, *Ger.* (fōr-ghī-ghĕr.) Leader, first violin.

Vortänzer, *Ger.* (fōr-tän-tsĕr.) Leader of a dance.

V. S. Abbreviation for *volti subito,* and for *violino secondo.*

Yang kin. A Chinese instrument with strings struck by two small hammers, like a dulcimer.

Zanze. A negro instrument consisting of a wooden box, on which a number of strips of wood or tongues of iron are fixed so as to vibrate by pressing them down with the thumb or with a stick.

Zeichen, *Ger.* (tsī-k'n.) A musical sign, note or character.

Ziffern, *Ger.* (tsĭf-fĕrn.) To cypher (as in an organ).

Zwölfachteltakt, *Ger.* (tsvölf-äkh-t'l-täkt.) Twelve-eight time.

www.ingramcontent.com/pod-product-compliance
Lightning Source LLC
Chambersburg PA
CBHW031816230426
43669CB00009B/1164